Praise for
Schizophrenia: Core Interventions in the Treatment and Management of Schizophrenia in Adults in Primary and Secondary Care
(Updated edition)

"There are still many inequalities that exist in mental health, some of which are particularly pertinent for people with schizophrenia, such as not getting access to effective and evidence based psychological and pharmacological treatments. These inequalities are even more difficult to overcome for people from ethnic minorities, who often gain access to help at a very late stage. This guideline is the first to tackle these problematic issues by undertaking a full evidence review of the problems faced by people from African Caribbean groups in accessing UK services. The guideline provides all the evidence underpinning which services and treatments work for people with schizophrenia, including people from black and minority ethnic groups, such as family interventions, cognitive behavioural therapy, arts therapies and careful use of antipsychotics. I can thoroughly recommend this world class guideline to anyone with an interest in the evidence about what works for people with schizophrenia."

Professor DINESH BHUGRA,
MA, MSc, MBBS, FRCPsych, MPhil, PhD,
President, Royal College of Psychiatrists

SCHIZOPHRENIA

CORE INTERVENTIONS IN THE TREATMENT AND MANAGEMENT OF SCHIZOPHRENIA IN ADULTS IN PRIMARY AND SECONDARY CARE (UPDATED EDITION)

National Clinical Guideline Number 82

National Collaborating Centre for Mental Health
commissioned by the

National Institute for Health &
Clinical Excellence

published by
The British Psychological Society and The Royal College of Psychiatrists

British Library Cataloguing-in-Publication Data

A catalogue record for this book is available from the British Library.

ISBN-: 978-1-85433-479-4

Printed in Great Britain by Stanley Hunt.

Additional material: data CD-Rom created by Pix18 (www.pix18.co.uk)

developed by   National Collaborating Centre for Mental Health
Royal College of Psychiatrists' Research Unit
4th Floor, Standon House
21 Mansell Street
London
E1 8AA
www.nccmh.org.uk

commissioned by   National Institute for Health and Clinical Excellence
MidCity Place, 71 High Holborn
London
WCIV 6NA
www.nice.org.uk

published by   The British Psychological Society
St Andrews House
48 Princess Road East
Leicester
LE1 7DR
www.bps.org.uk

The
British
Psychological
Society

and

The Royal College of Psychiatrists
17 Belgrave Square
London
SW1X 8PG
www.rcpsych.ac.uk

RC
PSYCH
ROYAL COLLEGE OF
PSYCHIATRISTS

CONTENTS

Contents

GUIDELINE DEVELOPMENT GROUP MEMBERS

Professor Elizabeth Kuipers (Chair, Guideline Development Group)
Professor of Clinical Psychology, Head of Department, Institute of Psychiatry,
King's College London
Honorary Consultant Clinical Psychologist, Maudsley Hospital, South London and
Maudsley NHS Foundation Trust

Dr Tim Kendall (Facilitator, Guideline Development Group)
Joint Director, The National Collaborating Centre for Mental Health
Deputy Director, Royal College of Psychiatrists' Research and Training Unit
Consultant Psychiatrist and Medical Director, Sheffield Health and Social Care
NHS Foundation Trust

Ms Janey Antoniou
Service user representative and freelance writer, trainer and researcher on mental
health issues

Professor Thomas Barnes
Professor of Clinical Psychiatry, Imperial College London

Professor Kamaldeep Bhui
Professor of Cultural Psychiatry and Epidemiology, Wolfson Institute of
Preventative Medicine, Barts and The London, Queen Mary University of London

Ms Victoria Bird
Research Assistant, The National Collaborating Centre for Mental Health

Dr Alison Brabban
Consultant Clinical Psychologist, Tees, Esk and Wear Valley NHS Trust

Ms Esther Flanagan
Guideline Development Manager, The National Collaborating Centre for Mental
Health (2008 to 2009)

Professor Philippa Garety
Professor of Clinical Psychology, Institute of Psychiatry, King's College London
Trust Head of Psychology, South London and Maudsley NHS Foundation Trust

Ms Sarah Hopkins
Project Manager, The National Collaborating Centre for Mental Health (2006 to 2008)

Mr Ryan Li
Research Assistant, The National Collaborating Centre for Mental Health (2007)

Ms Anna Maratos
Head of Profession, Arts Therapies, Central and North West London NHS Foundation Trust

Dr Ifigeneia Mavranezouli
Senior Health Economist, The National Collaborating Centre for Mental Health

Dr Jonathan Mitchell
Consultant Psychiatrist, Sheffield Health and Social Care NHS Foundation Trust
Honorary Systematic Reviewer, The National Collaborating Centre for Mental Health

Professor Irwin Nazareth
Professor of Primary Care and Population Sciences
Director, Medical Research Council General Practice Research Framework

Mr J Peter Pratt
Chief Pharmacist, Sheffield Health and Social Care NHS Foundation Trust and Doncaster and South Humber NHS Trust

Dr Robert Paul Rowlands
Consultant Psychiatrist, Derbyshire Mental Health Services NHS Trust

Ms Christine Sealey
Centre Manager, The National Collaborating Centre for Mental Health (2008 to 2009)

Ms Jacqueline Sin
Education and Practice Lead in Psychosocial Interventions, Berkshire Healthcare NHS Foundation Trust and Thames Valley University

Ms Sarah Stockton
Senior Information Scientist, The National Collaborating Centre for Mental Health

Dr Geraldine Strathdee
Trust Director of Clinical Services, Oxleas NHS Foundation Trust

Guideline development group members

Dr Clare Taylor
Editor, The National Collaborating Centre for Mental Health

Dr Clive Travis
Service user representative

Professor Douglas Turkington
Professor of Psychosocial Psychiatry, Newcastle University
Consultant Psychiatrist, Northumberland, Tyne and Wear NHS Trust

Dr Craig Whittington
Senior Systematic Reviewer, The National Collaborating Centre for Mental Health

Mr Peter Woodhams
Carer representative

ACKNOWLEDGEMENTS

The Schizophrenia Update Guideline Development Group (GDG) and the National Collaborating Centre for Mental Health (NCCMH) review team would like to thank the following people:

Those who acted as advisers on specialist topics or have contributed to the process by meeting with the Guideline Development Group:

Professor Tony Ades, University of Bristol
Dr Micol Ascoli, East London and The City Mental Health NHS Trust
Dr Patricia d'Ardenne, East London Foundation NHS Trust
Mr Peter Blackman, The Afiya Trust
Mr Gwynne Jones, General Social Care Council
Dr David Ndegwa, South London and Maudsley NHS Trust
Dr Clare Reeder, King's College London
Dr Nicky J. Welton, University of Bristol
Professor Til Wykes, King's College London

Those who have experiences of schizophrenia who contributed personal accounts that have been included in this guideline.

Technical assistance
Mr Simos Mavranezoulis

Editorial assistance
Ms Nuala Ernest

1   PREFACE

This guideline was first published as the NICE guideline in December 2002 and the full guideline in 2003 (NCCMH, 2003) (referred to as the 'previous guideline'). The present guideline (referred to as the 'update') updates most areas of the previous guideline, except some service-level interventions and the use of rapid tranquillisation. There are also two new chapters on service user and carer experience of schizophrenia (Chapter 4), and access and engagement for minority ethnic groups and people developing psychosis for the first time (Chapter 5). Recommendations categorised as 'good practice points' in the previous guideline were reviewed for their current relevance (including issues around consent and advance directives). Further details of what has been updated and what has been left unchanged can be found at the beginning of each evidence chapter. The scope for the update also included updating the National Institute for Health and Clinical Excellence (NICE) technology appraisal (TA43) on the use of newer (atypical) antipsychotics (NICE, 2002)[1]. See Appendix 1 for more details on the scope of this update. Sections of the guideline where the evidence has *not* been updated are marked by asterisks (**_**).

The previous guideline and this update have been developed to advise on the treatment and management of schizophrenia. The guideline recommendations have been developed by a multidisciplinary team of healthcare professionals, service users, a carer and guideline methodologists after careful consideration of the best available evidence. It is intended that the guideline will be useful to clinicians and service commissioners in providing and planning high-quality care for people with schizophrenia while also emphasising the importance of the experience of care for them and their carers.

Although the evidence base is rapidly expanding, there are a number of major gaps, and further revisions of this guideline will incorporate new scientific evidence as it develops. The guideline makes a number of research recommendations specifically to address gaps in the evidence base. In the meantime, it is hoped that the guideline will assist clinicians, people with schizophrenia and their carers by identifying the merits of particular treatment approaches where the evidence from research and clinical experience exists.

1.1   NATIONAL GUIDELINE

1.1.1   What are clinical practice guidelines?

Clinical practice guidelines are 'systematically developed statements that assist clinicians and patients in making decisions about appropriate treatment for specific

---

[1]Recommendations from TA43 were incorporated into the previous schizophrenia guideline according to NICE protocol.

conditions' (Mann, 1996). They are derived from the best available research evidence, using predetermined and systematic methods to identify and evaluate the evidence relating to the specific condition in question. Where evidence is lacking, the guidelines incorporate statements and recommendations based upon the consensus statements developed by GDG.

Clinical guidelines are intended to improve the process and outcomes of healthcare in a number of different ways. They can:

- provide up-to-date evidence-based recommendations for the management of conditions and disorders by healthcare professionals
- be used as the basis to set standards to assess the practice of healthcare professionals
- form the basis for education and training of healthcare professionals
- assist service users and their carers in making informed decisions about their treatment and care
- improve communication between healthcare professionals, service users and their carers
- help identify priority areas for further research.

1.1.2   Uses and limitations of clinical guidelines

Guidelines are not a substitute for professional knowledge and clinical judgement. They can be limited in their usefulness and applicability by a number of different factors: the availability of high-quality research evidence, the quality of the methodology used in the development of the guideline, the generalisability of research findings and the uniqueness of individuals with schizophrenia.

Although the quality of research in this field is variable, the methodology used here reflects current international understanding on the appropriate practice for guideline development (AGREE Collaboration, 2003 [Appraisal of Guidelines for Research and Evaluation Instrument]; www.agreecollaboration.org), ensuring the collection and selection of the best research evidence available and the systematic generation of treatment recommendations applicable to the majority of people with these disorders and situations. However, there will always be some people and situations where clinical guideline recommendations are not readily applicable. This guideline does not, therefore, override the individual responsibility of healthcare professionals to make appropriate decisions in the circumstances of the individual, in consultation with the person with schizophrenia or their carer.

In addition to the clinical evidence, cost-effectiveness information, where available, is taken into account in the generation of statements and recommendations in clinical guidelines. While national guidelines are concerned with clinical and cost effectiveness, issues of affordability and implementation costs are to be determined by the National Health Service (NHS).

In using guidelines, it is important to remember that the absence of empirical evidence for the effectiveness of a particular intervention is not the same as evidence for ineffectiveness. In addition, and of particular relevance to mental health, evidence-based treatments are often delivered within the context of an overall treatment programme including a range of activities, the purpose of which may be to help engage the person and to provide an appropriate context for the delivery of specific interventions. It is important to maintain and enhance the service context in which these interventions are delivered, otherwise the specific benefits of effective interventions will be lost. Indeed, the importance of organising care to support and encourage a good therapeutic relationship is at times as important as the specific treatments offered.

1.1.3   Why develop national guidelines?

NICE was established as a Special Health Authority for England and Wales in 1999, with a remit to provide a single source of authoritative and reliable guidance for patients, professionals and the public. NICE guidance aims to improve standards of care, to diminish unacceptable variations in the provision and quality of care across the NHS and to ensure that the health service is patient centred. All guidance is developed in a transparent and collaborative manner using the best available evidence and involving all relevant stakeholders.

NICE generates guidance in a number of different ways, three of which are relevant here. First, national guidance is produced by the Technology Appraisal Committee to give robust advice about a particular treatment, intervention, procedure or other health technology. Second, NICE commissions public health intervention guidance focused on types of activity (interventions) that help to reduce people's risk of developing a disease or condition or help to promote or maintain a healthy lifestyle. Third, NICE commissions the production of national clinical practice guidelines focused upon the overall treatment and management of a specific condition. To enable this latter development, NICE originally established seven National Collaborating Centres (NCCs) in conjunction with a range of professional organisations involved in healthcare.

1.1.4   The National Collaborating Centre for Mental Health

This guideline has been commissioned by NICE and developed within the National Collaborating Centre for Mental Health (NCCMH). The NCCMH is a collaboration of the professional organisations involved in the field of mental health, national patient and carer organisations, a number of academic institutions and NICE. The NCCMH is funded by NICE and is led by a partnership between the Royal College of Psychiatrists' Research Unit and the British Psychological Society's equivalent unit (Centre for Outcomes Research and Effectiveness).

1.1.5   From national guidelines to local protocols

Once a national guideline has been published and disseminated, local healthcare groups will be expected to produce a plan and identify resources for implementation, along with appropriate timetables. Subsequently, a multidisciplinary group involving commissioners of healthcare, primary care and specialist mental health professionals, service users and carers should undertake the translation of the implementation plan into local protocols taking into account both the recommendations set out in this guideline and the priorities set in the National Service Framework (NSF) for Mental Health (Department of Health, 1999) and related documentation. The nature and pace of the local plan will reflect local healthcare needs and the nature of existing services; full implementation may take considerable time, especially where substantial training needs are identified.

1.1.6   Auditing the implementation of guidelines

This guideline identifies key areas of clinical practice and service delivery for local and national audit. Although the generation of audit standards is an important and necessary step in the implementation of this guidance, a more broadly based implementation strategy will be developed. Nevertheless, it should be noted that the Care Quality Commission will monitor the extent to which Primary Care Trusts, trusts responsible for mental health and social care, and Health Authorities have implemented these guidelines.

1.2   THE NATIONAL SCHIZOPHRENIA GUIDELINE

1.2.1   Who has developed this guideline?

The GDG was convened by the NCCMH and supported by funding from NICE. The GDG included two service users and a carer, and professionals from psychiatry, clinical psychology, general practice, nursing and psychiatric pharmacy.

Staff from the NCCMH provided leadership and support throughout the process of guideline development, undertaking systematic searches, information retrieval, appraisal and systematic review of the evidence. Members of the GDG received training in the process of guideline development from NCCMH staff, and the service users and carer received training and support from the NICE Patient and Public Involvement Programme. The NICE Guidelines Technical Adviser provided advice and assistance regarding aspects of the guideline development process.

All GDG members made formal declarations of interest at the outset, which were updated at every GDG meeting. The GDG met a total of 14 times throughout the process of guideline development. It met as a whole, but key topics were led by a national expert in the relevant topic. The GDG was supported by the NCCMH technical team, with additional expert advice from special advisers where needed. The group oversaw the production and synthesis of research evidence before presentation. All statements and recommendations in this guideline have been generated and agreed by the whole GDG.

1.2.2   For whom is this guideline intended?

This guideline is relevant for adults with schizophrenia and covers the care provided by primary, community, secondary, tertiary and other healthcare professionals who have direct contact with, and make decisions concerning the care of, adults with schizophrenia.

The guideline will also be relevant to the work, but will not cover the practice, of those in:

● occupational health services
● social services
● forensic services
● the independent sector.

The experience of schizophrenia can affect the whole family and often the community. The guideline recognises the role of both in the treatment and support of people with schizophrenia.

1.2.3   Specific aims of this guideline

The guideline makes recommendations for the treatment and management of schizophrenia. It aims to:

● improve access and engagement with treatment and services for people with schizophrenia
● evaluate the role of specific psychological and psychosocial interventions in the treatment of schizophrenia
● evaluate the role of specific pharmacological interventions in the treatment of schizophrenia
● evaluate the role of specific service-level interventions for people with schizophrenia
● integrate the above to provide best-practice advice on the care of people with schizophrenia and their family and carers
● promote the implementation of best clinical practice through the development of recommendations tailored to the requirements of the NHS in England and Wales.

1.2.4   The structure of this guideline

The guideline is divided into chapters, each covering a set of related topics. The first three chapters provide an introduction to guidelines, the topic of schizophrenia and to the methods used to update this guideline. Chapters 5–9 provide the evidence that underpins the recommendations about the treatment and management of schizophrenia, with Chapter 4 providing personal accounts from service users and carers, which offer an insight into their experience of schizophrenia.

Each evidence chapter begins with a general introduction to the topic that sets the recommendations in context. Depending on the nature of the evidence, narrative reviews or meta-analyses were conducted, and the structure of the chapters varies accordingly. Where appropriate, details about current practice, the evidence base and any research limitations are provided. Where meta-analyses were conducted, information is given about the review protocol and studies included in the review. Clinical evidence summaries are then used to summarise the data presented (with forest plots and/or data tables in Appendix 16). Health economic evidence is then presented (where appropriate), followed by a section ('from evidence to recommendations') that draws together the clinical and health economic evidence and provides a rationale for the recommendations[2]. On the CD-ROM, further details are provided about included/excluded studies, the evidence and the previous guideline methodology (see Table 1 for details).

Table 1: Appendices on CD-ROM

Evidence tables for economic studies	Appendix 14
Study characteristics tables	Appendix 15
Clinical evidence forest plots and/or data tables	Appendix 16
Previous guideline methodology	Appendix 17

---

[2]Because of the nature of pharmacological evidence, the 'from evidence to recommendations' section and the recommendations can be found at the end of the chapter (rather than after each topic reviewed).

2   SCHIZOPHRENIA

This guideline is concerned with the treatment and management of what is called schizophrenia, and its related disorders. Although the precise terminology used for these disorders has been debated over the years, this updated guideline relates specifically to those identified by the tenth edition of the International Statistical Classification of Diseases and Related Health Problems (ICD–10; World Health Organization [WHO], 1992). These disorders are schizophrenia, schizoaffective disorder, schizophreniform disorder and delusional disorder. This updated guideline does not address the management of other psychotic disorders, such as bipolar disorder, mania or depressive psychosis, because they are covered by other guidelines.

2.1   THE DISORDER

2.1.1   Symptoms, presentation and patterns

Schizophrenia is one of the terms used to describe a major psychiatric disorder (or cluster of disorders) that alters an individual's perception, thoughts, affect and behaviour. Individuals who develop schizophrenia will each have their own unique combination of symptoms and experiences, the precise pattern of which will be influenced by their particular circumstances.

Typically, the problems of schizophrenia are preceded by a 'prodromal' period. This is often characterised by some deterioration in personal functioning. Difficulties may include memory and concentration problems, social withdrawal, unusual and uncharacteristic behaviour, disturbed communication and affect, bizarre ideas and perceptual experiences, poor personal hygiene, and reduced interest in and motivation for day-to-day activities. During this prodromal period, people with schizophrenia often feel that their world has changed, but their interpretation of this change may not be shared by others. Relatives and friends frequently report that the person with schizophrenia has changed 'in themselves'. These changes may well affect the person's ability to hold down a job, study, or relate to family and friends.

The prodromal period is typically followed by an acute phase marked by characteristic positive symptoms of hallucinations, delusions, and behavioural disturbances, such as agitation and distress. Following resolution of the acute phase, usually because of some treatment, positive symptoms diminish or disappear for many people, sometimes leaving a number of negative symptoms not unlike the early prodromal period. This third phase, which may last many years, is often interrupted by acute exacerbations or 'relapses', which may need additional interventions.

Although this is a common pattern, the course of schizophrenia varies considerably. For example, although some people may experience disturbing symptoms only briefly, others may live with them for months or years. A number of individuals experience no prodromal period, the disorder beginning with a sudden and often frightening acute episode. After an initial episode, between 14 and 20% of individuals will recover fully. Others will improve but have recurrences (see Section 2.1.3). Recurrence can be affected by stress, social adversity and isolation. In the longer term (up to 15 years), over half of those with these diagnoses will have episodic rather than continuous difficulties. As Harrow and colleagues (2005) have observed, 'some of these intervals of recovery will appear spontaneously and may be tied to individual patient factors, such as resilience'.

There is debate about the presentation of different symptoms and the prominence of affective symptoms among those diagnosed with schizophrenia from diverse cultural or ethnic backgrounds, and also over comorbidities and their prevalence across cultural and ethnic groups. There are few recent studies of such issues among populations in the UK, reflecting not only a serious omission but also that there may be reasons why people from specific ethnic backgrounds or socially excluded groups do not engage or benefit as much from services and treatments.

2.1.2   Impairment and disability

Although the problems and experiences associated with schizophrenia are often distressing, the effects of the disorder can be pervasive. A significant number of people continue to experience long-term impairments, and as a result schizophrenia can have a considerable effect on people's personal, social and occupational lives. A European study of six countries found that over 80% of adults with this diagnosis had some persistent problems with social functioning, though not all of them were severe. The best predictor of poorer functioning in the long term was poor functioning in the first 3 years post-diagnosis (Wiersma *et al.*, 2000). Thornicroft and colleagues (2004) found that 80% remained unemployed.

The disabilities experienced by people with schizophrenia are not solely the result of recurrent episodes or continuing symptoms. Unpleasant side effects of treatment, social adversity and isolation, poverty and homelessness also play a part. These difficulties are not made any easier by the continuing prejudice, stigma and social exclusion associated with the diagnosis (Sartorius, 2002; Thornicroft, 2006).

Worldwide, it has been estimated that schizophrenia falls into the top ten medical disorders causing disability (WHO, 1990). Mortality among people with schizophrenia is approximately 50% above that of the general population, partly as a result of an increased incidence of suicide (about 10% die by suicide) and violent death, and partly as a result of an increased risk of a wide range of physical health problems. These include those illnesses associated with cigarette smoking, obesity and diabetes, as recent research has shown. The precise extent to which this excess mortality and high rates of disability are, at least in part, a result of some of the medications given for schizophrenia is still not clear. Difficulties experienced by mental health service users in accessing general medical services in both primary and secondary care continue to contribute to reduced life expectancy. Recent work indicates that young Caribbean and African men, and middle-aged women from diverse ethnic or cultural backgrounds, are at higher risk of suicide, and that this may be because of differences in symptom presentation and conventional risk-factor profiles across ethnic groups (Bhui & McKenzie, 2008).

2.1.3   Prognosis, course and recovery

Historically, many psychiatrists and other healthcare professionals have taken a pessimistic view of the prognosis for schizophrenia, regarding it as a severe, intractable and often deteriorating lifelong illness. This negative view has failed to find confirmation from long-term follow-up studies, which have demonstrated considerable variations in long-term outcome. While it is estimated that around three quarters of people with schizophrenia will experience recurrent relapse and some continued disability (Nadeem *et al.*, 2004), the findings of follow-up studies over periods of 20 to 40 years suggest that there is a moderately good long-term global outcome in over half of people with schizophrenia, with a smaller proportion having extended periods of remission of symptoms without further relapses (Gaebel & Fromman, 2000; Harrison *et al.*, 2001; Jobe & Harrow, 2005). It should also be noted that some people who never experience complete recovery from their experiences nonetheless manage to sustain an acceptable quality of life if given adequate support and help.

The early stages of schizophrenia are often characterised by repeated exacerbation of symptoms such as hallucinations and delusions and disturbed behaviour. While a high proportion respond to initial treatment with antipsychotic medication, around 80% will relapse within 5 years of a treated first episode, which is partly explained by discontinuation of medication (Nadeem *et al.*, 2004; Robinson *et al.*, 1999a, 2002). There is some evidence that early involvement in a progressive therapeutic programme incorporating social and psychological interventions as well as medication might be an important factor in realising long-term gains (de Haan *et al.*, 2003; Harrison *et al.*, 2001; Linszen *et al.*, 2001). Research has also suggested that delayed access to mental health services in early schizophrenia – often referred to as the duration of untreated psychosis – is associated with slower or less complete recovery, and increased risk of relapse and poorer outcome in subsequent years (Bottlender *et al.*, 2003; Harrigan *et al.*, 2003). In the longer term, the factors that influence the differential recovery from schizophrenia are not well known. But recovery may happen at any time, even after many years (Harrison *et al.*, 2001).

A number of social and economic factors also appear to affect the course of schizophrenia. For example, in developed countries it is well established that schizophrenia is more common in lower socioeconomic groups. However, this appears to be partly reversed in some developing countries (Jablensky *et al.*, 1992), suggesting that the relationship between incidence, recovery rates, and cultural and economic factors is more complex than a simple correspondence with socioeconomic deprivation (Warner, 1994).

The risk factors for developing schizophrenia and the acceptability of interventions and the uptake of treatments have been shown to vary across ethnic groups. Although the focus in the UK has been on African and Caribbean populations, early evidence suggests other ethnic groups and migrants in general may be at risk; social risk factors may be expressed through an ethnic group, rather than being an intrinsic risk for that ethnic groups *per se*. However, the different pattern of service use, access to services and perceived benefits across ethnic groups is a cause of concern among service users.

The effects of schizophrenia on a person's life experience and opportunities are considerable; service users and carers need help and support to deal with their future and to cope with any changes that may happen.

2.1.4 Diagnosis

A full and proper discussion of the diagnosis and classification of schizophrenia is outside the scope of this updated guideline, although they are important issues in research and in clinical practice, and the impact of receiving a diagnosis of schizophrenia can have considerable social and personal consequences for the individual.

The wide variation in presentation, course and outcome in schizophrenia may reflect an underlying variation in the nature of the disorder, or even that schizophrenia is a cluster of different disorders with variable courses and outcomes (Gelder *et al.*, 1997). Equally, this variation may result from a complex interaction between biological, social, psychological, cultural and economic factors. Several models to explain this heterogeneity have been proposed, although none has been widely accepted. Moreover, prior to the establishment of diagnostic systems, such as the Diagnostic and Statistical Manual of Mental Disorders (DSM; American Psychiatric Association [APA], 1994) and the ICD (WHO, 1992), large variations in the incidence and prevalence of the disorder were reported. While DSM, ICD and similar systems have improved the reliability and consistency of diagnosis, considerable controversy exists as to whether a diagnosis of schizophrenia really represents a single underlying disorder.

Both ICD-10 and DSM-IV agree on the symptom clusters that confirm a diagnosis of schizophrenia. There are three main domains, including: psychotic symptoms, such as certain types of auditory hallucinations (hearing voices), delusions ('paranoia' and 'telepathy') and thought disorder (incomprehensible speech); negative symptoms, such as poor self-care, reduced motivation, reduced ability to experience pleasure, alogia (reduced production of thought), affective blunting (lack of emotional expression) and reduced social functioning; and the rarer symptom of catatonia. ICD-10 requires that at least one such diagnostic symptom from one of the three domains should be clearly present for 1 month. ICD-10 also confirms the diagnosis if two of these symptoms have been present in a less clear manner over the same time frame. The diagnosis is not made in the presence of prominent mood symptoms, such as depression or mania. In DSM-IV there is agreement with ICD-10 that diagnostic symptoms need to be present for at least 1 month. It also stipulates that there should be evidence of ongoing symptoms persisting for at least 6 months.

The uncertainty about diagnosis, and consequently its limited predictive validity, raises a number of important issues for service users. First, many clinicians in both primary and secondary care are reluctant to give this diagnosis, sometimes making it more difficult for people and their families to receive help early on. Second, some service users are reluctant to accept the diagnosis, and may reject suggestions that schizophrenia is an illness in need of treatment. Third, to receive a diagnosis of schizophrenia, with the stigma that this entails, seems to some a heavy price to pay given the diagnostic uncertainties that exist. Finally, some people diagnosed with schizophrenia object to receiving compulsory treatment for what they regard as no more than a putative illness.

That there are genuine problems with the diagnosis and classification of schizophrenia is not at question. However, for many people diagnosed with schizophrenia, the frequently painful and frightening experiences, and the disability often associated occur with or without the diagnosis. Moreover, to improve treatments and services for this group of people would be difficult without an operational diagnostic category with which to undertake research and the allocation of resources on the basis of proven need. Despite this practical requirement for diagnostic categories, caution is necessary to avoid making overly simplistic prognostications for individual service users. Professionals also have a duty to provide good, clear and honest information regarding schizophrenia, and about the treatments and services available.

2.1.5 Physical healthcare

The association between schizophrenia and poor physical health is well established (Marder & Wirshing, 2003). Poor health results in higher standardised mortality rates and increased morbidity for individuals with schizophrenia (Saha *et al.*, 2008). It is apparent from epidemiological work that this excess morbidity and mortality is the result of a range of physical disorders, and not simply because of the effects of long-term antipsychotic medication or other factors, such as substance misuse, which are also associated with schizophrenia.

Reports on the mortality of people with schizophrenia indicate that there is an increased risk of death from circulatory conditions, infections and endocrine disorders. Despite high reported rates of smoking in people with schizophrenia, rates of lung cancer do not appear to be raised (Gulbinat *et al.*, 1992; Harris & Barraclough, 1998; Jeste *et al.*, 1996; Osborn *et al.*, 2007b). People with schizophrenia have higher rates of cardiovascular disease, including myocardial infarction, than the general population (Hennekens *et al.*, 2005; Lawrence *et al.*, 2003; Osborn *et al.*, 2007b).

Patients with schizophrenia are more likely than the general population to have lifestyle risk factors for cardiovascular disease and mortality (de Leon & Diaz, 2005; McCreadie *et al.*, 2003; Osborn *et al.*, 2006). They were found to be more likely to smoke even when the study population was controlled for socioeconomic status (Brown *et al.*, 1999; Osborn *et al.*, 2006). It has been suggested that high smoking rates in people with schizophrenia can be explained by the therapeutic effect of nicotine on psychotic symptoms and the reduction in side effects of antipsychotic medication because of the enhanced metabolism of antipsychotic drugs in smokers (Jeste *et al.*, 1996). People with schizophrenia are also less likely to exercise and are more likely to have diets higher in fat and lower in fibre than the general population (Brown *et al.*, 1999; Osborn *et al.*, 2007a). People with schizophrenia are at increased risk of weight gain and this can be partly attributed to some of the newer antipsychotic drugs having a greater propensity to cause weight gain (American Diabetes Association *et al.*, 2004; Nasrallah, 2003, 2008). Recent evidence from a systematic review of trials on non-pharmacological treatments including individual or group interventions, cognitive behavioural therapy (CBT) and nutritional counselling indicated that these treatments were effective in reducing or attenuating antipsychotic-induced weight gain compared with treatment as usual (Álvarez-Jiménez *et al.*, 2008).

Antipsychotic medication may induce endocrine abnormalities (for example, diabetes and galactorrhoea), neurological disorders (for example, tardive dyskinesia), metabolic abnormalities (for example, lipid abnormalities and weight gain) and cardiovascular side effects (for example, lengthening of the QT interval on electro-cardiography) (American Diabetes Association *et al.*, 2004; Dinan, 2004; Holt *et al.*, 2005; Koro *et al.*, 2002; Lieberman *et al.*, 2005; Lindenmayer *et al.*, 2003; Nasrallah, 2003, 2008; Saari *et al.*, 2004; Thakore, 2005).

The fact that this excess mortality and morbidity has a range of causes – including dietary and behavioural ones – suggests that lifestyle factors have a significant part to play. It could be that some of the problems associated with the development of schizophrenia impair or otherwise affect people's ability to manage their own physical health effectively. It is also likely that socioeconomic factors, including social exclusion, have a significant role to play. Nevertheless, there is also convincing evidence that psychiatrists and general practitioners (GPs) are poor at recognising and treating physical conditions, such as cardiovascular disorders in psychiatric patients (for a review see Osborn, 2001). A direct comparison of cardiovascular screening (that is, blood pressure, lipid levels and smoking status) of people with asthma, people with schizophrenia and other attendees indicated that GPs were less likely to screen people with schizophrenia for cardiovascular risk compared with the other two groups (Roberts *et al.*, 2007).

The development of case registers and specific remuneration of GPs for the monitoring of physical health problems for those with mental disorders, are contained within the new General Medical Services contract (Department of Health, 2003b), and has encouraged focus on these issues. The contract certainly provides opportunity for increased cooperation across the primary/secondary care interface, but as yet, the evidence for such interventions remains uncertain. Some early findings suggest that quite simple interventions might have some impact on the lifestyle factors associated with increased morbidity, for example group interventions for smoking cessation (Addington *et al.*, 1998). There is also evidence to suggest that people with schizophrenia are just as likely as others to attend their GP for cardiovascular screening as others without this diagnosis (Osborn *et al.*, 2003). Given this, careful consideration should be given to the role of GPs in the management of physical health problems. This is discussed further in Chapter 9 (Section 9.2).

2.2 INCIDENCE AND PREVALENCE

Schizophrenia is a relatively common illness and it is certainly the most common form of psychotic disorder. The mean incidence of schizophrenia reported in epidemiological studies, when the diagnosis is limited to core criteria and corrected for age, is 0.11 per 1000 (range 0.07–0.17 per 1000); if broader criteria are used, this figure doubles to 0.24 per 1000 (range 0.07–0.52 per 1000) (Jablensky *et al.*, 1992). Average rates for men and women are similar, although the mean age of onset is about 5 years greater in women (hence a lower female rate in adolescence), with a second smaller peak after the menopause. The lifetime prevalence of schizophrenia is between 0.4 and 1.4% (Cannon & Jones, 1996). The National Survey of Psychiatric Morbidity in the UK found a population prevalence of probable psychotic disorder of 5 per 1000 in the age group 16 to 74 years (Singleton *et al.*, 2000).

2.3 POSSIBLE CAUSES OF SCHIZOPHRENIA

The possible causes of schizophrenia are not well understood. Research has attempted to determine the causal role of biological, psychological and social factors. The evidence does not point to any single cause. Increasingly, it is thought that schizophrenia and related psychoses result instead from a complex interaction of multiple factors (Broome *et al.*, 2005; Garety *et al.*, 2007). Much of the research evidence on the aetiology of schizophrenia is consistent with the long-standing 'vulnerability-stress' model (Nuechterlein & Dawson, 1984). This paradigm suggests that individuals possess different levels of vulnerability to schizophrenia, which are determined by a combination of biological, social and psychological factors. It is proposed that vulnerability results in the development of problems only when environmental stressors are present. If there is great vulnerability, relatively low levels of stress might be sufficient to cause problems. If there is less vulnerability, problems develop only with higher levels of stress. The model is consistent with a wide variety of putative causes of the disorder, as well as the differential relapse and readmission rates observed among people with schizophrenia.

Recent research has therefore attempted to specify more precisely the nature of any vulnerability and of types of environmental stress. This includes biological hypotheses about brain biochemistry and pathology (Broome *et al.*, 2005), and attempts to identify genes that confer susceptibility (Craddock *et al.*, 2005). Biochemical theories have centred mainly on the 'dopamine hypothesis', for which there is enduring support (Kapur, 2003). This argues that schizophrenia might be related to problems in the regulation of the neurotransmitter dopamine in the prefrontal cortex.

Psychological factors can be divided into problems with basic cognitive functions, such as learning, attention, memory or planning, and biases in emotional and reasoning processes. Problems in cognitive function are related to research in brain structure and function, while emotional processes may be linked to social factors. Studies of psychological factors thus provide a bridge between biological and social theories.

Both types of psychological factor have been implicated in the development of symptoms of schizophrenia (Frith, 1992; Garety *et al.*, 2001, 2007; Gray *et al.*, 1991; Green, 1992; Hemsley 1993). Recently depression and anxiety, which were previously considered unimportant by researchers, have been found to contribute to the symptoms of schizophrenia (Birchwood, 2003; Freeman & Garety, 2003; Krabbendam & van Os, 2005).

Recently there has been a resurgence of interest in investigating social and environmental factors. Evidence has been accumulating to suggest that urban birth and rearing, social adversity and trauma, heavy cannabis use, migration and stressful life events all increase the risk of schizophrenia (Arseneault *et al.*, 2004; Bebbington *et al.*, 2004; Moore *et al.*, 2007; Read *et al.*, 2005; van Os *et al.*, 2005). There is now consistent evidence that migrant populations experience raised rates and especially high rates have been found among certain minority ethnic groups (Cantor-Graae & Selten, 2005; Kirkbride *et al.*, 2006). It is thought that this is most likely related to the high rates of social adversity and family disruption experienced by some migrant populations (Selten & Cantor-Graae, 2005; Fearon *et al.*, 2006).

2.4   ASSESSMENT

Mental health assessments are conducted for a number of reasons: to reach a diagnosis, to develop a psychological formulation and identify strengths and needs, for screening purposes (including the detection of risk) and to measure outcomes. This guideline can only be implemented following a comprehensive biopsychosocial assessment. The assessment should provide an understanding of the presenting problems of the service user within the context of their life, both past and present, and should facilitate the development of a care plan that addresses a broad range of client needs beyond symptom reduction.

When comorbid conditions are identified, including substance misuse or physical illness, or if there is a forensic history, treatment and care plans that deal with these wider concerns will need to be developed, although these are outside the scope of this guideline.

Given the uncertainties surrounding the diagnosis of schizophrenia (see Section 2.1.4), it is important that following a full needs assessment, a comprehensive care plan is implemented whenever this diagnosis is suspected. Where a diagnosis has been reached, it should be fully explained and discussed with the service user (and with the carer where appropriate). The service user (and carer) may ask for a second opinion as many people are distressed about receiving the diagnosis and its potential implications.

2.5   ENGAGEMENT, CONSENT AND THERAPEUTIC ALLIANCE

People with schizophrenia and its related disorders may be intensely distressed, especially during acute phases. This can manifest as fear, agitation, suspicion or anger. The development of a constructive therapeutic relationship is crucial to assessing accurately the nature of a person's problems and provides the foundation of any subsequent plan of management. Managing the process of engagement requires professionals to have sensitivity to the perspective of the individual and to understand that the condition can have a profound effect on the person's judgment, their capacity to understand their situation and their capacity to consent to specific interventions.

The process of engaging successfully with individuals with schizophrenia may at times require considerable persistence and flexibility from professionals. Establishment of trust is crucial and reliability and constancy on the part of professionals is an important component of this. The individual with schizophrenia may not share the professionals' view of what the main problem is. Seeking out and assisting with what the individual regards as the main problem can provide a route towards 'common ground'. This common ground can establish trust and collaboration, allowing further collaborative care planning over time.

All approaches must, of course, take place within a framework that acknowledges appropriate risk assessment. At times, individuals with schizophrenia may present sufficient risk to themselves or others to justify detention under the Mental Health Act (HMSO, 2007). Although the Mental Health Act will extend the powers of compulsory treatment, it is essential that any individual detained under the Act continues to be engaged as far as possible in a collaborative approach to their difficulties. Again, the constant seeking out of common ground and common objectives from consistent, reliable professionals is a vital part of this process. Individuals subject to the provisions of the Mental Health Act should be entitled to the highest quality of care from the most experienced and trained staff, including consultant psychiatrists.

Both the short- and long-term engagement of the individual is the foundation stone of any specific intervention including pharmacological interventions, psychosocial interventions and interventions aimed at addressing physical health. Favourably altering the medium- to long-term prognosis of the condition requires the development of broad-based, acceptable care plans developed in cooperation with the individual and, frequently, their relatives and carers. Continuity of care from professionals capable of communicating warmth, concern and empathy is important, and frequent changes of key personnel threaten to undermine this process. At the same time, having services available at short notice is at times important to ensure that urgent assessments can be provided in a timely and appropriate fashion. The NHS Plan (Department of Health, 2000) instituted the development of separate teams, such as crisis and home treatment teams, to try to address this. While such teams can offer a responsive service, they can at times struggle to maintain continuity of care. Other service changes have seen the development in some areas of separate teams for inpatients and community-based individuals. These service changes present further potential seams and discontinuities, which need to be actively managed to ensure adequate continuity of care. Assertive outreach teams and early intervention services, with their small caseloads and team-based approaches based around the individual, are well placed to manage this continuity, especially if the consultant psychiatrist to the team remains involved in any inpatient or crisis care.

Carers, relatives and friends of individuals with schizophrenia are important both in the process of assessment and engagement, and in the long-term successful delivery of effective interventions. Their views and needs must be acknowledged and should not be minimised or ignored.

Effective communication of care plans that follow a clear structure, are written in understandable language and preferably typed, provides a crucial contribution to the successful delivery of management strategies. This is particularly so in respect of providing clear guidance for emergency contacts and an outline of risks with associated contingency planning. This process should be managed in secondary services through the Care Programme Approach (CPA). Increasingly, the voluntary sector is providing a strong role in delivery and it is important that there is close working between these providers and the NHS services and that specific roles are clearly identified within care plans.

Issues of consent remain important throughout the care pathway. Professionals must be fully aware of all appropriate legislation, particularly the Mental Health Act (HMSO, 2007) and the Mental Capacity Act (HMSO, 2005). All reasonable steps need to be taken to engage individuals in meaningful discussion about issues relating to consent, and discussion with individuals should include specific work around relapse signatures, crisis plans, advance statements and advance decisions. The above statutory framework does provide for individuals with schizophrenia to make a contemporaneous decision to refuse treatment, though this could potentially be overruled by detention under the Mental Health Act.

2.6   LANGUAGE AND STIGMA

Although treatment for schizophrenia has improved since the 1950s and 1960s, some people with this diagnosis still encounter difficulties finding employment and may feel excluded from society. In an editorial for the *British Medical Journal*, Norman Sartorius claimed that 'stigma remains the main obstacle to a better life for the many hundreds of millions of people suffering from mental disorders' (Sartorius, 2002). In part because of media coverage of events associated with schizophrenia, people with the condition live with the stigma of an illness often seen as dangerous and best dealt with away from the rest of society. In this regard, research has shown that while the number of psychiatrically unrelated homicides rose between 1957 and 1995, homicides by people sent for psychiatric treatment did not, suggesting that the public fear of violence arising from people with schizophrenia is misplaced (Taylor & Gunn, 1999).

Those with schizophrenia may also feel stigmatised because of mental health legislation, including compulsory treatment in the community, which may exacerbate their feelings of exclusion. The side effects of the medication, such as hypersalivation, involuntary movements, sedation and severe weight gain, and the less than careful use of diagnostic labels, can all contribute to singling out people with schizophrenia, marking them as different. In addition, people with this condition may find that any physical health problems they have are not taken as seriously by healthcare professionals.

In the view of many service users, clinical language is not always used in a helpful way, and may contribute to the stigma of schizophrenia. For example, calling someone a 'schizophrenic' or a 'psychotic' gives the impression that the person has been wholly taken over by an illness, such that no recognisable or civilised person remains. Many non-psychiatric health workers and many employers continue to approach people with schizophrenia in this way. There is a move away from using the word 'schizophrenia' for people with psychotic symptoms because the label is so unhelpful, especially in the early intervention services.

It is important that professionals are careful and considerate, but also clear and thorough in their use of clinical language and in the explanations they provide, not only to service users and carers but also to other healthcare professionals. Services should also ensure that all clinicians are skilled in working with people from diverse linguistic and ethnic backgrounds, and have a process by which they can assess cultural influences and address cumulative inequalities through their routine clinical practice (Bhui *et al.*, 2007). Addressing organisational aspects of cultural competence and capability is necessary alongside individual practice improvements.

Parents of people with schizophrenia often feel to blame, either because they have 'passed on the genes' causing schizophrenia, or because they are 'bad parents'. However, the families of people with schizophrenia often play an essential part in the treatment and care of their relative, and with the right support and help can positively contribute to promoting recovery. The caring role can come at a high cost of depression and strain, and services need to remain sensitive to the separate needs of carers (see Section 2.7).

2.7   ISSUES FOR FAMILIES AND CARERS

Carers, relatives and friends of people with schizophrenia are important both in the process of assessment and engagement in treatment and, in the long-term, successful delivery of effective interventions for people with schizophrenia. This guideline uses the term 'carer' to apply to all people who have regular close contact with the person, including advocates, friends or family members, although some family members may choose not to be carers.

As is explored in Chapter 4, carers have needs both in terms of providing support to the person with schizophrenia and requiring support for themselves. In their caring role, families and carers need detailed information about schizophrenia and many seek to be involved in some way in the person's treatment and care, if the person consents. (The Royal College of Psychiatrists' Partners in Care document on confidentiality contains useful guidance on the sharing of information; available from http://www.rcpsych.ac.uk/PDF/Carersandconfidentiality.pdf). But families and carers also need support for themselves, because they may be emotionally and psychologically affected by caring for someone with schizophrenia; they may be fearful, distressed and isolated, and these feelings can have a significant impact on their quality of life. As some personal accounts in Chapter 4 suggest, carers can feel neglected by health and social care services in terms of their own health and support needs and become frustrated by the lack of opportunities to contribute to the development of the care plan for the person for whom they care.

2.8   TREATMENT AND MANAGEMENT OF SCHIZOPHRENIA IN THE NHS

Until the 1950s, the treatment and management of schizophrenia generally took place in large asylums where people remained confined for much of their lives. Although government policy initiated a programme of gradual closure of these large hospitals and the rehousing of the residents in the community, this process was greatly assisted by the introduction of antipsychotic drugs, such as chlorpromazine, thioridazine and haloperidol. Antipsychotic medication would become the mainstay of treatment for the rest of the 20th century.

2.8.1   Pharmacological treatment

Today, within both hospital and community settings, antipsychotic medicines remain the primary treatment for schizophrenia. There is well-established evidence for their efficacy in both the treatment of acute psychotic episodes and relapse prevention over time (Janicak *et al.*, 1993). However, despite this, considerable problems remain. A significant proportion of service users – up to 40% (Kane *et al.*, 1996; Klein & Davis, 1969) – have a poor response to conventional antipsychotic drugs and continue to show moderate to severe psychotic symptoms (both positive and negative).

In addition, conventional or typical antipsychotic agents (more recently called first-generation antipsychotics [FGAs]) are associated with a high incidence and broad range of side effects including lethargy, sedation, weight gain and sexual dysfunction. Movement disorders, such as parkinsonism, akathisia and dystonia (often referred to as acute extrapyramidal side effects [EPS]), are common and can be disabling and distressing. A serious long-term side effect is tardive dyskinesia, which develops in around 20% of people receiving FGAs (Kane *et al.*, 1985); this is a late-onset EPS characterised by abnormal involuntary movements of the lips, jaw, tongue and facial muscles, and sometimes the limbs and trunk. Although a person who develops tardive dyskinesia is usually unaware of the movements, they are clearly noticed by others, and the condition has long been recognised as a severe social handicap (Barnes & Kidger, 1978).

In response to the limited effectiveness and extensive side effects of FGAs, considerable effort has gone into developing pharmacological treatments for schizophrenia that are more effective and produce fewer or less disabling side effects. The main advantage of these second-generation ('atypical') antipsychotics (SGAs) appears to be that they have a lower liability for acute EPS and tardive dyskinesia. However, in practice this must be balanced against other side effects, such as weight gain and other metabolic problems that may increase the risk of type-2 diabetes and cardiovascular disease (American Diabetes Association *et al.*, 2004; Lindenmayer *et al.*, 2003; Mackin *et al.*, 2007; Nasrallah, 2003, 2008; Suvisaari *et al.*, 2007).

Raised serum prolactin is also an important adverse effect of antipsychotic medication, which can lead to problems such as menstrual abnormalities, galactor-rhea and sexual dysfunction, and in the longer term to reduced bone mineral density (Haddad & Wieck, 2004, Meaney *et al.*, 2004).

In people with schizophrenia who have not responded well to other antipsy-chotics, only one antipsychotic drug, clozapine, has a specific license for the treatment of this group of people.

Further information about the antipsychotic medication reviewed for this update can be found in Chapters 6 and 7.

2.8.2   Psychological and psychosocial interventions

The use of specific psychological and psychosocial methods to help people with schizophrenia is relatively recent. Some of the earliest attempts included psycho-analysis (Fromm-Reichman, 1950), and a modification of psychoanalysis designed to enhance better integration into a hospital environment (Stack-Sullivan, 1947). These pioneering efforts increased awareness of the psychological processes and personal impact of schizophrenia.

Since then, a number of other psychological approaches have been introduced. Social skills training, developed in the 1970s, was derived from the recognition of the social difficulties that many people with schizophrenia face, especially those in insti-tutions, and used methods popular at the time based on learning theory and behav-iourism (Shepherd, 1978). As deinstitutionalisation gained ground in the 1970s, psychological and social research into factors that might contribute to relapse in people living in community settings, such as stressful life events and communication difficulties in families (high expressed emotion), stimulated the development of family interventions to prevent relapse (Leff *et al.*, 1982). Family interventions often included education for family members about schizophrenia (sometimes called 'psychoeducation') and, in time, research was conducted on the benefits of psychoe-ducation alone.

By the late 1980s, CBT approaches, originally developed in the 1970s for depres-sion, were first applied to aid the reduction of distressing psychotic symptoms and then broadened to work with emotional problems and functioning (Garety *et al.*, 2000). Another approach, cognitive remediation therapy (CRT), was also developed in the 1980s and 1990s, and differs from CBT in that it is not directed at distressing symptoms but is instead focused on training in cognitive functions, such as learning, planning, attention or memory (Green, 1993). A specific cognitive behavioural approach that aims to enhance compliance with medication was also developed towards the mid 1990s and is now commonly known as 'adherence therapy' (Kemp *et al.*, 1996).

Counselling and supportive psychotherapy, as well as various forms of group therapy and 'milieu' therapy, have long been practised with this client group. Finally, the four arts therapies that emerged as organised professions in the middle of the last century have in recent years begun to be evaluated formally in trials (Crawford & Patterson, 2007).

The psychological approaches considered in this updated guideline are reviewed, with further description and definitions, in Chapter 8.

2.8.3 Service-level interventions

Service-level interventions for people with schizophrenia include both 'inpatient' services and a variety of community team models. According to recent figures, services for people with schizophrenia account for 24% of the NHS spend on mental health (Mind, 2005). Two-thirds of that spend is on inpatient care where people with schizophrenia use over 60% of the provision (Knapp, 1997). The inpatient services comprise a range of statutory, independent and third sector provision ranging in degree of restriction and cost from high secure hospitals, medium secure and low secure units for mentally disordered offenders, through to intensive care, acute beds and rehabilitation units. The rates of use, care models and outcomes vary widely in these settings and there is no substantial evidence base for the optimal model, although a range of national regulators and peer review networks describe architectural 'healing' designs, standards and care pathways, for example, AIMS (Accreditation for Acute Inpatient Mental Health Services) initiated by the Royal College of Psychiatrists (2007) and the King's Fund's Enhancing the Healing Environment Programme (Waller & Finn, 2004).

Service-level interventions in the community include, most commonly, psychiatric outpatient clinics, generic locality community mental health teams (CMHTs), case management, acute day hospital care and non-acute day centre care. With the NSF policy directives and the various Mental Health Policy Implementation Guides being implemented in the past decade (for example, Department of Health, 1999; 2001), a growing number of crisis resolution and home treatment teams, assertive community treatment (ACT) or outreach teams and early intervention in psychosis services (EIPS) have been set up across the country. These new configurations in service delivery, though still evolving, have formed an increasingly important element in the management of all forms of severe mental illness, particularly psychoses. They emphasise an alternative to inpatient admission, with treatments and interventions focused on the service user's usual environment and context.

Social interventions for people with schizophrenia should strive to promote recovery. As the National Institute for Mental Health in England (NIMHE) states: 'Recovery is what people experience themselves as they become empowered to manage their lives in a manner that allows them to achieve a fulfilling, meaningful life and a contributing positive sense of belonging in their communities' (NIMHE, 2005). An integrated social programme for supporting access to work, education and recreation is regarded as essential in addressing the impact on social function and isolation caused by schizophrenia. Social support and services looking at independent accommodation/housing, fighting stigma, improving access to meaningful activities that address the individual's aspiration and strengths, and health promotion in the wider communities are all important considerations in realising the social inclusion principle (Repper & Perkins, 2003). Survey results amongst service users have also promoted the importance of social interventions that would improve/enhance more personal relationships, minimise discrimination, promote self-management, and ease social isolation through better availability of befriending and peer support schemes (Rethink, 2003).

2.8.4   Primary–secondary care interface

Most people with a diagnosis of schizophrenia in the care of the NHS are treated by secondary care mental health services. Surveys suggest that about 10 to 20% of service users are managed solely in primary care (Jeffreys *et al.*, 1997; Kendrick *et al.*, 2000; Rodgers *et al.*, 2003). This represents a significant shift from previous surveys (Johnstone *et al.*, 1984; Pantelis *et al.*, 1988) and may be an indication of the impact of recent changes in the structure and delivery of mental health services. This updated guideline therefore concentrates on the provision of care by secondary care services. It does not address the issue of the identification and initial diagnosis of schizophrenia, which is beyond its scope, although this is a key issue for primary care services.

Nevertheless, primary care services provide a vital service for people with schizophrenia, who consult primary care practitioners more frequently (Nazareth *et al.*, 1993) and are in contact with primary care services for a longer cumulative time than patients without mental health problems (Kai *et al.*, 2000; Lang *et al.*, 1997a, 1997b). A small percentage of service users have all their mental healthcare needs provided by primary care; this includes monitoring, treatment and support for their mental health problems in collaboration with secondary care services. Most receive much, if not all, of their physical care from primary care. Moreover, although most GPs regard themselves as involved in the monitoring and treatment of physical illness and prescribing for physical health problems, only a minority of GPs regard themselves as involved in the monitoring and treatment of mental health difficulties for people with schizophrenia (Bindman *et al.*, 1997; Burns *et al.*, 2000). Even fewer GPs are involved in secondary care CPA review meetings (Bindman *et al.*, 1997). Where possible, the guideline addresses these issues in its evidence-based recommendations. Where this is not possible, they are addressed through a number of good practice points, particularly in relation to the interface between primary and secondary care. Guidance on this interface has been incorporated into Chapter 9 on service interventions, with the aim of assisting primary care professionals in the management and referral of people with schizophrenia.

2.9   THE ECONOMIC COST OF SCHIZOPHRENIA

Schizophrenia places a heavy burden on individuals and their carers, as well as potentially large demands on the healthcare system. In 1990, WHO ranked schizophrenia as the ninth leading cause of disability among all diseases worldwide. When the burden of premature mortality and non-fatal health outcomes were combined and expressed in Disability Adjusted Life Years (DALYs), schizophrenia was the 26th leading cause of worldwide burden among all diseases and the ninth leading cause of DALYs at ages 15 to 44 years (Murray & Lopez, 1996).

A recent study estimated the total societal cost of schizophrenia at £6.7 billion (in 2004/2005 prices) only in England (Mangalore & Knapp, 2007). Of this, roughly £2 billion (about 30% of the total cost) comprised direct costs of treatment and care falling on the public purse, while the remaining £4.7 billion (70% of the total cost) constituted indirect costs to society. The cost of lost productivity of people with schizophrenia owing to unemployment, absence from work and premature mortality reached £3.4 billion, while the cost of lost productivity of carers was £32 million. The cost of informal care and private expenditures borne by families was reported to approximate £615 million. In addition, £1 million of the total cost was attributed to criminal justice system services, £570 million to benefit payments and another £14 million was associated with administration relating to these payments. Based on the above estimates, the average annual cost of a person with schizophrenia in England was calculated at approximately £55,000.

Davies and Drummond (1994) estimated that the lifetime total direct and indirect costs of a person with schizophrenia ranged from £8,000 (for a person with a single episode of schizophrenia) to £535,000 (for a person with multiple episodes lasting more than 2.5 years, requiring long-term care either in hospital or intensive community programmes) in 1990/1991 prices. Guest and Cookson (1999) estimated the average costs of a newly diagnosed person with schizophrenia at around £115,000 over the first 5 years following diagnosis, or approximately £23,000 annually (1997 prices). Of these, 49% were indirect costs owing to lost productivity.

Schizophrenia has been shown to place a substantial economic burden to the healthcare system and society worldwide: Wu and colleagues (2005) reported a total cost of schizophrenia in the US of US$62.7 billion (2002 prices). More than 50% of this cost was attributed to productivity losses, caused by unemployment, reduced workplace productivity, premature mortality from suicide and family caregiving; another 36% was associated with direct healthcare service use and the remaining 12% was incurred by other non-healthcare services. In Canada, Goeree and colleagues (2005) estimated the total cost of schizophrenia at approximately CA$2.02 billion (2002 prices). Again, productivity losses were by far the main component of this cost (70% of the total cost). In Australia, the total societal cost associated with schizophrenia reached AU$1.44 billion in 1997/1998 prices, with roughly 60% relating to indirect costs (Carr *et al.*, 2003). Finally, several national studies conducted in Europe in the 1990s showed that schizophrenia was associated with significant and long-lasting health, social and financial implications, not only for people with schizophrenia but also for their families, other caregivers and the wider society (Knapp *et al.*, 2004b).

The use of hospital inpatient care by people with schizophrenia is substantial. In the financial year 2006–2007, 34,407 admissions were reported for schizophrenia and related disorders in England, resulting in 2,232,724 inpatient bed days. This amounted to 16% of all admissions and 34% of all bed days related to psychiatric inpatient care (NHS, The Information Centre, 2008A). Inpatient care is by far the most costly healthcare component in the overall treatment of schizophrenia. Kavanagh and colleagues (1995) found that care in short- or long-stay psychiatric hospitals accounted for 51% of the total public expenditure on care for people with schizophrenia. Lang and colleagues (1997a) reported that provision of inpatient care for people with schizophrenia amounted to 59% of the total cost of health and social care for this population. A more recent estimate suggested that inpatient care accounted for 56.5% of the total treatment and care costs of schizophrenia, compared with 2.5% for outpatient care and 14.7% for day care (Knapp *et al.*, 2002).

Unemployment is a considerable burden for people with schizophrenia. A recent review reported a rate of employment among people with schizophrenia of between 4 and 27% in the UK, with stigmatisation being one of the main barriers to employment for this population. The rates of employment were higher for newly diagnosed people compared with those with established schizophrenia; however, the majority of people presenting to services for the first time were already unemployed (Marwaha & Johnson, 2004). According to Guest and Cookson (1999), between 15 and 30% of people with schizophrenia are unable to work at diagnosis, rising to 67% following a second episode. Overall, the estimates of total indirect costs of people with schizophrenia in the UK range from £412 million for newly diagnosed people over the first 5 years following diagnosis (Guest & Cookson, 1999) to £1.7 billion annually for people with chronic schizophrenia (Davies & Drummond, 1994).

Family members and friends often provide care and support to those with schizophrenia, which places significant burdens on them that impact upon their health, leisure time, employment and financial status. Guest and Cookson (1999) estimated that, in the UK, 1.2 to 2.5% of carers gave up work to care for dependants with schizophrenia. Measuring the total cost of informal care provided by family members and friends is difficult but it is important to highlight that it is a significant amount. Data on costs of informal care for people with schizophrenia are not available. Based on figures provided by the Office for National Statistics (ONS), the Sainsbury Centre for Mental Health (2003) estimated that in 2002/2003 the aggregate value of informal care provided by family members and friends in the UK to those with mental health problems was £3.9 billion.

It is therefore evident that efficient use of available healthcare resources is required to maximise the health benefit for people with schizophrenia and, at the same time, reduce the emotional distress and financial implications to society.

3 METHODS USED TO UPDATE THIS GUIDELINE

3.1 OVERVIEW

The update of this guideline drew upon methods outlined by NICE (*The Guidelines Manual* [NICE, 2007]). A team of healthcare professionals, lay representatives and technical experts known as the Guideline Development Group (GDG), with support from the NCCMH staff, undertook the update of a patient-centred evidence-based guideline. There are six basic steps in the process of updating a guideline:

● define the scope, which sets the parameters of the update and provides a focus and steer for the development work
● update the clinical questions developed for the previous guideline
● develop criteria for updating the literature search and conduct the search
● design validated protocols for systematic review and apply to evidence recovered by search
● synthesise and (meta-) analyse data retrieved, guided by the clinical questions, and produce evidence summaries (for both the clinical and health economic evidence)
● decide if there is sufficient new evidence to change existing recommendations, and develop new recommendations where necessary.

The update will provide recommendations for good practice that are based on the best available evidence of clinical and cost effectiveness. In addition, to ensure a service user and carer focus, the concerns of service users and carers regarding health and social care have been highlighted and addressed by recommendations agreed by the whole GDG.

3.2 THE SCOPE

NICE commissioned the NCCMH to review recent evidence on the management of schizophrenia and to update the existing guideline 'Schizophrenia: full national clinical guideline on core interventions in primary and secondary care' (NCCMH, 2003). The NCCMH developed a scope for the guideline update (see Appendix 1). The scope for the update of the guideline also included updating the NICE technology appraisal on the use of a typical antipsychotics (NICE, 2002), which had been incorporated into the previous guideline.

The purpose of the scope is to:

● provide an overview of what the guideline will include and exclude
● identify the key aspects of care that must be included

- set the boundaries of the development work and provide a clear framework to enable work to stay within the priorities agreed by NICE and the NCC, and the remit from the Department of Health/Welsh Assembly Government
- inform the development of updated clinical questions and search strategy
- inform professionals and the public about expected content of the guideline
- keep the guideline to a reasonable size to ensure that its development can be carried out within the allocated period.

The draft scope was subject to consultation with registered stakeholders over a 4-week period. During the consultation period, the scope was posted on the NICE website (www.nice.org.uk). Comments were invited from stakeholder organisations and Guideline Review Panel (GRP). Further information about the GRP can also be found on the NICE website. The NCCMH and NICE reviewed the scope in light of comments received, and the revised scope was signed off by the GRP.

3.3   THE GUIDELINE DEVELOPMENT GROUP

The GDG consisted of: professionals in psychiatry, psychiatric pharmacy, clinical psychology, nursing, arts therapies and general practice; academic experts in psychiatry and psychology; and service users and a carer. The guideline development process was supported by staff from the NCCMH, who undertook the clinical and health economics literature searches, reviewed and presented the evidence to the GDG, managed the process, and contributed to drafting the guideline.

3.3.1   Guideline Development Group meetings

Fourteen GDG meetings were held between June 2007 and December 2008. During each day-long GDG meeting, clinical questions and clinical and economic evidence were reviewed and assessed in a plenary session, and recommendations formulated. At each meeting, all GDG members declared any potential conflicts of interest, and service user and carer concerns were routinely discussed as part of a standing agenda.

3.3.2   Topic groups

The GDG divided its workload along clinically relevant lines to simplify the guideline development process, and GDG members formed smaller topic groups to undertake guideline work in that area of clinical practice. Four topic groups were formed to cover: (1) pharmacology interventions, (2) psychological and psychosocial interventions, (3) access and engagement with services and (4) primary and physical healthcare. These groups were designed to efficiently manage the large volume of evidence appraisal prior to presenting it to the GDG as a whole. Each topic group was chaired by a GDG member with expert knowledge of the topic area (one of the healthcare professionals). Topic groups refined the clinical questions, refined the clinical definitions of treatment interventions, reviewed and prepared the evidence with the systematic reviewer before presenting it to the GDG as a whole, and helped the GDG to identify further expertise in the topic. Topic group leaders reported the status of the group's work as part of the standing agenda. They also introduced and led the GDG discussion of the evidence review for that topic and assisted the GDG Chair in drafting the section of the guideline relevant to the work of each topic group.

3.3.3   Service users and carers

Individuals with direct experience of services gave an integral service-user focus to the GDG and the guideline. The GDG included two service users and a carer. They contributed as full GDG members to writing the clinical questions, helping to ensure that the evidence addressed their views and preferences, highlighting sensitive issues and terminology relevant to the guideline, and bringing service-user research to the attention of the GDG. In drafting the guideline, they contributed to writing the guideline's introduction and Chapter 4 and identified recommendations from the service user and carer perspective.

3.3.4   Special advisers

Special advisers, who had specific expertise in one or more aspects of treatment and management relevant to the guideline, or provided expertise in methodological aspects of evidence synthesis, assisted the GDG, commenting on specific aspects of the developing guideline and, where necessary, making presentations to the GDG. Appendix 3 lists those who agreed to act as special advisers.

3.3.5   National and international experts

National and international experts in the area under review were identified through the literature search and through the experience of the GDG members. These experts were contacted to recommend unpublished or soon-to-be published studies to ensure up-to-date evidence was included in the development of the guideline. They informed the group about completed trials at the pre-publication stage, systematic reviews in the process of being published, studies relating to the cost effectiveness of treatment and trial data if the GDG could be provided with full access to the complete trial report. Appendix 5 lists researchers who were contacted.

3.4   CLINICAL QUESTIONS

Clinical questions were used to guide the identification and interrogation of the evidence base relevant to the topic of the guideline. Before the first GDG meeting, an analytic framework (see Appendix 6) was prepared by NCCMH staff based on the scope and the clinical questions developed for the previous guideline. The framework was used to provide a structure from which the clinical questions were drafted. Both the analytic framework and the draft clinical questions were then discussed by the GDG at the first few meetings and amended as necessary. Where appropriate, the framework and questions were refined once the evidence had been searched and, where necessary, sub-questions were generated. Questions submitted by stakeholders were also discussed by the GDG and included where appropriate. For the purposes of the systematic review of clinical evidence, the questions were categorised as primary or secondary. The review focused on providing evidence to answer the primary questions. The final list of clinical questions can be found in Appendix 6.

For questions about interventions, the PICO (patient, intervention, comparison and outcome) framework was used. This structured approach divides each question into four components: the patients (the population under study), the interventions (what is being done), the comparisons (other main treatment options) and the outcomes (the measures of how effective the interventions have been) (see Table 2).

In some situations, the prognosis of a particular condition is of fundamental importance, over and above its general significance in relation to specific interventions. Areas where this is particularly likely to occur relate to assessment of risk, for example in terms of early intervention. In addition, questions related to issues of service delivery are occasionally specified in the remit from the Department of Health/Welsh Assembly Government. In these cases, appropriate clinical questions were developed to be clear and concise.

Table 2: Features of a well-formulated question on effectiveness intervention – the PICO (patient, intervention, comparison and outcome) guide

Patients/ population	Which patients or population of patients are we interested in? How can they be best described? Are there subgroups that need to be considered?
Intervention	Which intervention, treatment or approach should be used?
Comparison	What is/are the main alternative/s to compare with the intervention?
Outcome	What is really important for the patient? Which outcomes should be considered: intermediate or short-term measures; mortality; morbidity and treatment complications; rates of relapse; late morbidity and readmission; return to work, physical and social functioning and other measures, such as quality of life; general health status; costs?

Table 3: Best study design to answer each type of question

Type of question	Best primary study design
Effectiveness or other impact of an intervention	Randomised controlled trial; other studies that may be considered in the absence of a randomised controlled trial are the following: internally/externally controlled before and after trial, interrupted time-series
Accuracy of information (for example risk factor, test, prediction rule)	Comparing the information against a valid gold standard in a randomised trial or inception cohort study
Rates (of disease, patient experience, rare side effects)	Cohort, registry, cross-sectional study
Costs	Naturalistic prospective cost study

To help facilitate the literature review, a note was made of the best study design type to answer each question. There are four main types of clinical question of relevance to NICE guidelines. These are listed in Table 3. For each type of question, the best primary study design varies, where 'best' is interpreted as 'least likely to give misleading answers to the question'.

However, in all cases, a well-conducted systematic review of the appropriate type of study is always likely to yield a better answer than a single study.

Deciding on the best design type to answer a specific clinical or public health question does not mean that studies of different design types addressing the same question were discarded.

3.5   SYSTEMATIC CLINICAL LITERATURE REVIEW

The aim of the clinical literature review was to systematically identify and synthesise relevant evidence from the literature (updating the existing evidence base where appropriate) to answer the specific clinical questions developed by the GDG. Thus, clinical practice recommendations are evidence based where possible and, if evidence is not available, informal consensus methods are used (see Section 3.5.7) and the need for future research is specified.

3.5.1   Methodology

A stepwise, hierarchical approach was taken for locating and presenting evidence to the GDG. The NCCMH developed this process based on methods set out in

The Guidelines Manual (NICE, 2007) and after considering recommendations from a range of other sources. These sources included:

- Clinical Policy and Practice Program of the New South Wales Department of Health (Australia)
- Clinical Evidence online
- The Cochrane Collaboration
- New Zealand Guidelines Group
- NHS Centre for Reviews and Dissemination
- Oxford Centre for Evidence-Based Medicine
- Oxford Systematic Review Development Programme
- Scottish Intercollegiate Guidelines Network (SIGN)
- United States Agency for Healthcare Research and Quality.

3.5.2   The review process

During the development of the scope, a more extensive search was undertaken for systematic reviews and guidelines published since the previous schizophrenia guideline. These were used to inform the development of review protocols for each topic group. Review protocols included the relevant clinical question(s), the search strategy, the criteria for assessing the eligibility of studies and any additional assessments (see Appendix 7).

The initial approach taken to locating primary-level studies depended on the type of clinical question and potential availability of evidence. Based on the previous guideline and GDG knowledge of the literature, a decision was made about which questions were best addressed by good practice based on expert opinion, which questions were likely to have a good evidence base and which questions were likely to have little or no directly relevant evidence. Recommendations based on good practice were developed by informal consensus of the GDG. For questions with a good evidence base, the review process depended on the type of key question (see below). For questions that were unlikely to have a good evidence base, a brief descriptive review was initially undertaken by a member of the GDG (see Section 3.5.7).

Searches for evidence were updated between 6 and 8 weeks before the guideline consultation. After this point, studies were included only if they were judged by the GDG to be exceptional (for example, the evidence was likely to change a recommendation).

The search process for questions concerning interventions
For questions related to interventions, the initial evidence base (or updated evidence base) was formed from well-conducted randomised controlled trials (RCTs) that addressed at least one of the clinical questions. Although there are a number of difficulties with the use of RCTs in the evaluation of interventions in mental health, the RCT remains the most important method for establishing treatment efficacy. For other clinical questions, searches were for the appropriate study design (see above).

Standard mental health related bibliographic databases (that is, the Cumulative Index to Nursing and Allied Health Literature [CINAHL], Cochrane Library, Excerpta Medica Database [EMBASE], Medical Literature Analysis and Retrieval System Online [MEDLINE] and the Psychological Information Database [PsycINFO]) were used for the initial search for all studies potentially relevant to the guideline. Where the evidence base was large, recent high-quality English-language systematic reviews were used primarily as a source of RCTs (see Appendix 9 for quality criteria used to assess systematic reviews). However, in some circumstances existing data sets were utilised. Where this was the case, data were cross-checked for accuracy before use. New RCTs meeting inclusion criteria set by the GDG were incorporated into the existing reviews and fresh analyses performed.

After the initial search results were scanned liberally to exclude irrelevant papers, the review team used EPPI-Reviewer[3], a tool developed by the Evidence for Policy and Practice Information and Co-ordinating Centre (EPPI-Centre) for storing and analysing data for systematic reviews, to manage both the included and the excluded studies (eligibility criteria were developed after consultation with the GDG). Double checking of all excluded studies was not done routinely, but a selection of abstracts was checked to ensure reliability of the sifting. For questions without good-quality evidence (after the initial search), a decision was made by the GDG about whether to (a) repeat the search using subject-specific databases (for example, the Allied and Alternative Medicine Database [AMED], Educational Resources Information Center [ERIC], OpenSIGLE [System for information on Grey Literature in Europe] or Sociological Abstracts), (b) conduct a new search for lower levels of evidence or (c) adopt a consensus process (see Section 3.5.7).

In addition, searches were made of the reference lists of all eligible systematic reviews and included studies. Known experts in the field (see Appendix 5), based both on the references identified in early steps and on advice from GDG members, were sent letters requesting relevant studies that were in the process of being published[4]. In addition, the tables of contents of appropriate journals were periodically checked for relevant studies.

The search process for questions of prognosis
For questions related to prognosis, the search process was the same as described above, except that the initial evidence base was formed from studies with the most appropriate and reliable design to answer the particular question, that is, for cohort studies of representative patients. In situations where it was not possible to identify a substantial body of appropriately designed studies that directly addressed each clinical question, a consensus process was adopted (see Section 3.5.7).

---

[3]For further information see: http://eppi.ioe.ac.uk/cms/
[4]Unpublished full trial reports were also accepted where sufficient information was available to judge eligibility and quality (see section on unpublished evidence).

Search filters

Search filters developed by the review team consisted of a combination of subject heading and free-text phrases. Specific filters were developed for the guideline topic and, where necessary, for each clinical question. In addition, the review team used filters developed for systematic reviews, RCTs and other appropriate research designs (Appendix 8).

Study selection

All primary-level studies included after the first scan of citations were acquired in full and re-evaluated for eligibility (based on the relevant review protocol) at the time they were being entered into EPPI-Reviewer. Eligible systematic reviews and primary-level studies were critically appraised for methodological quality (see Appendix 9 for the quality checklists, and Appendix 15 for characteristics of each study including quality assessment). The eligibility of each study was confirmed by consensus during topic group meetings.

For some clinical questions, it was necessary to prioritise the evidence with respect to the UK context (that is, external validity). To make this process explicit, the topic groups took into account the following factors when assessing the evidence:

- participant factors (for example, gender, age and ethnicity)
- provider factors (for example, model fidelity, the conditions under which the intervention was performed and the availability of experienced staff to undertake the procedure)
- cultural factors (for example, differences in standard care and differences in the welfare system).

It was the responsibility of each topic group to decide which prioritisation factors were relevant to each clinical question in light of the UK context and then decide how they should modify their recommendations.

Unpublished evidence

The GDG used a number of criteria when deciding whether or not to accept unpublished data. First, the evidence must have been accompanied by a trial report containing sufficient detail to properly assess the quality of the research. Second, where evidence was submitted directly to the GDG, it must have been done so with the understanding that details would be published in the full guideline. However, the GDG recognised that unpublished evidence submitted by investigators might later be retracted by those investigators if the inclusion of such data would jeopardise publication of their research.

3.5.3 Data extraction

Outcome data were extracted from all eligible studies, which met the minimum quality criteria, using Review Manager 4.2.10 (The Nordic Cochrane Centre, 2003) or Review Manager 5 (The Nordic Cochrane Centre, 2008).

For each major area reviewed, the GDG distinguished between outcomes that they considered critical and those that were important but not critical for the purposes of updating the guideline. Only critical outcomes were initially extracted for data analysis (further details about the critical outcomes can be found in the review protocols in each evidence chapter).

In most circumstances, for a given outcome (continuous and dichotomous), where more than 50% of the number randomised to any group were lost to follow up, the data were excluded from the analysis (except for the outcome 'leaving the study early', in which case, the denominator was the number randomised). Where possible, dichotomous efficacy outcomes were calculated on an intention-to-treat basis (that is, a 'once-randomised-always-analyse' basis). Where there was good evidence that those participants who ceased to engage in the study were likely to have an unfavourable outcome, early withdrawals were included in both the numerator and denominator. Adverse events were entered into Review Manager as reported by the study authors because it was usually not possible to determine whether early withdrawals had an unfavourable outcome. Where there was limited data for a particular review, the 50% rule was not applied. In these circumstances the evidence was downgraded because of the risk of bias.

Where necessary, standard deviations (SDs) were calculated from standard errors, confidence intervals or p-values according to standard formulae (see the Cochrane Reviewers' Handbook 4.2.2 [Alderson *et al.*, 2004]). Data were summarised using the generic inverse variance method using Review Manager.

Consultation with another reviewer or members of the GDG was used to overcome difficulties with coding. Data from studies included in existing systematic reviews were extracted independently by one reviewer and cross-checked with the existing data set. Where possible, data extracted by one reviewer were checked by a second reviewer. Disagreements were resolved with discussion. Where consensus could not be reached, a third reviewer or GDG members resolved the disagreement. Masked assessment (that is, blinded to the journal from which the article comes, the authors, the institution and the magnitude of the effect) was not used since it is unclear that doing so reduces bias (Jadad *et al.*, 1996; Berlin, 2001).

3.5.4   Synthesising the evidence

Where possible, meta-analysis was used to synthesise the evidence using Review Manager. If necessary, re-analyses of the data or sub-analyses were used to answer clinical questions not addressed in the original studies or reviews.

Dichotomous outcomes were analysed as relative risks (RR) with the associated 95% confidence interval (CI) (for an example, see Figure 1). A relative risk (also called a risk ratio) is the ratio of the treatment event rate to the control event rate. An RR of 1 indicates no difference between treatment and control. In Figure 1, the overall RR of 0.73 indicates that the event rate (that is, non-remission rate) associated with intervention A is about three quarters of that with the control intervention or, in other words, the relative risk reduction is 27%.

Figure 1: Example of a forest plot displaying dichotomous data

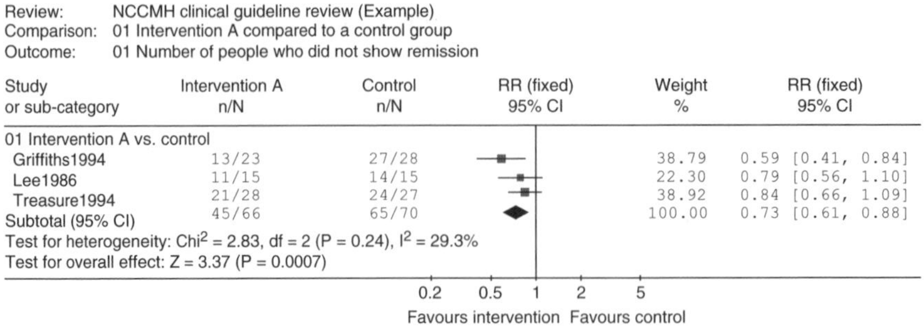

Review: NCCMH clinical guideline review (Example)
Comparison: 01 Intervention A compared to a control group
Outcome: 01 Number of people who did not show remission

Study or sub-category	Intervention A n/N	Control n/N	RR (fixed) 95% CI	Weight %	RR (fixed) 95% CI
01 Intervention A vs. control					
Griffiths1994	13/23	27/28		38.79	0.59 [0.41, 0.84]
Lee1986	11/15	14/15		22.30	0.79 [0.56, 1.10]
Treasure1994	21/28	24/27		38.92	0.84 [0.66, 1.09]
Subtotal (95% CI)	45/66	65/70		100.00	0.73 [0.61, 0.88]
Test for heterogeneity: Chi² = 2.83, df = 2 (P = 0.24), I² = 29.3%					
Test for overall effect: Z = 3.37 (P = 0.0007)					

```
                          0.2    0.5    1    2    5
                     Favours intervention  Favours control
```

The CI shows with 95% certainty the range within which the true treatment effect should lie and can be used to determine statistical significance. If the CI does not cross the 'line of no effect', the effect is statistically significant.

Continuous outcomes were analysed as weighted mean differences (WMDs) or as a standardised mean difference (SMD) when different measures were used in different studies to estimate the same underlying effect (for an example, see Figure 2). If provided, intention-to-treat data, using a method such as 'last observation carried forward', were preferred over data from completers.

To check for consistency between studies, both the I^2 test of heterogeneity and a visual inspection of the forest plots were used. The I^2 statistic describes the proportion of total variation in study estimates caused by heterogeneity (Higgins & Thompson, 2002). The I^2 statistic was interpreted in the following way:

- >50%: notable heterogeneity (an attempt was made to explain the variation by conducting sub-analyses to examine potential moderators. In addition, studies with effect sizes greater than two SDs from the mean of the remaining studies were excluded using sensitivity analyses. If studies with heterogeneous results were found to be comparable with regard to study and participant characteristics, a random-effects model was used to summarise the results [DerSimonian & Laird,

Figure 2: Example of a forest plot displaying continuous data

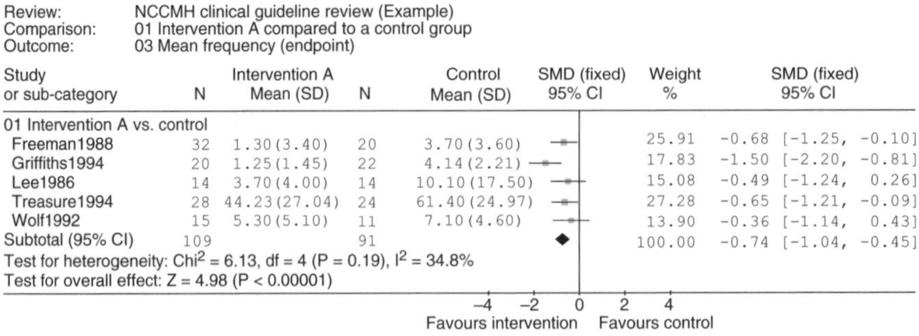

Review: NCCMH clinical guideline review (Example)
Comparison: 01 Intervention A compared to a control group
Outcome: 03 Mean frequency (endpoint)

Study or sub-category	Intervention A N Mean (SD)	Control N Mean (SD)	SMD (fixed) 95% CI	Weight %	SMD (fixed) 95% CI
01 Intervention A vs. control					
Freeman1988	32 1.30(3.40)	20 3.70(3.60)		25.91	-0.68 [-1.25, -0.10]
Griffiths1994	20 1.25(1.45)	22 4.14(2.21)		17.83	-1.50 [-2.20, -0.81]
Lee1986	14 3.70(4.00)	14 10.10(17.50)		15.08	-0.49 [-1.24, 0.26]
Treasure1994	28 44.23(27.04)	24 61.40(24.97)		27.28	-0.65 [-1.21, -0.09]
Wolf1992	15 5.30(5.10)	11 7.10(4.60)		13.90	-0.36 [-1.14, 0.43]
Subtotal (95% CI)	109	91		100.00	-0.74 [-1.04, -0.45]
Test for heterogeneity: Chi² = 6.13, df = 4 (P = 0.19), I² = 34.8%					
Test for overall effect: Z = 4.98 (P < 0.00001)					

```
                        -4    -2    0    2    4
                   Favours intervention   Favours control
```

1986]. In the random-effects analysis, heterogeneity is accounted for both in the width of CIs and in the estimate of the treatment effect. With decreasing heterogeneity the random-effects approach moves asymptotically towards a fixed-effects model).

- 30 to 50%: moderate heterogeneity (both the chi-squared test of heterogeneity and a visual inspection of the forest plot were used to decide between a fixed and random-effects model).
- <30%: mild heterogeneity (a fixed-effects model was used to synthesise the results).

3.5.5   Presenting the data to the Guideline Development Group

Study characteristics tables and, where appropriate, forest plots generated with Review Manager were presented to the relevant topic group.

Forest plots
Each forest plot displayed the effect size and CI for each study as well as the overall summary statistic. The graphs were organised so that the display of data in the area to the left of the 'line of no effect' indicated a 'favourable' outcome for the treatment in question.

3.5.6   Forming the clinical summaries and recommendations

After the presentation of evidence, members of the topic group discussed whether there was sufficient evidence to change existing recommendations or drafted new recommendations where necessary. One member of the review team in conjunction with the topic group lead then produced a clinical evidence summary based on the topic group discussion.

3.5.7   Method used to answer a clinical question in the absence of appropriately designed, high-quality research

In the absence of appropriately designed, high-quality research, or where the GDG were of the opinion (on the basis of previous searches or their knowledge of the literature) that there were unlikely to be such evidence, an informal consensus process was adopted. This process focused on those questions that the GDG considered a priority.

Informal consensus
The starting point for the process of informal consensus was that a member of the topic group identified, with help from the systematic reviewer, a narrative review that most directly addressed the clinical question. Where this was not possible, a brief descriptive review of the recent literature was initiated.

This existing narrative review or new review was used as a basis for beginning an iterative process to identify lower levels of evidence relevant to the clinical question and to lead to written statements for the guideline. The process involved a number of steps:

- A description of what is known about the issues concerning the clinical question was written by one of the topic group members.
- Evidence from the existing review or new review was then presented to the GDG and further comments were sought about the evidence and its perceived relevance to the clinical question.
- Based on the feedback from the GDG, additional information was sought and added to the information collected. This might have included studies that did not directly address the clinical question but were thought to contain relevant data.
- If, during the course of preparing the report, a significant body of primary-level studies (of appropriate design to answer the question) were identified, a full systematic review was carried out.
- At this time, possibly subject to further reviews of the evidence, a series of statements that directly addressed the clinical question was developed.
- Following this, on occasion and as deemed appropriate by the development group, the report was sent to appointed experts outside the GDG for peer review and comment. The information from this process was then fed back to the GDG for further discussion of the statements.
- Recommendations were then developed and could also be sent for further external peer review.
- After this final stage of comment, the statements and recommendations were again reviewed and agreed upon by the GDG.

3.6   HEALTH ECONOMICS METHODS

The aim of health economics was to contribute to the guideline's development by providing evidence on the cost effectiveness of interventions for people with schizophrenia covered in the guideline, in areas with likely major resource implications. This was achieved by:

- systematic literature review of existing economic evidence
- economic modelling, where economic evidence was lacking or was considered inadequate to inform decisions.

3.6.1   Key economic issues

Systematic search of the economic literature was undertaken on all areas that were updated since the previous guideline, that is:

- access to and engagement with services, including early intervention services for people with schizophrenia
- pharmacological interventions for people with schizophrenia (excluding rapid tranquillisation)
- psychological interventions for people with schizophrenia.

Moreover, literature on the health-related quality of life of people with schizophrenia was systematically searched to identify studies reporting appropriate utility weights that could be utilised in a cost-utility analysis.

In addition to the systematic review of economic literature, the following economic issues were identified by the GDG in collaboration with the health economist as key priorities for *de novo* economic modelling in the guideline update:

● cost effectiveness of psychological therapies/psychosocial interventions provided in addition to standard care versus standard care alone; CBT and family intervention were examined
● cost effectiveness of antipsychotic medications for people with schizophrenia that is in remission.

The rest of this section describes the methods adopted in the systematic literature review of economic studies undertaken for this guideline update. The respective methodology adopted in the previous guideline is provided in Appendix 17. Methods employed in *de novo* economic modelling carried out for this guideline update are described in the respective sections of the guideline.

3.6.2 Search strategy

For the systematic review of economic evidence the standard mental-health-related bibliographic databases (EMBASE, MEDLINE, CINAHL and PsycINFO) were searched. For these databases, a health economics search filter adapted from the Centre for Reviews and Dissemination at the University of York was used in combination with a general search strategy for schizophrenia. Additional searches were performed in specific health economics databases (economic evaluation database [NHS EED], Office of Health Economics – Health Economic Evaluations Database [OHE HEED]), as well as in the Health Technology Assessment (HTA) database. For the HTA and NHS EED databases, the general strategy for schizophrenia was used. OHE HEED was searched using a shorter, database-specific strategy. Initial searches were performed in June 2007. The searches were updated regularly, with the final search performed in November 2008. Details of the search strategy for economic studies on interventions for people with schizophrenia are provided in Appendix 10.

In parallel to searches of electronic databases, reference lists of eligible studies and relevant reviews were searched by hand. Studies included in the clinical evidence review were also screened for economic evidence.

The systematic search of the literature identified 10,425 references in total (stage 1). Publications that were clearly not relevant were first excluded (stage 2). The abstracts of all potentially relevant publications were then assessed against a set of selection criteria by the health economist (stage 3). Full texts of the studies potentially meeting the selection criteria (including those for which eligibility was not clear from the abstract) were obtained (stage 4). At this stage, 154 studies had been selected. Studies that did not meet the inclusion criteria, were duplicates, were secondary publications to a previous study, or had been updated in more recent publications were subsequently excluded (stage 5). Finally, 36 papers eligible for inclusion were assessed for internal validity and critically appraised (stage 6). The quality assessment was based on the checklists used by the *British Medical Journal* to assist referees in appraising full and partial economic analyses (Drummond & Jefferson, 1996) (Appendix 11).

3.6.3   Selection criteria

The following inclusion criteria were applied to select studies identified by the economic searches for further analysis:

- Only papers published in English language were considered.
- Studies published from 1996 onwards were included. This date restriction was imposed to obtain data relevant to current healthcare settings and costs.
- Only studies from Organisation for Economic Co-operation and Development countries were included, as the aim of the review was to identify economic information transferable to the UK context.
- Selection criteria based on types of clinical conditions and patients were identical to the clinical literature review.
- Studies were included provided that sufficient details regarding methods and results were available to enable the methodological quality of the study to be assessed, and provided that the study's data and results were extractable. Poster presentations and abstracts were excluded from the review.
- Full economic evaluations that compared two or more relevant options and considered both costs and consequences (that is, cost-consequence analysis, cost-effectiveness analysis, cost-utility analysis or cost-benefit analysis) were included in the review.
- Studies were included if they used clinical effectiveness data from an RCT, a prospective cohort study, or a systematic review and meta-analysis of clinical studies. Studies were excluded if they had a mirror-image or other retrospective design, or if they utilised efficacy data that were based mainly on assumptions.
- Studies were included only if pharmacological and psychological treatments were clearly described; antipsychotic medications had to be specifically defined so that it was clear which antipsychotic drugs were being compared, the dose and route of administration used, and the duration of treatment. In particular, evaluations in which two or more antipsychotic drugs were treated as a class, and in which comparisons between specific antipsychotic drugs were not provided, were excluded from further consideration. An exception was made in the case of the Cost Utility of the Latest Antipsychotic Drugs in Schizophrenia Study (CUtLASS, Lewis *et al.*, 2006a, 2006b; Jones *et al.*, 2006), two large effectiveness trials conducted in the UK that compared SGAs with FGAs and clozapine with SGAs; it was decided to describe these studies in the systematic economic literature review because their findings and conclusions, although non-informative on the cost effectiveness of specific antipsychotic drugs, were deemed by the GDG to be relevant and useful in decision-making.
- Studies comparing pharmacological interventions with no treatment/placebo were not considered in the review.

- Studies that adopted a very narrow perspective, ignoring major categories of costs to the NHS, were excluded; for example studies were not considered to be informative if they exclusively estimated drug acquisition, psychological intervention or hospitalisation costs.
- Cost effectiveness analyses were included only if their measure of outcome was considered relevant and was recorded in the guideline systematic literature review of clinical evidence; cost utility analyses were included if their measure of outcome was a validated measure, such as quality adjusted life years (QALYs) or DALYs. Health-related quality of life studies were included if they reported preference-based utility weights appropriate to use in a cost utility analysis.

3.6.4   Data extraction

Data were extracted by the health economist using a standard economic data extraction form (Appendix 12).

3.6.5   Presentation of economic evidence

The economic evidence identified by the health economics systematic review is summarised in the respective chapters of the guideline, following presentation of the clinical evidence. The references to included studies and to those potentially eligible that were excluded at stage 5 of the review, as well as the evidence tables with the characteristics and results of economic studies included in the review, are provided in Appendix 14. Methods and results of economic modelling on psychological therapies/ psychosocial interventions are reported in the respective economic sections of Chapter 8. Methods and results of economic modelling on pharmacological interventions aiming at prevention of relapse in people with schizophrenia are presented in Chapter 7.

3.7   STAKEHOLDER CONTRIBUTIONS

Professionals, service users and companies have contributed to and commented on the guideline at key stages in its development. Stakeholders for this guideline include:
- service user/carer stakeholders: the national service user and carer organisations that represent people whose care is described in this guideline
- professional stakeholders: the national organisations that represent healthcare professionals who are providing services to service users
- commercial stakeholders: the companies that manufacture medicines used in the treatment of schizophrenia
- Primary Care Trusts
- Department of Health and Welsh Assembly Government.

Stakeholders have been involved in the guideline's development at the following points:

- commenting on the initial scope of the guideline and attending a briefing meeting held by NICE
- contributing possible clinical questions and lists of evidence to the GDG
- commenting on the draft of the guideline.

3.8   VALIDATION OF THE GUIDELINE

Registered stakeholders had an opportunity to comment on the draft guideline, which was posted on the NICE website during the consultation period. Following the consultation, all comments from stakeholders and others were responded to, and the guideline updated as appropriate. The GRP also reviewed the guideline and checked that stakeholders' comments had been addressed.

Following the consultation period, the GDG finalised the recommendations and the NCCMH produced the final documents. These were then submitted to NICE. NICE then formally approved the guideline and issued its guidance to the NHS in England and Wales.

4   EXPERIENCE OF CARE

4.1   INTRODUCTION

This chapter is about the experiences of people who have been given a diagnosis of schizophrenia and their carers. It contains some personal accounts from users of mental health services and from their carers, which are illustrative only and not intended to be representative. The personal accounts are followed by a summary of themes and concerns identified in the accounts. In addition some experiences from Healthtalkonline (formerly DIPEx; www.healthtalkonline.org, 2008) and an NHS trust (Anonymous, 2008) are included to capture the voice of people from different ethnic minority backgrounds and from someone using an early intervention service. Findings from a survey conducted independently by Rethink relating to people with schizophrenia or psychosis are also incorporated (Borneo, 2008). In the final section are good practice points based on the previous guideline and current concerns of service users and carers.

4.2   METHODOLOGY

The writers of the personal accounts were contacted primarily through the GDG's service user and carer representatives. The people who were approached to write the accounts were asked to consider a number of questions when composing their narratives. These included:

- What is the nature of your experience of living with schizophrenia?
- When were you diagnosed and how old were you; how did you feel about the diagnosis or 'label'?
- Do you think that any life experiences led to the onset of the condition? If so, please describe if you feel able to do so.
- When did you seek help from the NHS and whom did you contact? (Please describe this first contact.)
- What possible treatments were discussed with you?
- What treatment(s) did you receive? Please describe both drug treatment and psychological therapy.
- Was the treatment(s) helpful? (Please describe what worked for you and what didn't work for you.)
- How would you describe your relationship with your practitioner(s)? (GP/community psychiatric nurse [CPN]/psychiatrist and so on.)
- Have you ever been violent or been a victim of violence? If you would like to explain the circumstances please do so.
- In the context of having schizophrenia, have you ever broken the law or been arrested? If you would like to explain the circumstances please do so if it led to you accessing treatment.

- Did you attend a support group and was this helpful? Did any people close to you help and support you?
- How has the nature of the condition changed over time?
- How do you feel now?
- If your condition has improved, do you use any strategies to help you to stay well? If so, please describe these strategies.

The questions for carers were based on the above.

The first two accounts from people with schizophrenia (A and B) are written by men who have been receiving treatment for nearly 15 years and more. The third account (C) is by a woman who was first diagnosed in the 1980s when she was in her mid-twenties. In the accounts from carers, one is written by the father (E) of the person in account A and another by the partner (H) of the person in account C. Carer accounts D and F are written by mothers of sons with schizophrenia. Account G is from a father.

The Rethink survey (Borneo, 2008) was conducted independently and some of its findings are included here. A questionnaire was distributed to its members and to services and support groups, with 959 service users completing the form. Thirty seven per cent of the respondents (357) had a diagnosis of schizophrenia (323), schizoaffective disorder (33) and delusional disorder (1). The results that are reported below relate to this sample of people alone. Men accounted for 65% and women 35%, while a large majority (89%) were white British/Irish (only 11% were other ethnic groups). Sixty-one per cent were aged 35 to 54 years, 25% were aged up to 34 years; and 14% were aged 55 years and over. The survey asked people about their experience of taking medication and any side effects, care planning and decision making by their healthcare team, physical healthcare and access to non-pharmacological treatment. Where the size of the sample was large enough, different demographic groups were compared as were people taking atypical and typical antipsychotics.

4.3 PERSONAL ACCOUNTS FROM PEOPLE WITH SCHIZOPHRENIA

4.3.1 Personal account A

I first became ill with paranoid schizophrenia in April 1994, aged nearly 33. I don't know why I got the illness – there are no reports of it in my family. However, my father has coeliac disease, which is thought to be linked with schizophrenia. I used to drink three pints of beer every night and had done for some years (more on Friday and Saturday), and that might not have helped, though I don't imagine smoking some weed 10 years earlier while travelling in Africa can have caused it, however bad the reaction at the time.

I became ill almost overnight although I had paid certain aspects of my life little attention for some time. (I was trying to launch a business in my spare time and this left no time to make myself at home and relax in my new flat or cook for myself). I felt wonderfully excited as though I was the only person in the country to be let in on a great secret. I spent that summer travelling around Britain, Ireland and parts of Europe in search of more delusional excitement. I thought I had become involved in the peace process in Ireland and, amusingly, that I had something to do with the disappearance of Prince Charles's dog, which had been announced in the national news. Nobody appeared to notice anything was wrong except, perhaps, one of my brothers who realised I had a strange obsession with dogs, which I thought I could hear barking on the radio!

I had had some trouble with panic attacks connected with my alcohol intake. I spent a few days in hospital due to the first one, but was given no diagnosis. At the end of the summer I was prescribed an antidepressant, following a further panic attack. It was like pouring petrol on a fire to put it out. A week or two later I caused £10,000 worth of damage in a few minutes and was sectioned in an old asylum, which was quite an experience. I was then prescribed chlorpromazine. No alternatives were mentioned or discussed. It made me suicidally depressed and caused retroejaculation. I knew I could not live my life feeling so low and as soon as I was released I stopped taking it, the schizophrenia having gone into remission. It was a lonely decision to stop taking the drug. I felt there would be no support if I told anyone. Nobody had given me any hope that I could either recover completely to the point of requiring no medication or find a medication I could reasonably be expected to take. I felt a great stigma towards myself and acute embarrassment at my diagnosis. It was not possible to really acknowledge to myself I had been ill as the consequences of that were unthinkable. It was a sort of protection mechanism in a way. Although I encountered one or two good nurses on the wards I was very unimpressed by almost all of the psychiatrists and this pattern would continue throughout my history.

I spent the next 10 years of my life in a cycle of gradually getting ill (which, in fact, I usually enjoyed), getting arrested, being sectioned, and feeling suicidal because of the side effects of the drugs I was prescribed – even one of the modern atypical drugs made me feel suicidally depressed. Even though I was at risk of suicide, I would be deemed 'well' and released from hospital because the schizophrenia was in remission. I would then stop my treatment because of the side effects and gradually get ill all over again over the following 6 months or so. There were three specific reasons or barriers why this cycle took me 10 years to break: firstly, I enjoyed the illness most of the time; secondly, I found all of the medications that I was given for 10 years intolerable to take because of the side effects; and finally, the stigma of the illness. These facts left me unable to accept that I had an illness.

I believe that since drugs were first introduced for paranoid schizophrenia in 1952 some patients have committed suicide, not because of the illness but because of the side effects, in particular depression. I was, and still am, absolutely staggered that I was given no warning or understanding regarding the depression many, but not all, of the drugs prescribed for schizophrenia can cause. How could a person be locked up and have chemicals forced into their bloodstream which made them suicidal? What misery of depression, akathisia and other side effects (for example, sexual) I had to put up with! Perhaps I only managed to keep going because my Dad asked me to promise that I would.

I escaped from hospital on the second occasion I was sectioned because I was so frightened of the side effects. I went on the run until the section had expired. My benchmark for happiness was not being medicated and so I was able to find joy as a street beggar. I disappeared from home for a whole year at one point to avoid treatment and later absconded, rightfully terrified of the injection I was to have had the next day. Again, I found some happiness on the run.

After a decade of this, I was told about an illness called post-psychotic depression. When, eventually, I was given a drug (first quetiapine fumarate, then clozapine) that did not list depression as a side effect I did not get depressed, which was a major advance in my treatment. So I wondered if there really was such an illness as post-psychotic depression as I had proved I did not suffer from it. The depressions I had were caused by the drugs I had been prescribed. Another step forward took place when I got a new CPN and she agreed to try and treat me without medication. It did not work, but it showed me (if only subconsciously) we could perhaps work together. She also helped me with my advance statement so I could set out that I did not want to have any of the drugs that had given me such serious side effects. Another key moment was when the mental health review tribunal released me from a section; this showed me that I could at least get some justice.

Some 10 years, and as many sections, after I first became ill I was released from hospital by the hospital managers. Before my release the patient in the next bed to me had told me he was getting no side effects from his treatment, which was olanzapine. As none of the hospital managers was a doctor I felt a particular responsibility to them for releasing me. I went to my GP (with whom I had generally maintained a good relationship) and told him it did not take a genius to see I would be back in hospital after a few months if I was not taking medication and asked him to at least try me on olanzapine. I have been on it now for 4 years and have stayed well and avoided hospital.

Generally, I enjoyed being ill because I felt very positive and purposeful. On the other hand the treatment was appalling: criminally and murderously shocking for 10 years until I found the drug I am currently taking. My family were all at their wits' end at my behaviour. I remain well although I have problems with mood, which I think are associated with my employment situation. This is greatly helped by going to the gym most days. I have also written a book about schizophrenia, which is something I would not have done had I not been ill. My family are very happy that I have avoided hospital for 4 years and don't look like I am going back. If I were to go back, what is there to fear? I have found a drug I take voluntarily and all the ones that have been unsuccessful are now excluded by my advance statement.

4.3.2   Personal account B

I was diagnosed with schizophrenia in 1975 when I was in my mid 20s. My experience of mental health has been determined by two care regimes, before and after the Community Care Act was passed in 1990. Before the Act it was very bad, after it there was an improvement. Strangely enough, given that she is popularly associated with the poll tax, benefit cuts, privatisation, and three million unemployed, I have Mrs Thatcher to thank for passing the community care legislation and in so doing freeing me from the revolving door system of the old asylums and giving me a dignified life.

I was a content but lonely child. I got seven 'O' levels and three 'A' levels, and then went to university in 1969 where I failed my finals in 1974 after two sabbatical years off. I feel I have constantly underachieved by many standards. In 1968 I lost a leg in a motorcycle accident.

I first became an inpatient before Christmas 1974. I had had difficulties at university, with smoking cannabis and with my parents' divorce, and the loss of my leg still troubled me physically and psychologically. I think one of my parents may have had something to do with the actual circumstances of the admission – I can't remember exactly. I was discharged before Christmas and then, after severe rows with my parents, I lived in my car and stole petrol. This led to my next admission in about February 1975. By this time I had a criminal record, and was sent to an asylum as a condition of a probation order from the magistrates.

I have been sectioned three times. The first of these was in about 1981 for a year, but I was resettled after about 9 months. My appeal was unsuccessful.

When I was first diagnosed with schizophrenia, I had no insight but was paranoid. By the time I had my house repossessed in 1986 after 3 years' ownership, I spent the next 5 years mainly living in bus shelters, and being victim to severe delusions. I had lots of delusory beliefs and was very unwell. I thought that Russians were sure to invade England. I thought there were leprechaun-like Irishmen creeping through Kent to do horrible things to the Archbishop of Canterbury. I thought there were people in the police in Newcastle who were supporting the IRA. At times when I was in custody for minor misdeeds, I thought the gaolers' keys were singing out signals and lots of other strange things. I neglected my welfare and did not attempt to get bail. When I left custody I went back to live in bus shelters. The second time I was sectioned was in 1989 when I was detained for a month. My appeal was allowed, and I went back to living in bus shelters again.

In the old asylums I was put in a male dormitory, given regular humiliating and debilitating injections in the backside and sent to the industrial therapy unit to pack soap for £1.75 a week. At this time I was worried about having to give information to the police about drug dealers who had corrupted me at university, having failed my finals while psychotic, and having to recover a substantial sum of money from a company who had borrowed money from me, using the county court. All of these concerns were ignored by the hospital; all I got was dormitory, needles in the rear, and days of menial slave labour, the proceeds of which went on tobacco. What followed, when I escaped from the routine of the asylum, was going into a low paid job, which led to vagrancy and custody before being returned to asylum care.

The last time I was an inpatient was in 1991 for 6 months. I negotiated a medication regime that did not include injections, because after I was injected I experienced 7 days and nights of extreme restlessness. I now know there is a name for the 'side effects' of the flupentixol and fluphenazine decanoate I was given previously, and that term is akathisia. I informed the staff in 1991 that I considered them to be using the British state to humiliate me and give me unbearable concoctions. I declared that if they injected me, I would do property damage to some part of the British state. When the nurses gave me an injection, I told them that I would be putting their names on the bricks that would go through some official windows when I had recovered from the week-long effects of the injection. They proceeded to give me the injection, and after a week had passed I duly smashed windows and that was the last psychiatric injection I have had. I have never refused to take tablets or liquid.

After this satisfactory outcome, I have lived in the community. During that time I have conscientiously taken my pills every day. For the last several years I have been put on atypical medication, olanzapine, which I find has even fewer sedative side effects than the chlorpromazine I was on when I left the asylum. I am satisfied with the therapeutic effect of that, as are my carers.

Since 1991 I have got an 'A' level, a BA, an MA, and have helped organise art shows and a digital art group both of which have featured in the local press. I have also helped in the garden of the local day centre where we have won many prizes over the last 6 years. I am active in a local church. This is a lot better than being allowed to become psychotic, which is what happened whenever I escaped from the asylum routine to become the revolving door patient.

Thanks to community care and no injections, I have a life and try to highlight the user voice. I get involved where I think a difference can be made. It is my ambition, even at 57, to become a fully paid-up member of the property-owning democracy. I have no idea how that might come about. I have in mind that I might attempt a PhD in my 60s.

Nowadays I fully participate in my own care and the medication that I take. I speak to a counsellor once a week and I have support (after the recovery model) from user groups and the day centre. My relationships with these people who help me (and do not stand in my way) are good and I do not feel they want to do anything but assist me to be the best I can be, through the ups and downs. No one has ever come up to me and abused me for being a schizophrenic. Neither do I know of anyone who has seriously done me down or stopped me doing something or getting somewhere. Yet with my qualifications, my years of non-offending and of not being an inpatient, people might have expected a different outcome from still being supported by mental health services. So there may be some residual stigma and covert discrimination after all. Maybe there is a glass ceiling.

4.3.3 Personal account C

I was diagnosed as having schizophrenia in the 1980s when I was in my mid 20s, although in retrospect I had some delusions and hallucinations when I was at university. I was hearing voices and was reading strange meanings into what was going on around me. At one point I ran away to Scotland because I was so scared of what was happening inside my head. I forgot to take money so had to hitchhike back to the south of England. In the end I took an overdose and was going to cut my wrists so friends called the campus doctor. At the time the campus GP made me see a psychiatrist but I managed to persuade him I was alright and later a stay in hospital for tonsillitis gave me the space to sort my head out. I went on to finish my degree and start work as a research scientist.

In my mid 20s, I was working in a research laboratory attached to a hospital when I started having both visual and auditory hallucinations. I mentioned the things I was seeing (because I didn't realise that other people couldn't see them) but did not talk about hearing voices because I thought everyone heard them and we were not supposed to discuss them. The occupational doctor made me see a psychiatrist and a few days later I was hospitalised for the first time after I took an overdose which had been triggered by my distress at what was happening.

I was put on antidepressants to start with, mainly, I think, because I was not mentioning the voices. But when I eventually did talk about them I was put on an antipsychotic. In neither case was there any discussion with me about the medication – the psychiatrist chose it, and I was just given it without being told about the possible side effects. It turned out that I had the misfortune to be very sensitive to those side effects and this was the start of a vicious cycle. I would be put on drugs, find it difficult to function in the real world (I was still a scientist), stop taking them and gradually get ill again until I was sectioned. I would then be put on a different medication.

Although I was on antipsychotics, to begin with I was never given a diagnosis. I think subconsciously I knew what was wrong with me but didn't ask. About 2 years after first being hospitalised, I was still working and finding it difficult so I asked the psychiatrist if he knew the contact details for any support group for people who had an illness like mine. He referred me to the 'Voices' group of the National Schizophrenia Fellowship (now Rethink). This was the first time I had heard the word 'schizophrenia' in association with me and, despite knowing what antipsychotics were for, it was all quite shocking. However, in the longer term, knowing the diagnosis meant that I could find out about schizophrenia and I went to the Voices group and made some good friends.

I come from a family where everyone was expected to sort out their own problems from a very early age. I don't think that this contributed to me developing schizophrenia but it has made a difference with treatment because I've always found it very difficult to ask for help. In the early days of my illness, I think this is why I was sectioned so many times. My background, and being a scientist, made me completely happy with the 'medical model' of my illness and very scared of the idea of any kind of counselling or psychotherapy for the first few years I was ill. I would tell myself that it was all the fault of my brain receptors and, other than taking medication, there was nothing I could do.

After several years like this I was lucky enough to get a care coordinator with whom I got on really well. She encouraged me to think more positively about counselling and helped me understand that asking for help was alright. The outcome of this was that I trained to become a person-centred therapist and eventually left molecular biology with the intention of becoming a counsellor. However, for various reasons this did not happen and I have since become a trainer, writer and researcher in the mental health area. I have applied for other jobs but have a feeling my diagnosis will make it hard to find one.

Over time, the nature of the condition has changed. I have had no visual hallucinations for many years and after working my way through 29 different antidepressants, antipsychotics, mood stabilisers and anxiolytics, I have found a combination that mostly works without giving me too many side effects. I think it also helps that I no longer have a stressful job in science, although I did enjoy it. I hear voices constantly but only sometimes do they give me real problems. I occasionally have to go into hospital but usually as a voluntary patient and only for a short time. I also sometimes take medication for the side effects, especially if I have to sit still for any length of time.

Interestingly I have chosen to take one of the older antipsychotics despite having tried some of the second generation ones, because it's the one that works best for my lifestyle. I often have to be up early, which rules out anything that is sedating, and I hate depot injections because then I don't feel master of my own destiny. I have been helped to make these choices by my psychiatrists and GP, who have allowed me to experiment. The GP and I made an agreement that I could try any appropriate medication I wanted but I was not allowed to complain about it for at least 6 weeks!

I have tried CBT but struggle with it. My main problem is that in an effort to find out what is going on when I become ill, I've been asked to keep records, but the first thing I do when I do start getting ill is to stop keeping records. Consequently I've never really managed to understand the details of becoming ill. I know stress is involved, that I'm affected by the societal mood (such as worries about world events) and sleep less, but other than that I'm not sure what causes it.

I have made a lot of friends in hospital who form an informal support group and we do look out for each other. However, I think it's very important for me to have friends outside the mental health system and I still see people I've met in science, from the counselling course and from singing in one of the big London choirs. They all know about my diagnosis and understand if I withdraw for a while to sort my head out.

In terms of my personal coping strategies, I do Transcendental Meditation, use some aromatherapy oils, try to get enough sleep and not get too stressed. I exercise using step-aerobic videos at home (cheaper than joining a gym) and walking a lot. I love singing in the choir, reading books and adore working in my garden. I'm still not allowed to drive but this is not really a problem where I live. I've also learned what it's not a good idea for me to do: things like going to the pub, watching too much television and working full time. I get on great with my GP and care coordinator and okay with my psychiatrist.

The voices are still awful when they are really loud. They discuss me, put me down, shout obscenities, comment on what is happening to me and tell me to do things that put me in danger. It is very difficult to remain communicating in the real world, and doing this leaves me exhausted. In addition I often end up seeing the world in a very different and frightening way, and at the time I'm having these delusions I really believe them. I can still get very distressed by it all, but these days living with schizophrenia is easier than it was when I was first ill.

4.4   PERSONAL ACCOUNTS FROM CARERS

4.4.1   Personal account D

My son, aged 43, was diagnosed with schizophrenia when he was 19 years old. He has two older sisters who are both married, work, and have children. My son had a disturbed childhood. He did not talk until he was 2 years old and had obsessional habits, such as constantly twirling objects and spinning around and around. When he went to school he had concentration difficulties and did not read until he was 8. However, he was very musical and played the trumpet and the guitar. He also enjoyed acting and played some leading parts in school plays. He was an excellent mimic.

When my son was 8 he was referred by his school to a clinic near where we lived. He received intensive psychotherapy and his therapist also saw and advised me. However, the therapy did not really improve his condition. I was not told of any diagnosis at this time. (However, after my son had received a diagnosis of schizophrenia I had a chance meeting with his therapist who told me that she had found that children exhibiting the behaviour he had displayed often developed psychotic symptoms in later life). When he was 13, he, along with friends, began smoking cannabis periodically. After gaining two 'O' levels, he left school and attended a further educational college. His behaviour became even more disturbed and he began to dabble in the occult, and became convinced he had cursed his best friend. He began talking to himself and writing 'I didn't curse Charles' on pieces of paper and in any book he was reading.

When my son was 18 years old we moved to a different part of the country and he obtained a place at theatre school, but after two terms he was asked to leave because of his disturbed and disruptive behaviour. We persuaded him to see his GP, who referred him to a consultant psychiatrist. The consultant, however, said there was nothing wrong with him and refused to speak to my husband or me.

During the following year my son's behaviour rapidly worsened. He spent long periods of the night pacing about, talking to himself. During the day he appeared to be listening to voices and swearing at them. He became self-destructive and tore up many of his favourite books. He also stamped on his guitar, kicked in radiators and broke mirrors. We received no support or advice from anyone during this time, but eventually managed to make another appointment to see the consultant and this time we were told his behaviour was psychotic. He was admitted to hospital and 2 weeks later was diagnosed as suffering from schizophrenia. He was given chlorpromazine and was told he could be discharged. There was of course no CPA at this time and we were given no advice on how to care for him. There was only one CPN in the town where we lived and all other services were hospital based.

When my son came home for a predischarge weekend we could see very little change in him and, with regret, refused to have him home. He then stayed in hospital for another 4 months before being admitted to a therapeutic community. My son was actually experiencing psychotic symptoms when he joined the therapeutic community, but these became very much worse during his stay. He was offered admission to a psychiatric unit but refused to go. The therapeutic community discharged him after a year and he returned home where he became steadily worse. He eventually agreed to return to our local psychiatric hospital. His current consultant told us that he thought it was a 'tragedy' that he had been referred to the therapeutic community because the stresses and challenges of life in the community had worsened his condition.

My son remained extremely ill and spent most of the next 8 years in hospital. We always had him home for weekends in spite of the fact that he was still extremely disturbed. In 1991, when the hospital he was in closed, he became a resident in an eight-bed high care home run by the National Schizophrenia Fellowship in the town where we lived. My son has lived there ever since. His schizophrenia has proved treatment resistant although many different medications have been tried. However, during this time he has managed to complete an Open University foundation course in maths and has also joined a supportive amateur dramatic society. He comes home for 2 or 3 hours every day and I am in close contact with the staff of the home and his consultant psychiatrist.

My one worry is that the admirable optimism of the 'recovery' concept has unwittingly disadvantaged people like my son. As well as the excellent highly supported unit he lives in, he would benefit from a creative sheltered activity scheme and a comfortable drop-in centre where he could relax with people who have similar mental health problems. Unfortunately, many excellent day and high care accommodation services are closing. The concept of sanctuary and asylum seem unfashionable today and families are often the only resource left to the sufferer, which places a heavy burden on often elderly carers.

Caring for my son over the years has not been easy. The most important thing I have had to remember is that coping with the often angry and derisory voices in his head, which take the form of spirits, take up most of his mental energy. In latter years he has talked to me about them, but in the beginning I was ignorant and confused over his behaviour and made too many demands on him.

What I try to cultivate is an attitude of loving tolerance, while encouraging anything positive he wants to do. As he grows older he seems to have less motivation to do anything, but he still plays his guitar and has become interested in blues music. I also try to actively listen whenever he wants to talk to me, which often occurs at quite inconvenient moments!

I joined the National Schizophrenia Fellowship when my son was diagnosed. I find the society, which is now called Rethink, extremely supportive and knowledgeable and have been an active member for many years. I belong to a local active carers group, have been a member of my local implementation team and sit on service development groups. I also take part, with mental health professionals, in facilitating educational and supportive courses for carers. I find this work extremely satisfying as it gives me the opportunity to put the experience and knowledge I have gained from caring for my son over the years to good use.

4.4.2   Personal account E

My son was first sectioned in 1994 after damaging some property and was placed in a Victorian 'lunatic asylum', which has since closed. Here he was given the diagnosis of paranoid schizophrenia. I visited him and was appalled by the primitive accommodation and the treatment he was receiving. The staff did not appear to be trained in dealing with psychiatric illness and the consultant seemed to lack all understanding of the extreme anguish and suffering my son was evidently enduring, due both to the illness and the side effects of the medication. All I could do was to ask if he could be transferred to the hospital in his home town, so that his family could visit him more easily. The request was denied.

Eventually my son was permitted to leave of his own accord and he came home and admitted himself to the local psychiatric ward. But, once again, I had little faith in the staff and their training. The greatest and most unfortunate difficulty was the failure to find a drug that as well as helping his condition would not make it worse in other ways, such as was the case with the chlorpromazine he was being given.

Later he would be given injections and I often wept at the brutal treatment meted out to my son by male nurses forcing him to have these drugs, which he soon learnt would give him suicidal clinical depression and other extremely unpleasant side effects. Can one imagine how terrifying this was for him?

From my subsequent reading, it seemed that there was great uncertainty about the treatment of schizophrenia regarding the choice of drugs; and while new ones were appearing regularly that promised better results, my son was also unable to tolerate these. At no time was I offered any professional guidance in helping my son. I felt sad, desperate and helpless in my role as carer.

In despair, he absconded from hospital, not returning at the agreed time, and even escaped from hospital and went missing for long periods in order to save himself from the unhelpful regime and find some happiness in his life as best he could. On one occasion he disappeared for over a year, and we were uncertain if he was still alive. Eventually he returned voluntarily, though he found himself back in the 'revolving door' of hospitalisation and treatment for a number of years.

During the latter part of his treatment, the standard of care from the CMHT improved considerably and this undoubtedly contributed to his recovery. Finally, after a decade-long battle, he arrived at the correct choice of drug, which he had found out about from another patient. My son has made heroic efforts to restore himself to normal life, and has received the Lilly 'Moving Life Forward' award for his spirit and determination.

If there are any useful lessons to be learned from this experience they are that, firstly, sufferers of schizophrenia must not be treated like animals in a zoo. Secondly, drugs must be used only if they are proven to be useful in the long term and not, as in my son's case, forcibly administered when they only make matters worse overall. My son often said he would happily go to prison if it meant he did not have to have an injection. Finally, treatment must be by trained professional staff who know what they are doing and who most of all will regularly communicate with the sufferer, to help them and give them hope in their struggle until they can cope on their own.

4.4.3   Personal account F

I came to England from Jamaica in 1957 and so my four sons and four daughters were all born and raised in the UK. Very sadly, two of my sons developed schizophrenia within a very short period of each other in the early 1980s when they were 18 and 17 years old. In the area we lived in at that time, it was easy for teenagers to drift towards the Rastafarian culture due to peer pressures and so this is what happened with my eldest boy. This culture was attractive to black teenagers who felt victimised in the 'white man's world' and targeted by the police. So, my son drifted into a drug culture and quickly this developed into trouble with the police. He was charged with stealing but due to his behavioural patterns he was seen in prison by a psychiatrist who assessed that my son was a fit person and so had to serve a prison sentence.

After my son's release his behavioural patterns continued to deteriorate and he became increasingly restless. On one particular occasion he had a crisis at home during the night and the following day he was found jumping from one car roof to another in the city centre. He was picked up by the police but on this occasion he was detained under the Mental Health Act. This at least meant that he was seen by a psychiatrist who realised that he had mental health problems and so he was sectioned and treated as someone with mental ill-health.

When I first went to meetings after my eldest son had been sectioned, there were so many people at the meeting that it was very confusing and nobody seemed to want to try and move my son forward. However, eventually, I was invited to attend a support group, albeit one where the members were mainly carers of people with learning difficulties. I found this group very helpful and supportive particularly when I was offered a place on a carer education course. It would have been so much more helpful if these things had been offered to me much earlier.

It has always been disappointing to me that my son's psychiatrist has seldom talked to me – I know his name, but that's all. Sometimes my eldest son has been in hospital and sometimes in his own accommodation, but on very few occasions have I, as his mother, been given any information about his medication or given advice or even treated as his carer. I have never really felt involved.

However, the GP has been very helpful because he knows our family well and I have always been able to talk to him. Our son's illness has been difficult for the family to deal with, particularly in talking about it outside of the family. Sadly he himself finds it difficult to cope with being in a family group.

Schizophrenia has destroyed my son's life. He is now 44 and he has been in and out of trouble with the police. Fortunately some police recognise him and understand that he has an illness, and so handle him appropriately. Voices continue to torment him and unfortunately sometimes he has found that drugs make him feel peaceful and good, and over the years he has sold most of his belongings to buy drugs. He has been prescribed many different medications, but has never been offered any psychological therapies or family interventions.

Things have been a little better for my younger son. The treatments for both of my sons have been very similar, but my younger son has more insight and takes greater responsibility for his own treatment. He is able to advocate for himself with professionals and he will not accept substandard accommodation. He attends college and has found a real interest in art and carpentry.

For the past 25 years or so, life has been really difficult for both of my sons and for my family. For all of us it has been distressing, uncomfortable and full of fear.

Overall we feel badly let down with the lack of consistency and appropriateness in mental health services and staff, and also by the lack of suitable accommodation available, some of which is quite disgraceful.

4.4.4   Personal account G

When he was a boy, our son was well presented and well balanced and seemed to be taking life and education in his stride. Although never strong academically, he coped well enough, but it was in sport that he really excelled. He represented his school in rugby, cricket and badminton, and outside of school he became a very competent squash player. However, it was on the hockey field that he really shone with his skilful play. He was also in the choir at a local church and with other typical boys' activities, such as cubs and scouts, he had a busy and active life. He had a laid-back and cheerful approach so it was difficult to gauge what his potential in life really was, or if he was capable of achieving more in any of these activities or in education.

His life seemed to be evolving quite straightforwardly, and with six GCSEs he went off at 16 to a local college to do a BTEC course and then in September 1993 he started his degree course in Wales. We had no hint of any problems or difficulties in his life. He settled into a bedsit quite quickly and became a regular first team player with the local hockey club.

It was in only his second term that there was any hint of a problem and it was during this period that we discovered that he was a regular user of cannabis (we later learnt he had started taking cannabis several years earlier). It transpired that he was not attending college courses and spent much of his time shut in his room. Then the phone calls home started; these were often made late at night or during the night with regular use of expletives (not previously a feature of his dialogue). He shouted and yelled accusations at us and indeed anyone who had any involvement in his life.

Appointments were made for him to either go to a doctor, or for a doctor to go to him, but neither came to fruition. The extent of the problem became clearer when eventually I was able to get access to his bedsit and he told me that he had just seen on TV that he was to become the next King of England.

It proved extremely difficult for us to ascertain what to do next because while it was possible to get very general information from libraries and the family GP, nobody actually offered advice on what to do. This was brought to a head when the landlord of the bedsit wanted him evicted due to a potential threat of violence to others living in the house.

We didn't know where to go for real help, but eventually a friend explained to us that we were entitled to request a mental health assessment. With this new information we were able to access a social worker who was the first person to offer practical help. He arranged for an assessment involving a really helpful psychiatrist, a GP, the social worker himself and with police in attendance. Thanks to the great skills of the psychiatrist, our son was admitted to a psychiatric unit as a voluntary patient.

He immediately chose not to recognise us as his parents and blamed us for his problems. Communication with him became virtually impossible and, although we travelled down each weekend to see him, he would never talk to us. While we were given an indication that he may be suffering from schizophrenia, at no stage was this confirmed and neither was he informed of this. We also didn't really know what treatment he was receiving at this time, other than that it was medication, but he wouldn't talk to us and he didn't really want the staff to talk to us. After a few months he was transferred to supported accommodation, and at this stage he became slightly more communicative and was showing signs of recovery. This progress continued and after a few more months he returned to live in the family home.

Everything seemed to be moving forward for him; he resumed college, he got a job relevant to his career ambitions and in hockey he represented the county at senior level. But then the roller coaster started, which was probably attributable to his own denial of the illness. He stopped taking his medication and returned to cannabis for comfort.

The next few years were a nightmare for all of us with difficult periods with him living at home, attempts to live in his own accommodation which highlighted his own fears, and several periods of hospitalisation. He blamed us for his problems, would not communicate with us rationally and yet it was still us he turned to when in difficulty. He couldn't live with us, but he couldn't live without us.

During this period, support from the CMHT was spasmodic and ineffective – the fact that he kept disappearing and was non-compliant contributed significantly to this. Eventually yet another major crisis arose while he was living at home: he would lock himself in his room and seldom come out; when he did come out he was threatening and aggressive, particularly to his mother. In addition, a neighbour complained that he was trespassing on their property and spending time in a shed they had in an adjacent field. The social worker (supported by the psychiatrist) considered that sectioning was the only way forward. This was the first time that his problems were addressed on a compulsory basis. A change in personnel also facilitated a different type of approach to his care and treatment, and also to the way in which we were treated and involved as his carers.

It was at this stage that it was suggested by a new CPN and the social worker that perhaps behavioural family therapy might be helpful to all of us. As his carers, we had received very little support and were still ignorant about the illness and its treatments and so when we were offered help as a family, we saw this as a potential lifeline – what could we lose?

We were given an outline of what the therapy consisted of and what the potential outcomes and benefits might be, but we really needed very little persuasion. The therapists felt that it would be a good idea for our family and that it was possible that the therapy would give us some of the information and support that we were looking for. In particular we were told that the communications aspects of the therapy might help the day-to-day relationships within the family.

Getting our son to buy in was a different matter. He was still in hospital at the time, although he was allowed home on leave one evening a week. He was ambivalent about getting involved in the programme himself but, very fortunately, did not put any barriers in the way for his Mum and me to get started. Although this was not ideal, the support team now engaged with our family had the foresight to agree to proceed on the basis that our son might join in later and, indeed, after a few weeks he gradually fully engaged with the family work.

The family work continued both formally and informally for several years and we used many of the techniques that we had learned within the family quite regularly. Although in the intervening years our son has had several relapses, his psychiatrists have shown a creative approach and have encouraged him to take medication (currently pipotiazine palmitate) in a depot form, and he has also taken fish oil tablets on a regular basis. Many of their meetings with him have been in informal settings which have made communication much easier.

We also have a daughter who throughout the period of our son's illness has been supportive, and yet keen to be at a certain distance from the immediate practicalities facing the family. In the early years she felt that her brother's behaviour was just that of a typical teenager and she sought to reassure herself that this was all the problem was. The realisation of a more serious health problem was more difficult for her to cope with, particularly when he would present himself at her front door to seek refuge. However as our son's mental health has improved, so she has offered more support. He is now very proud to be an uncle to her to her two little boys. She never actually participated in our behavioural family therapy sessions but there were a number of occasions when she joined our regular family meetings and actively participated.

At the time of writing it is 5 years since our son's last relapse and his progress has been such that we all have a comfortable and relatively stress-free life totally compatible with the objectives we set when we started the family intervention several years previously. He lives in a very nice flat provided through a social housing scheme and receives support through an assertive outreach team and a community support team in the voluntary sector. He has a part time job in a local garage which he thoroughly enjoys and which has been key to him feeling able to lead a normal life again; he has recently completed a related NVQ. He plays hockey and golf regularly.

All this progress is attributable to several things, not least of which are the efforts he has made himself to move his life forward. He has continued to receive great support and help from psychiatrists, assertive outreach staff and the visiting support team in his accommodation. However there is no doubt in my mind that the family intervention that we all participated in has also played a significant part in his treatment and progress, particularly in the development of his interpersonal skills and levels of activity. In our son's case, the effective family intervention has illustrated how psychological treatments can interface with medications to provide an holistic approach in the treatment of schizophrenia.

4.4.5   Personal account H

I am the husband of someone who was diagnosed with schizophrenia 20 years ago. When we got married I was aware that she had had minor problems with depression in the past, but did not think that this would cause any problems in our life together. We had been married 4 years when she first became ill – she had got antidepressants off the GP and took an overdose of them, and was taken to the psychiatric hospital for the first time. I had not realised how serious things had become and that her work colleagues had already insisted that she see a psychiatrist. After treating her for a mood disorder for over a year, the doctors eventually told us that she had schizophrenia.

In those early years, my thoughts were mainly disbelief and incomprehension at the diagnosis. I had no accurate idea of what schizophrenia was and thought it would soon blow over, and my wife would be alright again. The treatment seemed to revolve totally around medications, which, although they pacified the symptoms, gave her awful side effects. She would then be given medication to try to control the side effects but these had adverse effects of their own. It all made life very difficult. The worst time was when she was put on a depot injection – the side effects of this led to her being like a zombie; she had no personality, was emotionally flat and ended up sleeping her life away.

When my wife stopped taking the medication, things were also difficult because she would relapse and leave home and wander the streets, sometimes for days. I wouldn't know where she was and would be very worried. On numerous occasions I would return from a business trip abroad to find her in hospital as she had had a relapse. I knew she was in great danger during these wandering episodes and I realised that she might be seriously injured or even die; this was an extremely difficult reality that I had to come to terms with on an emotional level. At the height of my despair, I recall on one occasion coming home and finding that she was not there; she had wandered away on her way from work. I went out in the car and drove to where I thought she might be based on what she had told me previously of where she tended to go. We live in a big city and the chances of me finding her were very small but I felt desperate and felt I had to try something. I didn't find her and was really worried until she eventually turned up. She was also often arrested by the police on a Section 136 of the Mental Health Act and I would either get a phone call to tell me they had taken her to the hospital or they would bring her home. For a while I was anxious all my waking hours.

To begin with I tried very hard to help her remember to take the medication and to look after her but the episodic nature of the condition caused me much despair and frustration. Every time the symptoms receded, I thought that she would stay okay. We would plan things – holidays and evenings out – but she would become ill and they would have to be cancelled. In the end, on a day when she was sectioned yet again, I snapped and told her she would have to take more responsibility for herself, that I could not go on living like this. It seemed like a hurtful thing to do but she has managed to do it and our life together is now very much better.

I am a strong person who takes care of himself so have never felt the need to join a support group. I was also worried that they would be focused on the negative side of things in a self-pitying kind of way – 'Isn't it awful. . .' – and I did not want that. I have, however, had some support from my family, mostly my brother (because mental health problems are a taboo subject in my culture and my parents have found it difficult to deal with). I had a very good relationship with my wife's first psychiatrist and with her second care coordinator; but these days, because she manages the condition for herself, I have little contact with the psychiatric team. I prefer it this way – I would rather be her husband than her 'carer'.

I sometimes get the feeling that because most carers seem to be parents caring for children that some NHS staff can develop a one-size-fits-all approach to carers. As a partner, it is obviously very different for me and I feel things like family therapy are not appropriate for us. Also I would only want the care coordinator to send me a copy of a care plan if my wife wanted me to see it. I also sometimes wonder whether the patient's quality of life in the community is thought about sufficiently by the doctors. It is probably quite easy to control the symptoms by giving enough medication, but if you destroy the person's personality this curtails their enjoyment of life and causes a great deal of unhappiness for the people around them. My wife is naturally a very lively and stimulating person to be with, and seeing her pacified by the side effects of medication was heart breaking.

Looking back on events, we have both grown from having gone through these experiences. What I mean by this is that we have learned a lot about humility, compromise, patience, humour and how to live with things. The best strategy for both of us now is for my wife to be on the lowest possible dose of medication needed to keep things under control so that she doesn't have too many side effects. We both try to have a good routine, eat a healthy diet and enjoy ourselves; that is, we try to live as normal a life as possible despite my wife's condition. She still occasionally goes into the hospital but usually for a short time – in the past she could be in for many months. I think it is important for the people in the psychiatric team to work with the person rather than try and force treatment on them. I also think it is important for them to only take control when they absolutely have to. I know my wife still has some symptoms but if she can live her life around them I am happy.

4.5 SUMMARY OF THEMES FROM SERVICE USERS' AND CARERS' EXPERIENCES

4.5.1 Introduction

The personal accounts cover a wide range of experience and also extend across over 30 years of treatment and care of people with schizophrenia. While it is not possible to make any statements about effectiveness of individual interventions from these accounts, what is evident is the extent to which overall care of people with the condition has improved. This is because of a variety of factors, including the modernisation of services, greater choice of drugs, the introduction of the Community Care Act in 1990 and the National Service Framework for Mental Health in 1999, and also because of service users' individual efforts in terms of information sharing and peer support. There is a sense from the personal accounts and the wider literature that most service users feel that they have more dignity as they are gaining more responsibility for and agency regarding their own treatment.

However, there is not such an optimistic picture from the personal accounts from carers. Although treatments for schizophrenia may have improved, the carers whose voices are captured here expressed concern about being excluded from their family members' care and feeling generally unsupported. Greater emphasis on community care may also impact negatively on carers because more of the day-to-day responsibility of care will rest on their shoulders.

4.5.2 Service user experiences

Becoming ill and accessing services
The personal accounts from both people with schizophrenia and their carers express that when a person first becomes ill they can find everyday life a real struggle and very frightening. The symptoms of a first episode can be devastating (although one person found the symptoms exhilarating) and it can take a while to find the right strategies for coping. These strategies tend to be very individual, but having a good therapeutic relationship with mental health professionals is also crucial.

Some people become ill suddenly, while for others it can take weeks or even years. It is interesting that in the personal accounts from service users and carers, cannabis and other street drugs are often mentioned. However, because there are only eight accounts here it would not be appropriate to make a general statement about this. Some people are helped to access services by relatives, while others come to the attention of healthcare professionals after an 'incident' of some kind.

There may be a reluctance among people from ethnic minorities to become service users even if they think they have a mental health problem because they do not wish to be 'shunned' by their community (see account F).

One service user highlighted the positive aspects of an early intervention service that they had used after a psychotic episode. The service had helped them to talk about their experiences in an atmosphere that was non-judgemental and encouraging:

> *'Through opening up to someone and talking to them honestly without any fear of condemnation or reprisal, I was able to relieve the massive burden of anxiety that I was experiencing in the early stages of my recovery, a burden which was preventing me from moving forward and getting on with the rest of my life'* (Anonymous, 2008).

The service provided advice on practical issues, such as making applications for benefits, as well as helping the person cope with paranoid thoughts. They enabled the person to get involved in activities that interested them and provided company and transport so that the person could attend these activities: *'I began to realise that there was a life out there for me, full of possibilities and opportunities and my hopes and desires for the future were restored, even enhanced'* (Anonymous, 2008).

For respondents to the Rethink survey, their priorities regarding elements of their care were: (1) having concerns taken seriously (2) having a choice of medication and (3) being treated with respect (Borneo, 2008).

Medication
A major theme of the personal accounts was about finding the right medication and the struggle that service users underwent to find appropriate drug treatment that did

not cause debilitating side effects (over half of the respondents to the Rethink survey found the side effects of both typical and atypical antipsychotics *'quite bad'* or *'intolerable'*, with social life being the most affected domain [Borneo, 2008]). For example, one person preferred to be homeless or violent rather than take a specific drug. What is striking from the personal accounts is the degree to which people with schizophrenia felt compelled to try to take control of the situation and make their own choices or impose their own rules about how they were to be treated. This was done by making an advance statement (account A), outright refusal (account B) and careful negotiation (account C). It should be noted that this process of 'taking control' may take a long time, and indeed may not be possible in the early stages of the illness. The person may have been prescribed many different drugs before one is found that helps them to feel like they are regaining control. It is therefore of prime importance that healthcare professionals respect the views and wishes of service users regarding treatment, and their own assessments of the effectiveness of treatments.

What also emerges from the accounts is the fact that medication was rarely discussed with the person in advance of it being administered, and how important it is for professionals to give people with schizophrenia detailed information about the drugs and also options for different types of treatment. On the positive side, it is worth pointing out that over the last decade there has been a much greater choice of drugs and hence a greater likelihood that service users will find one to which they are suited. At least one of the service users above found a newly available drug that it was possible for them to take on an ongoing basis because they did not experience any side effects.

In the Rethink survey, 98% of people with a diagnosis of schizophrenia/schizo-affective disorder (345) were receiving pharmacological treatment, which was predominantly atypical antipsychotic medication (although for people taking typical antipsychotics, women were more likely to be prescribed these than men). Nine percent of people with schizophrenia/schizoaffective disorder who were taking medication (30) were prescribed more than one antipsychotic (but may have been in the process of changing drug). A large percentage of people (84%) recognised that that there were benefits to taking medication, including 'alleviation of symptoms', 'mood stabilisation', having a 'calming effect', 'aiding sleep' and 'preventing relapse'. Eight per cent said that they could identify no benefits to taking medication (Borneo, 2008).

In the personal accounts, the medication that was first administered was rarely discussed with the person. However, the situation had latterly improved and there had been discussion with the service user about their current treatment. In the Rethink survey there was some discussion about 'at least one aspect' of medication with 88% of service users; for the majority this was the dose (66%), followed by the type of medication (60%), followed by when the drug should be taken (59%). However, only half had been told about possible side effects. The Rethink survey also confirmed one theme from the personal accounts – that is, that people who had been taking medication for longer, and may have first been prescribed typical psychotics, were given less information about the medication (Borneo, 2008).

Another concerning amplification of some of the experiences in the personal accounts from the Rethink survey is that two thirds of the respondents said that they were not given any options about the medication they were prescribed. More people taking typical antipsychotics, when compared with atypicals, were offered a choice of medication (Borneo, 2008).

Psychological interventions

Few people in the accounts above mentioned individual psychological therapies – for them the issue of medication seemed to be of primary importance. One of the service users mentioned that CBT was not helpful because it required a degree of commitment and concentration that was just not possible during difficult phases of the illness. One of the carers highlighted the importance of a family intervention, which was an important step towards his son and the rest of the family making significant progress.

The Rethink survey echoes this prioritisation of medication over psychological therapy with only 14% of respondents having had CBT. Twenty two per cent had had other types of psychological therapy, but not all of these were available through the NHS. It was more likely that younger people (aged 18 to 34 years) would be offered non-pharmacological treatments. Fewer people who had had CBT found it helpful (69%) than arts therapies (83%) or 'other talking therapy' (80%) (Borneo, 2008).

For the person who used early intervention services, therapeutic intervention was invaluable for recovery (Anonymous, 2008). On the Healthtalkonline website (Healthtalkonline, 2008) although some service users wanted therapists who understood their culture and issues about race, others just wanted a good relationship with a therapist regardless of ethnicity.

Creative activities

Some interest in the arts is frequently mentioned as helping. For example, one service user was in a choir, while another ran an art group. The carers also mention that one family member had joined a drama group and another was interested in art and carpentry. One service user on the Healthtalkonline website said that '*writing gave her a reason to wake up in the morning*' and that '*art gives you your voice back*' (Healthtalkonline, 2008; transcript 14). Exercise is also viewed as helpful by respondents to the Rethink survey (Borneo, 2008).

Recovery

Some of the personal accounts pointed to the importance of being given hope and optimism by professionals that recovery is attainable. Recovery is a very individual process, and the factors that aided in the recovery of the people whose accounts are presented in this chapter, and helped them to break the cycle of episode-hospitalisation-discharge-relapse, are varied. Also, what one person may consider to be 'recovery' may be different from other people's concepts. For instance, it might mean taking responsibility for one's medication, being able to choose one's treatment, or finding a place where one can be as well as possible within certain constraints. Another point to bear in mind is the fact that, as the carer in account D points out, the recovery model may not be appropriate for some people like her son who may be treated with unrealistic expectations, or whose complex needs cannot be met solely in the community.

Having a good care coordinator or CPN, who the service user feels is listening to them, can mark the start of recovery, as can regular support and feeling that one is actively participating in one's own treatment and care rather than being 'coerced' down a particular treatment route. Finding a medication regime that minimised side effects and was reasonably flexible was important to many of the people in the personal accounts. People with schizophrenia also aided their own recovery by understanding their illness and knowing what may trigger an episode and engaging in occupations and meaningful activities. However, it should be emphasised that recovery has to happen at the person's own rate.

4.5.3   Carer experience

It is clear from the personal accounts that healthcare professionals do not always consider involving the family or carers, where appropriate, in care and treatment plans for people with schizophrenia, and they do not always communicate basic information about the condition when what families and carers often seek most in the care of their family member is information and involvement.

Families and carers often feel excluded from the care and treatment of the person with schizophrenia, yet if that person is to be cared for effectively in the community then the involvement of carers is of paramount importance.

Very often the cycle of patient care will mean that the person with schizophrenia may move from, for example, primary care into an acute unit and then into a community team, which results in several changes in the personnel of the care team. However, professionals often forget that in some circumstances families and carers generally remain constant and give a degree of permanency that services do not. Even if in acute stages of the illness the carer is rejected by the person with schizophrenia, it is important that the carer is kept informed because so often they will have an important role to play in the future.

Healthcare professionals should ensure, therefore, that family members and carers are involved in the development of the care programme as far as any confidentiality issues allow, and that carers are clear of their role in this programme. This should certainly be the case with regard to the new Care Programme Approach. Confidentiality issues should be fully explained to families and carers at an early stage and health and social care professionals should be proactive in ensuring that carers still receive the information that they need to be effective and supportive carers.

The personal accounts highlight that close contact between carers and healthcare professionals, and clear lines of communication, can have a positive impact on the treatment and care of the person with schizophrenia. Carers should be provided with information and support at an early stage, and this should include a structured carer education programme if possible.

It is important that carers know where to go for help and guidance, and that they are fully aware of all key local 'signposts' including where to go when there is a crisis. They might be encouraged to attend support groups and, indeed, some carers may go on to be active in the running and organisation of these groups on both a local and national level.

Without support, carers may feel overwhelmed and unable to cope, which may lead to a breakdown in the relationship between the family and the person with schizophrenia, or to the carer experiencing anxiety or depression. Moreover, because schizophrenia is often a long-term condition, this can impact on an increasingly elderly carer population. Carers should therefore be offered a carer's assessment and the benefits of this assessment should be fully explained. If requested by the carer, any interventions should take into account the carers' physical, social and mental health needs. Interventions that involve the whole family may be beneficial, depending on the family circumstances, because they provide support and help families to understand the issues surrounding schizophrenia and to be more effective in contributing to the care and recovery programme.

It should be recognised that the needs of carers who are partners may be very different from those of parental carers. Indeed it might be the case, as the husband in personal account H points out, that the partner may choose not to be seen as a 'carer' but as a supportive partner. This may fluctuate according to the course of the person's illness, with more support being offered during a crisis. If, however, a partner wishes to be more actively involved in the person's care, and the person consents to it, then means other than family intervention may have to be found to engage such carers.

The needs of young carers should also be recognised and addressed and recent publications from the Social Care Institute for Excellence and the Department of Health (Department of Health *et al.*, 2008; Greene *et al.*, 2008; Roberts *et al.*, 2008) provide guidance on how this can be achieved. It should be recognised that young carers may marginalise themselves from their peer group and experience other social and educational disadvantage. The report by Roberts and colleagues (2008) suggests that the needs of young carers could be more effectively addressed by respecting their anxieties and acknowledging their input and skills. It is also recommended that young carers should be included in their family member's care planning.

4.6   RECOMMENDATIONS

4.6.1   Optimism

4.6.1.1   Work in partnership with people with schizophrenia and their carers. Offer help, treatment and care in an atmosphere of hope and optimism. Take time to build supportive and empathic relationships as an essential part of care.

4.6.2   Getting help early

4.6.2.1   Healthcare professionals should facilitate access as soon as possible to assessment and treatment, and promote early access throughout all phases of care.

4.6.3   Assessment

4.6.3.1   Ensure that people with schizophrenia receive a comprehensive multidisciplinary assessment, including a psychiatric, psychological and physical health assessment. The assessment should also address the following:
- accommodation
- culture and ethnicity
- economic status
- occupation and education (including employment and functional activity)
- prescribed and non-prescribed drug history
- quality of life
- responsibility for children
- risk of harm to self and others
- sexual health
- social networks.

4.6.3.2   Routinely monitor for other coexisting conditions, including depression and anxiety, particularly in the early phases of treatment.

4.6.4   Working in partnership with carers

4.6.4.1   When working with carers of people with schizophrenia:
- provide written and verbal information on schizophrenia and its management, including how families and carers can help through all phases of treatment
- offer them a carer's assessment
- provide information about local carer and family support groups and voluntary organisations, and help carers to access these
- negotiate confidentiality and information sharing between the service user and their carers, if appropriate
- assess the needs of any children in the family, including young carers.

4.6.5   Consent, capacity and treatment decisions

4.6.5.1   Before each treatment decision is taken, healthcare professionals should ensure that they:
- provide service users and carers with full, patient-specific information in the appropriate format about schizophrenia and its management, to ensure informed consent before starting treatment
- understand and apply the principles underpinning the Mental Capacity Act, and are aware that mental capacity is decision specific (that is, if there is doubt about mental capacity, assessment of mental capacity should be made in relation to each decision)
- can assess mental capacity, if this is in doubt, using the test set out in the Mental Capacity Act.

These principles should apply whether or not people are being detained or treated under the Mental Health Act and are especially important for people from black and minority ethnic (BME) groups.

4.6.5.2   When the Mental Health Act is used, inform service users of their right to appeal to a first-tier tribunal (mental health). Support service users who choose to appeal.

4.6.5.3   After each acute episode, encourage people with schizophrenia to write an account of their illness in their notes.

4.6.6   Advance agreements

4.6.6.1   Advance decisions and advance statements should be developed collaboratively with people with schizophrenia, especially if their illness is severe and they have been treated under the Mental Health Act. Record the decisions and statements and include copies in the care plan in primary and secondary care. Give copies to the service user and their care coordinator, and their carer if the service user agrees.

4.6.6.2   Advance decisions and advance statements should be honoured in accordance with the Mental Capacity Act. Although decisions can be overridden using the Mental Health Act, healthcare professionals should endeavour to honour advance decisions and statements wherever possible.

4.6.7   Second opinion

4.6.7.1   A decision by the service user, and carer where appropriate, to seek a second opinion on the diagnosis should be supported, particularly in view of the considerable personal and social consequences of being diagnosed with schizophrenia.

4.6.8   Service-level interventions

4.6.8.1   All teams providing services for people with schizophrenia should offer social, group and physical activities to people with schizophrenia (including in inpatient settings) and record arrangements in their care plan.

4.6.9   Employment, education and occupational activities

4.6.9.1   Mental health services should work in partnership with local stakeholders, including those representing BME groups, to enable people with mental health problems, including schizophrenia, to access local employment and educational opportunities. This should be sensitive to the person's needs and skill level and is likely to involve working with agencies such as Jobcentre Plus, disability employment advisers and non-statutory providers.

4.6.9.2 Routinely record the daytime activities of people with schizophrenia in their care plans, including occupational outcomes.

5   ACCESS AND ENGAGEMENT

This chapter is new for the guideline update and focuses on two types of service organisation and clinical practice, with the aim of:

- promoting early intervention for all people developing psychosis for the first time
- ensuring that people from specific cultural or ethnic backgrounds who appear not to engage or access care are offered attractive and effective interventions.

Section 5.2 updates a review of early intervention that was reported in the chapter on service-level intervention in the previous guideline. Section 5.3 includes a new review of ethnic-specific services, a re-analysis of work undertaken for the NICE guideline on bipolar disorder (NCCMH, 2006) on services, and secondary sub-analyses of two service-level intervention studies.

5.1   INTRODUCTION

Although there is great emphasis on clinical practice and service organisation to deliver effective clinical interventions, it is well known that there are significant social and ethnic inequalities regarding access to and benefit from such effective clinical interventions. Schizophrenia is likely to impact negatively on finances, employment and relationships, especially if the illness begins when the person is very young, which is a vulnerable time and when the adverse social impact of an illness can be most devastating. More attention is now rightly focused on ensuring early access to effective interventions for psychosis, to reduce periods of untreated psychosis, and also to ensure prompt and precise diagnosis, and quicker recovery to minimise social deficits, following the onset of illness.

There is substantial evidence that patterns of inequality regarding access to and benefit from treatment show some ethnic groups are disadvantaged and might benefit from prompt and precise diagnosis and intervention. Furthermore, some people from specific ethnic groups may fear services, or respond to stigma, or find that services do not understand their personal, religious, spiritual, social and cultural needs or their cultural identity. These needs are important for them to sustain and maintain a healthy identity.

5.2   EARLY INTERVENTION

5.2.1   Introduction

The NHS Plan (Department of Health, 2000) set out a requirement for mental health services to establish early intervention services. Early intervention services are expected to provide care for: (a) people aged between 14 and 35 years with a first presentation of psychotic symptoms; and (b) people aged 14 to 35 years during the first 3 years of psychotic illness. *The Mental Health Policy Implementation Guide* (Department of Health, 2001) set out a wide range of tasks for early intervention services, including: reducing stigma and raising awareness of symptoms of psychosis to reduce the duration of untreated illness; developing engagement, providing evidence-based treatments and promoting recovery for young people who have experienced an episode of psychosis; and working across the traditional divide between child and adolescent services and adult services as well as in partnership with primary care, education, social services, youth and other services.

Early intervention is primarily concerned with identification and initial treatment of people with psychotic illnesses, such as schizophrenia. Identification may be directed either at people in the prodromal phase of the illness ('earlier early intervention') or at those who have already developed psychosis ('early intervention'). Providing treatment for people in a possible prodromal phase of schizophrenia is an interesting but potentially controversial area, which at present is outside the scope of this guideline. The GDG is, however, aware of developments in the field (for example, McGorry *et al.*, 2002; Morrison *et al.*, 2004), which may be reviewed in further updates of the guideline.

Early identification of people with psychotic disorders also does not fall within the scope of the guideline, but may be especially relevant to specific groups, for example, African–Caribbean people who are reported to have a higher incidence of schizophrenia, but whose treatment is not flexible to their cultural needs or based on choice. Central to the rationale for this type of early identification is the concept of duration of untreated psychosis (DUP). A number of researchers have reported that the longer the psychosis goes untreated, the poorer the prognosis becomes (for example, Loebel *et al.*, 1992; McGorry *et al.*, 1996). This finding has led them to argue that new services are required to reduce the length of time that people with psychosis remain undiagnosed and untreated. Moreover, these researchers have argued that such services should offer specialised, phase-specific treatment to their users, to maximise their chances of recovery.

Definitions

Early intervention services are defined as a service approach with focus on the care and treatment of people in the early phase (usually up to 5 years) and including the prodromal phase of the disorder. The service may be provided by a team or a specialised element of a team, which has designated responsibility for at least two of the following functions:

- early identification and therapeutic engagement of people in the prodromal phase
- provision of specialised pharmacological and psychosocial interventions during or immediately following a first episode of psychosis
- education of the wider community to reduce obstacles to early engagement in treatment.

5.2.2 Clinical review protocol

The review protocol, including the primary clinical question, information about the databases searched and the eligibility criteria can be found in Table 4. For the guideline update, a new systematic search was conducted for relevant RCTs published since the previous guideline (further information about the search strategy can be found in Appendix 8).

Table 4: Clinical review protocol for the review of early intervention services

Primary clinical question	For people with psychosis, do early intervention services improve outcomes when compared with standard care?
Subquestions	For all people with psychosis, do early intervention services improve the number of people remaining in contact with services?
	For African–Caribbean people with psychosis, do early intervention services improve the number of people remaining in contact with services?
Electronic databases	CINAHL, EMBASE, MEDLINE, PsycINFO
Date searched	1 January 2002 to 30 July 2008
Study design	RCTs
Patient population	People with psychosis
Interventions	An early intervention service
Outcomes	Any

Note: Studies (or outcomes from studies) were categorised as short term (12 weeks or fewer), medium term (12–51 weeks) and long term (52 weeks or more).

5.2.3 Studies considered for review[5]

In the previous guideline, no high-quality evaluation of the impact of early intervention services on the initial treatment of psychosis was available. The update search identified four RCTs (N = 800) relating to clinical evidence that met the inclusion criteria. All trials were published in peer-reviewed journals between 2004 and 2006. In addition, one study was excluded from the analysis because of the population

---

[5] Here and elsewhere in this chapter, each study considered for review is referred to by a study ID in capital letters (primary author and date of study publication). References for included studies denoted by study IDs can be found in Appendix 15a.

characteristics and primary focus of the intervention (further information about both included and excluded studies can be found in Appendix 15a).

5.2.4   Early intervention services versus standard care

For the update, four RCTs of an early intervention service versus standard care were included in the meta-analysis (see Table 5 for a summary of the study characteristics). Of the four included trials, three reported long-term outcomes of at least 18 months. A further trial (KUIPERS2004-COAST) reported outcomes at 6 and 9 months, but had more than 50% loss to follow-up and therefore only the outcome of leaving the study early was included in the meta-analysis. Forest plots and/or data tables for each outcome can be found in Appendix 16a.

5.2.5   Clinical evidence summary

In three RCTs including 741 participants with psychosis, there was consistent evidence at 18 to 24 months' follow-up that early intervention services, when compared with standard care, produced clinically significant benefits for a number of critical outcomes including relapse, rehospitalisation, symptom severity, satisfaction and quality of life. Early intervention services may also improve access and engagement with services as measured by the number leaving the study early and the number of service users receiving psychological treatments. However, there is currently insufficient evidence to determine whether these effects are sustained past 2 years, with one RCT (N = 547) failing to find consistent evidence of benefit at 5 years' follow-up.

5.2.6   Health economic evidence

No studies evaluating the cost effectiveness of early intervention services for people with schizophrenia met the set criteria for inclusion in the guideline systematic review of economic literature. However, the previous guideline, using more relaxed inclusion criteria, had identified one economic study on this area (Mihalopoulos *et al.*, 1999). Details on the methods used for the systematic search of the economic literature in the guideline update are described in Chapter 3; details on the respective methods in the previous NICE schizophrenia guideline are provided in Appendix 17. The following text marked by asterisks is derived from the full version of the previous NICE schizophrenia guideline (NCCMH, 2003):

**Early intervention services have been hypothesised to reduce long-term healthcare resource use and improved social functioning, leading to savings which may offset the cost of providing early intervention. This supposition is based on the evidence for a potential link between shorter duration of untreated psychosis and better outcome in schizophrenia.

Table 5: Summary of study characteristics for RCTs of early intervention services

Early intervention services versus standard care	
k (total N)	4 (800)
Study ID	CRAIG2004-LEO GRAWE2006-OTP KUIPERS2004-COAST PETERSEN2005-OPUS
Diagnosis	66–100% schizophrenia or other related diagnoses (DSM-III or IV)
Baseline severity	BPRS total: Mean (SD): 40 (7.6) (GRAWE2006)
Selected inclusion criteria	CRAIG2004: - Aged 16–40 years living in the London borough of Lambeth - Presenting to mental health services for the first time with non-affective psychosis (ICD-10) - People who had presented once but had subsequently disengaged without treatment from routine community services GRAWE2006: - Aged 18–35 - DSM-IV diagnosis of schizophrenic disorders - Recent onset (<2 years since first psychotic symptoms) KUIPERS2004: - First contact with mental health services within the past 5 years - Diagnosis of any functional psychosis PETERSEN2005: - Aged 18–45 years - ICD-10 diagnosis of schizophrenia spectrum diagnosis - Had not been given antipsychotic drugs for more than 12 weeks of continuous treatment
Treatment length	CRAIG2004-LEO: 78 weeks GRAWE2006-OTP: 104 weeks KUIPERS2004-COAST: 52 weeks PETERSEN2005-OPUS: 104 weeks

Note: Studies (or outcomes from studies) were categorised as short term (12 weeks or fewer), medium term (12–51 weeks) and long term (52 weeks or more).

The economic review identified one eligible study (Mihalopoulos *et al.*, 1999), which is a cost-effectiveness analysis from Australia based on a controlled study with historical controls. No RCTs addressing the cost-effectiveness question were identified. The results of the study by Mihalopoulos and colleagues (1999) have a low risk of bias, and the robustness of the findings was confirmed by sensitivity analysis. However, the authors costed only direct healthcare services, so it is impossible to estimate any broader economic effects of early intervention.

The results showed that the Early Psychosis Prevention and Intervention Centre (EPPIC) had a clear advantage over standard care in economic terms, being more effective and cost saving (Mihalopoulos *et al.*, 1999). Nevertheless, an interpretation of this result in the context of UK or other types of early intervention services should be treated with caution.**

The evidence table for the above study, as it appeared in the previous schizophrenia guideline, is included in Appendix 14.

5.2.7   From evidence to recommendations

In the previous guideline there was little high-quality evidence regarding the benefit of early intervention services; however, the GDG recognised that the rationale for an early intervention service is powerful, both ethically (helping people with serious mental health problems at an early stage to reduce distress and possibly disability) and in terms of flexibility and choice (service users and carers want help sooner than is usually available). New evidence from the clinical review clearly demonstrates that early intervention can be effective with benefits lasting at least 2 years. Further research is needed to establish longer-term effectiveness.

Early intervention services are potentially a cost-effective option for people with psychosis. Limited evidence from research undertaken in Australia has shown that the costs of providing early intervention services are likely to be offset by cost savings in other parts of the healthcare service.

5.2.8   Recommendations

5.2.8.1   Offer early intervention services to all people with a first episode or first presentation of psychosis, irrespective of the person's age or the duration of untreated psychosis. Referral to early intervention services may be from primary or secondary care.

5.2.8.2   Early intervention services should aim to provide a full range of relevant pharmacological, psychological, social, occupational and educational interventions for people with psychosis, consistent with this guideline.

5.3 ACCESS AND ENGAGEMENT TO SERVICE-LEVEL INTERVENTIONS

5.3.1 Introduction

Background and approach
Schizophrenia is known to be a devastating illness with significant social and psychological deficits, and it is crucial that service users receive treatments and services that are collectively sanctioned as appropriate approaches in the context of dominant ethical, clinical and legal frameworks of practice and service organisation. These frameworks and standards of care are informed by the evolving evidence base and expert opinion. African–Caribbean people in the UK have been shown to have a higher incidence of schizophrenia, while the treatment practices and service organisation for recovery have not been especially tailored to meet their needs (Kirkbride *et al.*, 2006). South Asian people may also have a higher incidence of schizophrenia, but there is less compelling evidence (Kirkbride *et al.*, 2006). Migrants, people living in cities, and those at the poorer and less advantaged end of society are also at risk (Cantor-Graae & Selten, 2005). Asylum seekers and refugees may face additional risks of poor mental health, but their experience, to date, has not been directly linked to a higher incidence of schizophrenia, although it is related to complex social and health needs among those developing schizophrenia (Royal College of Psychiatrists, 2007). More generally, culture is known to influence the content and, some would argue, the form and intensity of presentation of symptoms; it also determines what is considered to be an illness and who people seek out for remedy. Cultural practices and customs may well create contexts in which distress is generated; for example, where conformity to gender, age, and cultural roles is challenged.

Paradigms for quality improvement
The dominant paradigms for improved standards of care (including service organisation, effective interventions, and integrated care pathways and patterns of treatment received by ethnic groups and migrants) are the cultural psychiatry and equalities paradigms.

The cultural psychiatry paradigm tries to understand the cultural origins of symptoms, as well as: (a) how these symptoms are coloured when expressed across cultural boundaries; (b) which treatments are sanctioned; and (c) whether treatments themselves, ostensibly evidence-based, are really culturally constructed solutions that work best for people sharing the same cultural norms and expectations of what constitutes illness and treatment. This endeavour is largely clinically motivated and responds to frontline evidence of a lack of appropriate knowledge and skills to benefit all people equally using existing guidelines and treatment approaches. It also draws upon sociology and anthropology as key disciplines.

The equalities paradigm is heavily underpinned by two national policies: Inside Outside (NIMHE, 2003) and Delivering Race Equality (Department of Health, 2003a, 2005; Bhui *et al.*, 2004). These policies promote race equality through institutional and national programmes of actions with leadership from health authorities, mental health trusts and locally organised groups of stakeholders. These actions have not been specific to schizophrenia, but have certainly been motivated by the perceived crisis in the care and treatment of African–Caribbean people with schizophrenia, to which providers have not previously responded in a consistent and visibly effective manner. To date, results from the Care Quality Commission's patient census ('Count Me In') indicate that policies and programmes in this area have not yet had the desired effects (Healthcare Commission, 2008). Perceived, individual and institutional prejudice and racism are also tackled within a broader equalities framework that addresses multiple forms of social exclusion and stigma (Mckenzie & Bhui, 2007).

Cultural competence

Encompassed in the above two paradigms is the notion of cultural competence. A recent systematic review (Bhui *et al.*, 2007) suggested that staff cultural competence training may produce benefits in terms of cultural sensitivity, staff knowledge and staff satisfaction. However, despite these promising findings, clinicians should be aware of the problems and controversies surrounding the definition or current understandings of cultural competence. Kleinman and Benson (2006) propose that a cultural formulation, based upon a small scale ethnographic study of the individual or on the DSM-IV cultural formulation, should be written for each patient. This cultural formulation can then be used to help determine and inform appropriate clinical interventions at the individual patient level. On the other hand, others, such as Papadopoulous and colleagues (2004), have suggested a more model-based approach, in which cultural competence is seen as part of a four stage conceptual map, wherein competence is informed by and informs three other processes, namely cultural sensitivity, cultural knowledge and cultural awareness. Whichever approach is taken, it is clear from the literature that cultural competence is now recognised as a core requirement for mental health professionals. Yet despite this increased awareness of its importance, little evaluative work has been done to assess the effects of cultural competence (at both an individual and organisational level) on a range of service user, carer and healthcare professional outcomes.

The update: how did the Guideline Development Group take account of race, ethnicity and culture?

For the update, the GDG did not attempt to examine all evidence relevant to race, culture and ethnicity, but instead focused on three main approaches. First, the two topic groups examining psychological/psychosocial interventions and pharmacological interventions reviewed evidence of benefits for ethnic groups. Second, where there was little evidence for specific effects for ethnic groups, included studies (for the recommended interventions) were reviewed to assess the ethnic diversity of the samples. This was done to establish whether the findings may be of relevance to ethnic groups as well as the majority population. Third, a specific topic group examining clinical questions related to access and engagement was formed with input from special advisers. In particular, the group requested that the literature search should cover specialist ethnic mental health services, that studies of service-level interventions should be examined to assess the ethnic diversity of the samples and that preliminary subgroup analyses of existing datasets should be conducted to inform research recommendations (see Section 5.3.11).

Limitations of the update

The focus on race, culture and ethnicity in this schizophrenia guideline update is welcomed and groundbreaking, but there is a limitation in the sense that all mental healthcare should be similarly reviewed, with a broader focus. Regarding this guideline, the methodologies developed during the update have necessarily been targeted on some key issues and are not comprehensive in their actions. The update has also not been able to look at broader issues of pathways to care and effectiveness of psychological and pharmacological interventions on the basis of new and different levels of evidence. In part, this is because there is limited evidence. Furthermore, the update has not looked at issues that were not reviewed in the previous schizophrenia guideline. Therefore the following might be usefully accommodated in further reviews: matching the racial identity of the professional with the service user, ethnic matching (which is broader than matching racial identity and also encompasses cultural similarities), the impact of social exclusion and racism across generations, and the impact on young people of parents who have been socially excluded, subjected to prejudice and have a mental illness. All of these might seem imperative to service users from black and minority ethnic groups, but were not within the scope of the present update. It is vital that future guideline updates attend to these broader issues, perhaps additionally with a guideline for these issues across disease areas.

On evidence and ethnicity

There are general concerns that current evidence relating to ethnicity has not come from adequate samples of ethnic groups (or any socially excluded group). There are also concerns regarding the hierarchy of evidence. First, in the absence of high-quality evidence, expert opinion and the dominant paradigms of treatment are given preference over other forms of evidence (for example, qualitative evidence); second, clinical trials are given preference over other study designs. Thus, existing institutionalised practices are sustained. Research studies propose that there are pharmacokinetic and pharmacodynamic differences in drug handling across migrant, national and ethnic groups, but our scientific understanding of these at an ethnic-group level does not permit generalised statements to be made about a group that can then be applied to the individual from that group. Psychological therapies may privilege psychologised forms of mental distress, perhaps excluding those experiencing social manifestations of distress that is not so easily recognised as having a mental component. However, this update could not fully address these issues.

Assuming that service users from black and minority ethnic groups can benefit from the same interventions delivered in the same way, the next question is whether black and minority ethnic groups have equal access to these effective interventions and whether they remain in contact with services. The access and engagement topic group focused on this broad question of engagement and retained contact with existing innovative services that aim to be flexible and should be culturally appropriate, namely assertive community treatment (assertive outreach teams), crisis resolution and home treatment teams, and case management. For this work, existing reviews of these services were reanalysed for data on ethnic groups with loss to follow-up and contact with services as the primary outcome. The next part of the update involved reviewing the literature for evidence that ethnic-specific or culturally-adapted services were effective or more effective at preventing loss to follow-up, dropout and sustained contact over time. The interventions reviewed are defined below.

Definitions

Assertive community treatment (assertive outreach teams)

The bipolar disorder guideline (NCCMH, 2006) review of assertive community treatment (ACT) updated the review undertaken for the previous schizophrenia guideline, which was based on the review by Marshall and Lockwood (2002). This latter review identified the key elements of ACT as:

- a multidisciplinary team-based approach to care (usually involving a psychiatrist with dedicated sessions)
- care is exclusively provided for a defined group of people (those with serious mental illness)
- team members share responsibility for clients so that several members may work with the same client and members do not have individual caseloads (unlike case management)
- ACT teams attempt to provide all the psychiatric and social care for each client rather than referring on to other agencies
- care is provided at home or in the work place, as far as this is possible
- treatment and care is offered assertively to uncooperative or reluctant service users ('assertive outreach')
- medication concordance is emphasised by ACT teams.

The bipolar disorder guideline (NCCMH, 2006) adopted the definition of ACT used by Marshall and Lockwood (2002), which followed a pragmatic approach based upon the description given in the trial report. For a study to be accepted as ACT, Marshall and Lockwood (2002) required that the trial report had to describe the experimental intervention as 'Assertive Community Treatment, Assertive Case Management or PACT; or as being based on the Madison, Treatment in Community Living, Assertive Community Treatment or Stein and Test models.'

ACT and similar models of care are forms of long-term interventions for those with severe and enduring mental illnesses. Thus, the review did not consider the use of ACT as an alternative to acute hospital admission. The review also excluded studies of 'home-based care', as these were regarded as forms of crisis intervention, and are reviewed with crisis resolution and home treatment teams.

Crisis resolution and home treatment teams

The GDG for the bipolar disorder guideline (NCCMH, 2006) adopted the inclusion criteria developed by the Cochrane Review (Joy *et al.*, 2002) for studies of crisis resolution and home treatment teams (CRHTTs) in the management of people with schizophrenia. Crisis intervention for people with serious mental health problems was selected by the bipolar disorder GDG for review and further analysis.

Crisis intervention and the comparator treatment were defined as follows:

- Crisis resolution: any type of crisis-orientated treatment of an acute psychiatric episode by staff with a specific remit to deal with such situations, in and beyond 'office hours'.
- Standard care: the normal care given to those experiencing acute psychiatric episodes in the area concerned. This involved hospital-based treatment for all studies included.

The focus of the review was to examine the effects of CRHTT models for anyone with serious mental illness experiencing an acute episode when compared with the 'standard care' they would normally receive.

Case management

Given the variation in models of case management evaluated in the literature, the bipolar disorder GDG adopted the definition used in a Cochrane review (Marshall *et al.*, 2002), where an intervention was considered to be 'case management' if it was described as such in the trial report. In the original review no distinction, for eligibility purposes, was made between 'brokerage', 'intensive', 'clinical' or 'strengths' models. For the purposes of the bipolar disorder guideline (NCCMH, 2006) review, intensive case management (ICM) was defined as a caseload of less than or equal to 15. The UK terms 'care management' and 'care programme approach' were also treated as synonyms for case management. However, the review excluded studies of two types of intervention often loosely classed as 'case management', including ACT and 'home-based care'.

Specialist ethnic mental health services (culturally specific or culturally skilled)

Specialist ethnic mental health services aim, by definition, to offer a culturally appropriate service and effective interventions to either a specific racial, ethnic, cultural or religious group or to deliver an effective service to diverse ethnic groups (Bhui *et al.*, 2000; Bhui & Sashidharan, 2003). Models of specialist services have not been mapped recently but include cultural consultation service styles, and others outlined by Bhui and colleagues (2000).

5.3.2   Clinical review protocol

The review protocol, including the primary clinical question, information about the databases searched and the eligibility criteria can be found in Table 6. For the update, all studies were examined for information about ethnicity of the sample and numbers losing contact with services by ethnic group. The access and engagement topic group and special advisers developing the guideline proposed that a sample of which at least 20% of subjects were from black and minority ethnic groups could be considered 'ethnically diverse'. It was assumed that a decrease in the number of participants leaving the study early for any reason indicated that the service was more engaging.

Table 6: Clinical review protocol for the review of services

Primary clinical questions	For all people from black and minority ethnic groups (particularly, African–Caribbean people) with psychosis, do services, such as ACT, CRHTTs and case management improve the number of people remaining in contact with services? For all people from black and minority ethnic groups with psychosis, do specialist ethnic mental health services (culturally specific or culturally skilled) improve the number of people remaining in contact with services?
Electronic databases	MEDLINE, EMBASE, PsycINFO, CINAHL
Date searched	Database inception to 6 April 2008
Other resources searched	Bipolar disorder guideline (NCCMH, 2006) and reference lists of included studies
Study design	Any
Patient population	People with psychosis from a black and minority ethnic group in the UK
Interventions	1. ACT, CRHTTs and case management 2. Specialist ethnic mental health services (culturally specific or culturally skilled)
Outcomes	Number of people remaining in contact with services (measured by the number of people lost to follow-up or loss of engagement with services)

However, the GDG acknowledges that people may leave a study early for reasons other than a lack of engagement with the service.

5.3.3 Studies considered for review

Assertive community treatment (assertive outreach teams)
The bipolar disorder guideline (NCCMH, 2006) included 23 RCTs of ACT: 13 versus standard care (N = 2,244), four versus hospital-based rehabilitation (N = 286) and six versus case management (N = 890). Studies included had to conform to the definition

of ACT given above, and the inclusion criteria used by Marshall and Lockwood (2002) were widened to include populations with serious mental illness.

Of the 23 trials included in the bipolar disorder guideline (NCCMH, 2006), nine included adequate information about ethnicity of the sample, although none reported outcome data by ethnic group. Therefore, the GDG conducted a sensitivity analysis of seven studies that had an ethnically diverse sample (see Table 7 for further information).

Crisis resolution and home treatment teams
The bipolar disorder guideline (NCCMH, 2006) included seven RCTs of a CRHTT versus inpatient care (N = 1,207). Of these, three included an ethnically diverse sample, and one (MUIJEN1992) reported the number of people leaving the study early for any reason by ethnicity (see Table 7 for further information).

Case management
The bipolar disorder guideline (NCCMH, 2006) review updated the review under-taken for the previous schizophrenia guideline and included 17 RCTs of case manage-ment: 13 versus standard care (intensive and standard case management [SCM]), two intensive versus standard case management, one enhanced case management versus standard case management and one case management versus brokerage case manage-ment. One trial (BRUCE2004) was excluded from the present review as 100% of participants had a diagnosis of depression. Of the 16 remaining RCTs, six included an ethnically diverse sample, and three of these studies (FRANKLIN1987; MUIJEN1994; BURNS1999) reported the number of people leaving the study early for any reason by ethnicity (see Table 8 for further information).

Specialist ethnic mental health services
For the update, papers were included in the review if they reported comparisons of UK-based specialist mental-health service interventions and/or initiatives. An inclu-sive definition of 'specialist ethnic service' was used to include those services that were either culturally adapted or tailored to the needs of individual patients, includ-ing any religious or ethnic needs. To measure improved access and engagement, the numbers of people from different black and minority ethnic groups remaining in contact with services (as measured by loss to follow-up and loss of engagement) was the primary outcome. All study designs were considered and papers were included even if a formal evaluation of the service had not been intended.

Papers were excluded from the review if: (a) they only reported descriptions of current service use by different black and minority ethnic groups, (b) did not report any comparison between services, and (c) were non-UK based or did not report loss to follow-up/ loss of engagement within different black and minority ethnic groups. The reference lists of included papers and any relevant reviews were further checked for additional papers. The review was restricted to English language papers only.

The search identified 2,284 titles and abstracts, of which 19 were collected for further consideration. All 19 papers were excluded because of lack of comparator, failure to report loss to follow-up and/or loss of engagement by ethnicity or were non-UK interventions.

5.3.4   Assertive community treatment or crisis resolution and home treatment teams versus control

Table 7: Study information and evidence summary table for trials of ACT or CRHTTs

	ACT versus standard care	ACT versus hospital-based rehabilitation	ACT versus case management	CRHTTs versus standard care
k (total N)	5 RCTs (N = 684)	1 RCT (N = 59)	1 RCT (N = 28)	3 RCTs (N = 492)
Study ID	AUDINI1994 BOND1998 BOND1990 LEHMAN1997 MORSE1992	CHANDLER1997	BUSH1990	FENTON1998 MUIJEN1992 PASAMANICK 1964
Diagnosis	30–61% schizophrenia	61% schizophrenia	86% schizophrenia	49–100% schizophrenia
Ethnicity	AUDINI1994: 26% African–Caribbean BOND1998: 34% black, 2% Latino BOND1990: 30% black LEHMAN1997: 61% African–American (ACT), 84% African–American (control) MORSE1992: 52.5% non-white (mostly African–American)	40% African–American (ACT), 55.2% African–American (control)	50% black	FENTON1998: 14% black (CRHTTs), 28% black (control) MUIJEN1992: 25% African–Caribbean (CRHTTs), 21% African–Caribbean (control) PASAMANICK 1964: 32.9% non-white
Outcomes				
Leaving the study early for any reason	RR 0.63 (0.48, 0.82), *k* = 5, N = 684, I^2 = 0% Excluding studies targeting homeless people: RR 0.62 (0.44, 0.89), *k* = 3, N = 416, I^2 = 0%	RR 1.55 (0.28, 8.62), *k* = 1, N = 59	RR not estimable (nobody left the study early)	RR 0.73 (0.43, 1.25), *k* = 3, N = 492, I^2 = 57% Excluding PASAMANICK 1964: RR 0.66 (0.50, 0.88), *k* = 2, N = 374, I^2 = 0%
Leaving the study early for any reason by black and minority group				African–Caribbean: RR 1.12 (0.51, 2.45), *k* = 1, N = 43 Other non-white: RR 0.70 (0.21, 2.34), *k* = 1, N = 26

5.3.5 Case management versus control

Table 8: Study information and evidence summary table for trials of case management

	Standard case management (SCM) versus standard care	Intensive case management (ICM) versus standard care	ICM versus SCM
Total number of studies (number of participants)	1 RCT (N = 413)	4 RCTs (N = 362)	1 RCT (N = 708)
Study ID	FRANKLIN1987	FORD1995 HOLLOWAY1998 MUIJEN1994 SOLOMON1994	BURNS1999(UK700)[a]
Diagnosis	56% schizophrenia	66–83% schizophrenia	87% schizophrenia or schizoaffective disorder
Ethnicity	25% black, 2% Hispanic (SCM), 24% black, 6% Hispanic (control)	FORD1995: 23% black and minority ethnic groups (ICM), 37% black and minority ethnic groups (control) HOLLOWAY1998: 51% non-white (ICM), 57% non-white (control) MUIJEN1994: 29% African–Caribbean, 2% Asian (ICM), 17% African–Caribbean, 5% Asian (control) SOLOMON1994: 83% black, 3% Hispanic	29% African–Caribbean, 20% other black and minority ethnic groups (ICM) 26% African–Caribbean, 20% other black and minority ethnic groups (SCM)
Outcomes			
Leaving the study early for any reason	RR 0.95 (0.74, 1.23), $k = 1$, N = 413,	RR 0.76 (0.53, 1.09), $k = 4$, N = 362, $I^2 = 3.9\%$	RR 0.56 (0.38, 0.82), $k = 1$, N = 708
Leaving the study early for any reason by black and minority ethnic group	-	Black: RR 0.74 (0.48, 1.23), $k = 2$, N = 121	White: RR 0.73 (0.38, 1.40), $k = 1$, N = 267 African–Caribbean: RR 1.00 (0.53, 1.87), $k = 1$, N = 270
Lost contact with case manager	-	-	RR 1.71 (1.09, 2.69), $k = 1$, N = 708
Refused contact with case manager	-	-	RR 1.44 (0.55, 3.73), $k = 1$, N = 708

[a] Subgroup by ethnicity data obtained from authors.

5.3.6 Secondary subgroup analyses

Given the paucity of evidence available to answer questions about the use of, and engagement with, services by people from black and minority ethnic groups, the GDG examined data from two service-level intervention studies conducted in the UK (Johnson *et al.*, 2005; Killaspy *et al.*, 2006). Patient-level data were made available to the GDG during the development of the guideline for the purposes of conducting secondary *post hoc* analyses to examine loss of contact and engagement with the service by ethnicity of the participants. These analyses were exploratory in nature and were intended to be purely hypothesis generating as opposed to generating evidence to underpin recommendations. Both studies were non-blind RCTs (see Table 9 for further details).

In both trials, participants categorised as black African, black Caribbean or black other were included in the black and minority ethnic subgroup. Additionally, in the North Islington Crisis study (Johnson *et al.*, 2005) participants categorised as 'mixed race' were included in the subgroup analysis. As far as possible, the same procedures used in the primary papers were applied to the secondary analysis conducted for this guideline update. For example, where a primary paper excluded missing data, the same procedure was subsequently applied to the present analysis. In addition to looking at engagement with services as measured by numbers losing contact, other measures of access and engagement (including contact with forensic services and engagement rating scales) were included in the present analysis. For continuous measures, because of the high potential for skewed data, Mann Whitney-U tests were applied to test for differences in the median values. For dichotomous outcomes, Chi-squared tests were applied where appropriate to test for differences with relative risks calculated for variables such as relapse and rehospitalisation. Although the main findings are summarised below, more detailed evidence tables for each subgroup comparison can be found in Appendix 16b.

REACT (Killaspy et al., 2006)
The findings can be summarised as follows:
- In the whole sample, there was no difference in the proportion consenting to treatment in the group of participants allocated to ACT versus standard care. This finding was replicated in the subgroup of black and minority ethnic participants.
- In the whole sample, ACT was associated with reduced loss to follow-up at both 9 and 18 months. These findings were not demonstrated in the subgroup of black and minority ethnic participants.
- In the whole sample, ACT improved service user engagement, but this finding did not hold for black and minority ethnic subgroup.
- In both the whole sample and the black and minority ethnic subgroup, ACT increased the number of contacts with mental health professionals at both 9 and 18 months.
- ACT had no effect on any measure of detention or hospitalisation (including involuntary admissions) in both the whole sample and the black and minority ethnic subgroup.

Table 9: Details of studies included in the secondary subgroup analyses

Study	Objective	Design/ Setting	Participants	Groups	Main outcome measures
REACT (Killaspy et al., 2006)	To compare outcomes of care from ACT with care by CMHTs for people with serious mental illnesses	Non-blind RCT/two inner London boroughs	251 men and women under the care of adult secondary mental health services with recent high use of inpatient care and difficulties engaging with community services	Intervention = treatment from ACT team (127 participants) Comparator = continuation of care from CMHT (124 participants)	Primary outcome was inpatient bed use 18 months after randomisation. Secondary outcomes included symptoms, social function, client satisfaction, and engagement with services.
North Islington Crisis RCT (Johnson et al., 2005)	To evaluate the effectiveness of a crisis resolution team	Non-blind RCT/ London borough of Islington	260 residents of the inner London borough of Islington who were experiencing crises severe enough for hospital admission to be considered	Intervention = acute care including a 24-hour crisis resolution team (experimental group) Comparator = standard care from inpatient services and CMHTs (control group)	Primary outcome was hospital admission and number of inpatient bed use. Secondary outcomes included symptoms and client satisfaction.

North Islington Crisis team RCT (Johnson et al., 2005)
The findings can be summarised as follows:
- The crisis team intervention significantly reduced hospitalisation rates and number of inpatient bed days for both the whole sample and the black and minority ethnic subgroup.
- The crisis team intervention had no impact on treatment compliance or numbers lost to follow-up, for both the whole sample and the black and minority ethnic subgroup.
- The number of professional contacts, including contacts with GPs increased at 8 weeks and 6 months, and although the effect was not significant in the black and minority ethnic subgroup, the point estimate suggests this is because of a small sample size and resulting lack of statistical power, rather than the absence of an effect.
- For both the sample as a whole and the black and minority ethnic subgroup, the crisis team intervention did not impact upon any measure of involuntary detention or status under the Mental Health Act.

5.3.7   Other sources of evidence

The review of ethnically-specific or adapted services yielded no UK-based studies that investigated loss to follow-up. However, some of the studies, although falling outside the guideline's inclusion criteria, offer important lessons for clinical practice and research. Bhugra and colleagues (2004) demonstrated that black people in contact with mental health services via contact with either primary care or non-primary care services were equally as dissatisfied as a white group gaining access to services from outside primary care. The most satisfied group were identified as white people accessing mental health service following contact and referral from primary care. Mohan and colleagues (2006) showed, in a non-randomised study, that subsequent to the introduction of intensive case management, black patients were more likely to have greater contact with psychiatrists and nurses, while white patients more often had greater social care contact. Black patients were less likely to require hospital admission. Khan and colleagues (2003) showed in a small qualitative study that South Asian people receiving care from a home treatment team valued the intervention because of the cultural appropriateness in terms of language, religious needs, dietary needs and stigma, while hospitals were preferred for investigations (for example, blood tests).

A systematic review of interventions that improve pathways into care for people from black and minority ethnic groups was recently completed (Moffat *et al.*, 2009; Sass *et al.*, 2009). This was commissioned by the Department of Health through the Delivering Race Equality programme (established in 2005). The systematic grey literature search yielded 1,309 documents, of which eight fully met inclusion criteria. The main findings of the review indicated that:

'The key components of effective pathway interventions include specialist services for ethnic minority groups, collaboration between sectors, facilitating referral routes between services, outreach and facilitating access into care, and supporting access to rehabilitation and moving out of care. Services that support collaboration, referral between services, and improve access seem effective, but warrant further evaluation. Innovative services must ensure that their evaluation frameworks meet minimum quality standards if the knowledge gained from the service is to be generalised, and if it is to inform policy' (Moffat *el al.*, 2009).

The review of mainstream published literature identified 2,216 titles and abstracts with six studies meeting the review's inclusion criteria. In only one study was the initiative UK based, and included patients with depression as opposed to psychosis. The main findings of the review indicated that

'There was evidence that interventions led to three types of pathways change; accelerated transit through care pathways, removal of adverse pathways, and the addition of a beneficial pathway. Ethnic matching promoted desired pathways in many groups but not African Americans, managed care improved equity, a pre-treatment service improved access to detoxification and an education leaflet increased recovery' (Sass *et al.*, 2009).

In addition to these findings, the review concluded that further research is needed to facilitate evidence-based guidance for the development of services.

5.3.8   Clinical evidence summary

Although there were no RCTs assessing the effectiveness of ACT for specific ethnic groups, five RCTs including an ethnically diverse sample indicated that when compared with standard care ACT interventions were effective in reducing loss to follow-up. When compared with standard care alone, CRHTTs were also effective at reducing loss to follow-up. Only one RCT (MUIJEN1992) included in the review permitted stratification of these effects by ethnic group. The positive findings from this RCT regarding reduced loss to follow-up held most strongly for Irish people, but was not convincing for African–Caribbean subgroups. However, it must be noted that because of the limited sample size no firm conclusions can be drawn from this one RCT alone. The review of case management included more RCTs permitting stratification of outcomes by ethnicity. Despite this, there was no consistent evidence for the effectiveness of either intensive or standard case management when compared with standard care and other service configurations.

Although the search of specialist ethnic mental health services undertaken for the guideline update did not yield any eligible studies, recent reviews (Moffat *et al.*, 2009; Sass *et al.*, 2009) of both grey and mainstream literature provided some interesting examples of how cultural adaptations can lead to improved outcomes. However it must be noted that even within these reviews, there was paucity of information, with the majority of included studies being non-UK based, thus limiting the generalisability to specific black and minority ethnic populations within the UK.

5.3.9   From evidence to recommendations

The systematic review did not provide any robust evidence to warrant changing the service recommendations in the previous guideline for people with schizophrenia from black and minority ethnic groups. However, the GDG and the special advisers recognised that there were a number of problems specifically faced by people from different black and minority ethnic groups, including:

- People from black and minority ethnic groups with schizophrenia are more likely than other groups to be disadvantaged or have impaired access to and/or engagement with mental health services.
- People from black and minority ethnic groups may not benefit as much as they could from existing services and interventions, with the aforementioned problems in access and engagement further undermining any potential benefits.
- For all people with a first episode of psychosis or severe mental distress (including those from black and minority ethnic groups), fears about the safety of the intervention may not be appropriately addressed by the clinician.
- Conflict may arise when divergent explanatory models of illness and treatment expectations are apparent.
- Clinicians delivering psychological and pharmacological interventions may lack an understanding of the patient's cultural background.
- The lack of supportive and positive relationships may impact on the future engagement with services.
- Comprehensive written information may not be available in the appropriate language.
- Participants from black and minority ethnic groups may face additional language barriers with a lack of adequate interpretation services being available. Where such services are available, clinicians may lack the training to work proficiently with such services.
- Lack of knowledge about the quality of access for specific black and minority ethnic groups and inflexible approaches to service delivery may hamper continued engagement with treatment.
- There is often a lack of collaborative work between mental health service providers and local voluntary and charitable sectors that may have expertise in the provision of the best cultural or specific services.
- Race, culture, ethnicity or religious background may challenge the clarity with which assessments and decisions regarding the Mental Health Act are undertaken, especially where clinicians do not seek appropriate advice and/or consultation.

Therefore, based on informal consensus, the GDG made recommendations that address, in at least an initial way, the problems raised above. Additionally, where possible, specific problems faced by black and minority ethnic groups have been addressed in other parts of the guideline (for example, see Section 8.7.6). It was further acknowledged by the GDG that all of the recommendations in this section should be viewed as a foundation step in a longer process including the provision of good quality research and development. In particular, the GDG highlighted that the following points specifically need addressing through this process of research:

- RCTs of psychological and pharmacological interventions and service organisation have not been adequately powered to investigate effects in specific ethnic groups including African–Caribbean people with schizophrenia.
- There are no well-designed studies of specialist mental health services providing care to diverse communities or to specific communities.
- The effect of the cultural competence of mental health professionals on service user experience and recovery has not been adequately investigated in UK mental health settings.
- English language teaching may be an alternative to providing interpreters to reduce costs and to encourage integration. This has not been tested for feasibility or outcomes.
- The early diagnosis and assessment of psychosis and comorbid disorders across ethnic, racial and cultural groups needs to be systematically assessed, with research projects including adequate samples from different cultural and ethnic backgrounds.

5.3.10   Recommendations

5.3.10.1   When working with people with schizophrenia and their carers:
- avoid using clinical language, or keep it to a minimum
- ensure that comprehensive written information is available in the appropriate language and in audio format if possible
- provide and work proficiently with interpreters if needed
- offer a list of local education providers who can provide English language teaching for people who have difficulties speaking and understanding English.

5.3.10.2   Healthcare professionals inexperienced in working with people with schizophrenia from diverse ethnic and cultural backgrounds should seek advice and supervision from healthcare professionals who are experienced in working transculturally.

5.3.10.3   Healthcare professionals working with people with schizophrenia should ensure they are competent in:
- assessment skills for people from diverse ethnic and cultural backgrounds
- using explanatory models of illness for people from diverse ethnic and cultural backgrounds
- explaining the causes of schizophrenia and treatment options
- addressing cultural and ethnic differences in treatment expectations and adherence
- addressing cultural and ethnic differences in beliefs regarding biological, social and family influences on the causes of abnormal mental states

- negotiating skills for working with families of people with schizophrenia
- conflict management and conflict resolution.

5.3.10.4   Mental health services should work with local voluntary BME groups to jointly ensure that culturally appropriate psychological and psychosocial treatment, consistent with this guideline and delivered by competent practitioners, is provided to people from diverse ethnic and cultural backgrounds.

5.3.11   Research recommendations

5.3.11.1   For people with schizophrenia, RCTs of psychological and psychosocial interventions should be adequately powered to assess clinical and cost effectiveness in specific ethnic groups (or alternatively in ethnically diverse samples).

5.3.11.2   An adequately powered RCT should be conducted to investigate the clinical and cost effectiveness of CBT that has been culturally adapted for African–Caribbean people with schizophrenia where they are refusing or intolerant of medication.

5.3.11.3   Studies of ethnically specific and specialist services and new service designs should be appropriately powered to assess effectiveness. Studies should include sufficient numbers of specific ethnic groups and be evaluated using an agreed high quality evaluation framework (Moffat *et al.*, 2009).

5.3.11.4   For people with schizophrenia from black and minority ethnic groups living in the UK, does staff training in cultural competence at an individual level and at an organisational level (delivered as a learning and training process embedded in routine clinical care and service provision) improve the service user's experience of care and chance of recovery, and reduce staff burnout?[6]

5.3.11.5   An adequately powered proof of principle study should be conducted to investigate the feasibility of comparing language skills development for those with English as a second language against using interpreters.

5.3.11.6   A study should be conducted to investigate engagement and loss to follow-up, prospective outcomes and care pathways, and the factors that hinder engagement. For example, ethnic, religious, language or racial identity matching may be important. This is not the same as ethnic matching, but matching on ability to work with diverse identities.

5.3.11.7   A study should be conducted to investigate the use of pre-identification services, including assessment, diagnosis and early engagement, across racial and ethnic groups.

---

[6]For more details see Chapter 10 (recommendation 10.5.1.3).

6 PHARMACOLOGICAL INTERVENTIONS IN THE TREATMENT AND MANAGEMENT OF SCHIZOPHRENIA

For the guideline update, all sections of the previous guideline's chapter on pharmacological interventions were updated apart from the section on rapid tranquillisation, which was removed because it was updated by the NICE clinical guideline on violence[7]. The scope for the update also included updating the NICE technology appraisal (TA43) on the use of newer (atypical) antipsychotic drugs (NICE, 2002). In Section 6.9.2 of this chapter, new evidence is presented from economic modelling of pharmacological relapse prevention (the rationale for economic modelling, the methodology adopted, the results and the conclusions from this economic analysis are described in detail in Chapter 7).

For the guideline update the term 'first-generation antipsychotics' (FGAs) is used to refer to drugs that in the previous NICE guideline were called 'conventional' or 'typical' antipsychotics. Likewise, the term 'second-generation antipsychotics' (SGAs) is used to refer to drugs that were previously called 'atypical' antipsychotics. This terminology is used here because it is widely used in the literature; it should not be taken to suggest that FGAs and SGAs represent distinct classes of antipsychotics (see Section 6.4.1 for further discussion of this issue).

For this chapter, the review of evidence is divided into the following areas:
- initial treatment with oral antipsychotic medication (Section 6.2)
- oral antipsychotics in the treatment of the acute episode (Section 6.3)
- promoting recovery in people with schizophrenia that is in remission – pharmacological relapse prevention (Section 6.4)
- promoting recovery in people with schizophrenia whose illness has not responded adequately to treatment (Section 6.5)
- combining antipsychotic medication with another antipsychotic (Section 6.5.10)
- treatment with depot/long-acting injectable antipsychotic medication (Section 6.6)
- side effects of antipsychotic medication, focusing on metabolic and neurologic adverse events—these were considered a priority by the GDG and were also highlighted as areas of concern by service users (Section 6.7)
- effectiveness of antipsychotic medication (Section 6.8)
- health economics (Section 6.9).

Because of the nature of the evidence, all recommendations can be found in Section 6.11 at the end of the chapter (rather than after each subsection), preceded by Section 6.10 (from evidence to recommendations) that draws together the clinical and health economic evidence and provides a rationale for the recommendations.

---

[7]Available from http://www.nice.org.uk/Guidance/CG25

6.1   INTRODUCTION

Antipsychotic drugs have been the mainstay of treatment of schizophrenia since the 1950s. Initially used for the treatment of acute psychotic states, their subsequent use to prevent relapse led to these drugs being prescribed for long-term maintenance treatment, either as oral preparations or in the form of long-acting injectable preparations ('depots').

Although a number of different classes of drugs have antipsychotic activity, the primary pharmacological action of antipsychotic drugs is their antagonistic effect on the D2 dopamine receptors. Indeed, the potency of a drug's antipsychotic effect is at least in part determined by its affinity for the D2 receptor (Agid *et al.*, 2007; Kapur & Remington, 2001; Snyder *et al.*, 1974), an association that informed the dopamine hypothesis of schizophrenia. It is worth noting, however, that antipsychotic drugs are also of use in the treatment of other psychotic disorders, their dopamine-blocking activity probably again being central to their pharmacological efficacy.

Uses of antipsychotics

In the treatment and management of schizophrenia, antipsychotics are currently used for the treatment of acute episodes, for relapse prevention, for the emergency treatment of acute behavioural disturbance (rapid tranquillisation) and for symptom reduction. They are available as oral, intramuscular (IM) and intravenous (IV) preparations, or as medium- or long-acting depot IM preparations. In the UK, clozapine is only licensed for use in people with 'treatment-resistant' schizophrenia, defined by the manufacturers' Summary of Product Characteristics (SPC) as a 'lack of satisfactory clinical improvement despite the use of adequate doses of at least two different antipsychotic agents, including an atypical antipsychotic agent, prescribed for adequate duration'.

Antipsychotics are usually prescribed within the recommended SPC dosage range and there is little evidence to support the use of higher dosage or combination with another antipsychotic if monotherapy proves to be ineffective (Royal College of Psychiatrists, 2006; Stahl, 2004). Antipsychotics are also used in combination with a range of other classes of drugs, such as anticonvulsants, mood stabilisers, anticholinergics, antidepressants and benzodiazepines. Clinicians may augment antipsychotics with such drugs for several reasons:

- where there is a lack of effective response to antipsychotics alone
- for behavioural control
- for the treatment of the side effects of antipsychotics
- for the treatment of comorbid or secondary psychiatric problems, such as depression and anxiety.

Although such augmentation strategies are commonly used in clinical practice, they are outside the scope of this guideline. It is anticipated that a future guideline will address the evidence base for these interventions.

Antipsychotic dose

The current British National Formulary (BNF) is the most widely used reference for the prescription of medicines and the pharmacy industry within the UK, and a complete

SPC for all the drugs referred to in this guideline can be found in the Electronic Medicines Compendium (http://emc.medicines.org.uk/). The recommended dose ranges listed in the BNF normally echo the information contained in the manufacturers' SPC, as well as advice from an external panel of experts to ensure that the SPC recommendations on issues such as dose range reflect current good practice ('standard dosing'). 'Standard doses' are identified as doses that fall within the range likely to achieve the best balance between therapeutic gain and dose-related adverse effects. However, with up to a third of people with schizophrenia showing a poor response to antipsychotic medication, there has been a tendency for higher doses to be prescribed: surveys of prescribing practice suggest that doses of antipsychotics exceeding BNF limits, either for a single drug or through combining antipsychotics, continue to be commonly used (Harrington *et al.*, 2002; Lehman *et al.*, 1998; Paton *et al.*, 2008).

In an attempt to increase the rate or extent of response, 'loading doses' and rapid dose escalation strategies have been employed (Kane & Marder, 1993); studies have failed to show any advantage for such a strategy in terms of speed or degree of treatment response (Dixon *et al.*, 1995). The Schizophrenia Patient Outcomes Research Team (1998) concluded that in the treatment of acute episodes of schizophrenia 'massive loading doses of antipsychotic medication, referred to as "rapid neuroleptization," should not be used'.

Evidence suggests that drug-naïve patients and those experiencing their first episode of schizophrenia respond to doses of antipsychotic drugs at the lower end of the recommended dosage range (Cookson *et al.*, 2002; McEvoy *et al.*, 1991; Oosthuizen *et al.*, 2001; Remington *et al.*, 1998; Tauscher & Kapur, 2001).

Relapse prevention
For people with established schizophrenia, the chance of relapse while receiving continuous antipsychotic medication appears to be about a third of that on placebo (Marder & Wirshing, 2003). Risk factors for relapse of illness include the presence of persistent symptoms, poor adherence to the treatment regimen, lack of insight and substance use, all of which can be reasonable targets for intervention.

Stopping antipsychotic medication in people with schizophrenia, especially abruptly, dramatically increases the risk of relapse in the short to medium term, although even with gradual cessation about half will relapse in the succeeding 6 months (Viguera *et al.*, 1997). Low-dose prescribing and the use of intermittent dosing strategies (with medication prompted by the appearance of an individual's characteristic early signs of relapse) have also been suggested in the past as ways to minimise side effects in the long-term. However, when these were tested in controlled trials, the risks, particularly in terms of increased relapse, outweighed any benefits (Dixon *et al.*, 1995; Hirsch & Barnes, 1995).

The Schizophrenia Patient Outcomes Research Team (1998) concluded that 'targeted, intermittent dosage maintenance strategies should not be used routinely in lieu of continuous dosage regimens because of the increased risk of symptom worsening or relapse. These strategies may be considered for patients who refuse maintenance or for whom some other contraindication to maintenance therapy exists, such as side-effect sensitivity'.

Clozapine

The antipsychotic clozapine was introduced in the 1970s, only to be withdrawn soon after because of the risk of potentially fatal agranulocytosis. However, after further research revealed the drug's efficacy in treatment-resistant schizophrenia (for example, Kane *et al.*, 1988), clozapine was reintroduced in the 1980s with requirements for appropriate haematological monitoring. Clozapine was considered to have a novel mode of action. Its pharmacological profile includes a relatively low affinity for D2 receptors and a much higher affinity for D4 dopamine receptors, and for subtypes of serotonin receptors, although it is not clear exactly which aspects are responsible for its superior antipsychotic effect in treatment-resistant schizophrenia.

Side effects

Clinical issues relating to side effects were summarised by NICE (2002), as follows:

'All antipsychotic agents are associated with side effects but the profile and clinical significance of these varies among individuals and drugs. These may include EPS (such as parkinsonism, acute dystonic reactions, akathisia and tardive dyskinesia), autonomic effects (such as blurring of vision, increased intra-ocular pressure, dry mouth and eyes, constipation and urinary retention), increased prolactin levels, seizures, sedation and weight gain. Cardiac safety is also an issue because several antipsychotics have been shown to prolong ventricular repolarisation, which is associated with an increased risk of ventricular arrhythmias. Routine monitoring is a pre-requisite of clozapine use because of the risk of neutropenia and agranulocytosis. Prescribers are therefore required to ensure that effective ongoing monitoring is maintained as alternative brands of clozapine become available.

Individuals with schizophrenia consider the most troublesome side effects to be EPS, weight gain, sexual dysfunction and sedation. EPS are easily recognised, but their occurrence cannot be predicted accurately and they are related to poor prognosis. Akathisia is also often missed or misdiagnosed as agitation. Of particular concern is tardive dyskinesia (orofacial and trunk movements), which may not be evident immediately, is resistant to treatment, may be persistent, and may worsen on treatment withdrawal. Sexual dysfunction can be a problem, sometimes linked to drug-induced hyperprolactinaemia; it is likely to be an underreported side effect of antipsychotic treatment, as discussion of this issue is often difficult to initiate.'

Blockade of D2 receptors by antipsychotic drugs is responsible for EPS, such as parkinsonism, akathisia, dystonia and dyskinesia, but the therapeutic, antipsychotic effect may occur at a lower level of D2 receptor occupancy than the level associated with the emergence of EPS (Farde *et al.*, 1992). SGA drugs were introduced with claims for a lower risk of EPS. The individual SGAs differ in their propensity to cause EPS: for some SGAs (for example, clozapine and quetiapine), acute EPS liability does not differ from placebo across their full dose, while for some others the risk is dose dependent. These differences may reflect individual drug profiles in relation to properties such as selective dopamine D2-like receptor antagonism, potent 5-HT2A antagonism and rapid dissociation from the D2 receptor, and for aripiprazole, partial agonism at D2 and 5HT1A receptors. Interpretation of the RCT evidence for the superiority of SGAs regarding acute EPS should take into account the dosage and choice of FGA comparator, most commonly haloperidol, which is considered a high potency D2 antagonist with a relatively high liability for EPS.

Raised serum prolactin is also an important adverse effect of antipsychotic medication (Haddad & Wieck, 2004). It can lead to problems, such as menstrual abnormalities, galactorrhea and sexual dysfunction, and in the longer term to reduced bone mineral density (Haddad & Wieck, 2004; Meaney *et al.*, 2004). While the propensity for antipsychotic drugs to affect prolactin varies between agents, the extent to which an individual service user will be affected may be difficult to determine before treatment.

Antipsychotic drugs also have strong affinity for a range of other receptors, including histaminergic, serotonergic, cholinergic and alpha-adrenergic types, which may produce a number of other effects, such as sedation, weight gain and postural hypotension. As the various antipsychotic drugs possess different relative affinities for each receptor type, each drug will have its own specific profile of side effects. For example, antipsychotic drugs vary in their liability for metabolic side effects, such as weight gain, lipid abnormalities and disturbance of glucose regulation. These are side effects that have been increasingly recognised as problems that may impact on long-term physical health. Specifically, they increase the risk of the metabolic syndrome, a recognised cluster of features (hypertension, central obesity, glucose intolerance/insulin resistance and dyslipidaemia) (American Diabetes Association *et al.*, 2004; Mackin *et al.*, 2007), which is a predictor of type-2 diabetes and coronary heart disease. Even without antipsychotic treatment, people with schizophrenia may have an increased risk of such problems, which is partly related to lifestyle factors such as smoking, poor diet, lack of exercise, and also, possibly, the illness itself (Brown *et al.*, 1999; Holt *et al.*, 2005; Osborn *et al.*, 2007a, 2007b; Taylor *et al.*, 2005; van Nimwegen *et al.*, 2008). While there is some uncertainty about the precise relationship between schizophrenia, metabolic problems and antipsychotic medication, there is agreement that routine physical health screening of people prescribed antipsychotic drugs in the long term is required (Barnes *et al.*, 2007; Newcomer, 2007; Suvisaari *et al.*, 2007) (further information about physical health screening can be found in Chapter 9).

6.2 INITIAL TREATMENT WITH ANTIPSYCHOTIC MEDICATION

6.2.1 Introduction

Evidence published before the previous guideline suggests that drug-naïve patients may respond to doses of antipsychotic medication at the lower end of the recommended range (Cookson *et al.*, 2002; McEvoy *et al.*, 1991; Oosthuizen *et al.*, 2001; Tauscher & Kapur, 2001). This may have particular implications in the treatment of people experiencing their first episode of schizophrenia. Lehman and colleagues (1998) have suggested that the maximum dose for drug-naïve patients should be 500 mg chlorpromazine equivalents per day. This contrasts with a recommended optimal oral antipsychotic dose of 300 to 1000 mg chlorpromazine equivalents per day for the routine treatment of an acute episode in non-drug-naïve patients.

6.2.2   Clinical review protocol

The review protocol, including the primary clinical question, information about the databases searched and the eligibility criteria can be found in Table 10. For the guideline update, a new systematic search was conducted for relevant RCTs published since the previous guideline (further information about the search strategy can be found in Appendix 8).

6.2.3   Studies considered for review[8]

Nine RCTs (N = 1,801) met the inclusion criteria for the update. Of these, two trials (Emsley1995; Jones1998) were included in the previous guideline, but analysed with the acute treatment trials (that is, non-initial treatment). All included studies are now published in peer-reviewed journals between 1999 and 2008. Further information about both included and excluded studies can be found in Appendix 15b.

6.2.4   Antipsychotic drug treatment in people with first-episode or early schizophrenia

Of the nine RCTs included in the meta-analysis, two were multiple-arm trials and, therefore, there were a total of 12 evaluations: three of olanzapine versus haloperidol, one of olanzapine versus quetiapine, three of olanzapine versus risperidone, four of risperidone versus haloperidol, and one of risperidone versus quetiapine (see Table 11 for a summary of the study characteristics). Forest plots and/or data tables for each outcome can be found in Appendix 16c.

---

[8]Here and elsewhere in this chapter, each study considered for review is referred to by a study ID, with studies included in the previous guideline in lower case and new studies in upper case (primary author and date or study number for unpublished trials). References for included studies denoted by study IDs can be found in Appendix 15b.

Table 10: Clinical review protocol for the review of initial treatment with antipsychotic medication

Primary clinical question	For people with first-episode or early schizophrenia, what are the benefits and downsides of continuous oral antipsychotic drug treatment when compared with another oral antipsychotic drug at the initiation of treatment (when administered within the recommended dose range [BNF 54])?	
Electronic databases	CENTRAL, CINAHL, EMBASE, MEDLINE, PsycINFO	
Date searched	1 January 2002 to 30 July 2008	
Study design	Double-blind RCT (≥10 participants per arm and ≥4 weeks' duration)	
Patient population	Adults (18+) with first-episode or early schizophrenia (including recent onset/people who have never been treated with antipsychotic medication)[a]	
Excluded populations	Very late onset schizophrenia (onset after age 60). Other psychotic disorders, such as bipolar disorder, mania or depressive psychosis. People with coexisting learning difficulties, significant physical or sensory difficulties, or substance misuse.	
Interventions	FGAs: Benperidol Chlorpromazine hydrochloride Flupentixol Fluphenazine hydrochloride Haloperidol Levomepromazine Pericyazine Perphenazine Pimozide Prochlorperazine Promazine hydrochloride Sulpiride Trifluoperazine Zuclopenthixol acetate Zuclopenthixol dihydrochloride	SGAs[b]: Amisulpride Aripiprazole Olanzapine Paliperidone Quetiapine Risperidone Sertindole Zotepine
Comparator	Any relevant antipsychotic drug	
Critical outcomes	Mortality (suicide) Global state (CGI) Mental state (total symptoms, depression) Social functioning Leaving the study early for any reason Adverse events	

Note: Studies (or outcomes from studies) were categorised as short term (12 weeks or fewer), medium term (12–51 weeks) and long term (52 weeks or more); studies that used drug doses outside the recommended dose range were flagged during data analysis.

[a] Studies that included participants under the age of 18 were not excluded from the review unless all participants were less than 18 years old.

[b] Clozapine and sertindole were excluded from this analysis because they are not usually used to treat people with first-episode or early schizophrenia.

Table 11: Summary of study characteristics for RCTs of antipsychotic drugs in people with first-episode or early schizophrenia

	Olanzapine versus haloperidol	Olanzapine versus quetiapine	Olanzapine versus risperidone	Risperidone versus haloperidol	Risperidone versus quetiapine
k (total N)	3 (331)	1 (267)	3 (446)	5 (1102)	1 (267)
Study ID	DEHAAN2003 Jones1998 LIEBERMAN 2003A	MCEVOY2007A	Jones1998 MCEVOY2007A VANNIMWEGEN2008	Emsley1995 Jones1998 LEE2007 MOLLER2008 SCHOOLER2005	MCEVOY2007A
Diagnostic criteria	DSM-IV	DSM-IV	DSM-IV	DSM-III, DSM-IV	DSM-IV
Baseline severity	PANSS total: ~81 (SD 15) (LIEBERMAN 2003A)	PANSS total: mean ~74 (SD ~16)	PANSS total: mean ~74 (SD 16) (MCEVOY2007A)	PANSS total: range 77.3 to 94.2	PANSS total: mean ~74 (SD 16)
Selected inclusion criteria	DEHAAN2003: 1–2 psychotic episodes; aged 17–28 years Jones1998: first 5 years of illness; aged 18–65 years LIEBERMAN 2003A: experienced	Participants had to be in first episode of their psychotic illness, and had to be continuously ill for ≥1 month and no more than 5 months	Jones1998: first 5 years of illness MCEVOY2007A: participants had to be in first episode of their psychotic illness, and had to be continuously ill for ≥1 month and no more than 5 months	Emsley1995: first-episode Jones1998: first 5 years of illness; aged 18–65 years LEE2007: drug-naïve MOLLER2008: first episode; aged 18–60 years	Participants had to be in first episode of their psychotic illness, and had to be continuously ill for ≥1 month and no more than 5 months

Continued

103

Table 11: *(Continued)*

	Olanzapine versus haloperidol	Olanzapine versus quetiapine	Olanzapine versus risperidone	Risperidone versus haloperidol	Risperidone versus quetiapine
	psychotic symptoms for ≥1 month but not more than 60 months; aged 16–40 years		VANNIMWEGEN2008: recent onset; aged 18–30 years	SCHOOLER2005: schizophrenia,<1 year, during which there were no more than two psychiatric hospitalisations for psychosis and ≤12 weeks cumulative exposure to antipsychotics; aged 16–45 years	
Age of participants	DEHAAN2003: 17–26 years Jones1998: mean ~29 years LIEBERMAN 2003A: mean 23.9 (SD 4.6)	16–44 years, mean 24.5 (SD 5.8)	Jones1998: mean ~29 years MCEVOY2007A: 16–44 years, mean 24.5(SD 5.8) VANNIMWEGEN 2008: mean 25 years	Emsley1995: 15–50 years, median ~23 years Jones1998: mean ~29 years LEE2007: mean 32.6 (SD 1) years MOLLER2008: mean 30.1 (9.8) years SCHOOLER 2005: mean ~24 years	16–44 years, mean 24.5 (SD 5.8) years
Setting	Inpatient and outpatient	Inpatient and outpatient	Inpatient and outpatient	Inpatient and outpatient	Inpatient and outpatient
Duration of treatment	Short term: 6 weeks Medium term: 12 weeks Long term: 54–104 weeks	Long term: 52 weeks	Short term: 6 weeks Long term: 52–54 weeks	Short term: 6–8 weeks Medium term: 24–30 weeks Long term: 54–104 weeks	Long term: 52 weeks
Medication dose (mg/day)	Olanzapine: 5–20 (range) Haloperidol: 2.5–20 (range)	Olanzapine: 2.5–20 (range) Quetiapine: 100–800 (range)	Olanzapine: 2.5–20 (range) Risperidone: 0.5–10 (range)	Risperidone: 2–10 (range) Haloperidol: 1–20 (range)	Risperidone: 0.5–4 (range) Quetiapine: 100–800 (range)

6.2.5   Clinical evidence summary

In nine RCTs with a total of 1,801 participants with first-episode or early schizophrenia (including people with a recent onset of schizophrenia and people who have never been treated with antipsychotic medication), the evidence suggested there were no clinically significant differences in efficacy between the antipsychotic drugs examined. Most of the trials were not designed to examine differences in adverse effects of treatment, but metabolic and neurological side effects reported were consistent with those identified in the SPC for each drug.

6.3   ORAL ANTIPSYCHOTICS IN THE TREATMENT OF THE ACUTE EPISODE

6.3.1   Introduction

Early clinical studies established that antipsychotic medications are effective in the treatment of acute schizophrenic episodes (Davis & Garver, 1978), although they proved to be more effective at alleviating positive symptoms than negative symptoms, such as alogia or affective blunting. However, no consistent difference between the FGAs was demonstrated in terms of antipsychotic efficacy or effects on individual symptoms, syndromes or schizophrenia subgroups. Accordingly, the choice of drug for an individual was largely dependent on differences in side-effect profiles (Hollister, 1974; Davis & Garver, 1978). The limitations of these FGAs included heterogeneity of response in acute episodes, with a proportion of individuals showing little improvement (Kane, 1987), and a range of undesirable acute and long-term side effects. The search for better-tolerated and more effective drugs eventually generated a series of second-generation drugs, characterised by a lower liability for EPS (Barnes & McPhillips, 1999; Geddes *et al.*, 2000; Cookson *et al.*, 2002).

6.3.2   Clinical review protocol

The review protocol, including the primary clinical question, information about the databases searched and the eligibility criteria can be found in Table 12. A new systematic search for relevant RCTs, published since the previous guideline, was conducted for the guideline update (further information about the search strategy can be found in Appendix 8).

Table 12: Clinical review protocol for the review of oral antipsychotics in the treatment of the acute episode

Primary clinical question	For people with an acute exacerbation or recurrence of schizophrenia, what are the benefits and downsides of continuous oral antipsychotic drug treatment when compared with another oral antipsychotic drug (when administered within the recommended dose range [BNF 54])?	
Electronic databases	CENTRAL, CINAHL, EMBASE, MEDLINE, PsycINFO	
Date searched	1 January 2002 to 30 July 2008	
Study design	Double-blind RCT ($\geq$10 participants per arm and $\geq$4 weeks' duration)	
Patient population	Adults (18+) with an acute exacerbation or recurrence of schizophrenia	
Excluded populations	Very late onset schizophrenia (onset after age 60). Other psychotic disorders, such as bipolar disorder, mania or depressive psychosis. People with coexisting learning difficulties, significant physical or sensory difficulties, or substance misuse. People with schizophrenia who have met established criteria for treatment-resistant schizophrenia.	
Interventions	FGAs: Benperidol Chlorpromazine hydrochloride Flupentixol Fluphenazine hydrochloride Haloperidol Levomepromazine Pericyazine Perphenazine Pimozide Prochlorperazine Promazine hydrochloride Sulpiride Trifluoperazine Zuclopenthixol acetate Zuclopenthixol dihydrochloride	SGAs[a]: Amisulpride Aripiprazole Olanzapine Paliperidone Quetiapine Risperidone Sertindole Zotepine
Comparator	Any relevant antipsychotic drug	
Critical outcomes	Mortality (suicide) Global state (CGI) Mental state (total symptoms, depression) Social functioning Leaving the study early for any reason Adverse events	

Note: Studies (or outcomes from studies) were categorised as short term (12 weeks or fewer), medium term (12–51 weeks) and long term (52 weeks or more); studies that used drug doses outside the recommended dose range were flagged during data analysis.

[a] Clozapine was excluded from this analysis because it is not usually used to treat people with schizophrenia unless criteria for treatment-resistant schizophrenia are met (see Section 6.5).

6.3.3   Studies considered for review

In the previous guideline, 180 RCTs were included[9]. The update search identified ten papers providing follow-up or published data for existing trials and 19 new trials. Two trials (Klieser1996; Malyarov1999) were multi-arm and contributed to more than one comparison. Because of the large volume of evidence, the GDG excluded open-label studies, head-to-head comparisons of two FGAs and comparisons with placebo from the update, leaving 72 RCTs (N = 16,556) that met inclusion criteria. Further information about both included and excluded studies can be found in Appendix 15b.

6.3.4   Treatment with antipsychotic drugs in people with an acute exacerbation or recurrence of schizophrenia

Because most included studies involved olanzapine or risperidone, comparisons involving these drugs are reported first followed by comparisons involving other drugs. Twenty-six RCTs compared olanzapine with another antipsychotic (see Table 13 for a summary of the study characteristics) and 30 compared risperidone with another antipsychotic (see Table 14). Six RCTs were included in the analysis comparing amisulpride with an FGA, two in the analysis compared aripiprazole with an FGA and one compared aripiprazole with ziprasidone (see Table 15); seven compared quetiapine with an FGA and two compared sertindole with an FGA (see Table 16), and seven compared zotepine with an FGA (see Table 17). Forest plots and/or data tables for each outcome can be found in Appendix 16c.

6.3.5   Clinical evidence summary

In 72 RCTs involving 16,556 participants with an acute exacerbation or recurrence of schizophrenia, there was little evidence of clinically significant differences in efficacy between the oral antipsychotic drugs examined. Metabolic and neurological side effects were consistent with those reported in the SPC for each drug.

---

[9]Of these, 146 trials came from the following existing sources: NICE TA43 (NICE, 2002) and the Cochrane reviews of benperidol (Leucht & Hartung, 2002), loxapine (Fenton *et al.*, 2002), pimozide (Sultana & McMonagle, 2002), sulpiride (Soares *et al.*, 2002) and thioridazine (Sultana *et al.*, 2002). New systematic reviews were conducted for chlorpromazine, flupentixol, fluphenazine, oxypertine, pericyazine, perphenazine, prochlorperazine, promazine, trifluoperazine, and zuclopenthixol dihydrochloride. Data from poor quality trials, placebo comparisons and drugs not available in the UK were excluded.

Table 13: Summary of study characteristics for olanzapine versus another antipsychotic drug (acute treatment)

	Olanzapine versus haloperidol	Olanzapine versus another FGA	Olanzapine versus amisulpride	Olanzapine versus paliperidone
k (total N)	9 (3,071)	4 (249)	2 (429)	3 (1,090)
Study ID	Beasley1996a Beasley1997 HGCJ1999 (HK) HGCU1998 (Taiwan) Malyarov1999 Reams1998 Tollefson1997 KONGSAKON2006 ROSENHECK2003	HGBL1997 Loza1999 Jakovljevic1999 Naukkarinen 1999/ HGBJ (Finland)	MARTIN2002 WAGNER2005	DAVIDSON2007 KANE2007A MARDER2007
Diagnostic criteria	DSM-III-R, DSM-IV, ICD-10	DSM-IV	DSM-IV	DSM-IV
Setting	Inpatient and outpatient	Inpatient and outpatient	Inpatient and outpatient	Inpatient and outpatient
Duration of treatment	Short term: 6 weeks Medium term: 14–26 weeks Long term: 52 weeks	Short term: 4–6 weeks Medium term: 26 weeks	Short term: 8 weeks Medium term: 24 weeks	Short term: 6 weeks
Medication dose (mg/day)	Olanzapine: 5–20 (range) Haloperidol: 5–20 (range)	Olanzapine: 5–20 (range) Chlorpromazine hydrochloride: 200–800 (range) Flupentixol: 5–20 (range) Fluphenazine: 6–21 (range) Perphenazine: 8–32 (range)	Olanzapine: 5–20 (range) Amisulpride: 200–800 (range)	Olanzapine: 10 (range) Paliperidone: 6 or 9[a]

[a] For the purpose of the review, data from the 6 mg group (MARDER2007) and the 9 mg group (DAVIDSON2007) were used in the meta-analysis

Table 13: Summary of study characteristics for olanzapine versus another antipsychotic drug (acute treatment) (*Continued*)

	Olanzapine versus quetiapine	Olanzapine versus risperidone	Olanzapine versus ziprasidone
k (total N)	1 (52)	5 (928)	2 (817)
Study ID	RIEDEL2007B	Conley2001 Gureje1998 Malyarov1999 Tran1997 STUDY-S036	StudyR-0548 (SIMPSON2004) BREIER2005
Diagnostic criteria	DSM-IV	DSM-IV or ICD-10	DSM-IV
Setting	Inpatient	Inpatient and outpatient	Inpatient and outpatient
Duration of treatment	Short term: 8 weeks	Short term: 6–8 weeks Medium term: 26–30 weeks	Short term: 6 weeks Medium term: 28 weeks
Medication dose (mg/day)	Olanzapine: 15.82 (mean); 10–20 (range) Quetiapine: 586.86 (mean); 400–800 (range)	Olanzapine: 5–20 (range) Risperidone: 2–12 (range)	Olanzapine: 11.3–15.27 (range of means) Ziprasidone: 115.96–129.9 (range of means)

Table 14: Summary of study characteristics for risperidone versus another antipsychotic drug (acute treatment)

	Risperidone versus haloperidol	Risperidone versus another FGA	Risperidone versus amisulpride	Risperidone versus aripiprazole
k (total N)	14 (2,437)	2 (205)	3 (585)	2 (487)
Study ID	Blin1996 Ceskova1993 Cetin1999 Chouinard1993 Claus1991 Janicak1999 Liu2000 Malyarov1999 Marder1994 Mesotten1991 Min1993 Muller-Siecheneder1998 Peuskens1995 ZHANG2001	Hoyberg1993 Huttunen1995	Fleurot1997 Lecrubier2000 HWANG2003	CHAN2007B POTKIN2003A
Diagnostic criteria	DSM-III-R, DSM-IV, ICD-9, ICD-10	DSM-III-R	DSM-IV	DSM-IV
Setting	Inpatient	Not reported	Inpatient	Inpatient
Duration of treatment	Short term: 4–8 weeks Medium term: 12–26 weeks	Short term: 8 weeks	Short term: 6–8 weeks Medium term: 26 weeks	Short term: 4 weeks
Medication dose (mg/day)	Risperidone: 5.5–12 (range of means); 1–20 (range) Haloperidol: 9.2–20 (range of means); 2–20 (range)	Risperidone: 8–8.5 (range of means); 15–20 (max) Perphenazine: 28 (mean); 48 (max) Zuclopenthixol: 38 (mean); 100 (max)	Risperidone: 4–10 (range) Amisulpride: 400–1000 (range)	Risperidone: 6 (fixed) Aripiprazole: 15, 20, 30 (fixed)

Table 14: Summary of study characteristics for risperidone versus another antipsychotic drug (acute treatment) (*Continued*)

	Risperidone versus quetiapine	Risperidone versus sertindole	Risperidone versus ziprasidone	Risperidone versus zotepine
k (total N)	1 (673)	1 (187)	1 (296)	1 (59)
Study ID	ZHONG2006	AZORIN2006	Study128-302 (ADDINGTON2004)	Klieser1996
Diagnostic criteria	DSM-IV	DSM-IV	DSM-III-R	ICD-9
Setting	Inpatient and outpatient	Inpatient and outpatient	Not reported	Not reported
Duration of treatment	Short term: 8 weeks	Medium term: 12 weeks	Short term: 8 weeks	Short term: 4 weeks
Medication dose (mg/day)	Risperidone: 6.0 (mean); 2–8 (range) Quetiapine: 525 (mean); 200–800 (range)	Risperidone: 6.6 (mean); 4–10 (range) Sertindole: 16.2 (mean); 12–24 (range)	Risperidone: 7.4 (mean); 3–10 (range) Ziprasidone: 114 (mean); 80–160 (range)	Risperidone: 4 or 8 (fixed) Zotepine: 225 (fixed)

Table 15: Summary of study characteristics for amisulpride or aripiprazole versus another antipsychotic drug (acute treatment)

	Amisulpride versus haloperidol	Amisulpride versus another FGA	Aripiprazole versus haloperidol	Aripiprazole versus ziprasidone
k (total N)	5 (921)	1 (132)	2 (1,708)	1 (256)
Study ID	Carriere2000 Delcker1990 Moller1997 Puech1998 Ziegler1989	Hillert1994	KANE2002 KASPER2003	ZIMBROFF2007
Diagnostic criteria	DSM-III-R, DSM-IV, ICD-9	DSM-III-R	DSM-IV	DSM-IV
Setting	Inpatient and outpatient	Inpatient	Inpatient and outpatient	Inpatient and outpatient
Duration of treatment	Short term: 4–6 weeks Medium term: 16 weeks	Short term: 6 weeks	Short term: 4 weeks Long term: 52 weeks	Short term: 4 weeks
Medication dose (mg/day)	Amisulpride: 400–2,400 (range) Haloperidol: 10–40 (range)	Amisulpride: 956 (mean); 1000 (maximum) Flupentixol: 22.6 (mean); 25 (maximum)	Aripiprazole: 15 or 30 (fixed) Haloperidol: 10 (fixed)	Aripiprazole: 20.9 (mean modal) Ziprasidone: 149 (mean modal)

Table 16: Summary of study characteristics for quetiapine or sertindole versus an FGA (acute treatment)

	Quetiapine versus haloperidol	Quetiapine versus another FGA	Sertindole versus haloperidol
k (total N)	4 (818)	1 (201)	1 (617)
Study ID	Arvanitis1997 Fleischhacker1996 Purdon2000 ATMACA2002	Link1994	Hale2000
Diagnostic criteria	DSM-III-R, DSM-IV, ICD-10	DSM-III-R	DSM-III-R
Setting	Inpatient and outpatient	Not reported	Inpatient
Duration of treatment	Short term: 6 weeks Medium term: 26 weeks	Short term: 6 weeks	Short term: 8 weeks
Medication dose (mg/day)	Quetapine: 50–800 (range) Haloperidol: 1–16 (range)	Quetapine: 407 (mean) Chlorpromazine hydrochloride: 384 (mean)	Sertindole: 8, 16 or 20, 24 (fixed) Haloperidol: 10 (fixed)

Table 17: Summary of study characteristics for zotepine versus an FGA (acute treatment)

	Zotepine versus haloperidol	Zotepine versus another FGA
k (total N)	5 (386)	2 (146)
Study ID	Barnas1987 Fleischhacker1989 Klieser1996 Petit1996 KnollCTR (StudyZT4002)	Cooper1999a Dieterle1999
Diagnostic criteria	DSM-III, DSM-III-R, ICD-9	DSM-III-R, ICD-9
Setting	Inpatient	Mostly inpatient
Duration of treatment	Short term: 4–8 weeks Medium term: 26 weeks	Short term: 4–8 weeks
Medication dose (mg/day)	Zotepine: 94–309 (range of means); 150–300 (range) Haloperidol: 4–15 (range of means); 10–20 (range)	Zotepine: 241 (mean); 300 (max) Chlorpromazine hydrochloride: 600 (max) Perphenazine: 348 (mean)

6.4 PROMOTING RECOVERY IN PEOPLE WITH SCHIZOPHRENIA THAT IS IN REMISSION – PHARMACOLOGICAL RELAPSE PREVENTION

6.4.1 Introduction

Following their introduction into clinical practice in the early 1950s, chlorpromazine and related drugs rapidly became widely used for both acute treatment of people experiencing symptoms of psychosis and for prevention of relapse. By the 1980s, haloperidol (synthesised in 1959) became the most widely used drug for these purposes in the US (Davis *et al.*, 1993; Gilbert *et al.*, 1995; Hirsch & Barnes, 1995; Healy, 2002). A meta-analysis (Davis *et al.*, 1993) of 35 double-blind studies compared maintenance treatment using FGAs with placebo in over 3,500 service users. Relapse was reported in 55% of those who were randomised to receive placebo, but in only 21% of those receiving active drugs. Gilbert and colleagues (1995) reviewed 66 antipsychotic withdrawal studies, published between 1958 and 1993, and involving over 4,000 service users. The mean cumulative rate of relapse in the medication withdrawal groups was 53% (follow-up period 6 to 10 months) compared with 16% (follow-up of 8 months) in the antipsychotic maintenance groups. Over a period of several years, continuing treatment with conventional antipsychotics appears to reduce the risk of relapse by about two-thirds (Kissling, 1991).

When the effects of stopping antipsychotic drugs after an acute psychotic episode or after long-term maintenance treatment were examined, the subsequent rate of relapse seemed to be similar in both situations. Individuals who are well stabilised on maintenance medication show high rates of relapse when their antipsychotic therapy is discontinued (Kane, 1990) or switched to placebo (Hogarty *et al.*, 1976). A recent Cochrane review (Alkhateeb *et al.*, 2007) including ten trials of chlorpromazine cessation in stable participants (total N = 1,042) showed that those stopping chlorpromazine had a relative risk of relapse in the short term (up to 8 weeks) of 6.76 (95% CI, 3.37 to 13.54) and in the medium term (9 weeks to 6 months) of 4.04 (95% CI, 2.81 to 5.8). Relative risk of relapse after 6 months was 1.70 (95% CI, 1.44 to 2.01). Another meta-analysis of data from several large collaborative studies (Davis *et al.*, 1993) suggested that the number of people who survive without relapse after discontinuing drug treatment declines exponentially by around 10% a month.

Whether maintenance drug treatment is required for all people with schizophrenia is uncertain. Around 20% of individuals will only experience a single episode (Möller & van Zerssen, 1995). A recent pragmatic observational study analysing over 4,000 participants who achieved remission in the Schizophrenia Outpatient Health Outcomes study, showed that 25% relapsed over a 3-year follow-up period with a constant rate of relapse over this time (Haro *et al.*, 2007). It therefore appears that a proportion of people will experience a relapse despite continued antipsychotic drug treatment. It is unclear whether such people benefit from an increase in antipsychotic dosage during episodes of psychotic exacerbation (Steingard *et al.*, 1994).

Given that there are no consistent reliable predictors of prognosis or drug response, the previous schizophrenia guideline, as well as other consensus statements and guidelines, generally recommend that pharmacological relapse prevention is considered for every patient diagnosed with schizophrenia (for example, Dixon *et al.*, 1995; Lehman *et al.*, 1998). Possible exceptions are people with very brief psychotic episodes without negative psychosocial consequences, and the uncommon patient for whom all available antipsychotics pose a significant health risk (Fleischhacker & Hummer, 1997).

It is clear from the placebo-controlled RCTs and discontinuation studies cited above that the efficacy of antipsychotics in relapse prevention is established. However, it is also clear from recent pragmatic trials that switching of medication over time is common in clinical practice (Jones *et al.*, 2006; Lieberman *et al.*, 2005). In the Clinical Antipsychotic Trials of Intervention Effectiveness (CATIE) study (Lieberman *et al.*, 2005), 74% of participants discontinued their randomised treatment over 18 months (further information about this trial can be found in Section 6.8 on the effectiveness of antipsychotic medication). This may well reflect the need in clinical practice to search collaboratively for the drug that offers the best balance of efficacy and tolerability for the individual patient. The role of depot preparations in contributing to concordance and continuation on medication is discussed in Section 6.6.

All the antipsychotics identified for review have established supremacy over placebo in the prevention of relapse, although the evidence that any individual antipsychotic drug, or group of antipsychotics (FGAs and SGAs), has greater efficacy or better tolerability than another is still very uncertain. One of the main aims of antipsychotic drug development in recent decades has been to produce compounds with equivalent antipsychotic efficacy, but without troubling EPS. The doses of haloperidol that came to be used in routine clinical practice by the 1980s and early 1990s were higher than those required for its antipsychotic effect, and EPS were common. The trials conducted in the 1990s comparing SGAs and haloperidol often tested the latter at relatively high doses, arguably above the optimum for at least a proportion of the subjects treated, and highlighted the propensity of haloperidol to cause such side effects in comparison with SGAs. The widespread introduction of SGAs to clinical practice from the mid 1990s onwards thus appeared to offer a genuine therapeutic advance. However, more recent effectiveness (pragmatic) trials have suggested that the claimed advantages of these drugs may have been overstated, especially if their propensity to cause metabolic abnormalities and other side effects is taken into account, and if they are compared with FGAs (other than higher dose haloperidol) (Geddes *et al.*, 2000; Jones *et al.*, 2006; Lieberman *et al.*, 2005; NICE, 2002). SGAs are not a homogeneous class and may not deserve a group title. They differ widely in their pharmacology and side effect profile. There are unanswered questions regarding their relative efficacy and tolerability and their use over the long-term compared with FGAs. Their risks of long-term metabolic disturbance are not yet fully quantified and neither is the risk of movement disorders, such as tardive dyskinesia compared with FGAs, so any small advantage that may be offered by reduced EPS may be offset by these other adverse consequences not shown by the earlier drugs.

While evaluating each drug against each other would appear superficially the best way of approaching the question posed for this review, in reality the number of possible comparisons and the limited number of studies available would render this a meaningless task. Therefore, the GDG considered that comparing the individual

SGAs against all FGA comparators, primarily in terms of relapse, provided the most meaningful analysis of the available data.

Definitions
The definitions of relapse used in this review were those adopted by the individual studies. This definition varied between studies (see Sections 6.4.4 and 6.4.5), and therefore, caution should be exercised in the interpretation of the results.

6.4.2 Clinical review protocol

The review protocol, including the primary clinical question, information about the databases searched and the eligibility criteria used for this section of the guideline can be found in Table 18. A new systematic search for relevant RCTs, published since the previous guideline, was conducted for the guideline update (further information about the search strategy can be found in Appendix 8 and information about the search for health economic evidence can be found in Section 6.9.1).

6.4.3 Studies considered for review

In the previous guideline, nine RCTs comparing an SGA with an FGA were included (based on a then unpublished review by Leucht and colleagues). Since the publication of the previous guideline, Leucht and colleagues published their review in 2003; it included one additional trial and six trials comparing an SGA with placebo that were not included in the previous guideline. For the update, the review was limited to double-blind RCTs of antipsychotics used for relapse prevention; therefore, four studies (Daniel1998; Essock1996; Rosenheck1999; Tamminga1994) included in the previous guideline were excluded from the update. In addition, one trial of an SGA versus another SGA, included in the previous acute treatment review, met the criteria for inclusion in this review (Tran1997). The update search identified four additional RCTs (one comparing an SGA with an FGA, one comparing an SGA with an SGA, and one comparing an SGA with placebo). For the purposes of the health economic model (see Section 6.9.2), trials of ziprasidone versus placebo were included because this drug has been compared with a licensed SGA.

In total, 17 RCTs (N = 3,535) met the inclusion criteria for the update. Of these, one was unpublished (STUDY-S029) and the remainder were published in peer-reviewed journals between 1994 and 2007. Further information about both included and excluded studies can be found in Appendix 15b.

6.4.4 Second-generation antipsychotics versus placebo in people with schizophrenia that is in remission (relapse prevention)

Eight RCTs were included in the meta-analysis comparing an SGA (amisulpride, aripiprazole, olanzapine, paliperidone, ziprasidone, zotepine) with placebo (see Table 19). Forest plots and/or data tables for each outcome can be found in Appendix 16c.

Table 18: Clinical review protocol for the review of relapse prevention

Primary clinical question	For people with schizophrenia that is in remission, what are the benefits and downsides of continuous oral antipsychotic drug treatment when compared with another antipsychotic drug (when administered within the recommended dose range [BNF 54])?
Electronic databases	CENTRAL, CINAHL, EMBASE, MEDLINE, PsycINFO
Date searched	1 January 2002 to 30 July 2008
Study design	Double-blind RCT (≥10 participants per arm and ≥6 months' duration)
Patient population	Adults (age 18+) with schizophrenia that is in remission (for the purposes of the guideline, remission includes people who have responded fully or partially to treatment)
Excluded populations	Very late onset schizophrenia (onset after age 60). Other psychotic disorders, such as bipolar disorder, mania or depressive psychosis. People with coexisting learning difficulties, significant physical or sensory difficulties, or substance misuse.
Interventions	FGAs: Benperidol Chlorpromazine hydrochloride Flupentixol Fluphenazine hydrochloride Haloperidol Levomepromazine Pericyazine Perphenazine Pimozide Prochlorperazine Promazine hydrochloride Sulpiride Trifluoperazine Zuclopenthixol acetate Zuclopenthixol dihydrochloride	SGAs[a]: Amisulpride Aripiprazole Olanzapine Paliperidone Quetiapine Risperidone Zotepine
Comparator	Any relevant antipsychotic drug or placebo
Critical outcomes	Global state (relapse). Overall treatment failure (relapse or leaving the study early for any reason). Leaving the study early because of adverse events.

Note: Studies (or outcomes from studies) were categorised as short term (12 weeks or fewer), medium term (12–51 weeks) and long term (52 weeks or more); studies that used drug doses outside the recommended dose range were flagged during data analysis.

[a] Clozapine and sertindole were excluded from this analysis because they are not usually used to treat people with schizophrenia that is in remission (trials of ziprasidone were only included if a licensed SGA was used as the intervention).

Table 19: Summary of study characteristics for of an SGA versus placebo (relapse prevention)

	Amisulpride versus placebo	Aripiprazole versus placebo	Olanzapine versus placebo
k (total N)	1 (141)	1 (310)	3 (446)
Study ID	LOO1997	PIGOTT2003	BEASLEY2000 DELLVA1997 (study 1) DELLVA1997 (study 2)
Selected inclusion criteria	Residual or disorganised schizophrenia; predominant negative symptoms	Chronic schizophrenia with diagnosis made at least 2 years prior to entry and continued antipsychotic treatment during this period	BEASLEY2000[a] DELLVA1997 (studies 1 and 2)[b]
Diagnostic criteria	DSM-III-R	DSM-IV	DSM-III-R
Definition of relapse	Withdrawal because of inefficacy of treatment and PANSS >50	Impending decompensation based on one or more of the following: a CGI-I ≥5; a PANSS ≥5 on subscore items of hostility or uncooperativeness on 2 successive days; or a ≥20% increase in PANSS total score	BEASLEY2000: Hospitalisation for positive symptoms or ≥4 increase on BPRS positive score or increase of single BPRS item to 4 and increase from baseline ≥2 DELLVA1997: Hospitalisation for psychopathology
Duration of treatment	26 weeks	26 weeks	42–46 weeks
Setting	Outpatient	Inpatient and outpatient	Outpatient

Medication dose (mg/day)	Amisulpride: 100 (fixed)	Aripiprazole: 15 (fixed)	BEASLEY2000, olanzapine: 10–20 (range) DELLVA1997, olanzapine: ~12 (semi-fixed)
	Paliperidone versus placebo	**Ziprasidone versus placebo**	**Zotepine versus placebo**
k (total N)	1 (207)	1 (277)	1 (119)
Study ID	KRAMER2007	ARATO2002	COOPER2000
Selected inclusion criteria	Achieved stabilisation after 8-week hospitalisation for an acute episode, then further 6-week stabilisation	Lack of acute relapse, lack of treatment resistance, and living under medical supervision for at least 2 months	Rating of at least mildly ill according to CGI; relapse in the 18 months before inclusion
Diagnostic criteria	DSM-IV	DSM-III-R	DSM-III-R
Definition of relapse	Recurrent episode of schizophrenia	Hospitalisation for psychopathology	Hospitalisation for psychopathology
Duration of treatment	46 weeks	52 weeks	26 weeks
Setting	Inpatient initially, then outpatient	Inpatient	Inpatient/outpatient
Medication dose (mg/day)	Palperidone: 10.8 (mean); 3–15 (range)	Ziprasidone: 40, 80 or 160 (fixed)	Zotepine: 150 or 300 (fixed)

[a] Minimally symptomatic; negative symptoms; at least 6 weeks of stability; continued stability while taking olanzapine during an 8-week period.
[b] Responder from 6-week acute treatment phase (responders defined as ≥40% reduction in BPRS score or BPRS score ≤18).

6.4.5 Second-generation antipsychotics versus another antipsychotic drug in people with schizophrenia that is in remission (relapse prevention)

Nine RCTs were included in the meta-analysis comparing an SGA (amisulpride, olanzapine, risperidone) with an FGA (haloperidol) (see Table 20), and two were included in the analysis comparing an SGA (olanzapine) with another SGA (risperidone, ziprasidone) (see Table 21). Forest plots and/or data tables for each outcome can be found in Appendix 16c.

6.4.6 Clinical evidence summary

In 17 RCTs including 3,535 participants with schizophrenia, the evidence suggested that, when compared with placebo, all of the antipsychotics examined reduced the risk of relapse or overall treatment failure. Although some SGAs show a modest benefit over haloperidol, there is insufficient evidence to choose between antipsychotics in terms of relapse prevention.

6.5 PROMOTING RECOVERY IN PEOPLE WITH SCHIZOPHRENIA WHOSE ILLNESS HAS NOT RESPONDED ADEQUATELY TO TREATMENT

6.5.1 Introduction

The phrase 'treatment-resistant' is commonly used to describe people with schizophrenia whose illness has not responded adequately to treatment. The essence of treatment resistance in schizophrenia is the presence of poor psychosocial and community functioning that persists despite trials of medication that have been adequate in terms of dose, duration and adherence. While treatment resistance is sometimes conceptualised in terms of enduring positive psychotic symptoms, other features of schizophrenia can contribute to poor psychosocial and community functioning, including negative symptoms, affective symptoms, medication side effects, cognitive deficits and disturbed behaviour. Treatment resistance in schizophrenia is relatively common, in that between a fifth and a third of service users show a disappointing response to adequate trials of antipsychotic medication (Brenner et al., 1990; Lieberman et al., 1992; Conley & Buchanan, 1997). In a small proportion of people experiencing their first episode of schizophrenia, the illness will be resistant to antipsychotic medication, showing only a limited response (for example, precluding early discharge from hospital) (May, 1968; MacMillan et al., 1986; Lieberman et al., 1989, 1992, Lambert et al., 2008), but more commonly the illness becomes progressively more unresponsive to medication over time (Lieberman et al., 1993; Wiersma et al., 1998).

The definition of the term 'treatment-resistant schizophrenia' varies considerably in the studies covered in this review. Kane and colleagues (1988) introduced rigorous

Table 20: Summary of study characteristics for RCTs of an SGA versus another antipsychotic drug (relapse prevention)

	Amisulpride versus haloperidol	Olanzapine versus haloperidol	Risperidone versus haloperidol
k (total N)	1 (60)	4 (1082)	2 (428)
Study ID	Speller1997	Tran1998a Tran1998b Tran1998c STUDY-S029	Csernansky2000 MARDER2003[a]
Selected inclusion criteria	Chronic, long-term hospitalised inpatient; moderate to severe negative symptoms	Tran1998(a,b,c): Responder from a 6-week acute treatment (at least 40% reduction of BPRS score or BPRS score ≤18) STUDY-S029: Received a stable dose of the same conventional antipsychotic drug ≥8 weeks before visit 1; had a PANSS score ≥49 at visit 2; considered as possible patient in the patients with schizophrenia study (that is, patient global outcome improvement or benefit, such as optimisation of long-term therapy) who should benefit from a switch of current therapy based on investigator's judgment as a result of efficacy (PANSS score ≥49) or tolerability concerns.	Csernansky2000: Stability according to clinical judgment; receipt of the same medication for 30 days; same residence for 30 days MARDER2003: At least two acute episodes in last 2 years or 2 years of continuing symptoms; receipt of treatment as an outpatient for at least 1 month
Diagnostic criteria		DSM-III-R, DSM-IV	DSM-IV

Continued

Table 20: *(Continued)*

	Amisulpride versus haloperidol	Olanzapine versus haloperidol	Risperidone versus haloperidol
Definition of relapse	Increase of three or more BPRS positive symptom items that did not respond to a dose increase	Tran1998(a,b,c): Hospitalisation for psychopathology STUDY-S029: Psychiatric hospitalisation or 25% increase in the PANSS total score in relation to baseline or major deterioration in clinical condition defined by a CGI-I score of 6 or 7, or suicide attempt that required medical treatment and/or jeopardised vital prognosis	Csernansky2000: 1) Hospitalisation; 2) increase of level of care and 20% increase in PANSS score; 3) self-injury, suicidal or homicidal ideation, violent behaviour; 4) CGI rating >6 MARDER2003: Increase >3 in the BPRS scores for the thought disorder and hostile–suspiciousness clusters, or an increase >2 in the score for either of these clusters and a score >3 on at least one item of these clusters
Duration of treatment	52 weeks	22–84 weeks	52 weeks
Setting	Inpatient	Inpatient/outpatient	Outpatient
Medication dose (mg/day)	Amisulpride: 100–800; Haloperidol: 3–20[b]	Tran1998a and b Olanzapine: ~12 (semi-fixed) Haloperidol: ~14 (semi-fixed) Tran 1998c Olanzapine: 14 (mean); 5–20 (range) Haloperidol: 13 (mean); 5–20 (range)	Risperidone: ~5 (mean); 2–16 (range) Haloperidol: <5–12 (range of means); 2–20 (range)

[a] Duration was 2 years, but 1-year data was used for the review to enhance comparability.
[b] A minimum effective dose strategy was followed.

Table 21: Summary of study characteristics for RCTs of an SGA versus another SGA (relapse prevention)

	Olanzapine versus risperidone	Olanzapine versus ziprasidone
k (total N)	1 (339)	1 (126)
Study ID	Tran1997	SIMPSON2005
Selected inclusion criteria	Minimum BPRS of 42 and excluded for failure to show minimal clinical response with antipsychotics in three chemical classes dosed at ≥800 chlorpromazine hydrochloride equivalents/day or clozapine dosed at ≥400 mg/day for at least 6 weeks	Responders to 6-week acute treatment trial of olanzapine or risperidone (response defined as a CGI-I of ≤2 or a ≥20% reduction in PANSS at acute-study endpoint, and outpatient status)
Diagnostic criteria	DSM-IV	DSM-IV
Definition of relapse	20% or greater worsening in the PANSS total score along with a CGI-S score ≥3 after 8 weeks of therapy	≥20% worsening of PANSS total score and a CGI severity score ≥3
Duration of treatments	28 weeks	28 weeks
Setting	Inpatient or outpatient	Outpatient
Medication dose (mg/day)	Olanzapine: 17.2 (mean modal); 10–20 (range) Risperidone: 7.2 (mean modal); 4–12 (range)	Olanzapine: 12.6 (mean); 5–15 (range) Ziprasidone: 135.2 (mean); 78–162 (range)

criteria involving aspects of the clinical history, cross-sectional measures and prospective assessments. One trend has been a move towards broader definitions of treatment resistance that allow a larger number of individuals to be viewed as clinically eligible for treatment with clozapine. For example, Bondolfi and colleagues (1998) included in their trial people with chronic schizophrenia who 'had previously failed to respond to or were intolerant of at least two different classes of antipsychotic drugs given in appropriate doses for at least 4 weeks each'. Others have adopted an even wider clinical notion of 'incomplete recovery'(Pantelis & Lambert, 2003), which acknowledges the presence of lasting disability in functional and psychosocial aspects despite psychological/psychosocial and pharmacological interventions, while also recognising the potential for improvement.

6.5.2　Treatment-resistant schizophrenia and antipsychotic medication

High-dosage antipsychotic medication is commonly used for treatment-resistant schizophrenia, although there is little evidence to suggest any significant benefit with such a strategy (Royal College of Psychiatrists, 2006). Clinicians may also try switching to another antipsychotic, although similarly the research evidence on the possible value of such a strategy is not consistent or promising (Kinon *et al.*, 1993; Lindenmayer *et al.*, 2002; Shalev *et al.*, 1993). An alternative strategy has been to try to potentiate antipsychotics by combining them either with each other (see Section 6.5.3) or with other classes of drugs. Possible adjuncts to antipsychotic treatment include mood stabilisers and anticonvulsants, such as lithium, carbamazepine, sodium valproate, lamotrigine, antidepressants and benzodiazepines (Barnes *et al.*, 2003; Chong & Remington, 2000; Durson & Deakin, 2001). However, the use of such adjunctive treatments to augment the action of antipsychotics is beyond the scope of this guideline.

Kane and colleagues (1988, 2001) established the efficacy of clozapine over FGAs in strictly-defined treatment-resistant schizophrenia, and subsequent meta-analyses have confirmed the superiority of clozapine in terms of reducing symptoms and the risk of relapse (Chakos *et al.*, 2001; Wahlbeck *et al.*, 1999). However, Chakos and colleagues (2001) concluded from their meta-analysis that the evidence for clozapine when compared with the SGAs tested was inconclusive. Even with optimum clozapine treatment, the evidence suggests that only 30 to 60% of treatment-resistant schizophrenia will show a satisfactory response (Iqbal *et al.*, 2003). As clozapine is associated with severe and potentially life-threatening side effects, particularly the risk of agranulocytosis, the SPC states that drug should only be considered where there has been a lack of satisfactory clinical improvement despite adequate trials, in dosage and duration, of at least two different antipsychotic agents including an SGA.

Monitoring plasma clozapine concentration may be helpful in establishing the optimum dose of clozapine in terms of risk–benefit ratio, and also in assessing adherence (Gaertner *et al.*, 2001; Llorca *et al.*, 2002; Rostami-Hodjegan *et al.*, 2004), particularly for service users showing a poor therapeutic response or experiencing significant side effects despite appropriate dosage. An adequate trial will involve titrating the dosage to achieve a target plasma level, usually considered to be above 350mg/l, although response may be seen at lower levels (Dettling *et al.*, 2000; Rostami-Hodjegan *et al.*, 2004). If the response to clozapine monotherapy is poor, augmentation strategies may be considered (see Section 6.5.3 for a review of the evidence).

A number of patient-related factors have been reported to increase the variability of plasma clozapine concentrations, with gender, age and smoking behaviour being the most important (Rostami-Hodjegan *et al.* 2004). Smoking is thought to increase the metabolism of clozapine by inducing the cytochrome P450 1A2 (CYP1A2) and other hepatic enzymes (Flanagan, 2006; Ozdemir *et al.*, 2002). The metabolism of clozapine is mainly dependent on CYP1A2. This has several clinical implications. First, there is some evidence that smokers are prescribed higher doses by clinicians to compensate for higher clozapine clearance (Tang *et al.*, 2007). Secondly, plasma concentrations of clozapine and its active metabolite, norclozapine, vary considerably at a given dosage, and this variation may be greater in heavy smokers receiving lower doses of clozapine, increasing the risk of subtherapeutic concentrations (Diaz *et al.*, 2005). Thirdly, prompt adjustment of clozapine dosage in patients who stop smoking during treatment is important, to avoid the substantially elevated clozapine concentrations and increased risk of toxicity that would otherwise be expected (Flanagan, 2006; McCarthy, 1994; Zullino *et al.*, 2002).

6.5.3   Combining antipsychotic drugs

In clinical practice, the prescription of combined antipsychotics is relatively common. A multi-centre audit of the prescription of antipsychotic drugs for inpatients in 47 mental health services in the UK, involving over 3,000 inpatients, found that nearly half were receiving more than one antipsychotic drug (Harrington *et al.*, 2002). Similarly, prescription surveys in the UK by Taylor and colleagues (2000; 2002) and the Prescribing Observatory for Mental Health (Paton *et al.*, 2008) have confirmed a relatively high prevalence of combined antipsychotics for people with schizophrenia, including co-prescription of FGAs and SGAs.

The reasons for such prescriptions include as required ('p.r.n.') medication, a gradual switch from one antipsychotic drug to another and adding an oral antipsychotic to depot treatment to stabilise illness. A common rationale for combining antipsychotics is to achieve a greater therapeutic response when there has been an unsatisfactory response to a single antipsychotic. In this respect, there is little supportive evidence for superior efficacy (Chan & Sweeting, 2007; Chong & Remington, 2000), and Kreyenbuhl and colleagues (2007) reported that psychiatrists perceive antipsychotic polypharmacy to be generally ineffective for persistent positive psychotic symptoms. The concerns with combined antipsychotics include prescribing higher than necessary total dosage and an increased risk of side effects. If there is clinical benefit, one problem is the attribution of this to the combination rather than one or other of the individual antipsychotics, and thus uncertainty about the implications for optimal pharmacological treatment longer term.

For treatment-resistant schizophrenia that has proved to be unresponsive to clozapine alone, adding a second antipsychotic would seem to be a relatively common strategy. The prevalence of this augmentation strategy in people with schizophrenia on clozapine ranges from 18 to 44% depending on the clinical setting and country (Buckley *et al.*, 2001; Potter *et al.*, 1989; Taylor *et al.*, 2000).

The mechanisms that might underlie any increase in therapeutic effect with combined antipsychotics have not been systematically studied (McCarthy & Terkelsen, 1995). However, in relation to the strategy of adding an antipsychotic to clozapine, it has been hypothesised that any pharmacodynamic synergy might be related to an increased level of D2 dopamine receptor occupancy, above a threshold level (Chong & Remington, 2000; Kontaxakis *et al.*, 2005). However, such an increase might also be expected to be associated with an increased risk of EPS. An alteration of the interaction between serotonin (5-hydroxytryptamine) and D2 activity has also been suggested as a relevant mechanism (Shiloh *et al.*, 1997). Further, pharmacokinetic interactions might play a part, although there is no consistent evidence that adding an antipsychotic leads to increased clozapine plasma levels (Honer *et al.*, 2006; Josiassen *et al.*, 2005; Yagcioglu *et al.*, 2005).

RCTs and open studies have reported clozapine augmentation with a second antipsychotic to be relatively well tolerated. The main treatment-emergent side effects have been predictable from the pharmacology of the augmenting drug, with EPS and prolactin elevation among the most common problems. However, with risperidone as the augmenting antipsychotic there are isolated reports of problems such as agranulocytosis, atrial ectopics and possible neuroleptic malignant syndrome (Chong *et al.*, 1996; Godleski & Serynak, 1996; Kontaxakis *et al.*, 2002); with aripiprazole as the second antipsychotic, there are reports of nausea, vomiting, insomnia, headache and agitation in the first 2 weeks (Ziegenbein *et al.*, 2006) and also modest weight loss (Karunakaran *et al.*, 2006; Ziegenbein *et al.*, 2006).

6.5.4 Clinical review protocol

The clinical review protocol, including the primary clinical questions, information about the databases searched and the eligibility criteria, can be found in Table 22. A new systematic search for relevant RCTs, published since the previous guideline, was conducted for the guideline update (further information about the search strategy can be found in Appendix 8).

Table 22: Clinical review protocol for the review of interventions for people with schizophrenia whose illness has not responded adequately to treatment

Primary clinical questions	For people with schizophrenia whose illness has not responded adequately to treatment, what are the benefits and downsides of continuous oral antipsychotic drug treatment when compared with another antipsychotic drug (when administered within the recommended dose range [BNF 54])?
	For people with schizophrenia with persistent negative symptoms, what are the benefits and downsides of continuous oral antipsychotic drug treatment when compared with another antipsychotic drug (when administered within the recommended dose range [BNF 54])?
	For people with schizophrenia whose illness has not responded adequately to clozapine treatment, is augmentation of clozapine with another antipsychotic associated with an enhanced therapeutic response?
Electronic databases	CENTRAL, CINAHL, EMBASE, MEDLINE, PsycINFO
Date searched	1 January 2002 to 30 July 2008
Study design	Double-blind RCT (≥10 participants per arm and ≥4 weeks' duration)

Continued

Table 22: *(Continued)*

Patient population	Adults (18+) with schizophrenia whose illness has not responded adequately to treatment (including those with persistent negative symptoms[a])	
Excluded populations	Very late onset schizophrenia (onset after age 60). Other psychotic disorders, such as bipolar disorder, mania or depressive psychosis. People with coexisting learning difficulties, significant physical or sensory difficulties, or substance misuse.	
Interventions	FGAs: Benperidol Chlorpromazine hydrochloride Flupentixol Fluphenazine hydrochloride Haloperidol Levomepromazine Pericyazine Perphenazine Pimozide Prochlorperazine Promazine hydrochloride Sulpiride Trifluoperazine Zuclopenthixol acetate Zuclopenthixol dihydrochloride	SGAs: Amisulpride Aripiprazole Clozapine Olanzapine Paliperidone Quetiapine Risperidone Sertindole Zotepine
Comparator	Any relevant antipsychotic drug	
Critical outcomes	Mortality (suicide) Global state (relapse) Mental state (total symptoms, negative symptoms, depression) Social functioning Cognitive functioning Leaving the study early for any reason Adverse events	

Note: Studies (or outcomes from studies) were categorised as short term (12 weeks or fewer), medium term (12–51 weeks) and long term (52 weeks or more); studies that used drug doses outside the recommended dose range were flagged during data analysis.

[a] Studies that only included participants with persistent negative symptoms were analysed separately.

6.5.5   Studies considered for review

In the previous guideline, 19 RCTs were included in the review of antipsychotic medication for people with schizophrenia whose illness has not responded adequately to treatment. The update search identified five papers providing follow-up data or published versions of existing trials, and eight new trials (one trial [LIBERMAN2002] provided no useable outcome data and was excluded from the analysis). In addition, six trials (Altamura1999; Breier2000; Conley1998a; Emsley1999; Heck2000; Kern1998) previously analysed as acute phase studies were now included in this review, and three (Essock1996a; Gelenberg1979b; Wahlbeck2000) previously included were now excluded. In total, 26 trials (N = 3,932) met the inclusion criteria for the update. Further information about both included and excluded studies can be found in Appendix 15b.

A new analysis, not conducted for the previous guideline, examined RCTs of antipsychotic medication in people with persistent negative symptoms of schizophrenia. Three trials (Boyer1990; Lecrubier1999; Murasaki1999) included in the previous review of acute treatment are now included here, but excluded from the updated acute treatment review. One trial (OLIE2006[10]) excluded from the previous guideline is now included. One trial (Speller1997) included in the relapse prevention review also met the inclusion criteria for this review. The update search also identified five new RCTs that are included in this review, and one trial (HERTLING2003) that reported no appropriate data and so was excluded from the analysis. In total, ten RCTs (N = 1,200) met the inclusion criteria for the update. Further information about both included and excluded studies can be found in Appendix 15b.

For the review of clozapine augmentation, an existing systematic review and meta-analysis (Paton *et al.*, 2007), published since the previous guideline, was used as the basis for an updated meta-analysis. This published review focused on the augmentation of clozapine with another SGA and included four RCTs. The update search identified two further RCTs. In total, six trials (N = 252) met the inclusion criteria for the update. In addition, two small studies (Assion *et al.*, 2008; Mossaheb *et al.*, 2006) with fewer than ten participants in either arm were excluded, and one trial of clozapine plus amisulpride versus clozapine plus quetiapine (Genc *et al.*, 2007) was excluded. Further information about both included and excluded studies can be found in Appendix 15b.

6.5.6   Clozapine versus another antipsychotic drug in people with schizophrenia whose illness has not responded adequately to treatment

Seven RCTs were included in the analysis comparing clozapine with an FGA in people with schizophrenia whose illness has not responded adequately to treatment (see Table 23), and ten RCTs were included in the analysis of clozapine versus another SGA (see Table 24). Forest plots and/or data tables for each outcome can be found in Appendix 16c.

---

[10] In the previous guideline this trial was labelled as 'Study 128-305'.

Table 23: Summary of study characteristics for RCTs of clozapine versus an FGA in people with schizophrenia whose illness has not responded adequately to treatment

	Clozapine versus haloperidol	Clozapine versus a non-haloperidol FGA[a]
k (total N)	4 (607)	3 (459)
Study ID	Buchanan1998 Klieser1989 Rosenheck1997 VOLAVKA2002	Claghorn1987 Hong1997 Kane1988
Diagnostic criteria	DSM-III-R, DSM-IV	DSM-II, DSM-III, DSM-IV
Selected inclusion criteria	Buchanan1998: Non-complete response to at least two trials of therapeutic doses of antipsychotics for at least 6 weeks Klieser1989: Chronic treatment-resistant (no diagnostic criteria) Rosenheck1997: Treatment-resistant, high level use of inpatient services VOLAVKA2002: Suboptimal response to previous treatment, defined by history of persistent positive symptoms after at least 6 contiguous weeks of treatment with one or more typical antipsychotics at ≥600 mg/d in chlorpromazine hydrochloride equivalents, and a poor level of functioning over past 2 years	Claghorn1987: Intolerant to at least two prior antipsychotics Hong1997: Treatment-refractory (severe psychotic symptoms according to BPRS item scores for >6 months despite treatment with antipsychotics from at least two different classes at dosages of at least 1000 mg chlorpromazine hydrochloride equivalents) Kane 1988: ≥3 periods of antipsychotic treatment, 1000 mg/day of chlorpromazine hydrochloride equivalents without significant symptomatic relief and BPRS total score of at least 45
Setting	Inpatient/outpatient	Inpatient
Duration of treatment	Short term: 6–10 weeks Medium term: 14 weeks Long term: 52 weeks	Short term: 4–8 weeks Medium term: 12 weeks
Medication dose (mg/day)	Clozapine: 400–552 mg/day (range of means); 100–900 mg/day (range) Haloperidol: 20–28 mg/day (range of means); 5–30 mg/day (range)	Clozapine: 417–543 mg/d (range of means); 150–900 mg/d (range) Chlorpromazine hydrochloride: 798–1163 mg/day (range of means); 300–1800 mg/day (range)

[a]All three trials used chlorpromazine as the comparator.

Table 24: Summary of study characteristics for RCTs of clozapine versus another SGA in people with schizophrenia whose illness has not responded adequately to treatment

	Clozapine versus olanzapine	Clozapine versus risperidone	Clozapine versus zotepine
k (total N)	5 (485)	5 (529)	1 (50)
Study ID	Beuzen1998 Bitter1999 (BITTER2004) MELTZER2008 Oliemeulen2000 VOLAVKA2002	Anand1998 Bondolfi1998 Breier1999 Chowdhury1999 VOLAVKA2002	Meyer-Lindberg 1996
Diagnostic criteria	DSM-IV	DSM-III-R, DSM-IV, ICD-10	DSM-III-R
Selected inclusion criteria	Beuzen1998: Treatment resistant, >3 on at least two items of PANSS positive subscale Bitter1999: Treatment-resistant or intolerant individuals must have not responded adequately to standard acceptable antipsychotic medication, either because of ineffectiveness or because of intolerable side effects caused by the medication MELTZER2008: Documented history of treatment-resistant schizophrenia based on Kane and colleagues' (1988) criteria Oliemeulen2000: Therapy-resistant; schizophrenia or other psychotic disorders	Anand1998: Treatment resistant: severe, chronic disease and poor response to previous antipsychotics (no period of good functioning for at least 24 months despite the use of two antipsychotics, current episode without significant improvement for at least 6 months despite the use of an antipsychotic equivalent to haloperidol 20 mg for at least 6 weeks, total BPRS at least 45, and CGI at least 4 Bondolfi1998: Treatment resistant: failed to respond/intolerant to >2 different classes of antipsychotics in appropriate doses for >4 weeks Breier1999: Partial response to antipsychotics, defined as a history of	Unresponsive to >3 weeks of two FGAs in effective doses, BPRS >39

	VOLAVKA2002: Suboptimal response to previous treatment, defined by history of persistent positive symptoms after at least 6 contiguous weeks of treatment with one or more typical antipsychotics at ≥600 mg/day in chlorpromazine hydrochloride equivalents, and a poor level of functioning over past 2 years	residual positive and/or negative symptoms after at least a 6-week trial of a therapeutic dose of a antipsychotic and at least a minimum level of symptoms Chowdhury1999: Duration of illness >6 months and received at least one full course of FGA without adequate response, or cases intolerant to FGAs because of intractable neurological and non-neurological side effects, necessitating withdrawal of drug or inadequate dosing VOLAVKA2002: see left	
Setting	Inpatient/outpatient	Inpatient (not stated in three trials)	Not stated
Duration of treatment	Short term: 8 weeks Medium term: 14–26 weeks	Short term: 6–8 weeks Medium term: 12–16 weeks	Short term: 6 weeks
Medication dose (mg/day)	Clozapine: 564 mg/day (mean); 200–900 mg/day (range) Olanzapine: 33.6 mg/day (mean); 10–45 mg/day (range)	Clozapine: 291–597.5 mg/d (range of means); 150–900 mg/d (range) Risperidone: 5.8–8.3 mg/day (range of means); 2–16 mg/day (range)	Clozapine: 150–450 mg/day (range) Zotepine: 150–450 mg/d (range)

6.5.7 Second-generation antipsychotic drugs (other than clozapine) versus first-generation antipsychotic drugs in people with schizophrenia whose illness has not responded adequately to treatment

Ten RCTs were included in the analysis comparing clozapine with another antipsychotic in people with schizophrenia whose illness has not responded adequately to treatment (see Table 25). Forest plots and/or data tables for each outcome can be found in Appendix 16c.

6.5.8 Second-generation antipsychotic drugs (other than clozapine) versus second-generation antipsychotic drugs in people with schizophrenia whose illness has not responded adequately to treatment

Three RCTs were included in the analysis comparing an SGA (olanzapine and risperidone) with another SGA in people with schizophrenia whose illness has not responded adequately to treatment (see Table 26). Forest plots and/or data tables for each outcome can be found in Appendix 16c.

6.5.9 Second-generation antipsychotic drugs (other than clozapine) versus another antipsychotic in people who have persistent negative symptoms

Five RCTs were included in the analysis comparing an SGA (amisulpride, olanzapine, quetiapine, risperidone) with another SGA in people who have persistent negative symptoms (see Table 27). Five RCTs were included in the analysis comparing an SGA (amisulpride, olanzapine, quetiapine, risperidone) with another SGA in people who have persistent negative symptoms (see Table 28). Forest plots and/or data tables for each outcome can be found in Appendix 16c.

6.5.10 Combining antipsychotics (augmentation of clozapine with another second-generation antipsychotic drug)

One trial was included in the analysis comparing clozapine plus aripiprazole with clozapine plus placebo, four trials compared clozapine plus risperidone with clozapine plus placebo, and one trial compared clozapine plus sulpiride with clozapine plus placebo (see Table 29). Forest plots and/or data tables for each outcome can be found in Appendix 16c.

132

Table 25: Summary of study characteristics for RCTs of SGAs versus FGAs in people with schizophrenia whose illness has not responded adequately to treatment

	Aripiprazole versus a non-haloperidol FGA	Olanzapine versus haloperidol	Olanzapine versus a non-haloperidol FGA
k (total N)	1 (300)	3 (617)	1 (84)
Study ID	KANE2007B	Altamura1999 (ALTAMURA2002) Breier2000 BUCHANAN2005	Conley1998a
Diagnostic criteria	DSM-IV	DSM-IV	DSM-III-R
Selected inclusion criteria	Treatment resistant (defined as failure to experience satisfactory symptom relief despite at least two periods of treatment, each lasting ≥6 weeks with adequate doses of antipsychotics)	Altamura1999: Partial or non-responders to treatment according to preset criteria Breier2000: Sub-population from Tollefson1997 with treatment-resistant schizophrenia, defined as failure to respond to at least one neuroleptic over a period of at least 8 weeks during the previous 2 years BUCHANAN2005: Partial response to fluphenazine during 4-week open-label phase	Treatment resistant: Non-responders during haloperidol phase.
Setting	Inpatient/outpatient	Inpatient/outpatient	Inpatient
Duration of treatment	Short term: 6 weeks	Short term: 6 weeks Medium term: 14–16 weeks	Short term: 8 weeks
Medication dose (mg/day)	Aripiprazole: 15–30 mg/day (range) Perphenazine: 8–64mg/day (range)	Olanzapine: 11.1–12.4 mg/day (range of means); 5–30 mg/day (range) Haloperidol: 10–12.3 mg/day (range of means); 5–30 mg/day (range)	Olanzapine: 25 mg/day (fixed) Chlorpromazine hydrochloride: 1200 mg/day (fixed)

Continued

Table 25: Summary of study characteristics for RCTs of SGAs versus FGAs in people with schizophrenia whose illness has not responded adequately to treatment (*Continued*)

	Quetiapine versus haloperidol	Quetiapine versus a non-haloperidol FGA	Risperidone versus haloperidol	Risperidone versus a non-haloperidol FGA
k (total N)	1 (288)	1 (25)	3 (161)	1 (26)
Study ID	Emsley1999	CONLEY2005	Heck2000 Kern1998 SEE1999	CONLEY2005
Diagnostic criteria	DSM-IV	DSM-IV	DSM-III-R, DSM-IV	DSM-IV
Selected inclusion criteria	Persistent positive symptoms while previously taking antipsychotics	Treatment resistant [a]	Heck2000: Disturbing EPS during their previous neuroleptic treatment Kern1998: Treatment resistant according to the Kane criteria SEE1999: A history of partial responsiveness to FGAs and residual symptoms	Treatment resistant [a]
Setting	Not reported	Inpatient	Not reported	Inpatient
Duration of treatment	Short term: 8 weeks	Medium term: 12 weeks	Short term: 5–8 weeks	Medium term: 12 weeks
Medication dose (mg/day)	Quetiapine: 600 mg/day (fixed) Haloperidol: 20 mg/day (fixed)	Quetiapine: 400 mg/day (fixed) Fluphenazine hydrochloride: 12.5 mg/day (fixed)	Risperidone: 7 mg/day (mean) (Kern 1998); 16 mg/day (max) (Heck 2000) Haloperidol: 19 mg/day (mean) (Kern 1998); 24 mg/day (max) (Heck 2000)	Risperidone: 4 mg/day (fixed) Fluphenazine hydrochloride: 12.5 mg/day (fixed)

[a] Defined by: 1) Persistent positive symptoms (≥4 points on 2 of 4 BPRS psychosis items); 2) Persistent global illness severity (BPRS total ≥45 and CGI ≥4); 3) At least two prior failed treatment trials with two different antipsychotics at doses of ≥600 mg/day chlorpromazine hydrochloride equivalent each of at least 6 weeks' duration; 4) No stable period of good social/occupational functioning in past 5 years.

Table 26: Summary of study characteristics for RCTs of SGAs versus SGAs in people with schizophrenia whose illness has not responded adequately to treatment

	Olanzapine versus risperidone	Olanzapine versus ziprasidone	Risperidone versus quetiapine
k (total N)	1 (80)	1 (394)	1 (25)
Study ID	VOLAVKA2002	KINON2006A	CONLEY2005
Diagnostic criteria	DSM-IV	DSM-IV	DSM-IV
Selected inclusion criteria	Suboptimal response to previous treatment[a]	Prominent depressive symptoms[b]	Treatment resistant[c]
Setting	Inpatient	Outpatient	Inpatient
Duration of treatment	Medium term: 14 weeks	Medium term: 24 weeks	Medium term: 12 weeks
Medication dose (mg/day)	Olanzapine: 10–40 mg/day (range) Risperidone: 4–16 mg/day (range)	Olanzapine: 10, 15 or 20 mg/day (fixed) Ziprasidone: 80, 120 or 160 mg/day (fixed)	Risperidone: 4 mg/day (fixed) Quetiapine: 400 mg/day (fixed)

[a] Defined by history of persistent positive symptoms after at least 6 contiguous weeks of treatment with one or more typical antipsychotics at ≥600 mg/day chlorpromazine hydrochloride equivalent, and a poor level of functioning over past 2 years.

[b] Defined by a MADRS score ≥16 (mild depression) and a score ≥4 (pervasive feelings of sadness or gloominess) on item 2 (reported sadness) of the MADRS.

[c] Defined by: 1) Persistent positive symptoms (≥4 points on 2 of 4 BPRS psychosis items); 2) Persistent global illness severity (BPRS total ≥45 and CGI ≥4); 3) At least two prior failed treatment trials with two different antipsychotics at doses of ≥600 mg/day chlorpromazine hydrochloride equivalent each of at least 6 weeks' duration; 4) No stable period of good social/occupational functioning in past 5 years.

Table 27: Summary of study characteristics for RCTs of SGAs versus a FGA in people who have persistent negative symptoms

	Amisulpride versus haloperidol	Amisulpride versus a non-haloperidol FGA	Olanzapine versus haloperidol	Quetiapine versus Haloperidol	Risperidone versus a non-haloperidol FGA
k (total N)	1 (60)	1 (62)	1 (35)	1 (197)	1 (153)
Study ID	Speller1997	Boyer1990	LINDENMAYER2007	Murasaki1999	RUHRMANN2007
Diagnostic criteria	Not reported	DSM-III	DSM-IV	DSM-IV or ICD-10	ICD-10
Selected inclusion criteria	Chronic, long-term hospitalised inpatients with moderate to severe negative symptoms	All met Andreasen criteria for negative symptoms and absence of marked positive symptoms.	Fulfilled criteria for the Schedule for the Deficit Syndrome (SDS) which included negative symptoms that are stable rather than unstable-state manifestations	Predominantly negative symptoms	Negative symptoms (≥3 on PANSS negative subscale)
Setting	Not reported	Not reported	Inpatient/outpatient	Inpatient/outpatient	Inpatient/outpatient
Duration of treatment	Long term: 52 weeks	Short term: 6 weeks	Medium term: 12 weeks	Short term: 8 weeks	Medium term: 25 weeks
Medication dose (mg/day)	Amisulpride: 100–800 mg/day Haloperidol: 3–20 mg/day	Amisulpride: 225 mg/day (mean); 50–300 mg/day (range) Fluphenazine hydrochloride: 10 mg/day (mean); 2–12 mg/day (range)	Olanzapine: 15–20 mg/day (range) Haloperidol: 15–20 mg/day (range)	Quetiapine: 226 mg/day (mean); 600 mg/day (max) Haloperidol: 6.7 mg/day (mean); 18 mg/day (max)	Risperidone: 2–6 mg/day (range) Flupentixol: 4–12 mg/day (range)

Table 28: Summary of study characteristics for RCTs of SGAs versus another SGA in people who have persistent negative symptoms

	Amisulpride versus ziprasidone	Olanzapine versus amisulpride	Olanzapine versus quetiapine	Risperidone versus quetiapine
k (total N)	1 (123)	1 (140)	2 (386)	1 (44)
Study ID	OLIE2006	Lecrubier1999 (LECRUBIER2006)	KINON2006B SIROTA2006	RIEDEL2005
Diagnostic criteria	DSM-III-R	DSM-IV	DSM-IV	DSM-IV or ICD-10
Selected inclusion criteria	Negative symptoms (baseline scores on the PANSS negative subscale had to exceed the PANSS positive subscale by ≥6)	Primarily negative symptoms according to PANSS and SANS	Prominent negative symptoms according to PANSS and GAF/SANS.	Predominantly primary negative symptoms according to PANSS.
Setting	Outpatient	Inpatient/outpatient	Inpatient/outpatient	Inpatient/outpatient
Duration of treatment	Medium term: 12 weeks	Medium term: 26 weeks	Medium term: 12–26 weeks	Medium term: 12 weeks
Medication dose (mg/day)	Amisulpride: 144.7 mg/day (mean); 100–200 mg/day (range) Ziprasidone: 118 mg/day (mean); 80–160 mg/day (range)	Olanzapine: 5 or 20 mg/day (fixed) Amisulpride: 150 mg/day (fixed)	Olanzapine: 5–20 mg/day (range) Quetiapine: 200–800 mg/day (range)	Risperidone: 4.9 mg/day (mean); 2–6 mg/day (range) Quetiapine: 589.7 mg/day (mean); 50–600 mg/day (range)

Table 29: Summary of study characteristics for trials of clozapine augmentation

	Clozapine + aripiprazole versus clozapine + placebo	Clozapine + risperidone versus clozapine + placebo	Clozapine + sulpiride versus clozapine + placebo
k (total N)	1 (62)	4 (162)	1 (28)
Study ID	CHANG2008	FREUDENREICH2007 HONER2006 JOSIASSEN2005 YAGCIOGLU2005	SHILOH1997
Diagnostic criteria	DSM-IV	DSM-IV	DSM-IV
Inclusion criteria	1) Failure to respond to at least two previous antipsychotic drugs; 2) Clozapine treatment for more than 1 year with at least 8 weeks at a stable daily dose of 400mg or more, unless compromised by adverse effects; 3) No change in clozapine daily dose or other concomitant medication for more than 3 months, indicating a plateau of clinical response to clozapine; 4) Either a baseline BPRS total score of at least 35 or more than two SANS global rating item scores of at least 3	FREUDENREICH2007: 1) Failure to respond to at least two previous antipsychotics; 2) currently treated with clozapine monotherapy for at least 6 months, at a stable dose for at least 8 weeks and with clozapine plasma levels of at least 200ng/mL, unless the clozapine dose necessary to achieve that level was not tolerated HONER2006: 1) DSM diagnosis of schizophrenia; 2) 80 or more on PANSS and 4 or more on CGI; 3) 40 or less on Social and Occupational Functioning Assessment Scale; 4) Failure to respond (≥20% reduction in BPRS) after one placebo augmentation for 1 week	1) DSM diagnosis of schizophrenia; 2) Clozapine prescribed after failure to respond to three typical antipsychotics at adequate doses for at least 6 weeks each; 3) 25 or more on BPRS; 4) BPRS score stable for 5 weeks; 5) Inability to function as an outpatient

		JOSIASSEN2005: 1) DSM diagnosis of schizophrenia; 2) Continued significant psychotic symptoms; 3) Failure to respond to at least two previous antipsychotic drugs; 4) 45 or more on BPRS or 4 or more (moderately ill) on at least two BPRS positive symptoms subscale items (hallucinatory behaviour, conceptual disorganisation, unusual thought content, suspiciousness) — YAGCIOGLU2005: 1) DSM diagnosis of schizophrenia; 2) Failure to respond to at least two previous antipsychotic drugs; 3) 72 or more on PANSS or 4 or more on CGI (moderate level of psychopathology); 4) Prescribed clozapine because of failure to respond to other antipsychotic treatments	
Setting	Inpatient/outpatient	Inpatient/outpatient	Inpatient
Baseline severity	BPRS total 47.6 (clozapine + aripiprazole)/48.5 (clozapine + placebo)	Range of means: PANSS total 72.4–102.5 (clozapine + risperidone)/73.5–97.8 (clozapine + placebo)	BPRS total 41.9 (clozapine + sulpiride)/43.5 (clozapine + placebo)
Duration of treatment	8 weeks	FREUDENREICH2007: 6 weeks HONER2006: 8 weeks JOSIASSEN2005: 12 weeks YAGCIOGLU2005: 6 weeks	10 weeks

6.5.11　Clinical evidence summary

In 18 RCTs including 2,554 participants whose illness had not responded adequately to treatment, clozapine had the most consistent evidence for efficacy over the FGAs included in the trials. Further evidence is required to establish equivalence between clozapine and any other SGA, and to establish whether there are differences between any of the other antipsychotic drugs. Side effects were consistent with those reported in the SPC for each drug.

In 10 RCTs including 1,200 participants with persistent negative symptoms, there was no evidence of clinically significant differences in efficacy between any of the antipsychotic drugs examined. Careful clinical assessment to determine whether such persistent features are primary or secondary is warranted, and may identify relevant treatment targets, such as drug-induced parkinsonism, depressive features or certain positive symptoms.

In six RCTs including 252 participants with schizophrenia whose illness had not responded adequately to clozapine treatment, there was some evidence that clozapine augmentation with a second antipsychotic might improve both total and negative symptoms if administered for an adequate duration.

6.6　TREATMENT WITH DEPOT/LONG-ACTING INJECTABLE ANTIPSYCHOTIC MEDICATION

6.6.1　Introduction

The introduction of long-acting injectable formulations ('depot') of antipsychotic medication in the 1960s was heralded as a major advance in the treatment of established schizophrenia outside hospital. At the time it was hoped that depot preparations would lead to improved outcomes from antipsychotic pharmacotherapy. Consistent drug delivery and avoidance of the bioavailability problems that occur with oral preparations (such as gut wall and hepatic first-pass metabolism) were felt to be important factors. Other benefits include eliminating the risk of deliberate or inadvertent overdose. In the subsequent decades, the main practical clinical advantage to emerge has been the avoidance of covert non-adherence (both intentional and unintentional)[11] to antipsychotic drug treatment, where there is close nursing supervision and documentation of clinic attendance (Barnes & Curson, 1994; Patel & David, 2005). Service users who are receiving depot treatment and who decline their injection or fail to receive it (through forgetfulness or any other reason) can be immediately identified, allowing appropriate intervention, bearing in mind that poor adherence to the medication can be both a cause and consequence of worsening illness. In practice, the use of depot drugs does not guarantee good treatment adherence, with a significant number who are prescribed maintenance treatment with depot

---

[11] Further information about medicines concordance and adherence to treatment can be found in the NICE guideline on this topic (see http://www.nice.org.uk).

preparations after discharge from hospital failing to become established on the injections (Crammer & Eccleston, 1989; Young *et al.*, 1989, 1996). But for those who continue with long-acting injections, there may be some adherence advantage over oral antipsychotics, indicated by a longer time to medication discontinuation (Zhu *et al.*, 2008). There is also some evidence to suggest a better global outcome with depot as compared with oral antipsychotics (Adams *et al.*, 2001) with a reduced risk of rehospitalisation (Schooler, 2003, Tiihonen *et al.*, 2006). In 2002, a long-acting formulation of an SGA, risperidone, became available, offering the same advantages of convenience and the avoidance of covert non-adherence (Hosalli & Davis, 2003).

Information on the use of long-acting antipsychotic injections has been limited (Adams *et al.*, 2001), but relevant surveys and audits of antipsychotic prescription in the UK suggest that between a quarter and a third of psychiatric patients prescribed an antipsychotic may be receiving a long-acting injection, depending on the clinical setting (Barnes *et al.*, 2009; Foster *et al.*, 1996; Paton *et al.*, 2003).

6.6.2   Use of long-acting antipsychotic injections

Long-acting injectable antipsychotic formulations generally consist of an ester of the drug in an oily solution. Another way of formulating such a preparation is to use microspheres of the drug suspended in aqueous solution. These drugs are administered by deep intramuscular injection and are then slowly released from the injection site, giving relatively stable plasma drug levels over long periods, allowing the injections to be given every few weeks. However, this also represents a potential disadvantage because there is a lack of flexibility of administration, with adjustment to the optimal dosage being a protracted and uncertain process. The controlled studies of low-dose maintenance treatment with depot preparations suggest that any increased risk of relapse consequent upon a dose reduction may take months or years to manifest. Another disadvantage is that, for some people, receiving the depot injection is an ignominious and passive experience. Further, there have been reports of pain, oedema, pruritus and sometimes a palpable mass at the injection site. In some people, these concerns may lead service users to take active steps to avoid these injections and even disengage with services altogether rather than receive medication via this route. Nevertheless, a substantial proportion of people receiving regular, long-acting antipsychotic injections prefer them to oral therapy, largely because they consider them to be more convenient (Patel & David, 2005; Walburn *et al.*, 2001).

6.6.3   Clinical review protocol

The review protocol, including the primary clinical questions, information about the databases searched and the eligibility criteria, can be found in Table 30. A new systematic search for relevant RCTs, published since the previous guideline, was conducted for the guideline update (further information about the search strategy can be found in Appendix 8).

Table 30: Clinical review protocol for the review of depot/long-acting injectable antipsychotics

Primary clinical questions	For people with schizophrenia that is in remission, is any depot or long-acting antipsychotic medication associated with improved relapse prevention over time? For people with schizophrenia whose illness has not responded adequately to treatment and who have had long-term antipsychotic drug treatment, is there any evidence that patients have a preference for either depot/long-acting or oral preparations?
Electronic databases	CENTRAL, CINAHL, EMBASE, MEDLINE, PsycINFO
Date searched	1 January 2002 to 30 July 2008
Study design	Double-blind RCT (≥10 participants per arm and ≥4 weeks' duration)
Patient population	Adults (18+) with schizophrenia
Excluded populations	Very late onset schizophrenia (onset after age 60). Other psychotic disorders, such as bipolar disorder, mania or depressive psychosis. People with coexisting learning difficulties, significant physical or sensory difficulties, or substance misuse.
Interventions	FGAs: Flupentixol decanoate Fluphenazine decanoate Haloperidol (as decanoate) Pipotiazine palmitate Zuclopenthixol decanoate SGAs: Risperidone (long-acting injection)
Comparator	Any relevant antipsychotic drug or placebo
Critical outcomes	Mortality (suicide) Global state (CGI, relapse) Mental state (total symptoms, negative symptoms, depression) Social functioning Leaving the study early for any reason Adverse events

Note: Studies (or outcomes from studies) were categorised as short term (12 weeks or fewer), medium term (12–51 weeks) and long term (52 weeks or more).

6.6.4 Studies considered for review

In the previous guideline, the review of depot antipsychotic medication was based on a meta-review of five Cochrane Reviews (David & Adams, 2001), which included 13 RCTs of flupentixol decanoate, 48 of fluphenazine decanoate, 11 of haloperidol decanoate, ten of pipothiazine palmitate and three of zuclopenthixol decanoate.

Since publication of the previous guideline, the review of fluphenazine decanoate (David *et al.*, 2004) was updated and now includes 70 trials. The review of pipothiazine palmitate (Dinesh *et al.*, 2004) was also updated and now includes 18 trials. In addition, one SGA (long-acting injectable risperidone) has been licensed for use as a depot. A Cochrane review of this medication for people with schizophrenia was published in 2003 (Hosalli & Davis, 2003). The update search identified no additional trials that met the eligibility criteria. Because of the volume of evidence for FGA depots, the GDG checked the updated Cochrane reviews were consistent with the previous guideline and then focused on the evidence for long-acting risperidone, which had not previously been reviewed. In total, two trials (N = 1,042) met inclusion criteria (one trial of long-acting risperidone versus placebo, and one trial of long-acting risperidone versus oral risperidone). Both trials were published in peer-reviewed journals between 2003 and 2005. Further information about the included studies can be found in Appendix 15b.

6.6.5 Long-acting risperidone injection versus placebo or oral risperidone

One RCT was included in the analysis comparing long-acting risperidone injection with placebo injection, and one RCT was included in the analysis comparing long-acting risperidone with oral risperidone plus placebo injection (see Table 31). Forest plots and/or data tables for each outcome can be found in Appendix 16c.

6.6.6 Clinical evidence summary

The update search did not identify any new evidence for the efficacy and safety of depot FGAs beyond that included in the updated Cochrane Reviews (utilised in the previous guideline). These reviews did not indicate robust new evidence that would warrant changing the existing recommendations for depot antipsychotic medication.

Since publication of the previous guideline, the first depot SGA (risperidone) was licensed for use in the UK. However, there is currently only limited evidence from two double-blind RCTs regarding the efficacy and safety of long-acting injectable risperidone compared with placebo or oral antipsychotic medication (risperidone). The placebo controlled trial suggests that 25–75 mg of long-acting risperidone may improve the chance of response and produce a clinically significant reduction in the symptoms of schizophrenia, but larger doses carry an increased risk of neurological side effects. There is no evidence to suggest that long-acting risperidone has either greater efficacy or greater risk of adverse effects when compared with oral

Table 31: Summary of study characteristics for RCTs of long-acting risperidone versus placebo or oral risperidone

	Intramuscular injection of long-acting risperidone versus placebo injection	Intramuscular injection of long-acting risperidone versus oral risperidone + placebo injection
k (total N)	1 (400)	1 (642)
Study ID	KANE2003	CHUE2005
Diagnostic criteria	Schizophrenia (DSM-IV)	Schizophrenia (DSM-IV)
Baseline severity	25 mg long-acting risperidone: PANSS total: mean 81.7 (SD 12.5), n = 99 50 mg long-acting risperidone: PANSS total: mean 82.3 (SD 13.9), n = 103 75 mg long-acting risperidone: PANSS total: mean 80.1 (SD 14.0), n = 100 Placebo: PANSS total: mean 82.0 (SD 14.4), n = 98	Long-acting risperidone: PANSS total: mean 68.4 (SD 1.0), n = 319 Oral risperidone: PANSS total: mean 69.3(SD 0.9), n = 321 All participants were required to be symptomatically stable during the last 4 weeks of the run-in period
Run-in	1-week oral risperidone run-in period	8 weeks open-label period during which participants were stabilised on oral risperidone
Setting	Inpatient/outpatient	Inpatient/outpatient
Duration of treatment	12 weeks	12 weeks
Medication dose (mg/day)	Fixed dose of 25, 50 or 75 mg every 2 weeks	Long-acting risperidone: 88 participants received 25 mg every 2 weeks, 126 received 50 mg and 105 received 75 mg Oral risperidone: 86 participants received 2 mg/day, 126 received 4 mg/day and 109 received 6 mg/day

risperidone. However, as suggested by the trial authors, the trial was only designed to investigate the short-term switching of participants from oral medication to long-acting risperidone; further studies are needed to understand the effect of continuous delivery of this medication.

6.7 SIDE EFFECTS OF ANTIPSYCHOTIC MEDICATION

6.7.1 Introduction

Given that for some antipsychotics there was a paucity of side-effect data, the GDG decided to pool data, where appropriate, from the studies included in the other meta-analyses reported in this chapter and from any other relevant clinical trial. The review focused on metabolic and neurological side effects as these were considered a priority by the GDG and were also highlighted as areas of concern by service users.

6.7.2 Studies considered for review

All RCTs included in the efficacy reviews (except studies of depot/long-acting antipsychotics) were included in the overall side effects meta-analysis. In addition, four trials (ATMACA2003; LIEBERMAN2003B; MCQUADE2004; MELTZER2003) did not meet the inclusion criteria for any of the efficacy reviews, but reported relevant side effect data and so were included here.

6.7.3 Second-generation antipsychotic drugs versus another antipsychotic drug (overall analysis of side effects)

As shown in Table 32, 14 separate RCTs were included in the analysis of amisulpride against haloperidol ($k = 6$), a non-haloperidol FGA ($k = 2$), or an SGA ($k = 6$). Seven separate trials were included in the analysis of aripiprazole against haloperidol ($k = 2$), a non-haloperidol FGA ($k = 1$), or an SGA ($k = 4$). Sixteen separate trials were included in the analysis of clozapine against haloperidol ($k = 4$), a non-haloperidol FGA ($k = 4$), or an SGA ($k = 9$). Forty-one separate trials were included in the analysis of olanzapine against haloperidol ($k = 18$), a non-haloperidol FGA ($k = 5$), or an SGA ($k = 19$). Three trials were included in the analysis of paliperidone against an SGA ($k = 3$). Thirteen separate trials were included in the analysis of quetiapine against haloperidol ($k = 5$), a non-haloperidol FGA ($k = 2$), or an SGA ($k = 7$). Forty separate trials were included in the analysis of risperidone against haloperidol ($k = 20$), a non-haloperidol FGA ($k = 4$), or an SGA ($k = 18$). Three separate trials were included in the analysis of sertindole against haloperidol ($k = 2$), or an SGA ($k = 1$). Seven separate trials were included in the analysis of zotepine against haloperidol ($k = 5$), a non-haloperidol FGA ($k = 1$), or an SGA ($k = 1$). Forest plots and/or data tables for each outcome can be found in Appendix 16c.

Table 32: Summary of studies included in the overall analysis of side effects

Treatment	Comparator		
	Versus haloperidol (FGA)	**Versus non-haloperidol FGA**	**Versus SGA**
Amisulpride	Carriere2000 [16 weeks] Delcker1990 [6 weeks] Moller1997 [6 weeks] Puech1998 [4 weeks] Speller1997 [52 weeks] Ziegler1989 [4 weeks]	Boyer1990 (fluphenazine) [6 weeks] Hillert1994 (flupentixol) [6 weeks]	Fleurot1997 (risperidone) [8 weeks] HWANG2003 (risperidone) [6 weeks] Lecrubier1999 (olanzapine) [26 weeks] Lecrubier2000 (risperidone) [26 weeks] MARTIN2002 (olanzapine) [24 weeks] WAGNER2005 (olanzapine) [8 weeks]
	k = 6	*k* = 2	*k* = 6
Aripiprazole	KANE2002 [4 weeks] KASPER2003 [52 weeks]	KANE2007B (perphenazine) [6 weeks]	CHAN2007B (risperidone) [4 weeks] MCQUADE2004 (olanzapine) [26 weeks]* POTKIN2003A (risperidone) [4 weeks] ZIMBROFF2007 (ziprasidone) [4 weeks]
	k = 2	*k* = 1	*k* = 4

Clozapine	Buchanan1998 [10 weeks] Rosenheck1997 [52 weeks] Tamminga1994 [52 weeks] VOLAVKA2002 [14 weeks] *k* = 4	Claghorn1987 (chlorpromazine) [4–8 weeks] Hong1997 (chlorpromazine) [12 weeks] Kane1988 (chlorpromazine) [6 weeks] LIEBERMAN2003B [52 weeks]* *k* = 4	Anand1998 (risperidone) [12 weeks] ATMACA2003 (olanzapine/quetiapine/risperidone) [6 weeks]* Beuzen1998 (olanzapine) [18 weeks] Bitter1999 (olanzapine) [18 weeks] Bondolfi1998 (risperidone) [8 weeks] Breier1999 (risperidone) [18 weeks] Chowdhury1999 (risperidone) [16 weeks] MELTZER2003A (olanzapine) [104 weeks]* VOLAVKA2002 (olanzapine/risperidone) [14 weeks] *k* = 9
Olanzapine	Altamura1999 [14 weeks] Beasley1996a [6 weeks] Beasley1997	Conley1998a (chlorpromazine) [8 weeks] HGBL1997 (flupentixol) [4 weeks] Jakovljevic1999 (fluphenazine)	ATMACA2003 (quetiapine/risperidone) [6 weeks]* Conley 2001 (risperidone) [8 weeks]

Continued

147

Table 32: *(Continued)*

Treatment	Comparator		
	Versus haloperidol (FGA)	**Versus non-haloperidol FGA**	**Versus SGA**
	[6 weeks] Breier2000 [6 weeks] BUCHANAN2005 [16 weeks] HGCJ1999 (HK) [14 weeks] HGCU1998 (Taiwan) [14 weeks] Jones1998 [54 weeks] KONGSAKON2006 [24 weeks] LIEBERMAN2003A [24 weeks] LINDENMAYER2007 [12 weeks] ROSENHECK2003 [52 weeks] STUDY-S029 [52 weeks] Tollefson1997	[6 weeks] Loza1999 (chlorpromazine) [6 weeks] Naukkarinen1999/HGBJ (perphenazine) [26 weeks]	DAVIDSON2007 (paliperidone) [6 weeks] Gureje1998 (risperidone) [30 weeks] Jones1998 (risperidone) [54 weeks] KANE2007A (paliperidone) [6 weeks] KINON2006B (quetiapine) [26 weeks] Lecrubier1999 (amisulpride) [26 weeks] MARDER2007 (paliperidone) [6 weeks] MARTIN2002 (amisulpride) [24 weeks] MCEVOY2007A (quetiapine/ risperidone) [52 weeks] MCQUADE2004 (aripiprazole) [26 weeks]* RIEDEL2007B (quetiapine)

	[6 weeks] Tran1998a [52 weeks] Tran1998b [52 weeks] Tran1998c [22–84 weeks] VOLAVKA2002 [14 weeks] *k = 18*	[8 weeks] StudyS036 (risperidone) [6 weeks] SIROTA2006 (quetiapine) [26 weeks] Tran1997 (risperidone) [28 weeks] VANNIMWEGEN2008 (risperidone) [6 weeks] VOLAVKA2002 (risperidone) [14 weeks] WAGNER2005 (amisulpride) [8 weeks] *k = 19*
Paliperidone	- *k = 5*	DAVIDSON2007 (paliperidone) [6 weeks] KANE2007A (paliperidone) [6 weeks] MARDER2007 (paliperidone) [6 weeks] *k = 3*

Continued

Table 32: (*Continued*)

Treatment	Comparator		
	Versus haloperidol (FGA)	**Versus non-haloperidol FGA**	**Versus SGA**
Quetiapine	Arvanitis1997 [6 weeks] Emsley1999 [8 weeks] Fleischhacker1996 [6 weeks] Murasaki1999 [8 weeks] Purdon2000 [26 weeks]	CONLEY2005 (fluphenazine) [12 weeks] Link1994 (chlorpromazine) [6 weeks]	ATMACA2003 (clozapine/ olanzapine/ risperidone) [6 weeks]* CONLEY2005 (risperidone) [12 weeks] KINON2006B (olanzapine) [26 weeks] RIEDEL2005 (risperidone) [12 weeks] RIEDEL2007B (olanzapine) [8 weeks] SIROTA2006 (olanzapine) [26 weeks] ZHONG2006 (risperidone) [8 weeks]
	k = 5	*k* = 2	*k* = 7
Risperidone	Blin1996 [4 weeks] Ceskova1993 [8 weeks] Chouinard1993 [8 weeks]	CONLEY2005 (fluphenazine) [12 weeks] Hoyberg1993 (perphenazine) [8 weeks] Huttunen1995 (zuclopenthixol) [8 weeks]	ATMACA2003 (olanzapine/ quetiapine) [6 weeks]* AZORIN2006 (sertindole) [12 weeks] CHAN2007A (aripiprazole)

Continued

Claus1991 [12 weeks] Csernansky1999/ 2000 [52 weeks] Emsley1995 [6 weeks] Heck2000 [6 weeks] Janicak1999 [6 weeks] Jones1998 [54 weeks] Kern1998 [8 weeks] LEE2007 [24 weeks] Marder1994 [8 weeks] Mesotten1991 [8 weeks] Min1993 [8 weeks] MOLLER2008 [8 weeks] Peuskens1995 [8 weeks]	RUHRMANN2007 (flupentixol) [25 weeks]	[4 weeks] Conley2001 (olanzapine) [8 weeks] CONLEY2005 (quetiapine) [12 weeks] Fleurot1997 (amisulpride) [8 weeks] Gureje1998 (olanzapine) [30 weeks] HWANG2003 (amisulpride) [6 weeks] Jones1998 (olanzapine) [54 weeks] Klieser1996 (zotepine) [4 weeks] Lecrubier2000 (amisulpride) [26 weeks] MCEVOY2007A (olanzapine/ quetiapine) [52 weeks] POTKIN2003A (aripiprazole) [4 weeks] RIEDEL2005 (quetiapine) [12 weeks] StudyS036 (olanzapine) [6 weeks]

Table 32: (*Continued*)

Treatment	Comparator		
	Versus haloperidol (FGA)	**Versus non-haloperidol FGA**	**Versus SGA**
	SCHOOLER2005 [104 weeks] SEE1999 [5 weeks] ZHANG2001 [12 weeks] VOLAVKA2002 [14 weeks]		Tran1997 (olanzapine) [28 weeks] VANNIMWEGEN2008 (olanzapine) [6 weeks] VOLAVKA2002 (clozapine/ olanzapine) [14 weeks] ZHONG2006 (quetiapine) [8 weeks]
	k = 20	*k = 4*	*k = 19*
Sertindole	Hale 2000 [8 weeks] Daniel 1998 [52 weeks]*	-	AZORIN2006 (risperidone) [12 weeks]
	k = 2		*k = 1*

Zotepine	Barnas1987 [7 weeks] Fleischhacker1989 [6 weeks] Klieser1996 [4 weeks] KnollCTR (StudyZT4002) [26 weeks] Petit1996 [8 weeks]	Cooper1999a (chlorpromazine) [8 weeks]	Klieser1996 (risperidone) [4 weeks]
	$k = 5$	$k = 1$	$k = 1$

Note: *Study did not meet the inclusion criteria for any other review reported in this chapter.

153

6.7.4 Clinical evidence summary

Pooling data from 138 evaluations of one antipsychotic versus another antipsychotic did not reveal metabolic and neurological side effects that were inconsistent with those reported in the SPC for each drug. Because most trials were of relatively short duration and not designed to prospectively examine side effects, these trials provide little insight into the longer-term adverse effects of treatment or whether there are clinically significant differences between antipsychotic drugs.

6.8 EFFECTIVENESS OF ANTIPSYCHOTIC MEDICATION

6.8.1 Introduction

The RCT is widely recognised as the 'gold standard' for evaluating treatment efficacy, but some methodological issues may compromise the generalisability of the findings of research to the ordinary treatment setting. Nevertheless, it is still recognised that the RCT is an indispensable first step in the evaluation of interventions in mental health and provides the most valid method for determining the impact of two contrasting treatment conditions (treatment efficacy), while controlling for a wide range of participant factors including the effects of spontaneous remission.

Once an approach has been demonstrated as efficacious under the stringent conditions of an RCT, a next step is to examine its effectiveness in ordinary treatment conditions, including large-scale effectiveness (pragmatic) trials (very few of which were available when the previous guideline was developed).

In addition, the use of RCTs and other studies in the evaluation of interventions in the treatment of schizophrenia is limited in many cases by the absence of important outcome measures. For example, few trials report evidence on quality of life or satisfaction with services, despite the fact that service users and carers view these measures as very important. Effectiveness studies address this issue by focusing on patient-important outcomes.

6.8.2 Effectiveness (pragmatic) trials

Given the large scope of the guideline update, the GDG decided to focus on effectiveness trials that included a comparison between an SGA and an FGA. To ensure that the evidence was from high-quality research and reduce the risk of bias, studies were included only if they used a randomised design with an intention-to-treat analysis and at least independent rater-blinding (that is, the clinicians doing the assessment of outcome were independent and blind to treatment allocation). All studies identified during the searches for other sections of this chapter were considered for inclusion.

Two studies published since the previous guideline met the inclusion criteria for this review. These were the CATIE study (Lieberman *et al.*, 2005; Stroup *et al.*, 2003), funded by the National Institute of Mental Health, and the Cost Utility of the Latest Antipsychotic Drugs in Schizophrenia Study (CUtLASS 1) (Jones *et al.*, 2006;

Lewis *et al.*, 2006a), funded by the NHS Research and Development Health Technology Assessment Programme.

In the initial phase of CATIE (phase 1), which was conducted at 57 clinical sites in the US, 1,493 participants with chronic schizophrenia were randomised (double-blind) to one of four SGAs or an FGA (perphenazine) (see Table 33). Participants with current

Table 33: Summary of study characteristics for the initial phases of CATIE and CUtLASS

	CATIE (Phase 1)	**CUtLASS (Band 1)**
Total N	1,493[a]	227
Diagnostic criteria	DSM-IV	DSM-IV
Intervention	Number randomised (number that did not take drug): Olanzapine: 336 (6) Quetiapine: 337 (8) Risperidone: 341 (8) Perphenazine: 261 (4)	Number randomised (most common at 52 weeks): FGA: 118 (26% were taking sulpiride) SGA: 109 (34% were taking olanzapine)
Baseline severity – mean PANSS (SD)	Olanzapine: 76.1 (18.2) Quetiapine: 75.7 (16.9) Risperidone: 76.4 (16.6) Perphenazine: 74.3 (18.1)	FGA: 72.9 (17.2) SGA: 71.3 (16.5)
Selected inclusion criteria	Diagnosis of schizophrenia, no history of serious adverse reactions to study medications, not experiencing their first episode, not treatment-resistant.	Diagnosis of schizophrenia (or schizoaffective disorder or delusional disorder), requiring change of current FGA or SGA treatment because of inadequate clinical response or intolerance, at least 1 month since the first onset of positive psychotic symptoms.
Setting	Inpatient/outpatient	Inpatient/outpatient
Duration of treatment	Up to 18 months	Up to 12 months
Medication dose (mg/day)	Mean modal dose: Olanzapine: 20.1 (n = 312) Quetiapine: 534.4 (n = 309) Risperidone: 3.9 (n = 305) Perphenazine: 20.8 (n = 245)	Varied depending on drug taken

Note: In the CATIE trial, after ~40% of participants were enrolled, ziprasidone was added as treatment option and 185 participants were randomised to this arm. However, this drug is not licensed in the UK and is therefore not included in this review.

[a] Thirty-three participants from one site were excluded from the analysis because of concerns regarding the integrity of the data.

tardive dyskinesia could enrol, but were not able to be randomised to perphenazine. For the purposes of the guideline update, the GDG focused on the primary outcome (discontinuation of treatment for any reason), tolerability, and both metabolic and neurological side effects. An evidence summary table for these outcomes can be found in Appendix 16c (the section on effectiveness of antipsychotic drugs).

In the initial phase of CUtLASS (Band 1), 227 participants with schizophrenia (or a related disorder) were randomised to an FGA or SGA (the choice of individual drug was made by the psychiatrist responsible for the care of the patient). The study was conducted in 14 NHS trusts in England and was specifically designed to test effectiveness in routine NHS practice. For the purposes of the guideline update, the GDG focused on the primary outcome (the Quality of Life Scale; Heinrichs *et al.*, 1984), tolerability, and neurological side effects. An evidence summary table for these outcomes can be found in Appendix 16c (the section on effectiveness of antipsychotic drugs).

Further analysis of cost effectiveness, including Band 2 of the CUtLASS trial can be found in Section 6.9.

6.8.3 Clinical evidence summary

Two trials involving 1,720 participants failed to establish clinically significant differences in effectiveness between the oral (non-clozapine) antipsychotic drugs examined. Although both trials have limitations (for further information see Carpenter & Buchanan, 2008; Kasper & Winkler, 2006; Möller, 2008; Lieberman, 2006), it is clear that more effective medication is needed. Furthermore, neither study included participants experiencing their first episode of schizophrenia or examined depot/long-acting antipsychotic medication.

With regard to adverse effects of treatment, the diverse side effect profiles seen in the efficacy trials reported elsewhere in this chapter were supported by CATIE and CUtLASS and primarily confirmed differential metabolic effects. However, there were no consistent clinically significant differences between antipsychotics in terms of treatment-emergent EPS. It should be noted that the various FGAs tested (such as perphenazine and sulpiride) were generally not high-potency antipsychotics and were prescribed in standard doses. Further analyses of baseline data from CATIE also confirm other reports that people with schizophrenia are undertreated for metabolic disorders (Nasrallah *et al.*, 2006).

6.9 HEALTH ECONOMICS

6.9.1 Systematic literature review

The systematic search of the economic literature, undertaken for the guideline update, identified 33 eligible studies on pharmacological treatments for people with schizophrenia. Of these, one study assessed oral antipsychotic medications for initial treatment of schizophrenia (Davies & Lewis, 2000); 15 studies examined oral drug treatments for acute psychotic episodes (Alexeyeva *et al.*, 2001; Almond & O'Donnell, 2000; Bagnall *et al.*, 2003; Beard *et al.*, 2006; Bounthavong & Okamoto, 2007; Cummins *et al.*, 1998; Edgell *et al.*, 2000; Geitona *et al.*, 2008; Hamilton *et al.*, 1999; Jerrell, 2002; Lecomte *et al.*, 2000; Nicholls *et al.*, 2003; Palmer *et al.*, 1998, 2002; Rosenheck *et al.*, 2003); eight studies assessed oral antipsychotic medications aimed at promoting recovery (Davies *et al.*, 1998; Ganguly *et al.*, 2003; Knapp *et al.*, 2008; Launois *et al.*, 1998; Oh *et al.*, 2001; Rosenheck *et al.*, 2006; Tunis *et al.*, 2006; Vera-Llonch *et al.*, 2004); four studies examined pharmacological treatments aiming at promoting recovery in people with schizophrenia whose illness has not responded adequately to treatment (Rosenheck *et al.*, 1997; Tilden *et al.*, 2002; Lewis *et al.*, 2006a, 2006b; Davies *et al.*, 2008); and six studies evaluated depot antipsychotic treatments (Chue *et al.*, 2005; De Graeve *et al.*, 2005; Edwards *et al.*, 2005; Heeg *et al.*, 2008; Laux *et al.*, 2005; Oh *et al.*, 2001). Details on the methods used for the systematic review of the economic literature in the guideline update are described in Chapter 3; references to included and excluded studies and evidence tables for all economic evaluations included in the systematic literature review are provided in Appendix 14.

Initial treatment with antipsychotic medication
One study that assessed oral antipsychotics for the treatment of people with a first episode of schizophrenia was included in the systematic economic literature review (Davies & Lewis, 2000). The study, which was conducted in the UK, was a cost-utility analysis based on a decision-analytic model in the form of a decision tree. The antipsychotic treatments assessed were olanzapine, risperidone, chlorpromazine, haloperidol and clozapine. All drugs, with the exception of clozapine, were assessed as first, second, third or fourth lines of treatment, whereas clozapine was assessed as a third or fourth line of treatment only. According to the model structure, people switched to the next line of treatment when an antipsychotic was not acceptable to them; treatment unacceptability was defined as treatment intolerance (development of non-treatable or unacceptable side effects), inadequate response or non-compliance. People who found treatment acceptable were transferred to maintenance therapy. If they experienced a relapse during acceptable treatment over the time frame of the analysis, they were treated with the same antipsychotic. Acceptable side effects were treated without change in antipsychotic therapy. The adverse events considered in the analysis were EPS (except tardive dyskinesia, which was considered separately), tardive dyskinesia, neuroleptic malignant syndrome, hepatic dysfunction and agranulocytosis. Clinical efficacy data were derived from a systematic literature review and meta-analysis. The perspective of the analysis was that of health and social care services including expenses of people with schizophrenia. Resource use was based on published literature, other national sources and further assumptions. Prices were taken from national sources. The time horizon of the analysis was 3 years.

Results were reported separately for different scenarios regarding sequence of antipsychotic treatments. Olanzapine and haloperidol were dominated by chlorpromazine when used as any line of treatment. Risperidone was more effective than chlorpromazine, but always at an additional cost, which reached £34,241 per QALY when first-line treatment was assessed. Clozapine dominated olanzapine and

157

risperidone when used as third- or fourth-line treatment. It was shown to yield the highest number of QALYs out of all antipsychotics included in the analysis. Its incremental cost-effectiveness ratio (ICER) versus chlorpromazine was £35,689 and £47,980 per QALY, when they were compared as third- and fourth-line treatments, respectively.

The results of the analysis were statistically significant and indicated that olanzapine and haloperidol were not cost-effective options compared with the other antipsychotic drugs assessed for the treatment of people with a first episode of schizophrenia. The authors concluded that clozapine (as third- or fourth-line treatment) and risperidone might be more effective than chlorpromazine, but at a higher cost. However, they recognised that because multiple comparisons of costs and QALYs had been made, some statistically important differences might have occurred by chance rather than reflected real differences. Moreover, they recognised the limited availability of clinical data used in the model.

An additional limitation of the analysis was that efficacy data for each antipsychotic medication were apparently derived from 'naïve' addition of data across relevant treatment arms of all RCTs included in the systematic literature review. This method treats the data as if they came from a single trial and practically breaks the randomisation: data from treatment arms not directly relevant to the analysis are not taken into account and between-trial variance is completely ignored (Glenny *et al.*, 2005). Glenny and colleagues argue that such a method of combining trial data is liable to bias, highly unpredictable and also produces over-precise answers. They conclude that results of such analysis are completely untrustworthy and, therefore, naïve comparisons should never be made.

Furthermore, utility data used in the base-case analysis by Davis and Lewis (2000) were based on published utility values of seven people with schizophrenia in Canada (Glennie, 1997), which appeared to be favouring FGAs and clozapine. Overall, the conclusions of this analysis should be interpreted with caution.

Oral antipsychotics in the treatment of the acute episode
The systematic review of the economic literature considered 15 studies evaluating oral antipsychotic medications for the management of acute psychotic episodes (Alexeyeva *et al.*, 2001; Almond & O'Donnell, 2000; Bagnall *et al.*, 2003; Beard *et al.*, 2006; Bounthavong & Okamoto, 2007; Cummins *et al.*, 1998; Edgell *et al.*, 2000; Geitona *et al.*, 2008; Hamilton *et al.*, 1999; Jerrell, 2002; Lecomte *et al.*, 2000; Nicholls *et al.*, 2003; Palmer *et al.*, 1998, 2002; Rosenheck *et al.*, 2003). Of these, four were conducted in the UK (Almond & O'Donnell, 2000; Bagnall *et al.*, 2003; Cummins *et al.*, 1998; Nicholls *et al.*, 2003) and are described in more detail. Of the remaining 11 studies, seven were conducted in the US (Alexeyeva *et al.*, 2001; Bounthavong & Okamoto, 2007; Edgell *et al.*, 2000; Hamilton *et al.*, 1999; Jerrell, 2002; Palmer *et al.*, 1998; Rosenheck *et al.*, 2003), one in Germany (Beard *et al.*, 2006), one in Belgium (Lecomte *et al.*, 2000), one in Mexico (Palmer *et al.*, 2002) and one in Greece (Geitona *et al.*, 2008).

Bagnall and colleagues (2003), using the same economic model structure as Davies and Lewis (2000), evaluated the cost effectiveness of SGAs for the treatment of acute episodes in people with schizophrenia in the UK. Ten antipsychotic medications were included in a cost-utility analysis: olanzapine, risperidone, quetiapine, amisulpride, zotepine, sertindole, ziprasidone, clozapine, chlorpromazine and haloperidol. Clinical data were based on a systematic literature review and meta-analysis, and other published literature. The study adopted the perspective of health and social care services. Resource use was based on published literature and further assumptions. National unit costs were used. Outcomes were expressed in QALYs. Utility values in the base-case analysis were also taken from Glennie (1997). The time horizon of the analysis was 1 year.

Results were reported separately for first, second, third and fourth lines of treatment. The authors performed comparisons between each SGA and the other medications. Ziprasidone and amisulpride were associated with the highest costs and QALYs. According to the authors, amisulpride was the most cost-effective SGA drug if ziprasidone remained unlicensed. Amisulpride and ziprasidone were the most effective and costliest drugs, followed by risperidone, which was both the third most effective and costliest drug of those examined. Olanzapine was the least costly and least effective antipsychotic. The authors suggested that sertindole, zotepine and quetiapine were not superior to other SGAs in terms of cost effectiveness. However, the cost and the effectiveness results were characterised by high uncertainty. In addition, clinical data for haloperidol and chlorpromazine were taken from the control arms of SGA trials because no systematic review of the literature was undertaken for FGAs; this methodology may have introduced bias to the analysis. A further limitation of the study was that analysis of efficacy data utilised the 'naïve' method for data pooling, as described earlier, and therefore the analysis is subject to bias. For all of these reasons, no clear conclusions on the relative cost effectiveness of SGAs can be drawn from this analysis, and this was also the authors' conclusion.

Cummins and colleagues (1998) used the results of an RCT comparing olanzapine with haloperidol for acute treatment of people with schizophrenia (TOLLEFSON1997) to inform a decision tree that was constructed to assess the relative cost effectiveness of the two antipsychotic drugs in the UK. According to the model structure, people in an acute episode were started on one of the two evaluated drugs and followed up for 1 year. Those who did not respond to treatment, withdrew or relapsed following any response had their medication switched to haloperidol (if they had been started on olanzapine) or fluphenazine (if they had been started on haloperidol). The perspective of the analysis was that of the NHS. Resource use was based on published literature and further assumptions. Prices were taken from national sources. Outcomes were expressed in QALYs. Utility values were estimated using the index of health-related quality of life) (IHRQoL), a generic measure designed to capture social, psychological and physical functioning.

Olanzapine was found to dominate haloperidol because it produced more QALYs (0.833 versus 0.806) and resulted in lower costs (£26,200 versus £31,627). The results were robust in a number of sensitivity analyses carried out. Limitations of the analysis, as stated by the authors, were the weak evidence on longer-term effects of antipsychotics, which led to a number of assumptions in the model, and the simplicity of the model structure, which did not capture all events related to treatment of acute episodes with antipsychotics.

Almond and O'Donnell (2000) conducted an economic analysis to compare the costs and benefits associated with olanzapine, risperidone, and haloperidol in the treatment of acute psychotic episodes in the UK. Analysis was based on decision-analytic modelling. The economic model considered cycles of acute episodes, remission and relapse over a period of 5 years. Efficacy data were taken from two clinical trials (TOLLEFSON1997 and TRAN1997). The outcomes of the analysis were the percentage of people with a Brief Psychiatric Rating Scale (BPRS) score below 18 and the percentage of people without relapse over the time frame of the analysis. The study adopted the NHS perspective. Resource use estimates were based on published literature and further assumptions. UK national prices were used.

Olanzapine was reported to be less costly than both risperidone and haloperidol (costs of olanzapine, risperidone and haloperidol were £35,701, £36,590 and £36,653 respectively). In addition, olanzapine was found to be more effective (percentages of people with a BPRS score below 18 over 5 years for olanzapine, risperidone and haloperidol were 63.6%, 63.0%, and 52.2%, respectively; percentages of people without relapse over 5 years were 31.2%, 29.3% and 18.2%, respectively). These figures show that olanzapine and risperidone dominated haloperidol (olanzapine was more effective at a lower cost; risperidone was more effective at a similar cost). Olanzapine also dominated risperidone (it was slightly more effective at a lower cost). Cost results were sensitive to daily dosages, relapse rates and dropout rates. The authors reported as limitations of their analysis the assumptions needed to estimate resource utilisation and the omission of some categories of cost, such as the costs of monitoring drug therapy, owing to lack of relevant data.

Nicholls and colleagues (2003) performed a cost-minimisation analysis alongside an international, multicentre clinical trial that compared amisulpride with risperidone over a 6-month treatment period (LECRUBIER2000). The trial had demonstrated that amisulpride and risperidone had similar effectiveness, as measured using the Positive and Negative Syndrome Scale (PANSS), BPRS and Clinical Global Impression (CGI) scale scores. The economic analysis, which adopted the perspective of the NHS, utilised resource use estimates from the trial and UK unit costs.

Amisulpride was found to be overall less costly than risperidone by £2,145, but the result was not statistically significant (95% CI: −£5,379 to £1,089). The findings of the study are not directly applicable to the UK setting, as resource use was based on settings other than the UK, where clinical practice is likely to be different. For example, part-time hospitalisations were recorded in some settings; the authors stated that this type of care was not universally recognised in the NHS, and for this reason respective UK unit costs were not available and needed to be based on assumptions.

Of the further 11 studies included in the systematic review of the cost effectiveness of oral antipsychotics in the management of acute psychotic episodes, nine involved comparisons between olanzapine, risperidone and haloperidol. Relative cost effectiveness between olanzapine and risperidone cannot be established with certainty from the results of these studies: Beard and colleagues (2006) suggested that olanzapine was dominant over risperidone because it was shown to be more effective at a lower cost. The analysis, which was conducted from the perspective of the German healthcare system, was based on decision-analytic modelling. Other models of similar structure replicated this result in other countries: olanzapine dominated risperidone in the US (Palmer *et al.*, 1998) and in Mexico (Palmer *et al.*, 2002). On the other hand, the modelling studies by Bounthavong and Okamoto (2007) in the US and Lecomte and colleagues (2000) in Belgium indicated that risperidone might be marginally dominant over olanzapine because it was associated with better or similar outcomes at similar or slightly lower costs. Two economic analyses conducted alongside clinical trials in the US (Edgell *et al.*, 2000; Jerrell, 2002) were also unable to draw certain conclusions: in both trials, olanzapine appeared to be less costly than risperidone, but cost results were not statistically significant. In one of the trials, olanzapine was associated with longer maintenance of response and lower EPS rates (Edgell *et al.*, 2000) but the other trial (Jerrell, 2002) failed to demonstrate a superiority of olanzapine over risperidone in terms of clinical effectiveness.

With respect to the comparative cost effectiveness of olanzapine and haloperidol, there was less variety in the study results: two modelling studies (Bounthavong & Okamoto, 2007; Palmer *et al.*, 1998) and one economic analysis undertaken alongside a clinical trial (Hamilton *et al.*, 1999) demonstrated that olanzapine dominated haloperidol in the US because it was more effective at a lower cost. Another multicentre RCT conducted in the US (Rosenheck *et al.*, 2003) showed that olanzapine had similar effectiveness to haloperidol (measured by BPRS scores) and lower akathisia rates. It was more expensive than haloperidol, but cost results were not statistically significant. Finally, two modelling studies suggested that olanzapine was more effective than haloperidol at an additional cost approximating £3 per day with minimum symptoms and toxicity in Belgium (Lecomte *et al.*, 2000) and £11,350 per relapse avoided in Mexico (Palmer *et al.*, 2002). Overall, these results suggest that olanzapine may be more cost effective than haloperidol in the treatment of acute episodes.

Two of the comparisons of risperidone versus haloperidol showed that risperidone was the dominant option in the US (Bounthavong & Okamoto, 2007) and in Belgium (Lecomte *et al.*, 2000), while one economic model used to assessed the relative cost effectiveness of the two antipsychotics in two different countries found risperidone to be more effective than haloperidol at an additional cost that reached \$2,100/QALY in the US (Palmer *et al.*, 1998) and about £13,900 per relapse avoided in Mexico (Palmer *et al.*, 2002). These findings suggest that risperidone may be more cost effective than haloperidol.

Finally, of the remaining two studies included in the systematic economic literature review of acute treatment for people with schizophrenia, the study conducted by Alexeyeva and colleagues (2001) compared the cost effectiveness of olanzapine and ziprasidone in the US; the study, which was based on decision-analytic modelling, utilised published and unpublished clinical data and concluded that olanzapine dominated ziprasidone because it was more effective at a similar total cost. The other study (Geitona *et al.*, 2008) assessed the cost effectiveness of paliperidone relative to risperidone, olanzapine, quetiapine, aripiprazole and ziprasidone from the perspective of the Greek healthcare system. The study, which was also based on decision-analytic modelling, utilised efficacy data from selected placebo-controlled trials and other published sources. Resource utilisation estimates were based on expert opinion.

According to the authors' conclusions, paliperidone was the most cost-effective drug as it dominated all other treatment options assessed. This finding was reported to be robust in sensitivity analysis. However, dominance of paliperidone over olanzapine was only marginal (paliperidone resulted in 0.3 additional days free of symptoms per year and an annual extra saving of €4 compared with olanzapine).

It must be noted that the results of most modelling studies were sensitive to changes in response and dropout rates, drug acquisition costs, and hospitalisation rates for an acute episode. Most of these studies did not maintain randomisation effects because they used (and in some cases combined) efficacy data from arms of different trials for each antipsychotic drug evaluated, using a 'naïve' method of pooling. The impact of side effects on health related quality of life (HRQoL) was not explored in the majority of them.

Promoting recovery in people with schizophrenia that is in remission –
pharmacological relapse prevention
Eight studies that were included in the systematic economic literature review assessed oral antipsychotic medications for relapse prevention (Davies *et al.*, 1998; Ganguly *et al.*, 2003; Knapp *et al.*, 2008; Launois *et al.*, 1998; Oh *et al.*, 2001; Rosenheck *et al.*, 2006; Tunis *et al.*, 2006; Vera-Llonch *et al.*, 2004). None of the studies was undertaken in the UK.

The most relevant study to the UK context was that by Knapp and colleagues (2008); it evaluated the cost effectiveness of olanzapine versus a number of other antipsychotic medications (including risperidone, quetiapine, amisulpride and clozapine, as well as oral and depot FGAs) using clinical and resource use data from a multicentre prospective observational study conducted in outpatient settings in ten European countries. The analysis adopted the health service payer's perspective; costs were estimated by applying UK national unit cost data to recorded healthcare resource use. Outcomes were expressed in QALYs, estimated by recording and analysing participants' EQ-5D scores and linking them to respective UK population tariffs to determine utility values. The time horizon of the analysis was 12 months.

The study made separate comparisons of olanzapine with each of the other antipsychotic medications considered; no direct comparisons were made between the other antipsychotic medications. According to the performed comparisons, olanzapine dominated quetiapine and amisulpride; it was more effective than risperidone and clozapine at an additional cost reaching £5,156 and £775 per QALY, respectively. Compared with oral and depot FGAs, olanzapine was more effective and more costly, with an ICER of £15,696 and £23,331 per QALY respectively (2004 prices). However, FGAs were analysed together as a class, and no results from comparisons between olanzapine and specific FGAs were reported. Probabilistic sensitivity analysis conducted using bootstrap techniques revealed that the probability of olanzapine being more cost effective than quetiapine was 100% at a willingness-to-pay lower than £5,000/QALY; the probability of olanzapine being cost effective when compared with risperidone and amisulpride was 100% at a willingness-to-pay around £18,000/QALY; at a willingness-to-pay equalling £30,000 per QALY, the probability of olanzapine being more cost effective than clozapine, oral FGAs and depot FGAs was 81%, 98% and 79% respectively.

The results of the analysis indicated that olanzapine had a high probability of being cost effective relative to each of the other options assessed. However, no formal incremental analysis across all comparators was performed, as all comparisons involved olanzapine versus each of the other antipsychotics included in the analysis. The study conclusions may have limited applicability in the UK because reported healthcare resource use reflected average routine clinical practice in European countries and only unit costs were directly relevant to the UK health service.

The rest of the economic studies on pharmacological relapse prevention mainly included comparisons between olanzapine, risperidone and haloperidol. Two modelling studies, one in Australia (Davies *et al.*, 1998) and one in Canada (Oh *et al.*, 2001) concluded that risperidone was more cost effective than haloperidol because it was more effective at a lower cost. One US modelling study reported that risperidone was more effective and also more expensive than haloperidol (Ganguly *et al.*, 2003). The measure of outcome was the number of employable persons in each arm of the analysis; employability was determined by a PANSS score reduction of at least 20% from baseline and a WCST-Cat score of ≥3.5. The ICER of risperidone versus haloperidol was estimated at $19,609 per employable person.

An economic analysis undertaken alongside an open-label trial in the US (Tunis *et al.*, 2006) showed that olanzapine was associated with better outcomes and lower costs than risperidone in people with chronic schizophrenia, but results were statistically insignificant. Another study based on mainly unpublished data and employing Markov modelling techniques (Vera-Llonch *et al.*, 2004) came to different conclusions: according to this study, risperidone led to lower discontinuation rates, had overall lower side effect rates and was less costly than olanzapine. A modelling study carried out in France (Launois *et al.*, 1998) reported that sertindole dominated olanzapine and haloperidol; between olanzapine and haloperidol, the former was the cost-effective option. Overall, results of modelling studies were sensitive to changes in response rates, compliance rates and hospital discharge rates.

Finally, Rosenheck and colleagues (2006) performed an economic analysis alongside a large effectiveness trial in the US (CATIE, Lieberman *et al.*, 2005). The study compared olanzapine, quetiapine, risperidone, ziprasidone and perphenazine in people with chronic schizophrenia. It was demonstrated that perphenazine dominated all other antipsychotic medications, being significantly less costly than the other antipsychotics but with similar effectiveness expressed in QALYs (perphenazine was significantly more effective than risperidone at the 0.005 level in intention-to-treat analysis). Differences in total healthcare costs were mainly caused by differences in drug acquisition costs between perphenazine and the other antipsychotic drugs considered.

Promoting recovery in people with schizophrenia whose illness has not responded adequately to treatment (treatment resistance)
Four studies examining pharmacological treatments aiming at promoting recovery in people with schizophrenia whose illness has not responded adequately to treatment

were included in the systematic review (Davies *et al.*, 2008; Lewis *et al.*, 2006a, 2006b; Rosenheck *et al.*, 1997; Tilden *et al.*, 2002).

Tilden and colleagues (2002) constructed a Markov model to assess the cost effectiveness of quetiapine versus haloperidol in people with schizophrenia only partially responsive to FGAs, from the perspective of the UK NHS. The model was populated with clinical data taken from various sources: rates of response to treatment were taken from a multicentre RCT, which compared two antipsychotics in people with schizophrenia partially responsive to FGAs (EMSLEY1999). In this study, response to treatment was defined as an improvement in PANSS total score of at least 20% between the beginning and the end of the trial. Compliance rates in the economic model were estimated by linking non-compliance with the presence of EPS. Relapse rates were estimated by linking relapse with non-response to treatment. Other clinical data were derived from published literature. Resource use estimates were based on published studies and further assumptions; national unit costs were used. The measure of outcome for the economic analysis was the average number of relapses and the expected duration of time in response per person with schizophrenia, over the time horizon of the analysis, which was 5 years. Quetiapine was found to be more effective than haloperidol, at a slightly lower cost. Sensitivity analysis revealed that cost results were sensitive to differences in response rates between the two antipsychotic drugs, to the risk of relapse in non-responding and non-compliant individuals, and to the proportion of people requiring hospitalisation following relapse.

Rosenheck and colleagues (1997) assessed the cost effectiveness of clozapine relative to haloperidol in people with schizophrenia refractory to treatment and a history of high level use of inpatient services in the US, using a societal perspective. The analysis was based on clinical and resource use evidence from a multicentre RCT carried out in 15 Veterans Affairs medical centres. Clinical outcomes included PANSS scores, Quality of Life Scale (QLS) scores, side effect rates and compliance rates. Clozapine resulted in significantly lower mean PANSS scores, better compliance rates and lower rates of EPS compared with haloperidol. The total medical cost associated with clozapine was lower than the respective cost of haloperidol, but the difference in costs was not statistically significant.

In addition to the above two studies, Lewis and colleagues (2006a) described two effectiveness trials conducted in the UK that aimed at determining the clinical and cost effectiveness of SGAs versus FGAs and clozapine versus SGAs in people with schizophrenia responding inadequately to, or having unacceptable side effects from, their current medication (CUtLASS, Bands 1 and 2). The studies would normally have been excluded from the systematic review of the economic literature because they treated SGAs and FGAs as classes of antipsychotic medications; no data relating to specific antipsychotic drugs were reported. However, these studies were directly relevant to the UK context and their findings could lead to useful conclusions supporting formulation of guideline recommendations. Therefore, their methods and economic findings are discussed in this section.

Both trials were conducted in adult mental health settings in 14 NHS trusts in Greater Manchester, Nottingham and London. Participants in Band 1 (N = 227) were randomised to either an SGA (olanzapine, risperidone, quetiapine or amisulpride) or an FGA in oral or depot form. Participants in Band 2 (N = 136) were randomised to either clozapine or one of the four SGAs named above. The primary clinical outcome of the analyses was the QLS, with secondary outcomes PANSS scores, side effects from medication and participant satisfaction. The measure of outcome in economic analyses was the number of QALYs gained. QALYs were estimated by recording and analysing participants' EQ-5D scores and subsequently linking them to respective UK population tariffs to determine utility values. Costs were estimated from the perspective of health and social care services, and included medication, hospital inpatient and outpatient services, primary and community care services and social services. The time horizon of the analyses was 12 months.

According to the results for Band 1, FGAs dominated SGAs as they resulted in better outcomes at a lower total cost, but the results were not statistically significant. Bootstrap analysis of costs and QALYs, including imputed values for missing observations and censored cases, demonstrated that FGAs resulted in 0.08 more QALYs and net savings of £1,274 per person compared with SGAs (2001/02 prices). In univariate sensitivity analyses, FGAs dominated SGAs or had an ICER lower than £5,000 per QALY. Probabilistic sensitivity analysis (employing bootstrap techniques) showed that at a zero willingness-to-pay, FGAs had a 65% probability of being cost effective; this probability rose up to 91% at a willingness-to-pay equalling £50,000 per QALY. At a willingness-to-pay of £20,000 per QALY, the probability of FGAs being more cost effective than SGAs was roughly 80%. The results of the economic analysis indicate that FGAs are likely to be more cost effective than SGAs at the NICE cost-effectiveness threshold of £20,000–£30,000 per QALY (NICE, 2008b).

According to the results for Band 2, clozapine resulted in a statistically significant improvement in symptoms, but not in quality of life. Total costs associated with clozapine were also significantly higher than respective costs of SGAs. Updated bootstrap analysis of costs and QALYs showed that clozapine yielded 0.07 more QALYs per person relative to SGAs, at an additional cost of £4,904 per person (Davies *et al.*, 2007). The ICER of clozapine versus SGAs was estimated at £33,240 per QALY (2005/06 prices). This value ranged from approximately £23,000 to £70,000 per QALY in univariate sensitivity analyses. Probabilistic sensitivity analysis showed that at a zero willingness-to-pay, clozapine had a 35% probability of being cost effective compared with SGAs; this probability reached 50% at a willingness-to-pay ranging between £30,000 and £35,000 per QALY. Results indicate that clozapine is unlikely to be cost effective at the NICE cost-effectiveness threshold of £20,000 to £30,000 per QALY (NICE, 2008b).

Analysis of costs in both trials revealed that the vast majority of costs (approximately 90% of total costs) were incurred by psychiatric hospital attendances; only 2 to 4% of total costs constituted drug acquisition costs. Overall, there was great variance in the use of health services and associated costs among study participants. The significant difference in cost between clozapine and SGAs was caused by great difference in psychiatric hospital costs between the two arms, possibly reflecting the licensing requirement for inpatient admission for initiation of therapy with clozapine at the time of the study. Currently, such requirements are no longer in place; therefore, at present, the cost effectiveness of clozapine versus SGAs is likely to be higher than demonstrated in the analysis.

Treatment with depot/long-acting injectable antipsychotic medication
The systematic review of the economic literature identified six studies assessing the cost effectiveness of depot antipsychotic medications for people with schizophrenia (Chue *et al.*, 2005; De Graeve *et al.*, 2005; Edwards *et al.*, 2005; Heeg *et al.*, 2008; Laux *et al.*, 2005; Oh *et al.*, 2001). All studies were conducted outside the UK and employed modelling techniques.

According to the results of these studies, long-acting risperidone was dominant over haloperidol depot in Belgium (De Graeve *et al.*, 2005), Germany (Laux *et al.*, 2005), Portugal (Heeg *et al.*, 2008), Canada (Chue *et al.*, 2005) and the US (Edwards *et al.*, 2005). Risperidone was dominant over olanzapine in Belgium (De Graeve *et al.*, 2005), Germany (Laux *et al.*, 2005) and the US (Edwards *et al.*, 2005). Risperidone was dominant over oral risperidone in Portugal (Heeg *et al.*, 2008), Canada (Chue *et al.*, 2005) and the US (Edwards *et al.*, 2005). Finally, risperidone was also shown to dominate quetiapine, ziprasidone and aripiprazole in the US (Edwards *et al.*, 2005). In all of the studies, the cost effectiveness of long-acting risperidone was largely determined by its estimated higher compliance compared with oral antipsychotics. However, in most studies, the methodology used to estimate compliance as well as other clinical input parameters was not clearly described; a number of economic models were populated with estimates based to a great extent on expert opinion.

Oh and colleagues (2001), using data from published meta-analyses and expert opinion, reported that both haloperidol depot and fluphenazine depot were dominated by oral risperidone in Canada. Although the methodology adopted was clearly reported, the main limitation of this study was that randomisation effects from clinical trials were not maintained because clinical input parameters were estimated by pooling data from different clinical trials for each drug ('naïve' method of synthesis).

Overall, the quality of evidence on depot antipsychotic medications was rather poor and of limited applicability to the UK context, given that no study was conducted in the UK.

The impact of compliance with antipsychotic treatment on healthcare costs incurred by people with schizophrenia
The systematic search of economic literature identified a number of studies that assessed the impact of non-adherence to antipsychotic medication on healthcare costs incurred by people with schizophrenia. Although these studies did not evaluate the cost effectiveness of specific pharmacological treatments and therefore do not form part of the systematic review of economic evidence, they are described in this section because they provide useful data on the association between compliance, risk of relapse and subsequent healthcare costs. This information was considered by the GDG at formulation of the guideline recommendations.

Knapp and colleagues (2004a) analysed data from a national survey of psychiatric morbidity among adults living in institutions in the UK, conducted in 1994. Approximately 67% of the population surveyed had a diagnosis of schizophrenia.

According to the data analysis, non-adherence was one of the most significant factors that increased health and social care costs. Non-adherence predicted an excess annual cost reaching £2,500 per person for inpatient services and another £2,500 for other health and social care services, such as outpatient and day care, contacts with community psychiatric nurses, occupational therapists and social workers, and sheltered employment (2001 prices).

A modelling exercise that simulated the treated course of schizophrenia assessed the impact of compliance on health benefits and healthcare costs in people with schizophrenia in the UK over a period of 5 years (Heeg *et al.*, 2005). The study considered people experiencing a second or third episode of schizophrenia and took into account factors such as gender, disease severity, potential risk of harm to self and society, and social and environmental factors. Other factors, such as number of psychiatric consultations, presence of psychotic episodes, symptoms and side effects, were also incorporated into the model structure. People with a first episode of schizophrenia were excluded from the analysis. The analysis demonstrated that a 20% increase in compliance with antipsychotic treatment resulted in cost savings of £16,000 and in prevention of 0.55 psychotic episodes per person with schizophrenia over 5 years. Cost savings were almost exclusively attributed to the great reduction in hospitalisation costs following improved compliance. Higher levels of compliance were also associated with increased time between relapses, decreased symptom severity and improved ability of people to take care of themselves.

With regard to people experiencing a first episode of schizophrenia, Robinson and colleagues (1999b) assessed the rates of relapse following response to antipsychotic treatment in 104 people with a first episode of schizophrenia or schizoaffective disorder. The authors reported that, after initial recovery, the cumulative first-relapse rate was 82% over 5 years. Discontinuation of pharmacological treatment increased the risk of relapse by almost five times. The authors concluded that the risk of relapse within 5 years of recovery from a first episode of schizophrenia or schizoaffective disorder was high, but could be diminished with maintenance antipsychotic drug therapy. Although the study did not assess the costs associated with non-compliance, its results indicate that compliance with treatment can reduce healthcare costs considerably by reducing rates of relapse (relapse can lead to high hospitalisation costs).

Finally, two published reviews examined the impact of compliance with antipsychotic therapy on healthcare costs incurred by people with schizophrenia (Thieda *et al.*, 2003; Sun *et al.*, 2007). The reviews analysed data from 21 studies in total and concluded that antipsychotic non-adherence led to an increase in relapse and, subsequently, hospitalisation rates and hospitalisation costs.

Summary of findings and conclusions from systematic economic literature review
The economic literature review included 31 economic evaluations of specific antipsychotic treatments for the management of people with schizophrenia, plus two effectiveness trials conducted in the UK, which assessed antipsychotic medications grouped in classes. Twenty-two studies were based on decision-analytic modelling and were characterised by varying quality with respect to sources of clinical and utility data and methods of evidence synthesis. Clinical data were derived from a variety of sources,

ranging from published meta-analyses and RCTs to unpublished trials and expert opinion. Even when data were taken from meta-analyses of trial data, the effects of randomisation were not retained, because data were simply pooled (by using weighted mean values) from the respective trials evaluating the drug under assessment. This 'naïve' method is likely to have introduced strong bias in the analyses, and therefore is inappropriate for evidence synthesis of trial data (Glenny *et al.*, 2005). The impact of side effects on the HRQoL was explored in few studies, and even in these cases it was the decrement in HRQoL owing to the presence of EPS that was mostly considered. The impact of other side effects on HRQoL was not explored. The majority of the studies were funded by industry, which may have resulted in additional bias.

The included studies reported a variety of findings. The results of modelling exercises were sensitive, as expected, to a number of parameters, such as response and dropout rates, as well as rates and/or length of hospitalisation. Most of the cost results derived from clinical studies were statistically insignificant. With the exception of a few studies, the majority of economic evaluations included a very limited number of antipsychotic medications for the treatment of people in schizophrenia, mainly olanzapine, risperidone and haloperidol; however, a wider variety of antipsychotic medications has been shown to be clinically effective and is available in the market. Results of comparisons between the three most examined drugs were in some cases contradictory. Nevertheless, overall findings of the systematic review seem to suggest that olanzapine and risperidone may be more cost effective than haloperidol. Similarly, there is evidence that long-acting risperidone may lead to substantial cost-savings and higher clinical benefits compared with oral forms of antipsychotic medication because of higher levels of adherence characterising long-acting injectable forms. However, evidence on long-acting injectable forms comes from non-UK modelling studies that are characterised by unclear methods in estimating a number of crucial input parameters (such as levels of adherence).

The results of non-UK studies are not directly applicable to the UK context and therefore, although they may be indicative of trends in relative cost effectiveness of different antipsychotic drugs worldwide, they should not be used exclusively to inform decisions in the UK context. On the other hand, the results of UK studies were characterised by high uncertainty and several important limitations.

The results of the economic analyses alongside effectiveness trials in the UK (Lewis *et al.*, 2006a; Davies *et al.*, 2008) suggest that hospitalisation costs are the drivers of total costs associated with treatment of people with schizophrenia. Drug acquisition costs are only a small part of total costs, and are unlikely to affect significantly the cost effectiveness of antipsychotic medications. It could be hypothesised that in the short term and for people with schizophrenia treated as inpatients (for example, during an acute episode), there are no big differences in total costs between antipsychotic medications, unless there are differences in the length of hospital stays. It might be reasonable to argue that antipsychotic drugs that reduce the rate and length of hospital admissions (for example drugs that reduce the rate of future relapses and/or the length of acute episodes) are cost-saving options in the long term, despite potentially high acquisition costs. A related factor affecting the magnitude of healthcare costs and subsequently the cost effectiveness of antipsychotic medications is the level of adherence: according to published evidence, high levels of adherence to antipsychotic treatment can greatly reduce the risk of relapse and subsequent hospitalisation costs.

Details of the methods and the results of all economic evaluations described in this section are provided in Appendix 14.

6.9.2 Economic modelling

A decision-analytic model was developed to assess the relative cost effectiveness of antipsychotic medications aimed at promoting recovery (preventing relapse) in people with schizophrenia in remission. The rationale for economic modelling, the methodology adopted, the results and the conclusions from this economic analysis are described in detail in Chapter 7. This section provides a summary of the methods employed and the results of the economic analysis.

Overview of methods
A Markov model was constructed to evaluate the relative cost effectiveness of a number of oral antipsychotic medications over two different time horizons, that is, 10 years and over a lifetime. The antipsychotic drugs assessed were olanzapine, amisulpride, zotepine, aripiprazole, paliperidone, risperidone and haloperidol. The choice of drugs was based on the availability of relapse prevention data identified in clinical evidence review (see Section 6.4). The study population consisted of people with schizophrenia in remission. The model structure considered events such as relapse, discontinuation of treatment because of intolerable side effects and switching to another antipsychotic drug, discontinuation of treatment because of other reasons and moving to no treatment, development of side effects such as acute EPS, weight gain, diabetes and glucose intolerance, complications related to diabetes and death. Clinical data were derived from studies included in the guideline systematic review of clinical evidence and other published literature. Where appropriate, clinical data were analysed using mixed treatment comparison or standard meta-analytic techniques. The measure of outcome in the economic analysis was the number of QALYs gained. The perspective of the analysis was that of health and personal social care services. Resource use was based on published literature, national statistics and, where evidence was lacking, the GDG expert opinion. National UK unit costs were used. The cost year was 2007. Two methods were employed for the analysis of input parameter data and presentation of the results. First, a deterministic analysis was undertaken, where data were analysed as point estimates and results were presented in the form of ICERs following the principles of incremental analysis. A probabilistic analysis was subsequently performed in which most of the model input parameters were assigned probability distributions. This approach allowed more comprehensive consideration of the uncertainty characterising the input parameters and captured the non-linearity characterising the economic model structure. Results of probabilistic analysis were summarised in the form of cost effectiveness acceptability curves, which express the probability of each intervention being cost effective at

various levels of willingness-to-pay per QALY gained (that is, at various cost-effectiveness thresholds).

Overview of results
Results of deterministic analysis demonstrated that zotepine dominated all other treatment options, as it was less costly and resulted in a higher number of QALYs, both at 10 years and over a lifetime of antipsychotic medication use. After zotepine, olanzapine and paliperidone appeared to be the second and third most cost-effective drugs respectively, in both time horizons of 10 years and over a lifetime. Paliperidone and olanzapine dominated all other drugs (except zotepine) at 10 years; the ICER of paliperidone versus olanzapine was approximately £150,000/QALY. Over a lifetime, olanzapine was shown to be the least effective and least costly intervention among those examined, but according to incremental analysis it was still ranked as the second most cost-effective option following zotepine, using a cost-effectiveness threshold of £20,000/QALY (note that adopting a threshold of £30,000/QALY would result in paliperidone being ranked the second most cost-effective option and olanzapine third, as the ICER of paliperidone versus olanzapine was just above the £20,000/QALY threshold, at £20,872/QALY). According to sensitivity analysis, results were highly sensitive to the probability of relapse attached to each antipsychotic drug, but were not driven by the estimated probabilities of developing each of the side effects considered in the analysis.

Probabilistic analysis revealed that zotepine had the highest probability of being the most cost-effective option among those assessed, but this probability was rather low, roughly 27 to 30%, reflecting the uncertainty characterising the results of the analysis. This probability was practically independent of the cost-effectiveness threshold and the time horizon examined. The other antipsychotic medications had probabilities of being cost effective that ranged from approximately 5% (haloperidol) to 16% (paliperidone). Again, these probabilities were rather unaffected by different levels of willingness-to-pay and consideration of different time horizons.

The results of the economic analysis are characterised by substantial levels of uncertainty as illustrated in probabilistic analysis, indicating that no antipsychotic medication can be considered clearly cost effective compared with the other options included in the assessment. Moreover, it needs to be emphasised that the evidence base for the economic analysis was in some cases limited because clinical data in the area of relapse prevention for three medications (zotepine, paliperidone and aripiprazole) came from three single placebo-controlled trials.

6.10   FROM EVIDENCE TO RECOMMENDATIONS

In the previous guideline (which incorporated the recommendations from the NICE technology appraisal of SGAs [NICE, 2002]), SGAs were recommended in some situations as first-line treatment, primarily because they were thought to carry a lower potential risk of EPS. However, evidence from the updated systematic reviews of clinical evidence presented in this chapter, particularly with regard to other adverse effects such as metabolic disturbance, and together with new evidence from effectiveness (pragmatic) trials, suggest that choosing the most appropriate drug and formulation for an individual may be more important than the drug group.

Moreover, design problems in the individual trials continue to make interpretation of the clinical evidence difficult. Such problems include: (a) high attrition from one or both treatment arms in many studies; (b) differences between treatment arms in terms of medication dose; (c) small numbers of studies reporting the same outcomes for some drugs.

For people with schizophrenia whose illness has not responded adequately to antipsychotic medication, clozapine continues to have the most robust evidence for efficacy. In addition, evidence from the effectiveness studies (CATIE, Phase 2; CUtLASS, Band 2) suggests that in people who have shown a poor response to non-clozapine SGAs, there is an advantage in switching to clozapine rather than another SGA. Nevertheless, even with optimum clozapine treatment it seems that only 30 to 60% of treatment-resistant illnesses will respond satisfactorily (Chakos *et al.*, 2001, Iqbal *et al.*, 2003).

The systematic review of the economic literature identified a number of studies of varying quality and relevance to the UK setting. Results were characterised, in most cases, by high uncertainty. The majority of studies assessed the relative cost effectiveness between olanzapine, risperidone and haloperidol. Although study findings are not consistent, they seem to indicate that, overall, olanzapine and risperidone might be more cost effective than haloperidol.

In the area of antipsychotic treatment for first episode or early schizophrenia, the economic evidence is limited and characterised by important limitations, and therefore no safe conclusions on the relative cost effectiveness of antipsychotic medications can be drawn.

The amount of economic evidence is substantially higher in the area of pharmacological treatment for people with an acute exacerbation or recurrence of schizophrenia. However, the number of evaluated drugs is very limited and does not cover the whole range of drugs licensed for treatment of people with schizophrenia in the UK. In addition, existing studies are characterised by a number of limitations and, in many cases, by contradictory results. Available evidence indicates that olanzapine and risperidone may be more cost-effective options than haloperidol for acute exacerbation or recurrence of schizophrenia.

The economic literature in the area of relapse prevention is characterised by similar methodological limitations and also by the limited number of drugs assessed. Olanzapine and risperidone have been suggested to be more cost effective than haloperidol in preventing relapse, but these conclusions are based on results from analyses conducted outside the UK. On the other hand, evidence from CATIE suggests that perphenazine may be more cost effective than a number of SGAs (that is, olanzapine, quetiapine, risperidone and ziprasidone) in the US.

For people with schizophrenia whose illness has not responded adequately to treatment, sparse data on the cost effectiveness of specific antipsychotic medications are available. Evidence from CUtLASS, although not providing data on the cost effectiveness of individual drugs, provides useful insight into the factors that affect total costs incurred by people with schizophrenia. According to economic findings

171

from CUtLASS, psychiatric inpatient care costs are the drivers of total healthcare costs incurred by people with schizophrenia, with drug acquisition costs being only a small fraction of total costs.

CUtLASS Band 2 found that clozapine was more effective than SGAs in the treatment of people with inadequate response to, or unacceptable side effects from, current medication, but at a higher cost that reached £33,000/QALY (ranging from £23,000 to £70,000/QALY in univariate sensitivity analysis). It was suggested that the significant difference in cost between clozapine and SGAs might have been caused by a great difference in psychiatric hospital costs between clozapine and SGAs, possibly reflecting the licensing requirement for inpatient admission for initiation of therapy with clozapine at the time of the study. Currently, clozapine can be initiated in an outpatient setting; therefore, the current cost effectiveness of clozapine versus SGAs for people with inadequate response to treatment or unacceptable side effects is likely to be higher than was estimated when CUtLASS Band 2 was conducted.

Regarding depot/long-acting injectable antipsychotic medication, there is evidence that long-acting risperidone may lead to substantial cost savings and greater clinical benefits compared with oral forms of antipsychotic medication because of higher levels of adherence characterising long-acting injectable forms. However, this evidence comes from non-UK modelling studies that are characterised by unclear methods in estimating a number of crucial input parameters.

The economic analysis undertaken for this guideline estimated the cost effectiveness of oral antipsychotic medications for relapse prevention in people with schizophrenia. The results of the analysis suggest that zotepine is potentially the most cost-effective oral antipsychotic drug included in the model. However, results were characterised by high uncertainty and probabilistic analysis showed that no antipsychotic medication could be considered to be clearly cost effective compared with the other treatment options assessed: according to results of probabilistic analysis, the probability of each drug being cost effective ranged from roughly 5% (haloperidol) to about 27 to 30% (zotepine), and was independent of the cost effectiveness threshold used and the time horizon of the analysis (that is, 10 years or a lifetime). The probability of 27 to 30% assigned to zotepine, although indicative, is rather low and inadequate to be able to come to a safe conclusion regarding zotepine's superiority over the other antipsychotics assessed in terms of cost effectiveness. Moreover, clinical data for zotepine in the area of relapse prevention were exclusively derived from one small placebo-controlled RCT. Similarly, clinical data for paliperidone and aripiprazole were taken from two placebo-controlled trials. It must be noted that the economic analysis did not examine the cost effectiveness of quetiapine and any FGAs apart from haloperidol, owing to lack of respective clinical data in the area of relapse prevention.

An interesting finding of the economic analysis was that drug acquisition costs did not affect the cost effectiveness of antipsychotic medications: in fact haloperidol, which has the lowest price in the UK among those assessed, appeared to have the lowest probability (about 5%) of being cost effective at any level of willingness-to-pay. On the other hand, zotepine, which had the lowest average relapse rate across all evaluated treatments, dominated all other options in deterministic analysis and demonstrated the highest probability of being cost effective in probabilistic analysis;

this finding together with results of sensitivity analysis indicate that the effectiveness of an antipsychotic drug in preventing relapse is the key determinant of its relative cost effectiveness, apparently because relapse prevention, besides clinical improvement, leads to a substantial reduction in hospitalisation rates and respective costs.

Hospitalisation costs have been shown to drive healthcare costs incurred by people with schizophrenia, both in published evidence and in the economic analysis carried out for this guideline. It might be reasonable to argue that antipsychotic drugs that reduce the rate and length of hospital admissions (for example, drugs that reduce the rate of future relapses and/or the length of acute episodes) are cost-saving options in the long term, despite potentially high acquisition costs. This hypothesis is supported by published evidence, which shows that increased adherence to antipsychotic treatment is associated with a significant decrease in healthcare costs incurred by people with schizophrenia through a reduction in the risk of relapse and subsequent need for hospitalisation.

The GDG considered all clinical and economic evidence summarised in this section to formulate recommendations. In therapeutic areas where clinical and/or economic evidence on specific antipsychotic medications was lacking, as in the case of quetiapine and FGAs other than haloperidol in the area of relapse prevention, the GDG made judgements on the clinical and cost effectiveness of antipsychotic medication by extrapolating existing evidence and conclusions from other therapeutic areas.

Taking into account the findings from the systematic reviews of both the clinical and health economic literature, and the uncertainty characterising the results of economic modelling undertaken for this guideline, the evidence does not allow for any general recommendation for one antipsychotic to be preferred over another, but the evidence does support a specific recommendation for clozapine for people whose illness does not respond adequately to other antipsychotic medication.

Finally, the GDG noted that the following are the key points to be considered before initiating an antipsychotic medication in an acute episode of schizophrenia. First, there may be some lack of insight into the presence of a mental illness and the relevance of drug treatment. Careful explanation is needed regarding the rationale for antipsychotic medications and their modes of action. People with schizophrenia will usually accept that they have been stressed, experiencing insomnia and not eating well, so the acceptance of a tranquillising medication to help reduce stress and improve sleep and appetite might be acceptable. It can also be explained, if the patient is insightful enough, that the medication is antipsychotic and can help reduce the severity of distressing hallucinations, delusions and thought disorder.

Second, medication should always be started at a low dose if possible, after a full discussion of the possible side effects. Starting at a low dose allows monitoring for the early emergence of side effects, such as EPS, weight gain or insomnia. The dose can then be titrated upwards within the BNF treatment range. Although polypharmacy with antipsychotic medications is not recommended, it is equally important not to undertreat the acute psychotic episode.

Third, people with schizophrenia should be consulted on their preference for a more or less sedative medication option. Medication is ideally started following a period of antipsychotic-free assessment within an acute ward setting or under the supervision of a crisis home treatment team, early intervention in psychosis team or assertive outreach team.

6.11   RECOMMENDATIONS

6.11.1   Initiation of treatment (first episode)

6.11.1.1   For people with newly diagnosed schizophrenia, offer oral antipsychotic medication. Provide information and discuss the benefits and side-effect profile of each drug with the service user. The choice of drug should be made by the service user and healthcare professional together, considering:
- the relative potential of individual antipsychotic drugs to cause extra-pyramidal side effects (including akathisia), metabolic side effects (including weight gain) and other side effects (including unpleasant subjective experiences)
- the views of the carer if the service user agrees.

6.11.2   How to use oral antipsychotic medication

6.11.2.1   Before starting antipsychotic medication, offer the person with schizophrenia an electrocardiogram (ECG) if:
- specified in the SPC
- a physical examination has identified specific cardiovascular risk (such as diagnosis of high blood pressure)
- there is personal history of cardiovascular disease, or
- the service user is being admitted as an inpatient.

6.11.2.2   Treatment with antipsychotic medication should be considered an explicit individual therapeutic trial. Include the following:
- Record the indications and expected benefits and risks of oral antipsychotic medication, and the expected time for a change in symptoms and appearance of side effects.
- At the start of treatment give a dose at the lower end of the licensed range and slowly titrate upwards within the dose range given in the BNF or SPC.
- Justify and record reasons for dosages outside the range given in the BNF or SPC.
- Monitor and record the following regularly and systematically throughout treatment, but especially during titration:
  - efficacy, including changes in symptoms and behaviour
  - side effects of treatment, taking into account overlap between certain side effects and clinical features of schizophrenia, for example the overlap between akathisia and agitation or anxiety

- – adherence
- – physical health.
- Record the rationale for continuing, changing or stopping medication, and the effects of such changes.
- Carry out a trial of the medication at optimum dosage for 4–6 weeks.

6.11.2.3   Discuss any non-prescribed therapies the service user wishes to use (including complementary therapies) with the service user, and carer if appropriate. Discuss the safety and efficacy of the therapies, and possible interference with the therapeutic effects of prescribed medication and psychological treatments.

6.11.2.4   Discuss the use of alcohol, tobacco, prescription and non-prescription medication and illicit drugs with the service user, and carer if appropriate. Discuss their possible interference with the therapeutic effects of prescribed medication and psychological treatments.

6.11.2.5   'As required' (p.r.n.) prescriptions of antipsychotic medication should be made as described in recommendation 6.11.2.2. Review clinical indications, frequency of administration, therapeutic benefits and side effects each week or as appropriate. Check whether 'p.r.n.' prescriptions have led to a dosage above the maximum specified in the BNF or SPC.

6.11.2.6   Do not use a loading dose of antipsychotic medication (often referred to as 'rapid neuroleptisation').

6.11.2.7   Do not initiate regular combined antipsychotic medication, except for short periods (for example, when changing medication).

6.11.2.8   If prescribing chlorpromazine, warn of its potential to cause skin photosensitivity. Advise using sunscreen if necessary.

6.11.3   Acute treatment recommendations

6.11.3.1   For people with an acute exacerbation or recurrence of schizophrenia, offer oral antipsychotic medication. The choice of drug should be influenced by the same criteria recommended for starting treatment (see Section 6.11.1). Take into account the clinical response and side effects of the service user's current and previous medication.

6.11.4   Rapid tranquillisation

6.11.4.1   Occasionally people with schizophrenia pose an immediate risk to themselves or others during an acute episode and may need rapid tranquillisation. The management of immediate risk should follow the relevant NICE guidelines (see recommendations 6.11.4.2 and 6.11.4.5).

6.11.4.2   Follow the recommendations in 'Violence' (NICE clinical guideline 25[12]) when facing imminent violence or when considering rapid tranquillisation.

---

[12] Available from: http://www.nice.org.uk/Guidance/CG25

6.11.4.3 After rapid tranquillisation, offer the person with schizophrenia the opportunity to discuss their experiences. Provide them with a clear explanation of the decision to use urgent sedation. Record this in their notes.

6.11.4.4 Ensure that the person with schizophrenia has the opportunity to write an account of their experience of rapid tranquillisation in their notes.

6.11.4.5 Follow the recommendations in 'Self-harm' (NICE clinical guideline 16[13]) when managing acts of self-harm in people with schizophrenia.

6.11.5   Early post-acute period

6.11.5.1 Inform the service user that there is a high risk of relapse if they stop medication in the next 1–2 years.

6.11.5.2 If withdrawing antipsychotic medication, undertake gradually and monitor regularly for signs and symptoms of relapse.

6.11.5.3 After withdrawal from antipsychotic medication, continue monitoring for signs and symptoms of relapse for at least 2 years.

6.11.6   Promoting recovery recommendations

6.11.6.1 The choice of drug should be influenced by the same criteria recommended for starting treatment (see Section 6.11.2).

6.11.6.2 Do not use targeted, intermittent dosage maintenance strategies[14] routinely. However, consider them for people with schizophrenia who are unwilling to accept a continuous maintenance regimen or if there is another contraindication to maintenance therapy, such as side-effect sensitivity.

6.11.6.3 Consider offering depot/long-acting injectable antipsychotic medication to people with schizophrenia:
- who would prefer such treatment after an acute episode
- where avoiding covert non-adherence (either intentional or unintentional) to antipsychotic medication is a clinical priority within the treatment plan.

6.11.7   How to prescribe depot/long-acting injectable antipsychotic medication

6.11.7.1 When initiating depot/long-acting injectable antipsychotic medication:
- take into account the service user's preferences and attitudes towards the mode of administration (regular intramuscular injections) and organisational procedures (for example, home visits and location of clinics)

---

[13] Available from: http://www.nice.org.uk/Guidance/CG16
[14] Defined as the use of antipsychotic medication only during periods of incipient relapse or symptom exacerbation rather than continuously.

- take into account the same criteria recommended for the use of oral antipsychotic medication (see Section 6.11.2), particularly in relation to the risks and benefits of the drug regimen
- initially use a small test dose as set out in the BNF or SPC.

6.11.8   Interventions for people with schizophrenia who have an inadequate or no response to pharmacological or psychological treatment

6.11.8.1   For people with schizophrenia whose illness has not responded adequately to pharmacological or psychological treatment:
- review the diagnosis
- establish that there has been adherence to antipsychotic medication, prescribed at an adequate dose and for the correct duration
- review engagement with and use of psychological treatments and ensure that these have been offered according to this guideline. If family intervention has been undertaken suggest CBT; if CBT has been undertaken suggest family intervention for people in close contact with their families
- consider other causes of non-response, such as comorbid substance misuse (including alcohol), the concurrent use of other prescribed medication or physical illness.

6.11.8.2   Offer clozapine to people with schizophrenia whose illness has not responded adequately to treatment despite the sequential use of adequate doses of at least two different antipsychotic drugs. At least one of the drugs should be a non-clozapine second-generation antipsychotic.

6.11.8.3   For people with schizophrenia whose illness has not responded adequately to clozapine at an optimised dose, healthcare professionals should consider Recommendation 6.11.8.1 (including measuring therapeutic drug levels) before adding a second antipsychotic to augment treatment with clozapine. An adequate trial of such an augmentation may need to be up to 8–10 weeks. Choose a drug that does not compound the common side effects of clozapine.

6.11.9   Research recommendations

6.11.9.1   More long-term, head-to-head RCTs of the efficacy and safety/tolerability and patient acceptability of the available antipsychotic drugs are required, in individuals in their first episode of schizophrenia, testing the risk-benefit of dosage at the lower end of the recommended dosage range.

6.11.9.2   Large-scale, observational, survey-based studies, including qualitative components, of the experience of drug treatments for available antipsychotics should be undertaken. Studies should include data on service user satisfaction, side effects, preferences, provision of information and quality of life.

6.11.9.3   Quantitative and qualitative research is required to investigate the utility, acceptability and safety of available drugs for urgent sedation/control of acute behavioural disturbance (including benzodiazepines and antipsychotics), employing larger samples, in settings that reflect current clinical practice, and systematically manipulating dosage and frequency of drug administration.

6.11.9.4 Further work is required on the nature and severity of antipsychotic drug discontinuation phenomena, including the re-emergence of psychotic symptoms, and their relationship to different antipsychotic withdrawal strategies.

6.11.9.5 Direct comparisons between available oral antipsychotics are needed to establish their respective risk/long-term benefit, including effects upon relapse rates and persistent symptoms, and cost effectiveness. Trials should pay particular attention to the long-term benefits and risks of the drugs, including systematic assessment of side effects: metabolic effects (including weight gain), EPS (including tardive dyskinesia), sexual dysfunction, lethargy and quality of life.

6.11.9.6 Further RCT-based, long-term studies are needed to establish the clinical and cost effectiveness of available depot/long-acting injectable antipsychotic preparations to establish their relative safety, efficacy in terms of relapse prevention, side-effect profile and impact upon quality of life.

6.11.9.7 Further RCT-based, long-term studies are needed to establish the clinical and cost effectiveness of augmenting antipsychotic monotherapy with an antidepressant to treat persistent negative symptoms.

6.11.9.8 Controlled studies are required to test the efficacy and safety of combining antipsychotics to treat schizophrenia that has proved to be poorly responsive to adequate trials of antipsychotic monotherapy.

6.11.9.9 A randomised placebo-controlled trial should be conducted to investigate the efficacy and cost effectiveness of augmentation of clozapine monotherapy with an appropriate second antipsychotic where a refractory schizophrenic illness has shown only a partial response to clozapine.[15]

6.11.9.10 A randomised placebo-controlled trial should be conducted to investigate the efficacy and cost effectiveness of augmentation of antipsychotic monotherapy with lithium where a schizophrenic illness has shown only a partial response. The response in illness with and without affective symptoms should be addressed.

6.11.9.11 A randomised placebo-controlled trial should be conducted to investigate the efficacy and cost effectiveness of augmentation of antipsychotic monotherapy with sodium valproate where a schizophrenic illness has shown only a partial response. The response of illness in relation to behavioural disturbance, specifically persistent aggression, should be specifically addressed to determine if this is independent of effect on potentially confounding variables, such as positive symptoms, sedation, or akathisia.

6.11.9.12 Further controlled studies are required to test the claims that clozapine is particularly effective in reducing hostility and violence, and the inconsistent evidence for a reduction in suicide rates in people with schizophrenia.

---

[15]For more details see Chapter 10 (recommendation 10.5.1.1).

7 ECONOMIC MODEL – COST EFFECTIVENESS OF PHARMACOLOGICAL INTERVENTIONS FOR PEOPLE WITH SCHIZOPHRENIA

7.1 INTRODUCTION

7.1.1 Rationale for economic modelling – objectives

The systematic search of economic literature identified a number of studies on pharmacological treatments for the management of schizophrenia which were of varying quality and relevance to the UK setting. Results were characterised, in most cases, by high uncertainty and various levels of inconsistency. The number of antipsychotic medications assessed in this literature was limited and did not include the whole range of drugs available in the UK for the treatment of people with schizophrenia. These findings pointed to the need for *de novo* economic modelling for this guideline. The objective of economic modelling was to explore the relative cost effectiveness of antipsychotic medications for people with schizophrenia in the current UK clinical setting, using up-to-date appropriate information on costs and clinical outcomes, and attempting to include a wider choice of antipsychotic drugs than that examined in the existing economic literature as well as to overcome at least some of the limitations of previous models. Details on the guideline systematic review of economic literature on pharmacological interventions for people with schizophrenia are provided in Chapter 6 (Section 6.9.1).

7.1.2 Defining the economic question

The systematic review of clinical evidence covered four major areas of treating people with schizophrenia with antipsychotic drugs: initial treatment for people with first-episode or early schizophrenia; treatment of people with an acute exacerbation or recurrence of schizophrenia; promoting recovery in people with schizophrenia that is in remission (relapse prevention); and promoting recovery in people with schizophrenia whose illness has not responded adequately to treatment (treatment resistance). In deciding which area to examine in the economic model, the following criteria were considered:

- quality and applicability (to the UK context) of relevant existing economic evidence

- magnitude of resource implications expected by use of alternative pharmacological treatments in each area
- availability of respective clinical evidence that would allow meaningful and potentially robust conclusions to be reached that could inform formulation of recommendations.

Based on the above criteria, the economic assessment of antipsychotic medications aiming at promoting recovery (preventing relapse) in people with schizophrenia that is in remission was selected as a topic of highest priority for economic analysis: relevant existing economic evidence was overall rather poor and not directly transferable to the UK context. Resource implications associated with this phase of treatment were deemed major because treatment covers a long period that can extend over a lifetime. Finally, respective clinical evidence was deemed adequate to allow useful conclusions from economic modelling because it covered most (but not all) of the antipsychotic medications available in the UK and was derived from a sufficient number of trials (17) providing data on 3,535 participants.

7.2 ECONOMIC MODELLING METHODS

7.2.1 Interventions assessed

The choice of interventions assessed in the economic analysis was determined by the availability of respective clinical data included in the guideline systematic literature review. Only antipsychotic medications licensed in the UK and suitable for first-line treatment aiming at preventing relapse in people with schizophrenia that is in remission were considered. Depot/long-acting injectable antipsychotic medications were not included in the economic analysis because they were not deemed suitable for first-line treatment of people with schizophrenia. Consequently, the following seven oral antipsychotic medications were examined: olanzapine, amisulpride, zotepine, aripiprazole, paliperidone, risperidone and haloperidol. Quetiapine was not included in the economic analysis because no respective clinical data in the area of relapse prevention in people with schizophrenia that is in remission were identified in the literature. In addition, haloperidol was the only FGA evaluated because no clinical data on other FGAs were included in the guideline systematic review. Further clinical evidence on FGAs may exist, but may have not been identified because the guideline systematic search of the literature focused on clinical trials of SGAs. Non-inclusion of quetiapine and other FGAs is acknowledged as a limitation of the economic analysis.

7.2.2 Model structure

A decision-analytic Markov model was constructed using Microsoft Office Excel 2007. The model was run in yearly cycles. According to the model structure, seven hypothetical cohorts of people with schizophrenia that is in remission were initiated on each of the seven oral antipsychotic medications assessed (first-line antipsychotic). The age of the population was 25 years at the start of the model, as this is the mean age at onset of schizophrenia. Within each year, people either remained in remission, or experienced a relapse, or stopped the antipsychotic because of the presence of intolerable side effects, or stopped the antipsychotic for any other reason (except relapse or presence of intolerable side effects), or died. People who stopped the first-line antipsychotic because of the development of intolerable side effects switched to a second-line antipsychotic. People who stopped the first-line antipsychotic for any other reason were assumed to stop abruptly and move to no treatment; these people remained without antipsychotic treatment until they experienced a relapse. People discontinuing treatment because of side effects or other reasons were assumed not to experience relapse in the remaining time of the cycle within which discontinuation occurred. All people experiencing a relapse stopped any antipsychotic drug that they had been receiving while in remission and were treated for the acute episode; after achieving remission, they either returned to their previous antipsychotic medication aiming at promoting recovery (50% of people achieving remission), or switched to a second-line antipsychotic drug (the remaining 50%). People initiated on a second-line antipsychotic experienced the same events as described above. People who stopped the second-line antipsychotic medication either because of intolerable side effects or following a relapse (50% of people) were switched to a third-line antipsychotic drug. No further medication switches were assumed after this point. This means that people under the third-line antipsychotic were assumed not to stop medication because of side effects or for other reasons, and all of them returned to this antipsychotic after treatment of relapses. It must be noted that discontinuation of an antipsychotic because of intolerable side effects was assumed to occur only during the first year of use of this particular antipsychotic. Discontinuation of an antipsychotic for other reasons was assumed to occur over each year of use, at the same rate. People under first-, second- or third-line antipsychotic medication might experience side effects that do not lead to discontinuation (tolerable side effects). All transitions in the model, for purposes of estimation of costs and QALYs, were assumed to occur in the middle of each cycle. Two different time horizons were examined (10 years and over the lifetime of the study population), to allow exploration of the impact of long-term benefits and risks of antipsychotic medications on their relative cost effectiveness over time. A schematic diagram of the economic model is presented in Figure 3.

The first-line antipsychotic described in the model structure was one of the seven oral antipsychotics evaluated in the analysis. The second-line antipsychotic following first-line olanzapine, amisulpride, zotepine, aripiprazole, paliperidone or risperidone was an FGA; the second-line antipsychotic following first-line haloperidol was an SGA. The third-line antipsychotic was in all cases a depot antipsychotic medication. In terms of costs, relapse and discontinuation and side effect rates, the FGA used as second-line treatment was assumed to be haloperidol; the SGA used as second-line treatment was assumed to be olanzapine; the depot antipsychotic (third-line treatment) was assumed to be flupentixol decanoate, as this is the most

Figure 3: Schematic diagram of the economic model structure

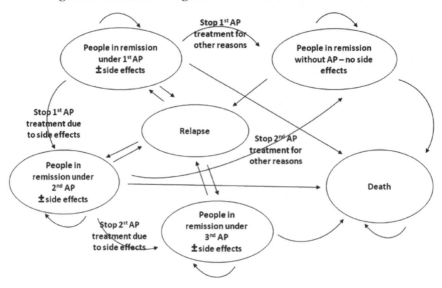

Note: AP = antipsychotic.

commonly used depot antipsychotic in UK clinical practice (NHS, The Information Centre, 2008b).

The aim of the consideration of three lines of treatment in the model structure was not to assess or recommend specific sequences of drugs. The model evaluated the relative cost effectiveness between the first-line antipsychotics only. The purpose of incorporating medication switching in the model structure was to assess the impact of lack of effectiveness in relapse prevention (expressed by relapse rates), intolerance (expressed by discontinuation rates because of side effects) and unacceptability (expressed by discontinuation rates because of other reasons) of the first-line antipsychotics on future costs and health outcomes, and to present a more realistic sequence of events related to treatment of people with schizophrenia with antipsychotic medication. The seven sequences of antipsychotic medications considered in the analysis are presented in Figure 4.

7.2.3   Costs and outcomes considered in the analysis

The economic analysis adopted the perspective of the NHS and personal social services, as recommended by NICE (2007). Costs consisted of drug acquisition costs, inpatient and outpatient secondary care costs, costs of primary and community healthcare, costs of treating side effects and related future complications, as well as costs of residential care. The measure of outcome was the QALY.

Figure 4: Sequences of antipsychotic treatment assumed in the model for each of the seven hypothetical cohorts of people with schizophrenia followed

First-line antipsychotic	Second-line antipsychotic	Third-line antipsychotic
Olanzapine	→ FGA	→ Depot antipsychotic medication
Amisulpride	→ FGA	→ Depot antipsychotic medication
Zotepine	→ FGA	→ Depot antipsychotic medication
Aripiprazole	→ FGA	→ Depot antipsychotic medication
Paliperidone	→ FGA	→ Depot antipsychotic medication
Risperidone	→ FGA	→ Depot antipsychotic medication
Haloperidol	→ SGA	→ Depot antipsychotic medication

7.2.4 Overview of methods employed for evidence synthesis

To populate the economic model with appropriate input parameters, the available clinical evidence from the guideline systematic review and meta-analysis needed to be combined in a way that would allow consideration of all relevant information on the antipsychotics assessed. The systematic review of clinical evidence in the area of relapse prevention identified 17 trials that made pair-wise comparisons between an SGA and another SGA, an FGA, or placebo. To take all trial information into consideration, without ignoring part of the evidence and without introducing bias by breaking the rules of randomisation (for example, by making 'naive' addition of data across relevant treatment arms from all RCTs as described in Glenny and colleagues, 2005), mixed treatment comparison meta-analytic techniques were employed. Mixed treatment comparison meta-analysis is a generalisation of standard pair-wise meta-analysis for A versus B trials to data structures that include, for example, A versus B, B versus C and A versus C trials (Lu & Ades, 2004). A basic assumption of mixed treatment comparison methods is that direct and indirect evidence estimate that the same parameter (that is, the relative effect between A and B measured directly from an A versus B trial) is the same with the relative effect between A and B estimated indirectly from A versus C and B versus C trials. Mixed treatment comparison techniques strengthen inference concerning the relative effect of two treatments by including both direct and indirect comparisons between treatments and, at the same time, allow simultaneous inference on all treatments examined in the pair-wise trial comparisons while respecting randomisation (Lu & Ades, 2004; Caldwell *et al.*, 2005). Simultaneous inference on the relative effect a number of treatments is possible provided that treatments participate in a single 'network of evidence', that is, every treatment is linked to at least one of the other treatments under assessment through direct or indirect comparisons.

Mixed treatment comparison methods were undertaken to make simultaneous inference for the antipsychotic drugs included in the economic analysis on the following five parameters: probability of relapse, probability of treatment discontinuation because of intolerable side effects, probability of treatment discontinuation because of any other reason, probability of weight gain and probability of acute EPS. Data on the first three parameters were analysed together using a mixed treatment comparison 'competing risks' logistic regression model appropriate for multinomial distribution of data. Data on probability of weight gain and probability of acute EPS were analysed using two separate logistic regression models for binomial distributions. All three models were constructed following principles of Bayesian analysis and were conducted using Markov Chain Monte Carlo simulation techniques implemented in WinBUGS 1.4 (Lunn *et al.*, 2000; Spiegelhalter *et al.*, 2001).

7.2.5   Relapse and discontinuation data

Data on (i) relapse, (ii) drug discontinuation because of intolerable side effects and (iii) drug discontinuation because of other reasons were taken from 17 RCTs included in the guideline systematic review of pharmacological treatments aiming at relapse prevention in people with schizophrenia that is in remission (details of this review are provided in Chapter 6, Section 6.4). All 17 RCTs reported data on the three outcomes considered in the analysis. The vast majority of the trials reported separately on the proportions of people that discontinued treatment because of relapse and of people discontinuing because of side effects, as well as of people discontinuing for any other reason; overall treatment failure was defined as the sum of these three outcomes. The outcomes were thus 'competing' or 'mutually exclusive', in the sense that within the time frame of the trials any person who did not remain under treatment and in remission (which would equal treatment success) was at risk of either relapsing or stopping treatment because of side effects, or stopping treatment because of other reasons. A small number of trials reported the numbers of people who experienced relapse within the time frame of analysis, without clarifying whether these people remained in the trial following relapse and could be potentially double-counted if they discontinued treatment because of side effects or other reasons at a later stage of the study. However, for the purpose of analysis of clinical data and to build the economic model, data on relapse, discontinuation because of side effects and discontinuation because of other reasons from all 17 RCTs were treated as competing, as described above. It must be noted that all 17 studies reported numbers of people that experienced relapse, but not the total number of relapses per such person. It is therefore not known whether some of the trial participants could have experienced more than one episode of relapse during the time frame of analyses. Consequently, clinical data have been analysed assuming that participants reported to have experienced relapse had only one episode of relapse over the time frame of each trial. A final limitation of the data analysis lay in the fact that the 17 RCTs used various definitions of relapse (described in Chapter 6, Sections 6.4.4 and 6.4.5) and therefore the reported relapse rates are not entirely comparable across studies.

Table 34: Summary of data reported in the RCTs included in the guideline systematic review on pharmacological relapse prevention that were utilised in the economic analysis

Study	Time horizon (weeks)	Comparators	Number of people relapsing (m1)	Number of people stopping because of side effects (m2)	Number of people stopping because of other reasons (m3)	Number of people in each arm (n)
1. BEASLEY2003	42	Placebo (1) Olanzapine (2)	28 9	12 2	15 19	102 224
2. DELLVA1997 (study 1)	46	Placebo (1) Olanzapine (2)	7 10	0 2	4 16	13 45
3. DELLVA1997 (study 2)	46	Placebo (1) Olanzapine (2)	5 6	2 10	5 15	14 48
4. LOO1997	26	Placebo (1) Amisulpride (3)	5 4	5 1	39 26	72 69
5. Cooper2000	26	Placebo (1) Zotepine (4)	21 4	4 16	24 21	58 61
6. PIGOTT2003	26	Placebo (1) Aripiprazole (5)	85 50	13 16	12 18	155 155
7. Arato2002	52	Placebo (1) Ziprasidone (6)	43 71	11 19	7 28	71 206
8. KRAMER2007[a]	47	Placebo (1) Paliperidone (7)	52 23	1 3	7 17	101 104

Continued

Table 34: *(Continued)*

Study	Time horizon (weeks)	Comparators	Number of people relapsing (m1)	Number of people stopping because of side effects (m2)	Number of people stopping because of other reasons (m3)	Number of people in each arm (n)
9. SIMPSON2005	28	Olanzapine (2) Ziprasidone (6)	11 8	6 5	44 33	71 55
10. Tran1998 (a + b + c)[b]	52	Olanzapine (2) Haloperidol (8)	87 34	54 20	170 50	627 180
11. STUDY-S029	52	Olanzapine (2) Haloperidol (8)	28 29	9 14	26 25	141 134
12. Tran1997	28	Olanzapine (2) Risperidone (9)	20 53	17 17	36 18	172 167
13. Speller1997	52	Amisulpride (3) Haloperidol (8)	5 9	3 5	2 2	29 31
14. Csernansky2000	52	Haloperidol (8) Risperidone (9)	65 41	29 22	80 60	188 177
15. MARDER2003	104	Haloperidol (8) Risperidone (9)	8 4	0 3	4 4	30 33

[a] Participants received treatment for up to 11 months (47 weeks).

[b] Data from the three RCTs with study ID Tran1998 (a + b + c) are presented together because discontinuation data were not reported separately for each trial. The time horizon for a + b studies was 52 weeks. In study c, participants completed between 22 and 84 weeks of therapy. For modelling purposes, the time horizon in all three studies was assumed to be 52 weeks.

Figure 5: Evidence network derived from data on relapse, treatment discontinuation because of intolerable side effects and treatment discontinuation for other reasons

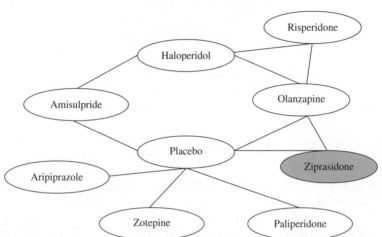

Note: Ziprasidone (in grey-shaded oval) was considered in the mixed treatment comparison analysis because it allowed indirect comparison between olanzapine and placebo, thus strengthening inference. However, it was not included in the economic analysis because it is not licensed in the UK.

The time horizon of the RCTs ranged from 26 to 104 weeks. Two of the trials assessed ziprasidone versus placebo and versus olanzapine. Ziprasidone is not licensed in the UK and for this reason was not considered in the economic analysis; nevertheless, data from these RCTs were utilised in the mixed treatment comparison model because they allowed indirect comparison between olanzapine and placebo, thus strengthening inference. Table 34 provides a summary of the data utilised in the mixed treatment comparison competing risks model. The network of evidence resulting from the available data is shown in Figure 5.

Mixed treatment comparisons – competing risks model for relapse
and discontinuation data
A random effects model was constructed to estimate for every antipsychotic drug evaluated the probabilities of relapse, treatment discontinuation because of intolerable side effects and treatment discontinuation because of other reasons over 52 weeks, using data from the 17 RCTs summarised in Table 34. The data for each trial j constituted a multinomial likelihood with four outcomes: $m = 1$ relapse, 2 = discontinuation because of intolerable side effects, 3 = discontinuation because of other reasons and 4 = none of these (treatment success). If r_{jm} is the number observed in each category and n_j is the total number at risk in trial j, then:

$$r_{j,m=1,2,3,4} \sim Multinomial\left(p_{j,m=1,2,3,4}, n_j\right) \quad \text{where} \quad \sum_{m=1}^{m=4} p_m = 1$$

Economic model – cost effectiveness of pharmacological interventions

Each of the three outcomes $m = 1, 2, 3$ was modelled separately on the log hazard rate scale. For outcome m, treatment k in trial j, and considering a trial j comparing treatments k and b,

$$\theta_{j,k,m} = \mu_{j,m} + \delta_{j,b,k,m} I(b \neq k), \quad m = 1, 2, 3$$

where $d_{j,b,k,m}$ is the trial-specific log hazard ratio of treatment k relative to treatment b. $\mu_{j,m}$ is the 'baseline' log hazard in that trial, relating to treatment b. The trial-specific log hazard ratios were assumed to come from a normal 'random effects' distribution:

$$\delta_{j,b,k,m} \sim Normal(d_{k,m} - d_{b,m}, \sigma_m^2)$$

The mean of this distribution is a difference between mean relative effects $d_{k,m}$ and $d_{b,m}$, which are the mean effects of treatments k and b respectively relative to treatment 1, which is placebo, for outcome m. This formulation of the problem expresses the consistency equations were assumed to hold (Lu & Ades, 2006). The between-trials variance of the distribution was specific to each outcome m.

Vague priors were assigned to trial baselines in the estimation of relative effects and to mean treatment effects, m_j, $d_{k,m} \sim N(0, 100^2)$.

A competing risks model was assumed, with constant hazards $\exp(\theta_{j,k,m})$ acting over the period of observation D_j in years. Thus, the probability of outcome m by the end of the observation period for treatment k in trial j was:

$$P_{j,k,m}(D_j) = \frac{\exp(\theta_{j,k,m})[1 - \exp(-\sum_{m=1}^{m=3} D_j \exp(\theta_{j,k,m})]}{\sum_{m=1}^{m=3} \exp(\theta_{j,k,m})}, \quad m = 1, 2, 3$$

To obtain absolute effects for use in the economic model requires an estimate of the baseline effect in the absence of treatment. While it is desirable to allow the baseline effects to be unconstrained so as to obtain unbiased estimates of relative effects, for the economic model in this guideline a baseline effect that represents the trial evidence was inputted. Therefore, a separate model was constructed for the response to placebo, based on the eight trials with a placebo arm. The response on each outcome was again modelled on a log hazard scale.

$$\xi_{j,m} \sim N(B, \omega_m^2), \quad B \sim N(0, 100^2)$$

$$P_{j,m}(D_j) = \frac{\exp(\xi_{j,m})[1 - \exp(-\sum_{m=1}^{m=3} D_j \exp(\xi_{j,m}))]}{\sum_{m=1}^{m=3} \exp(\xi_{j,m})}, \quad m = 1, 2, 3$$

Priors for the between-trials variation were constructed as follows. First, for the between-studies variation regarding placebo, each of the three outcomes was assigned vague inverse Gamma priors: $1/\omega_m^2 \sim Gamma(0.1, 0.1)$. Then, it was assumed that the variance of the treatment differences must be between zero (perfect correlation between arms) and unity (zero correlation between arms). Thus:

$$\sigma_m^2 = \omega_m^2 \sqrt{2(1-\rho)}, \quad \text{where } \rho \sim U(0,1)$$

For the economic analysis, the output from the model was the proportion of people reaching each outcome by 52 weeks on treatment. The absolute log hazard $\Theta_{k,m}$ for outcome m on treatment k was based on the mean treatment effect relative to treatment 1 (that is, placebo) and a random sample $X_{k,m}$ from the distribution of absolute log hazards on placebo:

$$X_m \sim N(\xi_m, \omega_m^2)$$
$$\Theta_{k,m} = X_m + d_{k,m}$$

$$P_{k,m} = \frac{\exp(\Theta_{k,m})[1 - \exp(-\sum_{m=1}^{m=3} \exp(\Theta_{k,m}))]}{\sum_{m=1}^{m=3} \exp(\Theta_{k,m})}, \quad m = 1, 2, 3$$

$$P_{k,4} = 1 - \sum_{m=1}^{m=3} P_{k,m}$$

Model parameters required for the economic analysis were estimated using Markov chain Monte Carlo simulation methods implemented in WinBUGS 1.4 (Lunn *et al.*, 2000; Spiegelhalter *et al.*, 2001). The first 60,000 iterations were discarded and 300,000 further iterations were run; because of high autocorrelation observed in some model parameters, the model was thinned so that every 30th simulation was retained. Consequently, 10,000 posterior simulations were recorded. To test whether prior estimates had an impact on the results, two chains with different initial values were run simultaneously. Convergence was assessed by inspection of the Gelman–Rubin diagnostic plot.

The Winbugs code used to estimate the 52-week probabilities of (i) relapse, (ii) treatment discontinuation because of side effects and (iii) treatment discontinuation because of other reasons is provided in Appendix 13, followed by summary statistics of a number of model parameters, including the log hazard ratios of all evaluated drugs relative to placebo on the three outcomes examined and the between-trials variation for each outcome. Results are reported as mean values with 95% credible intervals, which are analogous to confidence intervals in frequentist statistics. Table 35 presents the mean values and 95% credible intervals of the probabilities of each

Table 35: Results of mixed treatment comparison analysis – competing risks model

Treatment	Probability of relapse over 52 weeks			Probability that treatment is best in reducing relapse over 52 weeks
	Mean	Lower CI	Upper CI	
Olanzapine	0.1996	0.0146	0.7222	0.078
Amisulpride	0.2988	0.0197	0.9042	0.043
Zotepine	0.1067	0.0023	0.5601	0.486
Aripiprazole	0.2742	0.0130	0.8531	0.061
Paliperidone	0.1625	0.0025	0.7008	0.270
Risperidone	0.2761	0.0182	0.8785	0.044
Haloperidol	0.3317	0.0262	0.9028	0.018
Placebo	0.4361	0.0913	0.8613	0.000
	Probability of discontinuation because of side effects over 52 weeks			Probability that treatment is best in reducing discontinuation because of side effects over 52 weeks
	Mean	Lower CI	Upper CI	
Olanzapine	0.0783	0.0021	0.4784	0.152
Amisulpride	0.0554	0.0006	0.3721	0.444
Zotepine	0.3821	0.0120	0.9750	0.011
Aripiprazole	0.1582	0.0026	0.7847	0.084
Paliperidone	0.3287	0.0039	0.9770	0.053
Risperidone	0.1032	0.0020	0.6735	0.134
Haloperidol	0.0922	0.0017	0.5386	0.116
Placebo	0.1094	0.0088	0.4047	0.006
	Probability of discontinuation because of other reasons over 52 weeks			Probability that treatment is best in reducing discontinuation because of other reasons over 52 weeks
	Mean	Lower CI	Upper CI	
Olanzapine	0.2730	0.0207	0.8596	0.030
Amisulpride	0.2435	0.0139	0.8324	0.123
Zotepine	0.2253	0.0074	0.8189	0.229
Aripiprazole	0.3520	0.0202	0.9218	0.046
Paliperidone	0.3848	0.0090	0.9479	0.105
Risperidone	0.1761	0.0086	0.7141	0.390
Haloperidol	0.2516	0.0151	0.8290	0.069
Placebo	0.2754	0.0273	0.7849	0.008

Note: Mean values and 95% credible intervals (CIs) of probabilities of (i) relapse, (ii) treatment discontinuation because of side effects and (iii) treatment discontinuation because of other reasons and probabilities of each treatment being the best in ranking for each of the above outcomes (data on ziprasidone not reported – ziprasidone not considered in ranking).

outcome for each of the drugs evaluated in the economic analysis, as well as the probability of each treatment being the best with respect to each of the outcomes considered. It can be seen that results for all antipsychotic drugs and all outcomes are characterised by high uncertainty, as expressed by wide 95% credible intervals.

Goodness of fit was tested using the deviance information criterion (DIC) tool. Three different models were tested: a fixed effects model, a random effects model assuming the same between-trials variance of distribution for all three outcomes and the random effects model described above, which allowed between-trials variance of distribution specific for each outcome. The data showed a considerably worse fit in the fixed effects model (DIC = 676.7) compared with the random effects model with common between-trials variance for all three outcomes (DIC = 661.6) and the random effects model with between-trials variance specific for each outcome (DIC = 659.9). Data fit well in both random effects models.

The probability of relapse and the probability of treatment discontinuation because of other reasons over 52 weeks were assumed to apply to every (yearly) cycle of the economic model. The probability of treatment discontinuation because of intolerable side effects over 52 weeks was assumed to apply only to the first year following initiation of a particular antipsychotic drug.

Probability of relapse under no treatment
People discontinuing treatment because of other reasons and moving to no treatment were assumed to stop treatment abruptly, and were therefore at high risk of relapse, reaching 50%, in the first 7 months (Viguera *et al.*, 1997). The annual probability of relapse for no treatment (following treatment discontinuation because of other reasons) was assumed to be equal to that estimated in the mixed treatment comparison analysis for placebo, with the exception of the first year following treatment discontinuation: for this year a higher probability of relapse was estimated, taking into account the data reported in Viguera and colleagues (1997).

Probability of relapse for depot antipsychotic medication
The annual probability of relapse for the third-line depot antipsychotic medication was taken from data reported in a Cochrane Review on flupentixol decanoate (David *et al.*, 1999). The reported probability (29.77%) may seem rather high; however, this estimate was based on intention-to-treat analysis. Considering that the depot antipsychotic was the final line of treatment in the model and no further discontinuations (which indicate lower compliance) were allowed, the figure of 29.77% seemed reasonable and appropriate to use in the analysis, to reflect potential non-compliance associated with depot antipsychotic medication.

7.2.6   Side effect data

The choice of side effects for consideration in the economic analysis was based on a number of criteria, including the number of people affected in the study population, the impact of side effects on the HRQoL, the magnitude of costs incurred by their management and the availability of respective clinical data specific to the treatment options assessed. Based on the above criteria, three side effects were modelled: weight gain, acute EPS and glucose intolerance/insulin resistance as a representative feature of the metabolic syndrome. It must be noted that acute EPS did not include cases of tardive dyskinesia; the latter differs from acute EPS as it has lasting effects and was not considered in the analysis. Omission of tardive dyskinesia and other neurological side effects, as well as other side effects of antipsychotic medication that may lead to impairments in quality of life (such as sexual dysfunction, increase in prolactin levels, and cardiovascular and gastrointestinal side effects), is acknowledged as a limitation of the economic analysis.

Weight gain

Data on rates of weight gain were derived from the guideline systematic review of side effects of antipsychotic medication (details of this review are provided in Chapter 6, Section 6.7). Only data reported as 'number of people experiencing an increase in weight of at least 7% from baseline' were considered for the economic analysis because this measure ensured a consistent and comparable definition of weight gain across trials.

Table 36 presents a summary of the data included in the guideline systematic review and utilised in the mixed treatment comparison analysis. Data were available for six out of the seven antipsychotic medications evaluated in the economic analysis (that is, olanzapine, amisulpride, aripiprazole, paliperidone, risperidone and haloperidol). In addition, four trials that compared quetiapine with another antipsychotic drug were considered in the mixed treatment comparison analysis: two of the trials compared quetiapine with risperidone, one with haloperidol and one with olanzapine. Although quetiapine was not considered in the economic analysis because of lack of clinical data in the area of relapse prevention, quetiapine data on weight gain were considered in the respective mixed treatment comparison analysis as they allowed indirect comparisons across some antipsychotic medications, thus strengthening inference. Trials comparing an SGA with an FGA other than haloperidol were not considered in the mixed treatment comparison analysis as data on FGAs other than haloperidol were sparse; for this reason FGAs other than haloperidol have been treated as a class in the guideline meta-analysis. Nevertheless, such a methodology was considered inappropriate for mixed treatment comparison analysis. The network of evidence resulting from the available data is shown in Figure 6.

Mixed treatment comparisons – simple random effects model for data on weight gain

A simple random effects model was constructed to estimate the relative effect between the $k = 7$ antipsychotic drugs evaluated in terms of weight gain, using data from the 17 RCTs summarised in Table 36. The model is similar to that described by Hasselblad (1998). The data for each trial j comprised a binomial likelihood:

$$r_{jk} \sim \text{Bin} (p_{jk}, n_{jk})$$

Table 36: Summary of data reported in the RCTs included in the guideline systematic review on weight gain ('increase in weight ≥7% from baseline') that were utilised in the economic analysis

Study	Time horizon (weeks)	1. Haloperidol (r/n)	2. Olanzapine (r/n)	3. Aripiprazole (r/n)	4. Quetiapine (r/n)	5. Paliperidone (r/n)	6. Risperidone (r/n)	7. Amisulpride (r/n)
1. LIEBERMAN2003A	24	51/132	95/131	-	-	-	-	
2. KONGSAKON2006	24	30/94	51/113	-	-	-	-	
3. Study S029	52	23/128	46/134	-	-	-	-	
4. KANE2002	4	10/103	-	11/203	-	-	-	
5. Arvanitis1997	6	2/52	-	-	20/157	-	-	
6. MCQUADE2004	26	-	58/155	21/154	-	-	-	
7. RIEDEL2007B	8	-	8/17	-	8/16	-	-	
8. DAVIDSON2007	6	-	25/115	-	-	13/118	-	
9. KANE2007A	6	-	16/123	-	-	6/118	-	
10. MARDER2007	6	-	23/109	-	-	8/112	-	
11. Conley2001	8	-	44/161	-	-	-	18/155	
12. MARTIN2002	24	-	66/186	-	-	-	-	39/186
13. POTKIN2003A	4	-	-	22/201	-	-	11/99	
14. CHAN2007B	4	-	-	2/49	-	-	4/34	
15. RIEDEL2005	12	-	-	-	3/22	-	1/22	
16. ZHONG2006	8	-	-	-	35/338	-	35/334	
17. Lecrubier2000	26	-	-	-	-	-	18/100	32/95

Figure 6: Evidence network for data on weight gain (defined as an increase of at least 7% of baseline weight).

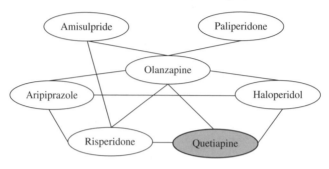

where p_{jk} is the probability of experiencing weight gain in trial j under treatment k, r_{jk} is the number of people experiencing weight gain in trial j under treatment k and n_{jk} is the total number of people at risk in trial j under treatment k.

Treatment effects were modelled on the log-odds scale and were assumed to be additive to the baseline treatment b in trial j:

$$logit(p_{jk}) = \mu_{jb} \quad \text{for } k = b;$$

$$logit(p_{jk}) = \mu_{jb} + \delta_{jkb} \quad \text{for } k \neq b$$

where μ_{jb} is the log odds of weight gain for baseline treatment b in trial j and δ_{jkb} is the trial-specific log-odds ratio of treatment k relative to treatment b.

By taking haloperidol (treatment A) as baseline, and the true mean treatment effects of the remaining six treatments B, C, D, *etc* relative to haloperidol as the basic parameters d_{AB}, d_{AC}, d_{AD}, the remaining functional parameters can be expressed in terms of these basic parameters, for example:

$$d_{BC} = d_{AC} - d_{AB}; \quad d_{BD} = d_{AD} - d_{AB}; \quad etc$$

The trial-specific log-odds ratios for every pair of treatments XY were assumed to come from normal random effects distributions:

$$\delta_{jXY} \sim N(d_{XY}, \sigma^2)$$

where d_{XY} is the true mean effect size between X and Y and σ^2 the variance of the normal distribution, which was assumed to be common in all pairs of treatments.

Vague priors were assigned to trial baselines, basic parameters and common variance:

$$\mu_{jb}, d_{AB}, d_{AC}, d_{AD}, \text{etc} \sim N(0, 100^2); \quad \sigma \sim \text{Uniform}(0, 2)$$

The results of mixed treatment comparison analysis were recorded as odds ratios (ORs) of weight gain for each of the six antipsychotics (olanzapine, amisulpride, aripiprazole, quetiapine, paliperidone and risperidone) versus haloperidol (which was used as baseline). Posterior distributions were estimated using Markov chain Monte Carlo simulation methods implemented in Winbugs 1.4 (Lunn *et al.*, 2000; Spiegelhalter *et al.*, 2001). The first 60,000 iterations were discarded and 300,000 further iterations were run; because of potentially high autocorrelation, the model was thinned so that every 30th simulation was retained. Consequently, 10,000 posterior simulations were recorded.

The Winbugs code used to estimate the ORs of weight gain for the six antipsychotic medications versus haloperidol is presented in Appendix 13, followed by summary statistics of a number of model parameters, including the ORs of each antipsychotic drug considered in the mixed treatment comparison model versus haloperidol and the between-trials variation.

Goodness of fit was tested using the residual deviance (resdev) and the deviance information criteria (DIC) tool. The simple random effects model demonstrated a better fit for the data (resdev = 45.06; DIC = 296.794) compared with a fixed effects model (resdev = 63.59; DIC = 306.519).

The probability of experiencing weight gain associated with haloperidol was calculated using data from RCTs included in the mixed treatment comparison analysis. The studies reporting increase in weight of at least 7% following use of haloperidol had time horizons ranging from 4 to 52 weeks. However, it was estimated that the rate of weight gain is not constant over time and that the majority of new cases of weight gain develop over the first 12 weeks following initiation of any particular antipsychotic drug. For this reason, only RCTs examining haloperidol with time horizons of up to 12 weeks were considered at the estimation of a weighted probability of weight gain for haloperidol. Rates of experiencing at least a 7% increase in weight reported in studies of duration shorter that 12 weeks were extrapolated to 12-week rates using exponential fit (assuming that the rate of experiencing an increase in weight of at least 7% remained stable over 12 weeks). The weighted average probability of weight gain for haloperidol was subsequently calculated from these estimates. The probabilities of weight gain (p_x) for each of the other antipsychotic medications included in the mixed treatment comparison analysis were then estimated using the following formulae:

$$p_x = odds_x \,/\, (1 + odds_x)$$

and

$$odds_x = OR_{x,b} * p_b \,/(1 - p_b)$$

where p_b is the probability of weight gain for haloperidol, $OR_{x,b}$ is the odds ratio for weight gain with each antipsychotic drug versus haloperidol as estimated in the mixed treatment comparison analysis, and $odds_x$ is the odds of each antipsychotic to cause weight gain.

Table 37: Increase in weight as a side effect of antipsychotic medications: ORs versus haloperidol, odds and absolute probabilities (mean values)

Antipsychotic drug	OR versus haloperidol	Odds	Probability of weight gain	Source
Haloperidol	1	0.2500	0.2000	Probability based on extrapolation of data from RCTs with time horizon up to 12 weeks included in the guideline systematic review
Olanzapine	2.8631	0.7158	0.4172	ORs versus haloperidol taken from mixed treatment comparison analysis (simple random effects model)
Amisulpride	1.8604	0.4651	0.3175	
Aripiprazole	0.7373	0.1843	0.1516	
Paliperidone	1.0779	0.2695	0.2123	
Risperidone	1.0895	0.2724	0.2141	

Table 37 provides the estimated probability of weight gain for haloperidol, the mean ORs of each antipsychotic drug examined in economic analysis versus haloperidol as derived from respective mixed treatment comparison analysis, as well as the estimated odds and probability of weight gain for each antipsychotic.

The drug-specific probabilities of experiencing weight gain derived from the above calculations were applied to the first year following initiation of a particular antipsychotic drug. In the following years, the probability of weight gain under this particular antipsychotic medication was assumed to be zero (for people at risk; that is, for those who had not already experienced weight gain).

Probability of experiencing weight gain under zotepine, depot antipsychotic medication and no treatment

The probability of experiencing weight gain for zotepine was assumed to equal the respective probability for risperidone; the probability for the third-line depot antipsychotic medication was assumed to equal that of haloperidol. People under no treatment were assumed to experience no increase in their weight equalling or exceeding 7% of their initial weight.

Acute extrapyramidal symptoms

Data on rates of acute EPS were derived from the guideline systematic review of side effects of antipsychotic medication (details of this review are provided in Chapter 6, Section 6.7). Of the available data, those expressing 'need for anticholinergic medication' were considered for the economic analysis as this measure was thought to capture more accurately the presence of acute EPS.

Table 38 presents a summary of the data on acute EPS included in the guideline systematic review and utilised in the mixed treatment comparison analysis.

Table 38: Summary of data reported in the RCTs included in the guideline systematic review on acute EPS ('need for anticholinergic medication') that were utilised in the economic analysis

Study	Time horizon (weeks)	1. Haloperidol (r/n)	2. Risperidone (r/n)	3. Olanzapine (r/n)	4. Zotepine (r/n)	5. Amisulpride (r/n)	6. Quetiapine (r/n)	7. Aripiprazole (r/n)	8. Paliperidone (r/n)
1. Claus1991	12	6/22	4/22	-	-	-	-	-	-
2. Mesotten1991	8	12/32	9/28	-	-	-	-	-	-
3. Chouinard1993	8	15/21	29/68	-	-	-	-	-	-
4. Marder1994	8	31/66	72/256	-	-	-	-	-	-
5. Peuskens1995	8	67/226	201/907	-	-	-	-	-	-
6. Blin1996	4	7/20	5/21	-	-	-	-	-	-
7. Janicak1999	6	22/32	12/30	-	-	-	-	-	-
8. Heck2000	6	10/37	11/40	-	-	-	-	-	-
9. Emsley1995	6	63/84	50/99	-	-	-	-	-	-
10. SCHOOLER2005	52	68/137	48/116	-	-	-	-	-	-
11. Csernansky2000	52	33/188	16/177	-	-	-	-	-	-
12. MARDER2003	104	26/30	23/33	-	-	-	-	-	-
13. Jones1998	54	17/23	9/21	3/21	-	-	-	-	-
14. Tollefson1997	6	315/660	-	228/1336	-	-	-	-	-
15. KONGSAKON2006	24	30/94	-	24/113	-	-	-	-	-
16. LIEBERMAN2003A	24	65/125	-	21/125	-	-	-	-	-
17. Klieser1996	4	25/45	-	-	6/20	-	-	-	-

Continued

Table 38: *(Continued)*

Study	Time horizon (weeks)	1. Haloperidol (r/n)	2. Risperidone (r/n)	3. Olanzapine (r/n)	4. Zotepine (r/n)	5. Amisulpride (r/n)	6. Quetiapine (r/n)	7. Aripiprazole (r/n)	8. Paliperidone (r/n)
18. Barnas1987	7	13/15	-	-	8/15	-	-	-	-
19. Petit1996	8	62/63	-	-	42/63	-	-	-	-
20. Delcker1990	6	13/20	-	-	-	11/21	-	-	-
21. Moller1997	6	54/96	-	-	-	28/95	-	-	-
22. Puech1998	4	26/64	-	-	-	45/194	-	-	-
23. Speller1997	52	25/31	-	-	-	10/29	-	-	-
24. Emsley1999	8	17/145	-	-	-	-	3/143	-	-
25. KANE2002	4	30/103	-	-	-	-	-	23/203	-
26. KASPER2003	52	245/430	-	-	-	-	-	196/853	-
27. Conley2001	8	-	61/188	53/189	-	-	-	-	-
28. Tran1997	28	-	55/167	34/172	-	-	-	-	-
29. Fleurot1997	8	-	26/113	-	-	35/115	-	-	-
30. Lecrubier2000	26	-	47/158	-	-	36/152	-	-	-
31. ZHONG2006	8	-	23/334	-	-	-	19/338	-	-
32. RIEDEL2005	12	-	9/22	-	-	-	2/22	-	-
33. CHAN2007B	4	-	14/34	-	-	-	-	12/49	-
34. SIROTA2006	26	-	-	6/21	-	-	5/19	-	-
35. KANE2007A	6	-	-	10/128	-	-	-	-	14/123
36. MARDER2007	6	-	-	13/109	-	-	-	-	10/112

Data on all seven antipsychotic medications evaluated in the economic analysis (olanzapine, amisulpride, zotepine, aripiprazole, paliperidone, risperidone and haloperidol) were available. In addition, four trials that compared quetiapine with another antipsychotic drug were considered in the mixed treatment comparison analysis: two of the trials compared quetiapine with risperidone, one with haloperidol and one with olanzapine. Although quetiapine was not considered in the economic analysis owing to lack of clinical data in the area of relapse prevention, quetiapine data on acute EPS were considered in the respective mixed treatment comparison analysis as they allowed indirect comparisons across drugs, thus strengthening inference. Trials comparing an SGA with an FGA other than haloperidol were not considered in the mixed treatment comparison analysis as data on FGAs other than haloperidol were sparse; for this reason FGAs other than haloperidol have been treated as a class in the guideline meta-analysis. Nevertheless, such a methodology was considered inappropriate for mixed treatment comparison analysis. The network of evidence constructed based on the available data is demonstrated in Figure 7.

Mixed treatment comparisons full random effects model for acute extrapyramidal side-effects data

A full random effects model was constructed to estimate the relative effect between the $k = 8$ antipsychotics evaluated in terms of development of acute EPS, using data from the 36 RCTs summarised in Table 38. The model is similar to that described above, utilised for the mixed treatment comparison analysis of data on weight gain, but takes into account the correlation structure induced by a three-arm trial (Jones1998) included in the 36 RCTs; this model structure relies on the realisation of

Figure 7: Evidence network for data on acute EPS (expressed as need for anticholinergic medication)

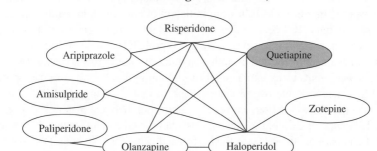

Note: Quetiapine (in grey-shaded oval) was considered in the mixed treatment comparison analysis because it allowed indirect comparisons between a number of medications, thus strengthening inference. However, it was not included in the economic analysis because no clinical data in the area of relapse prevention for people with schizophrenia that is in remission were available for quetiapine.

the bivariate normal distribution as a univariate marginal distribution and a univariate conditional distribution (Higgins & Whitehead, 1996):

$$\text{If} \quad \begin{pmatrix} x_1 \\ x_2 \end{pmatrix} \sim N\left[\begin{pmatrix} \mu_1 \\ \mu_2 \end{pmatrix}, \begin{pmatrix} \sigma^2 & \sigma^2/2 \\ \sigma^2/2 & \sigma^2 \end{pmatrix} \right]$$

$$\text{then} \quad x_1 \sim N(\mu_1, \sigma^2), \quad \text{and} \quad x_2 | x_1 \sim N\left(\mu_2 + \frac{1}{2}(x_1 - \mu_1), \frac{3}{4}\sigma^2 \right)$$

The results of this mixed treatment comparison analysis were also recorded as ORs of developing acute EPS for each of the seven antipsychotic drugs (olanzapine, amisulpride, aripiprazole, zotepine, quetiapine, paliperidone and risperidone) versus haloperidol (which was again used as baseline). Posterior distributions were estimated using Markov chain Monte Carlo simulation methods implemented in Winbugs 1.4 (Lunn *et al.*, 2000; Spiegelhalter *et al.*, 2001). The first 60,000 iterations were discarded, and 300,000 further iterations were run; because of potentially high autocorrelation, the model was thinned so that every 30th simulation was retained. Consequently, 10,000 posterior simulations were recorded.

The Winbugs code used to estimate the ORs of developing acute EPS for the seven antipsychotic medications versus haloperidol is presented in Appendix 13, followed by summary statistics of a number of model parameters, including the OR of each antipsychotic drug considered in the mixed treatment comparison model versus haloperidol and the between-trials variation. The resdev of the model was 75.93.

The probability of experiencing acute EPS for haloperidol was calculated using data from RCTs included in the mixed treatment comparison analysis. The studies reporting the need for anticholinergic medication following use of haloperidol had time horizons ranging from 4 to 104 weeks. However, it was estimated that the rate of developing acute EPS is not constant over time and that the majority of new cases of acute EPS develop over the first 8 weeks following initiation of any particular antipsychotic drug. For this reason, only RCTs examining haloperidol with time horizons of up to 8 weeks were considered at the estimation of a weighted probability of acute EPS for haloperidol. Rates of acute EPS reported in studies of duration shorter that 8 weeks were extrapolated to 8-week rates using exponential fit (assuming that the rate of development of acute EPS remained stable over 8 weeks). The weighted average probability of acute EPS for haloperidol was subsequently calculated from these estimates. The probability of acute EPS (p_x) for each of the other antipsychotic medications included in the mixed treatment comparison analysis was then estimated using the following formulae:

$$p_x = odds_x / (1 + odds_x)$$

and

$$odds_x = OR_{x,b} * p_b / (1 - p_b)$$

where p_b is the probability of acute EPS for haloperidol, $OR_{x,b}$ the odds ratio for acute EPS of each antipsychotic medication versus haloperidol as estimated in the mixed treatment comparison analysis, and $odds_x$ the odds of each antipsychotic leading to development of acute EPS.

Table 39 provides the estimated probability of weight gain for haloperidol, the mean ORs of each antipsychotic drug examined in economic analysis versus haloperidol as derived from respective mixed treatment comparison analysis, as well as the estimated odds and probability of weight gain for each antipsychotic.

The drug-specific probabilities of developing acute EPS derived from the above calculations were applied to the first year following initiation of a particular antipsychotic drug. In the following years, the probability of developing acute EPS under this particular antipsychotic medication was estimated to be 10% of the probability applied to the first year.

Probability of developing acute extrapyramidal side effects under depot antipsychotic medication and no treatment

The probability of developing acute EPS under the third-line depot antipsychotic medication was taken from data reported in a Cochrane Review on flupentixol decanoate (David *et al.*, 1999). People under no treatment were assumed to develop no acute EPS.

Glucose intolerance/insulin resistance and diabetes

Glucose intolerance/insulin resistance was modelled as a representative feature of the metabolic syndrome, the incidence of which is high in people taking antipsychotic

Table 39: Development of acute EPS as a side effect of antipsychotic medications: ORs versus haloperidol, odds and absolute probabilities (mean values)

Antipsychotic drug	OR versus haloperidol	Odds	Probability of weight gain	Source
Haloperidol	1	1.1586	0.5367	Probability based on extrapolation of data from RCTs with time horizon up to 8 weeks included in the guideline systematic review
Olanzapine	0.2631	0.3048	0.2336	ORs versus haloperidol taken from mixed treatment comparison analysis (full random effects model)
Amisulpride	0.3993	0.4626	0.3163	
Zotepine	0.1476	0.1710	0.1461	
Aripiprazole	0.2517	0.2916	0.2258	
Paliperidone	0.2983	0.3456	0.2569	
Risperidone	0.4743	0.5495	0.3546	

medication. The metabolic syndrome is a predictor of type-2 diabetes and coronary heart disease. Both conditions are associated with a number of events and complications that cause significant impairment in the HRQoL and incur substantial healthcare costs. Because there is a high correlation between the two conditions, it was decided to only model events (complications) resulting from the development of diabetes mellitus to avoid the double-counting of health events and the overestimation of the (negative) impact of metabolic syndrome on the cost effectiveness of antipsychotic drugs. Modelling health events as complications of diabetes was preferred to linking them to coronary heart disease because estimates of the incidence of diabetes complications have been reported in the literature, having been derived from a large prospective cohort study of people with diabetes mellitus in the UK (UK Prospective Diabetes Study [UKPDS]; Stratton *et al.*, 2000).

The relationship between specific antipsychotic medications, risk for metabolic syndrome and the development of type-2 diabetes has not been fully explored and relevant data that are appropriate for modelling are sparse. A systematic review of the metabolic effects of antipsychotic medications concluded that antipsychotics associated with greatest increases in body weight were also associated with a consistent pattern of clinically significant insulin resistance (Newcomer & Haupt, 2006). The authors noted that correlations between change in weight and change in plasma glucose values were weaker overall than correlations between weight change and change in insulin resistance, and that unchanged plasma glucose levels did not preclude clinically significant increases in insulin resistance. The results of the review indicated that the relative risk for diabetes mellitus during antipsychotic medication use generally matched the rank order of weight-gain potential for the different antipsychotics, although a significant minority of people taking antipsychotics might experience glucose dysregulation independent of weight gain.

A systematic review and meta-analysis of studies comparing the risk for diabetes between SGAs and FGAs in people with schizophrenia and related psychotic disorders found that SGAs led to a greater risk for diabetes compared with FGAs (Smith *et al.*, 2008). Besides being associated with impaired glucose levels and insulin resistance, antipsychotic drugs have been shown to lead directly to development of diabetes shortly after their initiation by people with schizophrenia (Saddichha *et al.*, 2008; van Winkel *et al.*, 2006, 2008).

Given that available data on the risk for glucose intolerance and/or diabetes associated with specific antipsychotic drugs are limited, the probability of developing glucose intolerance/insulin resistance (associated with greater future risk for developing diabetes) and the probability of developing diabetes directly in the first year of antipsychotic use were estimated as follows: first, estimates on these two probabilities specific to haloperidol were made, based on reported data in published literature. Second, drug-specific probabilities of weight gain, estimated as described in the previous section, were used to calculate relative risks of weight gain for each SGA included in the analysis versus haloperidol. Relative risks for weight gain were assumed to be equal to relative risks for developing glucose intolerance/insulin resistance and diabetes because existing evidence suggested a high correlation between increase in weight and insulin resistance, as discussed above (Newcomer & Haupt,

2006). Finally, relative risks of each SGA versus haloperidol were multiplied by the haloperidol-specific estimated probabilities of developing glucose intolerance/insulin resistance and diabetes to obtain respective probabilities for each SGA assessed in the economic analysis. The resulting estimates, based on the correlation between glucose intolerance/risk for diabetes and weight gain, may be potentially conservative because an additional mechanism leading to glucose dysregulation, independent of weight increases, appears to exist (Newcomer & Haupt, 2006). On the other hand, the fact that the rank order of relative risk for diabetes has been shown to match the rank order of weight-gain potential for the different antipsychotics, according to findings of the same study, does not guarantee that the relative risk of developing intolerance/insulin resistance and diabetes of each SGA versus haloperidol is actually equal to their in-between relative risk of weight-gain. The described method for estimating absolute probabilities for developing intolerance/insulin resistance and diabetes for each SGA in the model was deemed necessary because of a lack of other appropriate data, but is acknowledged as a limitation of the economic analysis.

The estimated probability of directly developing diabetes during the first year of initiation of haloperidol was based on respective rates reported in the literature for people with schizophrenia under antipsychotic medication (van Winkel *et al.*, 2006, 2008). Since these studies examined populations initiated on a number of antipsychotics, including SGAs, and the risk for developing diabetes is known to be higher for SGAs compared with FGAs (Smith *et al.*, 2008), the probability of developing diabetes within the first year of initiation of haloperidol was estimated to be lower than the respective figures reported in the literature associated with use of antipsychotics generally. Similarly, the probability of glucose intolerance/insulin resistance within the first year of initiation of haloperidol was estimated taking into account relevant data identified in the guideline systematic review of clinical evidence. The resulting estimates for haloperidol that were used in the economic analysis were 2% (first year probability of developing diabetes) and 15% (first year probability of developing glucose intolerance/insulin resistance).

The resulting probabilities of developing diabetes/glucose intolerance for all antipsychotics following the methodology described above, and the ranking of antipsychotics in terms of risk for diabetes, were consistent with evidence suggesting that olanzapine is strongly associated with diabetic events while aripiprazole, risperidone and haloperidol are poorly associated with such events (Dumouchel *et al.*, 2008).

The probability of developing diabetes directly was applied only to the first year of initiation of any particular antipsychotic. Similarly, it was assumed that development of glucose intolerance/insulin resistance occurred only within the first year of initiation of any specific drug. People who did not develop insulin resistance within the first year of initiation of a particular antipsychotic were assumed to develop no insulin resistance in the following years, provided that they remained on the same drug. However, insulin resistance that developed within the first year of initiation of a specific antipsychotic was assumed to be permanent and to result in an increased risk for diabetes over a lifetime. The annual transition probability from impaired glucose tolerance to developing diabetes was taken from Gillies and colleagues

(2008). It is acknowledged that applying the probabilities of developing diabetes and insulin resistance only to the first year of initiation of any particular antipsychotic is likely to be conservative and to underestimate the impact of the metabolic syndrome on the relative cost effectiveness of antipsychotics. On the other hand, insulin resistance that developed within the first year of initiation of a particular antipsychotic was assumed to be permanent and to lead to a lifetime risk of developing diabetes.

Complications from diabetes
The probabilities of complications following development of diabetes were estimated based on data reported in the UKPDS (Stratton *et al.*, 2000). This was a 20-year prospective study that recruited 5,102 people with type-2 diabetes in 23 clinical centres based in England, Northern Ireland and Scotland. The study reported incidence rates of complications for different levels of haemoglobin A_{1C} concentration (Hgb A_{1C}). Annual probabilities of complications were estimated based on the available data, assuming that 20% of people in the model had Hgb A_{1C} 7 to <8%, 30% of people had 8 to <9%, 30% of people had 9 to <10% and 20% of people had ≥10%. These assumptions took account of the clinical experience of the GDG, according to whom, people with schizophrenia in general do not have good glycaemic control. Incidence of complications in Stratton and colleagues (2000) were provided as aggregate figures of fatal and non-fatal events for each complication. To estimate the probability of fatal and non-fatal events for each complication separately in the economic model, the reported overall incidence of deaths related to diabetes at each level of Hgb A_{1C} was applied to the reported incidence of each complication at the same Hgb A_{1C} level to estimate the proportion of fatal events reported for each complication.

7.2.7   Mortality estimates

The risk of death is higher in people with schizophrenia than in the general population (McGrath *et al.*, 2008). Transition to death in the model occurred as a result of suicide or other reasons, including increased physical morbidity characterising people with schizophrenia that leads to increased mortality. It was assumed that the risk of death was independent of specific antipsychotic drug use, owing to lack of sufficient data to support the opposite hypothesis. Instead, all people in the model were subject to increased mortality relative to the general population, common to all antipsychotic drugs. To calculate the number of deaths occurring each year, the increased standardised mortality ratio (SMR) observed in people with schizophrenia (McGrath *et al.*, 2008) was multiplied by the age- and gender-specific mortality rates for people aged 25 years and above in the general population in England and Wales (Office for National Statistics, 2008). The number of deaths was calculated on the basis that the study population (people with schizophrenia) had a male to female ratio of 1.4 to 1 (McGrath, 2006).

Death was assumed to occur in the middle of every year (cycle); this means that over the year death occurred, people incurred half of the costs and gained half of the QALYs they were expected to incur and gain, respectively, had they not died.

7.2.8   Utility data and estimation of quality-adjusted life years

To express outcomes in the form of QALYs, the health states of the economic model needed to be linked to appropriate utility scores. Utility scores represent the HRQoL associated with specific health states on a scale from 0 (death) to 1 (perfect health); they are estimated using preference-based measures that capture people's preferences on, and perceptions of, HRQoL in the health states under consideration.

Systematic review of published utility scores for people with schizophrenia
The systematic search of the literature identified six studies that reported utility scores for specific health states and events associated with schizophrenia (Chouinard & Albright, 1997; Cummins *et al.*, 1998; Glennie, 1997; Lenert *et al.*, 2004; Revicki *et al.*, 1996; Sevy *et al.*, 2001).

Chouinard and Albright (1997) generated health states using data on PANSS scores from 135 people with schizophrenia participating in a Canadian multicentre RCT of risperidone versus haloperidol. Cluster analysis identified three clusters that included 130 of the participants with mild, moderate and severe symptomatology. A health-state profile was described for each cluster, including additional information on adverse events, obtained by assessing the average scores of Extrapyramidal Symptom Rating Scale (ESRS) subscales of parkinsonism, dyskinesia and dystonia in each treatment group. Subsequently, 100 psychiatric nurses in the US were asked to assign utility values to each of the three health states using standard gamble (SG) methods.

Glennie (1997) described the development of health-state profiles specific to antipsychotic medications, according to average PANSS scores reported in risperidone trials included in a systematic review. The impairment in HRQoL caused by the need for hospitalisation and the presence of EPS were also considered. In this case, seven people with schizophrenia in Canada who were in a stable state were asked to value the generated health states using the SG technique.

Lenert and colleagues (2004) valued health states associated with schizophrenia constructed from the results of principal component analysis of PANSS scores; the scores were obtained from people with schizophrenia participating in a large multi-centre effectiveness trial conducted in the US. This analysis led to the clustering of types of symptoms and the final development of eight health states describing different types and severity of schizophrenia symptoms. Moreover, the presence of common adverse events from antipsychotic medication was taken into account at valuation. The resulting health states were valued by a sample of 441 people from the general US population using the SG technique.

Revicki and colleagues (1996) developed five hypothetical health states (vignettes) describing various levels of schizophrenia symptoms, functioning and well-being in inpatient and outpatient settings, based on relevant descriptions available in the medical literature and expert opinion. The health states were subsequently valued by three different groups of people in the UK, using different valuation techniques: 49 people with schizophrenia in remission and their carers rated the health states using categorical rating scales (RS) and paired comparisons (PC);

a number of psychiatrists valued the health states using categorical RS and SG techniques. The study reported the psychiatrist-derived utility scores using SG, as well as the utility scores derived from people with schizophrenia and their carers using PC.

Cummins and colleagues (1998) linked health states observed in people with schizophrenia participating in an international RCT of olanzapine versus haloperidol with specific health states generated using the IHRQoL. The methodology used to link these two different sets of health state profiles was not clearly described. IHRQoL is a generic measure of HRQoL, consisting of three dimensions: disability, physical distress and emotional distress (Rosser *et al.*, 1992). The composite health states derived from this generic measure have been valued using the SG method. However, detailed description of the methods of valuation has not been made available and no other application of this instrument has been identified in the literature (Brazier *et al.*, 2007b).

Finally, Sevy and colleagues (2001) reported valuations of people with schizophrenia for a large number of side effects resulting from antipsychotic medication, using SG methods. The purpose of the study was to assess the relationship between the utility values obtained and the study population's willingness to pay to remove such side effects. The resulting scores were reported unadjusted because death was not used as anchor value 'zero' and are therefore not appropriate for use in economic modelling.

Table 40 summarises the methods used to derive health states and subsequent utility scores associated with schizophrenia health states and events, as well as the results of the first five studies described above, because these reported utility scores that could potentially be used in the guideline's economic analysis.

In addition to the above studies, a number of studies reported utility scores for people with schizophrenia that were generated using generic preference-based measures of HRQoL (Kasckow *et al.*, 2001; Knapp *et al.*, 2008; König *et al.*, 2007; Lewis *et al.*, 2006a; Sciolla *et al.*, 2003; Strakowski *et al.*, 2005; Tunis *et al.*, 1999). However, any utility scores reported in these studies expressed the overall HRQoL of the study population and were not linked to specific health states; consequently, they were not useful for economic modelling.

König and colleagues (2007) assessed and valued the HRQoL of people with schizophrenic, schizotypal or delusional disorders using the EQ-5D. They concluded that EQ-5D had reasonable validity in this group of people, but its association with the positive subscale of PANSS was rather weak. For this reason it was suggested that EQ-5D be used in combination with disease-specific instruments in such populations so that all aspects of HRQoL be captured. The study did not report utility scores relating to specific health states experienced by the study population. Lewis and colleagues (2006a) evaluated the cost effectiveness of FGAs versus SGAs, and clozapine versus SGAs, in people with schizophrenia responding poorly to, or being intolerant of, current antipsychotic treatment in two RCTs conducted in the UK (CUtLASS Bands 1 and 2). Health benefits from treatment were determined by measuring the participants' HRQoL using the EQ-5D at various points in the trials.

Table 40: Summary of studies reporting utility scores relating to specific health states and events associated with schizophrenia

Study	Definition of health states	Valuation method	Population valuing	Results
Chouinard & Albright, 1997	Based on cluster analysis of PANSS scores combined with information from data on ESRS subscales of parkinsonism, dyskinesia and dystonia, all obtained from 135 people with schizophrenia in Canada who participated in a multicentre three-arm RCT comparing risperidone versus haloperidol versus placebo	SG	100 psychiatric nurses in the US	Mild health state: 0.61 Moderate health state: 0.36 Severe health state: 0.29
Cummins et al., 1998	Health states of people with schizophrenia participating in a RCT linked with health states generated using the IHRQoL	SG	Unclear	Response – no EPS: 0.960 Response – EPS: 0.808 Need for acute treatment/relapse – no EPS: 0.762 Need for acute treatment/relapse – EPS: 0.631
Glennie, 1997	Based on average scores from each of the three PANSS subscales (positive, negative and general psychopathology) reported in risperidone trials included in a systematic review; need for hospitalisation and presence of EPS also considered	SG	7 people with stable schizophrenia in Canada	Mild delusional symptoms – risperidone: 0.89 Mild delusional symptoms – haloperidol: 0.86 Moderate delusional symptoms: 0.82 Hospitalisation: –0.07 Presence of EPS: –0.07
Lenert et al., 2004	Based on principal component analysis followed by cluster analysis of PANSS scores (positive, negative and general psychopathology subscales) obtained from people with schizophrenia participating in	SG	441 people from US general population	Mild (all areas low): 0.88 Moderate type I (negative predominant): 0.75 Moderate type II (positive predominant): 0.74

Continued

Table 40: *(Continued)*

Study	Definition of health states	Valuation method	Population valuing	Results
	an effectiveness trial in the US; presence of adverse events from medication also considered			Severe type I (negative predominant): 0.63 Severe type II (positive and cognitive predominant): 0.65 Severe type III (negative and cognitive predominant): 0.53 Severe type IV (positive predominant): 0.62 Extremely severe (all symptoms high): 0.42 Orthostatic hypotension: −0.912% Weight gain: −0.959% Tardive dyskinesia: −0.857% Pseudo-parkinsonism: −0.888% Akathisia: −0.898%
Revicki *et al.*, **1996**	Vignettes based on medical literature and expert opinion	SG	UK psychiatrists	Outpatient, excellent functioning: 0.83 Outpatient, good functioning: 0.73 Outpatient, moderate functioning: 0.70 Outpatient, negative symptoms: 0.60 Inpatient, acute positive symptoms: 0.56
		PC	49 people with schizophrenia in remission in the UK	Outpatient, excellent functioning: 0.77 Outpatient, good functioning: 0.57 Outpatient, moderate functioning: 0.49 Outpatient, negative symptoms: 0.30 Inpatient, acute positive symptoms: 0.19
		PC	Carers of people with schizophrenia in the UK	Outpatient, excellent functioning: 0.69 Outpatient, good functioning: 0.51 Outpatient, moderate functioning: 0.44 Outpatient, negative symptoms: 0.32 Inpatient, acute positive symptoms: 0.22

Knapp and colleagues (2008) also obtained EQ-5D scores from outpatients with schizophrenia participating in a European multicentre observational study to evaluate the cost effectiveness of olanzapine versus other oral and depot antipsychotics. In both of the above economic studies, the obtained EQ-5D scores were not attached to specific health states and therefore could not be applied to the health states described in the guideline economic analysis.

Sciolla and colleagues (2003) assessed the HRQoL of outpatients with schizophrenia aged over 45 years using the 36-item Short-Form health survey (SF-36). The authors stated that SF-36 adequately measured the impairment in HRQoL associated with schizophrenia in middle aged and older people. Strakowski and colleagues (2005) and Tunis and colleagues (1999) reported SF-36 scores in people with schizophrenia who participated in two different clinical trials of olanzapine versus haloperidol; both studies reported SF-36 scores at baseline and at end of treatment for each treatment group. None of the three studies that used the SF-36 linked the obtained scores to specific health states associated with schizophrenia; thus the data reported were not useful in the guideline economic analysis.

Kasckow and colleagues (2001) measured the quality of life of inpatients and outpatients with schizophrenia using the Quality of Well-Being Scale (QWB). Although hospitalisation and high levels of positive symptoms were shown to be associated with lower QWB scores, no health states that could be used in the guideline economic analysis were specified and linked with QWB-generated utility scores.

NICE recommends the EQ-5D as the preferred measure of HRQoL in adults for use in cost-utility analysis. NICE also suggests that the measurement of changes in HRQoL should be reported directly from people with the condition examined, and the valuation of health states should be based on public preferences elicited using a choice-based method, such as time trade-off (TTO) or SG, in a representative sample of the UK population. At the same time, it is recognised that EQ-5D data may not be available or may be inappropriate for the condition or effects of treatment (NICE, 2008a).

None of the studies summarised in Table 40 derived utility values using EQ-5D scores valued from members of the UK general population. Three of the five studies generated health states based on analysis of condition-specific PANSS scores (Chouinard & Albright, 1997; Glennie, 1997; Lenert *et al.*, 2004). Valuations in these three studies were made by healthcare professionals in the US (Chouinard & Albright, 1997), by people with schizophrenia in Canada (Glennie, 1997) or by members of the public in the US (Lenert *et al.*, 2004). All three studies used the SG technique. Revicki and colleagues (1996) developed health states based on vignettes, valued by people with schizophrenia and their carers using RS or PC, or by psychiatrists using SG. Finally, Cummins and colleagues (1998) linked health states associated with schizophrenia with health states generated using the IHRQoL. Although the last study used a generic measure to describe health states associated with schizophrenia, the methodology adopted in developing and valuing health states was not clear.

A comparison of data from the three studies that analysed PANSS scores to generate utility scores illustrated that Glennie (1997) reported the most conservative difference in utility scores between health states (difference between moderate and mild states 0.04–0.07; no severe state valued); Chouinard and Albright (1997) reported the greatest differences in utility between health states (difference between moderate and mild states 0.25; between severe and mild states 0.32); and Lenert and colleagues (2004) reported moderate changes in utility between health states (difference between moderate and mild states 0.13–0.14; between severe and mild states 0.22–0.35; and between very severe and mild states 0.46). It was therefore decided to use utility data from Lenert and colleagues (2004) in the base-case analysis and data from the other two studies that utilised PANSS scores (Chouinard & Albright, 1997; Glennie, 1997) in sensitivity analysis. The data by Lenert and colleagues (2004) were selected for the base-case analysis for a number of reasons: they were comprehensive, covering a wide range of health states of varying types and severity of symptoms; the described health states were derived from principal component analysis of condition-specific PANSS scores; the methodology was described in detail; the valuations were made by members of the general population using SG (although the population was from the US and not the UK); detailed utility data for a number of adverse events associated with antipsychotic medication were also reported; the study provided comprehensive data for linking PANSS scores to specific health states and subsequently to utility scores so that, apart from modelling exercises, these data may be used in cost-utility analyses conducted alongside clinical trials measuring PANSS scores, thus increasing comparability across economic evaluations of antipsychotic treatments for people with schizophrenia. There is at least one example where these data have been used in a cost-utility analysis undertaken alongside effectiveness trials (CATIE, Rosenheck *et al.*, 2006).

Development of health states from condition-specific instruments, such as PANSS, may be appropriate for people with schizophrenia because these are likely to capture more aspects of the HRQoL relating to emotional and mental status; they may also be more sensitive for a given dimension (Brazier *et al.*, 2007a). Generic measures, such as EQ-5D, could miss some dimensions of HRQoL associated with mental symptoms. EQ-5D has been demonstrated to associate weakly with the positive subscale of PANSS. For this reason, it has been suggested that EQ-5D be used in combination with disease-specific instruments in people with schizophrenia (König *et al.*, 2007).

The data reported in Revicki and colleagues (1996) were not considered further because they were based on vignettes, were not valued by members of the public and, in two of the participating groups, valuations were not made using choice-based methods. Data from Cummins and colleagues (1998) were also excluded from further consideration because the methods used for their derivation were not clearly reported.

Linking utility scores to health states of remission and relapse
To link the model states of remission and relapse with the utility scores reported for PANSS-generated health states in Lenert and colleagues (2004), the GDG estimated that the HRQoL of people in remission (model state) corresponded by 40% to HRQoL in the (PANSS-generated) mild state and by 60% to HRQoL in the moderate state (30% in moderate state type I and 30% in moderate state type II); the HRQoL of people in relapse corresponded by 60% to HRQoL in the severe state type IV and by 40% to HRQoL in the very severe state.

The GDG estimated that the decrement in HRQoL of people in schizophrenia while in acute episode (relapse) lasted for 6 months.

Utility scores for acute extrapyramidal symptoms and weight gain
The utility scores for acute EPS and weight gain were also taken from Lenert and colleagues (2004). The reduction in HRQoL caused by acute EPS corresponded to that reported for pseudo-parkinsonism and was estimated to last for 3 months, after which significant improvement in acute EPS symptoms was estimated to occur (either spontaneously after dose adjustment or following treatment). The reduction in HRQoL caused by weight gain was permanent because an increase in weight following use of antipsychotic medication was estimated to remain over a lifetime.

Utility scores for diabetes complications
Disutility owing to complications from diabetes was taken from the UKPDS (Clarke *et al.*, 2002). Utility scores in this study were generated using patient-reported EQ-5D scores; these were subsequently valued using EQ-5D UK tariff values. Disutility of diabetes without complications was not considered in the economic model as it was estimated to be negligible when compared with the impairment in HRQoL caused by schizophrenia.

7.2.9   Cost data

Costs associated with pharmacological treatment of people with schizophrenia and related events were calculated by combining resource-use estimates with respective national unit costs. Costs of the relapse and remission states consisted of relevant drug acquisition costs, outpatient, primary and community care costs, costs of treating acute episodes (relapse state only) and residential care costs. People under no treatment (following treatment discontinuation for reasons other than relapse or presence of intolerable side effects) were assumed to incur no costs until they experienced a relapse. Costs associated with baseline measurements and laboratory tests for monitoring purposes were omitted from the analysis, because they were estimated to be the same for all antipsychotic medications evaluated. All costs were uplifted to 2007 prices using the Hospital and Community Health Services (HCHS) Pay and Prices Index (Curtis, 2007). Costs were discounted at an annual rate of 3.5% annually, as recommended by NICE (NICE, 2008a).

Drug acquisition costs
Drug acquisition costs were taken from BNF 56 (British Medical Association & the Royal Pharmaceutical Society of Great Britain, 2008), with the exception of the cost of risperidone which was taken from the Electronic Drug Tariff (NHS, Business Services Authority, 2008) because risperidone recently became available in generic form but BNF 56 has not captured this information. The daily dosage of antipsychotic drugs was based on the national average daily quantity (ADQ) values reported by the NHS (NHS, The Information Centre, 2008c). In cases where no ADQ values were available, the average daily quantity was estimated based on BNF guidance. Some of the reported doses were slightly adjusted to match tablet/injection doses and usual injection intervals. The ADQs and the drug acquisition cost, as well as the monthly

ingredient cost for each drug included in the analysis, are reported in Table 41. Annual drug acquisition costs for people experiencing relapse were different because use of antipsychotic medication for relapse prevention was assumed to be interrupted during the acute episode and replaced with another antipsychotic (olanzapine) over this period of relapse.

Outpatient, primary and community care costs
Estimates on resource use associated with outpatient, primary and community care were based on data reported in a UK study (Almond *et al.*, 2004). The study collected information on healthcare resource use from 145 people with schizophrenia randomly selected from psychiatric caseloads drawn from urban and suburban areas of Leicester. Of the sample, 77 had experienced a recent relapse, defined as re-emergence or aggravation of psychotic symptoms for at least 7 days during the 6 months prior to the study ('relapse group'); the remaining 68 had not experienced such a relapse in the 6 months before the initiation of the study ('non-relapse group'). Healthcare resource use for each group over 6 months was collected prospectively from case notes and interviews with the study participants. The study also reported

Table 41: ADQs, drug acquisition costs and estimated monthly ingredient costs of antipsychotic medications included in the economic model

Drug	ADQ Unit	Unit cost (BNF 56, September 2008)	Monthly cost
Amisulpride	400 mg	Generic 400 mg, 60-tab = £114.45	£57.23
Haloperidol	8 mg	Generic 1.5 mg, 28-tab = £2.84; 5 mg, 28 = £7.71; 10 mg, 28 = £9.06	£14.35
Olanzapine	10 mg	Zyprexa 10 mg, 28-tab = £79.45; 15 mg, 28-tab = £119.18	£85.13
Aripiprazole	15 mg[a]	Abilify 15 mg, 28-tab = £101.63	£108.89
Paliperidone	9 mg[a]	Invega 9 mg, 28-tab = £145.92	£156.34
Risperidone	5 mg	Generic 1 mg, 60-tab = £28.38; 4 mg, 60-tab = £106.65[b]	£67.52
Zotepine	200 mg	Zoleptil 100 mg, 90-tab = £94.55	£63.03
Flupentixol decanoate	3.6 mg	Depixol Conc. 100 mg/mL, 1-mL amp = £6.25 (administered every 4 weeks)	£6.70

[a] No ADQ data available – daily dosage estimated based on BNF guidance.
[b] Based on the Electronic Drug Tariff as of 1 December 2008 (NHS, Business Services Authority, 2008).

inpatient care resource use for the two groups, but these data were not utilised in the economic model. It is acknowledged that the data reported in this study are not very recent (the study was conducted in the 1990s), but no more up-to-date data that were appropriate to inform the economic analysis were identified in the literature.

It was assumed that, over 1 year, people in the remission state in the model (including people who discontinued treatment because of side effects or any other reason for the cycle within which discontinuation occurred) consumed twice as much health resources as those reported for the 'non-relapse' group in Almond and colleagues (2004) over 6 months. Within a year, people in the relapse model state were assumed to consume the resources reported for the relapse group over 6 months and the resources reported for the non-relapse group over the remaining 6 months. Therefore, the annual resource use of outpatient, primary and community care for the relapse state consisted of the 6-month resource use reported for the relapse group (in Almond and colleagues, 2004), plus the 6-month resource use reported for the non-relapse group. Reported resource use in Almond and colleagues (2004) was combined with appropriate national unit costs (Curtis, 2007; Department of Health, 2008a) to estimate total annual outpatient, primary and community care costs for people in the model states of remission and relapse. The reported resource use for the relapse and the non-relapse groups in Almond and colleagues (2004) as well as the respective UK unit costs are presented in Table 42. Based on the above described methods and assumptions, the annual outpatient, primary and community care costs for the states of remission and relapse were estimated at £5,401 and £4,323, respectively (2007 prices).

Costs associated with management of acute episodes
People experiencing an acute episode (relapse) were assumed to be treated either as inpatients or by CRHTTs. Glover and colleagues (2006) examined the reduction in hospital admission rates in England, following implementation of CRHTT. They reported that the introduction of CRHTT was followed by a 22.7% reduction in hospital admission levels. Based on this data, the economic analysis assumed that 77.3% of people with schizophrenia experiencing a relapse would be admitted to hospital, and the remaining 22.7% would be seen by CRHTTs. However, all people under long-term hospital care while in remission (see costs of residential care in next subsection) were assumed to be treated as inpatients when they experienced an acute episode.

The average cost of hospitalisation for people in acute episode was estimated by multiplying the average duration of hospitalisation for people with schizophrenia, schizotypal and delusional disorders (F20-F29, according to ICD-10) in England in 2006/07 (NHS, The Information Centre, 2008a) by the national average unit cost per bed-day in a mental health acute care inpatient unit for adults in 2006/07 (Department of Health, 2008a).

Regarding the management of people with schizophrenia experiencing an acute episode by CRHTTs, the GDG estimated that treatment lasted 8 weeks. This period was multiplied by the unit cost of each case treated by CRHTTs per care staff per week (Curtis, 2007) to provide a total cost associated with the management of acute episodes by CRHTTs.

Table 42: Resource use over 6 months and unit costs associated with outpatient, primary and community care for people with schizophrenia

Service	Mean usage per person (Almond *et al.*, 2004)		Unit cost (2007 prices)	Sources of unit costs; comments
	Non-relapse	Relapse		
Outpatient psychiatric visits	1.4	2.1	£140	Department of Health, 2008a; cost per face-to-face contact in outpatient mental health services
Outpatient other visits	0.1	0.3	£93	Department of Health, 2008a; cost per attendance in day care
Day hospital visits	2.3	2.1	£93	Department of Health, 2008a; cost per attendance in day care
Community mental health centre visits	2.4	1.4	£124	Department of Health, 2008a; cost per contact with CMHTs
Day care centre visits	5.9	0.9	£93	Department of Health, 2008a; cost per attendance in day care
Group therapy	0.4	0.1	£93	Department of Health, 2008a; cost per attendance in day care
Sheltered workshop	1.1	0	£49	Curtis, 2007. Sheltered work schemes: £8.1 gross cost per hour; 6 hours per contact assumed
Specialist education	2.9	0	£93	Department of Health, 2008a; cost per attendance in day care

				Assumption
Other (not specified)	0.6	0	£50	
Psychiatrist visits	2.5	2.3	£240	Department of Health, 2008a; cost per domiciliary visit by psychiatrist
Psychologist visits	0	0	£196	Department of Health, 2008a; cost per domiciliary visit by psychologist
GP visits	1.8	1.6	£58	Curtis, 2007; cost per home visit £55 including travel, qualification and direct care staff costs – 2006 prices
District nurse visits	0.1	0	£24	Curtis, 2007; cost per home visit for community nurse including qualification costs and travelling
CPN visits	12.6	5.2	£26	Curtis, 2007; cost per hour of client contact for community nurse specialist £75; assuming 20 minutes' duration of visit; including qualification costs and travelling
Social worker visits	0.1	0.4	£41	Curtis, 2007; cost per hour of face-to-face contact £124; assuming 20 minutes' duration of visit – qualification costs not available
Occupational therapist visits	0	0.8	£39	Curtis, 2007; cost of community occupational therapist per home visit including qualification and travelling costs
Home help/care worker	0.4	0.6	£19	Curtis, 2007; cost of care worker per hour of face-to-face week day programme – qualification costs not available

Table 43: Hospital, and crisis resolution and home treatment team costs per person in acute episode (relapse)

Treatment	Duration	Unit cost (2007 prices)	Total cost	% of people treated
Acute hospital	111 days (NHS, 2008a)	£259/day (Department of Health, 2008a)	£28,645	77.3 (Glover *et al.*, 2006)
CRHTT	8 weeks (GDG estimate)	£264 per case per care staff per week (Curtis, 2007)	£2,112	22.7 (Glover *et al.*, 2006)
Olanzapine 15mg/day	111 days (NHS, 2008a)	£4.26/day (BNF 56)	£471	100 (assumption)

All people experiencing an acute episode were assumed to interrupt the antipsychotic medication they were taking during remission and receive olanzapine at a dose of 15mg/day (The Royal College of Psychiatrists, personal communication, 2008) for the duration of the acute episode, which was assumed to be equal to the duration of hospitalisation for people with schizophrenia (as reported by the NHS, The Information Centre, 2008a). Olanzapine was chosen as a representative SGA for the treatment of acute episodes; its selection was made only for modelling purposes and does not necessarily suggest use of olanzapine instead of other available antipsychotic drugs for the treatment of acute episodes in people with schizophrenia.

Table 43 presents the resource use and respective unit costs associated with management of acute episodes in people with schizophrenia, and the percentage of people receiving each intervention.

Residential and long-term hospital care costs

The percentage of people with schizophrenia living in private households, sheltered housing, group homes or under long-term hospital care were estimated using respective UK data (Mangalore & Knapp, 2007). The unit costs of residential care (sheltered housing and group homes) and long-term hospital care were taken from national UK sources (Curtis, 2007; Department of Health, 2008a). Residential and long-term hospital care costs in the model were assumed to be independent of the choice of antipsychotic drug and were incurred over all of the time that people were not hospitalised for an acute episode. For this reason, the costs somewhat differed between remission and relapse health states. Residential care costs were assumed to be zero during management of acute episodes for those people treated as inpatients. Long-term hospital care costs were assumed to be zero during management of acute episodes because all people under this type of care were assumed to be treated as inpatients once they experienced an acute episode.

The type of accommodation and the costs associated with residential and long-term hospital care in people with schizophrenia in the economic model are reported in Table 44.

Table 44: Type of accommodation and costs of residential and long-term hospital care in people with schizophrenia (remission state)

Type of accommodation	% of people[a]	Unit cost (2007 price)	Source of unit cost	Weighted annual cost
Private household	77	0	N/A	0
Residential care (sheltered housing)	18	£478/week	Curtis, 2007	£4,486
Residential care (group home)	2	£107/week	Curtis, 2007	£112
Long-term hospital care	3	£249/day	Department of Health, 2008a	£2,727
Total weighted residential cost per person in remission				£7,325

[a] Based on data reported in Mangalore & Knapp, 2007.

Costs incurred by switching between antipsychotic medications
People moving to next-line treatment (because of intolerable side effects or relapse) were assumed to incur additional costs, associated with three visits to a consultant psychiatrist lasting 20 minutes each, at a total cost of £435 (the unit cost of a consultant psychiatrist was £435 per hour of patient contact, including qualification costs [Curtis, 2007]).

Costs of managing side effects and related complications
Although acute EPS may be managed solely by dose adjustment or may improve spontaneously, people experiencing acute EPS were assumed to pay a visit to a consultant psychiatrist, lasting 20 minutes, and receive procyclidine at a daily dose of 15 mg for 3 months.

All people experiencing weight gain were assumed to pay two visits to their GP for general advice. In addition, 20% of them received special advice from a dietician. These methods of management were consistent with levels I and II of interventions for people with weight gain recommended by the NICE clinical guideline on obesity (NICE, 2006).

Resource use estimates and respective unit costs associated with management of acute EPS and weight gain in people with schizophrenia are reported in Table 45.

The annual cost of diabetes without complications, consisting of anti-diabetic and antihypertensive drug treatment and inclusive of implementation costs was estimated based on published data from UKPDS (Clarke *et al.*, 2005). Costs associated with management of complications from diabetes were taken from the same study.

Costs were uplifted to 2007 prices using the Hospital and Community Health Services Pay and Prices inflation index (Curtis, 2007). Costs and QALYs associated with each antipsychotic treatment were discounted at an annual rate of 3.5% as recommended by NICE (NICE, 2008a).

Table 45: Resource use and respective unit costs of managing acute EPS and weight gain

State – event	Resource use (GDG estimates)	Unit costs (2007 prices)
Acute EPS		
Procyclidine	5 mg/day for 3 months	5 mg, 28-tab = £3.35 (BNF 56)
Psychiatrist	1 visit of 20 minutes	Cost per hour of patient contact: £435 (qualification costs included – Curtis, 2007)
Weight gain		
100%[a] general advice	2 GP visits	Cost per clinic visit: £52 (qualification and direct care staff costs included – Curtis, 2007)
20%[a] diet and exercise	3 visits to dietician over 6 months (duration of first visit 1 hour; of next 2 visits 30 minutes)	Cost per hour of client contact: £32 (qualification costs included – Curtis, 2007)

[a] % based on GDG estimates.

Table 46 reports the mean (deterministic) values of all input parameters utilised in the economic model and provides information on the distributions assigned to specific parameters in probabilistic sensitivity analysis.

7.2.10   Data analysis and presentation of the results

Two methods were employed to analyse the input parameter data and present the results of the economic analysis.

First, a 'deterministic' analysis was undertaken, where data are analysed as point estimates; results are presented as mean total costs and QALYs associated with each treatment option are assessed. Relative cost effectiveness between alternative treatment options is estimated using incremental analysis: all options are initially ranked from most to least effective; any options that are more expensive than options that are ranked higher are dominated (because they are also less effective) and excluded from further analysis. Subsequently, ICERs are calculated for all pairs of consecutive options. ICERs express the additional cost per additional unit of benefit associated with one treatment option relative to its comparator. Estimation of such a ratio allows consideration of whether the additional benefit is worth the additional cost when choosing one treatment option over another.

Table 46: Input parameters utilised in the economic model

Input parameter	Deterministic value	Probabilistic distribution	Source of data – comments
Annual probability of relapse		**Distribution based on 10,000 mixed treatment comparison iterations**	Mixed treatment comparison competing risks model – analysis of data included in the guideline systematic review; results for 52 weeks assumed to reflect annual probability; results for placebo assumed to apply to no treatment in all years except the first year following the move to no treatment
		95% credible intervals	
Olanzapine	0.1996	0.0146 to 0.7222	
Amisulpride	0.2988	0.0197 to 0.9042	
Zotepine	0.1067	0.0023 to 0.5601	
Aripiprazole	0.2742	0.0130 to 0.8531	
Paliperidone	0.1625	0.0025 to 0.7008	
Risperidone	0.2761	0.0182 to 0.8785	
Haloperidol	0.3317	0.0262 to 0.9028	
No treatment – following years	0.4361	0.0913 to 0.8613	
Flupentixol decanoate	0.2977	**Beta distribution** ($\alpha = 39$, $\beta = 92$) according to data reported in David and colleagues, 1999)	David *et al.*, 1999. Meta-analysis of trials comparing flupentixol decanoate versus other depot antipsychotics; data on relapse
No treatment – first year following discontinuation of treatment	0.6062	**Distribution based on 10,000 mixed treatment comparison iterations** – results for placebo, adding the effect of abrupt discontinuation on the risk for relapse (Viguera *et al.*, 1997)	Mixed treatment comparison competing risks model – a higher probability of relapse over the first 7 months (50%) was taken into account (Viguera *et al.*, 1997)
Probability of discontinuation because of intolerable side effects – first year of initiation of a particular antipsychotic		**Distribution based on 10,000 mixed treatment comparison iterations**	Mixed treatment comparison competing risks model – analysis of data included in the guideline systematic review; results for 52 weeks assumed to apply to the first year within initiation of a particular antipsychotic only
		95% credible intervals	
Olanzapine	0.0783	0.0021 to 0.4784	
Amisulpride	0.0554	0.0006 to 0.3721	
Zotepine	0.3821	0.0120 to 0.9750	
Aripiprazole	0.1582	0.0026 to 0.7847	
Paliperidone	0.3287	0.0039 to 0.9770	
Risperidone	0.0994	0.0020 to 0.6471	
Haloperidol	0.0922	0.0017 to 0.5386	

Continued

Table 46: (*Continued*)

Input parameter	Deterministic value	Probabilistic distribution	Source of data – comments
Annual probability of discontinuation because of other reasons		**Distribution based on 10,000 mixed treatment comparison iterations** 95% credible intervals	Mixed treatment comparison competing risks model – analysis of data included in the guideline systematic review; results for 52 weeks assumed to reflect annual probability
Olanzapine	0.2730	0.0207 to 0.8596	
Amisulpride	0.2435	0.0139 to 0.8324	
Zotepine	0.2253	0.0074 to 0.8189	
Aripiprazole	0.3520	0.0202 to 0.9218	
Paliperidone	0.3848	0.0090 to 0.9479	
Risperidone	0.1761	0.0086 to 0.7141	
Haloperidol	0.2516	0.0151 to 0.8290	
Weight gain – first year of initiation of a particular antipsychotic ORs versus haloperidol		**Distribution based on 10,000 mixed treatment comparison iterations** 95% credible intervals	Mixed treatment comparison simple random-effects model – analysis of data from guide line meta-analysis of side effects; only data reported as 'increase in weight gain of ≥7% from baseline' were considered.
Olanzapine	2.8631	1.7050 to 4.5090	
Amisulpride	1.8604	0.7345 to 4.0360	
Aripiprazole	0.7373	0.3498 to 1.3990	
Paliperidone	1.0779	0.4405 to 2.1640	
Risperidone	1.0895	0.5214 to 2.0850	
Zotepine	1.0895	As for risperidone	
Probability of weight gain Haloperidol	0.2000	**Beta distribution** ($\alpha = 31$, $\beta = 124$ according to data reported in studies with time horizon up to 12 weeks included in the guideline meta-analysis of side effects)	OR of zotepine versus haloperidol assumed to be equal of that of risperidone versus haloperidol
Flupentixol decanoate	0.2000	As for haloperidol	Extrapolation of data reported in studies with time horizon up to 12 weeks included in the guideline meta-analysis of side effects; only data reported as 'increase in weight gain of ≥7% from baseline' were considered. Assumed to equal that for haloperidol

Acute EPS			
First year of initiation of a particular antipsychotic ORs versus haloperidol		**Distribution based on 10,000 mixed treatment comparison iterations** 95% credible intervals	Mixed treatment comparison full random effects model – analysis of data from guide line meta-analysis of side effects; only data on 'need for anticholinergic medication' were considered
Olanzapine	0.2631	0.1832 to 0.3641	
Amisulpride	0.3993	0.2587 to 0.5836	
Zotepine	0.1476	0.0517 to 0.3132	
Aripiprazole	0.2517	0.1505 to 0.4002	
Paliperidone	0.2983	0.1179 to 0.6214	
Risperidone	0.4743	0.3680 to 0.5994	
Probability of acute EPS Haloperidol	0.5367	**Beta distribution** ($\alpha = 928$, $\beta = 801$ according to data reported in RCTs with time horizon up to 8 weeks included in the guideline meta-analysis of side effects)	Extrapolation of data reported in studies with time horizon up to 8 weeks included in the guideline meta-analysis of side effects; only data on 'need for anticholinergic medication' were considered
Flupentixol decanoate	0.4891	**Beta distribution** ($\alpha = 45$, $\beta = 47$ according to data reported in David and colleagues, 1999)	David et al., 1999. Meta-analysis of trials comparing flupentixol decanoate versus other depot antipsychotics; data on need for anti cholinergic medication
Following years Probability of acute EPS All antipsychotics	10% of first year estimate	N/A (no distribution assigned)	GDG expert opinion

Continued

Table 46: *(Continued)*

Input parameter	Deterministic value	Probabilistic distribution	Source of data – comments
Probability of diabetes – first year of initiation of a particular antipsychotic		**Distribution based on 10,000 mixed treatment comparison iterations of data on weight gain**	Probability of haloperidol estimated from data reported in van Winkel *et al.*, 2006 and 2008 and considering the increased RR for diabetes of SGAs versus FGAs; the remaining probabilities were calculated by multiplying respective RRs for weight gain of each SGA versus haloperidol by the probability of diabetes for haloperidol
Olanzapine	0.0417	Relative risk of each SGA versus haloperidol for diabetes was assumed to equal their in-between relative risk for weight gain; the latter was determined by the posterior distribution of ORs of weight gain for each SGA and haloperidol	
Amisulpride	0.0317		
Zotepine	0.0214		
Aripiprazole	0.0156		
Paliperidone	0.0212		
Risperidone	0.0214		
Haloperidol	0.0200	**Beta distribution ($\alpha = 2$, $\beta = 98$** based on assumption)	
Flupentixol decanoate	0.0200	As for haloperidol	
Probability of glucose intolerance – first year of initiation of a particular antipsychotic		**Distribution based on 10,000 mixed treatment comparison iterations of data on weight gain**	Probability of haloperidol estimated from data identified in the guideline systematic review; the remaining probabilities were calculated by multiplying respective RRs for weight gain of each SGA versus haloperidol by the probability of glucose intolerance for haloperidol
Olanzapine	0.3129	Relative risk of each SGA versus haloperidol for glucose intolerance was assumed to equal their in-between relative risk for weight gain; the latter was determined by the posterior distribution of ORs of weight gain for each SGA and haloperidol, respectively	
Amisulpride	0.2381		
Zotepine	0.1606		
Aripiprazole	0.1167		
Paliperidone	0.1592		
Risperidone	0.1606		
Haloperidol	0.1500	**Beta distribution ($\alpha = 15$, $\beta = 85$** based on assumption)	
Flupentixol decanoate	0.1500	As for haloperidol	

Annual transition probability of impaired glucose tolerance to diabetes	0.0196	**Beta distribution** Standard error 0.0025 (Gillies et al., 2008)	Gillies et al., 2008
Annual probability of diabetes complications Fatal myocardial infarction Non-fatal myocardial infarction Non-fatal stroke Amputation Macrovascular events – heart failure Microvascular events – ischaemic heart disease	0.0042 0.0130 0.0039 0.0023 0.0040 0.0157	**Beta distribution** Determined from the numbers of people experiencing each of the complications at each level of Hgb A_{1C} concentration in the UKPDS (Stratton et al., 2000)	Based on UKPDS data (Stratton et al., 2000), assuming that 20% of people with schizophrenia and diabetes in the model had Hgb A_{1C} concentration 7 to <8%, 30% of people had 8 to <9%, 30% of people had 9 to <10% and 20% of people had ≥10%
Standardised mortality ratio – all cause mortality	2.6	N/A (no distribution assigned)	McGrath et al., 2008
Mortality rates per 1000 people in general population by age	25–34 years: 0.69 35–44 years: 1.29 45–54 years: 3.10 55–64 years: 7.53 65–74 years: 20.48 75–84 years: 59.36 ≥85 years: 164.02	N/A (no distribution assigned)	Office for National Statistics, 2008; mortality rates for England and Wales, 2005, estimated based on a male to female ratio 1.4 to 1, characterising people with schizophrenia (McGrath, 2006)
Utility scores Model health states Remission Relapse Death	0.799 0.670 0.000	**Beta distribution** Determined using the reported numbers of people valuing each PANSS-generated health state as in Lenert and colleagues (2004)	Lenert et al., 2004; linking between model states and states described in the study based on GDG estimates – see the main text for details. Duration of decrement in HRQoL caused by relapse: 6 months

Continued

Table 46: *(Continued)*

Input parameter	Deterministic value	Probabilistic distribution	Source of data – comments
Side effects		Estimated from the number of people valuing the presence of each side effect, as reported in Lenert and colleagues (2004)	Lenert *et al.*, 2004; acute EPS causes HRQoL reduction corresponding to that of pseudo-parkinsonism, lasting 3 months; weight gain causes permanent reduction in HRQoL
Acute EPS	–0.888%		
Weight gain	–0.959%		
		95% credible intervals	
Diabetes complications			Clarke *et al.*, 2002: utility scores based on patient-reported EQ-5D scores, valued using EQ-5D UK tariff values
Myocardial infarction	–0.055	–0.067 to –0.042	
Stroke	–0.164	–0.222 to –0.105	
Amputation	–0.280	–0.389 to –0.170	
Macrovascular events – heart failure	–0.108	–0.169 to –0.048	
Microvascular events – ischaemic heart disease	–0.090	–0.126 to –0.054	
Annual drug acquisition costs (remission state)		N/A (no distribution assigned)	BNF 56 (British Medical Association & the Royal Pharmaceutical Society of Great Britain, 2008), except risperidone cost, which was taken from the Electronic Drug Tariff (NHS, Business Services Authority, 2008). Average daily dosage taken from respective NHS data (NHS, The Information Centre, 2008c) and BNF guidance when no other data were available
Olanzapine	£1,036		
Amisulpride	£696		
Zotepine	£767		
Aripiprazole	£1,325		
Paliperidone	£1,902		
Risperidone	£821		
Haloperidol	£175		
Flupentixol decanoate	£81		
Annual costs of remission		**Gamma distribution** Standard error of all costs: 70% of mean value (assumption)	Details on outpatient, primary and community care cost reported in Table 42; details on costs of residential and long-term hospital care reported in Table 44; 2007 prices
Outpatient, primary and community care	£5,401		
Residential and long-term hospital care	£7,325		
Total (cost of antipsychotic medication for relapse prevention excluded)	£12,726		

Annual costs of relapse Outpatient, primary and community care Residential and long-term hospital care Acute treatment (including olanzapine) *Total* (cost of antipsychotic medication for relapse prevention excluded)	£4,323 £5,421 £23,274 £33,018	**Gamma distribution** Standard error of all costs: 70% of mean value (assumption)	Details on outpatient, primary and community care cost reported in Table 42; details on costs of treating acute episode reported in Table 43; details on costs of residential and long-term hospital care reported in Table 44; 2007 prices
Cost of switching between antipsychotics	£435	**Gamma distribution** Standard error: 70% of mean value (assumption)	3 visits to consultant psychiatrist, lasting 20 minutes each; unit cost from Curtis, 2007; 2007 prices
Cost of treating side effects Acute EPS Weight gain Diabetes (without complications) – annual Fatal myocardial infarction Non-fatal myocardial infarction first year/following years Non-fatal stroke first year/following years Amputation first year/following years Macrovascular events-heart failure first year/following years Microvascular events-ischaemic heart disease first year/following years	£177 £117 £199 £1,531 £5,407/£616 £3,144/£331 £11,238/£401 £418/£343 £363/£271	**Gamma distribution** Standard error of all costs: 70% of the respective mean value (assumption)	Details on resource use and unit costs associated with acute EPS and weight gain reported in Table 45; 2007 prices UKPDS (Clarke *et al.*, 2005); 2007 prices
Discount rate (for both costs and outcomes)	0.035	N/A (no distribution assigned)	Recommended by NICE (NICE, 2008a)

If the ICER for a given option is higher than the ICER calculated for the previous intervention in ranking, then this strategy is also excluded from further analysis, on the basis of extended dominance. After excluding cases of extended dominance, ICERs are recalculated. The treatment option with the highest ICER below the cost effectiveness threshold is the most cost-effective option.

A number of sensitivity analyses explored the impact of the uncertainty characterising model input parameters on the results of the deterministic analysis. The following scenarios were tested:

● Unit cost per bed-day in an adult mental health acute care inpatient unit of £235, according to the reported lower quartile of the NHS reference unit cost (Department of Health, 2008a)
● Duration of hospitalisation for people experiencing an acute episode of 69 days, taken from an effectiveness trial of clozapine versus SGAs conducted in the UK (CUtLASS Band 2, Davies *et al.*, 2008)
● Combination of the two scenarios above.

The following three scenarios attempted to investigate the impact of hospitalisation costs on the results of the analysis:

● Use of alternative utility scores for schizophrenia health states, as reported in Chouinard and Albright (1997) and Glennie (1997)
● Probability of side effects assumed to be common for all antipsychotic drugs: probabilities of acute EPS, weight gain and, subsequently, glucose intolerance and diabetes were assumed to be the same for all drugs. This scenario aimed at exploring the importance of side effects in determining total QALYs, costs and relative cost effectiveness between antipsychotic medications over time
● Probability of relapse assumed to be common for all antipsychotic drugs. The objective of this sensitivity analysis was to explore whether the effectiveness in preventing relapse was the driver of the cost effectiveness results, as expected.

In addition to deterministic analysis, a 'probabilistic' analysis was also conducted. In this case, most of the model input-parameters were assigned probability distributions (rather than being expressed as point estimates), to reflect the uncertainty characterising the available clinical and cost data. Subsequently, 10,000 iterations were performed, each drawing random values out of the distributions fitted onto the model input parameters. This exercise provided more accurate estimates of mean costs and benefits for each antipsychotic (averaging results from the 10,000 iterations) by capturing the non-linearity characterising the economic model structure (Briggs *et al.*, 2006).

The probabilistic distributions of data on relapse, discontinuation and side effects that were analysed using mixed treatment comparison techniques (that is, annual probability of relapse, probability of treatment discontinuation because of intolerable side effects and annual probability of treatment discontinuation because of any other reason, ORs of weight gain versus haloperidol and ORs of acute EPS versus haloperidol) were defined directly from random values recorded for each of the 10,000 respective mixed treatment comparison iterations performed in Winbugs. To maintain the correlation between the posterior estimates for (i) probability of relapse, (ii) probability of treatment discontinuation because of intolerable side effects and (iii) probability of treatment discontinuation because of any other reason, data from each of the common mixed treatment comparison simulations for these parameters were exported jointly and fitted into the Excel file of the economic model where the probabilistic analysis was carried out.

The probability of relapse and acute EPS for the depot antipsychotic, and of acute EPS and weight gain for haloperidol, were given a beta distribution. Beta distributions were also assigned to utility scores and rates of complications from diabetes. The estimation of distribution ranges in all these cases was based on available data in the published sources of evidence or from the guideline meta-analysis.

The probabilities of developing diabetes and glucose impairment following use of haloperidol were also given a beta distribution; the ranges of values attached to these parameters were based on assumptions.

All costs (except drug acquisition costs) were assigned a gamma distribution; to take account of their likely high skewness and variability, the standard errors associated with costs were assumed to equal 70% of the values used in deterministic analysis.

Table 46 shows which input parameters were assigned distributions in the probabilistic analysis, and gives more details on the types of distributions and the methods employed to define their range.

Results of probabilistic analysis are presented in the form of cost-effectiveness acceptability curves (CEACs), which demonstrate the probability of each treatment option being the most cost effective among the strategies assessed at different levels of willingness-to-pay per unit of effectiveness (that is, at different cost-effectiveness thresholds the decision-maker may set). In addition, the cost effectiveness acceptability frontier (CEAF) is provided alongside CEACs, showing which treatment option among those examined offers the highest average net monetary benefit (NMB) at each level of willingness-to-pay (Fenwick *et al.*, 2001). The NMB of a treatment option at different levels of willingness-to-pay is defined by the following formula:

$$NMB = E \cdot \lambda - C$$

where E and C are the effectiveness (number of QALYs) and costs associated with the treatment option, respectively, and λ is the level of the willingness-to-pay per unit of effectiveness.

7.3   RESULTS

7.3.1   Results of deterministic analysis

According to deterministic analysis, zotepine was the most cost-effective option among those assessed because it produced the highest number of QALYs and was associated with the lowest costs (dominant option). This result was observed for both time horizons of the analysis; that is, 10 years and lifetime.

Table 47 provides mean costs and QALYs for every antipsychotic drug assessed in the economic analysis, as well as the results of incremental analysis, over a time horizon of 10 years. The seven drugs have been ranked from the most to the least

Table **47:** Mean costs and QALYs per person for each antipsychotic drug used for relapse prevention in people with schizophrenia that is in remission – time horizon of 10 years. Incremental analysis undertaken in steps, after excluding the most cost-effective option of the previous step, to enable ranking of medications in terms of cost effectiveness

Antipsychotic drug	QALYs	Cost	Incremental analysis (cost per QALY gained)				
			All options	Excluding zotepine and olanzapine	Excluding paliperidone	Excluding haloperidol	Excluding aripiprazole
Zotepine	6.468	£139,170	Dominant				
Paliperidone	6.427	£142,173	Dominated	£150,159			
Olanzapine	6.420	£141,212	Dominated				
Risperidone	6.417	£149,112	Dominated	Dominated	£1,600,986	£204,529	£48,961
Haloperidol	6.413	£143,406	Dominated	Dominated			
Aripiprazole	6.400	£145,697	Dominated	Dominated	Dominated		
Amisulpride	6.392	£147,920	Dominated	Dominated	Dominated	Dominated	

effective in terms of number of QALYs gained. Zotepine is associated with lowest costs and highest benefits (QALYs) and consequently dominates all other treatment options. It can be seen that paliperidone and olanzapine dominate all drugs except zotepine; therefore, if zotepine is not an option for the treatment of people with schizophrenia that is in remission, then the decision (solely in terms of cost effectiveness) would have to be made between paliperidone and olanzapine. The ICER of paliperidone versus olanzapine is £150,159/QALY; this figure is much higher than the cost effectiveness threshold of £20,000–£30,000/QALY set by NICE (NICE, 2008b). Therefore, at 10 years of antipsychotic medication use, according to the results of deterministic analysis, olanzapine is the second most cost-effective option following zotepine, and paliperidone is the third (because it dominates all other options). If paliperidone and olanzapine are excluded from analysis (in addition to zotepine), then four drugs remain for further analysis: two of them, aripiprazole and amisulpride, are dominated by haloperidol. The ICER of risperidone to haloperidol exceeds £1,600,000/QALY, and therefore haloperidol is the most cost-effective option among the four remaining drugs. By repeating this process in steps, and excluding in each new incremental analysis all options found to be cost effective in previous ones, it is possible to rank all medications in terms of cost effectiveness. This incremental analysis 'in steps' resulted in the following ranking of antipsychotics in terms of cost effectiveness: (1) zotepine; (2) olanzapine; (3) paliperidone; (4) haloperidol; (5) aripiprazole; (6) amisulpride; (7) risperidone.

Table 48 provides mean costs and QALYs for each antipsychotic drug assessed in the economic model as well as results of incremental analysis in steps over a lifetime. The seven drugs have again been ranked from the most to the least effective. Zotepine dominates all other options in this analysis, too. If zotepine is excluded from the analysis, then paliperidone dominates all other drugs except haloperidol and olanzapine. The ICER of paliperidone versus haloperidol is £11,458 per QALY; the ICER of haloperidol versus olanzapine is £41,129 per QALY. Consequently, haloperidol is excluded from consideration on the basis of extended dominance. The ICER of paliperidone versus olanzapine is £20,872 per QALY. These figures suggest that, if zotepine is not an option, then olanzapine is the second best option in terms of cost effectiveness (using the lower, £20,000/QALY, threshold set by NICE [2008b]), and paliperidone third (however, it must be noted that the figure of £20,872/QALY is very close to the lower threshold and if the upper NICE cost effectiveness threshold of £30,000/QALY is used, then paliperidone is ranked second best option in terms of cost effectiveness and olanzapine third). If incremental analysis in steps is undertaken, as shown in Table 48, then the ranking of antipsychotic medications in terms of cost effectiveness is the following: (1) zotepine; (2) olanzapine; (3) paliperidone; (4) haloperidol; (5) aripiprazole; (6) risperidone; (7) amisulpride.

A comparison of rankings in terms of QALYs between Table 47 and Table 48 shows that olanzapine and haloperidol appear in low places in the lifetime horizon (seventh and fifth, respectively), compared with their ranking at 10 years where they are ranked third and fourth, respectively. This finding is explained by the higher risk for weight gain and diabetes characterising olanzapine (olanzapine was the second-line antipsychotic in the cohort initiated on haloperidol); eventually, the (permanent)

Table 48: Mean costs and QALYs per person for each antipsychotic drug used for relapse prevention in people with schizophrenia that is in remission – lifetime horizon. Incremental analysis undertaken in steps, after excluding the most cost-effective option of the previous step, to enable ranking of medications by cost effectiveness

Antipsychotic drug	QALYs	Cost	Incremental analysis (cost per QALY gained)					
			All options	Excluding zotepine	Excluding olanzapine	Excluding paliperidone	Excluding haloperidol	Excluding aripiprazole
Zotepine	16.849	£397,247	Dominant					
Paliperidone	16.804	£402,288	Dominated	£20,872	£11,458			
Risperidone	16.791	£409,083	Dominated	Dominated	Dominated	£191,056	£118,464	£12,809
Aripiprazole	16.767	£406,195	Dominated	Dominated	Dominated	Ext. domin.		
Haloperidol	16.753	£401,702	Dominated	Ext. domin.				
Amisulpride	16.733	£408,332	Dominated	Dominated	Dominated	Dominated	Dominated	
Olanzapine	16.729	£400,725	Dominated					

Note: Ext. domin. = extendedly dominated.

increase in weight and the incidence of complications from diabetes, which was higher in the cohorts receiving olanzapine as first or second-line treatment, reduced the overall HRQoL and the total number of QALYs gained relative to other treatment options. Nonetheless, the ranking of olanzapine and haloperidol in terms of cost effectiveness was not affected: they were ranked second and fourth cost-effective options, respectively, over 10 years, and this ranking order remained over a lifetime. It must be noted that, with the exception of the last two places, the ranking of antipsychotic medications in terms of cost effectiveness was not affected by the time horizon used.

Figure 8 and Figure 9 present the cost effectiveness planes for the two time horizons of the analysis, showing the incremental costs and benefits (QALYs) of all SGAs versus haloperidol. In both cases, it can be seen that zotepine is in the southeast quadrant and has the highest number of QALYs and the lowest costs relative to all other options assessed.

Results of deterministic sensitivity analysis

Results were very sensitive to annual probabilities of relapse, as expected. When all antipsychotic medications were assumed to have equal probabilities of relapse, the ranking of medications in terms of effectiveness was significantly affected. In general, this ranking by effectiveness was predicted by the ranking of medications in terms of discontinuation to other reasons, with options with lower probabilities of discontinuation ranking more highly in terms of effectiveness. Regarding cost effectiveness, the ranking of treatment options at 10 years following incremental analysis

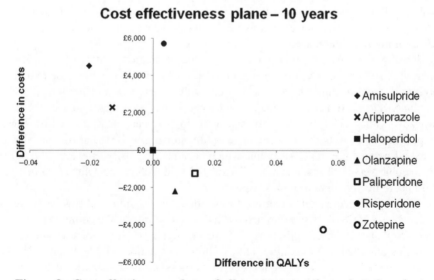

Figure 8: Cost-effectiveness plane of all treatment options plotted against haloperidol, at 10 years of antipsychotic medication use

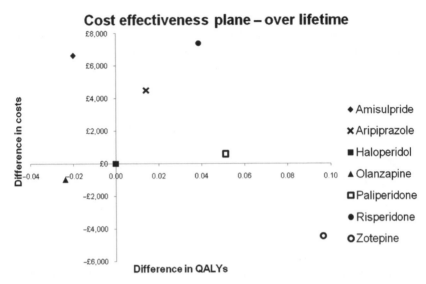

Figure 9: Cost-effectiveness plane of all treatment options plotted against haloperidol, over a lifetime of antipsychotic medication use

in steps was: (1) haloperidol; (2) amisulpride; (3) olanzapine; (4) aripiprazole; (5) risperidone; (6) zotepine; (7) paliperidone. Over a lifetime, the ranking of antipsychotic medications in terms of cost effectiveness was: (1) risperidone; (2) amisulpride; (3) haloperidol; (4) olanzapine; (5) aripiprazole; (6) zotepine; (7) paliperidone. It is obvious that results were greatly affected by this scenario, with options that were ranked highly in base-case deterministic analysis, such as zotepine and paliperidone, occupying the last two places in ranking when relapse rates were assumed to be the same for all treatment options.

Results were, overall, robust under the other scenarios explored in sensitivity analysis. In all cases, zotepine was the most cost-effective option: zotepine remained dominant under all other hypotheses tested, with the exception of the scenario that combined a low estimate of inpatient stay for people having an acute episode (69 days instead of 111, which was the estimate used in base-case analysis) with a lower respective unit cost. In this case, and over a time horizon of 10 years, zotepine dominated all treatment except olanzapine which became less costly. However, the ICER of zotepine versus olanzapine was £7,751/QALY; therefore, zotepine remained the most cost-effective option of those assessed.

Ranking of medications in terms of cost effectiveness did not change at 10 years under any scenario of those examined (with the exception of using common probabilities of relapse, as discussed above). However, over a lifetime, some of the tested scenarios did affect the ranking of antipsychotic medications. Table 49 provides the ranking of medications in terms of cost effectiveness for those scenarios that affected ranking over a lifetime (the scenario of using common probabilities of relapse has not been presented in this table, as it has been discussed above).

Table 49: Ranking of antipsychotic medications in terms of cost effectiveness over a lifetime under: (1) base-case analysis; (2) use of a lower estimate of inpatient stay; (3) use of a lower estimate of inpatient stay and a lower unit cost of mental health inpatient bed-day; (4) use of utility scores reported in Glennie (1997); (5) assumption of common probabilities of side effects for all antipsychotic medications

Base-case analysis	Scenario tested in sensitivity analysis			
1	**2**	**3**	**4**	**5**
Zotepine	Zotepine	Zotepine	Zotepine	Zotepine
Olanzapine	Paliperidone	Paliperidone	Paliperidone	Olanzapine
Paliperidone	Olanzapine	Haloperidol	Olanzapine	Haloperidol
Haloperidol	Haloperidol	Olanzapine	Haloperidol	Paliperidone
Aripiprazole	Aripiprazole	Aripiprazole	Aripiprazole	Aripiprazole
Risperidone	Amisulpride	Amisulpride	Risperidone	Amisulpride
Amisulpride	Risperidone	Risperidone	Amisulpride	Risperidone

It must be noted that using common probabilities of side effects (that is, acute EPS, weight gain, glucose intolerance and diabetes) for all antipsychotic medications did not significantly affect the results of the analysis. Ranking medications in terms of QALYs changed, as expected, with olanzapine being ranked in second place in both of the time horizons examined. However, the first two ranked places in terms of cost effectiveness were not affected, with zotepine remaining the most cost-effective option followed by olanzapine, as in base-case analysis.

7.3.2 Results of probabilistic analysis

Results of probabilistic analysis did not differ significantly from those of deterministic analysis: as in deterministic analysis, zotepine dominated all other options because it was associated with the lowest total costs and highest total QALYs (that is, mean values from 10,000 iterations) compared with the other six antipsychotic medications assessed. Regarding the ranking of medications in order of cost effectiveness, this was the same for deterministic and probabilistic analysis over 10 years. Over a lifetime, cost-effectiveness ranking of antipsychotic drugs in probabilistic analysis differed from respective ranking in deterministic analysis to some extent; probabilistic analysis ranking was as follows: (1) zotepine; (2) olanzapine; (3) haloperidol; (4) paliperidone; (5) risperidone; (6) amisulpride; (7) aripiprazole.

Probabilistic analysis demonstrated that zotepine had the highest probability of being the most cost-effective option among all antipsychotic medications examined,

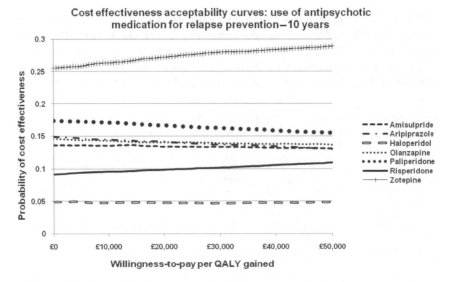

Figure 10: Cost-effectiveness acceptability curves of all treatment options at 10 years of antipsychotic medication use

at any level of willingness-to-pay per additional QALY gained of those explored; that is, from zero to £50,000 per QALY gained. However, this probability was low, ranging between 25 and 29% at 10 years, and 28 and 33% over a lifetime, and remained virtually unaffected by the cost-effectiveness threshold examined. The other antipsychotic medications had probabilities of being the most cost-effective options that ranged from approximately 5% (haloperidol) to 16% (paliperidone) and were also almost independent of the cost-effectiveness threshold and the time horizon examined. The cost effectiveness acceptability frontier coincided with the CEAC for zotepine, because zotepine produced the highest average net benefit at any level of willingness to pay.

Figure 10 and Figure 11 show the CEACs generated for each of the seven antipsychotic medications examined, over 10 years and a lifetime of antipsychotic medication use, respectively.

Table 50 and Table 51 show the probabilities of each antipsychotic medication being cost effective at various levels of willingness-to-pay per QALY gained.

7.4   DISCUSSION OF FINDINGS – LIMITATIONS OF THE ANALYSIS

The results of the economic analysis suggest that zotepine is potentially the most cost-effective pharmacological treatment of those examined for relapse prevention in people with schizophrenia that is in remission. Zotepine dominated all other

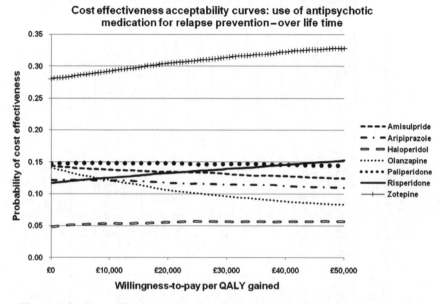

Figure 11: Cost-effectiveness acceptability curves of all treatment options over a lifetime of antipsychotic medication use

treatment options in deterministic analysis. In probabilistic analysis, use of zotepine yielded the maximum average net benefit and demonstrated the highest probability of being the most cost-effective option at any level of willingness-to-pay per unit of effectiveness. However, because of the high uncertainty characterising model input parameters, the probability of zotepine being the most cost-effective option was low at approximately 27 to 30% and remained virtually unaffected by the level of willingness-to-pay. The probability of zotepine being the most cost-effective antipsychotic medication at the NICE cost-effectiveness threshold of £20,000 per QALY was 27.17% at 10 years and 30.46% over a lifetime.

One of the major drawbacks of the economic analysis was the omission of a number of antipsychotic drugs that are potentially effective in preventing relapse in people with schizophrenia in remission. Quetiapine and FGAs other than haloperidol were not assessed in the economic analysis because no relevant clinical data in the area of relapse prevention were identified in the systematic review of relevant literature.

The clinical data on relapse and discontinuation utilised in the economic model were limited in some cases: data on zotepine, which was shown to be the dominant option in deterministic analysis, were derived exclusively from a placebo-controlled RCT. Respective data on aripiprazole and paliperidone were also taken from two trials that assessed each of these two antipsychotic drugs versus placebo. Therefore, the results of the economic analysis should be interpreted with caution.

Table 50: Probability of each antipsychotic intervention being cost effective at various levels of willingness-to-pay per QALY gained (WTP) – 10 years

WTP	Olanzapine	Amisulpride	Zotepine	Aripiprazole	Paliperidone	Risperidone	Haloperidol
0	0.1457	0.1363	0.2552	0.1492	0.1736	0.0911	0.0489
£5,000	0.1436	0.1364	0.2582	0.1466	0.1726	0.0939	0.0487
£10,000	0.1427	0.1357	0.2633	0.1442	0.1710	0.0955	0.0476
£15,000	0.1410	0.1364	0.2675	0.1420	0.1686	0.0967	0.0478
£20,000	0.1407	0.1341	0.2717	0.1413	0.1666	0.0982	0.0474
£25,000	0.1404	0.1341	0.2757	0.1387	0.1641	0.0998	0.0472
£30,000	0.1390	0.1338	0.2795	0.1370	0.1626	0.1014	0.0467
£35,000	0.1389	0.1333	0.2806	0.1357	0.1607	0.1034	0.0474
£40,000	0.1381	0.1324	0.2835	0.1343	0.1586	0.1054	0.0477
£45,000	0.1377	0.1322	0.2861	0.1323	0.1566	0.1072	0.0479
£50,000	0.1369	0.1312	0.2887	0.1301	0.1553	0.1092	0.0486

Table 51: Probability of each antipsychotic intervention being cost effective at various levels of willingness-to-pay per QALY gained (WTP) – over a lifetime

WTP	Olanzapine	Amisulpride	Zotepine	Aripiprazole	Paliperidone	Risperidone	Haloperidol
0	0.1412	0.1440	0.2801	0.1216	0.1476	0.1172	0.0483
£5,000	0.1294	0.1402	0.2863	0.1213	0.1488	0.1218	0.0522
£10,000	0.1218	0.1381	0.2924	0.1203	0.1484	0.1257	0.0533
£15,000	0.1143	0.1363	0.2984	0.1196	0.1483	0.1289	0.0542
£20,000	0.1060	0.1349	0.3046	0.1171	0.1485	0.1331	0.0558
£25,000	0.1007	0.1340	0.3092	0.1161	0.1464	0.1364	0.0572
£30,000	0.0960	0.1316	0.3140	0.1146	0.1471	0.1399	0.0568
£35,000	0.0921	0.1288	0.3182	0.1145	0.1472	0.1425	0.0567
£40,000	0.0882	0.1281	0.3224	0.1125	0.1458	0.1461	0.0569
£45,000	0.0853	0.1260	0.3261	0.1109	0.1449	0.1497	0.0571
£50,000	0.0831	0.1245	0.3279	0.1100	0.1443	0.1531	0.0571

Moreover, definition of relapse varied across the 17 trials that provided data on relapse; this is another factor that should be taken into account when interpreting the economic findings. Data on relapse, discontinuation because of side effects and discontinuation because of other reasons were treated as mutually exclusive in analysis. Although the majority of the 17 RCTs that formed the evidence-base for the economic analysis reported these outcomes as such (that is, trial participants could either stay in remission, or relapse, or discontinue because of side effects, or discontinue because of other reasons), a small number of trials did not clarify whether some participants could have been double-counted in the reporting of outcomes and an assumption of mutual exclusiveness of such outcomes also in these studies had to be made. Results of the mixed treatment comparison analysis of clinical data on relapse prevention were characterised by high uncertainty, as demonstrated by the wide 95% credible intervals of the respective posterior distributions; this uncertainty was reflected in the results of the probabilistic economic analysis: the probability of zotepine being the most cost-effective option was roughly 27 to 30%, with the probabilities of the remaining options being cost effective ranging from around 5% (haloperidol) to 16% (paliperidone), regardless of the level of willingness-to-pay per QALY gained.

The mixed treatment comparison analysis of the available clinical data, including relapse and discontinuation rates as well as rates of side effects, overcame the major limitation characterising previous economic models that assessed the cost effectiveness of pharmacological treatments for people with schizophrenia: most of those analyses synthesised trial-based evidence by naive addition of clinical data across relevant treatment arms, thus breaking randomisation rules and introducing bias into the analysis (Glenny *et al.*, 2005). On the other hand, mixed treatment comparison techniques enable evidence synthesis from both direct and indirect comparisons between treatments, and allow simultaneous inference on all treatments examined in pair-wise trial comparisons while respecting randomisation (Lu & Ades, 2004; Caldwell *et al.*, 2005).

The guideline economic analysis, in contrast to previous economic studies, considered a lifetime horizon (in addition to a time horizon of 10 years); this was deemed appropriate and relevant for the economic question, given the potential need for long-term (likely to be over a lifetime) use of antipsychotic drugs by people with schizophrenia in remission, and the nature of schizophrenia, which is often characterised by phases of remission alternating with phases of relapse over a lifetime. However, one limitation of the analysis was the extrapolation of relatively short-term clinical data over a lifetime because no appropriate long-term data were available to inform the economic model: clinical data on relapse and discontinuation were taken from trials with time horizons ranging between 26 and 104 weeks. The 52-week probability of relapse, the 52-week probability of treatment discontinuation because of intolerable side effects and the 52-week probability of treatment discontinuation because of any other reason were estimated in most cases by extrapolating the available clinical data; the estimated probability of relapse and of treatment discontinuation because of other reasons were then assumed to apply to every yearly cycle in the model, over a lifetime of the hypothetical study cohorts. Although such an extrapolation of the data was required to populate the economic model, no robust evidence exists to confirm that such extrapolation accurately reflects the long-term effectiveness of antipsychotic medication and its impact on the course of schizophrenia in real life. If the effectiveness of antipsychotic drugs in preventing relapse is maintained over time, then the results of the economic analysis more closely reflect a realistic situation. If, however, the effectiveness of antipsychotic drugs in preventing relapse is reduced over time, then this analysis has overestimated the cost effectiveness of antipsychotic medication, especially of those treatments that have been demonstrated to be the most effective in preventing relapse in the short term, such as zotepine.

The economic model structure incorporated three side effects: acute EPS, weight gain, and diabetes/glucose intolerance potentially leading to diabetes. The choice of side effects was based on their expected impact on the relative cost effectiveness of antipsychotic medications and the availability of relevant data. However, it should be emphasised that antipsychotic drugs are characterised overall by a wider range of side effects, such as other neurologic side effects including tardive dyskinesia, sexual dysfunction, increase in prolactin levels, as well as cardiovascular and gastrointestinal side effects, the omission of which may have affected the results of the economic analysis. In particular, lack of consideration of tardive dyskinesia, which has lasting effects and causes a significant impairment in HRQoL, is acknowledged as a limitation of the analysis. Inclusion of tardive dyskinesia in the model structure might disfavour haloperidol, given that clinical evidence indicates that haloperidol is associated with a higher risk for neurologic side effects.

To populate the economic model using the available data on side effects, a number of GDG estimates and further assumptions were required, including selection of data for analysis and extrapolation of available evidence over the time horizon of the analysis. Data on acute EPS were more comprehensive compared with data on weight gain and data on the risk for diabetes and glucose intolerance. Data on weight gain were not available for zotepine; for this reason the risk of weight gain for zotepine was assumed to be equal to the respective risk for risperidone. Data on the risk for diabetes and glucose intolerance associated with antipsychotic medication and appropriate for the economic analysis were very sparse and not available for all drugs assessed in the analysis. However, these parameters were considered to be important for inclusion in the model structure, as use of antipsychotic medication is associated with increased risk for development of diabetes, the complications of which have been shown to affect quality of life considerably and to incur substantial costs in the long term; therefore, to explore the impact of such parameters on the relative cost effectiveness of antipsychotic medications over time, a number of assumptions were made. It is acknowledged that the estimates used in the model regarding diabetes and glucose intolerance could be potentially conservative and may not fully reflect the negative effect of antipsychotic medication on glucose metabolism.

Deterministic analysis showed that although olanzapine was ranked second in terms of effectiveness (number of QALYs gained) at 10 years of antipsychotic medication use, it was placed last in the ranking when a lifetime horizon was considered. This change in ranking over time was probably caused by the eventual impairment in HRQoL of people taking olanzapine, owing to the estimated higher levels of permanent weight increase and the frequent presence of complications because of diabetes associated with use of olanzapine compared with other antipsychotic medications. Nevertheless, despite being the least effective option over a lifetime, olanzapine was still ranked second in terms of cost effectiveness among the antipsychotic drugs assessed in deterministic analysis. It must be emphasised that deterministic sensitivity analysis revealed that the probabilities of side effects used in the economic model had no significant impact on the overall conclusions of the incremental analysis, because assuming equal probabilities for side effects for all medications did not change their ranking in terms of cost effectiveness at 10 years and led to minor changes in ranking over a lifetime (zotepine and olanzapine were still ranked first and second most cost-effective options, respectively). However, if the estimates used in the model regarding diabetes and glucose intolerance are conservative and do not fully capture the negative impact of antipsychotic medication on HRQoL and associated costs, then the relative cost effectiveness of drugs with more significant metabolic implications, such as olanzapine, may have been overestimated.

Data on treatment discontinuation because of intolerable side effects and side-effect data were analysed separately. In probabilistic economic analysis, the probability of treatment discontinuation because of intolerable side effects was varied independently from the probability of developing each of the three side effects examined. However, there is a possible correlation between these probabilities; for example, treatment discontinuation because of intolerable side effects is likely to be related to the risk for acute EPS. Such potential correlation between these parameters has not been considered in the analysis. On the other hand, the correlations across probability of relapse, probability of treatment discontinuation because of intolerable side effects and probability of treatment discontinuation because of other reasons have been taken fully into account because data on these three parameters were analysed together in a competing risks mixed treatment comparison model. The posterior simulations resulting from this exercise were then exported jointly and fitted into the Excel file of the economic model where the probabilistic analysis was implemented.

The analysis adopted the perspective of the NHS and personal social services, as recommended by NICE. Costs associated with the pharmacological treatment of people with schizophrenia were estimated by combining data from the NHS and other national sources of healthcare resource utilisation, as well as information from published studies conducted in the UK, with national unit costs. A number of further GDG estimates and assumptions were required to inform the cost parameters of the economic model. The results of the economic analysis demonstrated that drug acquisition costs do not determine the relative cost effectiveness of antipsychotic medications: haloperidol had the lowest probability of being cost effective in probabilistic analysis, despite the fact that it is by far the cheapest drug among those assessed. On the other hand, paliperidone was ranked highly in terms of cost effectiveness (the third best option in deterministic analysis at 10 years and over a lifetime; and the second highest probability of being cost effective in probabilistic analysis), despite having the highest acquisition cost. Although drug acquisition costs seem to be unimportant in determining cost effectiveness, it must be noted that the prices of a number of antipsychotic medications are expected to fall in the future because more drugs will be available in generic form.

Deterministic analysis showed that the probability of relapse was the key driver of cost effectiveness. It is not surprising, therefore, that zotepine, which was shown to be the most cost-effective option in both deterministic and probabilistic analyses, had the lowest average probability of relapse and the highest probability of being the most effective drug in reducing relapse in the mixed treatment comparison analysis; olanzapine and paliperidone, which were the second and third most cost-effective options in deterministic analysis, respectively, had the third and second lowest relapse rates, respectively, and were ranked third and second best drugs in reducing relapse, respectively (details of effectiveness ranking in mixed treatment comparison analysis are provided in Table 35). These findings indicate that it is the effectiveness of an antipsychotic drug in preventing relapse that primarily affects its cost effectiveness, especially considering that the rates of side effects were not shown to have any significant impact on the cost-effectiveness results; such a hypothesis seems reasonable, given that relapse prevention greatly improves the HRQoL of people with schizophrenia and, simultaneously, leads to a substantial reduction in hospitalisation rates and associated high costs. In fact, reduction in inpatient costs associated with the development of acute episodes affects the level of total costs associated with antipsychotic medication and the ranking of options in terms of cost effectiveness in the long term, as shown in sensitivity analysis.

Besides the health and social care costs that were considered in this analysis, according to the NICE recommended economic perspective, wider societal costs (such as costs borne to the criminal justice system, personal expenses of people with schizophrenia and their carers, productivity losses of people with schizophrenia, carers' time spent with people with schizophrenia, which may also translate to productivity losses for carers, as well as the emotional burden associated with schizophrenia) need to be taken into account when the cost effectiveness of antipsychotic medications is assessed.

7.5   CONCLUSIONS

The economic analysis undertaken for this guideline showed that zotepine may be potentially the most cost-effective antipsychotic medication among those assessed for relapse prevention in people with schizophrenia in remission. However, results were characterised by high uncertainty, and probabilistic analysis showed that no antipsychotic medication can be considered to be clearly cost effective compared with the other options included in the assessment: the probability of each intervention being cost effective ranged from roughly 5% (haloperidol) to about 27 to 30% (zotepine), and was independent of the cost-effectiveness threshold used and the time horizon of the analysis (that is, 10 years or a lifetime). The probability of 27 to 30% assigned to zotepine, although indicative, is rather low and inadequate to lead to a safe conclusion regarding zotepine's superiority over the other antipsychotic medications assessed in terms of cost effectiveness. In addition, clinical data for zotepine in the area of relapse prevention (as well as for paliperidone and aripiprazole) came from a single placebo-controlled trial. Data on side effects were not comprehensive; in particular, data on the risk for diabetes and glucose intolerance associated with use of antipsychotic medications were sparse, so that the impact of the risk for diabetes and its complications on the relative cost effectiveness of antipsychotic drugs could not be determined accurately. It has to be noted, however, that the estimated rates of side effects considered in the analysis did not significantly affect the cost effectiveness results.

Further research is needed on the benefits and patterns of use of antipsychotic medications in the area of relapse prevention in people with schizophrenia that is in remission, as well as on the rates of associated long-term metabolic side effects, to address the uncertainty characterising the results of the economic analysis. Moreover, clinical data in the area of relapse prevention are needed for quetiapine and FGAs other than haloperidol, to enable a more comprehensive assessment of the relative cost effectiveness of antipsychotic medications in relapse prevention for people with schizophrenia that is in remission.

8   PSYCHOLOGICAL THERAPY AND PSYCHOSOCIAL INTERVENTIONS IN THE TREATMENT AND MANAGEMENT OF SCHIZOPHRENIA

For the guideline update, all sections of the psychology chapter in the previous guideline were updated, including the following evidence reviews of psychological therapies and psychosocial interventions:
- cognitive behavioural therapy (Section 8.4)
- cognitive remediation (Section 8.5)
- counselling and supportive therapy (Section 8.6)
- family intervention (Section 8.7)
- psychodynamic and psychoanalytic therapies (Section 8.8)
- psychoeducation (Section 8.9)
- social skills training (Section 8.10).
    In addition, new reviews were conducted for the following interventions:
- adherence therapy (Section 8.2)
- arts therapies (Section 8.3).

8.1   INTRODUCTION

Psychological therapies and psychosocial interventions in the treatment of schizophrenia have gained momentum over the past 3 decades. This can be attributed to at least two main factors. First, there has been growing recognition of the importance of psychological processes in psychosis, both as contributors to onset and persistence, and in terms of the negative psychological impact of a diagnosis of schizophrenia on the individual's well-being, psychosocial functioning and life opportunities. Psychological and psychosocial interventions for psychosis have been developed to address these needs. Second, although pharmacological interventions have been the mainstay of treatment since their introduction in the 1950s, they have a number of limitations. These include limited response of some people to antipsychotic medication, high incidence of disabling side effects and poor adherence to treatment. Recognition of these limitations has paved the way for acceptance of a more broadly-based approach, combining different treatment options tailored to the needs of individual service users and their families. Such treatment options include psychological therapies and psychosocial interventions. Recently, emphasis has also been placed on the value of multidisciplinary formulation and reflective practice, particularly where psychologists and allied mental health professionals operate within multidisciplinary teams (British Psychological Society, 2007).

The 'New Ways of Working' report (British Psychological Society, 2007) also details the increasing demand by both service users and carers to gain access to psychological interventions, and the increasing recognition of these interventions in the treatment and management of serious mental illnesses including schizophrenia. The report proposes that a large expansion of training of psychologists and psychological therapists is needed to increase the workforce competent in the provision of psychological therapies. This chapter addresses the evidence base for the application of psychological and psychosocial treatments, generally in combination with antipsychotic medication, in the treatment of schizophrenia, for individuals, groups and families.

8.1.1   The stress-vulnerability model

Although the rationales for medical, psychological and psychosocial interventions are derived from a variety of different biological, psychological and social theories, the development of the stress-vulnerability model (Zubin & Spring, 1977; Nuechterlein, 1987) has undoubtedly facilitated the theoretical and practical integration of disparate treatment approaches (see Chapter 2). In this model, individuals develop vulnerability to psychosis attributable to biological, psychological and/or social factors; treatments, whether pharmacological or psychological, then aim to protect a vulnerable individual and reduce the likelihood of relapse, reduce the severity of the psychotic episode and treat the problems associated with persisting symptoms. Psychological interventions may, in addition, aim to improve specific psychological or social aspects of functioning and to have a longer-term effect upon an individual's vulnerability.

8.1.2   Engagement

A prerequisite for any psychological or other treatment is the effective engagement of the service user in a positive therapeutic or treatment alliance (Roth *et al.*, 1996). Engaging people effectively during an acute schizophrenic illness is often difficult and demands considerable flexibility in the approach and pace of therapeutic working. Moreover, once engaged in a positive therapeutic alliance, it is equally necessary to maintain this relationship, often over long periods, with the added problem that such an alliance may wax and wane, especially in the event of service users becoming subject to compulsory treatment under the Mental Health Act. Special challenges in the treatment of schizophrenia include social withdrawal, cognitive and information-processing problems, developing a shared view with the service user about the nature of the illness, and the impact of stigma and social exclusion.

8.1.3   Aims of psychological therapy and psychosocial interventions

The aims of psychological and psychosocial interventions in the treatment of a person with schizophrenia are numerous. Particular treatments may be intended to improve one or more of the following outcomes: to decrease the person's vulnerability; reduce the impact of stressful events and situations; decrease distress and disability; minimise symptoms; improve quality of life; reduce risk; improve communication and coping skills; and/or enhance treatment adherence. As far as possible, research into psychological interventions needs to address a wide range of outcomes.

8.1.4   Therapeutic approaches identified

The following psychological therapies and psychosocial interventions were reviewed:
- adherence therapy
- arts therapies
- cognitive behavioural therapy
- cognitive remediation
- counselling and supportive therapy
- family intervention
- psychodynamic and psychoanalytic therapies
- psychoeducation
- social skills training.

The primary clinical questions addressed in this chapter can be found in Box 1.

Box 1:   Primary clinical questions addressed in this chapter

Initial treatment

For people with first-episode or early schizophrenia, what are the benefits and downsides of psychological/psychosocial interventions when compared with alternative management strategies at initiation of treatment?

Acute treatment

For people with an acute exacerbation or recurrence of schizophrenia, what are the benefits and downsides of psychological/psychosocial interventions when compared with alternative management strategies?

Promoting recovery in people with schizophrenia that is in remission

For people with schizophrenia that is in remission, what are the benefits and downsides of psychological/psychosocial interventions when compared with alternative management strategies?

Promoting recovery in people with schizophrenia who have had an inadequate or no response to treatment

For people with schizophrenia who have an inadequate or no response to treatment, what are the benefits and downsides of psychological/ psychosocial interventions when compared with alternative management strategies?

8.1.5   Multi-modal interventions

Some researchers have combined two psychological and/or psychosocial interventions to attempt to increase the effectiveness of the intervention. For example, a course of family intervention may be combined with a module of social skills training. The combinations are various and thus these multi-modal interventions do not form a homogenous group of interventions that can be analysed together. Therefore, multi-modal interventions that combined psychological and psychosocial treatments within the scope of this review were included in the primary analysis for each intervention review. Sensitivity analyses were conducted to test the effect, if any, of removing these multi-modal interventions. Where papers reported more than two treatment arms (for example, family intervention only versus social skills training only versus family intervention plus social skills training), only data from the single intervention arms was entered into the appropriate analysis (for example, family intervention only versus social skills training only). Papers assessing the efficacy of psychological treatments as adjuncts to discrete treatments outside the scope of the present update (for example, supported employment and pre-vocational training) were excluded from the analysis.

It is, however, worth noting that although some of the papers included in the previous guideline can be classed as multi-modal treatments because they systematically combine elements such as, for example, family intervention, social skills training and CBT, this needs to be understood in the context of the standard care available at the time. In particular, there has been a recent emphasis on incorporating active elements, particularly psychoeducation, into a more comprehensive package of standard care. Elements included in the experimental arms of older studies may now be considered routine elements of good standard care. It should also be noted that standard care differs across countries.

Definition
To be classified as multi-modal, an intervention needed to be composed of the following:
- a treatment programme where two or more specific psychological interventions (as defined above) were combined in a systematic and programmed way; and
- the intervention was conducted with the specific intention of producing a benefit over and above that which might be achieved by a single intervention alone.

In addition, multi-modal treatments could provide specific interventions, either concurrently or consecutively.

8.1.6   Competence to deliver psychological therapies

For the purpose of implementing the current guidelines, it is important to have an understanding of the therapists' level of competence in the psychological therapy trials that were included. Each of the psychological therapy papers was reviewed for details of training or level of competence of the therapists delivering the intervention[16].

8.2   ADHERENCE THERAPY

8.2.1   Introduction

Pharmacological interventions have been the mainstay of treatment since their introduction in the 1950s; however, about 50% of people with schizophrenia and schizophreniform disorder are believed to be non-adherent to (or non-compliant with) their medication (Nosě *et al.*, 2003). It is estimated that non-adherence to medication leads to a higher relapse rate, repeated hospital admissions, and therefore increased economic and social burden for the service users themselves as well as for mental health services (Gray *et al.*, 2006; Robinson *et al.*, 1999a)[17].

Against this background, 'compliance therapy' was first developed by Kemp and colleagues (1996, 1998) to target service users with schizophrenia and psychosis. The therapy aims to improve service users' attitude to medication and treatment adherence, and thus hypothetically enhance their clinical outcomes, and prevent potential and future relapse (Kemp *et al.*, 1996, 1998). Recently, the terms 'adherence' and 'concordance' have been used synonymously to denote 'compliance therapy' and its major aim (that is, adherence to medication), as reflected in emerging literature (McIntosh *et al.*, 2006). Overall, 'adherence therapy' is the commonly accepted term used contemporarily.

Adherence therapy is designed as a brief and pragmatic intervention, borrowing techniques and principles from motivational interviewing (Miller & Rollnick, 1991), psychoeducation and cognitive therapy (Kemp *et al.*, 1996). A typical adherence therapy course offered to a service user with psychosis usually comprises four to eight sessions, each lasting from roughly 30 minutes to 1 hour (Kemp *et al.*, 1996; Gray *et al.*, 2006). The intervention uses a phased approach to:

- assess and review the service user's illness and medication history
- explore his or her ambivalence to treatment, maintenance medication and stigma
- conduct a medication problem-solving exercise to establish the service user's attitude to future medication use.

Definition
Adherence therapy was defined as:

- any programme involving interaction between service provider and service user, during which service users are provided with support, information and management strategies to improve their adherence to medication and/or with the specific aim of improving symptoms, quality of life and preventing relapse.

---

[16] Training and competency reviews are presented only for recommended interventions.
[17] Further information about medicines concordance and adherence to treatment can be found in the NICE guideline on this topic (see http://www.nice.org.uk).

To be considered as well defined, the strategy should be tailored to the needs of individuals.

8.2.2   Clinical review protocol

The review protocol, including information about the databases searched and the eligibility criteria can be found in Table 52. The primary clinical questions can be found in Box 1. A new systematic search for relevant studies was conducted for the guideline update. The search identified an existing Cochrane review (McIntosh *et al.*, 2006), which was used to identify papers prior to 2002 (further information about the search strategy can be found in Appendix 8).

Table 52: Clinical review protocol for the review of adherence therapy

Electronic databases	CINAHL, CENTRAL, EMBASE, MEDLINE, PsycINFO
Date searched	1 January 2002 to 30 July 2008
Study design	RCT ($\geq$10 participants per arm)
Patient population	Adults (18+) with schizophrenia (including schizophrenia-related disorders)
Excluded populations	Very late onset schizophrenia (onset after age 60) Other psychotic disorders, such as bipolar disorder, mania or depressive psychosis People with coexisting learning difficulties, significant physical or sensory difficulties, or substance misuse
Interventions	Adherence therapy
Comparator	Any alternative management strategy
Critical outcomes	Mortality (suicide) Global state (relapse, rehospitalisation,) Mental state (total symptoms, depression) Psychosocial functioning Adherence to antipsychotic treatment Insight Quality of life Leaving the study early for any reason Adverse events

8.2.3   Studies considered for review[18]

Five RCTs (N = 649) met the inclusion criteria for the update. Although broadly based on a cognitive behavioural approach, KEMP1996 was reclassified as an adherence therapy paper because the primary aim of the intervention was to improve adherence and attitudes towards medication. All of the trials were published in peer-reviewed journals between 1996 and 2007. In addition, two studies were excluded from the analysis because they failed to meet the intervention definition (further information about both included and excluded studies can be found in Appendix 15c).

8.2.4   Adherence therapy versus control

For the update, five RCTs of adherence therapy versus any type of control were included in the meta-analysis (see Table 53 for a summary of the study characteristics). Forest plots and/or data tables for each outcome can be found in Appendix 16d.

8.2.5   Clinical evidence summary

The limited evidence from KEMP1996 regarding improvements in measures of compliance and insight has not been supported by new studies, including those with follow-up measures. Although there is limited and inconsistent evidence of improved attitudes towards medication, adherence therapy did not have an effect on symptoms, quality of life, relapse or rehospitalisation.

8.2.6   Health economic evidence

The systematic search of the economic literature identified one study that assessed the cost effectiveness of adherence therapy for people with acute psychosis treated in an inpatient setting in the UK (Healey *et al.*, 1998). The study was conducted alongside the RCT described in KEMP1996. The comparator of adherence therapy was supportive counselling. The study sample consisted of 74 people with schizophrenia, affective disorders with psychotic features or schizoaffective disorder who were hospitalised for psychosis. The time horizon of the economic analysis was 18 months (RCT period plus naturalistic follow-up). Costs consisted of those to the NHS (inpatient, outpatient, day-hospital care, accident and emergency services, primary and community care) and criminal justice system costs incurred by arrests, court

---

[18] Here and elsewhere in this chapter, each study considered for review is referred to by a study ID, with studies included in the previous guideline in lower case and new studies in upper case (primary author and date). References for included studies denoted by study IDs can be found in Appendix 15c.

Table 53: Summary of study characteristics for adherence therapy

Adherence therapy versus any control	
k (total N)	5 (649)
Study ID	GRAY2006 KEMP1996 MANEESAKORN2007 ODONNELL2003 TSANG2005
Diagnosis	58–100% schizophrenia or other related diagnoses (DSM-III or IV)
Baseline severity	*BPRS total*: Mean (SD) ~45 (13) GRAY2006 Mean (SD) ~58 (14) KEMP1996 Mean (SD) ~69 (20) ODONNELL2003 Mean (SD) ~44 (8) TSANG2005 *PANSS total*: Mean (SD) ~59 (13) MANEESAKORN2007
Number of sessions	*Range*: 4–8
Length of treatment	*Range*: Maximum 3–20 weeks (GRAY2006, KEMP1996; MANEESAKORN2007)
Length of follow-up	*Up to 12 months*: GRAY2006 ODONNEL2003 TSANG2005 *Up to 18 months*: KEMP1996
Setting	*Inpatient*: KEMP1996 MANEESAKORN2007 ODONNELL2003 TSANG2005 *Inpatient and outpatient*: GRAY2006

appearances, probation, and so on. Outcomes included relapse rates, BPRS and GAF scores, Drug Attitude Inventory (DAI) scores, Insight scale scores and levels of compliance with antipsychotic medication. Adherence therapy was reported to have a significant positive effect over supportive counselling in terms of relapse, GAF, DAI and Insight scale scores as well as compliance at various follow-up time points. The two interventions were associated with similar costs: mean weekly cost per person over 18 months was £175 for adherence therapy and £193 for supportive counselling in 1995/96 prices (p = 0.92). Because of high rates of attrition, the sample size at endpoint (N = 46) was adequate to detect a 30% difference in costs at the 5% level of significance. The authors suggested that adherence therapy was a cost-effective intervention in the UK because it was more effective than supportive counselling at a similar cost.

Details on the methods used for the systematic search of the economic literature are described in Chapter 3. References to included/excluded studies and evidence tables for all economic studies included in the guideline systematic literature review are presented in the form of evidence tables in Appendix 14.

8.2.7 From evidence to recommendations

The current review found no consistent evidence to suggest that adherence therapy is effective in improving the critical outcomes of schizophrenia when compared with any other control. Although one UK-based study (KEMP1996) reported positive results for measures of adherence and drug attitudes, these findings have not been supported in recent, larger-scale investigations. It is also noteworthy that a proportion of participants in the KEMP1996 study had a primary diagnosis of a mood disorder and that, in an 18-month follow-up paper, the authors stated that 'subgroup analyses revealed the following: patients with schizophrenia tended to have a less favourable outcome in terms of social functioning, symptom level, insight and treatment attitudes'

One economic analysis, conducted alongside KEMP1996, suggested that adherence therapy could be a cost-effective option for people experiencing acute psychosis in the UK because it was more effective than its comparator at a similar total cost. In addition to the aforementioned limitations of the KEMP1996 study, because of high attrition rates the sample was very small, making it difficult to establish such a hypothesis.

Based on the limited health economic evidence and lack of clinical effectiveness, the GDG therefore concluded that there is no robust evidence for the use of adherence therapy as a discrete intervention.

8.2.8 Recommendations

8.2.8.1 Do not offer adherence therapy (as a specific intervention) to people with schizophrenia.

8.3 ARTS THERAPIES

8.3.1 Introduction

The arts therapy professions in the US and Europe have their roots in late 19th and early 20th century hospitals, where involvement in the arts was used by patients and interested clinicians as a potential aid to recovery. This became more prevalent after the influx of war veterans in the 1940s, which led to the emergence of formal training and professional bodies for art, music, drama and dance movement therapies. These treatments were further developed in psychiatric settings in the latter half of the 20th century (Bunt, 1994; Wood, 1997).

While the four modalities use a variety of techniques and arts media, all focus on the creation of a working therapeutic relationship in which strong emotions can be expressed and processed. The art form is also seen as a safe way to experiment with relating to others in a meaningful way when words can be difficult. A variety of psychotherapeutic theories are used to understand the interactions between patient(s) and therapist but psychodynamic models (see Section 8.8) tend to predominate in the UK (Crawford & Patterson, 2007).

More recently, approaches to working with people with psychosis using arts therapies have begun to be more clearly defined, taking into consideration the phase and symptomatology of the illness (Gilroy & McNeilly, 2000; Jones, 1996). The arts therapies described in the studies included in this review have predominantly emphasised expression, communication, social connection and self-awareness through supportive and interactive experiences, with less emphasis on the use of 'uncovering' psychoanalytic approaches (Green, 1987; Rohricht & Priebe, 2006; Talwar *et al.*, 2006; Ulrich, 2007; Yang *et al.*, 1998).

Art, music, drama and dance movement therapists[19] practising in the UK are state registered, regulated by the Health Professions Council, which requires specialist training at Master's level.

Definition

Arts therapies are complex interventions that combine psychotherapeutic techniques with activities aimed at promoting creative expression. In all arts therapies:

● the creative process is used to facilitate self-expression within a specific therapeutic framework
● the aesthetic form is used to 'contain' and give meaning to the service user's experience
● the artistic medium is used as a bridge to verbal dialogue and insight-based psychological development if appropriate
● the aim is to enable the patient to experience him/herself differently and develop new ways of relating to others.

Arts therapies currently provided in the UK comprise: art therapy or art psychotherapy, dance movement therapy, body psychotherapy, dramatherapy and music therapy.

8.3.2   Clinical review protocol

The review protocol, including information about the databases searched and the eligibility criteria, can be found in Table 54. The primary clinical questions can be found

---

[19] Registration pending.

Table 54: Clinical review protocol for the review of arts therapies

Electronic databases	CINAHL, CENTRAL, EMBASE, MEDLINE, PsycINFO
Date searched	Database inception to 30 July 2008
Study design	RCT (≥10 participants per arm)
Patient population	Adults (18+) with schizophrenia (including schizophrenia-related disorders)
Excluded populations	Very late onset schizophrenia (onset after age 60) Other psychotic disorders, such as bipolar disorder, mania or depressive psychosis People with coexisting learning difficulties, significant physical or sensory difficulties, or substance misuse
Interventions	Arts therapies
Comparator	Any alternative management strategy
Critical outcomes	Mortality (suicide) Global state (relapse, rehospitalisation) Mental state (total symptoms, depression) Psychosocial functioning Quality of life Leaving the study early for any reason Adverse events

in Box 1. A new systematic search for relevant RCTs was conducted for the guideline update (further information about the search strategy can be found in Appendix 8).

8.3.3   Studies considered for review

Seven RCTs (N = 406) met the inclusion criteria for the update. All trials were published in peer-reviewed journals between 1974 and 2007 (further information about both included and excluded studies can be found in Appendix 15c).

8.3.4   Arts therapies versus any control

For the update, six out of the seven RCTs were included in the meta-analysis of arts therapies versus any type of control (see Table 55 for a summary of the study characteristics). One of the included studies (NITSUN1974) did not provide any useable

Table 55: Summary of study characteristics for arts therapies

Arts therapies versus any control	
k (total N)	6 (382)
Study ID	GREEN1987 RICHARDSON2007 ROHRICHT2006 TALWAR2006 ULRICH2007 YANG1998
Diagnosis	50–100% schizophrenia or other related diagnoses (DSM-III or IV)
Baseline severity	*BPRS total*: Mean (SD): ~16 (9) RICHARDSON2007 Mean (SD) ~40 (8) YANG1998 *PANSS total*: Mean (SD): ~78 (18) ROHRICHT2006 Mean (SD): ~72 (13) TALWAR2006
Treatment modality	*Art*: GREEN1987 RICHARDSON2007 *Body-orientated*: ROHRICHT2006 *Music*: TALWAR2006 ULRICH2007 YANG1998
Length of treatment	Range: 5–20 weeks
Length of follow-up	*Up to 6 months*: RICHARDSON2007 ROHRICHT2006
Setting	*Inpatient*: TALWAR2006 ULRICH2007 YANG1998 *Outpatient*: GREEN1987 RICHARDSON2007 ROHRICHT2006

data for any of the critical outcomes listed in the review protocol. Sub-analyses were used to examine treatment modality and setting. Forest plots and/or data tables for each outcome can be found in Appendix 16d.

8.3.5   Clinical evidence summary

The review found consistent evidence that arts therapies are effective in reducing negative symptoms when compared with any other control. There was some evidence indicating that the medium to large effects found at the end of treatment were sustained at up to 6 months' follow-up. Additionally, there is consistent evidence to indicate a medium effect size regardless of the modality used within the intervention (that is, music, body-orientated or art), and that arts therapies were equally as effective in reducing negative symptoms in both inpatient and outpatient populations.

8.3.6   Health economic considerations

No evidence on the cost effectiveness of arts therapies for people with schizophrenia was identified by the systematic search of the economic literature. Details on the methods used for the systematic search of the economic literature are described in Chapter 3.

The clinical studies on arts therapies included in the guideline systematic litera-ture review described interventions consisting of 12 sessions on average. These programmes are usually delivered by one therapist to groups of six to eight people in the UK and have an average duration of 1 hour.

Arts therapies are provided by therapists with a specialist training at Master's level. The unit cost of a therapist providing arts therapies was not available. The salary scale of an arts therapist lies across bands 7 and 8a, which is comparable to the salary level of a clinical psychologist. The unit cost of a clinical psychologist is £67 per hour of client contact in 2006/07 prices (Curtis, 2007). This estimate has been based on the mid-point of Agenda for Change salaries band 7 of the April 2006 pay scale according to the National Profile for Clinical Psychologists, Counsellors and Psychotherapists (NHS Employers, 2006). It includes salary, salary oncosts, overheads and capital overheads, but does not take into account qualification costs because the latter are not available for clinical psychologists.

Based on the estimated staff time associated with an arts therapy programme (as described above) and the unit cost of a clinical psychologist, the average cost of arts therapy per person participating in such a programme would range between £100 and £135 in 2006/07 prices.

Using the lower cost-effectiveness threshold of £20,000 per QALY set by NICE (NICE, 2008b), a simple threshold analysis indicated that arts therapies are cost effective if they improve the HRQoL of people with schizophrenia by 0.005 to

0.007 annually, on a scale of 0 (death) to 1 (perfect health). Using the upper cost-effectiveness threshold of £30,000 per QALY, the improvement in HRQoL of people in schizophrenia required for arts therapies to be cost effective fell by 0.003 to 0.004 annually.

8.3.7 From evidence to recommendations

The clinical review indicated that arts therapies are effective in reducing negative symptoms across a range of treatment modalities, and for both inpatient and outpatient populations. The majority of trials included in the review utilised a group-based approach. It is noteworthy that in all of the UK-based studies the therapists conducting the intervention were all Health Professions Council (HPC) trained and accredited, with the equivalent level of training occurring in the non-UK based studies.

The cost of arts therapies was estimated at roughly £100 to £135 per person with schizophrenia (2006/07 prices); a simple threshold analysis showed that if arts therapies improved the HRQoL of people with schizophrenia by approximately 0.006 annually (on a scale of 0 to 1) then they would be cost effective, according to the lower NICE cost-effectiveness threshold. Using the upper NICE cost-effectiveness threshold, improvement in HRQoL would need to approximate 0.0035 annually for the intervention to be considered cost effective. Use of this upper cost-effectiveness threshold can be justified because arts therapies are the only interventions demonstrated to have medium to large effects on negative symptoms in people with schizophrenia. The GDG estimated that the magnitude of the improvement in negative symptoms associated with arts therapies (SMD -0.59 with 95% CIs -0.83 to -0.36) could be translated into an improvement in HRQoL probably above 0.0035, and possibly even above 0.006 annually, given that the therapeutic effect of arts therapies was shown to last (and was even enhanced) at least up to 6 months following treatment (SMD -0.77 with 95% CIs -1.27 to -0.26).

At present, the data for the effectiveness of arts therapies on other outcomes, such as social functioning and quality of life, is still very limited and infrequently reported in trials. Consequently, the GDG recommends that further large-scale investigations of arts therapies should be undertaken to increase the current evidence base. Despite this small but emerging evidence base, the GDG recognise that arts therapies are currently the only interventions (both psychological and pharmacological) to demonstrate consistent efficacy in the reduction of negative symptoms. This, taken in combination with the economic analysis, has led to the following recommendations.

8.3.8 Recommendations

Treatment of acute episode
8.3.8.1   Consider offering arts therapies to all people with schizophrenia, particularly for the alleviation of negative symptoms. This can be started either during the acute phase or later, including in inpatient settings.

8.3.8.2   Arts therapies should be provided by an HPC registered arts therapist, with previous experience of working with people with schizophrenia. The intervention should be provided in groups unless difficulties with acceptability and access and engagement indicate otherwise. Arts therapies should combine psychotherapeutic techniques with activity aimed at promoting creative expression, which is often unstructured and led by the service user. Aims of arts therapies should include:

- enabling people with schizophrenia to experience themselves differently and to develop new ways of relating to others
- helping people to express themselves and to organise their experience into a satisfying aesthetic form
- helping people to accept and understand feelings that may have emerged during the creative process (including, in some cases, how they came to have these feelings) at a pace suited to the person.

Promoting recovery
8.3.8.3   Consider offering arts therapies to assist in promoting recovery, particularly in people with negative symptoms.

8.3.9   Research recommendations

8.3.9.1   An adequately powered RCT should be conducted to investigate the clinical and cost effectiveness of arts therapies compared with an active control (for example, sham music therapy) in people with schizophrenia.
8.3.9.2   An adequately powered RCT should be conducted to investigate the most appropriate duration and number of sessions for arts therapies in people with schizophrenia.

8.4   COGNITIVE BEHAVIOURAL THERAPY

8.4.1   Introduction

CBT is based on the premise that there is a relationship between thoughts, feelings and behaviour. Although Albert Ellis first developed CBT (which he called rational emotive behaviour therapy) in the 1960s, most CBT practiced in the present day has its origins in the work of Aaron T. Beck. Beck developed CBT for the treatment of depression in the 1970s (Beck, 1979), but since then it has been found to be an effective treatment in a wide range of mental health problems including anxiety disorders, obsessive compulsive disorder, bulimia nervosa and post-traumatic stress disorder. In the early 1990s, following an increased understanding of the cognitive psychology of psychotic symptoms (Frith, 1992; Garety & Hemsley, 1994; Slade & Bentall, 1988), interest grew in the application of CBT for people with psychotic disorders. Early CBT trials tended to be particularly symptom focused, helping service users develop coping strategies to manage hallucinations (Tarrier *et al.*, 1993). Since then, however, CBT for psychosis (CBTp) has evolved and now tends to be formulation based.

As with other psychological interventions, CBT depends upon the effective development of a positive therapeutic alliance (Roth *et al.*, 1996). On the whole, the aim is to help the individual normalise and make sense of their psychotic experiences, and to reduce the associated distress and impact on functioning. CBTp trials have investigated a range of outcomes over the years; these include symptom reduction (positive, negative and general symptoms) (Rector *et al.*, 2003), relapse reduction (Garety *et al.*, 2008), social functioning (Startup *et al.*, 2004), and insight (Turkington *et al.*, 2002). More recently, researchers have shown an interest in the impact of CBTp beyond the sole reduction of psychotic phenomena and are looking at changes in distress and problematic behaviour associated with these experiences (Trower *et al.*, 2004). Furthermore, the populations targeted have expanded, with recent developments in CBTp focusing on the treatment of first episode psychosis (Jackson *et al.*, 2005, 2008), and people with schizophrenia and comorbid substance use disorders (Barrowclough *et al.*, 2001).

Definition
CBT was defined as a discrete psychological intervention where service users:
- establish links between their thoughts, feelings or actions with respect to the current or past symptoms, and/or functioning, and
- re-evaluate their perceptions, beliefs or reasoning in relation to the target symptoms.

In addition, a further component of the intervention should involve the following:
- service users monitoring their own thoughts, feelings or behaviours with respect to the symptom or recurrence of symptoms, and/or
- promotion of alternative ways of coping with the target symptom, and/or
- reduction of distress, and/or
- improvement of functioning.

8.4.2   Clinical review protocol

The review protocol, including information about the databases searched and the eligibility criteria, can be found in Table 56. The primary clinical questions can be found in Box 1. For the guideline update, a new systematic search was conducted for relevant RCTs published since the previous guideline (further information about the search strategy can be found in Appendix 8 and information about the search for health economic evidence can be found in Section 8.4.8).

8.4.3   Studies considered for review

In the previous guideline, 13 RCTs (N = 1,297) of CBT were included. One RCT from the previous guideline (KEMP1996) was removed from the update analysis and re-classified by the GDG as adherence therapy and a further three studies were

Table 56: Clinical review protocol for the review of CBT

Electronic databases	CINAHL, CENTRAL, EMBASE, MEDLINE, PsycINFO
Date searched	1 January 2002 to 30 July 2008
Study design	RCT (≥10 participants per arm)
Patient population	Adults (18+) with schizophrenia (including schizophrenia-related disorders)
Excluded populations	Very late onset schizophrenia (onset after age 60) Other psychotic disorders, such as bipolar disorder, mania or depressive psychosis People with coexisting learning difficulties, significant physical or sensory difficulties, or substance misuse
Interventions	CBT
Comparator	Any alternative management strategy
Critical outcomes	Mortality (suicide) Global state (relapse, rehospitalisation,) Mental state (total symptoms, depression) Psychosocial functioning Adherence to antipsychotic treatment Insight Quality of life Leaving the study early for any reason Adverse events

removed because of inadequate numbers of participants (Garety1994; Levine1996; Turkington2000). The update search identified six papers providing follow-up data to existing RCTs and 22 new RCTs, including those with CBT as part of a multi-modal intervention. In total, 31 RCTs (N = 3,052) met the inclusion criteria for the update. Of these, one was currently unpublished and 30 were published in peer-reviewed journals between 1996 and 2008 (further information about both included and excluded studies can be found in Appendix 15c).

8.4.4 Cognitive behavioural therapy versus control

For the update, 31 RCTs of CBT versus any type of control were included in the meta-analysis (see Table 57 for a summary of the study characteristics). However, this comparison was only used for outcomes in which there were insufficient studies to allow for separate standard care and other active treatment arms.

Table 57: Summary of study characteristics for CBT

	CBT versus any control[a]	CBT versus standard care	CBT versus other active treatments	CBT versus non-standard care
k (total N)	31 (3052)	19 (2118)	14 (1029)	3 (136)
Study ID	BACH2002 BARROW-CLOUGH2006 BECHDOLF2004 Bradshaw2000 CATHER2005 Drury1996 DURHAM2003 ENGLAND2007 GARETY2008[b] GRANHOLM2005[c] GUMLEY2003 Haddock1999 Hogarty1997[e] JACKSON2005 JACKSON2007 JENNER2004[c] Kuipers1997 LECLERC2000 LECOMTE2008 Lewis2002[d] MCLEOD2007	BACH2002 BARROW-CLOUGH2006 DURHAM2003 ENGLAND2007 GARETY2008 GRANHOLM2005[c] GUMLEY2003 JACKSON2005 JENNER2004[c] Kuipers1997 LECLERC2000 LECOMTE2008 Lewis2002 MCLEOD2007 STARTUP2004 Tarrier1998 TROWER2004 Turkington2002 WYKES2005	BECHDOLF2004 CATHER2005 DURHAM2003 GARETY2008 Haddock1999 Hogarty1997 JACKSON2007 LECOMTE2008 Lewis2002 PENADES2006 PINTO1999[c] Sensky2000 Tarrier1998 VALMAGGIA2005	Drury1996 Bradshaw2000 RECTOR2003

	PENADES2006 PINTO1999c RECTOR2003 Sensky2000 STARTUP2004 Tarrier1998 TROWER2004 Turkington2002 VALMAGGIA2005 WYKES2005		
Diagnosis	58–100% schizophrenia or other related diagnoses (DSM or ICD-10)	58–100% schizophrenia or other related diagnoses (DSM or ICD-10)	64–100% schizophrenia or other related diagnoses (DSM or ICD-10)	100% schizophrenia or other related diagnoses (DSM or ICD-10)
Baseline severity	*BPRS total:* Mean (SD) range: ~17 (7) to ~82 (21) *PANSS total:* Mean (SD) range: ~25 (7) to ~96 (16) *CPRS total:* Mean (SD) ~24 (14) to ~36 (14)	*BPRS total:* Mean (SD) range: ~17 (7) to ~82 (21) *PANSS total:* Mean (SD) range: ~25 (7) to ~96 (16) *CPRS total:* Mean (SD) range: ~24 (14)	*PANSS total:* Mean (SD) range: ~51 (13) to ~96 (16) *CPRS total:* Mean (SD) ~36 (14)	Not reported

Continued

Table 57: *(Continued)*

	CBT versus any control[a]	CBT versus standard care	CBT versus other active treatments	CBT versus non-standard care
Number of sessions	*Range: 4–156*	*Range: 4–24*	*Range: 10–156*	*Range: 20–156*
Length of treatment	*Range: 2–156 weeks*	*Range: 2–52 weeks*	*Range: 8–156 weeks*	*Range: 24–156 weeks*
Length of follow-up (only including papers reporting follow-up measures)	*Range: 3–60 months*	*Range: 3–60 months*	*Range: 3–60 months*	*Range: 6–24 months*
Setting	*Inpatient:* BECHDOLF2004 Bradshaw2000 Drury1996 Haddock1999 Hogarty1997[e] Lewis2002[f] STARTUP2004 VALMAGGIA2005 *Outpatient:* BARROW-CLOUGH2006 CATHER2005 ENGLAND2007 GRANHOLM2005[c] GUMLEY2003	*Inpatient:* Lewis2002[f] STARTUP2004 *Outpatient:* BARROW-CLOUGH2006 ENGLAND2007 GRANHOLM2005[c] GUMLEY2003 JACKSON2005	*Inpatient:* BECHDOLF2004 Haddock1999 Hogarty1997[e] Lewis2002[f] VALMAGGIA2005 *Outpatient:* CATHER2005 LECOMTE2008 Sensky2000 Tarrier1998	*Inpatient:* Bradshaw2000 Drury1996 *Outpatient:* RECTOR2003

JACKSON2005	JENNER2004[c]	
JENNER2004[c]	Kuipers1997	
Kuipers1997	LECOMTE2008	
LECOMTE2008	Sensky2000	
RECTOR2003	Tarrier1998	
Sensky2000	WYKES2005	
Tarrier1998		
WYKES2005		
Inpatient and outpatient:	*Inpatient and outpatient:*	*Inpatient and outpatient:*
BACH2002	BACH2002	DURHAM2003
DURHAM2003	DURHAM2003	GARETY2008
GARETY2008	GARETY2008	PINTO1999[c]
LECLERC2000	LECLERC2000	
MCLEOD2007	MCLEOD2007	
PINTO1999[c]	TROWER2004	
TROWER2004	Turkington2002	
Turkington2002		
EIS setting:		*EIS setting:*
JACKSON2007		JACKSON2007

Note: Studies were categorised as short (fewer than 12 weeks), medium (12–51 weeks) and long (52 weeks or more).

[a] CBT versus any control was only used for outcomes in which there were insufficient studies to allow for separate standard care and other active treatment arms.

[b] The primary GARETY2008 paper reports data separately for the carer and non-carer pathways of the study. Although the dichotomous data has been combined across pathways, data for the continuous measures are presented separately. In the main and subgroup analyses GARETY2008 appears as GARETY2008C (carer pathway) and GARETY2008NC (non-carer pathway).

[c] Multi-modal interventions.

[d] Follow-up papers to Lewis2002 report the data separately for the three study sites, hence in the analysis Lewis2002 appears as LEWIS2002L (Liverpool), LEWIS2002M (Manchester) and LEWIS2002N (Nottingham).

[e] Participants were recruited in the inpatient setting with the intervention starting shortly before discharge.

[f] Participants were recruited from inpatient wards and day hospitals.

For the primary analysis, 19 RCTs were included comparing CBT with standard care, 14 comparing CBT with other active treatments and three comparing CBT with non-standard care. Forest plots and/or data tables for each outcome can be found in Appendix 16d.

In addition to the primary analyses, subgroup analyses were used to explore certain characteristics of the trials[20] (see Table 58 for a summary of the studies included in each subgroup comparison). Five RCTs were included in the analysis comparing CBT with any control in participants experiencing a first episode of schizophrenia; eight compared CBT with any control in participants experiencing an acute-episode; 11 compared CBT with any control in participants during the promoting recovery phase; six compared group CBT with any control; and 19 compared individual CBT with any control. Multi-modal trials were not included in the subgroup analyses. Forest plots and/or data tables for each outcome can be found in Appendix 16d.

8.4.5   Training

The inconsistency in reporting what training the therapists in the trials had received meant it was impossible to determine the impact of level of training on the outcomes of the trial. Less than half (15/31) of the included CBT papers made reference to specific CBT-related training. In early CBTp trials this is not surprising because the researchers were at the forefront of the development of the therapy and no specific psychosis-related CBT training would have been available. In studies where training was mentioned, it was often vague in terms of the length of training therapists had received and whether the training had been specifically focused on CBT for psychosis. Moreover, where details of training programmes associated with the trial were provided, previous experience and training did not always appear to have been controlled for. This means that therapists could have entered the study with different levels of competence, making it impossible to determine the impact of the specified training programme. Of the 25 trials reporting the professional conducting the intervention, the majority utilised clinical psychologists (14/25). However, a proportion of trials utilised different professionals including psychiatrists (3/25), psychiatric nurses (7/25), social workers (2/25), Master's level psychology graduates and/or interns (1/25), occupational therapists (1/24) and local mental health workers (2/25). Within some trials, a number of professionals may have delivered the intervention (for example, two psychologists and one psychiatrist). Often, where the professional conducting the intervention was not a clinical psychologist, reference was made to specific training in CBTp or extensive experience working with people with psychosis.

---

[20] Existing subgroup comparisons assessing the country of the trial, number of treatment sessions and duration of treatment were also updated. However, there was insufficient data to draw any conclusions based on these subgroups. Please refer to Appendix 16d for the forest plots and/or data tables for all subgroup comparisons conducted.

Table 58: Summary of study characteristics for CBT subgroup analyses

	CBT versus any control – first episode[a]	CBT versus any control – acute episode	CBT versus any control – promoting recovery	Group CBT versus any control	Individual CBT versus any control
k (total N)	5 (618)	8 (695)	11 (1093)	6 (534)	19 (2082)
Study ID	Haddock1999 JACKSON2005 JACKSON2007 LECOMTE2008 Lewis2002	BACH2002 BECHDOLF2004 Bradshaw2000 Drury1996 ENGLAND2007 GARETY2008 MCLEOD2007 STARTUP2004	BARROW-CLOUGH2006 CATHER2005 DURHAM2003 Kuipers1997 PENADES2006 Sensky2000 Tarrier1998 TROWER2004 Turkington2002 VALMAGGIA2005 WYKES2005	BARROW-CLOUGH2006 BECHDOLF2004 LECOMTE2008 LECLERC2000 MCLEDO2007 WYKES2005	BACH2002 Bradshaw1999 CATHER2005 DURHAM2003 ENGLAND2007 GARETY2008 GUMLEY2003 Haddock1999 JACKSON2005 JACKSON2007 Kuipers1997 Lewis2002 PENADES2006 Sensky2000 STARTUP2004 Tarrier1998 TROWER2004 Turkington2002 VALMAGGIA2005

Note: Studies were categorised as short (<12 weeks), medium (12–51 weeks) and long (52 weeks or more).
[a] A number of trials included participants in all phases of illness (for example, 20% first episode, 60% acute and 20% promoting recovery) and hence could not be included in the subgroup analysis.

Competence does not appear to be directly correlated with training and a number of additional variables play a part. The Durham and colleagues' (2003) study indicated that training in general CBT did not necessarily produce proficient CBTp therapists. Although the therapists in the study had undergone CBT training, when their practice was assessed on a CBTp fidelity measure, they did not appear to be using specific psychosis-focused interventions. A number of studies included in the CBTp meta-analyses used CBT fidelity measures to determine the quality of the therapy that was being delivered. Again, there were inconsistencies between studies. Three different fidelity measures were used and there was no agreed standard as to what the cut-off score for demonstrating competence should be. Moreover, Durham and colleagues (2003) used two of these scales in their trial and found that therapy ratings did not correlate.

With regard to the use of treatment manuals, however, there was more consistent reporting across the trials, with the majority of papers (24/31) making reference to either a specific treatment manual or to a manualised approach. Reporting of supervision was also more consistent, with both peer- and senior-supervision evident in over two-thirds of the trials.

8.4.6   Ethnicity

Only one follow-up paper (Rathod *et al.*, 2005) assessed changes in insight and compliance in the Black Caribbean and African–Caribbean participants included in the Turkington2002 study. The subgroup analysis indicated a higher dropout rate among both black and ethnic minority groups. Additionally, compared with their white counterparts, the black and minority ethnic participants demonstrated significantly smaller changes in insight. Although these are potentially interesting findings, it must be noted that black and minority ethnic participants comprised only 11% of the study population, with Black African and African–Caribbean participants representing 3 and 5% of the sample, respectively. With regard to the other studies included in the review, there was a paucity of information on the ethnicity of participants. Because of the lack of information, the GDG were unable to draw any conclusions from the data or make any recommendations relating to practice. However, the GDG acknowledge that this is an area warranting further research and formal investigation.

8.4.7   Clinical evidence summary

The review found consistent evidence that, when compared with standard care, CBT was effective in reducing rehospitalisation rates up to 18 months following the end of treatment. Additionally, there was robust evidence indicating that the duration of hospitalisation was also reduced (8.26 days on average). Consistent with the previous guideline, CBT was shown to be effective in reducing symptom severity as measured by total scores on items, such as the PANSS and BPRS, both at end of treatment and at up to 12 months' follow-up. Robust small to medium effects (SMD ~0.30) were also demonstrated for reductions in depression when comparing CBT with both standard care and other active treatments. Furthermore, when compared with any control, there was some evidence for improvements in social functioning up to 12 months.

Although the evidence for positive symptoms was more limited, analysis of PSYRATS data demonstrated some effect for total hallucination measures at the end of treatment. Further to this, there was some limited but consistent evidence for symptom-specific measures including voice compliance, frequency of voices and believability, all of which demonstrated large effect sizes at both end of treatment and follow-up. However, despite these positive effects for hallucination-specific measures, the evidence for there being any effect on delusions was inconsistent.

Although no RCTs directly compared group-based with individual CBT, indirect comparisons indicated that only the latter had robust effects on rehospitalisation, symptom severity and depression. Subgroup analyses also demonstrated additional effects for people with schizophrenia in the promoting recovery phase both with and without persistent symptoms. In particular, when compared with any other control, studies recruiting people in the promoting recovery phase demonstrated consistent evidence for a reduction in negative symptoms up to 24 months following the end of treatment.

8.4.8   Health economic evidence

Systematic literature review

The systematic literature search identified two economic studies that assessed the cost effectiveness of CBT for people with schizophrenia (Kuipers *et al.*, 1998; Startup *et al.*, 2005). Both studies were undertaken in the UK. Details on the methods used for the systematic search of the economic literature are described in Chapter 3. References to included/excluded studies and evidence tables for all economic studies included in the guideline systematic literature review are presented in the form of evidence tables in Appendix 14.

Kuipers and colleagues (1998) evaluated the cost effectiveness of CBT added to standard care compared with standard care alone in 60 people with medication-resistant psychosis participating in an RCT conducted in the UK (KUIPERS1997). The time horizon of the analysis was 18 months (RCT period plus naturalistic follow-up). The study estimated NHS costs (inpatient, outpatient, day hospital, primary and community services) and costs associated with specialist, non-domestic accommodation. Medication costs were not considered. The primary outcome of the analysis was the mean change in BPRS score. CBT was shown to be significantly more effective than its comparator in this respect, with the treatment effect lasting 18 months after the start of the trial (p < 0.001). The costs between the two treatment groups were similar: the mean monthly cost per person over 18 months was £1,220 for CBT added to standard care and £1,403 for standard care alone (p = 0.416, 1996 prices). The study had insufficient power to detect significant differences in costs. The authors suggested that CBT might be a cost-effective intervention in medication-resistant psychosis, as the clinical benefits gained during the 9 months of CBT were maintained and even augmented 9 months later, while the extra intervention costs seemed to be offset by reduced utilisation of health and social care services.

Startup and colleagues (2005) conducted a cost-consequence analysis to measure the cost effectiveness of CBT on top of treatment as usual versus treatment as usual alone in 90 people hospitalised for an acute psychotic episode participating in an RCT in North Wales (STARTUP2004). The time horizon of the analysis was 2 years; the perspective was that of the NHS and Personal Social Services (PSS). Costs included hospital, primary, community and residential care and medication. Health outcomes were measured using the Scale for the Assessment of Positive Symptoms (SAPS), the Scale for the Assessment of Negative Symptoms (SANS), the Social Functioning Scale (SFS) and the GAF scale. CBT showed a significant effect over control in SANS and SFS scores, at no additional cost: the mean cost per person over 24 months was £27,535 for the CBT group and £27,956 for the control group (p = 0.94). The study had insufficient power for economic analysis.

The above results indicate that CBT is potentially a cost-effective intervention for people with acute psychosis or medication-resistant schizophrenia. However, the study samples were very small in both studies and insufficient to establish such a hypothesis with certainty.

Economic modelling
Objective
The guideline systematic review and meta-analysis of clinical evidence demonstrated that provision of CBT to people with schizophrenia results in clinical benefits and reduces the rates of future hospitalisation. A cost analysis was undertaken to assess whether the costs to the NHS of providing CBT in addition to standard care to people with schizophrenia are offset by future savings resulting from reduction in hospitalisation costs incurred by this population.

Intervention assessed
According to the guideline systematic review and meta-analysis of clinical evidence, group-based CBT is not an effective intervention. Therefore, the economic analysis compared individually-delivered CBT added to standard care versus standard care alone.

Methods
A simple economic model estimated the net total costs (or cost savings) to the NHS associated with provision of individual CBT in addition to standard care to people with schizophrenia. Two categories of costs were assessed: intervention costs of CBT, and cost savings resulting from the expected reduction in hospitalisation rates in people with schizophrenia receiving CBT, estimated based on the guideline meta-analysis of respective clinical data. Standard care costs were not estimated, because these were common to both arms of the analysis.

Cost data
Intervention costs (costs of providing cognitive behavioural therapy) The clinical studies on individual CBT included in the guideline systematic review described programmes

of varying numbers of sessions. The resource use estimate associated with provision of CBT in the economic analysis was based on the average resource use reported in these studies, confirmed by the GDG expert opinion to be consistent with clinical practice in the UK. According to the reported resource use data, CBT in the economic analysis consisted of 16 individually-delivered sessions lasting 60 minutes each.

CBT can be delivered by a variety of mental health professionals with appropriate training and supervision. The salary level of a mental health professional providing CBT was estimated by the GDG to range between bands 6b and 8. This is comparable with the salary level of a clinical psychologist. Therefore, the unit cost of clinical psychologists was used to estimate an average intervention cost. The unit cost of a clinical psychologist has been estimated at £67 per hour of client contact in 2006/07 prices (Curtis, 2007). This estimate has been based on the mid-point of Agenda for Change salary band 7 of the April 2006 pay scale according to the National Profile for Clinical Psychologists, Counsellors and Psychotherapists (NHS Employers, 2006). It includes salary, salary oncosts, overheads and capital overheads but does not take into account qualification costs because the latter are not available for clinical psychologists. The same source of national health and social care unit costs reports the cost of CBT as £67 per hour of face-to-face contact (Curtis, 2007; 2006/07 price). This latter unit cost has been estimated on the basis that CBT is delivered by a variety of health professionals, including specialist registrars, clinical psychologists and mental health nurses, and is equal to the unit cost of a clinical psychologist per hour of client contact.

Based on the above resource use estimates and the unit cost of clinical psychologists, the cost of providing a full course of CBT to a person with schizophrenia was estimated at £1,072 in 2006/07 prices.

Costs of hospitalisation / cost savings from reduction in hospitalisation rates   The average cost of hospitalisation for a person with schizophrenia was estimated by multiplying the average duration of hospitalisation for people with schizophrenia, schizotypal and delusional disorders in England in 2006/07 (NHS, The Information Centre, 2008a) by the national average unit cost per bed-day in an inpatient mental health acute care unit for adults for 2006/07 (NHS Reference Costs; Department of Health, 2008a).

Hospital Episode Statistics (HES) is a service providing national statistical data of the care provided by NHS hospitals and for NHS hospital patients treated elsewhere in England (NHS, The Information Centre, 2008a). With respect to inpatient data, HES records episodes (periods) of continuous admitted patient care under the same consultant. In cases where responsibility for a patient's care is transferred to a second or subsequent consultant, there will be two or more episodes recorded relating to the patient's stay in hospital. This means that, for any condition leading to hospital admission, the average length of inpatient stay as measured and reported by HES may be an underestimation of the actual average duration of continuous hospitalisation. Based on HES, the average duration of hospitalisation for people with schizophrenia, schizotypal and delusional disorders (F20–F29 according to ICD-10) in England was 110.6 days in 2006/07. Based on the annually collected NHS Reference Costs (Department of Health, 2008a), the cost per bed-day in a mental health acute care inpatient unit was £259 in 2006/07. By multiplying these figures, the average cost of hospitalisation per person with schizophrenia was estimated at £28,645 in 2006/07 prices.

Clinical data on hospitalisation rates following provision of cognitive behavioural therapy   The guideline meta-analysis of CBT data on hospitalisation rates showed that providing CBT in addition to standard care to people with schizophrenia significantly reduces the rate of future hospitalisations compared with people receiving standard care alone. Table 59 shows the CBT studies included in the meta-analysis of hospitalisation-rate data up to 18 months following treatment (whether these studies were conducted in the UK or not), the hospitalisation rates for each treatment arm reported in the individual studies and the results of the meta-analysis.

The results of meta-analysis show that CBT, when added to standard care, reduces the rate of future hospitalisations in people with schizophrenia (RR of hospitalisation of CBT added to standard care versus standard care alone: 0.74). This result was statistically significant at the 0.05 level (95% CIs of RR: 0.61 to 0.94).

The baseline rate of hospitalisation in the economic analysis was taken from the overall rate of hospitalisation under standard care alone as estimated in the guideline meta-analysis of CBT data on hospitalisation rates; that is, a 29.98% baseline hospitalisation rate was used. The rate of hospitalisation when CBT was added to standard care was calculated by multiplying the estimated RR of hospitalisation of CBT plus standard care versus standard care alone by the baseline hospitalisation rate.

Details on the clinical studies considered in the economic analysis are available in Appendix 15c. The forest plots of the respective meta-analysis are provided in Appendix 16d.

Table 59: Studies considered in the economic analysis of CBT in addition to standard care versus standard care alone and results of meta-analysis

Study ID	Country	Total events (n) in each treatment arm (N)	
		CBT plus standard care (n/N)	Standard care alone (n/N)
TARRIER1998	UK	16/33	9/28
BACH2002	Non-UK	12/40	19/40
LEWIS2002	UK	33/101	37/102
TURKINGTON2002	UK	36/257	38/165
GUMLEY2003	UK	11/72	19/72
Total		108/503 (21.47%)	122/407 (29.98%)
Meta-analysis results		RR: 0.74 95% CI: 0.61–0.94	

Sensitivity analysis

One-way sensitivity analyses were undertaken to investigate the robustness of the results under the uncertainty characterising some of the input parameters and the use of different data and assumptions in the estimation of total net costs (or net savings) associated with provision of CBT to people with schizophrenia. The following scenarios were explored:

- use of the 95% CIs of the RR of hospitalisation of CBT added to standard care versus standard care alone
- exclusion of TARRIER1998 from the meta-analysis. TARRIER1998 was carried out before the National Service Framework was implemented, and therefore the way the study was conducted in terms of hospitalisation levels may have been different from current clinical practice. The baseline rate of hospitalisation used in the analysis was the pooled, weighted, average hospitalisation rate of the control arms of the remaining studies
- exclusion of BACH2002 from the meta-analysis as this was a non-UK study and clinical practice regarding hospital admission levels may have been different from that in the UK. The baseline rate of hospitalisation used in the analysis was the pooled, weighted, average hospitalisation rate of the control arms of the remaining studies
- exclusion of both TARRIER1998 and BACH2002 from the meta-analysis. The baseline rate of hospitalisation used in the analysis was the pooled, weighted, average hospitalisation rate of the control arms of the remaining studies
- change in the number of CBT sessions (16 in the base-case analysis) to a range between 12 and 20
- change in the baseline rate of hospitalisation (that is, the hospitalisation rate for standard care which was 29.98% in the base-case analysis) to a range between 20 and 40%
- use of a more conservative value of duration of hospitalisation. The average duration of hospitalisation for people with schizophrenia (ICD F20-F29) reported by HES (NHS, The Information Centre, 2008a) was 110.6 days, which was deemed high by the GDG. Indeed, HES reported a median duration of hospitalisation for this population of 36 days. HES data were highly skewed, apparently from a number of people with particularly long hospital stays. An alternative, lower length of hospitalisation of 69 days was tested, taken from an effectiveness trial of clozapine versus SGAs in people with schizophrenia with inadequate response or intolerance to current antipsychotic treatment conducted in the UK (CUtLASS Band 2, Davies *et al.*, 2008).

Results

Base-case analysis

The reduction in the rates of future hospitalisation achieved by offering CBT to people with schizophrenia in addition to standard care yielded cost savings equalling £2,061 per person. Given that provision of CBT costs £1,072 per person, CBT results in an overall net saving of £989 per person with schizophrenia. Full results of the base-case analysis are reported in Table 60.

Table 60: Results of cost analysis comparing CBT in addition to standard care versus standard care alone per person with schizophrenia

Costs	CBT plus standard care	Standard care alone	Difference
CBT cost	£1,072	0	£1,072
Hospitalisation cost	£6,526	£8,587	−£2,061
Total cost	£7,598	£8,587	−£989

Sensitivity analysis

The results of the base-case analysis were overall robust to the different scenarios explored in sensitivity analysis. When the 95% CIs of the RR of hospitalisation were used, then the total net cost of providing CBT ranged from −£2,277 (that is a net saving) to £557 per person. When the more conservative value of 69 days length of hospitalisation (instead of 110.6 days used in the base-case analysis) was tested, the net cost of providing CBT ranged between −£1,017 (net saving) to £751 per person. In all scenarios, using the relevant mean RR of hospitalisation taken from the guideline meta-analysis, addition of CBT to standard care resulted in overall cost savings because of a substantial reduction in hospitalisation costs. It must be noted that when BACH2002 was excluded from analysis, then the results of meta-analysis were insignificant at the 0.05 level; consequently, when the upper 95% CI of RR of hospitalisation was used, CBT added to standard care incurred higher hospitalisation costs relative to standard care alone.

Full results of sensitivity analysis are presented in Table 61.

Discussion

The economic analysis showed that CBT is likely to be an overall cost-saving intervention for people with schizophrenia because the intervention costs are offset by savings resulting from a reduction in the number of future hospitalisations associated with this therapy. The net cost of providing CBT was found to lie between −£2,277 (overall net saving) and £557 per person with schizophrenia (for a mean duration of hospitalisation of 110.6 days) or −£1,017 to £751 per person (for a mean duration of hospitalisation of 69 days), using the 95% CIs of RRs of hospitalisation, as estimated in the guideline meta-analysis. It must be noted that possible reduction in other types of health and social care resource use and subsequent cost savings to the NHS and social services, as well as broader financial implications to society (for example, potential increased productivity) associated with the provision of CBT to people with schizophrenia, have not been estimated in this analysis. In addition, clinical benefits associated with CBT, affecting both people with schizophrenia and their families/carers, such as symptom improvement and enhanced HRQoL following reduction in future inpatient stays, should also be considered when the cost effectiveness of CBT is assessed. Taking into account such benefits, even a (conservative) net cost of £751 per person can be probably justified.

Table 61: Results of sensitivity analysis of offering CBT in addition to standard care to people with schizophrenia

Scenario	Total net cost (negative cost implies net saving)
Use of 95% CIs of RR of hospitalisation	−£2,277 (lower CI) to £557 (upper CI)
Exclusion of TARRIER1998 from meta-analysis	−£1,490 (−£2,771 to £47 using the 95% CIs of RR of hospitalisation)
Exclusion of BACH2002 (non-UK study) from meta-analysis	−£375 (−£2,465 to £2,599 using the 95% CIs of RR of hospitalisation)
Exclusion of TARRIER1998 and BACH2002 from meta-analysis	−£1,231 (−£2,502 to £437 using the 95% CIs of RR of hospitalisation)
CBT sessions between 12 and 20	−£1,257 to −£721, respectively
Hospitalisation rate under standard care between 40 and 20%	−£1,678 to −£303, respectively
Mean length of hospitalisation 69 days	−£214 (−£1,017 to £751 using the 95% CIs of RR of hospitalisation)

8.4.9   From evidence to recommendations

The conclusions drawn in the previous guideline regarding the efficacy of CBT have been supported by the updated systematic review. The data for the reduction in rehospitalisation rates and duration of admission remains significant even when removing non-UK and pre-National Service Framework for Mental Health (Department of Health, 1999) papers in a sensitivity analysis, suggesting that these findings may be particularly robust within the current clinical context. The effectiveness of CBT has been corroborated by the evidence for symptom severity, which included reductions in hallucination-specific measures and depression in addition to total symptom scores. However, it must be noted that despite general confirmation of the previous recommendations, following the reclassification and subsequent removal of KEMP1996, there was no robust evidence for the efficacy of CBT on measures of compliance or insight. Consequently, the GDG concluded that there is insufficient evidence to support the previous recommendation about the use of CBT to assist in the development of insight or in the management of poor treatment adherence.

The systematic review of economic evidence showed that provision of CBT to people with schizophrenia in the UK improved clinical outcomes at no additional cost. This finding was supported by economic modelling undertaken for this guideline, which suggested that provision of CBT might result in net cost savings to the NHS, associated with a reduction in future hospitalisation rates. The results of both the systematic literature review and the economic modelling indicate that providing individual CBT to people with schizophrenia is likely to be cost effective in the UK setting, especially when clinical benefits associated with CBT are taken into account.

Although the GDG were unable to draw any firm conclusions from subgroup analyses assessing the impact of treatment duration and number of sessions, they did note that the evidence for CBT is primarily driven by studies that included at least 16 planned sessions. To incorporate the current state of evidence and expert consensus, the GDG therefore modified the previous recommendation relating to the duration and number of treatment sessions.

There was, however, more reliable evidence to support the provision of CBT as an individual-based therapy, a finding largely consistent with current therapeutic practice within the UK.

From the CBTp studies included in the meta-analyses, it is not possible to make any recommendations on the specific training requirements or competencies required to deliver effective CBTp. In particular, papers varied widely in the degree to which they reported details about the training and experience of the person delivering the intervention. However, the GDG felt that this is an important area for future development and have made a research recommendation. Despite not being able to make any specific recommendations for the types of training required at this stage, it was noted that, overall, the majority of trials used either clinical psychologists or registered and/or accredited psychological therapists to deliver the CBTp. In addition, regular clinical supervision was provided in two thirds of the trials and treatment manuals utilised in nearly all of the trials. From this evidence, and based upon expert opinion, the GDG included a number of recommendations relating to the delivery of CBT for people with schizophrenia.

Both the consistency with which CBT was shown to be effective across multiple critical outcomes and the potential net cost-savings to the NHS support the previous recommendations regarding the provision of CBT to people with schizophrenia.

8.4.10   Recommendations

8.4.10.1   Offer cognitive behavioural therapy (CBT) to all people with schizophrenia. This can be started either during the acute phase[21] or later, including in inpatient settings.

How to deliver psychological interventions
8.4.10.2   CBT should be delivered on a one-to-one basis over at least 16 planned sessions and:
  ● follow a treatment manual[22] so that:
    – people can establish links between their thoughts, feelings or actions and their current or past symptoms, and/or functioning
    – the re-evaluation of people's perceptions, beliefs or reasoning relates to the target symptoms

---

[21] CBT should be delivered as described in recommendation 8.4.10.2.
[22] Treatment manuals that have evidence for their efficacy from clinical trials are preferred.

- also include at least one of the following components:
  - people monitoring their own thoughts, feelings or behaviours with respect to their symptoms or recurrence of symptoms
  - promoting alternative ways of coping with the target symptom
  - reducing distress
  - improving functioning.

Promoting recovery

8.4.10.3 Offer CBT to assist in promoting recovery in people with persisting positive and negative symptoms and for people in remission. Deliver CBT as described in recommendation 8.4.10.2.

8.4.11 Research recommendations

8.4.11.1 An adequately powered RCT should be conducted to investigate the most appropriate duration and number of sessions for CBT in people with schizophrenia.

8.4.11.2 An adequately powered RCT should be conducted to investigate CBT delivered by highly trained therapists and mental health professionals compared with brief training of therapists in people with schizophrenia.

8.4.11.3 Research is needed to identify the competencies required to deliver effective CBT to people with schizophrenia.

8.5 COGNITIVE REMEDIATION

8.5.1 Introduction

The presence of cognitive impairment in a proportion of people with schizophrenia has been recognised since the term 'schizophrenia' was first coined (Bleuler, 1911). The precise cause of these deficits (such as structural brain changes, disruptions in neuro-chemical functions or the cognitive impact of the illness and/or of medication) remains contentious, whereas progress on characterising the cognitive problems that arise in schizophrenia has been substantial. Major domains identified include memory problems (Brenner, 1986), attention deficits (Oltmanns & Neale, 1975) and problems in executive function, such as organisation and planning (Weinberger *et al.*, 1988). A recent initiative to promote standardisation of methods for evaluating research on cognitive outcomes (the Measurement and Treatment Research to Improve Cognition in Schizophrenia consensus panel [MATRICS; Nuechterlein *et al.*, 2004]) has identified eight more specific domains: attention/vigilance; speed of processing; working memory; verbal learning and memory; visual learning and memory; reasoning and problem solving; verbal comprehension; and social cognition. Few studies as yet examine changes in all these domains. Cognitive impairment is strongly related to functioning in areas such as work, social relationships and independent living

(McGurk *et al.*, 2007). Because of the importance of cognitive impairment in terms of functioning, it has been identified as an appropriate target for interventions.

Currently available pharmacological treatments have limited effects on cognitive impairments (see Chapter 6). Cognitive remediation programmes have therefore been developed over the past 40 years with the goal of testing whether direct attempts to improve cognitive performance might be more effective (McGurk *et al.*, 2007). The primary rationale for cognitive remediation is to improve cognitive functioning, with some papers also stating improved functioning as an additional aim (Wykes & Reeder, 2005). Approaches adopted have ranged from narrowly defined interventions, which involve teaching service users to improve their performance on a single neuropsychological test, to the provision of comprehensive remediation programmes, increasingly using computerised learning (Galletly *et al.*, 2000). The programmes employ a variety of methods, such as drill and practice exercises, teaching strategies to improve cognition, suggesting compensatory strategies to reduce the effects of persistent impairments and group discussions (McGurk *et al.*, 2007).

Because the use of these methods in the treatment of schizophrenia is still developing and early studies had mixed results (Pilling *et al.*, 2002), there remains uncertainty over which techniques should be used (Wykes & van der Gaag, 2001) and whether the outcomes are beneficial, both in terms of sustained effects on cognition and for improving functioning. Reports of combinations of cognitive remediation with other psychosocial interventions, such as social skills training, or vocational interventions, such as supported employment programmes, have been increasing in the literature. In this review, the focus is on cognitive remediation as a single-modality intervention except where it has been combined with another of the psychological or psychosocial interventions updated within the current review. In these cases, the intervention has been classified as multi-modal intervention and subjected to sensitivity analyses (see Section 8.1.5).

Definition
Cognitive remediation was defined as:
- an identified procedure that is specifically focused on basic cognitive processes, such as attention, working memory or executive functioning, and
- having the specific intention of bringing about an improvement in the level of performance on that specified cognitive function or other functions, including daily living, social or vocational skills.

8.5.2 Clinical review protocol

The review protocol, including information about the databases searched and the eligibility criteria, can be found in Table 62. The primary clinical questions can be found in Box 1. For the guideline update, a new systematic search was conducted for relevant RCTs published since the previous guideline (further information about the search strategy can be found in Appendix 8). It must be acknowledged that some cognitive remediation studies cite improvements to cognition/cognitive measures as their primary outcome. However, it is the view of the GDG that only sustained improvements in cognition, as measured at follow-up, should be considered as clinically important. The rationale for this is that only sustained improvement would be likely to have an impact on other critical outcomes, such as mental state, psychosocial functioning, hospitalisation and relapse.

8.5.3   Studies considered for review

In the previous guideline, seven RCTs of cognitive remediation were included. Two trials (Bellack2001 and Tompkins1995) were removed from the update analysis as the GDG felt that they did not meet the definition of cognitive remediation. The update search identified 15 papers providing follow-up data to existing trials and 15 new trials. A recent meta-analysis (McGurk *et al.*, 2007) identified three additional trials and a number of other studies that did not meet inclusion criteria. The cognitive remediation studies included in the trials employed a variety of different methods and in some cases applied cognitive remediation in combination with a variety of other psychological or psychosocial interventions[23]. In total, 25 trials (N = 1,390) met the inclusion criteria. All of the trials were published in peer-reviewed journals between 1994 and 2008 (further information about both included and excluded studies can be found in Appendix 15c).

8.5.4   Cognitive remediation versus control

For the update, six of the included studies (Benedict1994; BURDA1994; EACK2007 KURTZ2007; SATORY2005; VOLLEMA1995) did not provide useable data for any of the critical outcomes listed in Table 62. Consequently, 20 RCTs of cognitive remediation versus any type of control were included in the meta-analysis (see Table 63 for a summary of the study characteristics). Where there was sufficient data, subanalyses were used to examine cognitive remediation versus standard care and versus other active treatment. Forest plots and/or data tables for each outcome can be found in Appendix 16d.

8.5.5   Clinical evidence summary

In the six RCTs (out of 17 included in the meta-analysis) that reported cognitive outcomes at follow-up, there was limited evidence that cognitive remediation produced sustained benefits in terms of cognition. However, these effects were driven primarily by two studies (HOGARTY2004; PENADES2006); therefore, sensitivity analyses were used to explore how robust the findings were. Removal of these

---

[23] Trials assessing the efficacy of cognitive remediation as an adjunct to non-psychological or psychosocial interventions, such as vocational rehabilitation programmes, were outside the scope of the review.

Table 62: Clinical review protocol for the review of cognitive remediation

Electronic databases	Databases: CINAHL, CENTRAL, EMBASE, MEDLINE, PsycINFO
Date searched	Database inception to 30 July 2008
Study design	RCT (≥10 participants per arm)
Patient population	Adults (18+) with schizophrenia (including schizophrenia-related disorders)
Excluded populations	Very late onset schizophrenia (onset after age 60) Other psychotic disorders, such as bipolar disorder, mania or depressive psychosis People with coexisting learning difficulties, significant physical or sensory difficulties, or substance misuse
Interventions	Cognitive remediation
Comparator	Any alternative management strategy
Critical outcomes	Mortality (suicide) Global state (relapse, rehospitalisation) Mental state (total symptoms, depression) Psychosocial functioning Quality of life Cognitive outcomes (at follow-up only)[a] Leaving the study early for any reason Adverse events

[a] Cognitive measures were categorised into the following cognitive domains based upon Nuechterlein and colleagues, 2004: attention/vigilance, speed of processing, working memory, verbal learning and memory, visual learning and memory, reasoning and problem solving, verbal comprehension, and social cognition. The effect sizes for each individual measure were pooled to produce one effect size per domain for each study.

studies led to the loss of effects for all but one cognitive domain (reasoning and problem solving). There was limited evidence suggesting that cognitive remediation when compared with standard care may improve social functioning. However, this effect was driven by a range of studies conducted by Velligan and colleagues (VELLIGAN2000, 2002, 2008A, 2008B), in which the intervention was more comprehensive than typical cognitive remediation programmes in the UK, and included the use of individually tailored environmental supports to ameliorate areas in addition to basic cognitive functions. The UK-based studies, although well-conducted, did not report evidence of improvement in social or vocational functioning or symptoms at either end of treatment or follow-up.

Table 63: Summary of study characteristics for cognitive remediation

	Cognitive remediation versus any control	Cognitive remediation versus standard care	Cognitive remediation versus other active treatments
k (total N)	17 (1084)	10 (522)	9 (605)
Study ID	BELLUCCI2002 Hadaslidor2001 HOGARTY2004 Medalia1998 Medalia2000 PENADES2006 SILVERSTEIN2005[a] SPAULDING1999 TWAMLEY2008 VANDERGAAG2002 VELLIGAN2000 VELLIGAN2002 VELLIGAN2008A VELLIGAN2008B Wykes1999 WYKES2007A WYKES2007B	BELLUCCI2002 Medalia2000 SILVERSTEIN2005[a] TWAMLEY2008 VELLIGAN2000 VELLIGAN2002 VELLIGAN2008A VELLIGAN2008B WYKES2007A WYKES2007B	Hadaslidor2001 HOGARTY2004 Medalia1998 PENADES2006 SPAULDING1999 VANDERGAAG2002 VELLIGAN2008A VELLIGAN2008B Wykes1999

Continued

279

Table 63: *(Continued)*

	Cognitive remediation versus any control	Cognitive remediation versus standard care	Cognitive remediation versus other active treatments
Diagnosis	83–100% schizophrenia or other related diagnoses (DSM or ICD-10)	95–100% schizophrenia or other related diagnoses (DSM or ICD-10)	83–100% schizophrenia or other related diagnoses (DSM or ICD-10)
Baseline severity	*BPRS total:* Mean (SD) ~30 (4) Medalia1998 Mean (SD) ~37 (9) WYKES2007B *PANSS total:* Mean (SD) ~60 (15) WYKES2007A	*BPRS total:* Mean (SD) ~37 (9) WYKES2007B *PANSS total:* Mean (SD) ~60 (15) WYKES2007A	*BPRS total:* Mean (SD) ~30 (4) Medalia1998
Length of treatment	*Range:* 5–104 weeks	*Range:* 5–104 weeks	*Range:* 6–104 weeks
Length of follow-up	*Up to 3 months:* TWAMLEY2008 WYKES2007B *Up to 6 months:* PENADES2006 Wykes1999 WYKES2007A *Up to 12 months:* HOGARTY2004	*Up to 3 months:* TWAMLEY2008 WYKES2007B *Up to 6 months:* WYKES2007A	*Up to 6 months:* PENADES2006 Wykes1999 *Up to 12 months:* HOGARTY2004

Setting		
Inpatient[b]: Medalia1998 Medalia2000 SILVERSTEIN2005 SPAULDING1999 VANDERGAAG2002 WYKES2007B *Outpatient:* BELLUCCI2002 HOGARTY2004 VELLIGAN2000[c] VELLIGAN2002 VELLIGAN2008A VELLIGAN2008B Wykes1999 WYKES2007A *Day rehabilitation centre:* Hadaslidor2001	*Inpatient*[b] : Medalia2000 SILVERSTEIN2005 WYKES2007B *Outpatient:* BELLUCCI2002 VELLIGAN2000[c] VELLIGAN2002 VELLIGAN2008A VELLIGAN2008B WYKES2007A	*Inpatient*[b]: Medalia1998 SPAULDING1999 VANDERGAAG2002 *Outpatient:* HOGARTY2004 VELLIGAN2008A VELLIGAN2008B Wykes1999 *Day rehabilitation centre:* Hadaslidor2001

[a] The study included an attentional module for both cognitive remediation and waiting list control participants. The attentional module started after the completion of the cognitive remediation intervention and after testing at time point two. Only data from time point two were used in the analysis as this represented cognitive remediation versus standard care alone.

[b] Included inpatient rehabilitation units.

[c] Participants in the Velligan papers were recruited following discharge from an inpatient setting.

Overall, there was no consistent evidence that cognitive remediation alone is effective in improving the critical outcomes, including relapse rates, rehospitalisation, mental state and quality of life. Furthermore, where effects of treatment were found, the evidence is difficult to interpret as many studies report non-significant findings without providing appropriate data for the meta-analysis. Thus, the magnitude of the effect is likely to be overestimated for all outcomes.

8.5.6 From evidence to recommendations

The previous guideline found no consistent evidence for the effectiveness of cognitive remediation versus standard care or any other active treatment in improving targeted cognitive outcomes or other critical outcomes, such as symptom reduction. It is noteworthy that although the McGurk and colleagues' (2007) review suggested positive effects for symptoms and functioning, this may be, in part, attributed to the fact that their review included a number of studies that failed to meet the inclusion criteria set out by the GDG (for example, minimum number of participants or cognitive remediation as an adjunct to vocational rehabilitation).

Although limited evidence of efficacy has been found in a few recent well-conducted studies, there is a distinct lack of follow-up data and various methodological problems in the consistency with which outcomes are reported. Where studies comprehensively reported outcomes at both ends of treatment and follow-up, there was little consistent advantage of cognitive remediation over standard care and attentional controls. Consequently, although there are some positive findings, the variability in effectiveness suggests that the clinical evidence as a whole is not robust enough to change the previous guideline.

The GDG did note, however, that a number of US-based studies have shown sustained improvements in vocational and psychosocial outcomes when cognitive remediation is added to vocational training and/or supported employment services. Despite the emerging evidence within this context, the effectiveness of psychological and psychosocial interventions as adjuncts to supported employment services was outside the scope of the guideline update and, therefore, has not been reviewed systematically. Given this finding and the variability in both the methodological rigour and effectiveness of cognitive remediation studies, it was the opinion of the GDG that further UK-based research is required. In particular, RCTs of cognitive remediation should include adequate follow-up periods to comprehensively assess its efficacy as a discrete and/or adjunctive intervention.

8.5.7 Research recommendations

8.5.7.1 An adequately powered RCT with longer-term follow-up should be conducted to investigate the clinical and cost effectiveness of cognitive remediation compared with an appropriate control in people with schizophrenia.

8.5.7.2   An adequately powered RCT with longer-term follow-up should be conducted to investigate the clinical and cost effectiveness of vocational rehabilitation plus cognitive remediation compared with vocational rehabilitation alone in people with schizophrenia.

8.6   COUNSELLING AND SUPPORTIVE THERAPY

8.6.1   Introduction

In the 1950s Carl Rogers, a pioneering US psychologist influenced by Alfred Adler and Otto Rank, devised 'client-centred' and later 'person-centred' counselling. This was a reaction against the behaviourist and psychodynamic schools that had emerged from late 19th century Freudian psychoanalysis. Unlike the early behaviourists, Rogers accepted the importance of a client's internal emotional world, but this centred on the lived experience of the person rather than empirically untestable psychoanalytic theories of unconscious drives and defences of unconscious processes (Thorne, 1992). Rogerian counselling has since been the starting point for newer therapies, such as humanistic counselling, psychodynamic counselling, psychodrama and Gestalt psychotherapy. In the UK, counselling is most likely to be offered to people with common mental illnesses within a primary care setting.

Supportive therapy has been cited as the individual psychotherapy of choice for most patients with schizophrenia (Lamberti & Hertz, 1995). It is notable that most trials involving this intervention have used it as a comparison treatment for other more targeted psychological approaches, rather than investigating it as a primary intervention. This may be because supportive therapy is not a well-defined unique intervention, has no overall unifying theory and is commonly used as an umbrella term describing a range of interventions from befriending to a type of formal psychotherapy (Buckley *et al.*, 2007). More formal supportive therapy approaches tend to be flexible in terms of frequency and regularity of sessions, and borrow some components from Rogerian counselling (namely an emphasis on empathic listening and 'non-possessive warmth'). These may be called 'supportive psychotherapy' and also tend to rely on an active therapist who may offer advice, support and reassurance with the aim of helping the patient adapt to present circumstances (Crown, 1988). This differs from the dynamic psychotherapist, who waits for material to emerge and retains a degree of opacity to assist in the development of a transference relationship.

Undoubtedly there are overlaps between counselling, supportive therapy and the other psychotherapies; known as 'non-specific factors', these are necessary for the development of a positive treatment alliance and are a prerequisite for any psychological intervention to stand a chance of success (Roth *et al.*, 1996). Many of these factors are also part of high-quality 'standard care', as well as forming the key elements of counselling and supportive therapy. Fenton and McGlashan (1997) reported that a patient's feeling of being listened to and understood is a strong predictor of, for example, medication compliance. Also, according to McCabe and Priebe (2004), the therapeutic relationship is a reliable predictor of patient outcome in mainstream psychiatric care.

Definition
Counselling and supportive therapy were defined as discrete psychological interventions that:
- are facilitative, non-directive and/or relationship focused, with the content largely determined by the service user, and
- do not fulfil the criteria for any other psychological intervention.

8.6.2   Clinical review protocol

The review protocol, including information about the databases searched and the eligibility criteria used for this section of the guideline, can be found in Table 64. The primary clinical questions can be found in Box 1. A new systematic search for

Table 64: Clinical review protocol for the review of counselling and supportive therapy

Electronic databases	Databases: CINAHL, CENTRAL, EMBASE, MEDLINE, PsycINFO
Date searched	1 January 2002 to 30 July 2008
Study design	RCT ($\geq$10 participants per arm)
Patient population	Adults (18+) with schizophrenia (including schizophrenia-related disorders)
Excluded populations	Very late onset schizophrenia (onset after age 60) Other psychotic disorders, such as bipolar disorder, mania or depressive psychosis People with coexisting learning difficulties, significant physical or sensory difficulties, or substance misuse
Interventions	Counselling and supportive therapy
Comparator	Any alternative management strategy
Critical outcomes	Mortality (suicide) Global state (relapse, rehospitalisation) Mental state (total symptoms, depression) Psychosocial functioning Quality of life Leaving the study early for any reason Adverse events

relevant RCTs published since the previous guideline was conducted for the guideline update (further information about the search strategy can be found in Appendix 8).

8.6.3   Studies considered for review

In the previous guideline, 14 RCTs (N = 1,143) of counselling and supportive therapy were included. Two studies included in the previous guideline (Levine1998; Turkington2000) were excluded from the update because of inadequate numbers of participants. The update search identified four papers providing follow-up data to existing trials and six new trials. In total, 18 RCTs (N = 1,610) met the inclusion criteria for the update. All were published in peer-reviewed journals between 1973 and 2007 (further information about both included and excluded studies can be found in Appendix 15c).

8.6.4   Counselling and supportive therapy versus control

For the update, 17 RCTs of counselling and supportive therapy versus any type of control were included in the meta-analysis. One included trial (Donlon1973) did not provide any useable data for the analysis. Sub-analyses were then used to examine counselling and supportive therapy versus standard care, versus other active treatment and versus CBT[24] (see Table 65 for a summary of the study characteristics). Forest plots and/or data tables for each outcome can be found in Appendix 16d.

8.6.5   Clinical evidence summary

In 17 RCTs comprising 1,586 participants there was evidence to suggest that counselling and supportive psychotherapy do not improve outcomes in schizophrenia when compared with standard care and other active treatments, most notably CBT. A subgroup analysis of counselling and supportive therapy versus CBT favoured CBT for a number of outcomes including relapse. However, it must be noted that in these studies, counselling and supportive therapy was used as comparators to control primarily for therapist time and attention, and thus were not the focus of the research.

---

[24] Existing subgroup comparisons exploring the format of the interention (group versus individual sessions) was also updated. However, there was insufficient data to draw any conclusions based on this subgroup. Please refer to Appendix 16d for the forest plots and/or data tables for all subgroup comparisons conducted.

Table 65: Summary of study characteristics for counselling and supportive therapy

	Counselling and supportive therapy versus any control	Counselling and supportive therapy versus standard care	Counselling and supportive therapy versus other active treatment	Counselling and supportive therapy versus CBT
k (total N)	17 (1586)	2 (262)[e]	17 (1452)	9 (678)
Study ID	Eckman1992 Falloon1981 Haddock1999 Herz2000 Hogarty1997 JACKSON2007 Kemp1996 Lewis2002[a] Marder1996 PATTERSON2006 PINTO1999 ROHRICHT2006 Sensky2000 SHIN2002 Stanton1984 Tarrier1998 VALMAGGIA2005	Tarrier1998 Lewis2002[a]	Eckman1992 Falloon1981 Haddock1999 Herz2000 Hogarty1997 JACKSON2007 Kemp1996 Lewis2002[a] Marder1996 PATTERSON2006 PINTO1999 ROHRICHT2006 Sensky2000 SHIN2002 Stanton1984 Tarrier1998 VALMAGGIA2005	Haddock1999 Hogarty1997 Kemp1996 JACKSON2007 Lewis2002[a] PINTO1999 Sensky2000 Tarrier1998 VALMAGGIA2005

Diagnosis	58–100% schizophrenia or other related diagnoses (DSM or ICD-10)	88–98% schizophrenia or other related diagnoses (DSM or ICD-10)	58–100% schizophrenia or other related diagnoses (DSM or ICD-10)	58–100% schizophrenia or other related diagnoses (DSM or ICD-10)
Baseline severity	*BPRS total:* Mean (SD) range: ~32 (8) to ~92 (8) *PANSS total:* Mean (SD) range: ~61 (27) to ~87 (17) *CPRS total:* Mean (SD) ~36 (14) Sensy2000	*PANSS total:* Mean (SD) ~87 (17) Lewis2000	*BPRS total:* Mean (SD) range: ~32 (8) to ~92 (8) *PANSS total:* Mean (SD) range: ~61 (27) to ~87 (17) *CPRS total:* Mean (SD) ~36 (14) Semsky2000	*BPRS total:* Mean (SD) range: ~32 (8) to ~92 (8) *PANSS total:* Mean (SD) range: ~61(27) to ~87 (17) *CPRS total:* Mean (SD) ~36 (14) Sensky2000
Length of treatment	*Range:* 5 to 156 weeks	*Range:* 5 to 10 weeks	*Range:* 5 to 156 weeks	*Range:* 5 to 156 weeks
Length of follow-up (only including papers reporting follow-up measures)	*Range:* 4 to 24 months	*Range:* up to 24 months	*Range:* 4 to 156 months	*Range:* 4 to 24 months

Continued

Table 65: *(Continued)*

Setting	Counselling and supportive therapy versus any control	Counselling and supportive therapy versus standard care	Counselling and supportive therapy versus other active treatment	Counselling and supportive therapy versus CBT
	Inpatient: Haddock1999 Hogarty1997[b] Kemp1996 Lewis2002[c] Stanton1984 VALMAGGIA2005	*Inpatient:* Lewis2002[c]	*Inpatient:* Haddock1999 Hogarty1997[b] Kemp1996 Lewis2002[c] Stanton1984 VALMAGGIA2005	*Inpatient:* Haddock1999 Hogarty1997[b] Lewis2002[c] VALMAGGIA2005
	Outpatient: Falloon1981 Herz2000 Marder1996 ROHRICHT2006 SHIN2002 Sensky2000 Tarrier1998	*Outpatient:* Tarrier1998	*Outpatient:* Falloon1981 Herz2000 Marder1996 ROHRICHT2006 SHIN2002 Sensky2000 Tarrier1998	*Outpatient:* Sensky2000 Tarrier1998

Inpatient and outpatient: Eckmann1992 PINTO1999 Other[d]: JACKSON2007 PATTERSON2006	Inpatient and outpatient: Eckmann1992 PINTO1999 Other[d]: JACKSON2007 PATTERSON2006	Inpatient and outpatient: PINTO1999 Other[d]: JACKSON2007

[a] Follow-up papers to Lewis2002 report the data separately for the three study sites, hence in the analysis Lewis2002 appears as LEWIS2002L (Liverpool), LEWIS2002M (Manchester) and LEWIS2002N (Nottingham).

[b] Participants were recruited in the inpatient setting with the intervention starting shortly before discharge.

[c] Participants were recruited from inpatient wards and day hospitals.

[d] Other settings included Board and Care facilities and EIS settings.

[e] Both studies included multiple treatment arms; only the numbers in the counselling and supportive therapy and standard care arms have been included in this count.

8.6.6   From evidence to recommendations

In the previous guideline, the GDG found no clear evidence to support the use of counselling and supportive therapy as a discrete intervention. The limited evidence found for this update does not justify changing this recommendation. The GDG do, however, acknowledge the preference that some service users and carers may have for these interventions, particularly when other more efficacious psychological treatments are not available in the local area. Furthermore, the GDG recognise the importance of supportive elements in the provision of good quality standard care.

8.6.7   Recommendations

8.6.7.1   Do not routinely offer counselling and supportive psychotherapy (as specific interventions) to people with schizophrenia. However, take service user preferences into account, especially if other more efficacious psychological treatments, such as CBT, family intervention and arts therapies, are not available locally.

8.7   FAMILY INTERVENTION

8.7.1   Introduction

Family intervention in the treatment of schizophrenia has evolved from studies of the family environment and its possible role in affecting the course of schizophrenia (Vaughn & Leff, 1976) after an initial episode. It should be noted that in this context, 'family' includes people who have a significant emotional connection to the service user, such as parents, siblings and partners. Brown and colleagues (Brown *et al.*, 1962; Brown & Rutter, 1966) developed a measure for the level of 'expressed emotion' within families and were able to show that the emotional environment within a family was an effective predictor of relapse in schizophrenia (Bebbington & Kuipers, 1994; Butzlaff & Hooley, 1998). The importance of this work lay in the realisation that it was possible to design psychological methods (in this case, family intervention) that could change the management of the illness by service users and their families, and influence the course of schizophrenia.

Family intervention in schizophrenia derives from behavioural and systemic ideas, adapted to the needs of families of those with psychosis. More recently, cognitive appraisals of the difficulties have been emphasised. Models that have been developed aim to help families cope with their relatives' problems more effectively, provide support and education for the family, reduce levels of distress, improve the ways in which the family communicates and negotiates problems, and try to prevent relapse by the service user. Family intervention is normally complex and lengthy (usually more than ten sessions) but delivered in a structured format with the individual family, and tends to include the service user as much as possible.

Definition

Family intervention was defined as discrete psychological interventions where:

- family sessions have a specific supportive, educational or treatment function and contain at least one of the following components:
  - problem solving/crisis management work, or
  - intervention with the identified service user.

8.7.2   Clinical review protocol

The review protocol, including information about the databases searched and the eligibility criteria used for this section of the guideline, can be found in Table 66. The primary clinical questions can be found in Box 1. A new systematic search for relevant RCTs published since the previous guideline was conducted for the guideline update (further information about the search strategy can be found in Appendix 8 and information about the search for health economic evidence can be found in Section 8.7.8).

Table 66: Clinical review protocol for the review of family intervention

Electronic databases	Databases: CINAHL, CENTRAL, EMBASE, MEDLINE, PsycINFO
Date searched	1 January 2002 to 30 July 2008
Study design	RCT ($\geq$10 participants per arm and $\geq$6 weeks' duration)
Patient population	Adults (18+) with schizophrenia (including schizophrenia-related disorders)
Excluded populations	Very late onset schizophrenia (onset after age 60) Other psychotic disorders, such as bipolar disorder, mania or depressive psychosis People with coexisting learning difficulties, significant physical or sensory difficulties, or substance misuse
Interventions	Family intervention
Comparator	Any alternative management strategy
Critical outcomes	Mortality (suicide) Global state (relapse, rehospitalisation,) Mental state (total symptoms, depression) Psychosocial functioning Family outcomes (including burden) Quality of life Leaving the study early for any reason Adverse events

8.7.3 Studies considered for review

In the previous guideline, 18 RCTs (N = 1,458) of family intervention were included. One study (Posner1992) included in the previous guideline was re-classified as 'psychoeducation' for the update and two previous trials were classified as having family intervention as part of a multi-modal treatment (Herz2000 and Lukoff1986). The update search identified five papers providing follow-up data to existing trials and 19 new trials. In total, 38 trials (N = 3,134) met the inclusion criteria for the update. All were published in peer-reviewed journals between 1978 and 2008 (further information about both included and excluded studies can be found in Appendix 15c).

8.7.4 Family intervention versus control

For the update, one of the included studies (CHENG2005) did not provide useable data for any of the critical outcomes listed in Table 66, thus 32 RCTs of family intervention versus any type of control were included in the meta-analysis. Of these, 26 trials compared family intervention with standard care and eight compared family intervention with other active treatments. Additionally, five trials directly compared a multiple family intervention with a single family intervention (see Table 67 for a summary of the study characteristics). Forest plots and/or data tables for each outcome can be found in Appendix 16d.

Subgroup analyses were also used to examine whether the format of the family intervention had an impact on outcome (ten trials were included in the analysis of multiple family interventions versus any control and 11 trials were included in the analysis of single family interventions versus any control). Additional subgroup analyses were used to explore certain characteristics of the trials, such as the inclusion of the person with schizophrenia, patient characteristics and the length of the intervention[25] (see Table 68 for a summary of the studies included in each subgroup comparison).

8.7.5 Training

Although there was a paucity of information on training and/or competence of the therapists in the RCTs of family intervention, 28 trials reported the profession of the therapist. In these trials, the professional background varied, with the most commonly reported professions being clinical psychologist (14/28) or psychiatric nurse (12/28). In addition, the following professionals also conducted the intervention in a number of papers: psychiatrist (10/28), social workers (3/28), Masters' level

---

[25] Existing subgroup comparisons exploring the country of the trial, the number of treatment sessions, and the family characteristics (high emotional expression versus everything) were also updated. However, there was insufficient data to draw any conclusions based on these subgroups. Please refer to Appendix 16d for the forest plots and/or data tables for all subgroup comparisons conducted.

Table 67: Summary of study characteristics for family intervention

	Family intervention versus any control	Family intervention versus standard care	Family intervention versus other active treatments	Multiple family versus single family intervention (direct format comparison)
k (total N)	32 (2429)	26 (1989)	8 (417)	5 (641)
Study ID	Barrowclough1999 Bloch1995 BRADLEY2006 BRESSI2008 Buchkremer1995 CARRA2007 CHIEN2004A CHIEN2004B CHIEN2007 Dyck2000 Falloon1981 GARETY2008[a] Glynn1992 Goldstein1978 Herz2000[b] Hogarty1997	Barrowclough1999 Bloch1995 BRADLEY2006 BRESSI2008 Buchkremer1995 CARRA2007 CHIEN2004A CHIEN2004B CHIEN2007 Dyck2000 GARETY2008[a] Glynn1992 Goldstein1978 JENNER2004[b] KOPELOWICZ2003 LEAVEY2004	CARRA2007 Falloon1981 GARETY2008[a] Herz2000[b] Hogarty1997 LINSZEN1996[b] Lukoff1986[b] SZMUKLER2003	Leff1989 McFarlane1995a McFarlane1995b MONTERO2001 Schooler1997

Continued

Table 67: (*Continued*)

	Family intervention versus any control	Family intervention versus standard care	Family intervention versus other active treatments	Multiple family versus single family intervention (direct format comparison)
	JENNER2004[b] KOPELOWICZ2003 LEAVEY2004 Leff1982 LI2005 LINSZEN196[b] Lukoff1986[b] MAGLIANO2006 RAN2003 SO2006 SZMUKLER2003 Tarrier1988 VALENCIA2007[b] Vaughan1992 Xiong1994 Zhang1994	Leff1982 LI2005 MAGLIANO2006 RAN2003 SO2006 Tarrier1988 VALENCIA2007[b] Vaughan1992 Xiong1994 Zhang1994		
Diagnosis	93–100% schizophrenia or other related diagnoses (DSM or ICD-10)	93–100% schizophrenia or other related diagnoses (DSM or ICD-10)	98–100% schizophrenia or other related diagnoses (DSM or ICD-10)	100% schizophrenia or other related diagnoses (DSM or ICD-10)

Baseline severity	*BPRS total:* Mean (SD) range: ~27 (3) to ~48 (10) *PANSS total:* Mean (SD) range: ~53 (1) to 112 (26)	*BPRS total:* Mean (SD) range: ~27 (3) to ~48 (10) *PANSS total:* Mean (SD) range: ~60 (14) to 112 (26)	*PANSS total:* Mean (SD) range: ~53 (17) to ~67 (14)	*BPRS total:* Mean (SD): 29 (7) Schooler1997
Length of treatment	*Range:* 6–156 weeks	*Range:* 12–104 weeks	*Range:* 6–156 weeks	*Range:* 52–104 weeks
Length of follow-up (only including papers reporting follow-up measures)	*Range:* 3–60 months	*Range:* 3–60 months	*Range:* 12–60 months	*Range:* 24–60 months
Setting	*Inpatient:* Bloch1995[c] BRESSI2008 Glynn1992 Hogarty1997[d] LINSZEN1996[b] Lukoff1986[b] Vaughan1992	*Inpatient:* Bloch1995[c] BRESSI2008 Glynn1992 Vaughan1992	*Inpatient:* Hogarty1997[d] LINSZEN1996[b] Lukoff1986[b]	*Inpatient:* Leff1989 McFarlane1995a

Continued

Table 67: *(Continued)*

Family intervention versus any control	Family intervention versus standard care	Family intervention versus other active treatments	Multiple family versus single family intervention (direct format comparison)
Outpatient: Barrowclough1999 BRADLEY2006 Buchkremer1995 CARRA2007 CHIEN2004A CHIEN2004B CHIEN2007 Dyck2000 Falloon1981 Goldstein1978[e] Herz2000[b] JENNER2004[b] KOPELOWICZ2003	*Outpatient:* Barrowclough1999 BRADLEY2006 Buchkremer1995 CARRA2007 CHIEN2004A CHIEN2004B CHIEN2007 Dyck2000 Goldstein1978[e] JENNER2004[b] KOPELOWICZ2003 Leff1982 MAGLIANO2006	*Outpatient:* CARRA2007 Falloon1981 Herz2000[b] SZMUKLER2003	*Outpatient:* McFarlane1995b MONTERO2001 Schooler1997

Leff1982	RAN2003	
MAGLIANO2006	SO2006	
RAN2003	Tarrier1998	
SO2006	VALENCIA2007[b]	
SZMUKLER2003	Xiong1994	
Tarrier1998	Zhang1994	
VALENCIA2007[b]		
Xiong1994		
Zhang1994		
Inpatient and outpatient:	*Inpatient and outpatient:*	*Inpatient and outpatient:*
GARETY2008[a]	GARETY2008[a]	GARETY2008[a]
LEAVEY2004	LEAVEY2004	
LI2005	LI2005	

Note: Studies were categorised as short (12 weeks or fewer), medium (12–51 weeks) and long (52 weeks or more).

[a] Only the carer pathway was included in the present analysis.

[b] Multi-modal interventions.

[c] Carers of patients admitted to the ward were recruited to take part in the study.

[d] Participants were recruited in the inpatient setting with the intervention starting shortly before discharge.

[e] Participants were recruited following discharge to an aftercare outpatient programme.

Table 68: Summary of study characteristics for family intervention subgroup comparisons

	Single family intervention versus any control	Multiple family intervention versus any control	Family intervention including service user versus any control	Family intervention excluding service user versus any control
k (total N)	11 (864)	10 (651)	18 (1319)	9 (622)
Study ID	Barrowclough1999	BRADLEY2006	Barrowclough1999	Bloch1995
	Bloch1995	Buchkremer1995	BRADLEY2006	Buchkremer1995
	BRESSI2008	CARRA2007	BRESSI2008	CARRA2007
	Falloon1981	CHIEN2004A	CHIEN2004B	CHIEN2004A
	GARETY2008	CHIEN2004B	CHIEN2007	Dyck2000
	Glynn1992	CHIEN2007	Falloon1981	LEAVEY2004
	Hogarty1997	Dyck2000	GARETY2008	SO2006
	LEAVEY2004	KOPELOWICZ2003	Glynn1992	SZMUKLER2003
	MAGLIANO2006	SO2006	Goldstein1978	Vaughan1992
	RAN2003	Xiong1994	Hogarty1997	
	Vaughan1992		KOPELOWICZ2003	
			Leff1982	
			LI2005	
			MAGLIANO2006	
			RAN2003	
			Tarrier1988	
			Xiong1994	
			Zhang1994	

Table 68: (*Continued*)

	Short-term family intervention versus any control	Medium-term family intervention versus any control	Long-term family intervention versus any control
k (total N)	4 (248)	12 (1056)	10 (660)
Study ID	Bloch1995 Goldstein1978 SO2006 Vaughan1992	Barrowclough1999 CHIEN2004A CHIEN2004B CHIEN2007 GARETY2008 KOPELOWICZ2003 LEAVEY2004 Leff1982 MAGLIANO2006 RAN2003 SZMUKLER2003 Tarrier1988	BRADLEY2006 BRESSI2008 Buchkremer1995 CARRA2007 Dyck2000 Falloon1981 Glynn1992 Hogarty1997 Xiong1994 Zhang1994
	Family intervention versus any control– first episode[a]	Family intervention versus any control – acute episode	Family intervention versus any control – promoting recovery
k (total N)	4 (333)	12 (673)	9 (702)
Study ID	Goldstein1978 LEAVEY2004 SO2006 Zhang1994	Bloch1995 BRADLEY2006 BRESSI2008 Falloon1981 GARETY2008 Glynn1992 Hogarty1997 KOPELOWICZ2003 Leff1982 Tarrier1988 Vaughan1992 Xiong1994	Barrowclough1999 Buchkremer1995 CARRA2007 CHIEN2004A CHIEN2004B CHIEN2007 Dyck2000 LI2005 MAGLIANO2006

[a] A number of trials included participants across different phases of illness (for example, first episode, acute and promoting recovery) and hence could not be included in the subgroup analysis.

psychology graduates (2/28) and local mental health workers (1/28). In many trials a number of therapists, often across different disciplines, conducted the interventions, with some trials emphasising collaboration between the therapists and the participant's key worker.

8.7.6   Ethnicity

Although the data on ethnicity was limited, a subgroup analysis looking at the efficacy of family intervention in an ethnically diverse population was conducted (see Chapter 5 for definition of ethnically diverse sample). For critical outcomes including relapse, rehospitalisation and symptoms, family intervention was shown to have clinically significant benefits within studies including an ethnically diverse sample. One UK study (LEAVEY2004) assessed the impact of a brief family intervention for families of patients with first episode psychosis. Participants were drawn from a multicultural and ethnically diverse population, with the researchers attempting to match the ethnicity of the family worker with the ethnicity of the carer. LEAVEY2004 failed to demonstrate any significant impact on ether patient outcomes or carer level of satisfaction. However, the authors note that the high proportion failing to take up the intervention may have had a detrimental impact upon the results.

A number of papers have assessed the effectiveness of adapting a Western family intervention approach to better suit non-Western populations. For example, both RAN2003 and LI2005 adapted the content of the intervention to better match the cultural needs and family structures of people living in different communities in mainland China. Further to this, researchers have started to assess the impact of cultural modifications aimed at tailoring an intervention to better suit the cultural and ethnic needs of minority populations. For instance, BRADLEY2006 assessed the effectiveness of a modified intervention approach that included the use of language matching and ethno-specific explanatory models in a sample of Vietnamese speaking migrants living in Australia. Although both types of cultural modifications were shown to be effective across critical outcomes, none of the RCTs was conducted with black and minority ethnic participants from the UK; therefore the generalisability of such findings is limited. Furthermore, at present little research exists that directly compares the efficacy and acceptability of culturally and non-culturally modified approaches.

8.7.7   Clinical evidence summary

In 32 RCTs including 2,429 participants, there was robust and consistent evidence for the efficacy of family intervention. When compared with standard care or any other control, there was a reduction in the risk of relapse with numbers needed to treat (NNTs) of 4 (95% CIs 3.23 to 5.88) at the end of treatment and 6 (95% CIs 3.85 to 9.09) up to 12 months following treatment. In addition, family intervention also reduced hospital admission during treatment and the severity of symptoms both during and up to 24 months following the intervention. Family intervention may also be effective in improving additional critical outcomes, such as social functioning and the patient's knowledge of the disorder. However, it should be noted that evidence for the latter is more limited and comes from individual studies reporting multiple outcomes across a range of scale based measures.

The subgroup analyses conducted for the update to explore the variation in terms of intervention delivery consistently indicated that where practicable the service user should be included in the intervention. Although direct format comparisons did not indicate any robust evidence for single over multiple family intervention in terms of total symptoms, single family intervention was seen as more acceptable to service users and carers as demonstrated by the numbers leaving the study early. Additionally, subgroup comparisons that indirectly compared single with multiple family intervention demonstrated some limited evidence to suggest that only the former may be efficacious in reducing hospital admission.

8.7.8 Health economic evidence

Systematic literature review

No studies evaluating the cost effectiveness of family intervention for people with schizophrenia met the set criteria for inclusion in the guideline systematic review of economic literature. However, the previous NICE schizophrenia guideline, using more relaxed inclusion criteria, had identified a number of economic studies on family intervention for people with schizophrenia. Details on the methods used for the systematic search of the economic literature in the guideline update are described in Chapter 3; details on the respective methods in the previous NICE schizophrenia guideline are provided in Appendix 17. The following text marked by asterisks is derived from the previous schizophrenia guideline:

**The economic review identified five eligible studies, and a further two studies were not available. All five included studies were based on RCTs. Three papers adapted simple costing methods (Goldstein, 1996; Leff *et al.*, 2001; Tarrier *et al.*, 1991), while two studies were economic evaluations (Liberman *et al.*, 1987; McFarlane *et al.*, 1995a). Of these, two economic analyses were conducted in the UK (Tarrier *et al.*, 1991; Leff *et al.*, 2001) and two others were based on clinical data from the UK, but the economic analyses were conducted within a US context (Goldstein, 1996; Liberman *et al.*, 1987). Most of these studies are methodologically weak, with the potential for a high risk of bias in their results. Another common problem was the low statistical power of the studies to show cost differences between the comparators. All studies focused narrowly on direct medical costs. As such, economic evaluation of family interventions from a broader perspective is impossible.

One study (Tarrier *et al.*, 1991) compared family intervention with standard care and concluded that family intervention is significantly less costly than standard care. Two analyses compared family intervention with individual supportive therapy (Goldstein, 1996; Liberman *et al.*, 1987). Both studies used clinical data from the same RCT, but their evaluation methodology differed. They concluded that the treatment costs of family intervention are higher than those of individual supportive therapy, but cost savings relating to other healthcare costs offset the extra treatment costs. One study (Leff *et al.*, 2001) showed economic benefits of family intervention combined with two psychoeducational sessions over psychoeducation alone. However, the difference was not significant. One study (McFarlane *et al.*, 1995a) demonstrated that multi-family group intervention is more cost effective than single-family intervention.

The quality of the available economic evidence is generally poor.

The evidence, such as it is, suggests that providing family interventions may represent good 'value for money'.

There is limited evidence that multi-family interventions require fewer resources and are less costly than single-family interventions.**

The evidence table for the above studies as it appeared in the previous schizophrenia guideline is included in Appendix 14.

Economic modelling
Objective
The guideline systematic review and meta-analysis of clinical evidence demonstrated that provision of family intervention is associated with a reduction in relapse and hospitalisation rates of people with schizophrenia. A cost analysis was undertaken to assess whether the costs of providing family intervention for people with schizophrenia are offset by cost savings to the NHS following this decrease in relapse and hospitalisation rates.

Intervention assessed
Family intervention can be delivered to single families or in groups. The guideline meta-analysis included all studies of family intervention versus control in its main analysis, irrespective of the mode of delivery, because it was difficult to distinguish between single and multiple programmes. The majority of studies described family intervention programmes that were predominantly single or multiple, but might have some multiple or single component, respectively; some of the interventions combined single and multiple sessions equally.

Apart from the main meta-analysis, studies of family intervention versus control were included in additional sub-analyses in which studies comparing (predominantly) single family intervention versus control were analysed separately from studies comparing (predominantly) multiple family intervention versus control. These sub-analyses demonstrated that single family intervention significantly reduced the rates of hospital admission of people with schizophrenia up to 12 months into therapy, whereas multiple family intervention was not associated with a statistically significant respective effect. On the other hand, single and multiple family intervention had a significant effect of similar magnitude in reducing the rates of relapse.

A small number of studies compared directly (exclusively) single with (exclusively) multiple family intervention. Meta-analysis of these studies showed that single and multiple family intervention had no significant difference in clinical outcomes. However, participants showed a clear preference for single interventions, as expressed in dropout rates.

It was decided that the economic analysis would utilise evidence from the main meta-analysis of all studies on family intervention versus control (irrespective of the model of delivery) but, in terms of intervention cost, would consider single family intervention; this would produce a conservative cost estimate per person with schizophrenia, given that in multiple family intervention the intervention cost is spread over more than one family.

Methods

A simple economic model estimated the total net costs (or cost savings) to the NHS associated with provision of single family therapy, in addition to standard care, to people with schizophrenia and their families/carers. Two categories of costs were assessed: costs associated with provision of family intervention, and cost savings from the reduction in relapse and hospitalisation rates in people with schizophrenia receiving family intervention, estimated based on the guideline meta-analysis of respective clinical data. Standard care costs were not estimated because these were common to both arms of the analysis.

Cost data

Intervention costs (costs of providing family intervention) The single family intervention programmes described in the clinical studies included in the guideline systematic review were characterised by a wide variety in terms of number of sessions and duration of each session. The resource use estimate associated with provision of single family intervention in the economic analysis was based on the expert opinion of the GDG regarding optimal clinical practice in the UK, and was consistent with average resource use reported in these studies. Single family intervention in the economic analysis consisted of 20 hours and was delivered by two therapists.

As with CBT, the GDG acknowledge that family intervention programmes can be delivered by a variety of mental health professionals with appropriate training and supervision. The salary level of a mental health professional providing family intervention was estimated to be similar to that of a mental health professional providing CBT, and comparable with the salary level of a clinical psychologist. Therefore, the unit cost of a clinical psychologist was used to estimate an average intervention cost. The unit cost of a clinical psychologist is estimated at £67 per hour of client contact in 2006/07 prices (Curtis, 2007). This estimate is based on the mid-point of Agenda for Change salaries Band 7 of the April 2006 pay scale, according to the National Profile for Clinical Psychologists, Counsellors and Psychotherapists (NHS Employers, 2006). It includes salary, salary oncosts, overheads and capital overheads, but does not take into account qualification costs because the latter are not available for clinical psychologists.

Based on the above resource use estimates and the unit cost of a clinical psychologist, the cost of providing a full course of family intervention was estimated at £2,680 per person with schizophrenia in 2006/07 prices.

Costs of hospitalisation/cost-savings from reduction in hospitalisation rates As described in Section 8.4.8, the average cost of hospitalisation per person with schizophrenia was estimated at £28,645 in 2006/07 prices, based on national statistics on the mean length of hospitalisation for people with schizophrenia (NHS, The Information Centre, 2008a) and the NHS reference cost per bed-day of an inpatient mental health acute care unit for adults, in 2006/07 prices (Department of Health, 2008a).

Clinical data on hospitalisation rates following provision of family intervention
The guideline meta-analysis provided pooled data on both hospitalisation and relapse rates associated with provision of family intervention in addition to standard care versus standard care alone. The analyses showed that adding family intervention to standard care significantly reduced the rates of both hospitalisation and relapse in people with schizophrenia. The vast majority of these data came from studies conducted outside the UK. The GDG expressed the view that hospitalisation levels may differ significantly across countries, depending on prevailing clinical practice, and therefore data on hospitalisation rates derived from non-UK countries might not be applicable to the UK setting. On the other hand, the definition of relapse was more consistent across studies (and countries). For this reason, it was decided to use pooled data on relapse rather hospitalisation rates for the economic analysis; these data would be used, subsequently, to estimate hospitalisation rates relevant to people with schizophrenia in the UK to calculate cost savings from reducing hospital admissions following provision of family intervention.

The guideline meta-analysis of family intervention data on relapse rates included two analyses: one analysis explored the effect on relapse rates during treatment with family intervention, and another analysis estimated the effect on relapse rates at follow-up, between 4 and 24 months after completion of family intervention. Ideally, both analyses should be taken into account at the estimation of total savings associated with family intervention. However, follow-up data were not homogeneous: some studies reported relapse data during treatment separately from respective data after treatment, but other studies included events that occurred during treatment in the reported follow-up data. Taking into account both sets of data might therefore double-count events occurring during treatment and would consequently overestimate the value of cost savings associated with family intervention. It was decided to use relapse data during treatment in the analysis, because these data were homogeneous and referred to events that occurred within the same study phase. It is acknowledged, however, that the cost savings estimated using data exclusively reported during treatment are probably underestimates of the true cost savings because the beneficial effect of family intervention on relapse remains for a substantial period after completing treatment.

Table 69 shows the family intervention studies included in the meta-analysis of relapse rate data for 1 to 12 months into treatment, the relapse rates for each treatment arm reported in the individual studies and the results of the meta-analysis.

The results of the meta-analysis show that family intervention, when added to standard care, reduces the rate of relapse in people with schizophrenia during the intervention period (the RR of relapse of family intervention added to standard care versus standard care alone is 0.52). This result was significant at the 0.05 level (95% CIs of RR: 0.42 to 0.65). It must be noted that the meta-analysis of relapse follow-up data showed that this beneficial effect remains significant up to at least 24 months

Table 69: Studies considered in the economic analysis of family intervention added to standard care versus standard care alone and results of the meta-analysis (1 to 12 months into treatment)

Study ID	Total events (n) in each treatment arm (N)	
	Family intervention plus standard care (n/N)	Standard care alone (n/N)
GOLDSTEIN1978	7/52	12/52
LEFF1982	1/12	6/12
TARRIER1988	13/32	20/32
GLYNN1992	3/21	11/20
XIONG1994	12/34	18/29
BARROWCLOUGH1999	9/38	18/39
RAN2003	22/57	32/53
BRADLEY2006	8/30	13/29
BRESSI2008	3/20	13/20
TOTAL	78/296 (26.35%)	143/286 (50.00%)
Meta-analysis results	RR: 0.52 95% CI: 0.42–0.65	

after the end of therapy (respective RR up to 24 months following provision of family intervention 0.63, with 95% CIs 0.52 to 0.78).

The baseline rate of relapse in the economic analysis was taken from the overall rate of relapse under standard care alone, as estimated in the guideline meta-analysis of family intervention data on relapse; that is, a 50% baseline relapse rate was used. The rate of relapse when family intervention was added to standard care was calculated by multiplying the estimated RR of relapse of family intervention plus standard care versus standard care alone by the baseline relapse rate.

Details on the studies considered in the economic analysis are available in Appendix 15c. The forest plots of the respective meta-analysis are provided in Appendix 16d.

Association between relapse and hospitalisation rates
In the UK, people with schizophrenia experiencing a relapse are mainly treated either as inpatients or by CRHTTs. Glover and colleagues (2006) examined the reduction in hospital admission rates in England following the implementation of CRHTTs. They reported that the introduction of CRHTTs was followed by a 22.7% reduction in hospital admission levels. Based on this data, the economic analysis assumed that 77.3% of people with schizophrenia experiencing a relapse would be admitted in hospital, and the remaining 22.7% would be seen by CRHTTs.

Sensitivity analysis

One- and two-way sensitivity analyses were undertaken to investigate the robustness of the results under the uncertainty characterising some of the input parameters and the use of different assumptions in the estimation of total net costs (or net savings) associated with provision of family intervention for people with schizophrenia. The following scenarios were explored:

- Use of the 95% CIs of the RR of relapse of family intervention added to standard care versus standard care alone.
- Change in the total number of hours of a course of family intervention (20 hours in the base-case analysis) to between a range of 15 and 25 hours.
- Change in the baseline rate of relapse (that is, the relapse rate for standard care) from 50% (that is, the baseline relapse rate in the base-case analysis) to a more conservative value of 30%.
- Change in the rate of hospitalisation following relapse (77.3% in base-case analysis) to 61.6% (based on the upper 95% CI of the reduction in hospital admission levels following the introduction of CRHTTs which, according to Glover and colleagues [2006], was 38.4%).
- Simultaneous use of a 30% relapse rate for standard care and a 61.6% hospitalisation rate following relapse.
- Use of a lower value for duration of hospitalisation. A value of 69 days was tested, taken from an effectiveness trial of clozapine versus SGAs conducted in the UK (CUtLASS Band 2, Davies *et al.*, 2008).

Results

Base-case analysis Providing family intervention cost £2,680 per person. The reduction in the rates of relapse in people with schizophrenia during treatment with family intervention in addition to standard care resulted in cost savings equalling £5,314 per person. Thus, family intervention resulted in an overall net saving of £2,634 per person with schizophrenia. Full results of the base-case analysis are reported in Table 70.

Table 70: Results of cost analysis comparing family intervention in addition to standard care with standard care alone per person with schizophrenia

Costs	Family intervention plus standard care	Standard care alone	Difference
Family intervention cost	£2,680	0	£2,680
Hospitalisation cost	£5,757	£11,071	−£5,314
Total cost	£8,437	£11,071	−£2,634

Sensitivity analysis   The results of the base-case analysis were overall found to be robust to the different scenarios explored in sensitivity analysis. Family intervention remained cost saving when the 95% CIs of the RR of relapse during treatment were used. In most scenarios, using the mean RR of relapse taken from the guideline meta-analysis, the addition of family intervention to standard care resulted in overall cost savings because of a substantial reduction in relapse and subsequent hospitalisation costs. The only scenario in which family intervention was not cost saving (instead incurring a net cost of £139 per person) was when a 30% baseline relapse rate was assumed, combined with a 61.6% rate of hospitalisation following relapse (in this scenario, the overall cost ranged between a net saving of £390 and a net cost of £827 when the 95% CIs of RR of relapse were used). Full results of sensitivity analysis are presented in Table 71.

Discussion

The economic analysis showed that family intervention for people with schizophrenia is likely to be an overall cost-saving intervention because the intervention costs are offset by savings resulting from a reduction in the rate of relapses experienced during therapy. The net cost saving of providing family intervention ranged between £1,195 and £3,741 per person with schizophrenia, using a mean duration of hospitalisation of 110.6 days and the 95% CIs of RRs of relapse, as estimated in the guideline meta-analysis. When a mean length of hospital stay of 69 days was used, the net cost of providing family intervention was found to lie between –£1,326 (overall net saving) and £263 per person with schizophrenia.

Table 71: Results of sensitivity analysis of providing family intervention in addition to standard care for people with schizophrenia

Scenario	Total net cost (negative cost implies net saving)
Use of 95% CIs of RR of relapse	–£3,741 (lower CI) to –£1,195 (upper CI)
Family intervention hours between 15 and 25	–£3,304 to –£1,964 respectively
Relapse rate under standard care 30%	–£509 (–£1,173 to £355 using the 95% CIs of RR of relapse)
Rate of hospitalisation following relapse 61.6%	–£1,555 (–£2,437 to –£408 using the 95% CIs of RR of relapse)
Relapse rate under standard care 30% and rate of hospitalisation following relapse 61.6%	£139 (–£390 to £827 using the 95% CIs of RR of relapse)
Mean length of hospitalisation 69 days	–£635 (–£1,326 to £263 using the 95% CIs of RR of relapse)

The economic analysis estimated cost savings related exclusively to a decrease in hospitalisation costs following reduction in relapse rates associated with family intervention. Consideration of further potential cost savings, such as savings resulting from an expected reduction in contacts with CRHTTs following reduction in relapse rates, would further increase the cost savings associated with family intervention. Moreover, meta-analysis of follow-up data demonstrated that the beneficial effect of family intervention on relapse rates observed in people with schizophrenia remains significant for a period at least 24 months following treatment. This means that the cost savings associated with family intervention are even higher. Finally, the expected improvement in HRQoL of people with schizophrenia and their carers following a reduction in relapse rates further strengthens the argument that family intervention is likely to be a cost-effective option for people with schizophrenia in the UK.

8.7.9   From evidence to recommendations

There was sufficient evidence in the previous guideline for the GDG to recommend family intervention in the treatment of schizophrenia. Recent studies have corroborated these conclusions and have consistently shown that family intervention may be particularly effective in preventing relapse.

Further analyses undertaken for the update continue to support the evidence demonstrated in the previous guideline with regard to the duration of treatments and the inclusion of the person with schizophrenia, where practicable. Although the evidence is more limited for the advantages of single compared with multiple family interventions, this must be considered in the context of current practice as well as service user and carer preferences. Furthermore, the GDG noted that the majority of UK-based studies were conducted as single family interventions, with the non-UK studies contributing more to the multiple family intervention evidence base. Thus, the evidence for single family intervention may additionally be more generalisable to UK settings.

Existing economic evidence on family intervention is poor. A simple economic analysis undertaken for this guideline demonstrated that, in the UK setting, family intervention is associated with net cost savings when offered to people with schizophrenia in addition to standard care, owing to a reduction in relapse rates and subsequent hospitalisation. The findings of the economic analysis used data on relapse that referred to the period during treatment with family intervention. However, there is evidence that family intervention also reduces relapse rates for a period after completion of the intervention. Therefore, net cost savings from family intervention are probably higher than those estimated in the guideline economic analysis.

With regard to the training and competencies required by the therapist to deliver family intervention to people with schizophrenia and their carers, there was a paucity of information reported throughout the trials. Consequently, the GDG were unable to form any conclusions or make any recommendations relating to practice. However, the GDG acknowledges that the training and competencies of the therapist is an important area, and one that warrants further research.

The robust evidence presented in the current clinical and health economic evaluation of family intervention further supports the conclusions and recommendations in the previous guideline. Although there was a lack of evidence for the use of culturally adapted family interventions within the UK, the GDG acknowledges that this is an important area warranting further investigation given the evidence previously discussed relating to inequality of access for people from black and minority ethnic groups (see Chapter 5).

8.7.10 Recommendations

Treatment of acute episode

8.7.10.1 Offer family intervention to all families of people with schizophrenia who live with or are in close contact with the service user. This can be started either during the acute phase[26] or later, including in inpatient settings.

8.7.10.2 Family intervention should:
- include the person with schizophrenia if practical
- be carried out for between 3 months and 1 year
- include at least ten planned sessions
- take account of the whole family's preference for either single-family intervention or multi-family group intervention
- take account of the relationship between the main carer and the person with schizophrenia
- have a specific supportive, educational or treatment function and include negotiated problem solving or crisis management work.

Promoting recovery

8.7.10.3 Offer family intervention to families of people with schizophrenia who live with or are in close contact with the service user. Deliver family intervention as described in recommendation 8.7.10.2.

8.7.10.4 Family intervention may be particularly useful for families of people with schizophrenia who have:
- recently relapsed or are at risk of relapse
- persisting symptoms.

8.7.11 Research recommendations

8.7.11.1 For people with schizophrenia from black and minority ethnic groups living in the UK, does ethnically adapted family intervention for schizophrenia (adapted in consultation with black and minority ethnic groups to better suit different cultural and ethnic needs) enable more people in black and minority ethnic groups to engage with this therapy, and show concomitant reductions in patient relapse rates and carer distress?[27]

---

[26] Family intervention should be delivered as described in recommendation 8.7.10.2.
[27] For more details see Chapter 10 (recommendation 10.5.1.2).

8.7.11.2   Research is needed to identify the competencies required to deliver effective family intervention to people with schizophrenia and their carers.

8.8   PSYCHODYNAMIC AND PSYCHOANALYTIC THERAPIES

8.8.1   Introduction

Psychoanalysis and its derivatives, often termed psychoanalytic and psychodynamic psychotherapies, originate from the work of Freud in the first quarter of the 20th century. These approaches assume that humans have an unconscious mind where feelings that are too painful to face are often held. A number of psychological processes known as defences are used to keep these feelings out of everyday consciousness. Psychoanalysis and psychodynamic psychotherapy aim to bring unconscious mental material and processes into full consciousness so that the individual can gain more control over his or her life. These approaches were originally regarded as unsuitable for the treatment of the psychoses (Freud, 1914, p. 74; 1933, p. 155). However, a number of psychoanalysts have treated people with schizophrenia and other psychoses using more or less modified versions of psychoanalysis (Fromm-Reichmann, 1950; Stack-Sullivan, 1974). Psychoanalytically-informed approaches to psychotherapy continue to be accessed by people with schizophrenia today, though the actual psychoanalytic technique is rarely used (Alanen, 1997). Approaches tend to be modified to favour relative openness on the part of the therapist, flexibility in terms of content and mode of sessions, holding off from making interpretations until the therapeutic alliance is solid, and building a relationship based on genuineness and warmth while maintaining optimal distance (Gabbard, 1994).

RCTs were undertaken in the 1970s and 1980s to investigate the use of psychoanalytically-orientated psychotherapy. Research into the effects of psychoanalytic approaches in the treatment of schizophrenia has been repeated more recently, with mixed results (Fenton & McGlashan, 1995; Jones *et al.*, 1999; Mari & Streiner, 1999), leading to the publication of a Cochrane Review on the subject (Malmberg & Fenton, 2001).

Definition
Psychodynamic interventions were defined as having:
● regular therapy sessions based on a psychodynamic or psychoanalytic model; and
● sessions that could rely on a variety of strategies (including explorative insight-orientated, supportive or directive activity), applied flexibly.

To be considered as well-defined psychodynamic psychotherapy, the intervention needed to include working with transference and unconscious processes.

Psychoanalytic interventions were defined as having:
● regular individual sessions planned to continue for at least 1 year; and
● analysts required to adhere to a strict definition of psychoanalytic technique.

To be considered as well-defined psychoanalysis, the intervention needed to involve working with the unconscious and early child/adult relationships.

8.8.2 Clinical review protocol

The review protocol, including information about the databases searched and the eligibility criteria used for this section of the guideline, can be found in Table 72. The primary clinical questions can be found in Box 1. A new systematic search for relevant RCTs, published since the previous guideline, was conducted for the guideline update (further information about the search strategy can be found in Appendix 8).

8.8.3 Studies considered for review

In the previous guideline, three RCTs (N = 492) of psychodynamic and psycho-analytic therapies were included. The update search identified one new trial. In total, four RCTs (N = 558) met the inclusion criteria for the update. All of the trials were

Table 72: Clinical review protocol for the review of psychodynamic and psychoanalytic therapies

Electronic databases	Databases: CINAHL, CENTRAL, EMBASE, MEDLINE, PsycINFO
Date searched	1 January 2002 to 30 July 2008
Study design	RCT (≥10 participants per arm)
Patient population	Adults (18+) with schizophrenia (including schizophrenia-related disorders)
Excluded populations	Very late onset schizophrenia (onset after age 60) Other psychotic disorders, such as bipolar disorder, mania or depressive psychosis People with coexisting learning difficulties, significant physical or sensory difficulties, or substance misuse
Interventions	Psychodynamic and psychoanalytic therapies
Comparator	Any alternative management strategy
Critical outcomes	Mortality (suicide) Global state (relapse, rehospitalisation,) Mental state (total symptoms, depression) Psychosocial functioning Quality of life Leaving the study early for any reason Adverse events

published in peer-reviewed journals between 1972 and 2003. In addition, one study identified in the update search was excluded from the analysis because of an inadequate method of randomisation (further information about both included and excluded studies can be found in Appendix 15c).

8.8.4   Psychodynamic and psychoanalytic therapies versus control

For the update, two RCTs of psychodynamic and psychoanalytic therapies versus any type of control were included in the meta-analysis. Additionally, two trials included in the previous guideline directly compared the format of the intervention; one trial compared insight-orientated with reality-adaptive therapy and another trial compared individual with group therapy[28] (see Table 73 for a summary of the study characteristics). Forest plots and/or data tables for each outcome can be found in Appendix 16d.

8.8.5   Clinical evidence summary

Only one new RCT was identified for the update (DURHAM2003), which used a psychodynamic-based intervention as a comparator for CBT. The new study did not provide any evidence for the effectiveness of psychodynamic approaches in terms of symptoms, functioning or quality of life.

8.8.6   From evidence to recommendations

In the previous guideline, the GDG found no clear evidence to support the use of psychodynamic and psychoanalytic therapies as discrete interventions. The limited evidence found for the update does not justify changing this conclusion. However the GDG did acknowledge the use of psychoanalytic and psychodynamic principles to help healthcare professionals understand the experience of people with schizophrenia and their interpersonal relationships, including the therapeutic relationship. Furthermore, the GDG noted that the majority of trials included in the review assessed the efficacy of classic forms of psychodynamic and psychoanalytic therapy. However, these approaches have evolved in recent years, partly in response to a lack of demonstrable efficacy when compared with other interventions in research trials. At present, the GDG are not aware of any well-conducted RCTs assessing the efficacy of newer forms of psychodynamic and psychoanalytic therapy. It is therefore the view of the GDG that further well-conducted research is warranted.

---

[28] Existing subgroups comparing psychodynamic and psychoanalytic therapies with standard care and other active treatments and psychodynamic therapy with group psychodynamic therapy were also updated. However, there was insufficient data to draw any conclusions based on these subgroups. Please refer to Appendix 16d for the forest plots and/or data tables for all subgroup comparisons conducted.

Table 73: Summary of study characteristics for psychodynamic and psychoanalytic therapies

	Psychodynamic and psychoanalytic therapies versus any control	Insight-orientated therapy versus reality adaptive therapy	Individual therapy versus group therapy
k (total N)	2 (294)	1 (164)	1 (100)
Study ID	DURHAM2003 May1976	Gunderson1984	O'Brien1972
Diagnosis	100% schizophrenia or other related diagnoses (DSM or ICD-10)	100% schizophrenia or other related diagnoses (DSM II or III)	100% schizophrenia or other related diagnoses (DSM II or III)
Baseline severity	BPRS: Mean (SD) ~96 (17) DURHAM2003	Not reported	Not reported
Length of treatment	*Range:* 36–104 weeks	Up to 2 years	20 months
Length of follow-up	*Up to 3 months:* DURHAM2003 *Up to 5 years:* May1976		
Setting	*Inpatient:* May1976 *Inpatient and outpatient:* DURHAM2003	*Inpatient:* Gunderson1984[a]	*Outpatient:* O'Brien1972[b]

[a] Treatment was initiated in the inpatient setting and continued in a community setting upon discharge.
[b] All participants were newly discharged.

8.8.7 Recommendations

8.8.7.1 Healthcare professionals may consider using psychoanalytic and psycho-dynamic principles to help them understand the experiences of people with schizophrenia and their interpersonal relationships.

8.8.8 Research recommendations

8.8.8.1 A pilot RCT should be conducted to assess the efficacy of contemporary forms of psychodynamic therapy when compared with standard care and other active psychological and psychosocial interventions.

8.9 PSYCHOEDUCATION

8.9.1 Introduction

Psychoeducation, in its literal definition, implies provision of information and education to a service user with a severe and enduring mental illness, including schizophrenia, about the diagnosis, its treatment, appropriate resources, prognosis, common coping strategies and rights (Pekkala & Merinder, 2002).

In his recent review of the NHS, Darzi (2008) emphasised the importance of 'empowering patients with better information to enable a different quality of conversation between professionals and patients'. Precisely what and how much information a person requires, and the degree to which the information provided is understood, remembered or acted upon, will vary from person to person. Frequently, information giving has to be ongoing. As a result, psychoeducation has now been developed as an aspect of treatment in schizophrenia with a variety of goals over and above the provision of accurate information. Some psychoeducation involves quite lengthy treatment and runs into management strategies, coping techniques and role-playing skills. It is commonly offered in a group format. The diversity of content and information covered, as well as the formats of delivery, vary considerably, so that psychoeducation as a discrete treatment can overlap with family intervention, especially when families and carers are involved in both. Desired outcomes in studies have included improvements in insight, treatment adherence, symptoms, relapse rates, and family knowledge and understanding (Pekkala & Merinder, 2002).

Definition
Psychoeducational interventions were defined as:
- any programme involving interaction between an information provider and service users or their carers, which has the primary aim of offering information about the condition; and
- the provision of support and management strategies to service users and carers.

To be considered as well defined, the educational strategy should be tailored to the need of individuals or carers.

8.9.2   Clinical review protocol

The review protocol, including information about the databases searched and the eligibility criteria used for this section of the guideline, can be found in Table 74. The primary clinical questions can be found in Box 1. A new systematic search for relevant RCTs, published since the previous guideline, was conducted for the guideline update (further information about the search strategy can be found in Appendix 8).

8.9.3   Studies considered for review

In the previous guideline, ten RCTs (N = 1,070) of psychoeducation were included. The update search identified three papers providing follow-up data to existing trials

Table 74: Clinical review protocol for the review of psychoeducation

Electronic databases	Databases: CINAHL, CENTRAL, EMBASE, MEDLINE, PsycINFO
Date searched	1 January 2002 to 30 July 2008
Study design	RCT (≥10 participants per arm and ≥6 weeks' duration)
Patient population	Adults (18+) with schizophrenia (including schizophrenia-related disorders)
Excluded populations	Very late onset schizophrenia (onset after age 60) Other psychotic disorders, such as bipolar disorder, mania or depressive psychosis People with coexisting learning difficulties, significant physical or sensory difficulties, or substance misuse
Interventions	Psychoeducation
Comparator	Any alternative management strategy
Critical outcomes	Mortality (suicide) Global state (relapse, rehospitalisation,) Mental state (total symptoms, depression) Psychosocial functioning Quality of life Leaving the study early for any reason Adverse events

and ten new trials. In the previous guideline, one study (Posner1992) included in the family intervention review was reclassified as psychoeducation for the update. In total, 21 trials (N = 2,016) met the inclusion criteria for the update. All were published in peer-reviewed journals between 1987 and 2008 (further information about both included and excluded studies can be found in Appendix 15c).

8.9.4   Psychoeducation versus control

For the update, four of the included studies (Jones2001; SIBITZ2007; Smith1987; XIANG2007) only included a direct comparison of different types of psychoeducation and one trial (AGARA2007) did not provide any useable data, so 16 trials of psychoeducation versus any type of control were included in the meta-analysis (see Table 75 for a summary of the study characteristics). Subgroup analyses were used to examine the impact of the type of comparator (eight trials used standard care as the comparator and eight trials used another active treatment[29]). Forest plots and/or data tables for each outcome can be found in Appendix 16d.

8.9.5   Clinical evidence summary

There is no new robust evidence for the effectiveness of psychoeducation on any of the critical outcomes. In particular, there are no new UK-based RCTs meeting the GDG's definition of psychoeducation.

8.9.6   From evidence to recommendations

In the previous guideline, the GDG found it difficult to distinguish psychoeducation from the provision of good-quality information as required in standard care, and from good-quality family engagement, where information is provided with family members also present. There is clearly an overlap between good standard care and psychoeducation, and between psychoeducation and family intervention. It is noteworthy that most of the studies reviewed did not take place in the UK, and the nature and quality of the information provision in standard care may differ from services in the UK setting. The evidence found for the update does not justify making a recommendation. However, the GDG acknowledges the importance of providing good quality and accessible information to all people with schizophrenia and their carers, and have hence made a number of related recommendations (see Chapter 4, 4.6.4.1, 4.6.5.1 and Chapter 5, 5.3.10.1).

---

[29] Existing subgroup comparisons exploring the country of the trial, format of the intervention, number of treatment sessions, duration of treatment and patient characteristics were also updated. However, there was insufficient data to draw any conclusions based on these subgroups. Please refer to Appendix 16d for the forest plots and/or data tables for all subgroup comparisons conducted.

Table 75: Summary of study characteristics for psychoeducation

	Psychoeducation versus any control	Psychoeducation versus standard care	Psychoeducation versus other active treatments
k (total N)	16 (1610)	8 (966)	8 (644)
Study ID	Atkinson1996 Bauml1996 BECHDOLF2004 CATHER2005 CHABANNES2008 CHAN2007A CunninghamOwens2001 Hayashi2001 Hornung1995[a] Lecompte1996 Macpherson1996 Merinder1999 Posner1992 SHIN2002 VREELAND2006 XIANG2006	Atkinson1996 Bauml1996 CHABANNES2008 CunninghamOwnes2001 Hayashi2001 Macpherson1996 Posner1992 VREELAND2006	BECHDOLF2004 CATHER2005 CHAN2007A Hornung1995[a] Lecompte1996 Merinder1999 SHIN2002 XIANG2006
Diagnosis	100% schizophrenia or other related diagnoses (DSM or ICD-10)	100% schizophrenia or other related diagnoses (DSM or ICD-10)	100% schizophrenia or other related diagnoses (DSM or ICD-10)

Continued

Table 75: *(Continued)*

	Psychoeducation versus any control	Psychoeducation versus standard care	Psychoeducation versus other active treatments
Baseline severity	*BPRS total:* Mean (SD) range: ~29 (7) to ~92 (8) *PANSS total:* Mean (SD) range: ~14 (5) to ~51 (13)	Not reported	*BPRS total:* Mean (SD) range: ~29 (7) to ~92 (8) *PANSS total:* Mean (SD) range: ~14 (5) to ~51 (13)
Length of treatment	*Range:* 2–52 weeks	*Range:* 4–52 weeks	*Range:* 2–16 weeks
Length of follow-up	*Range:* 3–60 months	*Range:* 3–24 months	*Range:* 12–60 months
Setting	*Inpatient:* BECHDOLF2004 CHAN2007A CunninghamOwens2001[b] Hayashi2001 VREELAND2006	*Inpatient:* CunninghamOwens2001[b] Hayashi2001 VREELAND2006	*Inpatient:* BECHDOLF2004 CHAN2007A

Outpatient: Atkinson1996 Bauml1996 CATHER2005 Hornung1995[a] Macpherson1996 Merinder1999 Posner1992 SHIN2002 XIANG2006 Inpatient and outpatient: CHABANNES2008	Outpatient: Atkinson1996 Bauml1996 Macpherson1996 Posner1992 Inpatient and outpatient: CHABANNES2008	Outpatient: CATHER2005 Hornung1955[a] Merinder1999 SHIN2002 XIANG2006

[a] Multi-modal intervention.
[b] Participants were recruited as inpatients prior to discharge.

319

8.10   SOCIAL SKILLS TRAINING

8.10.1   Introduction

An early psychological approach to the treatment of schizophrenia involved the application of behavioural theory and methods with the aim of normalising behaviour (Ayllon & Azrin, 1965), improving communication or modifying speech (Lindsley, 1963). Given the complex and often debilitating behavioural and social effects of schizophrenia, social skills training was developed as a more sophisticated treatment strategy derived from behavioural and social learning traditions (see Wallace and colleagues [1980] for a review). It was designed to help people with schizophrenia regain their social skills and confidence, improve their ability to cope in social situations, reduce social distress, improve their quality of life and, where possible, to aid symptom reduction and relapse prevention.

Social skills training programmes begin with a detailed assessment and behavioural analysis of individual social skills, followed by individual and/or group interventions using positive reinforcement, goal setting, modelling and shaping. Initially, smaller social tasks (such as responses to non-verbal social cues) are worked on, and gradually new behaviours are built up into more complex social skills, such as conducting a meaningful conversation. There is a strong emphasis on homework assignments intended to help generalise newly learned behaviour away from the treatment setting.

Although this psychosocial treatment approach became very popular in the US and has remained so (for example, Bellack, 2004), since the 1980s it has had much less support in the UK, at least in part as a result of doubts in the UK about the evidence of the capacity of social skills training to generalise from the treatment situation to real social settings (Hersen & Bellack, 1976; Shepherd, 1978). No new studies, therefore, have been conducted of social skills training in the UK. Instead, the evidence base is largely derived from North America and, increasingly, from China and Southeast Asia.

Definition
Social skills training was defined as:
● a structured psychosocial intervention (group or individual) that aims to:
  – enhance social performance, and
  – reduce distress and difficulty in social situations.
  The intervention must:
● include behaviourally-based assessments of a range of social and interpersonal skills, and
● place importance on both verbal and non-verbal communication, the individual's ability to perceive and process relevant social cues, and respond to and provide appropriate social reinforcement.

8.10.2   Clinical review protocol

A new systematic search for relevant RCTs published since the previous guideline was conducted for the guideline update. Information about the databases searched and the eligibility criteria used for this section of the guideline can be found in Table 76 (further information about the search strategy can be found in Appendix 8).

8.10.3   Studies considered for review

In the previous guideline, nine RCTs (N = 436) of social skills training were included. One RCT from the previous guideline (Finch1977) was removed from the update analysis because of inadequate numbers of participants, and one RCT (Eckmann 1992) was reclassified as social skills training and included in the analysis. The update search identified 14 new trials. In total, 23 trials (N = 1,471) met the inclusion criteria for the update. All were published in peer-reviewed journals

Table 76: Clinical review protocol for the review of social skills training

Electronic databases	Databases: CINAHL, CENTRAL, EMBASE, MEDLINE, PsycINFO
Date searched	1 January 2002 to 30 July 2008
Study design	RCT (≥10 participants per arm and ≥6 weeks' duration)
Patient population	Adults (18+) with schizophrenia (including schizophrenia-related disorders)
Excluded populations	Very late onset schizophrenia (onset after age 60) Other psychotic disorders, such as bipolar disorder, mania or depressive psychosis People with coexisting learning difficulties, significant physical or sensory difficulties, or substance misuse
Interventions	Social skills training
Comparator	Any alternative management strategy
Critical outcomes	Mortality (suicide) Global state (relapse, rehospitalisation) Mental state (total symptoms, depression) Psychosocial functioning Quality of life Leaving the study early for any reason Adverse events

between 1983 and 2007 (further information about both included and excluded studies can be found in Appendix 15c).

8.10.4 Social skills training versus control

For the update, one of the included studies (GLYNN2002) only included a direct comparison of different types of social skills and two trials (GUTRIDE1973, KERN2005) did not provide any useable data for any of the critical outcomes listed in the review protocol. Thus, in total 20 trials of social skills training versus any type of control were included in the meta-analysis (see Table 77 for a summary of the study characteristics). Subgroup analyses were used to examine the impact of the type of comparator[30] (ten trials used standard care as the comparator and ten trials used another active treatment). Forest plots and/or data tables for each outcome can be found in Appendix 16d.

8.10.5 Clinical evidence summary

The review found no evidence to suggest that social skills training is effective in improving the critical outcomes. None of the new RCTs were UK based, with most new studies reporting non-significant findings. There was limited evidence for the effectiveness of social skills training on negative symptoms. However this evidence is primarily drawn from non-UK studies and is largely driven by one small study (RONCONE2004) that contains multiple methodological problems.

8.10.6 From evidence to recommendations

In the previous guideline, the GDG found no clear evidence that social skills training was effective as a discrete intervention in improving outcomes in schizophrenia when compared with generic social and group activities, and suggested that the evidence shows little if any consistent advantage over standard care. It is noteworthy that although a recent review (Kurtz & Mueser, 2008) indicated effects for social functioning, symptom severity and relapse, this may be attributed to the inclusion of a number of studies that are beyond the scope of the current definition of social skills used in the present review. In particular, a number of papers were included that assessed vocational and supported employment-based interventions. Consequently, the evidence found for the update does not justify changing the conclusions drawn in the previous guideline.

---

[30] Existing subgroup comparisons exploring the duration of treatment and treatment setting were also updated. However, there was insufficient data to draw any conclusions based on these subgroups. Please refer to Appendix 16d for the forest plots and/or data tables for all subgroup comparisons conducted.

Table 77: Summary of study characteristics for social skills training

	Social skills training versus any control	Social skills training versus standard care	Social skills training versus other active treatments
k (total N)	20 (1215)	10 (541)	10 (674)
Study ID	Bellack1994	Bellack1984	BROWN1983
	BROWN1983	CHIEN2003	Dobson1995
	CHIEN2003	CHOI2006	Eckmann1992
	CHOI2006	Daniels1998	Hayes1995
	Daniels1998	GRANHOLM2005[a]	Liberman1998
	Dobson1995	PATTERSON2003	Lukoff1986
	Eckmann1992	Peniston1988	Marder1996
	GRANHOLM2005[a]	RONCONE2004	NG2007
	Hayes1995	UCOK2006	PATTERSON2006
	Liberman1998	VALENCIA2007[a]	PINTO1999[a]
	Lukoff1986[a]		
	Marder1996		
	NG2007		
	PATTERSON2003		
	PATTERSON2006		
	PINTO1999[a]		
	Peniston1988		
	RONCONE2004		
	UCOK2006		
	VALENCIA2007[a]		

Continued

323

Table 77: (Continued)

	Social skills training versus any control	Social skills training versus standard care	Social skills training versus other active treatments
Diagnosis	100% schizophrenia or other related diagnoses (DSM or ICD-10)	100% schizophrenia or other related diagnoses (DSM or ICD-10)	100% schizophrenia or other related diagnoses (DSM or ICD-10)
Baseline severity	*BPRS total:* Mean (SD) ~47 (10) Hayes1995 Mean (SD) ~40 (10) NG2007 Mean (SD) ~82 (21) PINTO1999[a] Mean (SD) ~41 (7) UCOK2006 *PANSS total:* Mean (SD) ~54 (14) GRANHOLM2005[a] Mean (SD) ~61 (3) PATTERSON2006	*BPRS total:* Mean (SD) ~41 (7) UCOK2006 *PANSS total:* Mean (SD) ~54 (14) GRANHOLM2005[a] Mean (SD) ~112 (27) VALENCIA2007[a]	*BPRS total:* Mean (SD) ~47 (10) Hayes1995 Mean (SD) ~40 (10) NG2007 Mean (SD) ~82 (21) PINTO1999[a] *PANSS total:* Mean (SD) ~61 (3) PATTERSON2006

	Range: 4–104 weeks	Range: 4–52 weeks	Range: 8–104 weeks
Length of treatment			
Length of follow-up	*Up to 12 months:* Bellack1984 CHIEN2003 Hayes1995 PATTERSON2003 PATTERSON2006 *Up to 24 months:* Liberman1998 Lukoff1986	*Up to 12 months:* Bellack1984 CHIEN2003 PATTERSON2003	*Up to 12 months:* Hayes1995 PATTERSON2006 *Up to 24 months:* Liberman1998 Lukoff1986
Setting	*Inpatient:* BROWN1983 CHIEN2003 Lukoff1986 NG2007 Peniston1988 RONCONE2004 *Outpatient:* CHOI2006 GRANHOLM2005[a] Liberman1998	*Inpatient:* CHIEN2003 Peniston1988 RONCONE2004 *Outpatient:* CHOI2006 GRANHOLM2005[a] UCOK2006	*Inpatient:* BROWN1983 Luckoff1986 NG2007 *Outpatient:* Liberman1998 Marder1996

Continued

Table 77: *(Continued)*

Social skills training versus any control	Social skills training versus standard care	Social skills training versus other active treatments
Marder1996 UCOK2006 VALENCIA2007[a]	VALENCIA2007[a]	
Inpatient and outpatient: Daniels1998 Eckmann1992 Hayes1995 PINTO1999[a]	*Inpatient and outpatient:* Daniels1998	*Inpatient and outpatient:* Eckmann1992 Hayes1995 PINTO1999[a]
Other[b]: Bellack1984 Dobson1995 PATTERSON2003 PATTERSON2006	*Other*[b]: Bellack1984 PATTERSON2003	*Other*[b]: Dobson1995 PATTERSON2006

[a] Multi-modal interventions.
[b] Other settings include board and care facilities, and day hospitals.

8.10.7   Recommendations

8.10.7.1   Do not routinely offer social skills training (as a specific intervention) to people with schizophrenia.

8.11   RECOMMENDATIONS (ACROSS ALL TREATMENTS)[31]

8.11.1   Principles in the provision of psychological therapies

8.11.1.1   When providing psychological interventions, routinely and systematically monitor a range of outcomes across relevant areas, including service user satisfaction and, if appropriate, carer satisfaction.

8.11.1.2   Healthcare teams working with people with schizophrenia should identify a lead healthcare professional within the team whose responsibility is to monitor and review:
- access to and engagement with psychological interventions
- decisions to offer psychological interventions and equality of access across different ethnic groups.

8.11.1.3   Healthcare professionals providing psychological interventions should:
- have an appropriate level of competence in delivering the intervention to people with schizophrenia
- be regularly supervised during psychological therapy by a competent therapist and supervisor.

8.11.1.4   Trusts should provide access to training that equips healthcare professionals with the competencies required to deliver the psychological therapy interventions recommended in this guideline.

8.11.1.5   When psychological treatments, including arts therapies, are started in the acute phase (including in inpatient settings), the full course should be continued after discharge without unnecessary interruption.

---

[31] Recommendations for specific interventions can be found at the end of each review (see the beginning of this chapter for further information).

9 SERVICE-LEVEL INTERVENTIONS IN THE TREATMENT AND MANAGEMENT OF SCHIZOPHRENIA

For the guideline update, only the reviews of early intervention services (EIS) and primary care and physical health were updated. The review of EIS can now be found in Chapter 5 (Section 5.2). The following service reviews were not updated and therefore these sections of the chapter remain unchanged: community mental health teams (CMHTs), assertive outreach (ACT), acute day hospital care, vocational rehabilitation, non-acute day hospital care, crisis resolution and home treatment teams (CHRTTs) and intensive case management (ICM).

9.1   INTRODUCTION

Until the 1950s, most people with a diagnosis of schizophrenia were treated in large mental hospitals where they resided for much of their lives. It was not until most Western governments began to implement a policy of de-institutionalisation that other types of services began to develop, such as outpatient clinics, day hospitals, CMHTs and community mental health centres. However, by the 1970s the new community services that had been developed as a response to long-stay hospital closures failed to meet the needs of those most needing care (Audit Commission, 1986; Melzer *et al.*, 1991), evidenced by sharply rising readmission rates (Rossler *et al.*, 1992; Ellison *et al.*, 1995).

In recognition of the limitations of community-based service provision, a second generation of teams and services was developed. These aimed to: (a) prevent or reduce readmission, by providing more home- and community-based treatment; (b) improve engagement with service users; and (c) improve clinical, social and occupational outcomes.

In reviewing the evidence for the effectiveness of different services in the previous guideline, the GDG decided to focus on RCTs. By using this type of study design to evaluate service-level interventions there are specific problems relating to defining such interventions precisely; for example, the 'intervention' and 'standard care' may vary between studies, between countries and over time; and experimental interventions have a tendency to overlap with standard care. However, service-level interventions that claim superiority over other methods of care delivery must be able to characterise clearly what they do, how they do it, and how they differ from alternative types of service and from the standard care they hope to replace. For these reasons, it is essential for new services to be subjected to the rigour of evaluation through RCTs. Although other types of study might help to differentiate, evaluate and refine services and the ways in which they operate, services must be able to demonstrate their overall value in comparison with other interventions to remain a supportable component of care within the NHS.

9.2   INTERFACE BETWEEN PRIMARY AND SECONDARY CARE

This section has particular focus on the management of people with schizophrenia presenting to primary care with no past history of the disorder (first-episode schizophrenia) and those with an established diagnosis managed either partially or wholly in primary care, including those with a history of schizophrenia who have recently moved into a new primary care catchment area. The recommendations are based on an updated narrative review conducted for the previous guideline (further information about the review process can be found in Section 3.5.7).

9.2.1   First-episode schizophrenia

At the onset of a psychotic illness, people are frequently seen by their GP. Schizophrenia is often characterised by a long prodromal phase with a range of ill-defined, insidious and non-specific symptoms, and a gradual change in psychosocial functioning. The symptoms could include changes in affect (such as anxiety, irritability and depression), cognition (such as difficulty in concentration or memory), thought content (such as preoccupation with new ideas), physical state (such as sleep disturbance and loss of energy), social withdrawal and impairment of role functioning. The majority of such presentations, however, do not develop into schizophrenia. It is beyond the scope of this guideline to deal with the identification of people with schizophrenia. Nevertheless, people presenting with these types of symptoms to primary care should be monitored there and referred to an early intervention service if a diagnosis of schizophrenia is suspected or if referral to secondary care is requested.

A minority of people with what appear to be possible prodromal symptoms of schizophrenia will develop 'attenuated' positive symptoms, such as mild thought disorder, ideas of reference, suspiciousness, odd beliefs and perceptual distortion of a milder variety than that observed in established schizophrenia. In these instances, referral to an early intervention service is advisable. Some will develop more florid symptoms, including delusions, hallucinations, disturbed behaviour, and disrupted family and social relationships, which are suggestive of an acute episode of schizophrenia. For these people, urgent referral to secondary mental health services should be arranged at the earliest opportunity. This might involve the local early intervention service, CRHTT, CMHT or other similar community-based service.

Sometimes people will present to primary care at a stage when they are already experiencing an acute episode of schizophrenia and informed discussion is not possible. In these circumstances it is essential for primary care workers to contact relatives or arrange for an advocate to help, in the hope of persuading the person to accept referral to secondary care. If it is considered necessary to initiate antipsychotic medication before referral to secondary care, then this should be done by a GP with experience in the pharmacological treatment of schizophrenia and the recommendations in the chapter on pharmacological treatment should be followed. Urgent referral for people at this stage of the illness may involve use of the Mental Health Act, arranged in conjunction with secondary services.

After the first episode, some people refuse to accept the diagnosis and sometimes also reject the treatment offered. Bearing in mind the consequences of a diagnosis of schizophrenia, many people in this position, perhaps unsurprisingly, want a second opinion from another consultant psychiatrist and this should be requested as soon as possible.

9.2.2 People with an established diagnosis of schizophrenia in primary care

People with an established diagnosis of schizophrenia who are managed in primary care require regular assessment of their health and social needs. This should include monitoring of mental state, medication use and adherence, side effects, social isolation, access to services and occupational status. All such people should have a care plan developed jointly between primary care and secondary mental health services. Regular monitoring of physical health is also essential. With consent from service users, non-professional carers should also be seen at regular intervals for assessment of their health and social care needs. Carers should also be offered an assessment of their needs.

Advance statements and advance decisions about treatment should be documented in the service user's notes. These should be copied from secondary services to the responsible GP. If no secondary service is involved in the service user's care (because they have recently moved to the area, for example), the GP should ensure that any existing advance decisions or statements are copied to the secondary services to whom referral is made.

When a person with schizophrenia is planning on moving to the catchment area of a different NHS trust, their current secondary care provider should contact the new secondary and primary care providers, and send them the current care plan.

People presenting to primary care services who are new to the area (not known to local services) with previously diagnosed psychosis should be referred to secondary care mental health services for assessment, subject to their agreement. The GP should attempt to establish details of any previous treatment and pass on any relevant information about this to the CMHT.

When a person with schizophrenia is no longer being cared for in secondary care, the primary care clinician should consider re-referral of the service user to secondary care. When referring a service user to secondary mental health services, primary care professionals should take the following into account:

- Previous history: if a person has previously responded effectively to a particular treatment without experiencing unwanted side effects and is considered safe to manage in primary care, referral may not be necessary.

- Views about referral: the views of the mental health service user should be fully taken into account before making a referral. If the service user wants to be managed in primary care, it is often necessary to work with the family and carers. Sharing confidential information about the service user with carers raises many ethical issues, which should be dealt with through full discussion with the service user.

- Non-adherence to treatment: this may be the cause of the relapse, possibly as a result of lack of concordance between the views of the service user and of the healthcare professionals, with the former not recognising the need for medication. Alternatively, non-adherence might be the consequence of side effects. Finding the right antipsychotic drug specifically suited to the service user is an important aim in the effective management of schizophrenia.

- Side effects of medication and poor response to treatment: the side effects of antipsychotic drugs are personally and socially disabling, and must be routinely monitored. Side effects are also a cause of poor response to treatment. For about 40% of people given antipsychotics, their symptoms do not respond effectively.

- Concerns about comorbid drug and alcohol misuse: substance misuse by people with schizophrenia is increasingly recognised as a major problem, both in terms of its prevalence and its clinical and social effects (Banerjee *et al.*, 2001). Monitoring drug and alcohol use is an essential aspect of the management of people with schizophrenia in primary and secondary care.

- Level of risk to self and others: people with schizophrenia, especially when relapse is impending or apparent, are at risk of suicide and are often vulnerable to exploitation or abuse. During an acute episode of illness, conflicts and difficulties may manifest themselves through social disturbances or even violence.

As described in Chapter 2 (Section 2.1.5), people with schizophrenia have a higher rate of physical illness than many others. Just as with other groups at high risk, regular physical checks and health advice are an essential contribution of primary care to the treatment and management of people with schizophrenia. GPs and other primary healthcare workers should monitor the physical health of people with schizophrenia, and follow the appropriate NICE guidance. The results of physical health checks should be clearly documented by the primary care clinician. These results should be communicated to the care coordinator and/or psychiatrist, and recorded in the secondary care notes. The effectiveness of these screening and monitoring procedures in people with schizophrenia has yet to be tested in an RCT.

The identification of patients with schizophrenia in a well-organised computerised practice is feasible (Kendrick *et al.*, 1991; Nazareth *et al.*, 1993). The organisation and development of practice case registers is to be encouraged because it is often the first step in monitoring people with schizophrenia in general practice. There is evidence that providing payment incentives to GPs leads to improved monitoring of people with schizophrenia (Burns & Cohen, 1998). In 2004, as a part of the GP contract, the Quality and Outcomes Framework was introduced in English general practice as a voluntary process for all general practices – schizophrenia is one of the medical conditions to be monitored as part of this framework.

9.2.3   Recommendations

Transfer between services

9.2.3.1   Discuss transfer from one service to another in advance with the service user, and carer if appropriate. Use the care programme approach (CPA) to help ensure effective collaboration with other care providers during transfer. Include details of how to access services in times of crisis.

Early referral

9.2.3.2   Urgently refer all people with first presentation of psychotic symptoms in primary care to a local community-based secondary mental health service (for example, crisis resolution and home treatment team, early intervention service, community mental health team). Referral to early intervention services may be from primary or secondary care. The choice of team should be determined by the stage and severity of illness and the local context.

9.2.3.3   Carry out a full assessment of people with psychotic symptoms in secondary care, including an assessment by a psychiatrist. Write a care plan in collaboration with the service user as soon as possible. Send a copy to the primary healthcare professional who made the referral and the service user.

9.2.3.4   Include a crisis plan in the care plan, based on a full risk assessment. The crisis plan should define the role of primary and secondary care and identify the key clinical contacts in the event of an emergency or impending crisis.

Early treatment

9.2.3.5   If it is necessary for a GP to start antipsychotic medication, they should have experience in treating and managing schizophrenia. Antipsychotic medication should be given as described in Section 6.11.1 and Section 6.11.2.

Promoting recovery

9.2.3.6   Develop and use practice case registers to monitor the physical and mental health of people with schizophrenia in primary care.

9.2.3.7   GPs and other primary healthcare professionals should monitor the physical health of people with schizophrenia at least once a year. Focus on cardiovascular disease risk assessment as described in 'Lipid modification' (NICE clinical guideline 67) but bear in mind that people with schizophrenia are at higher risk of cardiovascular disease than the general population. A copy of the results should be sent to the care coordinator and/or psychiatrist, and put in the secondary care notes.

9.2.3.8   People with schizophrenia at increased risk of developing cardiovascular disease and/or diabetes (for example, with elevated blood pressure, raised lipid levels, smokers, increased waist measurement) should be identified at the earliest opportunity. Their care should be managed using the appropriate NICE guidance for prevention of these conditions[32].

9.2.3.9   Treat people with schizophrenia who have diabetes and/or cardiovascular disease in primary care according to the appropriate NICE guidance[33].

9.2.3.10   Healthcare professionals in secondary care should ensure, as part of the CPA, that people with schizophrenia receive physical healthcare from primary care as described in recommendations 9.2.3.6–9.2.3.9.

9.2.3.11   When a person with an established diagnosis of schizophrenia presents with a suspected relapse (for example, with increased psychotic symptoms or a significant increase in the use of alcohol or other substances), primary healthcare professionals should refer to the crisis section of the care plan. Consider referral to the key clinician or care coordinator identified in the crisis plan.

9.2.3.12   For a person with schizophrenia being cared for in primary care, consider referral to secondary care again if there is:
● poor response to treatment
● non-adherence to medication
● intolerable side effects from medication
● comorbid substance misuse
● risk to self or others.

9.2.3.13   When re-referring people with schizophrenia to mental health services, take account of service user and carer requests, especially for:
● review of the side effects of existing treatments
● psychological treatments or other interventions.

9.2.3.14   When a person with schizophrenia is planning to move to the catchment area of a different NHS trust, a meeting should be arranged between the services involved and the service user to agree a transition plan before transfer. The person's current care plan should be sent to the new secondary care and primary care providers.

Return to primary care

9.2.3.15   Offer people with schizophrenia whose symptoms have responded effectively to treatment and remain stable the option to return to primary care for further management. If a service user wishes to do this, record this in their notes and coordinate transfer of responsibilities through the CPA.

Service-level interventions

9.2.3.16   All teams providing services for people with schizophrenia should offer a comprehensive range of interventions consistent with this guideline.

---

[32] See 'Lipid modification' (NICE clinical guideline 67), 'Type 1 diabetes' (NICE clinical guideline 15), 'Type 2 diabetes' (NICE clinical guideline 66). Further guidance about treating cardiovascular disease and diabetes is available from www.nice.org.uk
[33] Ibid.

9.2.4 Research recommendations

9.2.4.1 Cardiovascular disease risk assessment prediction tools specific to people with schizophrenia should be developed.

9.2.4.2 An RCT should be conducted to investigate the clinical and cost effectiveness of cardiovascular screening of people with schizophrenia in primary care.

9.2.4.3 An RCT should be conducted to investigate the clinical and cost effectiveness of monitoring the physical health of people with schizophrenia.

9.2.4.4 An RCT should be conducted to investigate the clinical and cost effectiveness of interventions for weight management for people with schizophrenia in primary care.

9.2.4.5 An RCT should be conducted to investigate the clinical and cost effectiveness of primary prevention of coronary heart disease for people with schizophrenia in primary care.

9.2.4.6 An RCT should be conducted to investigate the clinical and cost effectiveness of delivering recommended psychological interventions in general practice (especially CBT and family intervention).

9.2.4.7 A study should be conducted to investigate the role of GPs in early diagnosis of schizophrenia and management of first-episode psychosis.

9.3 COMMUNITY MENTAL HEALTH TEAMS

The following section marked by asterisks has not been updated from the previous guideline.

9.3.1 Introduction

**One of the earliest service developments in community-based care was that of the community mental health team (CMHT; Merson *et al.*, 1992). CMHTs are multidisciplinary teams, comprising all the main professions involved in mental health, including nursing, occupational therapy, psychiatry, psychology and social work. Having developed in a relatively pragmatic way, CMHTs have become the mainstay of community-based mental health work in developed countries (Bouras *et al.*, 1986; Bennett & Freeman, 1991), as well as in many other nations (Pierides, 1994; Slade *et al.*, 1995; Isaac, 1996). Nevertheless, concerns about CMHTs have been raised, particularly regarding the incidence of violence (Coid, 1994), the quality of day-to-day life for people with serious mental health problems and their carers, and the impact upon society (Dowell & Ciarlo, 1983).

Definition
The GDG used the Cochrane Review (Tyrer *et al.*, 2002) of the effects of CMHT management when compared with non-team community management for people with

serious mental health problems. The definitions used in this review for CMHTs and the comparator 'standard care' or 'usual care' were as follows:

- CMHT care was 'management of care from a multidisciplinary, community-based team (that is, more than a single person designated to work within a team)'
- 'standard care' or 'usual care' must be stated to be the normal care in the area concerned, non-team community care, outpatient care, admission to hospital (where acutely ill people were diverted from admission and allocated to CMHT or inpatient care) or day hospital care.

The review specifically focused upon CMHT management, and therefore excluded studies that involved any additional method of management in the CMHT.

9.3.2 Studies considered for review

The review by Tyrer and colleagues (2002) included five studies of CMHTs, three undertaken in London (MERSON1992 [London]; BURNS1993 [London]; TYRER1998 [London]), one from Australia (HOULT1981 [Sydney]) and one from Canada (FENTON1979 [Montreal]). For the purposes of the GDG review, however, BURNS1993 was excluded on the grounds of inadequate allocation concealment, and the Canadian and Australian studies were excluded because the GDG regarded them to be primarily studies of crisis intervention teams rather than CMHTs. An additional search by the review team for recent RCTs evaluating CMHTs identified one suitable study, which was set in Manchester (GATER1997).

The review team conducted a new analysis using the three studies selected (MERSON1992 [London]; GATER1997 [Manchester]; TYRER1998 [London]), with data for 334 participants. All studies were undertaken in urban or inner-city settings. Only published data were used for analysis, except in the case of the MERSON1992 (London) study, for which unpublished data were available for further analysis. In all three studies the most common diagnosis was schizophrenia, but each study also included a significant minority of participants with non-psychotic disorders.

Studies included varied in the following ways:
- follow-up period (3 months to 2 years)
- proportion of individuals with schizophrenia (38% to 55%)
- type of interventions used by the CMHT.

9.3.3 Results

The studies considered in this review included people with a variety of diagnoses, making recommendations specifically for people with schizophrenia tentative. With this caveat in mind, the review found the evidence insufficient to determine whether CMHTs, when compared with 'standard care', reduced admission rates or death rates, improved the mental state of service users, improved contact with services, or improved social functioning. The review did not combine data from the studies by

335

MERSON1992 (London) and TYRER1998 (London), because in the latter study the service was dealing with discharged psychiatric patients who presumably are more likely to be readmitted to hospital and to be more severely ill than those seen in the other two trials. This would appear to be confirmed by the enormously high admission rates in the Tyrer study.

Based on two studies (which could not be combined in a meta-analysis), there is insufficient evidence to determine if CMHTs reduce admission rates to hospital, compared with standard care (MERSON1992 [London]: n = 100, RR = 0.71, 95% CI: 0.42 to 1.19; TYRER1998 [London]: n = 155, RR = 0.88, 95% CI: 0.76 to 1.01). (Ib)[34]

There is insufficient evidence to determine if CMHTs are associated with increased death rates (MERSON1992 [London]: n = 100, RR = 0.54, 95% CI: 0.05 to 5.78; TYRER1998 [London]: n = 155, RR = 0.89, 95% CI: 0.06 to 13.98). (Ib)

There is insufficient evidence to determine if CMHTs are associated with a loss of contact with services (MERSON1992 [London]: n = 100, RR = 1.24, 95% CI: 0.49 to 3.16; TYRER1998 [London]: n = 155, RR = 1.04, 95% CI: 0.60 to 1.79). (Ib)

There is insufficient evidence to determine if CMHTs are associated with improvements in mental state (CPRS: n = 100, WMD = –0.80, 95% CI: –5.74 to 4.14). (Ib)

There is insufficient evidence to determine if CMHTs are associated with improvements in social functioning (Social Functioning Questionnaire: n = 100, WMD = 0.70, 95% CI: –1.18 to 2.58). (Ib)

9.3.4   Clinical summary

Despite the fact that CMHTs remain the mainstay of community mental healthcare, there is surprisingly little evidence to show that they are an effective way of organising services. As such, evidence for or against the effectiveness of CMHTs in the management of schizophrenia is insufficient to make any evidence-based recommendations.

9.3.5   Health economic evidence

It has been hypothesised that the provision of services by CMHTs has the potential for cost saving, resulting from better organisation of the delivery of care and the low establishment costs of community teams.

The economic review identified five eligible studies, all of which were conducted in the UK. Four studies were based on RCTs (Burns & Raftery, 1993; Gater *et al.*, 1997; Merson *et al.*, 1996; Tyrer *et al.*, 1998), while another reported data from a controlled study with concurrent controls (McCrone *et al.*, 1998). Four

---

[34] Ib refers to the levels of evidence used in the previous guideline: evidence obtained from a small RCT or a meta-analysis of fewer than three RCTs.

studies evaluated only costs and one study was a cost-minimisation analysis estimating the cost difference between interventions (Burns & Raftery, 1993). All studies contained a low risk of bias, with the exception of the study by Tyrer and colleagues (1998).

Four studies compared CMHTs with 'standard care'. The study by Gater and colleagues (1997) found standard care to be less costly both for the healthcare system and for families, although none of the cost differences was significant. Three studies showed that CMHTs are cheaper than standard care. However, Merson and colleagues (1996) did not calculate the significance of the difference, and the other two savings were not statistically significant (Burns & Raftery, 1993; Tyrer *et al.*, 1998). One study compared CMHTs with intensive case management (McCrone *et al.*, 1998), and found that none of the interventions resulted in significant cost savings compared with the costs in the period before the introduction of the new services. The result of the between-intervention comparison was not reliable, owing to differences in the disability status of the comparison populations.

Health economic conclusions
The available evidence on health economics is unclear. The non-significant differences between standard care and CMHTs, and between pre-intervention period and intervention period, suggest that CMHTs provide no real cost savings or extra costs.

9.3.6   Recommendations

9.3.6.1   Consider community mental health teams alongside other community-based teams as a way of providing services for people with schizophrenia.

9.3.7   Research recommendations

9.3.7.1   High-quality research, including health economic outcomes, should be conducted to establish the clinical and economic effectiveness, including the impact upon quality of life, of community mental health teams compared with other ways of delivering care for people with schizophrenia.

9.3.7.2   Studies are needed to establish the relative effectiveness of specialist teams (for example crisis resolution and home treatment, and early intervention) compared with community mental health teams augmented or enhanced to deliver these functions.**

9.4   ASSERTIVE OUTREACH (ASSERTIVE COMMUNITY TREATMENT)

The following section marked by asterisks has not been updated from the previous guideline.

9.4.1 Introduction

**Assertive outreach, usually known outside the UK as assertive community treatment (ACT), is a method of delivering treatment and care for people with serious mental health problems in the community (Thompson *et al.*, 1990). First developed in the 1970s as a means of preventing or reducing admission to hospital, the model of care has since been defined and validated, based upon the consensus of an international panel of experts (McGrew *et al.*, 1994; McGrew & Bond, 1995). Assertive outreach is now a well-defined model of service delivery, with the following aims:

- to keep people with serious mental health problems in contact with services
- to reduce the extent (and cost) of hospital admissions
- to improve outcomes (particularly quality of life and social functioning).

Definition
The GDG adopted the definition used in a systematic review of ACT by Marshall and Lockwood (2002), which identified the following key elements:

- care is provided by a multidisciplinary team (usually involving a psychiatrist with dedicated sessions)
- care is exclusively provided for a defined group of people (those with serious mental illness)
- team members share responsibility for clients, so that several members may work with the same client, and members do not have individual caseloads (unlike case management)
- the team attempts to provide all the psychiatric and social care for each service user, rather than making referrals to other agencies
- care is provided at home or in the workplace, as far as possible
- treatment and care are offered assertively to uncooperative or reluctant service users ('assertive outreach')
- medication concordance is emphasised.

For a study intervention to be accepted as ACT, Marshall and Lockwood (2002) required that the trial report described the experimental intervention as 'Assertive Community Treatment, Assertive Case Management or PACT; or as being based on the Madison, Treatment in Community Living, Assertive Community Treatment or Stein and Test models.' Assertive community treatment and similar models of care are long-term interventions for those with severe and enduring mental illnesses, and so the review did not consider ACT as an alternative to acute hospital admission. The review also excluded studies of 'home-based care', as this was regarded as a form of crisis intervention; these studies are reviewed in the section on crisis resolution and home treatment teams (Section 9.8).

9.4.2 Studies considered for review

The review team undertook a search for recent RCTs, locating two further studies (CHANDLER [California; 2]; FEKETE [Indiana]) for inclusion and reanalysis with the Marshall and Lockwood (2002) review. Studies included had to conform to the definition of ACT given above and comparator treatments were standard community care, hospital-based rehabilitation and case management. A total of 22 trials were incorporated for review, including data on 3,722 participants.

The included studies varied in the following ways:
- follow-up period (up to 2.4 years)
- country of study (Sweden 1, UK 1, US 18, Canada 2)
- gender of participants (mixed, male)
- setting (urban, rural, inner city)
- comparator treatment (standard community care, hospital-based rehabilitation, case management).

Trials were only included if the participants were described as having a 'severe mental disorder', defined as a schizophrenia-like disorder, bipolar disorder or depression with psychotic features.

9.4.3 Results

Effect of assertive community treatment on use of services
Most of the studies reviewed here were undertaken in the US and, although the ACT model is well defined, comparisons with standard care must limit our confidence in generalising findings to the UK. Nevertheless, the evidence is persuasive in the American context and shows that for people with severe mental disorders, ACT improves contact with services, reduces bed usage and hospital admission, and increases satisfaction with services, when compared with standard community care.

There is strong evidence suggesting that those receiving ACT were more likely to remain in contact with services than people receiving standard community care (number lost to follow-up: n = 1757, RR = 0.62, 95% CI: 0.52 to 0.74). (Ia)[35]

There is strong evidence suggesting that ACT teams decrease the likelihood of hospital admission, compared with standard care (n = 1047, random effects RR = 0.71, 95% CI: 0.52 to 0.97; NNT = 7, 95% CI: 4 to 100). (Ia)

There is limited evidence suggesting that ACT teams decrease the likelihood of hospital admission, compared with hospital-based rehabilitation (n = 185, RR = 0.47, 95% CI: 0.33 to 0.66; NNT = 3, 95% CI: 3 to 5). (Ib)

ACT is associated with an average 40% reduction in bed usage. (Ia)

There is limited evidence suggesting that ACT is associated with increased satisfaction with services, compared with standard care (Client Satisfaction Scale: n = 120, WMD = –0.56, 95% CI: –0.77 to –0.36). (Ib)

---

[35] Ia refers to the levels of evidence used in the previous guideline: evidence obtained from a single, large randomised trial or a meta-analysis of at least three RCTs.

Effect of assertive community treatment on accommodation and work
Service users receiving ACT are less likely to be homeless, are more likely to be living independently and are less likely to be unemployed than those receiving standard care. However, these data include a study that specifically targeted homeless people and people at risk of being homeless.

There is strong evidence that ACT decreases the likelihood that service users would be homeless, compared with standard care (n = 374, RR = 0.22, 95% CI: 0.09 to 0.56; NNT = 10, 95% CI: 7 to 20). (Ia)

There is strong evidence suggesting that those receiving ACT were more likely to live independently than people receiving standard community care (not living independently at end of study: n = 362, RR = 0.70, 95% CI: 0.57 to 0.87; NNT = 7, 95% CI: 5 to 17). (Ia)

There is strong evidence suggesting that people receiving ACT were less likely to be unemployed at the end of the study than people receiving standard community care (n = 604, RR = 0.86, 95% CI: 0.80 to 0.91; NNT = 8, 95% CI: 6 to 13). (Ia)

Effect of assertive community treatment on symptoms and quality of life
Service users receiving ACT are more likely to experience modest improvements in both mental state and quality of life than those receiving standard care.

There is strong evidence suggesting a statistically significant difference in mental state between those receiving ACT and those receiving standard care, but this difference is small in terms of clinical significance (BPRS/Brief Symptom Inventory/Colorado Symptom Index: n = 255, SMD = –0.16, 95% CI: –0.41 to –0.08). (Ia)

There is limited evidence suggesting that homeless people receiving ACT are more likely to experience a clinically significant improvement in quality of life, compared with standard care (General Wellbeing in Quality of Life Scale: n = 125, WMD = –0.52, 95% CI: –0.99 to –0.05). (Ib)

9.4.4   Clinical summary

Caution is necessary in the interpretation and translation of these findings for application in a UK context. Also, when assertive outreach is targeted at people who tend not to receive services and have little social support or help, such as the homeless, improvements in areas, such as quality of life will be measured from a very low baseline. Generalising such findings to people with better access to services and/or better social support is problematic. With these caveats in mind, this review found evidence that for people with severe mental disorders, ACT compared with standard care is more likely to improve contact and satisfaction with services, decrease the use of hospital services, improve quality of life, and improve work and accommodation status.

9.4.5   Health economic evidence

It has been hypothesised that assertive outreach achieves significant cost reduction by shifting the focus of care into the community, reducing hospital admissions and improving concordance with the provided services. The cost effectiveness of assertive outreach compared with other forms of service provision, such as case management and CMHTs, was also of interest.

The economic review identified 11 eligible studies, none of which originated in the UK. All studies were based on RCTs, with the exception of one study by Preston and Fazio (2000), which used data from a study with concurrent controls. Five studies adapted simple costing methods (Bond *et al.*, 1988; Hu & Jerrell, 1998; Preston & Fazio, 2000; Quinlivan *et al.*, 1995; Salkever *et al.*, 1999) and six studies were economic evaluations (Chandler *et al.*, 1999; De Cangas, 1994; Essock *et al.*, 1998; Lehman *et al.*, 1999; Rosenheck & Neale, 1998; Wolff *et al.*, 1997). Six studies demonstrated a high risk of bias and none of the studies used sensitivity analyses to investigate the robustness of their findings. Although the international results are unambiguous, interpretation of them within a UK context should be treated with caution.

Six studies compared ACT with 'standard care'. Bond and colleagues (1988) found discrepancies in the cost-saving characteristics of ACT between the three participating study sites. All the remaining studies demonstrated that ACT was a cost-saving form of service provision (Quinlivan *et al.*, 1995) or that ACT was more cost effective than standard care (De Cangas, 1994; Lehman *et al.*, 1999; Rosenheck & Neale, 1998).

Six studies compared ACT with different approaches to case management. The study by Preston and Fazio (2000) demonstrated intensive care management to be more cost saving than ACT, relative to the costs measured in the period before the introduction of these new forms of service provision. However, baseline data suggest a difference between the two comparison groups and the analysis focused only on narrow cost components. Salkever and colleagues (1999) found no significant cost difference between standard case management and ACT, but the study suffered from flaws similar to those of the analysis by Preston and Fazio (2000). A more reliable result by Essock and colleagues (1998) showed equal cost effectiveness of the two forms of service provision. Hu and Jerrell (1998) demonstrated that ACT was more cost saving in the long term, while Quinlivan and colleagues (1995) also found ACT to be less costly, although the difference was not significant. Another study showed that ACT is equally as costly but more effective than case management (Wolff *et al.*, 1997). None of the studies compared ACT with CMHTs.

Two studies investigated the cost effectiveness of ACT specifically for homeless people with severe mental illness and found that ACT was more cost effective than standard care (Lehman *et al.*, 1999) and more cost effective than case management (Wolff *et al.*, 1997).

Health economic conclusions

There is evidence that assertive community treatment is more cost effective than standard care, representing a good 'value for money' form of service provision.

Comparing ACT with case management, the evidence suggests that there is no significant cost difference between the two forms of service provision.

There is evidence that ACT is a cost-effective form of service provision for homeless people with severe mental illness.

9.4.6   Recommendations

9.4.6.1   Assertive outreach teams should be provided for people with serious mental disorders, including for people with schizophrenia, who make high use of inpatient services and who have a history of poor engagement with services leading to frequent relapse and/or social breakdown (as manifest by homelessness or seriously inadequate accommodation).

9.4.7   Research recommendations

9.4.7.1   Adequately powered RCTs reporting all relevant outcomes, including quality of life, are needed to establish the efficacy of assertive outreach teams for people with schizophrenia (and other serious mental disorders) in the UK. Studies should evaluate the suitability and efficacy of assertive outreach for different service user subgroups, and include economic analyses applicable to the UK setting.**

9.5   ACUTE DAY HOSPITAL CARE

The following section marked by asterisks has not been updated from the previous guideline.

9.5.1   Introduction

**Given the substantial costs and high level of use of inpatient care, the possibility of day hospital treatment programmes acting as an alternative to acute admission gained credence in the early 1960s, initially in the US (Kris, 1965; Herz *et al.*, 1971), and later in Europe (Wiersma *et al.*, 1989) and the UK (Creed *et al.*, 1990; Dick *et al.*, 1985).

Definition
Acute psychiatric day hospitals were defined by the GDG as units that provided 'diagnostic and treatment services for acutely ill individuals who would otherwise be treated in traditional psychiatric inpatient units'. Thus, trials would only be eligible for inclusion if they compared admission to an acute day hospital with admission to an inpatient unit. Participants were people with acute psychiatric disorders (all diagnoses) who would have been admitted to inpatient care had the acute day hospital not

been available. Studies were excluded if they were largely restricted to people who were under 16 years or over 65 years old, or to those with a primary diagnosis of substance misuse or organic brain disorder.

9.5.2 Studies considered for review

The GDG selected a Health Technology Assessment (Marshall *et al.*, 2001) as the basis for a fresh systematic review and meta-analysis. This assessment reviewed nine trials of acute day hospital treatment published between 1966 and 2000, including data for 1,568 participants. A search for recent RCTs did not uncover any suitable new studies of acute day hospital treatment. Some difficulties were encountered in synthesising the outcome data because a number of similar outcomes were presented in slightly different formats.

The included studies varied in the following ways:

- country of study (UK 3, the Netherlands 2, US, 4)
- follow-up (2 months to 2 years)
- patient mix by diagnosis (schizophrenia 23.5 to 39%; in one RCT all patients had been treated for a psychosis previously; in two trials the exact diagnostic composition of the samples was unknown)
- additional services (none, out-of-hours back-up, 'back-up bed')
- point of randomisation (unsuitable patients excluded prior to randomisation or randomisation at referral)
- outcomes recorded.

9.5.3 Results

The studies included in this review examined the use of acute day hospitals as an alternative to acute admission to an inpatient unit. The individuals involved in the studies were a diagnostically mixed group, including between a quarter and just over a third of people with a diagnosis of schizophrenia. Moreover, acute day hospitals are not suitable for people subject to compulsory treatment, and some studies explicitly excluded people with families unable to provide effective support at home. Clearly, the findings from this review, and the recommendations based upon them cannot be generalised to all people with schizophrenia who present for acute admission.

The review found strong evidence that people attending acute day hospitals, when compared with inpatient care, spend fewer days in hospital and do not recover more slowly. The review also found that the burden on families was no greater than for inpatient care and that social functioning of service users is much the same in either treatment setting. Insufficient evidence was found to ascertain whether treatment in an acute day hospital led to a reduction in readmission, compared with inpatient care.

There is insufficient evidence to determine whether there was a significant difference in readmission rates between acute day hospital patients and inpatients (n = 667, RR = 0.91, 95% CI: 0.72 to 1.15). (Ia)

There is strong evidence suggesting that people attending acute day hospitals are more likely to spend fewer days in inpatient care than those admitted directly to inpatient units (inpatient days per month: n = 465, WMD = –2.75, 95% CI: –3.63 to –1.87). (Ia)

There is strong evidence suggesting that acute day hospitals do not lead to slower rates of recovery than inpatient care (all hospital days per month: n = 465, WMD = –0.38, 95% CI: –1.32 to 0.55). (Ia)

There is limited evidence suggesting that there is no clinically significant difference between acute day hospitals and inpatient care on a measure of family burden (for example Social Behaviour Assessment Scale Burden Score at 3 months: n = 160, WMD = –0.59, 95% CI: –1.62 to 0.44). (Ib)

There is limited evidence suggesting that there is no clinically significant difference between acute day hospital patients and inpatients on a measure of social functioning at 12 months and 24 months (Groningen Social Disabilities Schedule overall role score at 24 months: n = 95, WMD = –0.19, 95% CI: –0.58 to 0.20). (Ib)

9.5.4   Clinical summary

For a mixed population of service users, including those with a diagnosis of schizophrenia, acute day hospital care is a viable alternative to inpatient care, reducing hospital bed use without adversely affecting the family, the rate of recovery, or social functioning.

9.5.5   Health economic evidence

Given the large direct medical costs associated with relapse in schizophrenia, primarily resulting from expensive inpatient treatment, it has been suggested that the lower operational cost of acute day hospitals could result in substantial savings for the health service. On the other hand, there have been fears that these savings would be achieved by shifting the cost burden to families and carers, offering no real reduction in the overall cost to society.

The economic review identified three eligible studies. Two economic analyses were based on RCTs (Sledge et al., 1996; Creed *et al.*, 1997); the third used data from a controlled study with concurrent controls (Francois *et al.*, 1993). The UK-based study (Creed *et al.*, 1997) adapted a cost-consequences method with a broad societal perspective; the other two studies were simple cost analyses focusing on direct medical care costs. All three studies reported results with a low risk of bias.

Each of the studies compared acute day hospitals with routine inpatient treatment and concluded that acute day hospitals are less costly than inpatient care. In the UK study, the significant median cost saving for the health trust using acute day hospitals was £1,923 per patient (95% CI: 750 to 3,174). The savings mainly originated from reduced operational costs (Creed *et al.*, 1997). Moreover, Creed and colleagues (1997) demonstrated that acute day hospitals are both cheaper and more effective than inpatient treatment. Those caring for day hospital patients may bear additional costs, but other sources of caregiver burden are reduced. Accordingly, for society as a whole, acute day hospitals remain a more cost-effective alternative than routine inpatient services, with significant cost savings of £1,994 per patient at 1994/95 prices (Creed *et al.*, 1997). Although some cost savings for acute day hospitals were reported in the US study by Sledge and colleagues (1996), this was not of statistical significance for the subgroup of service users with psychosis.

Health economic conclusions
There are few economic studies of acute day hospitals. There is evidence that acute day hospital care is more cost effective than routine inpatient care, saving nearly £2,000 per patient per year for the NHS.

Carers of day hospital patients may bear additional costs, although other caregiver burden is significantly less.

9.5.6   Recommendations

9.5.6.1   Acute day hospitals should be considered alongside crisis resolution and home treatment teams as an alternative to acute admission to inpatient care and to help early discharge from inpatient care.

9.5.7   Research recommendations

9.5.7.1   More high-quality, direct economic evaluations are necessary to establish the cost effectiveness of acute day hospitals compared with other acute service provisions, such as crisis resolution and home treatment teams.**

9.6   VOCATIONAL REHABILITATION

The following sections marked by asterisks have not been updated from the previous guideline.

9.6.1   Introduction

**Most people with mental health problems want to work (Hatfield *et al.*, 1992; Shepherd *et al.*, 1994), yet unemployment rates among mental health service users are extremely high, both in the UK (61 to 73%; McCreadie, 1992; Meltzer *et al.*, 1995) and in the US (75 to 85%; Lehman *et al.*, 1995; Ridgeway & Rapp, 1998). These high rates of unemployment are only in part a reflection of the disability experienced by people with schizophrenia, as suggested by evidence that other disabled groups experience lower unemployment than people with severe mental health problems (Office of National Statistics, 1998). Other factors contributing to high unemployment include discrimination by employers and the low priority given to employment status by mental health services (Lehman *et al.*, 1998). Nevertheless, work and employment schemes (vocational rehabilitation) have an established place in the history of contemporary psychiatry. The development of these schemes has been motivated partly by a belief that work itself can be therapeutic, and partly to help service users develop the skills and gain the confidence to re-enter competitive employment (for a brief review, see Marshall *et al.*, 2001).

Two models of vocational rehabilitation have emerged over recent years, using different methods and principles, both aiming to improve employment outcomes. In prevocational training programmes, service users undergo a preparation phase and sometimes a transitional employment phase, intended to help them become re-accustomed to working and to develop the skills necessary for later competitive employment. There are both traditional (sheltered workshop) and 'clubhouse' versions of this approach. In supported employment programmes, on the other hand, service users are placed as quickly as possible in competitive employment, with training and support provided by 'job coaches' (Anthony & Blanch, 1987) in the real work setting, without a lengthy, prevocational preparation phase. Ordinary service provision is tailored to meet the needs and work situation of the individual.

In the UK, it is estimated that there are about 135 organisations offering prevocational training schemes and 77 offering supported employment programmes (ERMIS European Economic Interest Grouping database, 1998, cited by Marshall *et al.*, 2001). Proponents of each model (or variants thereof) have claimed superiority with varying degrees of evidential support. The GDG therefore elected to review the evidence base for each form of vocational rehabilitation compared with standard community care and with each other, and to examine specific modifications (such as payment or psychological interventions) designed to enhance motivation and improve outcomes.

Definitions

For this review, the GDG used the following definitions:

● Prevocational training is defined as any approach to vocational rehabilitation in which participants are expected to undergo a period of preparation before being encouraged to seek competitive employment. This preparation phase could involve either work in a sheltered environment (such as a workshop or work unit), or some form of pre-employment training or transitional employment. This included both traditional (sheltered workshop) and 'clubhouse' approaches.

● Supported employment is any approach to vocational rehabilitation that attempts to place service users immediately in competitive employment. It was acceptable for supported employment to begin with a short period of preparation, but this had to be of less than 1 month's duration and not involve work placement in a sheltered setting, training, or transitional employment.

- Modifications of vocational rehabilitation programmes are defined as either prevocational training or supported employment that has been enhanced by some technique to increase participants' motivation. Typical techniques consist of payment for participation in the programme or some form of psychological intervention.

- Standard care is defined as the usual psychiatric care for participants in the trial without any specific vocational component. In all trials where an intervention was compared with standard care, unless otherwise stated participants would have received the intervention in addition to standard care. Thus, for example, in a trial comparing prevocational training and standard community care, participants in the prevocational training group would also have been in receipt of standard community services, such as outpatient appointments.

9.6.2   Studies considered for review

The GDG selected a Cochrane review (Crowther *et al.*, 2001) of 18 RCTs, updated with two new RCTs (MUESER [Hartford]; LEHMAN [Baltimore]), for further systematic review and meta-analysis. All included trials fulfilled the GDG definitions for the different types of vocational rehabilitation. Trials primarily evaluating case management or assertive outreach were excluded.

Specific inclusion criteria were age 16 to 65 years and a diagnosis of severe mental disorder, including schizophrenia and schizophrenia-like disorders, bipolar disorder and depression with psychotic features. Trials were excluded if the majority of participants had a learning disability or substance misuse as their primary or sole diagnosis. Trials involving people with substance misuse as a secondary diagnosis to a mental disorder were included.

The included studies varied in the following ways:
- follow-up period (5 months to 4 years)
- numbers lost to follow-up (0 to 37%, some unclear)
- rater independence (independent, not independent, unclear)
- diagnostic mix of clients (27 to 100% for schizophrenia and schizophrenia-like disorders; not clearly specified in three studies)
- mean age (19 to 46 years)
- history of employment (variable or unknown)
- country of study (US 19, UK 1)
- outcomes recorded.

9.6.3   Results

All except one of the studies considered in this review were conducted in the US, where employment practices, employment law, social structures, and health and social care services are substantially different from those of the UK. Nevertheless, cautious translation of the findings of this review into a UK context is defensible.

Supported employment versus prevocational training
There is strong evidence that supported employment is superior to prevocational training, improving employment prospects and hours per week spent in competitive employment significantly more when the two are compared.

In studies from the US, supported employment, when compared with prevocational training, strongly increases the likelihood that people with serious mental health problems will gain competitive employment at 4, 6, 9, 12, 15, 18 and 24 months (for example, numbers not in competitive employment at 18 months: n = 718, RR = 0.82, 95% CI: 0.77 to 0.88; NNT = 7, 95% CI: 5 to 9; at 24 months: n = 290, RR = 0.81, 95% CI: 0.73 to 0.89; NNT = 6, 95% CI: 4 to 10). (Ia)

Supported employment increases the likelihood of people with serious mental health problems spending more time in competitive employment; for example, in three trial reports (DRAKE [New Hampshire; 1]; DRAKE [Washington]; GERVEY [New York]) service users in supported employment spent on average significantly more hours per month in competitive employment than those receiving prevocational training (for example DRAKE [New Hampshire; 1]: supported employment group mean 33.7 hours, prevocational training group mean 11.4 hours; t = 3.7, p < 0.001). (Ib)

Prevocational training versus standard care; modified prevocational training versus standard prevocational training
There is insufficient evidence to determine whether prevocational training confers any additional benefit on employment prospects for people with serious mental health problems when compared with standard care. However, the addition of either payment or psychological interventions to prevocational training results in a limited but clinically significant improvement in outcomes.

In one study from the US there is limited evidence to suggest that prevocational training does not increase the likelihood that people with serious mental health problems will enter competitive employment when compared with standard care (not in competitive employment at 18 to 24 months: n = 243, RR = 0.99, 95% CI: 0.82 to 1.18). (Ib)

In US studies there is insufficient evidence to determine if there is a clinically significant difference between prevocational training and standard care in admission rates (by 1 year: n = 887, random effects RR = 0.71, 95% CI: 0.48 to 1.04). (Ia)

There is limited evidence that combining prevocational training with a psychological intervention improves the chances of entering competitive employment, compared with prevocational training alone at 9 months (not in competitive employment: n = 122, RR = 0.90, 95% CI: 0.83 to 0.98; NNT = 10, 95% CI: 6 to 50). Another very small study failed to detect this difference at 6 months, although the confidence intervals are wide (n = 20, RR = 0.56, 95% CI: 0.29 to 1.07). (Ib)

There is limited evidence that combining prevocational training with payment improves the chances of gaining any form of employment, compared with prevocational training alone, at 6 months (not in competitive employment: n = 150, RR = 0.40, 95% CI: 0.28 to 0.57; NNT = 3, 95% CI 2 to 4). (Ib)

Supported employment versus standard care
The evidence from this review suggests that supported employment has a significant additional effect on employment prospects for people with serious mental health problems, compared with standard care.

There is limited evidence that supported employment significantly increases the likelihood that people with serious mental health problems will return to employment of any kind, compared with standard care alone (n = 256, RR = 0.79, 95% CI: 0.70 to 0.90; NNT = 6, 95% CI: 4 to 12). (Ib)

Supported employment increases the likelihood that people with serious mental health problems will enter competitive employment, compared with standard care, at 24 months' follow-up (n = 256, RR = 0.92, 95% CI: 0.85 to 0.99; NNT = 13, 95% CI: 7 to 100) and at 36 months follow-up (n = 256, RR = 0.88, 95% CI: 0.82 to 0.96; NNT = 10, 95% CI: 6 to 25), but not at 12 months' follow-up (not in competitive employment: n = 256; RR = 1.01, 95% CI: 0.93 to 1.09). (Ib)

9.6.4   Clinical summary

There is evidence from studies in the US to suggest that supported employment is superior to prevocational training programmes in helping people with serious mental health problems gain competitive employment.

9.6.5   Health economic evidence

One way in which schizophrenia imposes a heavy burden on families and broader society is in the form of additional unemployment resulting from the illness. Interventions aiming to improve employment outcomes, such as vocational rehabilitation programmes, have been hypothesised to provide cost savings to society through reduced productivity losses, as well as additional economic benefits associated with improved social functioning (for example housing, legal and social benefit costs). Improved employment status might also have indirect effects on health service use. Vocational rehabilitation programmes may be delivered in several different ways, which may differ in their cost effectiveness.

The economic review identified seven eligible studies, while a further study was not available. Three studies were based on RCTs (Bell & Lysaker, 1995; Bond *et al.*, 1995; Clark *et al.*, 1998): one was a controlled study with concurrent controls (Warner *et al.*, 1999), two were mirror-image studies based on before-and-after data (Rogers *et al.*, 1995; Clark *et al.*, 1996) and one was an observational study

(Hallam & Schneider, 1999). Three studies adapted simple costing methods, while four could be considered as economic evaluations. Only the study by Hallam and Schneider (1999) was conducted in the UK. One study was prone to a high risk of bias because of its validity (Warner *et al.*, 1999), but the studies were generally not without methodological flaws. Common problems were small study samples, known biasing effects and the lack of sensitivity analyses to confirm the robustness of the results. Results should be treated with caution when interpreted within a UK context.

One study compared the 'clubhouse' approach to prevocational training with standard care (Warner *et al.*, 1999) and another compared supported employment with standard care (Rogers *et al.*, 1995). Warner and colleagues (1999) showed prevocational training to be less costly, but the result was not adjusted to the difference in disease severity between the two groups. Rogers and colleagues (1995) found standard care to be more efficient. When supported employment was compared with historical rehabilitative day treatment, the former seemed to improve vocational outcomes without increasing costs (Clark *et al.*, 1996).

When different forms of vocational rehabilitation were compared, two studies found supported employment to be more cost saving than prevocational training, although the differences were not significant and the direct programme cost was estimated to be greater for supported employment (Bond *et al.*, 1995; Clark *et al.*, 1998). One study compared the sheltered workshop form of prevocational training with the 'clubhouse' approach in the UK, and showed that the sheltered workshop form is cheaper. Its net cost per placement was £3,449, compared with £6,172 per placement for the 'clubhouse' approach, in the year 1994–1995 (Hallam & Schneider, 1999). Bell and Lysaker (1995) compared the cost effectiveness of prevocational training including payment to the participants with prevocational training without payment and found that the paid form of prevocational training was more cost effective.

Health economic conclusions
It is impossible to draw any firm conclusion about the cost effectiveness of vocational rehabilitation programmes compared with standard forms of service provision on the basis of the available evidence.

It seems that supported employment is equally cost saving or more cost saving than prevocational training.

There is limited evidence that the paid form of prevocational training is more cost effective than unpaid prevocational training.

The available evidence suggests that the 'clubhouse' approach is more costly than the sheltered workshop form.

9.6.6   Recommendations

9.6.6.1   Supported employment programmes should be provided for those people with schizophrenia who wish to return to work or gain employment. However, they should not be the only work-related activity offered when individuals are unable to work or are unsuccessful in their attempts to find employment.

9.6.7   Research recommendations

9.6.7.1   RCTs, recording all relevant outcomes, including quality of life and self-esteem, should be conducted to establish the clinical, economic and occupational effectiveness of supported employment in the UK.

9.6.7.2   Research should be conducted, recording all relevant outcomes, including quality of life and self-esteem, to identify the most beneficial types of work-related daytime activity for people with schizophrenia and other serious mental health problems.**

9.7   NON-ACUTE DAY HOSPITAL CARE

The following sections marked by asterisks have not been updated from the previous guideline.

9.7.1   Introduction

**Although the earliest use of day hospitals in mental healthcare was to provide an alternative to inpatient care (Cameron, 1947), non-acute day hospitals have also been used for people with refractory mental health problems unresponsive to treatment in outpatient clinics. Two broad groups of people have been referred for non-acute day hospital care: those with anxiety and depressive disorders who have residual or persistent symptoms, and those with more severe and enduring mental disorders such as schizophrenia. For the latter group, day hospital care has been used to improve outcomes, reduce admission rates and enhance engagement (Marshall *et al.,* 2001). The evidence for the effectiveness of non-acute day hospital care in improving clinical outcomes for people with severe mental illness has been challenged (Hoge *et al.,* 1992), and indeed some think such centres may even be doing harm (Tantam & McGrath, 1989).

Given the need for services for people with severe and enduring mental health problems who are refractory to other forms of treatment, the GDG undertook a review of the evidence comparing the efficacy of non-acute day hospitals with that of traditional outpatient treatment programmes.

Definition
For this review, and following the Cochrane review by Marshall and colleagues (2001), the GDG agreed the following definition for non-acute day hospitals, in so far as they apply to people with serious mental health problems, including schizophrenia:
● psychiatric day hospitals offering continuing care to people with severe mental disorders.

Studies were excluded if the participants were predominantly either over 65 years or under 18 years of age.

9.7.2   Studies considered for review

A systematic (Cochrane) review of non-acute day hospitals and outpatient clinics, recently published as a Health Technology Assessment (Marshall *et al.*, 2001), was selected for reanalysis. Of the eight original trials, four were excluded because more than 80% of the participants in each study had been given diagnoses other than schizophrenia. The excluded studies were those by Bateman and Fonagy (1999) in London, Dick and colleagues (1991) in Dundee, Piper and colleagues (1993) in Alberta, and Tyrer and Remington (1979) in Southampton. No additional trial was found suitable for inclusion for further analysis. Three of the four studies included were set in New York (MELTZOFF1966; WELDON1979; GLICK1986), and one (LINN1979) was conducted elsewhere in the US.

The included studies varied in the following ways:
- follow-up period (3 to 24 months)
- diagnosis of participants (schizophrenia: 47% up to 100%)
- gender of participants (male 2, mixed 2)
- comparator treatments (standard outpatient care, outpatient care plus additional psychotherapy input).

9.7.3   Results

As all the studies in this review were conducted in the US, application of their findings to the UK should be tentative. Also, it should be borne in mind that the people referred to psychiatric day hospitals, both in the US and the UK, are those whose symptoms have responded less than optimally to standard treatment. The review found no evidence to suggest that non-acute day hospitals increased the likelihood of improving outcomes when compared with standard outpatient care.

There is insufficient evidence to determine if there is a clinically significant difference between non-acute day hospital care and outpatient care for people with severe mental disorders on numbers lost to follow-up (at 18 months: n = 80, RR = 1.75, 95% CI: 0.56 to 5.51). (Ib)

There is insufficient evidence to determine if there is a clinically significant difference between day care centres and outpatient care on admission rates (at 12 months: n = 162, RR = 0.86, 95% CI: 0.61 to 1.23; at 24 months: n = 162, RR = 0.82, 95% CI: 0.64 to 1.05). (Ib)

There is insufficient evidence to determine whether there is a clinically significant difference between day care centres and outpatient care on a measure of mental state (Symptom Checklist-90: n = 30, WMD = 0.31, 95% CI: –0.20 to 0.82). (Ib)

There is insufficient evidence to determine if there is a clinically significant difference between day care centres and outpatient care on social functioning (Community Adaptation Scale: n = 30, WMD = –0.03, 95% CI: –0.30 to 0.24). (Ib)

9.7.4   Clinical summary

The limited evidence found at review suggests that non-acute day hospital care offers no discernible advantage over standard outpatient care for people with serious mental health problems whose symptoms have responded less than optimally to standard care.

9.7.5   Recommendations

There was insufficient evidence to make any recommendation about day care activities in a day hospital setting.**

9.8   CRISIS RESOLUTION AND HOME TREATMENT TEAMS

The following sections marked by asterisks have not been updated from the previous guideline.

9.8.1   Introduction

**Traditionally, a first episode or acute exacerbation of schizophrenia is managed by admission to an acute inpatient unit. However, in recent years there has been growing interest in attempting to manage such episodes in the community. If this could be done safely, it might avoid the stigma and costs associated with hospital admission, thus providing benefits to both service users and service providers. Crisis resolution and home treatment teams (CRHTTs) are a form of service that aims to avoid admitting acutely ill people to hospital by providing intensive home-based support. A Cochrane review of crisis intervention for people with serious mental health problems (Joy *et al.*, 2002) was selected by the GDG for review and further analysis.

Definition
The GDG adopted the inclusion criteria developed by the Cochrane review team for studies of CRHTTs in the management of people with schizophrenia. Crisis intervention and the comparator treatment were defined as follows:
● crisis resolution is any type of crisis-orientated treatment of an acute psychiatric episode by staff with a specific remit to deal with such situations, in and beyond 'office hours'

● 'standard care' is the normal care given to those experiencing acute psychiatric episodes in the area concerned; this involved hospital-based treatment for all studies included.

The focus of the review was to examine the effects of CRHTT care for people with serious mental illness experiencing an acute episode, compared with the standard care they would normally receive.

9.8.2 Studies considered for review

The Cochrane review of CRHTTs (Joy *et al.*, 2002) included five RCTs (PASAMANICK1964 [Ohio], FENTON1979 [Montreal], HOULT1981 [Sydney], MUIJEN [UK; 2], STEIN1975 [Madison, Wisconsin]). A further search identified one new RCT (FENTON1998 [Maryland]) not included in the Cochrane review and suitable for inclusion for this guideline. Data from these six studies, including 883 participants, were pooled and reanalysed. All studies selected participants on the basis of their referral for acute admission and treatment.

The included studies varied in the following ways:
● follow-up (6 months to 2 years)
● diagnosis of participants (schizophrenia: 41.9 to 100%)
● participants excluded (three studies excluded people with organic brain syndrome, three excluded alcoholism or dual diagnosis, one made no exclusion on the basis of psychopathology, and one study excluded participants who were suicidal, homicidal or whose family were unable to provide support at home)
● setting (inner city, urban, suburban, mixed)
● outcomes recorded.

9.8.3 Results

Effects of crisis resolution and home treatment teams on admission
Evidence from this review suggests that CRHTTs, when compared with standard care, decrease the likelihood of people with serious mental health problems being admitted while being treated by the CRHTT, and increase the likelihood of shorter admissions.

Compared with standard care:
● there is strong evidence that CRHTTs substantially decrease the likelihood of admission (admission rates at 12 months: n = 400, RR = 0.39, 95% CI: 0.33 to 0.47; NNT = 2, 95% CI: 2 to 2) (Ia)
● there is limited evidence that for service users cared for by CRHTTs there is a clinically significant reduction in the duration of acute inpatient care (all admissions) after 3 to 4 months (n = 122, WMD = −19.61, 95% CI: −24.99 to −14.23), 8 months (n = 122, WMD = −10.25, 95% CI: −16.12 to −4.38) and 12 months (n = 121, WMD = −8.42, 95% CI: −16.36 to −0.48). (Ib)

Effects of crisis resolution and home treatment teams on readmission
It appears that CRHTTs do not change the likelihood of people with serious mental health problems being readmitted, or reduce the duration of inpatient treatment (for non-index admissions), when compared with standard care.

Compared with standard care:

- there is insufficient evidence to determine whether CRHTTs alter the likelihood of people being readmitted to acute care by 12 months (n = 601, random effects RR = 0.51, 95% CI: 0.21 to 1.20) and by 24 months (n = 306, random effects RR = 0.76, 95% CI: 0.36 to 1.63) (Ia)
- there is insufficient evidence to determine whether CRHTTs affect the duration of acute inpatient care (non-index admissions only) by 6 months (n = 108, WMD = –0.74, 95% CI: –18.15 to 16.67). (Ib)

Other effects of crisis resolution and home treatment teams
People found treatment by CRHTTs to be more acceptable (participant more satisfied, less likely to leave the study early) than standard care. The review found insufficient evidence to determine the effect of CRHTTs on death rates, and evidence for CRHTTs improving mental state and global functioning was either limited or insufficient to determine, compared with standard care.

There is limited evidence that people cared for by CRHTTs are more satisfied with services at 6 months, 12 months and 20 months (for example, Satisfaction Scale at 20 months: n = 137, WMD = –5.40, 95% CI: –6.89 to –3.91). (Ib)

There is strong evidence that people cared for by CRHTTs are less likely to leave treatment early (leaving the study early at 12 months: n = 600, RR = 0.72, 95% CI: 0.55 to 0.95; NNT = 13, 95% CI: 7 to 100). (Ia)

There is insufficient evidence to determine if CRHTTs are associated with an increase in the rate of attempted suicide (n = 250, RR = 1.33, 95% CI: 0.87 to 2.03). (Ib)

There is insufficient evidence to determine if the mental state of people cared for by CRHTTs is improved at 6 months and 12 months. However, at 20 months there is limited evidence of significant improvement in mental state (BPRS at 6 months: n = 129, WMD = –2.10, 95% CI: –6.40 to 2.20; at 12 months: n = 131, WMD = –2.00, 95% CI: –6.03 to 2.03; at 20 months: n = 142, WMD = –4.50, 95% CI: –8.68 to –0.32). (Ib)

There is limited evidence suggesting that CRHTTs lead to a small improvement in global functioning at 6 months, but the evidence is insufficient at 12 months and 20 months (PEF/GAS end-point scores at 6 months: n = 226, SMD = –0.32, 95% CI: –0.59 to –0.06; at 12 months: n = 231, SMD = –0.07, 95% CI: –0.33 to –0.19; at 20 months: n = 142, SMD = –0.31, 95% CI: –0.64 to –0.02). (Ib)

9.8.4   Clinical summary

For people with schizophrenia and other serious mental health problems in an acute crisis, CRHTT care is superior to standard hospital-based care in reducing admissions and shortening stay in hospital, and appears to be more acceptable than hospital-based care for acute crises. CRHTTs are less likely to lose contact with service users, and may also have a marginally better effect on some clinical outcomes.

9.8.5   Health economic evidence

It has been hypothesised that community treatment of acutely ill people with schizophrenia might reduce admissions and shorten hospital stays, enabling savings in expensive inpatient treatment that might offset the extra costs of running the CRHTT service. On the other hand, there have been fears that these savings would be achieved by shifting the cost burden to families and carers, offering no real reduction in the cost to society.

The economic review identified four eligible studies, three based on RCTs (Weisbrod *et al,* 1980; Fenton *et al.,* 1984; Knapp *et al.,* 1998) and one based on a controlled study with concurrent controls (Ford *et al.,* 2001). One study was a simple cost analysis (Fenton *et al.,* 1984), while the others were in the form of economic evaluations. All studies reported results with a low risk of bias, except the study by Weisbrod and colleagues (1980).

The study by Fenton and colleagues (1984) showed that CRHTTs are cost saving from a narrow healthcare provider perspective. This result is in agreement with the conclusions of studies employing broader costing perspectives, which demonstrated that CRHTTs are significantly more cost effective than standard care (Weisbrod *et al.,* 1980; Knapp *et al.,* 1998) or hospital-based acute psychiatric treatment (Ford *et al.,* 2001). Ford and colleagues estimated that the annual cost of providing the service was £481,000. Knapp and colleagues (1998) estimated the cost difference to be £236 per week during the first year (fiscal year 1996–1997). The UK-based studies by Ford and colleagues (2001) and Knapp and colleagues (1998) also confirmed the cost effectiveness of CRHTTs by sensitivity analysis and by the analysis of biasing effects. Two studies investigated the long-term outcomes of CRHTT care (Fenton *et al.,* 1984; Knapp *et al.,* 1998) and found that the difference in cost between CRHTTs and standard care decreased continuously after 12 months. Family burden costs were not measured systematically in any of the studies, but analyses showed no difference between subsamples for which data were available (Weisbrod *et al.,* 1980; Knapp *et al.,* 1998).

Health economic conclusions
There is evidence that CRHTTs are cost saving for at least 1 year compared with standard care and for at least 6 months compared with hospital-based acute psychiatric treatment.

There is evidence that CRHTTs lose their cost effectiveness in the long term.

9.8.6   Recommendations

9.8.6.1   Crisis resolution and home treatment teams should be used to support people with schizophrenia during an acute episode in the community.

Teams should pay particular attention to risk monitoring as a high-priority routine activity.

9.8.6.2 Crisis resolution and home treatment teams should be considered for people with schizophrenia who may benefit from early discharge from hospital following a period of inpatient care.

9.8.7 Research recommendations

9.8.7.1 Adequately powered RCTs recording all relevant clinical, social and economic outcomes, including quality of life and the methods and effects of risk monitoring, are needed to compare the effectiveness of treatment by acute day hospitals, inpatient units, and crisis resolution and home treatment teams.**

9.9 INTENSIVE CASE MANAGEMENT

The following sections marked by asterisks have not been updated from the previous guideline.

9.9.1 Introduction

**Many people who develop schizophrenia have a wide range of needs for health and social care. For most people this will be provided by family and carers, primary care health workers, secondary mental health services, social services, legal and forensic services, and work and education organisations. Each individual service user will have a unique combination of needs. Moreover, each service user's health and social care needs will vary, often considerably, over time. For the delivery of variable and often complex treatment and care arrangements in a flexible and well-integrated way, especially when service users live in the community outside psychiatric institutions, services need systematic methods of coordinating care reliably. Case management (CM) was introduced as a means of ensuring that people with serious mental health problems remain in contact with services, and of improving the coordination of the provision of treatment across services and between agencies.

Although CM always involves allocating each service user a named and known professional to act as a case manager, whose role is to maintain contact with the service user and to individually arrange and coordinate care across all agencies, numerous models of this approach exist. These include 'brokerage', intensive case management (ICM) and the care programme approach (CPA). Also, studies of case management often use the same term for rather different approaches, sometimes describing assertive outreach or 'home-based' care as case management. Nevertheless, case management, in the form of the CPA, has been formally endorsed as the preferred method of coordinating care by the Department of Health (2002).

Definition
The GDG identified a Cochrane review of case management (Marshall *et al.*, 2002) for updating and reanalysis. Given the variation in the models studied, the GDG followed the Cochrane review team's approach: an intervention was considered to be 'case management' if it was described as such in the trial report. In the original review no distinction, for eligibility purposes, was made between 'brokerage', 'intensive', 'clinical' or 'strengths' models. For the purposes of the current review, ICM was defined as a case-load of 15 or fewer. The UK terms 'care management' and 'care programme approach' were also treated as synonyms for case management. However, the review excluded studies of two types of intervention often loosely classed as case management: ACT and 'home-based care'.

9.9.2   Studies considered for review

The Cochrane review (Marshall *et al.*, 2002) incorporated ten trials of CM published between 1966 and 1997 (CURTIS [New York]; FRANKLIN [Houston]; JERRELL [Carolina]; MACIAS [Utah]; QUINLIVAN [California]; SOLOMON [Philadelphia]; MUIJEN [London; 2]; FORD [London]; TYRER [London]; MARSHALL [Oxford]). The GDG undertook a further search for additional trials published since the review and found three trials of case management that fulfilled the definition and passed quality criteria. The additional studies were: BURNS (UK700); HOLLOWAY (London); ISSAKIDIS (Sydney). This gave a total of 13 trials, with data for 2,546 participants, for review and meta-analysis.

The included studies varied in the following ways:
- country of study (UK 6, US 6, Australia 1)
- follow-up period (6 to 52 months)
- participants with diagnosis of schizophrenia (38 to 89%; two studies unknown/unclear)
- gender of participants (mixed 12, all male 1)
- mean age for trial (36 to 49 years)
- experimental group (ICM, CM)
- comparator treatments (standard care, CM, ACT)
- case-loads for case managers (1:4 to 1:40)
- setting (inner city, urban, suburban, men discharged from prison to urban centre)
- inclusion criteria (however, most services included people with serious mental health problems and excluded people presenting with organic brain disorder, learning disabilities or drug misuse problems).

9.9.3   Results

There is strong evidence suggesting that ICM is associated with increased contact with services, compared with that provided by standard CM (number lost to follow-up after 2 years: n = 1060, RR = 0.54, 95% CI: 0.39 to 0.74). (Ia)

There is insufficient evidence to determine whether there is a clinically significant difference between ICM and standard CM in terms of numbers of participants who lost contact with their case manager (n = 780, RR = 1.27, 95% CI: 0.85 to 1.90). (Ia)

There is insufficient evidence to be able to differentiate ICM and standard CM with regard to admission rates or adherence to medication, but there was strong evidence that there was no difference between ICM and standard CM in their effects upon the mental state and social function of those in either service. There was insufficient evidence to determine any difference between ICM and CM with regard to suicide (of 780 participants only, there was one suicide in each group).

There is insufficient evidence to determine whether there is a clinically significant difference between ICM and standard CM in terms of admission rates (n = 747, RR = 0.95, 95% CI: 0.85 to 1.05). (Ia)

There is insufficient evidence to determine if there is a clinically significant difference in adherence to medication regimens between ICM and standard CM (non-adherence: n = 68, RR = 1.32, 95% CI: 0.46 to 3.75). (Ib)

There is strong evidence that there is no clinically significant difference between ICM and standard CM in terms of mental state (BPRS/CPRS end-point score: n = 823, SMD = 0.02, 95% CI: –0.12 to 0.16). (Ia)

There is strong evidence that there is no clinically significant difference between ICM and standard CM in terms of social functioning (Disability Assessment Schedule/Life Skills Profile: n = 641, SMD = –0.08, 95% CI: –0.24 to 0.07). (Ia)

The review found inconsistent evidence when comparing ICM with standard CM, with regard to contact with services. Compared with standard CM, there was strong evidence that ICM reduced the likelihood that service users would be lost to follow-up, but it was unclear whether people in ICM services were any less likely to lose contact with their case manager.

9.9.4 Clinical summary

The review found insufficient evidence to make an adequate comparison between the impact of ICM and that of standard CM. Where sufficient evidence was available, the review found little to differentiate ICM from standard CM.

9.9.5 Health economic evidence

It has been suggested that case management might reduce costs by providing an efficient way of coordinating treatment and care, and by ensuring that people with schizophrenia remain in contact with services, thereby reducing the likelihood of hospital admission. The cost effectiveness of CM compared with other forms of service provision, such as assertive outreach and CMHTs, was also of interest.

359

The economic review identified 12 eligible studies, of which nine were based on RCTs and three used data from controlled studies with concurrent controls (Galster *et al.*, 1995; McCrone *et al.*, 1998; Preston & Fazio, 2000). Four studies were conducted in the UK (Byford *et al.*, 2000; McCrone *et al.*, 1994, 1998; Ford *et al.*, 1997). Six of the studies used simple costing methods, while the others were economic evaluations (Byford *et al.*, 2000; Essock *et al.*, 1998; Ford *et al.*, 1997; Johnston *et al.*, 1998; McCrone *et al.*, 1994; Wolff *et al.*, 1997). The results of four studies were prone to a high risk of bias. In addition, only three of the studies carried out sensitivity analyses (Ford *et al.*, 1997; Johnston *et al.*, 1998; Byford *et al.*, 2000).

Three of the eligible studies compared case management with standard care. Two studies showed no significant differences in costs (McCrone *et al.*, 1994; Quinlivan *et al.*, 1995), although both studies demonstrated some cost savings in the case of CM, and McCrone and colleagues (1994) found CM to be more cost effective during the first 6 months. Both studies had small sample sizes. Ford and colleagues (1997) showed that ICM is more costly than standard care, with only limited extra benefits.

Six studies compared different approaches to CM with assertive outreach (ACT). The study by Preston and Fazio (2000) demonstrated ICM to be more cost saving than ACT, in relation to the costs measured in the period prior to the introduction of these new forms of service provision. However, baseline data suggest a difference between the two comparison groups, and the analysis focused only on narrow cost components. Salkever and colleagues (1999) found no significant cost difference between standard CM and ACT, but the study suffered from flaws similar to those of the analysis by Preston and Fazio (2000). A more reliable result by Essock and colleagues (1998) showed the two forms of service provision to be equally cost effective. Hu and Jerrell (1998) demonstrated that CM was less cost saving in the long term, while Quinlivan and colleagues (1995) also found that CM was more costly than ACT, although the difference was not significant. One study showed that CM was as costly as ACT but less effective (Wolff *et al.*, 1997). One study compared ICM with CMHTs (McCrone *et al.*, 1998), and found that none of the interventions resulted in significant savings relative to the costs in the period before the introduction of the new services.

Three studies compared standard CM with ICM. One study found that standard CM was significantly cheaper than ICM (Galster *et al.*, 1995); another found standard CM to be not only cheaper but also more effective (Johnston *et al.*, 1998). A large-scale RCT from the UK showed the two approaches to be equally cost effective, and sensitivity analysis confirmed this conclusion (Byford *et al.*, 2000).

Health economic conclusions
It is difficult to draw any firm conclusion about the cost-saving characteristics of case management compared with standard care on the basis of the available evidence.

Comparing CM with assertive community treatment or care by CMHTs, the evidence suggests that there is no significant cost difference between these forms of service provision. There is evidence that reduced case-loads have no clear beneficial effect on the cost effectiveness of CM.

9.9.6   Recommendations

There is insufficient evidence to make any recommendation about ICM for routine use in the NHS in England and Wales.**

10 SUMMARY OF RECOMMENDATIONS

10.1 CARE ACROSS ALL PHASES

10.1.1 Optimism

10.1.1.1 Work in partnership with people with schizophrenia and their carers. Offer help, treatment and care in an atmosphere of hope and optimism. Take time to build supportive and empathic relationships as an essential part of care.

10.1.2 Race, culture and ethnicity

10.1.2.1 When working with people with schizophrenia and their carers:
- avoid using clinical language, or keep it to a minimum
- ensure that comprehensive written information is available in the appropriate language and in audio format if possible
- provide and work proficiently with interpreters if needed
- offer a list of local education providers who can provide English language teaching for people who have difficulties speaking and understanding English.

10.1.2.2 Healthcare professionals inexperienced in working with people with schizophrenia from diverse ethnic and cultural backgrounds should seek advice and supervision from healthcare professionals who are experienced in working transculturally.

10.1.2.3 Healthcare professionals working with people with schizophrenia should ensure they are competent in:
- assessment skills for people from diverse ethnic and cultural backgrounds
- using explanatory models of illness for people from diverse ethnic and cultural backgrounds
- explaining the causes of schizophrenia and treatment options
- addressing cultural and ethnic differences in treatment expectations and adherence
- addressing cultural and ethnic differences in beliefs regarding biological, social and family influences on the causes of abnormal mental states
- negotiating skills for working with families of people with schizophrenia
- conflict management and conflict resolution.

10.1.2.4 Mental health services should work with local voluntary BME groups to jointly ensure that culturally appropriate psychological and psychosocial treatment, consistent with this guideline and delivered by competent practitioners, is provided to people from diverse ethnic and cultural backgrounds.

10.1.3 Getting help early

10.1.3.1 Healthcare professionals should facilitate access as soon as possible to assessment and treatment, and promote early access throughout all phases of care.

10.1.4 Assessment

10.1.4.1 Ensure that people with schizophrenia receive a comprehensive multidisciplinary assessment, including a psychiatric, psychological and physical health assessment. The assessment should also address the following:
- accommodation
- culture and ethnicity
- economic status
- occupation and education (including employment and functional activity)
- prescribed and non-prescribed drug history
- quality of life
- responsibility for children
- risk of harm to self and others
- sexual health
- social networks.

10.1.4.2 Routinely monitor for other coexisting conditions, including depression and anxiety, particularly in the early phases of treatment.

10.1.5 Comprehensive services provision

10.1.5.1 All teams providing services for people with schizophrenia should offer a comprehensive range of interventions consistent with this guideline.

10.1.5.2 All teams providing services for people with schizophrenia should offer social, group and physical activities to people with schizophrenia (including in inpatient settings) and record arrangements in their care plan.

10.1.6 Working in partnership with carers

10.1.6.1 When working with carers of people with schizophrenia:
- provide written and verbal information on schizophrenia and its management, including how families and carers can help through all phases of treatment

- offer them a carer's assessment
- provide information about local carer and family support groups and voluntary organisations, and help carers to access these
- negotiate confidentiality and information sharing between the service user and their carers, if appropriate
- assess the needs of any children in the family, including young carers.

10.1.7 Consent, capacity and treatment decisions

10.1.7.1 Before each treatment decision is taken, healthcare professionals should ensure that they:
- provide service users and carers with full, patient-specific information in the appropriate format about schizophrenia and its management, to ensure informed consent before starting treatment
- understand and apply the principles underpinning the Mental Capacity Act, and are aware that mental capacity is decision specific (that is, if there is doubt about mental capacity, assessment of mental capacity should be made in relation to each decision)
- can assess mental capacity, if this is in doubt, using the test set out in the Mental Capacity Act.

These principles should apply whether or not people are being detained or treated under the Mental Health Act and are especially important for people from BME groups.

10.1.7.2 When the Mental Health Act is used, inform service users of their right to appeal to a first-tier tribunal (mental health). Support service users who choose to appeal.

10.1.8 Advance decisions and statements

10.1.8.1 Advance decisions and advance statements should be developed collaboratively with people with schizophrenia, especially if their illness is severe and they have been treated under the Mental Health Act. Record the decisions and statements and include copies in the care plan in primary and secondary care. Give copies to the service user and their care coordinator, and their carer if the service user agrees.

10.1.8.2 Advance decisions and advance statements should be honoured in accordance with the Mental Capacity Act. Although decisions can be overridden using the Mental Health Act, healthcare professionals should endeavour to honour advance decisions and statements wherever possible.

10.1.9 Second opinion

10.1.9.1 A decision by the service user, and carer where appropriate, to seek a second opinion on the diagnosis should be supported, particularly in view of the considerable personal and social consequences of being diagnosed with schizophrenia.

10.1.10   Transfer between services

10.1.10.1 Discuss transfer from one service to another in advance with the service user, and carer if appropriate. Use the care programme approach (CPA) to help ensure effective collaboration with other care providers during transfer. Include details of how to access services in times of crisis.

10.2   INITIATION OF TREATMENT (FIRST EPISODE)

10.2.1   Early referral

10.2.1.1 Urgently refer all people with first presentation of psychotic symptoms in primary care to a local community-based secondary mental health service (for example, crisis resolution and home treatment team, early intervention service, community mental health team). Referral to early intervention services may be from primary or secondary care. The choice of team should be determined by the stage and severity of illness and the local context.

10.2.1.2 Carry out a full assessment of people with psychotic symptoms in secondary care, including an assessment by a psychiatrist. Write a care plan in collaboration with the service user as soon as possible. Send a copy to the primary healthcare professional who made the referral and the service user.

10.2.1.3 Include a crisis plan in the care plan, based on a full risk assessment. The crisis plan should define the role of primary and secondary care and identify the key clinical contacts in the event of an emergency or impending crisis.

10.2.2   Early intervention services

10.2.2.1 Offer early intervention services to all people with a first episode or first presentation of psychosis, irrespective of the person's age or the duration of untreated psychosis. Referral to early intervention services may be from primary or secondary care.

10.2.2.2 Early intervention services should aim to provide a full range of relevant pharmacological, psychological, social, occupational and educational interventions for people with psychosis, consistent with this guideline.

10.2.3   Early treatment

10.2.3.1 If it is necessary for a GP to start antipsychotic medication, they should have experience in treating and managing schizophrenia. Antipsychotic medication should be given as described in Section 10.2.4.

10.2.4 Pharmacological interventions

10.2.4.1 For people with newly diagnosed schizophrenia, offer oral antipsychotic medication. Provide information and discuss the benefits and side-effect profile of each drug with the service user. The choice of drug should be made by the service user and healthcare professional together, considering:
- the relative potential of individual antipsychotic drugs to cause extrapyramidal side effects (including akathisia), metabolic side effects (including weight gain) and other side effects (including unpleasant subjective experiences)
- the views of the carer if the service user agrees.

10.2.4.2 Before starting antipsychotic medication, offer the person with schizophrenia an electrocardiogram (ECG) if:
- specified in the SPC
- a physical examination has identified specific cardiovascular risk (such as diagnosis of high blood pressure)
- there is personal history of cardiovascular disease, or
- the service user is being admitted as an inpatient.

10.2.4.3 Treatment with antipsychotic medication should be considered an explicit individual therapeutic trial. Include the following:
- Record the indications and expected benefits and risks of oral antipsychotic medication, and the expected time for a change in symptoms and appearance of side effects.
- At the start of treatment give a dose at the lower end of the licensed range and slowly titrate upwards within the dose range given in the BNF or SPC.
- Justify and record reasons for dosages outside the range given in the BNF or SPC.
- Monitor and record the following regularly and systematically throughout treatment, but especially during titration:
  - efficacy, including changes in symptoms and behaviour
  - side effects of treatment, taking into account overlap between certain side effects and clinical features of schizophrenia, for example the overlap between akathisia and agitation or anxiety
  - adherence
  - physical health.
- Record the rationale for continuing, changing or stopping medication, and the effects of such changes.
- Carry out a trial of the medication at optimum dosage for 4 to 6 weeks.

10.2.4.4 Discuss any non-prescribed therapies the service user wishes to use (including complementary therapies) with the service user, and carer if appropriate. Discuss the safety and efficacy of the therapies, and possible interference with the therapeutic effects of prescribed medication and psychological treatments.

10.2.4.5 Discuss the use of alcohol, tobacco, prescription and non-prescription medication, and illicit drugs with the service user, and carer if appropriate. Discuss their possible interference with the therapeutic effects of prescribed medication and psychological treatments.

10.2.4.6 'As required' (p.r.n.) prescriptions of antipsychotic medication should be made as described in recommendation 10.2.4.3. Review clinical indications, frequency of administration, therapeutic benefits and side effects each week or as appropriate. Check whether 'p.r.n.' prescriptions have led to a dosage above the maximum specified in the BNF or SPC.

10.2.4.7 Do not use a loading dose of antipsychotic medication (often referred to as 'rapid neuroleptisation').

10.2.4.8 Do not initiate regular combined antipsychotic medication, except for short periods (for example, when changing medication).

10.2.4.9 If prescribing chlorpromazine, warn of its potential to cause skin photosensitivity. Advise using sunscreen if necessary.

10.3   TREATMENT OF THE ACUTE EPISODE

10.3.1   Service-level interventions

10.3.1.1 Consider community mental health teams alongside other community-based teams as a way of providing services for people with schizophrenia.

10.3.1.2 Crisis resolution and home treatment teams should be used to support people with schizophrenia during an acute episode in the community. Teams should pay particular attention to risk monitoring as a high-priority routine activity.

10.3.1.3 Crisis resolution and home treatment teams should be considered for people with schizophrenia who may benefit from early discharge from hospital following a period of inpatient care.

10.3.1.4 Acute day hospitals should be considered alongside crisis resolution and home treatment teams as an alternative to acute admission to inpatient care and to help early discharge from inpatient care.

10.3.2   Pharmacological interventions

10.3.2.1 For people with an acute exacerbation or recurrence of schizophrenia, offer oral antipsychotic medication. The choice of drug should be influenced by the same criteria recommended for starting treatment (see Section 10.2.4). Take into account the clinical response and side effects of the service user's current and previous medication.

10.3.3   Rapid tranquillisation

10.3.3.1 Occasionally people with schizophrenia pose an immediate risk to themselves or others during an acute episode and may need rapid tranquillisation.

367

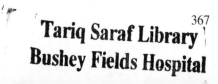

The management of immediate risk should follow the relevant NICE guidelines (see recommendations 10.3.3.2 and 10.3.3.5).

10.3.3.2 Follow the recommendations in 'Violence' (NICE clinical guideline 25) when facing imminent violence or when considering rapid tranquillisation.

10.3.3.3 After rapid tranquillisation, offer the person with schizophrenia the opportunity to discuss their experiences. Provide them with a clear explanation of the decision to use urgent sedation. Record this in their notes.

10.3.3.4 Ensure that the person with schizophrenia has the opportunity to write an account of their experience of rapid tranquillisation in their notes.

10.3.3.5 Follow the recommendations in 'Self-harm' (NICE clinical guideline 16) when managing acts of self-harm in people with schizophrenia.

10.3.4 Psychological and psychosocial interventions

10.3.4.1 Offer cognitive behavioural therapy (CBT) to all people with schizophrenia. This can be started either during the acute phase[36] or later, including in inpatient settings.

10.3.4.2 Offer family intervention to all families of people with schizophrenia who live with or are in close contact with the service user. This can be started either during the acute phase[37] or later, including in inpatient settings.

10.3.4.3 Consider offering arts therapies to all people with schizophrenia, particularly for the alleviation of negative symptoms. This can be started either during the acute phase or later, including in inpatient settings.

10.3.4.4 Do not routinely offer counselling and supportive psychotherapy (as specific interventions) to people with schizophrenia. However, take service user preferences into account, especially if other more efficacious psychological treatments, such as CBT, family intervention and arts therapies, are not available locally.

10.3.4.5 Do not offer adherence therapy (as a specific intervention) to people with schizophrenia.

10.3.4.6 Do not routinely offer social skills training (as a specific intervention) to people with schizophrenia.

Principles for providing psychological interventions

10.3.4.7 When providing psychological interventions, routinely and systematically monitor a range of outcomes across relevant areas, including service user satisfaction and, if appropriate, carer satisfaction.

10.3.4.8 Healthcare teams working with people with schizophrenia should identify a lead healthcare professional within the team whose responsibility is to monitor and review:

- access to and engagement with psychological interventions

---

[36] CBT should be delivered as described in recommendation 10.3.4.12.

[37] Family intervention should be delivered as described in recommendation 10.3.4.13.

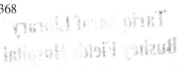

- decisions to offer psychological interventions and equality of access across different ethnic groups.

10.3.4.9 Healthcare professionals providing psychological interventions should:
- have an appropriate level of competence in delivering the intervention to people with schizophrenia
- be regularly supervised during psychological therapy by a competent therapist and supervisor.

10.3.4.10 Trusts should provide access to training that equips healthcare professionals with the competencies required to deliver the psychological therapy interventions recommended in this guideline.

10.3.4.11 When psychological treatments, including arts therapies, are started in the acute phase (including in inpatient settings), the full course should be continued after discharge without unnecessary interruption.

Delivering psychological interventions

10.3.4.12 CBT should be delivered on a one-to-one basis over at least 16 planned sessions and:
- follow a treatment manual[38] so that:
  - people can establish links between their thoughts, feelings or actions and their current or past symptoms, and/or functioning
  - the re-evaluation of people's perceptions, beliefs or reasoning relates to the target symptoms,
- also include at least one of the following components:
  - people monitoring their own thoughts, feelings or behaviours with respect to their symptoms or recurrence of symptoms
  - promoting alternative ways of coping with the target symptom
  - reducing distress
  - improving functioning.

10.3.4.13 Family intervention should:
- include the person with schizophrenia if practical
- be carried out for between 3 months and 1 year
- include at least 10 planned sessions
- take account of the whole family's preference for either single-family intervention or multi-family group intervention
- take account of the relationship between the main carer and the person with schizophrenia
- have a specific supportive, educational or treatment function and include negotiated problem solving or crisis management work.

10.3.4.14 Arts therapies should be provided by a Health Professions Council (HPC) registered arts therapist, with previous experience of working with people with schizophrenia. The intervention should be provided in

---

[38] Treatment manuals that have evidence for their efficacy from clinical trials are preferred.

groups unless difficulties with acceptability and access and engagement indicate otherwise. Arts therapies should combine psychotherapeutic techniques with activity aimed at promoting creative expression, which is often unstructured and led by the service user. Aims of arts therapies should include:

- enabling people with schizophrenia to experience themselves differently and to develop new ways of relating to others
- helping people to express themselves and to organise their experience into a satisfying aesthetic form
- helping people to accept and understand feelings that may have emerged during the creative process (including, in some cases, how they came to have these feelings) at a pace suited to the person.

10.3.5 Early post-acute period

10.3.5.1 After each acute episode, encourage people with schizophrenia to write an account of their illness in their notes.

10.3.5.2 Healthcare professionals may consider using psychoanalytic and psychodynamic principles to help them understand the experiences of people with schizophrenia and their interpersonal relationships.

10.3.5.3 Inform the service user that there is a high risk of relapse if they stop medication in the next 1 to 2 years.

10.3.5.4 If withdrawing antipsychotic medication, undertake gradually and monitor regularly for signs and symptoms of relapse.

10.3.5.5 After withdrawal from antipsychotic medication, continue monitoring for signs and symptoms of relapse for at least 2 years.

10.4 PROMOTING RECOVERY

10.4.1 Primary care

10.4.1.1 Develop and use practice case registers to monitor the physical and mental health of people with schizophrenia in primary care.

10.4.1.2 GPs and other primary healthcare professionals should monitor the physical health of people with schizophrenia at least once a year. Focus on cardiovascular disease risk assessment as described in 'Lipid modification' (NICE clinical guideline 67) but bear in mind that people with schizophrenia are at higher risk of cardiovascular disease than the general population. A copy of the results should be sent to the care coordinator and/or psychiatrist, and put in the secondary care notes.

10.4.1.3 People with schizophrenia at increased risk of developing cardiovascular disease and/or diabetes (for example, with elevated blood pressure, raised lipid levels, smokers, increased waist measurement) should be identified at the earliest opportunity. Their care should be managed using the appropriate NICE guidance for prevention of these conditions[39].

10.4.1.4 Treat people with schizophrenia who have diabetes and/or cardiovascular disease in primary care according to the appropriate NICE guidance[40].

10.4.1.5 Healthcare professionals in secondary care should ensure, as part of the CPA, that people with schizophrenia receive physical healthcare from primary care as described in recommendations 10.4.1.1–10.4.1.4.

10.4.1.6 When a person with an established diagnosis of schizophrenia presents with a suspected relapse (for example, with increased psychotic symptoms or a significant increase in the use of alcohol or other substances), primary healthcare professionals should refer to the crisis section of the care plan. Consider referral to the key clinician or care coordinator identified in the crisis plan.

10.4.1.7 For a person with schizophrenia being cared for in primary care, consider referral to secondary care again if there is:
- poor response to treatment
- non-adherence to medication
- intolerable side effects from medication
- comorbid substance misuse
- risk to self or others.

10.4.1.8 When re-referring people with schizophrenia to mental health services, take account of service user and carer requests, especially for:
- review of the side effects of existing treatments
- psychological treatments or other interventions.

10.4.1.9 When a person with schizophrenia is planning to move to the catchment area of a different NHS trust, a meeting should be arranged between the services involved and the service user to agree a transition plan before transfer. The person's current care plan should be sent to the new secondary care and primary care providers.

10.4.2   Service-level interventions

10.4.2.1 Assertive outreach teams should be provided for people with serious mental disorders, including for people with schizophrenia, who make high use of inpatient services and who have a history of poor engagement with services leading to frequent relapse and/or social breakdown (as manifest by homelessness or seriously inadequate accommodation).

---

[39] See 'Lipid modification' (NICE clinical guideline 67), 'Type 1 diabetes' (NICE clinical guideline 15) and 'Type 2 diabetes' (NICE clinical guideline 66). Further guidance about treating cardiovascular disease and diabetes is available from www.nice.org.uk

[40] Ibid.

10.4.3 Psychological interventions

10.4.3.1 Offer CBT to assist in promoting recovery in people with persisting positive and negative symptoms and for people in remission. Deliver CBT as described in recommendation 10.3.4.12.

10.4.3.2 Offer family intervention to families of people with schizophrenia who live with or are in close contact with the service user. Deliver family intervention as described in recommendation 10.3.4.13.

10.4.3.3 Family intervention may be particularly useful for families of people with schizophrenia who have:
  ● recently relapsed or are at risk of relapse
  ● persisting symptoms.

10.4.3.4 Consider offering arts therapies to assist in promoting recovery, particularly in people with negative symptoms.

10.4.4 Pharmacological interventions

10.4.4.1 The choice of drug should be influenced by the same criteria recommended for starting treatment (see Section 10.2.4).

10.4.4.2 Do not use targeted, intermittent dosage maintenance strategies[41] routinely. However, consider them for people with schizophrenia who are unwilling to accept a continuous maintenance regimen or if there is another contraindication to maintenance therapy, such as side-effect sensitivity.

10.4.4.3 Consider offering depot/long-acting injectable antipsychotic medication to people with schizophrenia:
  ● who would prefer such treatment after an acute episode
  ● where avoiding covert non-adherence (either intentional or unintentional) to antipsychotic medication is a clinical priority within the treatment plan.

10.4.5 Using depot/long-acting injectable antipsychotic medication

10.4.5.1 When initiating depot/long-acting injectable antipsychotic medication:
  ● take into account the service user's preferences and attitudes towards the mode of administration (regular intramuscular injections) and organisational procedures (for example, home visits and location of clinics)
  ● take into account the same criteria recommended for the use of oral antipsychotic medication (see Section 10.2.4), particularly in relation to the risks and benefits of the drug regimen
  ● initially use a small test dose as set out in the BNF or SPC.

---

[41] Defined as the use of antipsychotic medication only during periods of incipient relapse or symptom exacerbation rather than continuously.

10.4.6   Interventions for people with schizophrenia whose illness has not responded adequately to treatment

10.4.6.1   For people with schizophrenia whose illness has not responded adequately to pharmacological or psychological treatment:
- review the diagnosis
- establish that there has been adherence to antipsychotic medication, prescribed at an adequate dose and for the correct duration
- review engagement with and use of psychological treatments and ensure that these have been offered according to this guideline. If family intervention has been undertaken suggest CBT; if CBT has been undertaken suggest family intervention for people in close contact with their families
- consider other causes of non-response, such as comorbid substance misuse (including alcohol), the concurrent use of other prescribed medication or physical illness.

10.4.6.2   Offer clozapine to people with schizophrenia whose illness has not responded adequately to treatment despite the sequential use of adequate doses of at least two different antipsychotic drugs. At least one of the drugs should be a non-clozapine second-generation antipsychotic.

10.4.6.3   For people with schizophrenia whose illness has not responded adequately to clozapine at an optimised dose, healthcare professionals should consider recommendation 10.4.6.1 (including measuring therapeutic drug levels) before adding a second antipsychotic to augment treatment with clozapine. An adequate trial of such an augmentation may need to be up to 8–10 weeks. Choose a drug that does not compound the common side effects of clozapine.

10.4.7   Employment, education and occupational activities

10.4.7.1   Supported employment programmes should be provided for those people with schizophrenia who wish to return to work or gain employment. However, they should not be the only work-related activity offered when individuals are unable to work or are unsuccessful in their attempts to find employment.

10.4.7.2   Mental health services should work in partnership with local stakeholders, including those representing BME groups, to enable people with mental health problems, including schizophrenia, to access local employment and educational opportunities. This should be sensitive to the person's needs and skill level and is likely to involve working with agencies, such as Jobcentre Plus, disability employment advisers and non-statutory providers.

10.4.7.3   Routinely record the daytime activities of people with schizophrenia in their care plans, including occupational outcomes.

10.4.8   Return to primary care

10.4.8.1   Offer people with schizophrenia whose symptoms have responded effectively to treatment and remain stable the option to return to primary care for further management. If a service user wishes to do this, record this in their notes and coordinate transfer of responsibilities through the CPA.

10.5   RESEARCH RECOMMENDATIONS

10.5.1.1   Clozapine augmentation
For people with treatment-resistant schizophrenia whose illness has shown only a partial response to clozapine, is augmentation of clozapine monotherapy with an appropriate second antipsychotic clinically and cost effective?

Why is this important?
Clinicians commonly use a second antipsychotic to augment clozapine when the response has been unsatisfactory, but the findings from clinical trials so far are inconclusive. There is some indication that an adequate trial of such a strategy may be longer than the 6 to 8 weeks usually considered adequate for a treatment study of an acute psychotic episode. The pharmacological rationale for the choice of a second antipsychotic should be tested, that is:

- potent dopamine D2 receptor blockade, as a hypothesised mechanism of pharmacodynamic synergy, and
- a low liability for compounding the characteristic side effects of clozapine.

10.5.1.2   Family intervention
For people with schizophrenia from BME groups living in the UK, does ethnically adapted family intervention for schizophrenia (adapted in consultation with BME groups to better suit different cultural and ethnic needs) enable more people in BME groups to engage with this therapy, and show concomitant reductions in patient relapse rates and carer distress?

Why is this important?
Family intervention has a well-established evidence base from the last 30 years, and proven efficacy in reducing relapse rates in schizophrenia. However, most recent studies applying cultural modification to the intervention have been conducted in non-UK service settings and set against relatively undeveloped treatment as usual services. Thus, the efficacy of culturally adapted family intervention has not been established within UK NHS settings. BME groups are over-represented in schizophrenia diagnoses, and in some inner city settings make up at least 50% of admissions and crisis care. These groups are also less likely to be offered psychological interventions and may thus remain more vulnerable to relapse, despite larger networks and potentially

more family support, than those who are living with family carers. Engaging BME families in suitable adaptations of family intervention would expand the evidence base for family intervention in the UK and be an important way to improve experiences and outcomes for both carers and service users.

10.5.1.3   Cultural competence training for staff

For people with schizophrenia from BME groups living in the UK, does staff training in cultural competence at an individual level and at an organisational level (delivered as a learning and training process embedded in routine clinical care and service provision) improve the service user's experience of care and chance of recovery, and reduce staff burnout?

Why is this important?

Culture is known to influence the content and, some would argue, the form and intensity of presentation of symptoms; it also determines what is considered illness and the remedies people seek. Cultural practices and customs may create contexts in which distress is generated – for example, where conformity to gender, age and cultural roles is challenged. It is important that professionals are not only careful and considerate, but clear and thorough in their use of clinical language and in the explanations they provide, not just to service users and carers, but also to other health professionals. It is important that all clinicians are skilled in working with people from diverse linguistic and ethnic backgrounds, and have a process by which they can assess cultural influences and address cumulative inequalities through their routine clinical practice. Addressing organisational aspects of cultural competence and capability is necessary alongside individual practice improvements. Although cultural competence is now recognised as a core requirement for mental health professionals, little evaluative work has been done to assess the effects of cultural competence at both an individual and organisational level, on service user, carer and mental health professional outcomes. A recent systematic review (Bhui *et al.*, 2007) suggested that staff cultural competence training may produce benefits in terms of cultural sensitivity and staff knowledge and satisfaction; however, the included studies did not assess the impact on service users and carers, and all were conducted outside the UK, thus limiting their generalisability to UK mental health settings.

11 APPENDICES

APPENDIX 1:
SCOPE FOR THE DEVELOPMENT OF THE
CLINICAL GUIDELINE

Final version

December 2007

GUIDELINE TITLE

Schizophrenia: core interventions in the treatment and management of schizophrenia in adults in primary and secondary care (update)

Short title

Schizophrenia (update)

BACKGROUND

The National Institute for Health and Clinical Excellence ('NICE' or 'the Institute') has commissioned the National Collaborating Centre for Mental Health to review recent evidence on the management of schizophrenia and to update the existing guideline 'Schizophrenia: core interventions in the treatment and management of schizophrenia in primary and secondary care' (NICE clinical guideline 1, 2002). The update will provide recommendations for good practice that are based on the best available evidence of clinical and cost effectiveness.

The Institute's clinical guidelines will support the implementation of National Service Frameworks (NSFs) in those aspects of care where a Framework has been published. The statements in each NSF reflect the evidence that was used at the time the Framework was prepared. The clinical guidelines and technology appraisals published by the Institute after an NSF has been issued will have the effect of updating the Framework.

NICE clinical guidelines support the role of healthcare professionals in providing care in partnership with service users, taking account of their individual needs and preferences, and ensuring that service users (and their carers and families, where appropriate) can make informed decisions about their care and treatment.

Appendix 1

CLINICAL NEED FOR THE GUIDELINE

Schizophrenia is a term used to describe a major psychiatric disorder (or cluster of disorders) that alters an individual's perception, thoughts, affect and behaviour. The symptoms of schizophrenia are usually divided into positive symptoms, including hallucinations and delusions, and negative symptoms, such as emotional apathy, lack of drive, poverty of speech, social withdrawal and self-neglect. Nevertheless, people who develop schizophrenia will have their own unique combination of symptoms and experiences, the precise pattern of which will be influenced by their own particular circumstances.

The symptoms and experience of schizophrenia are often distressing and the effects of the illness are pervasive, with a significant number of people continuing to experience long-term disability. Schizophrenia can have a major detrimental effect on people's personal, social and occupational functioning, placing a heavy burden on individuals and their carers and dependents, as well as making potentially large demands on the social and healthcare system.

The lifetime prevalence of schizophrenia and schizophrenia-related disorders is approximately 14.5 per 1000 people, although there is considerable variation between estimates. The National Survey of Psychiatric Morbidity in the UK found a population prevalence of probable psychotic disorder of 5 per 1000 in people aged 16 to 74 years.

The cumulative cost of the care of individuals with schizophrenia is high. In 1992–3 the direct cost of health and social care for people with schizophrenia was estimated to be 2.8% of the total NHS expenditure, and 5.4% of NHS inpatient costs. Health and social services costs alone amounted to £810 million, of which inpatient care cost more than £652 million.

Two UK studies found that after the first episode of illness, unemployment rates for people with schizophrenia increased from on average 42 to 63%. Other UK studies have found that unemployment rates may be as high as 96% in some areas. Carers also have a very significant burden socially, financially and personally.

A systematic review of ethnic variations in pathways to and use of specialist mental health services in the UK found higher rates of inpatient admission among black patients than white patients. In addition, black people on inpatient units were four times more likely to experience a compulsory admission than white people. Variations in gaining access to mental health services may explain some of these differences. Furthermore, other studies suggest that there may be variation in response to treatment among people with schizophrenia from different ethnic groups.

Data from the Prescription Cost Analysis (PCA) system show that in the 12 months to March 2006, 'atypical' antipsychotic drugs accounted for 63% of all antipsychotic items dispensed in the community in England, at a net ingredient cost of £196 million, with non-atypical drugs accounting for £11 million.

The NICE clinical guideline 'Schizophrenia: core interventions in the treatment and management of schizophrenia in primary and secondary care' (NICE clinical guideline 1) was published in December 2002. The guideline incorporated a NICE technology appraisal on atypical antipsychotic drugs (NICE technology appraisal 43) that was published in June 2002. New evidence about the use of some psychological and psychosocial interventions and antipsychotic drugs to treat schizophrenia means that both the guideline and the technology appraisal need updating. After consultation with stakeholders, the decision was made by NICE that the technology appraisal guidance be updated as part of the update of the clinical guideline.

THE GUIDELINE

The guideline development process is described in detail in two publications that are available from the NICE website (see 'Further information'). 'The guideline development process: an overview for stakeholders, the public and the NHS' describes how organisations can become involved in the development of a guideline. 'The guidelines manual' provides advice on the technical aspects of guideline development.

This document is the scope. It defines exactly what this guideline will (and will not) examine, and what the guideline developers will consider.

The areas that will be addressed by the guideline are described in the following sections.

POPULATION

Groups that will be covered:

● Adults (18 and older) who have a clinical working diagnosis of schizophrenia, including those with an established diagnosis of schizophrenia (with onset before age 60) who require treatment beyond age 60. This will include specific consideration of the needs of black and minority ethnic people with schizophrenia.

Groups that will not be covered:

● Very late onset schizophrenia (onset after age 60).
● Other psychotic disorders, such as bipolar disorder, mania or depressive psychosis.
● People with coexisting learning difficulties, significant physical or sensory difficulties, or substance misuse.

HEALTHCARE SETTING

Care that is received from healthcare professionals in primary and secondary care who have direct contact with and make decisions concerning the care of people with schizophrenia.

Appendix 1

The guideline will also be relevant to the work of, but will not cover the practice of A&E departments, paramedic services, prison medical services, the police and those who work in the criminal justice and education sectors.

CLINICAL MANAGEMENT – AREAS THAT WILL BE COVERED BY THE GUIDELINE

- Initiation of treatment with antipsychotic medication and/or a psychological or psychosocial intervention.
- The use of antipsychotic medication and/or a psychological or psychosocial intervention for the treatment of an acute psychotic episode.
- The use of antipsychotic medication and/or a psychological or psychosocial intervention to promote recovery after an acute psychotic episode.
- The assessment and management of the known side effects of antipsychotic medication (for example, diabetes).
- Treatment options if antipsychotic medication or a psychological intervention is effective but not tolerated.
- Treatment options will also be informed by a review of the evidence on variation in response to antipsychotic medication between people with schizophrenia from different ethnic groups.
- The use of early intervention services in the early treatment of people with schizophrenia (studies that include people with psychosis who are younger than 18 will not be excluded from the review).
- Ways to improve access to mental health services for people from black and minority ethnic communities (this will include issues concerned with engagement with services).
- Recommendations categorised as good practice points in the original guideline will be reviewed for their current relevance (including issues around consent and advance directives).

Advice on treatment options will be based on the best evidence available to the Guideline Development Group. The recommendations will be based on effectiveness, safety and cost effectiveness. Note that guideline recommendations for pharmacological interventions will normally fall within licensed indications; exceptionally, and only where clearly supported by evidence, use outside a licensed indication may be recommended. The guideline will assume that prescribers will use a drug's summary of product characteristics to support joint clinical decision making between service users and prescribers.

The guideline will not cover:
- diagnosis
- primary prevention
- assessment
- management of schizophrenia in people with coexisting learning difficulties, significant physical or sensory difficulties, or significant substance misuse
- management of violence in people with schizophrenia.

The GDG will take reasonable steps to identify ineffective interventions and approaches to care. If robust and credible recommendations for re-positioning the intervention for optimal use, or changing the approach to care to make more efficient use of resources, can be made, they will be clearly stated. If the resources released are substantial, consideration will be given to listing such recommendations in the 'Key priorities for implementation' section of the guideline.

STATUS

This is the final version of the scope.

The guideline will update the following NICE guidance:
- Schizophrenia: core interventions in the treatment and management of schizophrenia in primary and secondary care (NICE clinical guideline 1, 2002).
- Guidance on the use of newer (atypical) antipsychotic drugs for the treatment of schizophrenia (NICE technology appraisal guidance 43, 2002).

GUIDELINE

The development of the guideline recommendations will begin in June 2007.

FURTHER INFORMATION

Information on the guideline development process is provided in:
- 'The guideline development process: an overview for stakeholders, the public and the NHS'
- 'The guidelines manual'.

These booklets are available as PDF files from the NICE website (www.nice.org.uk/guidelinesmanual). Information on the progress of the guideline will also be available from the website.

APPENDIX 2:

DECLARATIONS OF INTERESTS BY GUIDELINE

DEVELOPMENT GROUP MEMBERS[42]

With a range of practical experience relevant to schizophrenia in the GDG, members were appointed because of their understanding and expertise in healthcare for people with schizophrenia and support for their families and carers, including: scientific issues; health research; the delivery and receipt of healthcare, along with the work of the healthcare industry; and the role of professional organisations and organisations for people with schizophrenia and their families and carers.

To minimise and manage any potential conflicts of interest, and to avoid any public concern that commercial or other financial interests have affected the work of the GDG and influenced guidance, members of the GDG must declare as a matter of public record any interests held by themselves or their families which fall under specified categories (see below). These categories include any relationships they have with the healthcare industries, professional organisations and organisations for people with schizophrenia and their families and carers.

Individuals invited to join the GDG were asked to declare their interests before being appointed. To allow the management of any potential conflicts of interest that might arise during the development of the guideline, GDG members were also asked to declare their interests at each GDG meeting throughout the guideline development process. The interests of all the members of the GDG are listed below, including interests declared prior to appointment and during the guideline development process.

Categories of interest

- Paid employment.
- Personal pecuniary interest: financial payments or other benefits from either the manufacturer or the owner of the product or service under consideration in this guideline, or the industry or sector from which the product or service comes. This includes holding a directorship, or other paid position; carrying out consultancy or fee paid work; having shareholdings or other beneficial interests; receiving expenses and hospitality over and above what would be reasonably expected to attend meetings and conferences.
- Personal family interest: financial payments or other benefits from the healthcare industry that were received by a member of your family.

---

[42] Only declarations of interest from the GDG members involved in the update are published.

- Non-personal pecuniary interest: financial payments or other benefits received by the GDG member's organisation or department, but where the GDG member has not personally received payment, including fellowships and other support provided by the healthcare industry. This includes a grant or fellowship or other payment to sponsor a post, or contribute to the running costs of the department; commissioning of research or other work; contracts with, or grants from, NICE.
- Personal non-pecuniary interest: these include, but are not limited to, clear opinions or public statements you have made about schizophrenia, holding office in a professional organisation or advocacy group with a direct interest in schizophrenia, other reputational risks relevant to schizophrenia.

Declarations of interest	
Professor Elizabeth Kuipers – Chair, Guideline Development Group	
Employment	Professor of Clinical Psychology, Head of Department, Institute of Psychiatry, King's College London; Honorary Consultant Clinical Psychologist and Director of Psychological Intervention Clinic for Outpatients with Psychosis (PICuP), Maudsley Hospital, South London and Maudsley (SLAM) NHS Foundation Trust.
Personal pecuniary interest	Talk for AstraZeneca on CBT for psychosis, fee received for research support account (2008).
	Article updated for *Psychiatry* on pathways to psychological treatments for psychosis, fee paid to research support account (2008).
	Talk on CBT for psychosis at the 13th Annual Symposium of the North Yorkshire Rotational Training Scheme in Psychiatry, paid expenses and a speaker fee to research support account (2007).
Personal family interest	None
Non-personal pecuniary interest	Recent grants: Professors P. Garety and E. Kuipers (joint PIs) with Professors D. Fowler, G. Dunn and P. Bebbington, and Dr D. Freeman. Wellcome Trust Project Grant. Cognitive mechanisms of change in delusions.

Continued

Declarations of interest *(Continued)*

	Amount: £455,511.00. Period: 2008–2011. Professors E. Kuipers and G. Thornicroft, and Miss S. Gentleman. Wellcome Trust Public Engagement Activity Award. Amount: £59,905.00. Period: 2008–2009. Professor E. Kuipers jointly with S. Jolley & S. Hodgins. BRC Pump Priming. Developing CBT intervention for 9- to 12-year-old children displaying the putative antecedents of schizophrenia. Amount: £19,331. Period: 01/04/2008–31/03/2009. Professor E. Kuipers jointly with Professors T. Fahy and S. Hodgins. Department of Health. Reasoning and rehabilitation in mentally disordered offenders; a pilot RCT. Amount: £150,000. Period: 2004–09/2007. Professors E. Kuipers and P. Garety (joint PIs), with Professors Fowler, Dunn and Bebbington. Wellcome Trust Programme Grant No. 062452. Cognitive and Social Processes in Psychosis: developing more effective treatment approaches. Amount: £1,632,207. Period: 2001–2006 (extended to 09/2007). Professor E. Kuipers jointly with Dr E. Peters, Dr K. Greenwood, Professors P. Garety and Scott. SLAM R&D Funding. Pilot Project: Evaluating CBT for Psychosis: a new approach. Amount: £49,870. Period: 2004–2006.

Continued

Declarations of interest *(Continued)*	
	Professor E. Kuipers in conjunction with Health Service and Population Research Department, V. Pinfold and colleagues. SDO bid. Aiming to evaluate and develop models of information sharing with carers in collaboration with Rethink. Amount: £80,000. Period: 2003–2005. Professor E. Kuipers jointly with Professor P. Garety. Wellcome Trust Prize Studentship. Understanding persecutory ideation: testing a new cognitive model. Amount: £88,652. Period: 2003–2006. Professor E. Kuipers jointly with Professor V. Kumari and Dr E. Peters. Wellcome Trust Prize Studentship. Relationship to deficits in brain functions and structures, and responsiveness to cognitive behaviour therapy in psychosis. Amount: £77,178. Period: 2003–2006. Professor E. Kuipers with Professor R. Murray and Dr E. Peters. Study of olanzapine and CBT for psychosis. Using a donation from Eli Lilly of £60,000. Period: 2003–2005.
Personal non-pecuniary interest	Member of the management board of NCCMH since 2001 on behalf of the BPS (stepped down during guideline development). Published widely on family interventions for psychosis and CBT for psychosis and completed RCTs in both areas.

Continued

Declarations of interest *(Continued)*	
	Patron of Making Space.
	Keynote speech on family interventions for Making Space for role as Patron (2008).
	Talk on psychological interventions for psychosis at the World Psychiatric Association (WPA) and World Organisation of General Practitioners (WONCA) conference on Depression and other common mental illnesses, Granada, Spain (2008).
	Giving lecture entitled 'CBT for psychosis: potential mechanisms of action' at the Symposium 'Psychological approaches to the study of schizophrenia' at the ICP Congress, July 2008, Berlin, Germany.
	Organising a mini-workshop with Drs B. Smith and J. Onwumere on Family Interventions in Psychosis at the 38th EABCT Annual Congress, September 2008, Helsinki, Finland.
	Family Interventions workshop in Helsinki.
Ms Janey Antoniou	
Employment	Freelance trainer and writer on mental health service user issues.
Personal pecuniary interest	Talk on mental health service user issues to social workers at Heathrow, paid £300 by BAA (2008).
	Talk on the Prescribing Observatory for Mental Health – UK (POMH-UK) at a Rethink National Advice Service event, payment received from Jenssen Cilag (2008).
	Freelance work for Rethink (providing advice from a mental heath service user viewpoint) using money from pharmaceutical industry (2007).

Continued

Declarations of interest *(Continued)*	
	Freelance work and training with medical and social services professionals (2007 and 2008).
	Work for Rethink and The Cochrane Library schizophrenia group on making reviews accessible to mental health service users, 1 day per week (2007).
	Work on self-help information provided by pharmacists, paid for by PriMHE and CSIP (2007).
	Interview for Radio 4 'All in the Mind' paid by the BBC (2007).
	Work with East of England Ambulance Service.
	Talk for Barnet, Enfield and Haringey clinicians.
	Work for POMH-UK.
	Talk to 'A'-level psychology students in Stoke Newington.
	Talk for Camphill Trust.
Personal family interest	None
Non-personal pecuniary interest	None
Personal non-pecuniary interest	Service user on steering group for POMH-UK funded by The Health Foundation, topics include antipsychotic medication. Member of Rethink, Mind, UKAN and Harrow User Group, Pan-London Early Interventions Steering Group. Trustee of ISPS. Talk at ISPS UK conference on service user views (2008).

Continued

Declarations of interest (*Continued*)	
	Talk for Rethink/Common Purpose on service user views (2008).
Professor Thomas Barnes	
Employment	Professor of Clinical Psychiatry, Imperial College London.
Personal pecuniary interest	Consultant/advisory board member for Bristol-Myers Squibb, Johnson and Johnson and Servier (all in relation to antipsychotic medication).
Personal family interest	None
Non-personal pecuniary interest	Cognitive and neuroimaging abnormalities in psychosis: The West London longitudinal first episode study. Co-applicant with Dr E. Joyce, Professor M. Ron and Dr G. Barker. Programme grant from the Wellcome Trust. Amount: £1,547,518.
	Co-applicant with Professor G. Lewis and others. Cannabis and psychosis – expert briefing paper. Department of Health. Amount: £66,404.
	Principal investigator for North London Hub, and Professor P. Tyrer, co-investigator. PsyGrid: E-Science to improve the understanding and treatment of people in their first episode of psychosis. Institute of Psychiatry. Amount: £123,047.
	POMH-UK funded by the Health Foundation. Amount: £465,000.
	Interactive group art therapy as an adjunctive treatment for people with schizophrenia, known as the MATISSE study. Co-applicant with Dr M. Crawford and others. NHS Health Technology Assessment programme. Amount: £620,000. Period: 2006.

Continued

Declarations of interest *(Continued)*	
	Co-applicant on UK MHRN grant for using POMH-UK to generate data on prescribing practice relating to people with schizophrenia and bipolar disorder. Amount: £40,000. Period: 2008.
Personal non-pecuniary interest	Invited to update review articles for *Psychiatry* on treatment–resistant schizophrenia and relapse prevention. Invited to co-author a review article on the use of depot antipsychotic medication for a *British Journal of Psychiatry* supplement, sponsored by a pharmaceutical company. Member of NICE schizophrenia GDG (2001–2002). Talk on 'treatment resistant schizophrenia' to the Alpenlandisches Psychiatrie Symposium, Austria (September 2008). Talk on British Association for Psychopharmacology Masterclass (November 2008).
Professor Kamaldeep Bhui	
Employment	Professor of Cultural Psychiatry and Epidemiology, Wolfson Institute of Preventative Medicine, Barts and The London, Queen Mary, University of London.
Personal pecuniary interest	None
Personal family interest	None
Non-personal pecuniary interest	None
Personal non-pecuniary interest	Publicly expressed views about institutional and individual racism as risk factors for common mental disorders and for psychotic symptoms. Published widely on black and minority ethnic issues in schizophrenia.

Continued

Declarations of interest *(Continued)*	
	Director of an MSc in Transcultural Mental Healthcare, at Barts & The London, Queen Mary University of London. Trustee of Careif, an international mental health charity. Chair of Afiya, a national black and minority ethnic health charity. Board member of WACP.
Dr Alison Brabban	
Employment	Consultant Clinical Psychologist, Tees, Esk and Wear Valley NHS Trust.
Personal pecuniary interest	Four talks for Bristol-Meyers Squibb on CBT. Amount: £250 or £300 per talk Period: 2007 and 2008. Provided 5 days of training for staff at Harvard University Medical School on CBT for psychosis. Amount: $2,500 Period: 2008. Lecturing on CBT for psychosis in Oslo Amount: £1000.
Personal family interest	None
Non-personal pecuniary interest	None
Personal non-pecuniary interest	Chair, NIMHE Psychosocial Intervention Implementation Group.
Professor Philippa Garety	
Employment	Professor of Clinical Psychology, Institute of Psychiatry, King's College London; Trust Head of Psychology, South London and Maudsley NHS Foundation Trust.
Personal pecuniary interest	None

Continued

Declarations of interest *(Continued)*	
Personal family interest	None
Non-personal pecuniary interest	Wellcome Programme Grant, cognitive and social processes in psychosis with Professors Fowler, Dunn and Bebbington. Amount: £1.6 million. Period: 2001–2007.
	SLAM Trustees, Evaluation of implementation of NICE schizophrenia guideline. Amount: £152,000 Period: 2004–2007.
	Wellcome Trust, Research career development fellowship funding. Amount: £568,079. Period: 2006–2010.
	1-day workshop on 'A cognitive behavioural approach to overcoming paranoid and suspicious thoughts', received payment to institution from South Wales branch of the British Association of Behavioural and Cognitive Psychotherapy (2007).
	Keynote talk at World Congress of Behavioural and Cognitive Therapies, paid £500 expenses, no direct payment (2007).
	Keynote talk on CBT and early intervention for treatment and relapse prevention in psychosis at the Cyprus Mental Health Commission conference on community psychiatry in the EU and Cyprus, expenses paid, no direct payment (2008).
	Wellcome Trust Project grant, 'Cognitive mechanisms of change in delusions' with Professors Kuipers, Fowler, Bebbington and Dunn, and Dr Freeman. Amount: £455,511. Period: 2008–2011.

Continued

Declarations of interest *(Continued)*	
	Keynote lecture – Meriden Family Programme 'Implementation of evidence based practice for schizophrenia'. Expenses paid and £600 to King's College London.
Personal non-pecuniary interest	Member of NICE schizophrenia guideline development group (2001–2002).
	Publications arising from research on early interventions services for psychosis and CBT for psychosis.
	Keynote lecture–Spanish Association of Clinial Psychology and Psychopathy: 'Cognitive models and cognitive therapy of psychosis'.
Ms Anna Maratos	
Employment	Head of Profession – Arts Therapies, Central and North West London NHS Foundation Trust.
Personal pecuniary interest	Talk entitled 'How can clinical guidelines be credible and useful?' at psychological therapies conference (November 2008). Free delegate pass was received.
Personal family interest	None
Non-personal pecuniary interest	Interactive group art therapy as an adjunctive treatment for people with schizophrenia, known as the MATISSE study. Co-applicant with Dr M. Crawford and others. NHS Health Technology Assessment programme. Amount: £620,000 Period: 2006.
Personal non-pecuniary interest	Published paper advocating the use of music therapy for inpatients experiencing an acute psychotic episode (2006).
	Executive committee member of the Association of Professional Music Therapists (2007).
	Member of ISPS (2007).

Continued

Declarations of interest *(Continued)*	
Professor Irwin Nazareth	
Employment	Professor of Primary Care and Population Sciences; Director, MRC General Practice Research Framework.
Personal pecuniary interest	MRC funded grant on schizophrenia and physical health.
Personal family interest	None
Non-personal pecuniary interest	None
Personal non-pecuniary interest	Special interest in schizophrenia in general practice and expressed opinions about research experience on this topic and cardiovascular prevention in people with schizophrenia. Member of NICE schizophrenia guideline development group (2001–2002). Talk on primary care and schizophrenia at the WPA and WONCA conference on Depression and other common mental illnesses, Granada, Spain (2008).
Mr J. Peter Pratt	
Employment	Chief Pharmacist, Sheffield Health and Social Care NHS Foundation Trust and Doncaster and South Humber NHS Trust.
Personal pecuniary interest	Participation in telephone interview conducted by Brintnall & Nicolini Inc. for a study on the treatment of schizophrenia. Amount: $500. Period: 2006. Speaking and chairing Janssen-Cilag sponsored education meeting on treatments in schizophrenia. Amount: £400. Period: 2006.

Continued

Declarations of interest (*Continued*)
Participation at Eli Lilly Advisory Board meeting, travel expenses and consultation fee of £802 received. Period: 2006. Accepted invite from Shire Pharmaceuticals and The Dementia Link Faculty to attend Advisory Board meeting. Amount: travel expenses and £400 honorarium. Period: 2006. Telephone interview with Adelphi International Research undertaken to understand the views of policy makers in relation to their views on services and support programmes offered by external suppliers/companies. Amount: £60. Period: 2006. Teaching session for MSc Psychosocial Interventions (PSI) course for Sunderland University, travel expenses and standard university honorarium received. Period: 2006. Talk to undergraduate students at Liverpool John Moores University. Amount: travel expenses and £30 honorarium. Period: 2006. Asked to comment on changes to first draft of article to be published in March 2007 issue of *Drug and Therapeutics Bulletin* (buprenorphine for opioid dependence). Amount: £25 charitable donation paid to St Wilfred's Day Centre. Period: 2007. Participation in market research on management of depression for Cam Market Research. Amount: £80. Period: 2007.

Continued

Declarations of interest *(Continued)*	
	Telephone interview for Adelphi Marketing on the pharmacist's view of schizophrenia treatment. Amount: £100. Period: 2008. Participated in a workshop on the effects of prescribed drugs organised by the Diocese of Hallam Caring Services, Sheffield. Amount: £50 book token. Period: 2008. Two lectures on Psychosis on behalf of CPPE. Amount: £240. Review of schizophrenia guideline for Map of Medicine. Amount: £150 expected.
Personal family interest	Wife's family received a benefit (share prize) as a result of Lloyds Pharmacy LTD take over of Independent Pharmacy Care Centres plc (IPCC) (2007).
Non-personal pecuniary interest	None
Personal non-pecuniary interest	Widely known view on the role of specialist pharmacists in psychiatry. Speaking at Rethink Mental Health Awareness Day (2006). Member of NICE schizophrenia guideline development group (2001–2002).
Dr Robert Paul Rowlands	
Employment	Consultant Psychiatrist, Derbyshire Mental Health Services NHS Trust.
Personal pecuniary interest	Fee for talk on Modernising Medical Careers at Eisai funded conference, paid expenses. Period: 2007.

Continued

Declarations of interest *(Continued)*	
	Two lectures to Specialist Registrars at the Centre for Management at Keele University. Amount: £200. Period: 2007.
Personal family interest	None
Non-personal pecuniary interest	None
Personal non-pecuniary interest	Talk to local GPs sponsored by Merck (2007). Published article in Advances in Psychiatric Treatment on implementation of schizophrenia guideline (2004). Member of NICE schizophrenia guideline development group (2001–2002).
Ms Jacqueline Sin	
Employment	Education and Practice Lead in Psychosocial Interventions, Berkshire Healthcare NHS Foundation Trust and Thames Valley University.
Personal pecuniary interest	None
Personal family interest	None
Non-personal pecuniary interest	None
Personal non-pecuniary interest	Published articles on issues relating to implementation of evidence-based interventions for people with severe and enduring mental health illness (for example, family interventions, CBT, workforce education and training). Explicit opinion that implementation of evidence-based interventions as recommended by NICE schizophrenia guideline 2002 is in need of further investment and investigation in the clinical arena. Active clinical practice, academic and research collaboration with Berkshire Healthcare NHS Trust (my employer) Family Work for Psychosis Service as well as the Berkshire Healthcare NHS

Continued

Declarations of interest *(Continued)*	
	Trust Post-Traumatic Stress Disorder Clinic with a specialist clinical interest in providing clinical service for people with severe mental illness and complex needs, and their families/carers.
	Coordinates the BSc(Hons)/HEDip Psychosocial Interventions for Psychosis Programme for the Thames Valley region funded by the South-Central Strategic Health Authority.
	Member of the NIMHE PSI group and National THORN Steering Group.
Dr Geraldine Strathdee	
Employment	Trust Director of Clinical Services, Oxleas NHS Foundation Trust.
Personal pecuniary interest	None
Personal family interest	None
Non-personal pecuniary interest	Advice to Servier, one-off consultancy monies paid to service user empowerment fund (2007).
	Presentations to Care Quality Commision medicines management audit, funding paid to HCC (2007).
	Current service development funding from Department of Health for Information Prescriptions pilot (2007).
Personal non-pecuniary interest	Lectures and public presentations on NICE implementation and outcomes measurement for people with schizophrenia (2007).
Dr Clive Travis	
Employment	University of Bedfordshire.
Personal pecuniary interest	Freelance speaker about experiences as a service user.
	Talk at University of Bedfordshire – social work students. Amount: £189.30.

Continued

Declarations of interest *(Continued)*	
	Talk at Herts/North London – AMHP training consortium. Amount: £250.
Personal family interest	None
Non-personal pecuniary interest	None
Personal non-pecuniary interest	Spoken about experiences as a service user to Approved Social Worker trainees (General Social Care Council). Public opinions expressed on website www.paranoidschizophrenia.co.uk.
Professor Douglas Turkington	
Employment	Professor of Psychosocial Psychiatry, Newcastle University; Consultant Psychiatrist, Northumberland, Tyne and Wear NHS Trust.
Personal pecuniary interest	Fees for CBT lectures: AstraZeneca, £1000. BMS/Otsuka, £1800. Janssen, £1600. Period: 2007 and 2008. Talk on CBT in schizophrenia in Preston and Lancaster for which payment was received from AstraZeneca. Amount: £800. Period: 2008. Two day workshop on CBT for psychosis sponsored by Eli-Lilly and AstraZeneca. Amount: $2000. Period: 2008. Lecture for AstraZeneca on CBT for psychosis in Preston, funded by pharmaceutical companies. 2-day workshop in Oslo on CBT for psychosis.

Continued

Declarations of interest *(Continued)*	
	Evening lecture in Bradford on CBT for psychosis, funded by Janssen.
Personal family interest	None
Non-personal pecuniary interest	None
Personal non-pecuniary interest	Clear public opinion on the effectiveness of CBT in treating persistent symptoms of schizophrenia.
Mr Peter Woodhams	
Employment	Carer consultancy work on a self-employed basis.
Personal pecuniary interest	Ongoing paid work for Meriden Family Programme primarily on carer education programmes (2007–2008).
Personal family interest	None
Non-personal pecuniary interest	None
Personal non-pecuniary interest	Chair of Meriden Family Programme Advisory Group.

National Collaborating Centre for Mental Health staff

Dr Tim Kendall – Facilitator, Guideline Development Group	
Employment	Joint Director, National Collaborating Centre for Mental Health; Deputy Director, Royal College of Psychiatrists' Research and Training Unit; Consultant Psychiatrist and Medical Director, Sheffield Health and Social Care NHS Foundation Trust.
Personal pecuniary interest	None
Personal family interest	None
Non-personal pecuniary interest	Annual grant to develop guidelines (NICE, c£1,200,000).

Continued

	Funding for attendance at a 2-day symposium on evidence-based medicine in psychiatry at the London School of Economics (Economic and Social Research Council). Funding for attendance at a symposium on problems with the evidence base in the pharmaceutical industry at Nottingham University (Economic and Social Research Council).
Personal non-pecuniary interest	On behalf of the NCCMH, met with Jan Balmer of ABPI to discuss Department of Health/Industry proposals for developing implementation tools for the schizophrenia guideline. Expressed views on a number of news and current affairs television and radio programmes on the following topics: the role of selective publishing in the pharmaceutical industry; improving access to psychological therapies; use of Seroxat in children and adults; use of SSRIs in adults; use of antipsychotics for the treatment of dementia; use of cholinesterase inhibitors for the treatment of dementia.
Ms Victoria Bird	
Employment	Research Assistant, NCCMH.
Personal pecuniary interest	None
Personal family interest	None
Non-personal pecuniary interest	None
Personal non-pecuniary interest	None
Ms Sarah Hopkins	
Employment	Project Manager, NCCMH.
Personal pecuniary interest	None
Personal family interest	None
Non-personal pecuniary interest	None
Personal non-pecuniary interest	None

Continued

Ms Esther Flanagan	
Employment	Project Manager, NCCMH.
Personal pecuniary interest	None
Personal family interest	None
Non-personal pecuniary interest	None
Personal non-pecuniary interest	None
Mr Ryan Li	
Employment	Research Assistant, NCCMH.
Personal pecuniary interest	None
Personal family interest	None
Non-personal pecuniary interest	None
Personal non-pecuniary interest	None
Dr Ifigeneia Mavranezouli	
Employment	Senior Health Economist, NCCMH.
Personal pecuniary interest	None
Personal family interest	None
Non-personal pecuniary interest	None
Personal non-pecuniary interest	None
Dr Jonathan Mitchell	
Employment	Consultant Psychiatrist, Sheffield Health and Social Care NHS Foundation Trust; Honorary Systematic Reviewer, NCCMH.
Personal pecuniary interest	Received payment for chairing a meeting on behalf of Lilly (2006).
Personal family interest	None
Non-personal pecuniary interest	None
Personal non-pecuniary interest	None

Continued

Ms Sarah Stockton	
Employment	Senior Information Scientist, NCCMH.
Personal pecuniary interest	None
Personal family interest	None
Non-personal pecuniary interest	None
Personal non-pecuniary interest	None
Dr Clare Taylor	
Employment	Editor, NCCMH.
Personal pecuniary interest	None
Personal family interest	None
Non-personal pecuniary interest	None
Personal non-pecuniary interest	None
Dr Craig Whittington	
Employment	Senior Systematic Reviewer, NCCMH.
Personal pecuniary interest	None
Personal family interest	None
Non-personal pecuniary interest	None
Personal non-pecuniary interest	None

APPENDIX 3:

SPECIAL ADVISERS TO THE GUIDELINE DEVELOPMENT GROUP

Professor Tony Ades	University of Bristol
Dr Patricia d'Ardenne	East London Foundation NHS Trust
Dr Micol Ascoli	East London and The City Mental Health NHS Trust
Mr Peter Blackman	The Afiya Trust
Mr Gwynne Jones	General Social Care Council
Dr David Ndegwa	South London and Maudsley NHS Trust
Dr Clare Reeder	King's College London
Dr Nicky J. Welton	University of Bristol
Professor Til Wykes	King's College London

APPENDIX 4:

STAKEHOLDERS AND EXPERTS WHO SUBMITTED COMMENTS IN RESPONSE TO THE CONSULTATION DRAFT OF THE GUIDELINE

STAKEHOLDERS

Alder Hey Children's NHS Foundation Trust
Association for Dance Movement Psychotherapy UK
Association for Family Therapy and Systemic Practice in the UK (AFT)
Association of Professional Music Therapists
AstraZeneca UK Ltd
Bristol-Myers Squibb Pharmaceuticals Ltd
British Association of Art Therapists
British Association of Dramatherapists
British Psychological Society
Care Quality Commision
Care Services Improvement Partnership
Central and North West London Foundation Trust
College of Occupational Therapists
Department of Health
Eli Lilly
GE Healthcare
Gloucestershire Partnership NHS Trust (Now called 2gether NHS Trust)
Hafal
Hampshire Partnership NHS Trust
International Society for the Psychological Treatments of the Schizophrenias and Other Psychoses (ISPS UK)
Janssen-Cilag Ltd
Lundbeck Ltd
Meriden Programme
Mind
National Prescribing Centre
NIMHE (CSIP)
North Yorkshire and York PCT
Nottinghamshire Healthcare NHS Trust
Novartis Pharmaceuticals UK Ltd

Oxfordshire and Buckinghamshire Mental Health Partnership NHS Trust
Oxleas NHS Foundation Trust
Rethink
Royal College of Nursing
Royal College of Paediatrics and Child Health
Royal College of Pathologists
Royal College of Psychiatrists
Royal College of Speech and Language Therapists
Schering-Plough Ltd
schizophreniawatch
Sheffield Care Mental Health Trust
South London and Maudsley NHS Foundation Trust
Sussex Partnership NHS Trust
Tees, Esk and Wear Valleys NHS Trust
UK Psychiatric Pharmacy Group (UKPPG)
United Kingdom Council for Psychotherapy

EXPERTS

Gwynne Jones
Dr David Ndegwa
Dr Clare Reeder
Professor Peter Tyrer
Dr Chee-wing Wong
Professor Til Wykes

APPENDIX 5:
RESEARCHERS CONTACTED TO REQUEST INFORMATION ABOUT UNPUBLISHED OR SOON-TO-BE PUBLISHED STUDIES

Dr Han Boter
Professor Tom Craig
Dr Mike Crawford
Dr Kimberlie Dean
Chris Evans
Professor Philippa Garety
Professor Martin Knapp
Dr Tania Lecomte
Dr Stefan Leucht
Professor Philip McGuire
Ms Fiona Nolan
Dr Frank Rohricht
Dr Saddichha Sahoo
Ms Amber Shingleton-Smith
Professor Švestka
Professor Nicholas Tarrier
Professor Douglas Turkington
Gunnar Ulrich
Dr Hidehisa Yamashita

APPENDIX 6:

ANALYTIC FRAMEWORK AND CLINICAL

QUESTIONS

ACCESS AND ENGAGEMENT

No.	Primary clinical questions
1.1.1	For people with psychosis, do early intervention services improve outcomes when compared with standard care?
1.1.1a	For all people with psychosis, do early intervention services improve the number of people remaining in contact with services?
1.1.1b	For African–Caribbean people with psychosis, do early intervention services improve the number of people remaining in contact with services?
1.1.2	For all people from black and minority ethnic groups (particularly, African–Caribbean people) with psychosis, do services, such as assertive outreach teams, crisis teams, and home treatment teams improve the number of people remaining in contact with services?
1.1.3	For all people from black and minority ethnic groups with psychosis, do specialist ethnic mental health services (culturally specific or culturally skilled) improve the number of people remaining in contact with services?

Appendix 6

Initial treatment

This is concerned with appropriate treatment and management when a person first comes to the attention of services with a clinical picture indicating a probable diagnosis of schizophrenia.

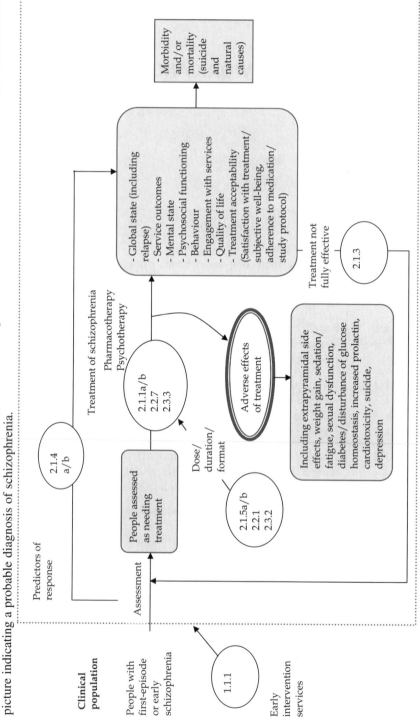

Initial treatment with antipsychotic medication

No.	Primary clinical question
2.1.1a	For people with first-episode or early schizophrenia, what are the benefits and downsides of continuous oral antipsychotic drug[43] treatment when compared with another oral antipsychotic drug at the initiation of treatment[44]?
	Secondary clinical questions
2.1.3	For people with first-episode or early schizophrenia in whom initial oral antipsychotic medication is not fully effective, what is the most effective treatment strategy and when do you decide to alter initial treatment?
2.1.4a	For people with first-episode or early schizophrenia, are there any relevant factors (including patient populations) which predict the nature and degree of response to initial antipsychotic medication?
2.1.5a	For people with first-episode or early schizophrenia, what should be the dose/duration (and where relevant frequency) of initial antipsychotic medication?
2.2.1	When antipsychotic-naïve patients are started on antipsychotic medication, are relatively low doses required for a therapeutic response?
2.2.5	For people with first-episode or early schizophrenia, what is the most appropriate treatment strategy to manage known side effects of antipsychotic medication?
2.2.6	For people with first-episode or early schizophrenia, what is the most appropriate treatment strategy if antipsychotic medication is effective but not tolerated?
2.2.7	For people with first-episode or early schizophrenia, what baseline measurements should be taken before initiating antipsychotic medication?

---

[43] The analysis will compare each of the SGAs (amisulpride, aripiprazole, olanzapine, paliperidone, quetiapine, sertindole and zotepine) with each other, as well as with haloperidol and any non-haloperidol FGA.
[44] When administered within the recommended dose range (BNF 54).

Appendix 6

Initial treatment with a psychological/psychosocial intervention

No.	Primary clinical question
2.1.1b	For people with first-episode or early schizophrenia, what are the benefits and downsides of psychological/psychosocial interventions[45] when compared with alternative management strategies at initiation of treatment?
	Secondary clinical questions
2.1.4b	For people with first-episode or early schizophrenia, are there any relevant factors (including patient populations) that predict the nature and degree of response to an initial psychological/psychosocial intervention?
2.1.5b	For people with first-episode or early schizophrenia, what should be the dose/duration (and where relevant frequency) of an initial psychological/psychosocial intervention?
2.3.2	For people with first-episode or early schizophrenia, what is the most effective format for particular psychological/psychosocial interventions (for example, group or individual)?
2.3.3	For people with first-episode or early schizophrenia, are there any advantages of combining particular psychological/psychosocial interventions with an antipsychotic, either concurrently or sequentially?

---

[45] The analysis will be conducted separately for each intervention (CBT, cognitive remediation, counselling and supportive psychotherapy, family intervention, psychodynamic psychotherapy and psychoanalysis, psychoeducation, social skills training and arts therapies).

Acute treatment

This is concerned with the management and treatment of any acute exacerbation or recurrence of schizophrenia.

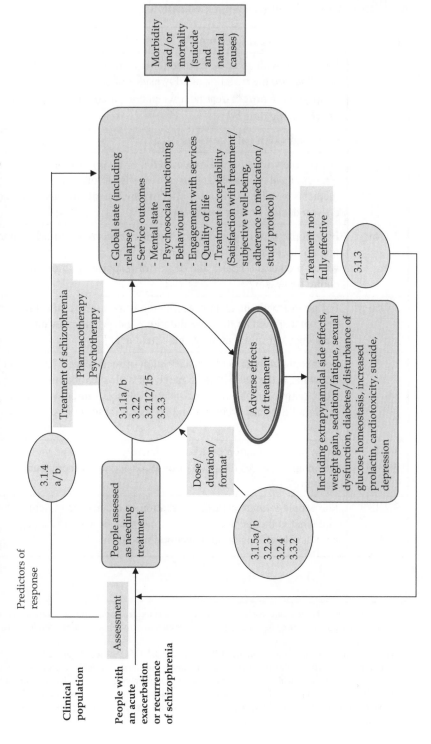

Appendix 6

Acute treatment with antipsychotic medication

No.	Primary clinical question
3.1.1a	For people with an acute exacerbation or recurrence of schizophrenia, what are the benefits and downsides of continuous oral antipsychotic drug[46] treatment when compared with another oral antipsychotic drug[47]?
	Secondary clinical questions
3.1.3	For people with an acute exacerbation or recurrence of schizophrenia who have an inadequate or no response to oral antipsychotic medication, what is the most effective treatment strategy and when do you decide to alter treatment?
3.1.4a	For people with an acute exacerbation or recurrence of schizophrenia, are there any relevant factors (including patient populations) which predict the nature and degree of response to initial antipsychotic treatment?
3.1.5a	For people with an acute exacerbation or recurrence of schizophrenia, what should be the dose/duration (and, where relevant, frequency) of initial antipsychotic treatment?
3.2.3	For people with an acute exacerbation or recurrence of schizophrenia, what is the optimal dose range for antipsychotic medication (for example, in chlorpromazine equivalents, milligrams per day for conventional antipsychotics and on a drug-by-drug basis for the SGAs)?
3.2.4	Does rapid escalation of dosage/relatively high dosage yield any advantage in terms of speed of onset or degree of therapeutic response?
3.2.13	For people with an acute exacerbation or recurrence of schizophrenia, what is the most appropriate treatment strategy to manage known side effects of antipsychotic medication?

[46] The analysis will be compare each of the SGAs (amisulpride, aripiprazole, clozapine, olanzapine, paliperidone, quetiapine, sertindole and zotepine) with each other, as well as with haloperidol and any non-haloperidol FGA.

[47] When administered within the recommended dose range (BNF 54). *Note.* Clozapine is only licensed in the UK for people with treatment-resistant schizophrenia and in people with schizophrenia who have severe, untreatable neurological adverse reactions to other antipsychotic agents, including atypical antipsychotics. Treatment-resistance is defined as a lack of satisfactory clinical improvement despite the use of adequate doses of at least two different antipsychotic agents, including an atypical antipsychotic agent, prescribed for adequate duration.

	Secondary clinical questions
3.2.14	For people with an acute exacerbation or recurrence of schizophrenia, what is the most appropriate treatment strategy if antipsychotic medication is effective but not tolerated?
3.2.15	For people with an acute exacerbation or recurrence of schizophrenia, what baseline measurements should be taken before initiating antipsychotic medication?

Acute treatment with a psychological/ psychosocial intervention

No.	**Updated clinical question**
3.1.1b	For people with an acute exacerbation or recurrence of schizophrenia, what are the benefits and downsides of psychological/psychosocial interventions[48] when compared with alternative management strategies?
	Secondary clinical questions
3.1.4b	For people with an acute exacerbation or recurrence of schizophrenia, are there any relevant factors (including patient populations) that predict the nature and degree of response to an initial psychological/psychosocial intervention?
3.1.5b	For people with an acute exacerbation or recurrence of schizophrenia, what should be the dose/duration (and, where relevant, frequency) of an initial intervention?
3.3.2	For people with an acute exacerbation or recurrence of schizophrenia, what are the most effective formats for psychological/psychosocial interventions (for example, group or individual)?
3.3.3	For people with an acute exacerbation or recurrence of schizophrenia, are there any advantages of combining a psychological/psychosocial intervention with an antipsychotic, either concurrently or sequentially?

[48] The analysis will be conducted separately for each intervention (CBT, cognitive remediation, counselling and supportive psychotherapy, family interventions, psychodynamic psychotherapy and psychoanalysis, psychoeducation, social skills training and arts therapies).

Promoting recovery in people with schizophrenia that is in remission
This is concerned with the continuing management and treatment of schizophrenia.

Promoting recovery with antipsychotic medication in people with schizophrenia that is in remission[49]

No.	Primary clinical questions
4.1.1a	For people with schizophrenia that is in remission, what are the benefits and downsides of continuous oral antipsychotic drug[50] treatment when compared with another oral antipsychotic drug[51]?
4.2.4	For people with schizophrenia that is in remission, is any depot or long-acting antipsychotic medication associated with improved relapse prevention over time?
	Secondary clinical questions
4.1.4a	For people with schizophrenia that is in remission, are there any relevant factors (including patient populations) that predict continuing remission?
4.1.5a	For people with schizophrenia that is in remission, what should be the dose/duration (and, where relevant, frequency) of antipsychotic medication?
4.1.6a	For people with schizophrenia that is in remission, is antipsychotic medication acceptable to the person being treated?
4.2.2	For people with schizophrenia that is in remission, how long should antipsychotic medication be continued for prevention of relapse?
4.2.6	For people with schizophrenia that is in remission, who have had long-term antipsychotic drug treatment, is there any evidence that patients have a preference for either depot/long-acting or oral preparations?
4.2.11	For people with schizophrenia that is in remission and comorbid depressive features, is antipsychotic medication associated with an enhanced therapeutic response?
4.2.15	For people with schizophrenia that is in remission, is any antipsychotic medication associated with improved cognitive function in relevant domains?

---

[49] For the purposes of the guideline, the definition of remission includes people who have responded fully or partially to treatment.

[50] The analysis will compare each of the SGAs (amisulpride, aripiprazole, clozapine, olanzapine, paliperidone, quetiapine, sertindole and zotepine) with each other, as well as with placebo, haloperidol and any non-haloperidol FGA. *Note.* Clozapine is only licensed in the UK for people with treatment-resistant schizophrenia and in people with schizophrenia who have severe, untreatable neurological adverse reactions to other antipsychotic agents, including atypical antipsychotics. Treatment resistance is defined as a lack of satisfactory clinical improvement despite the use of adequate doses of at least two different antipsychotic agents, including an atypical antipsychotic agent, prescribed for adequate duration.

[51] When administered within the recommended dose range (BNF 54).

	Secondary clinical questions
4.2.17	For people with schizophrenia that is in remission, is there any evidence that switching to a particular antipsychotic medication is associated with a lower liability for tardive dyskinesia?
4.2.18	For people with schizophrenia that is in remission, is augmentation of antipsychotic medication with another antipsychotic associated with an increased risk of/severity of treatment-emergent adverse events?
4.2.19	For people with schizophrenia that is in remission, what is the most appropriate treatment strategy to manage known side effects of antipsychotic medication?
4.2.20	For people with schizophrenia that is in remission, what is the most appropriate treatment strategy if antipsychotic medication is effective but not tolerated?

Promoting recovery with a psychological/psychosocial intervention in people with schizophrenia that is in remission

No.	Primary clinical question
4.1.1b	For people with schizophrenia that is in remission, what are the benefits and downsides of psychological/psychosocial interventions[52] when compared with alternative management strategies?
	Secondary clinical questions
4.1.5b	For people with schizophrenia that is in remission, what should be the dose/duration (and, where relevant, frequency) of a psychological/psychosocial intervention?
4.3.2	For people with schizophrenia that is in remission, what is the most effective format for psychological/psychosocial interventions (for example, group or individual)?
4.3.3	For people with schizophrenia that is in remission, is there any advantage in terms of preventing relapse of combining psychological/psychosocial interventions with an antipsychotic drug, either concurrently or sequentially?
4.3.4	For people with schizophrenia that is in remission and comorbid depressive features, is any psychological/psychosocial intervention associated with an enhanced therapeutic response?

---

[52] The analysis will be conducted separately for each intervention (CBT, cognitive remediation, counselling and supportive psychotherapy, family interventions, psychodynamic psychotherapy and psychoanalysis, psychoeducation, social skills training and arts therapies).

Promoting recovery in people with schizophrenia whose illness has not responded adequately to treatment
This is concerned with the continuing management and treatment of schizophrenia.

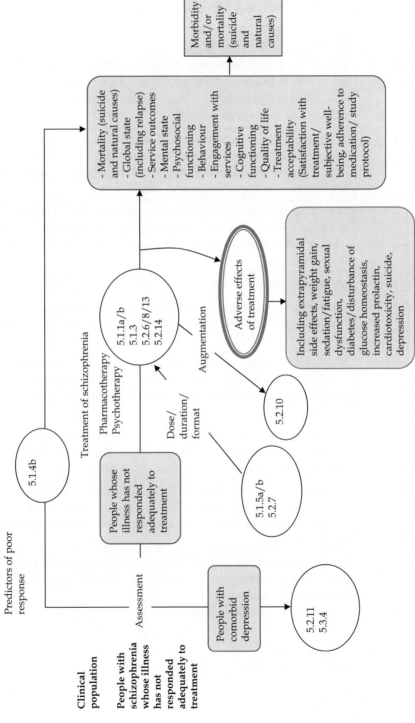

Promoting recovery with antipsychotic medication in people with schizophrenia whose illness has not responded adequately to treatment

No.	Primary clinical questions
5.1.1a	For people with schizophrenia whose illness has not responded adequately to treatment, what are the benefits and downsides of continuous oral antipsychotic drug[53] treatment when compared with another oral antipsychotic drug[54]?
5.2.6	For people with schizophrenia whose illness has not responded adequately to treatment and who have had long-term antipsychotic drug treatment, is there any evidence that patients have a preference for either depot/long-acting or oral preparations?
5.2.10	For people with schizophrenia whose illness has not responded adequately to clozapine treatment, is augmentation of clozapine with another antipsychotic medication associated with an enhanced therapeutic response?
	Secondary clinical questions
5.1.3	For people with schizophrenia whose illness has not responded adequately to treatment, when do you decide to change antipsychotic medication?
5.1.4a	For people with schizophrenia whose illness has not responded adequately to treatment, are there any relevant factors (including patient populations) that predict poor response to antipsychotic medication?
5.1.5a	For people with schizophrenia whose illness has not responded adequately to treatment, what should be the dose/duration (and, where relevant, frequency) of antipsychotic medication?
5.2.7	For people with schizophrenia whose illness has not responded adequately to treatment, do high (mega) doses of antipsychotic medication offer any therapeutic advantage over standard (recommended) dosage?
5.2.8	For people with schizophrenia whose illness has not responded adequately to treatment, is clozapine more effective than other antipsychotic medications?

---

[53] The analysis will be compare each of the SGAs (amisulpride, aripiprazole, clozapine, olanzapine, paliperidone, quetiapine, sertindole and zotepine) with each other, as well as with placebo, haloperidol and any non-haloperidol FGA.

[54] When administered within the recommended dose range (BNF 54).

	Secondary clinical questions
5.2.11	For people with schizophrenia and comorbid depressive features whose illness has not responded adequately to treatment, is antipsychotic medication associated with an enhanced therapeutic response?
5.2.13	For people with schizophrenia with persistent negative symptoms, is any antipsychotic medication (including adjunctive treatments) associated with an enhanced therapeutic response?
5.2.14	For people with schizophrenia with persistent symptoms of irritability, hostility and aggression, is any antipsychotic medication (including adjunctive treatments) associated with an enhanced therapeutic response?
5.2.15	For people with schizophrenia whose illness has not responded adequately to treatment, is any antipsychotic medication associated with improved cognitive function in relevant domains?
5.2.18	For people with schizophrenia whose illness has not responded adequately to treatment, is augmentation of antipsychotic medication with another antipsychotic associated with an increased risk of/severity of treatment-emergent adverse events?

Promoting recovery with a psychological/psychosocial intervention in people with schizophrenia whose illness has not responded adequately to treatment

No.	Primary clinical question
5.1.1b	For people with schizophrenia whose illness has not responded adequately to treatment, what are the benefits and downsides of psychological/psychosocial interventions[55] when compared with alternative management strategies?
	Secondary clinical questions
5.1.5b	For people with schizophrenia whose illness has not responded adequately to treatment, what should be the dose/duration (and where relevant frequency) of a psychological/psychosocial intervention?
5.3.4	For people with schizophrenia and comorbid depressive features whose illness has not responded adequately to treatment, are psychological/psychosocial interventions associated with an enhanced therapeutic response?

---

[55] The analysis will be conducted separately for each intervention (CBT, cognitive remediation, counselling and supportive psychotherapy, family interventions, psychodynamic psychotherapy and psychoanalysis, psychoeducation, social skills training and arts therapies).

APPENDIX 7:
CLINICAL REVIEW PROTOCOL TEMPLATE

Primary clinical question(s)	
Subquestions	
Search strategy	
Existing reviews	
Updated	
Not updated	
Search filters used	
Question specific search filter	
Amendments to filter/ search strategy	
Eligibility criteria	
Intervention	
Comparator	
Population (including age, gender, etc)	
Outcomes	
Study design	
Publication status	
Year of study	
Dosage	
Minimum sample size	
Study setting	
Additional assessments	

APPENDIX 8:

SEARCH STRATEGIES FOR THE IDENTIFICATION OF CLINICAL STUDIES

1. Guideline topic search strategies

   a.   MEDLINE, EMBASE, PsycINFO, CINAHL – Ovid SP interface

Version 1
1   exp schizophrenia/
2   (paranoid schizophrenia or paranoid psychosis).sh,id.
3   (schizo$ or hebephreni$).mp.
4   or/1-3

Version 2
1   exp paranoid psychosis/ or exp schizophrenia/ or 'schizophrenia and disorders with psychotic features'/
2   ('paranoia (psychosis)' or paranoid disorders or psychotic disorders or psychosis).sh,id.
3   (schizo$ or hebephreni$ or oligophreni$ or psychotic$ or psychosis or psychoses).mp.
4   exp movement disorders/ or exp motor dysfunction/
5   exp dyskinesia/ or exp dyskinesias/ or (akathisia, drug-induced or akathisia or dyskinesia, drug-induced).sh,id.
6   neuroleptic malignant syndrome.sh,id.
7   (tardiv$ and dyskine$).mp.
8   (akathisi$ or acathisi$).mp.
9   (neuroleptic$ and ((malignant and syndrome) or (movement and disorder))).mp.
10   (parkinsoni$ or neuroleptic induc$).mp. not (parkinson$ and disease).ti.
11   ((chronic$ or sever$) and mental$ and (ill$ or disorder$)).mp.
12   or/1-11

b. Cochrane Database of Systematic Reviews, Database of Abstracts of Reviews of Effects, Cochrane Central Register of Controlled Trials – Wiley Interscience interface

Version 1

#1 MeSH descriptor Schizophrenia explode all trees

#2 (schizo* or hebephreni*):ti or (schizo* or hebephreni*):ab or (schizo* or hebephreni*):kw

#3 (#1 OR #2)

Version 2

#1 MeSH descriptor Schizophrenia explode all trees

#2 MeSH descriptor Paranoid Disorders, this term only

#3 MeSH descriptor Psychotic Disorders, this term only

#4 MeSH descriptor Schizophrenia and Disorders with Psychotic Features, this term only

#5 (schizo* or hebephreni* or oligophreni* or psychotic* or psychosis or psychoses):ti or (schizo* or hebephreni* or oligophreni* or psychotic* or psychosis or psychoses):ab

#6 MeSH descriptor Movement Disorders explode all trees

#7 MeSH descriptor Dyskinesias explode all trees

#8 MeSH descriptor Neuroleptic Malignant Syndrome, this term only

#9 (tardiv* and dyskine*) or (akathisi* or acathisi*) or (neuroleptic* and ((malignant and syndrome) or (movement and disorder))) or (parkinsoni* or neuroleptic induc*) or ((chronic* or sever*) and mental* and (ill* or disorder*)):ti or (tardiv* and dyskine*) or (akathisi* or acathisi*) or (neuroleptic* and ((malignant and syndrome) or (movement and disorder))) or (parkinsoni* or neuroleptic induc*) or ((chronic* or sever*) and mental* and (ill* or disorder*)):ab

#10 (#1 OR #2 OR #3 OR #4 OR #5 OR #6 OR #7 OR #8 OR #9)

2. Systematic review search filters

a. MEDLINE, EMBASE, PsycINFO, CINAHL – Ovid SP interface

1 cochrane library/ or exp literature searching/ or exp literature review/ or exp review literature/ or systematic review/ or meta analysis/ or meta-nalysis as topic/

2 ((systematic or quantitative or methodologic$) adj5 (overview$ or review$)).mp.

3 (metaanaly$ or meta analy$ or metasynthesis or meta synethesis).mp.

4 (research adj (review$ or integration)).mp.

5 reference list$.ab.

6 bibliograph$.ab.

7 published studies.ab.

8 relevant journals.ab.

9 selection criteria.ab.

10   (data adj (extraction or synthesis)).ab.
11   (handsearch$ or ((hand or manual) adj search$)).tw.
12   (mantel haenszel or peto or dersimonian or der simonian).tw.
13   (fixed effect$ or random effect$).tw.
14   ((bids or cochrane or index medicus or isi citation or psyclit or psychlit or scisearch or science citation or (web adj2 science)) and review$).mp.
15   (systematic$ or meta$).pt. or (literature review or meta analysis or systematic review).md.
16   (pooled or pooling).tw.
17   or/1-16

3. RCT search filters

    a.   MEDLINE, EMBASE, PsycINFO, CINAHL – Ovid SP interface

1   exp clinical trials/ or exp clinical trial/ or exp controlled clinical trials/
2   exp crossover procedure/ or exp cross over studies/ or exp crossover design/
3   exp double blind procedure/ or exp double blind method/ or exp double blind studies/ or exp single blind procedure/ or exp single blind method/ or exp single blind studies/
4   exp random allocation/ or exp randomization/ or exp random assignment/ or exp random sample/ or exp random sampling/
5   exp randomized controlled trials/ or exp randomized controlled trial/ or randomized controlled trials as topic/
6   (clinical adj2 trial$).tw.
7   (crossover or cross over).tw.
8   (((single$ or doubl$ or trebl$ or tripl$) adj5 (blind$ or mask$ or dummy)) or (singleblind$ or doubleblind$ or trebleblind$)).tw.
9   (placebo$ or random$).mp.
10   (clinical trial$ or random$).pt. or treatment outcome$.md.
11   animals/ not (animals/ and human$.mp.)
12   (animal/ or animals/) not ((animal/ and human/) or (animals/ and humans/))
13   (animal not (animal and human)).po.
14   (or/1-10) not (or/11-13)

Details of additional searches undertaken to support the development of this guideline are available on request.

APPENDIX 9:

QUALITY CHECKLISTS FOR CLINICAL STUDIES AND REVIEWS

The methodological quality of each study was evaluated using dimensions adapted from SIGN (SIGN, 2001). SIGN originally adapted its quality criteria from checklists developed in Australia (Liddel *et al.*, 1996). Both groups reportedly undertook extensive development and validation procedures when creating their quality criteria.

Quality Checklist for a Systematic Review or Meta-analysis		
Study ID:		
Guideline topic:	Key question no:	
Checklist completed by:		
SECTION 1: INTERNAL VALIDITY		
In a well-conducted systematic review:	In this study this criterion is: (Circle one option for each question)	
1.1	The study addresses an appropriate and clearly focused question.	Well covered Adequately addressed Poorly addressed	Not addressed Not reported Not applicable
1.2	A description of the methodology used is included.	Well covered Adequately addressed Poorly addressed	Not addressed Not reported Not applicable
1.3	The literature search is sufficiently rigorous to identify all the relevant studies.	Well covered Adequately addressed Poorly addressed	Not addressed Not reported Not applicable
1.4	Study quality is assessed and taken into account.	Well covered Adequately addressed Poorly addressed	Not addressed Not reported Not applicable
1.5	There are enough similarities between the studies selected to make combining them reasonable.	Well covered Adequately addressed Poorly addressed	Not addressed Not reported Not applicable
SECTION 2: OVERALL ASSESSMENT OF THE STUDY		
2.1	How well was the study done to minimise bias? *Code ++, + or –*		

Notes on the use of the methodology checklist: systematic reviews and meta-analyses

Section 1 identifies the study and asks a series of questions aimed at establishing the internal validity of the study under review – that is, making sure that it has been carried out carefully and that the outcomes are likely to be attributable to the intervention being investigated. Each question covers an aspect of methodology that research has shown makes a significant difference to the conclusions of a study.

For each question in this section, one of the following should be used to indicate how well it has been addressed in the review:

- well covered
- adequately addressed
- poorly addressed
- not addressed (that is, not mentioned or indicates that this aspect of study design was ignored)
- not reported (that is, mentioned but insufficient detail to allow assessment to be made)
- not applicable.

1.1   The study addresses an appropriate and clearly focused question

Unless a clear and well-defined question is specified in the report of the review, it will be difficult to assess how well it has met its objectives or how relevant it is to the question to be answered on the basis of the conclusions.

1.2   A description of the methodology used is included

One of the key distinctions between a systematic review and a general review is the systematic methodology used. A systematic review should include a detailed description of the methods used to identify and evaluate individual studies. If this description is not present, it is not possible to make a thorough evaluation of the quality of the review, and it should be rejected as a source of level-1 evidence (though it may be useable as level-4 evidence, if no better evidence can be found).

1.3   The literature search is sufficiently rigorous to identify all the relevant studies

A systematic review based on a limited literature search – for example, one limited to MEDLINE only – is likely to be heavily biased. A well-conducted review should as a minimum look at EMBASE and MEDLINE and, from the late 1990s onward, the Cochrane Library. Any indication that hand searching of key journals, or follow-up of reference lists of included studies, were carried out in addition to electronic database searches can normally be taken as evidence of a well-conducted review.

1.4   Study quality is assessed and taken into account

A well-conducted systematic review should have used clear criteria to assess whether individual studies had been well conducted before deciding whether to include or exclude them. If there is no indication of such an assessment, the review should be rejected as a source of level-1 evidence. If details of the assessment are poor, or the methods are considered to be inadequate, the quality of the review should be downgraded. In either case, it may be worthwhile obtaining and evaluating the individual studies as part of the review being conducted for this guideline.

1.5   There are enough similarities between the studies selected to make combining them reasonable

Studies covered by a systematic review should be selected using clear inclusion criteria (see question 1.4 above). These criteria should include, either implicitly or explicitly, the question of whether the selected studies can legitimately be compared. It should be clearly ascertained, for example, that the populations covered by the studies are comparable, that the methods used in the investigations are the same, that the outcome measures are comparable and the variability in effect sizes between studies is not greater than would be expected by chance alone.

Section 2 relates to the overall assessment of the paper. It starts by rating the methodological quality of the study, based on the responses in Section 1 and using the following coding system:

++	All or most of the criteria have been fulfilled. Where they have not been fulfilled, the conclusions of the study or review are thought **very unlikely** to alter.
+	Some of the criteria have been fulfilled. Those criteria that have not been fulfilled or not adequately described are thought **unlikely** to alter the conclusions.
–	Few or no criteria fulfilled. The conclusions of the study are thought **likely or very likely** to alter.

Quality Checklist for an RCT	
Study ID:	
Guideline topic:	Key question no:
Checklist completed by:	

SECTION 1: INTERNAL VALIDITY

In a well-conducted RCT study:		In this study this criterion is: (Circle one option for each question)	
1.1	The study addresses an appropriate and clearly focused question.	Well covered Adequately addressed Poorly addressed	Not addressed Not reported Not applicable
1.2	The assignment of subjects to treatment groups is randomised.	Well covered Adequately addressed Poorly addressed	Not addressed Not reported Not applicable
1.3	An adequate concealment method is used.	Well covered Adequately addressed Poorly addressed	Not addressed Not reported Not applicable
1.4	Subjects and investigators are kept 'blind' about treatment allocation.	Well covered Adequately addressed Poorly addressed	Not addressed Not reported Not applicable
1.5	The treatment and control groups are similar at the start of the trial.	Well covered Adequately addressed Poorly addressed	Not addressed Not reported Not applicable
1.6	The only difference between groups is the treatment under investigation.	Well covered Adequately addressed Poorly addressed	Not addressed Not reported Not applicable
1.7	All relevant outcomes are measured in a standard, valid and reliable way.	Well covered Adequately addressed Poorly addressed	Not addressed Not reported Not applicable
1.8	What percentage of the individuals or clusters recruited into each treatment arm of the study dropped out before the study was completed?		

SECTION 1: INTERNAL VALIDITY			
1.9	All the subjects are analysed in the groups to which they were randomly allocated (often referred to as intention-to-treat analysis).	Well covered Adequately addressed Poorly addressed	Not addressed Not reported Not applicable
1.10	Where the study is carried out at more than one site, results are comparable for all sites.	Well covered Adequately addressed Poorly addressed	Not addressed Not reported Not applicable
SECTION 2: OVERALL ASSESSMENT OF THE STUDY			
2.1	How well was the study done to minimise bias? *Code ++, + or –*		

Notes on the use of the methodology checklist: RCTs

Section 1 identifies the study and asks a series of questions aimed at establishing the internal validity of the study under review – that is, making sure that it has been carried out carefully and that the outcomes are likely to be attributable to the intervention being investigated. Each question covers an aspect of methodology that research has shown makes a significant difference to the conclusions of a study.

For each question in this section, one of the following should be used to indicate how well it has been addressed in the review:

- well covered
- adequately addressed
- poorly addressed
- not addressed (that is, not mentioned or indicates that this aspect of study design was ignored)
- not reported (that is, mentioned but insufficient detail to allow assessment to be made)
- not applicable.

1.1   The study addresses an appropriate and clearly focused question

Unless a clear and well-defined question is specified, it will be difficult to assess how well the study has met its objectives or how relevant it is to the question to be answered on the basis of its conclusions.

1.2   The assignment of subjects to treatment groups is randomised

Random allocation of patients to receive one or other of the treatments under investigation, or to receive either treatment or placebo, is fundamental to this type of study.

If there is no indication of randomisation, the study should be rejected. If the description of randomisation is poor, or the process used is not truly random (for example, allocation by date or alternating between one group and another) or can otherwise be seen as flawed, the study should be given a lower quality rating.

1.3 An adequate concealment method is used

Research has shown that where allocation concealment is inadequate, investigators can overestimate the effect of interventions by up to 40%. Centralised allocation, computerised allocation systems or the use of coded identical containers would all be regarded as adequate methods of concealment and may be taken as indicators of a well-conducted study. If the method of concealment used is regarded as poor or relatively easy to subvert, the study must be given a lower quality rating and can be rejected if the concealment method is seen as inadequate.

1.4 Subjects and investigators are kept 'blind' about treatment allocation

Blinding can be carried out up to three levels. In single-blind studies, patients are unaware of which treatment they are receiving; in double-blind studies, the doctor and the patient are unaware of which treatment the patient is receiving; in triple-blind studies, patients, healthcare providers and those conducting the analysis are unaware of which patients receive which treatment. The higher the level of blinding, the lower the risk of bias in the study.

1.5 The treatment and control groups are similar at the start of the trial

Patients selected for inclusion in a trial should be as similar as possible in order to eliminate any possible bias. The study should report any significant differences in the composition of the study groups in relation to gender mix, age, stage of disease (if appropriate), social background, ethnic origin or comorbid conditions. These factors may be covered by inclusion and exclusion criteria, rather than being reported directly. Failure to address this question, or the use of inappropriate groups, should lead to the study being downgraded.

1.6 The only difference between groups is the treatment under investigation

If some patients receive additional treatment, even if of a minor nature or consisting of advice and counselling rather than a physical intervention, this treatment is a potential confounding factor that may invalidate the results. If groups are not treated equally, the study should be rejected unless no other evidence is available.

If the study is used as evidence, it should be treated with caution and given a low quality rating.

1.7 All relevant outcomes are measured in a standard, valid and reliable way

If some significant clinical outcomes have been ignored or not adequately taken into account, the study should be downgraded. It should also be downgraded if the measures used are regarded as being doubtful in any way or applied inconsistently.

1.8 What percentage of the individuals or clusters recruited into each treatment arm of the study dropped out before the study was completed?

The number of patients that drop out of a study should give concern if the number is very high. Conventionally, a 20% dropout rate is regarded as acceptable, but this may vary. Some regard should be paid to why patients drop out, as well as how many. It should be noted that the dropout rate may be expected to be higher in studies conducted over a long period of time. A higher dropout rate will normally lead to downgrading, rather than rejection, of a study.

1.9 All the subjects are analysed in the groups to which they were randomly allocated (often referred to as intention-to-treat analysis)

In practice, it is rarely the case that all patients allocated to the intervention group receive the intervention throughout the trial, or that all those in the comparison group do not. Patients may refuse treatment or contraindications may arise that lead them to be switched to the other group. If the comparability of groups through randomisation is to be maintained, however, patient outcomes must be analysed according to the group to which they were originally allocated irrespective of the treatment they actually received (this is known as intention-to-treat analysis.) If it is clear that analysis is not on an intention-to-treat basis, the study may be rejected. If there is little other evidence available, the study may be included but should be evaluated as if it were a non-randomised cohort study.

1.10 Where the study is carried out at more than one site, results are comparable for all sites

In multi-site studies, confidence in the results should be increased if it can be shown that similar results have been obtained at the different participating centres.

Section 2 relates to the overall assessment of the paper. It starts by rating the methodological quality of the study, based on the responses in Section 1 and using the following coding system:

+ +	All or most of the criteria have been fulfilled.
	Where they have not been fulfilled, the conclusions of the study or review are thought **very unlikely** to alter.
+	Some of the criteria have been fulfilled.
	Those criteria that have not been fulfilled or not adequately described are thought **unlikely** to alter the conclusions.
−	Few or no criteria fulfilled.
	The conclusions of the study are thought **likely or very likely** to alter.

APPENDIX 10:
SEARCH STRATEGIES FOR THE
IDENTIFICATION OF HEALTH
ECONOMICS EVIDENCE

1. Guideline topic search strategies

    a.   MEDLINE, EMBASE, PsycINFO, CINAHL – Ovid SP interface

Version 1
1   exp schizophrenia/
2   (paranoid schizophrenia or paranoid psychosis).sh,id.
3   (schizo$ or hebephreni$).mp.
4   or/1-3

Version 2
1   exp paranoid psychosis/ or exp schizophrenia/ or 'schizophrenia and disorders with psychotic features'/
2   ('paranoia (psychosis)' or paranoid disorders or psychotic disorders or psychosis).sh,id.
3   (schizo$ or hebephreni$ or oligophreni$ or psychotic$ or psychosis or psychoses).mp.
4   exp movement disorders/ or exp motor dysfunction/
5   exp dyskinesia/ or exp dyskinesias/ or (akathisia, drug-induced or akathisia or dyskinesia, drug-induced).sh,id.
6   neuroleptic malignant syndrome.sh,id.
7   (tardiv$ and dyskine$).mp.
8   (akathisi$ or acathisi$).mp.
9   (neuroleptic$ and ((malignant and syndrome) or (movement and disorder))).mp.
10   (parkinsoni$ or neuroleptic induc$).mp. not (parkinson$ and disease).ti.
11   ((chronic$ or sever$) and mental$ and (ill$ or disorder$)).mp.
12   or/1-11

b. NHS Economic Evaluation Database, Health Technology Assessment Database – Wiley interface

Version 1

\#1   MeSH descriptor Schizophrenia explode all trees

\#2   (schizo* or hebephreni*):ti or (schizo* or hebephreni*):ab or (schizo* or hebephreni*):kw

\#3   (#1 OR #2)

Version 2

\#1   MeSH descriptor Schizophrenia explode all trees

\#2   MeSH descriptor Paranoid Disorders, this term only

\#3   MeSH descriptor Psychotic Disorders, this term only

\#4   MeSH descriptor Schizophrenia and Disorders with Psychotic Features, this term only

\#5   (schizo* or hebephreni* or oligophreni* or psychotic* or psychosis or psychoses):ti or (schizo* or hebephreni* or oligophreni* or psychotic* or psychosis or psychoses):ab

\#6   MeSH descriptor Movement Disorders explode all trees

\#7   MeSH descriptor Dyskinesias explode all trees

\#8   MeSH descriptor Neuroleptic Malignant Syndrome, this term only

\#9   (tardiv* and dyskine*) or (akathisi* or acathisi*) or (neuroleptic* and ((malignant and syndrome) or (movement and disorder))) or (parkinsoni* or neuroleptic induc*) or ((chronic* or sever*) and mental* and (ill* or disorder*)):ti or (tardiv* and dyskine*) or (akathisi* or acathisi*) or (neuroleptic* and ((malignant and syndrome) or (movement and disorder))) or (parkinsoni* or neuroleptic induc*) or ((chronic* or sever*) and mental* and (ill* or disorder*)):ab

\#10   (#1 OR #2 OR #3 OR #4 OR #5 OR #6 OR #7 OR #8 OR #9)

c. OHE HEED – Wiley interface

1   AX = hebephreni* or oligophreni* or psychoses or psychosis or psychotic* or schizo*

2   AX = tardiv* and dyskine*

3   AX = akathisi* or acathisi*

4   AX = (neuroleptic* and ((malignant and syndrome) or (movement and disorder)))

5   AX = (parkinsoni* or (neuroleptic and induc*))

6   AX = ((chronic* or sever*) and mental* and (ill* or disorder*))

7   CS = 1 or 2 or 3 or 4 or 5 or 6

2. *Health economics and quality-of-life search filters*

    a. MEDLINE, EMBASE, PsycINFO, CINAHL – Ovid SP interface

1   exp 'costs and cost analysis'/ or 'healthcare costs'/
2   exp health resource allocation/ or exp health resource utilization/
3   exp economics/ or exp economic aspect/ or exp health economics/
4   exp value of life/
5   (burden adj5 (disease or illness)).tw.
6   (cost or costs or costing or costly or economic$ or or expenditure$ or price or prices or pricing or pharmacoeconomic$).tw.
7   (budget$ or financ$ or fiscal or funds or funding).tw.
8   (resource adj5 (allocation$ or utilit$)).tw.
9   or/1-8
10   (value adj5 money).tw.
11   exp quality of life/
12   (qualit$3 adj5 (life or survival)).tw.
13   (health status or QOL or wellbeing or well being).tw.
14   or/9-13

Details of additional searches undertaken to support the development of this guideline are available on request.

APPENDIX 11:

QUALITY CHECKLIST FOR ECONOMIC STUDIES

Author: **Date:**

Title:

	Study design	Yes	No	NA
1	The research question is stated	❑	❑	
2	The economic importance of the research question is stated	❑	❑	
3	The viewpoint(s) of the analysis are clearly stated and justified	❑	❑	
4	The rationale for choosing the alternative programmes or interventions compared is stated	❑	❑	
5	The alternatives being compared are clearly described	❑	❑	
6	The form of economic evaluation is stated	❑	❑	
7	The choice of form of economic evaluation used is justified in relation to the questions addressed	❑	❑	
	Data collection			
1	The source of effectiveness estimates used is stated	❑	❑	
2	Details of the design and results of effectiveness study are given (if based on a single study)	❑	❑	❑
3	Details of the method of synthesis or meta-analysis of estimates are given (if based on an overview of a number of effectiveness studies)	❑	❑	❑
4	The primary outcome measure(s) for the economic evaluation are clearly stated	❑	❑	
5	Methods to value health states and other benefits are stated	❑	❑	❑
6	Details of the subjects from whom valuations were obtained are given	❑	❑	❑

7	Indirect costs (if included) are reported separately	❑	❑	❑
8	The relevance of indirect costs to the study question is discussed	❑	❑	❑
9	Quantities of resources are reported separately from their unit costs	❑	❑	
10	Methods for the estimation of quantities and unit costs are described	❑	❑	
11	Currency and price data are recorded	❑	❑	
12	Details of currency, price adjustments for inflation or currency conversion are given	❑	❑	
13	Details of any model used are given	❑	❑	❑
14	The choice of model used and the key parameters on which it is based are justified	❑	❑	❑
	Analysis and interpretation of results			
1	The time horizon of costs and benefits is stated	❑	❑	
2	The discount rate(s) is stated	❑	❑	❑
3	The choice of rate(s) is justified	❑	❑	❑
4	An explanation is given if costs or benefits are not discounted	❑	❑	❑
5	Details of statistical tests and confidence intervals are given for stochastic data	❑	❑	❑
6	The approach to sensitivity analysis is given	❑	❑	❑
7	The choice of variables for sensitivity analysis is given	❑	❑	❑
8	The ranges over which the variables are varied are stated	❑	❑	❑
9	Relevant alternatives are compared	❑	❑	
10	Incremental analysis is reported	❑	❑	❑
11	Major outcomes are presented in a disaggregated as well as aggregated form	❑	❑	
12	The answer to the study question is given	❑	❑	
13	Conclusions follow from the data reported	❑	❑	
14	Conclusions are accompanied by the appropriate caveats	❑	❑	

Validity score: Yes/No/NA:

APPENDIX 12:
DATA EXTRACTION FORM FOR ECONOMIC STUDIES

Reviewer: **Date of review:**

Authors:

Publication Date:

Title:

Country:

Language:

Economic study design:

- ❑ CEA   ❑ CCA
- ❑ CBA   ❑ CA
- ❑ CUA   ❑ CMA

Modelling:

- ❑ No   ❑ Yes

Source of data for effect size measure(s):

- ❑ Meta-analysis   ❑ Cohort study
- ❑ RCT   ❑ Mirror image (before-after) study
- ❑ Quasi experimental study   ❑ Expert opinion

Comments _____

Primary outcome measure(s) (please list):

_____

Interventions compared (please describe):

Treatment: _____

Comparator: _____

Setting (please describe):

_____

_____

Patient population characteristics (please describe):

_____

_____

_____

Perspective of analysis:

❑ Societal   ❑ Other: _____

❑ Patient and family

❑ Healthcare system

❑ Healthcare provider

❑ Third party payer

Time frame of analysis: _____

Cost data:

❑ Primary   ❑ Secondary

If secondary please specify: _____

Costs included:

Direct medical	Direct non-medical	Lost productivity
❑ direct treatment	❑ social care	❑ income forgone due
❑ inpatient	❑ social benefits	to illness
❑ outpatient	❑ travel costs	❑ income forgone due to
❑ day care	❑ caregiver	death
❑ community healthcare	out-of-pocket	❑ income forgone by
❑ medication	❑ criminal justice	caregiver
	❑ training of staff	

Or

❑ staff

❑ medication

❑ consumables

❑ overhead

❑ capital equipment

❑ real estate   Others: _____

Currency: _____   **Year of costing:** _____

Was discounting used?

❏ Yes, for benefits and costs   ❏ Yes, but only for costs   ❏ No

       Discount rate used for costs: _____

       Discount rate used for benefits: _____

Result(s):

_____

_____

_____

_____

Comments, limitations of the study:

_____

_____

_____

Quality checklist score (Yes/NA/All): ....../....../......

APPENDIX 13:

WINBUGS CODES USED FOR MIXED TREATMENT COMPARISONS IN THE ECONOMIC MODEL OF PHARMACOLOGICAL TREATMENTS FOR RELAPSE PREVENTION

A. Competing risks model for relapse rates, rates of discontinuation because of side effects and rates of discontinuation because of other reasons (random effects model)

```
model{

# code for treatment effects relative to placebo (treatment 1)
for(i in 1:30){ # LOOP OVER ARMS
r[i,1:4] ~ dmulti(p[i,1:4],n[i]) # likelihood
slam[i] <- sum(lam[,i]) # sum of the 3 hazard rates

for (m in 1:3) { # LOOP OVER 3 ENDPOINTS
p[i,m] <- lam[m,i] * (1-exp(-slam[i]*w[i]/52)) / slam[i] # cumulative pr(failed) at
    each end point
log(lam[m,i]) <- theta[m,i] # log rates for each arm, each end point
theta[m,i] <- mu[m,s[i]] + delta[m,i]*(1-equals(t[i],b[i])) # baseline & treatment effects
delta[m,i] ~ dnorm(md[m,i],pr[m]) # random outcome- & trial-specific relative effect
md[m,i] <- d[m,t[i]] - d[m,b[i]] # mean of the random effect
} # END LOOP OVER 3 ENDPOINTS
p[i,4] <- 1- sum(p[i,1:3]) # pr(no failure)
} # END LOOP OVER ARMS

for (m in 1:3) {d[m,1] <- 0
for (k in 2:9) {d[m,k] ~ dnorm(0,.0001) # priors for treatment effects
log(hazr[m,k]) <- d[m,k] # hazard ratios
}
for (j in 1:15) {mu[m,j] ~ dnorm(0,.0001) } # priors for baselines
}

for (m in 1:3) {pr[m] <- pow(sd[m],-2)
sd[m] <- sdb[m] * sqrt(2*(1-rho[m])) }
```

```
# code for absolute effects on baseline (Treatment 1)
for (i in 1:9) { rb[i,1:4] ~ dmulti(pb[i,1:4],nb[i]) # likelihood
for (m in 1:3) { # LOOP OVER 3 ENDPOINTS
pb[i,m] <- lamb[m,i] * (1-exp(-slamb[i]*wb[i]/52)) / slamb[i]
log(lamb[m,i]) <- mub[m,sb[i]]
} # END LOOP OVER 3 ENDPOINTS
slamb[i] <- sum(lamb[,i]) # sum of the 3 hazard rates
pb[i,4] <- 1- sum(pb[i,1:3]) # pr(no failure)
} # END LOOP OVER ARMS
for (m in 1:3) { for (j in 1:9) {mub[m,j] ~ dnorm(mb[m],prb[m]) } # priors for
    outcome- & trial-specific effects
mb[m] ~ dnorm(0,.001) } # common means
for (m in 1:3) {prb[m] ~ dgamma(.1,.1)
sdb[m] <- pow(prb[m],-.5)
rho[m] ~dbeta(1,1) }
u1 <-tb[1]
u2 <-bb[1]


# code for predicted effects at 52 weeks, on a probability scale. baseline risks in
    mub[1:3,9]
for (m in 1:3) {d.new[m,1] <- 0
for (k in 2:9) {d.new[m,k] ~ dnorm(d[m,k],pr[m]) }
for (k in 1:9) {theta52[m,k] <- mub[m,9] + d.new[m,k]
log(lam52[m,k]) <- theta52[m,k]
p52[m,k] <- lam52[m,k] * (1-exp(-slam52[k])) / slam52[k]
}
}
for (k in 1:9) {slam52[k] <- sum(lam52[1:3,k])
p52[4,k] <- 1-sum(p52[1:3,k])
}
for (k in 1:8){
        ind[k] <- k + step(k-6)
        for (m in 1:4){
                p52.rk[m,k] <- p52[m,ind[k]]        #Omits treatment 6, & moves
    treatments 7-9 down to indices 6-8
                rank52[m,k] <- rank(p52.rk[m,],k)    #Smallest is best (i.e. rank 1)
        }
        for (m in 1:3){ best[m,k] <- equals(rank52[m,k],1)}    #Record    whether
    best (rank=1 for outcomes m = 1,2,3)
        best[4,k] <- equals(rank52[4,k],8)    #Record    whether    best    (rank = 8    for
    outcome m = 4)
}
}
```

Appendix 13

```
# initial values 1
list(d=structure(.Data=c(NA,0,0,0, 0,0,0,0,0,
    NA,0,0,0, 0,0,0,0,0,
    NA,0,0,0, 0,0,0,0,0),.Dim=c(3,9)),
mu=structure(.Data=c(0,0,0,0,0, 0,0,0,0,0, 0,0,0,0,0,
    0,0,0,0,0, 0,0,0,0,0, 0,0,0,0,0,
    0,0,0,0,0, 0,0,0,0,0, 0,0,0,0,0),.Dim=c(3,15)),
mb=c(0,0,0),prb=c(1,1,1), rho=c(.2,.2,.6)
)

# initial values 2
list(d=structure(.Data=c(NA,-1,-1,-1, -1,-1,-1,-1,-1,
    NA,-1,-1,-1, -1,-1,-1,-1,-1,
    NA,-1,-1,-1, -1,-1,-1,-1,-1),.Dim=c(3,9)),
mu=structure(.Data=c(-1,-1,-1,-1,-1, -1,-1,-1,-1,-1, -1,-1,-1,-1,-1,
    -1,-1,-1,-1,-1, -1,-1,-1,-1,-1, -1,-1,-1,-1,-1,
    -1,-1,-1,-1,-1, -1,-1,-1,-1,-1, -1,-1,-1,-1,-1),.Dim=c(3,15)),
mb=c(-2,-2,-2), prb=c(3,3,3), rho=c(.5,.5,.5)
)
```

Summary statistics

Node	Mean	SD	MC error	2.5%	Median	97.5%	Start	Sample
d[1,2]	−1.468	0.4232	0.003149	−2.302	−1.474	−0.627	60001	10000
d[1,3]	−0.9755	0.722	0.005072	−2.397	−0.9758	0.4687	60001	10000
d[1,4]	−2.105	0.887	0.005918	−3.91	−2.083	−0.4041	60001	10000
d[1,5]	−0.7272	0.6881	0.004969	−2.104	−0.7243	0.6635	60001	10000
d[1,6]	−1.227	0.5577	0.003978	−2.366	−1.22	−0.1202	60001	10000
d[1,7]	−1.022	0.7104	0.005406	−2.451	−1.024	0.4045	60001	10000
d[1,8]	−0.7058	0.5631	0.004189	−1.804	−0.7139	0.4421	60001	10000
d[1,9]	−1.127	0.6388	0.004798	−2.382	−1.13	0.1351	60001	10000
d[2,2]	−1.167	0.6127	0.005447	−2.317	−1.192	0.1243	60001	10000
d[2,3]	−1.718	1.012	0.008357	−3.807	−1.695	0.1862	60001	10000
d[2,4]	1.147	1.059	0.009187	−0.9445	1.126	3.323	60001	10000
d[2,5]	0.0208	0.9386	0.00601	−1.88	0.0304	1.934	60001	10000
d[2,6]	−1.02	0.7491	0.005658	−2.499	−1.03	0.5075	60001	10000
d[2,7]	1.333	1.679	0.01896	−1.704	1.208	5.037	60001	10000
d[2,8]	−0.8596	0.7718	0.006442	−2.415	−0.8648	0.6964	60001	10000
d[2,9]	−0.9484	0.9093	0.007632	−2.58	−1.01	1.06	60001	10000
d[3,2]	−0.4861	0.3061	0.002925	−1.08	−0.4863	0.1248	60001	10000

Continued

443

Summary statistics *(Continued)*

Node	Mean	SD	MC error	2.5%	Median	97.5%	Start	Sample
d[3,3]	−0.5919	0.4205	0.003346	−1.435	−0.5906	0.2445	60001	10000
d[3,4]	−0.4769	0.489	0.003619	−1.449	−0.4748	0.4982	60001	10000
d[3,5]	0.2254	0.5352	0.004616	−0.8364	0.2306	1.262	60001	10000
d[3,6]	−0.3937	0.4045	0.003791	−1.175	−0.3992	0.4275	60001	10000
d[3,7]	0.7269	0.5973	0.006136	−0.4142	0.716	1.941	60001	10000
d[3,8]	−0.4185	0.3861	0.003207	−1.189	−0.4155	0.345	60001	10000
d[3,9]	−1.05	0.4485	0.003855	−1.912	−1.058	−0.1139	60001	10000
sd[1]	0.6343	0.1926	9.11E-04	0.324	0.6115	1.078	60001	10000
sd[2]	0.7626	0.3672	0.002587	0.1953	0.7128	1.622	60001	10000
sd[3]	0.3164	0.2131	0.001434	0.0460	0.27	0.8539	60001	10000
sdb[1]	0.6666	0.1996	9.76E-04	0.3884	0.6314	1.147	60001	10000
sdb[2]	0.8122	0.3471	0.002161	0.3387	0.7504	1.662	60001	10000
sdb[3]	0.955	0.2781	0.001428	0.5676	0.9046	1.628	60001	10000

B. Simple random effects model for rates of weight gain

```
model{
for(i in 1:34){
                r[i] ~ dbin(p[i],n[i])
                logit(p[i]) <-mu[s[i]]+delta[i]*(1-equals(t[i],b[i]))
#Random effects model for log-odds ratios
                delta[i] ~ dnorm(md[i],prec)
                md[i] <- d[t[i]] - d[b[i]]
#Deviance residuals for data i
rhat[i] <- p[i] * n[i]
dev[i] <- 2 * (r[i] * (log(r[i])-log(rhat[i])) + (n[i]-r[i]) * (log(n[i]-r[i]) - log(n[i]-rhat[i])))
                }
sumdev <- sum(dev[])

#priors
for(j in 1:17){ mu[j] ~ dnorm(0,.0001)}
prec <- 1/(sd*sd)
sd ~ dunif(0,2)

#Give priors for log-odds ratios
        d[1] <-0
        for (k in 2:7){d[k] ~ dnorm(0,.001) }

#All pairwise odds ratios
for (c in 1:6){
        for (k in (c + 1):7){
                or[c,k] <- exp(d[k] - d[c]) }}
}

# initial values
list(
d = c(NA,0,0,0,0,0,0),sd = 1,mu = c(0,0,0,0,0, 0,0,0,0,0, 0,0,0,0,0, 0,0),
delta = c(0,0,0,0,0, 0,0,0,0,0, 0,0,0,0,0, 0,0,0,0,0, 0,0,0,0,0, 0,0,0,0,0, 0,0,0,0)
)
```

Appendix 13

Summary statistics

Node	Mean	SD	MC error	2.5%	Median	97.5%	Start	Sample
or[1,2]	2.8631	0.7454	0.007843	1.705	2.771	4.509	60001	10000
or[1,3]	0.7373	0.2767	0.003196	0.3498	0.693	1.399	60001	10000
or[1,4]	1.8321	1.009	0.01043	0.7807	1.602	4.284	60001	10000
or[1,5]	1.0779	0.4967	0.005028	0.4405	0.9904	2.164	60001	10000
or[1,6]	1.0895	0.4294	0.004114	0.5214	1.013	2.085	60001	10000
or[1,7]	1.8604	0.989	0.01032	0.7345	1.674	4.036	60001	10000
Sd	0.3218	0.1934	0.002541	0.02308	0.3004	0.7511	60001	10000
sumdev	33.32	7.786	0.0865	19.7	32.77	50.09	60001	10000

C. Full random effects model for rates of acute extrapyramidal side effects

```
model{
sw[1] <- 0
for(i in 1:73){
                r[i] ~ dbin(p[i],n[i])
                logit(p[i]) <-mu[s[i]]+delta[i]*(1-equals(t[i],b[i]))

#Random effects model for log-odds ratios
                delta[i] ~ dnorm(md[i],taud[i])
                taud[i] <- tau * (1 + equals(m[i],3) /3)
                md[i] <- d[t[i]] - d[b[i]] + equals(m[i],3) * sw[i]

#Deviance residuals for data i
rhat[i] <- p[i] * n[i]
dev[i] <- 2 * (r[i] * (log(r[i])-log(rhat[i])) + (n[i]-r[i]) * (log(n[i]-r[i]) - log(n[i]-rhat[i])))
                }
sumdev <- sum(dev[])

#Adjustment for 3 arm trials
for (i in 2:73) { sw[i] <- (delta[i-1] - d[t[i-1]] + d[b[i-1]] ) /2}

#priors
for(j in 1:36){ mu[j]~dnorm(0,.0001)}
tau <- 1/(sd*sd)
sd~dunif(0,2)
#Give priors for log-odds ratios
        d[1] <-0
        for (k in 2:8){d[k] ~ dnorm(0,.001) }

#All pairwise odds ratios
for (c in 1:7){
        for (k in (c+1):8){
                or[c,k] <- exp(d[k] - d[c]) }}
}

#initial values
list(
d=c(NA,0,0,0,0,0,0,0),sd=1,mu=c(0,0,0,0,0,0, 0,0,0,0,0,0, 0,0,0,0,0,0, 0,0,0,0,0,0, 0,0,0,0,0,0,
0,0,0,0,0,0, 0,0,0,0,0,0, 0),delta=c(0,0,0,0,0,0, 0,0,0,0,0,0, 0,0,0,0,0,0, 0,0,0,0,0,0, 0,0,0,0,0,0,
0,0,0,0,0,0, 0,0,0,0,0,0, 0,0,0,0,0,0, 0,0,0,0,0,0, 0,0,0,0,0,0, 0,0,0,0,0,0, 0,0,0,0,0,0, 0,0,0,0,0,0,
0,0,0,0,0,0, 0,0,0)
)
```

Summary statistics

Node	Mean	SD	MC error	2.5%	Median	97.5%	Start	Sample
or[1,2]	0.4743	0.05824	5.87E-04	0.368	4.72E-01	0.5994	60001	10000
or[1,3]	0.2631	0.04556	4.71E-04	0.1832	2.60E-01	0.3641	60001	10000
or[1,4]	0.1476	0.06829	7.77E-04	0.05171	1.35E-01	0.3132	60001	10000
or[1,5]	0.3993	0.08162	8.73E-04	0.2587	0.3928	0.5836	60001	10000
or[1,6]	0.2405	0.07893	8.70E-04	0.1147	0.2316	0.4221	60001	10000
or[1,7]	0.2517	0.06318	6.28E-04	0.1505	0.2438	0.4002	60001	10000
or[1,8]	0.2983	0.1333	1.26E-03	0.1179	0.2719	0.6214	60001	10000
sd	0.292	0.1132	0.001455	0.08428	0.2859	0.5386	60001	10000
sumdev	75.93	11.79	0.1198	54.13	75.6	100.5	60001	10000

12   REFERENCES

Adams, C. E., Fenton, M. K. P., Quiraishi, S., *et al.* (2001) Systematic meta-review of depot antipsychotic drugs for people with schizophrenia. *British Journal of Psychiatry*, *179*, 290–299.

Addington, J., el-Guebaly, N., Campbell, P., *et al.* (1998) Smoking cessation treatment for patients with schizophrenia. *American Journal of Psychiatry*, *155*, 974–976.

Agid, O., Mamo, D., Ginovart, N., *et al.* (2007) Dopamine D2 receptors in antipsychotic response – a double-blind PET study in schizophrenia. *Neuropsychopharmacology*, *32*, 1209–1215.

AGREE Collaboration (2003) Development and validation of an international appraisal instrument for assessing the quality of clinical practice guidelines: the AGREE project. *Quality and Safety in Health Care*, *12*, 18–23.

Alanen, Y. O. (1997) *Schizophrenia: Its Origins and Need-Adapted Treatment.* London: Karnac Books.

Alderson, P., Green, S., Higgins, J. P. T. (editors) (updated March 2004). Cochrane Reviewers' Handbook 4.2.2. *The Cochrane Library*, Issue 1. Chichester: John Wiley & Sons, Ltd.

Alexeyeva, I., Mauskopf, J., Earnshaw, S. R., *et al.* (2001) Comparing olanzapine and ziprasidone in the treatment of schizophrenia: a case study in modeling. *Journal of Drug Assessment*, *4*, 275–288.

Alkhateeb, H., Essali, A., Matar, H. E. D., *et al.* (2007) Cessation of medication for people with schizophrenia already stable on chlorpromazine (Cochrane review). *The Cochrane Library*, Issue 1. Oxford: Update Software.

Almond, S. & O'Donnell, O. (2000) Cost analysis of the treatment of schizophrenia in the UK. A simulation model comparing olanzapine, risperidone and haloperidol. *Pharmacoeconomics*, *17*, 383–389.

Almond, S., Knapp, M., Francois, C., *et al.* (2004) Relapse in schizophrenia: costs, clinical outcomes and quality of life. *British Journal of Psychiatry*, *184*, 346–351.

Álvarez-Jiménez, M., Hetrick, S., González-Blanch, C., *et al.* (2008) Non-pharmacological management of antipsychotic-induced weight gain: systematic review and meta-analysis of randomised controlled trials. *British Journal of Psychiatry*, *193*, 101–107.

American Diabetes Association, American Psychiatric Association, American Association of Clinical Endocrinologists & North American Association for the Study of Obesity (2004) Consensus Development Conference on Antipsychotic Drugs and Obesity and Diabetes. *Journal of Clinical Psychiatry*, *65*, 267–272.

American Psychiatric Association (1994) *Diagnostic and Statistical Manual of Mental Disorders*, 4th edn (DSM–IV). Washington, DC: APA.

Anonymous (2008) 'My early intervention experience'. Available at: http://www.kmpt.nhs.uk/Recovery_stories/My_Early_Intervention_Experience/index.html [accessed August 2008]

References

Anthony, W. A. & Blanch, A. (1987) Supported employment for persons who are psychiatrically disabled: an historical and conceptual perspective. *Psychosocial Rehabilitation Journal, 11*, 5–23.

Arseneault, L., Cannon, M., Witton, J., *et al.* (2004) Causal association between cannabis and psychosis: examination of the evidence. *British Journal of Psychiatry, 184*, 110–117.

Assion, H. J., Reinbold, H., Lemanski, S., *et al.* (2008) Amisulpride augmentation in patients with schizophrenia partially responsive or unresponsive to clozapine. A randomized, double-blind, placebo-controlled trial. *Pharmacopsychiatry, 41*, 24–28.

Audit Commission (1986) *Making a Reality of Community Care.* London: HMSO.

Ayllon, T. & Azrin, N. H. (1965) The measurement and reinforcement of behaviour of psychotics. *Journal of Experimental Analysis of Behavior, 8*, 357–383.

Bagnall, A.-M., Jones, L., Ginnelly, L., *et al.* (2003) A systematic review of atypical antipsychotic drugs in schizophrenia. *Health Technology Assessment, 7*, 1–193.

Banerjee, S., Clany, C. & Crome, I. (2001) *Coexisting Problems of Mental Disorder and Substance Misuse (Dual Diagnosis). An Information Manual.* London: Royal College of Psychiatrists' Research Unit.

Barnes, T. R. & Curson, D. A. (1994) Long-term depot antipsychotics. A risk-benefit assessment. *Drug Safety, 10*, 464–479.

Barnes, T. R. E. & Kidger, T. (1978) Tardive dyskinesia and problems of assessment. In *Current Themes in Psychiatry.* Vol. 2 (eds R.N. Gaind & B.L. Hudson). London: Macmillan.

Barnes, T. R. & McPhillips, M. A. (1999) Critical analysis and comparison of the side-effect and safety profiles of the new antipsychotics. *British Journal of Psychiatry* (Suppl. 38), 34–43.

Barnes, T. R. E., Buckley, P. & Schulz, S.C. (2003) Treatment-resistant schizophrenia. In *Schizophrenia.* Second Edition (eds S. R. Hirsch & D. R. Weinberger). Oxford: Blackwell Publishing.

Barnes, T. R. E., Paton, C., Cavanagh, M.-R., *et al.* on behalf of the UK Prescribing Observatory for Mental Health (2007) A UK audit of screening for the metabolic side effects of antipsychotics in community patients. *Schizophrenia Bulletin, 33*, 1397–1401.

Barnes, T. R. E., Shingleton-Smith, A. & Paton, C. (2009) Antipsychotic long-acting injections: prescribing practice in the UK. *British Journal of Psychiatry, 195*, S37–S42.

Barrowclough, C., Haddock, G., Tarrier, N., *et al.* (2001) Randomized controlled trial of motivational interviewing, cognitive behavior therapy, and family intervention for patients with comorbid schizophrenia and substance use disorders. *American Journal of Psychiatry, 158*, 1706–1713.

Bateman, A. & Fonagy, P. (1999) Effectiveness of partial hospitalization in the treatment of borderline personality disorder: a randomized controlled trial. *American Journal of Psychiatry, 156*, 1563–1569.

Beard, S. M., Maciver, F., Clouth, J., *et al.* (2006) A decision model to compare health care costs of olanzapine and risperidone treatment for schizophrenia in Germany. *European Journal of Health Economics*, 7, 165–172.

Bebbington, P. E. & Kuipers, E. (1994) The predictive utility of expressed emotion in schizophrenia. *Psychological Medicine*, 24, 707–718.

Bebbington, P. E., Bhugra, D., Brugha, T., *et al.* (2004) Psychosis, victimisation and childhood disadvantage: evidence from the second British National Survey of Psychiatric Morbidity. *British Journal of Psychiatry*, 185, 220–226.

Beck, A. T. (1979) *Cognitive Therapy and the Emotional Disorders.* New York: International Universities Press.

Bell, M. & Lysaker, P. (1995) Paid work activity in schizophrenia: program costs offset by costs of rehospitalizations. *Psychosocial Rehabilitation Journal*, 18, 25–34.

Bell, M. D., Milstein, R. M. & Lysaker, P. H. (1993) Pay as an incentive in work participation by patients with severe mental illness. *Hospital and Community Psychiatry, 44*, 684–686.

Bellack, A. S. (2004) Skills training for people with severe mental illness. *Psychiatric Rehabilitation Journal*, 27, 375–391.

Bennett, D. & Freeman, H. (1991) Principles and prospect. In *Community Psychiatry* (eds D. Bennett & H. Freeman), pp. 1–39. Edinburgh: Churchill Livingstone.

Berlin, J. A. (2001) Does blinding of readers affect the results of meta-analyses? *Lancet*, 350, 185–186.

Bhugra, D., Harding, C. & Lippett, R. (2004) Pathways into care and satisfaction with primary care for black patients in South London. *Journal of Mental Health*, 13, 171–183.

Bhui, K. S. & McKenzie, K. (2008) Rates and risk factors by ethnic group for suicides within a year of contact with mental health services in England and Wales. *Psychiatric Services*, 59, 414–420.

Bhui, K. & Sashidharan, S. P. (2003) Should there be separate psychiatric services for ethnic minority groups? *British Journal of Psychiatry*, 182, 10–12.

Bhui, K., Bhugra, D. & McKenzie, K. (2000) Specialist services for minority ethnic groups? *Maudsley Discussion Paper no. 8.* Available at: http://admin.iop. kcl.ac.uk/maudsley-publications/maudsley-discussion-papers/mdp08.pdf [accessed 2008]

Bhui, K., McKenzie, K. & Gill, P. (2004) Delivering mental health services for a diverse society. *British Medical Journal*, 14, 363–364.

Bhui, K. S., Warfa, N., Edonya, P., *et al.* (2007) Cultural competence in mental health care: a review of model evaluations. *BMC Health Services Research*, 31, 7–15.

Bindman, J., Johnson, S., Wright, S., *et al.* (1997) Integration between primary and secondary services in the care of the severely mentally ill: patients' and general practitioners' views. *British Journal of Psychiatry*, 171, 169–174.

Birchwood, M. (2003) Pathways to emotional dysfunction in first-episode psychosis. *British Journal of Psychiatry*, 182, 373–375.

Bleuler, E. (1911) *Dementia Praecox or the Group of Schizophrenias* (translated by J.J. Zinkin, 1950). New York: International Universities Press.

Bond, G. R., Miller, L. D., Krumwied, R. D., *et al.* (1988) Assertive case management in three CMHCs: a controlled study. *Hospital and Community Psychiatry*, *39*, 411–418.

Bond, G. R., Dietzen, L. L., Vogler, K., *et al.* (1995) Toward a framework for evaluating cost and benefits of psychiatric rehabilitation: three case examples. *Journal of Vocational Rehabilitation*, *5*, 75–88.

Bondolfi, G., Dufour, H., Patris, M., *et al.* (1998) Risperidone versus clozapine in treatment-resistant chronic schizophrenia: a randomized double-blind study. The Risperidone Study Group. *American Journal of Psychiatry*, *155*, 499–504.

Borneo, A. (2008) 'Your choice: results from the Your Treatment, Your Choice survey 2008 – final report'. Available at: http://www.rethink.org/how_we_can_help/campaigning_for_change/opening_doors/your_treatment_your.html [accessed August 2008]

Bottlender, R., Sato, T., Jager, M., *et al.* (2003) The impact of the duration of untreated psychosis prior to first psychiatric admission on the 15-year outcome in schizophrenia. *Schizophrenia Research*, *62*, 37–44.

Bounthavong, M. & Okamoto, M. P. (2007) Decision analysis model evaluating the cost-effectiveness of risperidone, olanzapine and haloperidol in the treatment of schizophrenia. *Journal of Evaluation in Clinical Practice*, *13*, 453–460.

Bouras, N., Tufnell, G., Brough, D. I., *et al.* (1986) Model for the integration of community psychiatry and primary care. *Journal of the Royal College of General Practice*, *36*, 62–66.

Brazier, J., Ratcliffe, J., Salomon, J. A., *et al.* (2007a) Describing health. In *Measuring and Valuing Health Benefits for Economic Evaluation* (eds J. Brazier, J. Ratcliffe, J. A. Salomon, *et al.*). Oxford & New York: Oxford University Press.

Brazier, J., Ratcliffe, J., Salomon, J. A., *et al.* (2007b) Methods for obtaining health state values: generic preference-based measures of health and the alternatives. In *Measuring and Valuing Health Benefits for Economic Evaluation* (eds. J. Brazier, J. Ratcliffe, J. A. Salomon, *et al.*). Oxford & New York: Oxford University Press.

Brenner, H. D. (1986) On the importance of cognitive disorders in treatment and rehabilitation. In *Psychosocial Treatment of Schizophrenia* (eds J. S. Strauss, W. Boker & H. D. Brenner), pp. 136–151. Toronto: Hans Huber.

Brenner, H. D., Dencker, S. J., Goldstein, M. J., *et al.* (1990) Defining treatment refractoriness in schizophrenia. *Schizophrenia Bulletin*, *16*, 551–561.

Briggs, A., Sculpher, M. & Claxton, C. (2006) Making decision models probabilistic. In *Decision Modelling for Health Economic Evaluation* (eds. A. Briggs, M. Sculpher & C. Claxton). New York: Oxford University Press.

British Medical Association & the Royal Pharmaceutical Society of Great Britain (2008) *British National Formulary (BNF) 56* London: Pharmaceutical Press. Avaliable at: http://www.bnf.org/bnf/bnf/56/104945.htm

British Psychological Society (2007) *New Ways of Working for Applied Psychologists in Health and Social Care – The End of the Beginning*. Leicester: British Psychological Society, Leicester.

Broome, M. R., Woolley, J. B., Tabraham, P., *et al.* (2005) What causes the onset of psychosis? *Schizophrenia Research*, *79*, 23–34.

Brown, G. W. & Rutter, M. (1966) The measurement of family activities and relationships: a methodological study. *Human Relations, 19,* 241–263.

Brown, G. W., Monck, E. M., Carstairs, G. M., *et al.* (1962) Influence of family life on the course of schizophrenic illness. *British Journal of Preventive and Social Medicine, 16,* 55–68.

Brown, S., Birtwhistle, J., Row, L., *et al.* (1999) The unhealthy lifestyle of people with schizophrenia. *Psychological Medicine, 29,* 697–701.

Buckley, L. A, Pettit, T. A. C. L. & Adams, C. E. (2007) Supportive therapy for schizophrenia. (Cochrane review). *The Cochrane Library,* Issue 3. Oxford: Update Software.

Buckley, P., Miller, A., Olsen, J., *et al.* (2001) When symptoms persist: clozapine augmentation strategies. *Schizophrenia Bulletin, 27,* 615–628.

Bunt, L. (1994) *Music Therapy: An Art Beyond Words.* London: Routledge.

Burns, T. & Cohen, A. (1998) Item-of-service payments for general practitioner care of severely mentally ill persons: does the money matter? *British Journal of General Practice, 48,* 1415–1416.

Burns, T. & Raftery, J. (1993) A controlled trial of home-based acute psychiatric services. II: Treatment patterns and costs. *British Journal of Psychiatry, 163,* 55–61.

Burns, T., Greenwood, N., Kendrick, T., *et al.* (2000) Attitudes of general practitioners and community mental health team staff towards the locus of care for people with chronic psychotic disorders. *Primary Care Psychiatry, 6,* 67–71.

Butzlaff, A. M. & Hooley, J. M. (1998) Expressed emotion and psychiatric relapse. *Archives of General Psychiatry, 55,* 547–552.

Byford, S., Fiander, M., Barber, J. A., *et al.* (2000) Cost-effectiveness of intensive v. standard case management for severe psychotic illness. UK700 case management trial. *British Journal of Psychiatry, 176,* 537–543.

Caldwell, D. M., Ades, A. E. & Higgins, J. P. (2005) Simultaneous comparison of multiple treatments: combining direct and indirect evidence. *British Medical Journal, 331,* 897–900.

Cameron, E. (1947) The day hospital. An experimental form of hospitalization for psychiatric patients. *Modern Hospital, 69,* 60–63.

Cannon, M. & Jones, P. (1996) Schizophrenia. *Journal of Neurology, Neurosurgery and Psychiatry, 60,* 604–613.

Cantor-Graae, E. & Selten, J. P. (2005) Schizophrenia and migration: a meta-analysis and review. *American Journal of Psychiatry, 162,* 12–24.

Carpenter, W. T. & Buchanan, R. W. (2008) Lessons to take home from CATIE. *Psychiatric Services, 59,* 523–525.

Carr, V. J., Neil, A. L., Halpin, S., *et al.* (2003) Costs of schizophrenia and other psychoses in urban Australia: findings from the Low Prevalence (Psychotic) Disorders Study. *Australian and New Zealand Journal of Psychiatry, 37,* 31–40.

Chakos, M., Lieberman, J., Hoffman, E., *et al.* (2001) Effectiveness of second-generation antipsychotics in patients with treatment-resistant schizophrenia: a review and meta-analysis of randomized trials. *American Journal of Psychiatry, 158,* 518–526.

Chan, J. & Sweeting, M. (2007) Review: combination therapy with non-clozapine atypical antipsychotic medication a review of current evidence. *Journal of Psychopharmacology, 21*, 657–664.

Chandler, D., Spicer, G., Wagner, M., *et al.* (1999) Cost-effectiveness of a capitated assertive community treatment program. *Psychiatric Rehabilitation Journal, 22*, 327–336.

Chong, S. A. & Remington, G. (2000) Clozapine augmentation: safety and efficacy. *Schizophrenia Bulletin, 26*, 421–440.

Chong, S. A., Tan, C. H. & Lee, H. S. (1996) Hoarding and clozapine–risperidone combination. *Canadian Journal of Psychiatry, 41*, 315–316.

Chouinard, G. & Albright, P. S. (1997) Economic and health state utility determinations for schizophrenic patients treated with risperidone or haloperidol. *Journal of Clinical Psychopharmacology, 17*, 298–307.

Chue, P. S., Heeg, B. M. S., Buskens, E., *et al.* (2005) Modelling the impact of compliance on the costs and effects of long-acting risperidone in Canada. *Pharmacoeconomics, 23*, 62–74.

Clark, R. E., Bush, P. W., Becker, D. R., *et al.* (1996) A cost-effectiveness comparison of supported employment and rehabilitative day treatment. *Administration and Policy in Mental Health, 24*, 63–77.

Clark, R. E., Xie, H., Becker, D. R., *et al.* (1998) Benefits and costs of supported employment from three perspectives. *Journal of Behavioral Health Services and Research, 25*, 22–34.

Clarke, P., Gray, A. & Holman, R. (2002) Estimating utility values for health states of type 2 diabetic patients using the EQ-5D (UKPDS 62). *Medical Decision Making, 22*, 340–349.

Clarke, P. M., Gray, A. M., Briggs, A., *et al.* (2005) On behalf of the UK Prospective Diabetes Study (UKPDS). Cost-utility analyses of intensive blood glucose and tight blood pressure control in type 2 diabetes (UKPDS 72). *Diabetologia, 48*, 868–877.

Cochrane Collaboration (2004) *Review Manager* (RevMan) [Computer program]. Version 4.2.7 for Windows. Oxford: The Cochrane Collaboration.

Coid, J. (1994) Failure in community care: psychiatry's dilemma. *British Medical Journal, 308*, 805–806.

Conley, R. R. & Buchanan, R. W. (1997) Evaluation of treatment-resistant schizophrenia. *Schizophrenia Bulletin, 23*, 663–674.

Cookson, J., Taylor, D. & Katona, C. (2002) *Use of Drugs in Psychiatry* (5th edn). London: Gaskell.

Craddock, N., O'Donovan, M. C. & Owen, M. J. (2005) The genetics of schizophrenia and bipolar disorder: dissecting psychosis. *Journal of Medical Genetics, 42*, 193–204.

Crammer, J. & Eccleston, D. A. (1989) Survey of the use of depot neuroleptics in a whole region. *Psychiatric Bulletin, 13*, 517–520.

Crawford, M. J. & Patterson, S. (2007) Arts therapies for people with schizophrenia: an emerging evidence base. *Evidence-Based Mental Health, 10*, 69–70.

Creed, F., Black, D., Anthony, P., *et al.* (1990) Randomised controlled trial of day patient versus in-patient psychiatric treatment. *British Medical Journal, 300,* 1033–1037.

Creed, F., Mbaya, P., Lancashire, S., *et al.* (1997) Cost effectiveness of day and in-patient psychiatric treatment. *British Medical Journal, 314,* 1381–1385.

Crown, S. (1988) Supportive psychotherapy: a contradiction in terms? *British Journal of Psychiatry, 152,* 266–269.

Crowther, R., Marshall, M., Bond, G., *et al.* (2001) Vocational rehabilitation for people with severe mental illness (Cochrane review). *The Cochrane Library,* Issue 4. Oxford: Update Software.

Cummins, C., Stevens, A. & Kisely, S. (1998) *The Use of Olanzapine as a First and Second Choice Treatment in Schizophrenia.* A West Midlands Development and Evaluation Committee report. Birmingham: Development and Evaluation Service, Department of Public Health and Epidemiology, University of Birmingham.

Curtis, L. (2007) *Unit Costs of Health and Social Care 2007.* Canterbury: Personal Social Services Research Unit, University of Kent.

Darzi, A. R (2008) *High Quality Care for All: NHS Next Stage Review Final Report.* London: Department of Health. Available at: http://www.dh.gov.uk/en/Publicationsandstatistics/Publications/PublicationsPolicyAndGuidance/DH_0 85825 [accessed August 2008]

David, A. S. & Adams, C. (2001) Depot antipsychotic medication in the treatment of patients with schizophrenia: (1) meta-review; (2) patient and nurse attitudes. *Health Technology Assessment, 5,* 1–61.

David, A., Adams, C. E. & Quraishi, S. N. (1999) Depot flupenthixol decanoate for schizophrenia or other similar psychotic disorders. (Cochrane review). *The Cochrane Library.* Issue 2. Oxford: Update Software.

David, A., Adams, C. E., Eisenbruch, M., *et al.* (2004) Depot fluphenazine decanoate and enanthate for schizophrenia. (Cochrane review). *The Cochrane Library.* Issue 3. Oxford: Update Software.

Davies, A., Langley, P. C., Keks, N., *et al.* (1998) Risperidone versus haloperidol: II. Cost-effectiveness. *Clinical Therapeutics, 20,* 196–213.

Davies, L. M. & Drummond, M. F. (1994) Economics and schizophrenia: the real cost. *British Journal of Psychiatry, 165* (Suppl. 25), 18–21.

Davies, L. & Lewis, S. (2000) *Antipsychotic Medication for People with First Episode Schizophrenia: an Exploratory Economic Analysis of Alternative Treatment Algorithms.* Discussion Paper 178, 1–51. York: Centre for Health Economics, University of York.

Davies, L. M., Lewis, S., the CUtLASS team, *et al.* (2007) Cost-effectiveness of first-v. second-generation antipsychotic drugs: results from a randomised controlled trial in schizophrenia responding poorly to previous therapy. *British Journal of Psychiatry, 191,* 14–22.

Davies, L. M., Barnes, T. R. E., Jones, P. B., *et al.* (2008) A randomised controlled trial of the cost-utility of second-generation antipsychotics in people with psychosis and eligible for clozapine. *Value in Health, 11,* 549–562.

Davis, J. M. & Garver, D. L. (1978) Neuroleptics: clinical use in psychiatry. In *Handbook of Psychopharmacology* (eds L. Iversen, S. Iversen & S. Snyder). New York: Plenum Press.

Davis, J. M., Kane, J. M, Marder, S. R., *et al.* (1993) Dose response of prophylactic antipsychotics. *Journal of Clinical Psychiatry*, *54* (Suppl.), 24–30.

De Cangas, J. P. C. (1994) Le 'case management' affirmatif: une evaluation complete d'un programme du genre en milieu hospitalier. *Sante mentale au Quebec*, *19*, 75–92.

De Graeve, D., Smet, A., Mehnert, A., *et al.* (2005) Long-acting risperidone compared with oral olanzapine and haloperidol depot in schizophrenia: a Belgian cost-effectiveness analysis. *Pharmacoeconomics 2005*, *23* (Suppl. 1), 35–47.

De Haan, L., Linszen, D., Lenoir, M., *et al.* (2003) Duration of untreated psychosis and outcome of schizophrenia: delay in intensive psychosocial treatment versus delay in treatment with antipsychotic medication. *Schizophrenia Bulletin*, *29*, 341–348.

De Leon, J. & Diaz, F. J. (2005) A meta-analysis of worldwide studies demonstrates an association between schizophrenia and tobacco smoking behaviors. *Schizophrenia Research*, *76*, 135–157.

Department of Health (1999) *NSF for Mental Health: Modern Standards and Service Models*. London: Department of Health.

Department of Health (2000) *The NHS Plan: a Plan for Investment, a Plan for Reform*. London: Department of Health.

Department of Health (2001) *The Mental Health Policy Implementation Guide*. London: Department of Health.

Department of Health (2002) *National Service Framework for Mental Health: Modern Standards and Service Models*. London: Department of Health. Available at: http://www.doh.gov.uk/pub/docs/doh/mhmain.pdf

Department of Health (2003a) *Delivering Race Equality: a Framework for Action*. London: Department of Health. www.doh.gov.uk/deliveringraceequality/77951-del_race_equality.pdf [accessed February 2004]

Department of Health (2003b) *General Medical Services Contract for General Practices*. London: NHS. Available at: http://www.dh.gov.uk/en/Healthcare/Primarycare/Primarycarecontracting/GMS/DH_4125637

Department of Health (2005) *Delivering Race Equality in Mental Health Care: an Action Plan for Reform Inside and Outside Services and the Government's Response to the Independent Inquiry Into the Death Of David Bennett*. London: Department of Health. Available at: http://www.dh.gov.uk/assetRoot/04/10/07/75/04100775.pdf

Department of Health (2007) *Mental Health Act 2007*. London: Department of Health.

Department of Health (2008a) *NHS Reference Costs 2006–07*. London: Department of Health. Available at: www.hesonline.nhs.uk [accessed July 2008]

Department of Health, Social Care Institute for Excellence & Care Services Improvement Partnership (2008b) *Care Programme Approach (CPA) Briefing: Parents with Mental Health Problems and Their Children*. Available at: http://www.cpaa.co.uk/cpa-briefing

DerSimonian, R. & Laird, N. (1986) Meta-analysis in clinical trials. *Controlled Clinical Trials*, *7*, 177–188.

Dettling, M., Sachse, C., Brockmoller, J., *et al.* (2000) Long-term therapeutic drug monitoring of clozapine and metabolites in psychiatric in- and outpatients. *Psychopharmacology*, *152*, 80–86.

Diaz F. J., de Leon, J., Josiassen, R. C., *et al.* (2005) Plasma clozapine concentration coefficients of variation in a long-term study. *Schizophrenia Research*, *72*, 131–135.

Dick, P., Ince, A. & Barlow, M. (1985) Day treatment: suitability and referral procedure. *British Journal of Psychiatry*, *147*, 250–253.

Dick, P., Sweeney, M. L. & Crombie, I. K. (1991) Controlled comparison of day-patient and outpatient treatment for persistent anxiety and depression. *British Journal of Psychiatry*, *158*, 24–27.

Dinan, T. G. (2004) Schizophrenia and diabetes 2003: an expert consensus meeting. Introduction. *British Journal of Psychiatry*, *184* (Suppl. 47), S53–54.

Dinesh, M., David, A. & Quraishi, S. N. (2004) Depot pipotiazine palmitate and undecylenate for schizophrenia. (Cochrane review). *The Cochrane Library*, Issue 4. Oxford: Update Software.

Dixon, L. B., Lehman, A. F. & Levine, J. (1995) Conventional antipsychotic medications for schizophrenia. *Schizophrenia Bulletin*, *21*, 567–577.

Donlon, P. T., Swaback, D. O. & Osborne, M. L. (1977) Pimozide versus fluphenazine in ambulatory schizophrenics: a 12-month comparison study. *Diseases of the Nervous System*, *38*, 119–123.

Dorevitch, A., Katz, N., Zemishlany, Z., *et al.* (1999) Intramuscular flunitrazepam versus intramuscular haloperidol in emergency treatment of aggressive psychotic behavior. *American Journal of Psychiatry*, *156*, 142–144.

Dowell, D. A. & Ciarlo, J. A. (1983) Overview of the community mental health centres program from an evaluation perspective. *American Journal of Psychiatry*, *19*, 95–125.

Drake, R. E., Becker, D. R. & Anthony, W. A. (1994) A research induction group for clients entering a mental health research project. *Hospital and Community Psychiatry*, *45*, 487–489.

Drake, R. E., McHugo., G. J., Becker, D. R., *et al.* (1996) The New Hampshire Study of supported employment for people with severe mental illness. *Journal of Consulting and Clinical Psychology*, *64*, 391–399.

Drummond, M. F. & Jefferson, T. O. (1996) Guidelines for authors and peer reviewers of economic submissions to the BMJ. *British Medical Journal*, *313*, 275–283.

Dumouchel, W., Mahmoud, R. A., Engelhart, L., *et al.* (2008) Antipsychotics, glycemic disorders, and life-threatening diabetic events: a Bayesian data-mining analysis of the FDA Adverse Event Reporting System (1968–2004). *Annals of Clinical Psychiatry*, *20*, 21–31.

Durham, R. C., Guthrie, M., Morton, R. V., *et al.* (2003) Tayside-Fife clinical trial of cognitive-behavioural therapy for medication-resistant psychotic symptoms. *British Journal of Psychiatry*, *182*, 303–311.

Durson, S. M. & Deakin, J. F. (2001) Augmenting antipsychotic treatment with lamotrigine or topiramate in patients with treatment-resistant schizophrenia: a naturalistic case-series outcome study. *Journal of Psychopharmacology, 15,* 297–301.

Edgell, E. T., Andersen, S. W., Johnstone, B. M., *et al.* (2000) Olanzapine versus risperidone. A prospective comparison of clinical and economic outcomes in schizophrenia. *Pharmacoeconomics, 18,* 567–579.

Edwards, N. C., Locklear, J. C., Rupnow, M. F., *et al.* (2005) Cost effectiveness of long-acting risperidone injection versus alternative antipsychotic agents in patients with schizophrenia in the USA. *Pharmacoeconomics, 23* (Suppl. 1), 75–89.

Ellison, M. L., Rogers, E. S., Sciarappa, K., *et al.* (1995) Characteristics of mental health case management: results of a national survey. *Journal of Mental Health Administration, 22,* 101–112.

Essock, S. M. & Kontos, N. (1995) Implementing assertive community treatment teams. *Psychiatric Services, 46,* 679–683.

Essock, S. M., Frisman, L. K. & Kontos, N. J. (1998) Cost-effectiveness of assertive community treatment teams. *American Journal of Orthopsychiatry, 68,* 179–190.

Falloon, I. R., Boyd, J. L., McGill, C. W., *et al.* (1985) Family management in the prevention of morbidity of schizophrenia. Clinical outcome of a two-year longitudinal study. *Achives of General Psychiatry, 42,* 887–896.

Farde, L., Nordstrom, A. L., Wiesel, F. A., *et al.* (1992) Positron emission tomographic analysis of central D1 and D2 dopamine receptor occupancy in patients treated with classical neuroleptics and clozapine. Relation to extrapyramidal side-effects. *Archives of General Psychiatry, 49,* 538–544.

Fearon, P., Kirkbride, J. B., Morgan, C., *et al.* (2006) Incidence of schizophrenia and other psychoses in ethnic minority groups: results from the MRC AESOP Study. *Psychological Medicine, 36,* 1–10.

Fenton, F. R., Tessier, L. & Struening, E. L. (1979) A comparative trial of home and hospital psychiatric care: one year follow-up. *Archives of General Psychiatry, 36,* 1073–1079.

Fenton, F. R., Tessier, L., Struening, E. L., *et al.* (1984) A two-year follow-up of a comparative trial of the cost-effectiveness of home and hospital psychiatric treatment. *Canadian Journal of Psychiatry, 29,* 205–211.

Fenton, M., Murphy, B., Wood, J., *et al.* (2002) Loxapine for schizophrenia (Cochrane review). *The Cochrane Library,* Issue 2. Oxford: Update Software.

Fenton, W. S. & McGlashan, T. H. (1995) Schizophrenia: individual psychotherapy. In *Comprehensive Textbook of Psychiatry* (eds. H. Kaplan & B. Sadock), pp. 1007–1018. Baltimore, Maryland: Williams & Wilkins.

Fenton, W. S. & McGlashan, T. H. (1997) 'We can talk: individual psychotherapy for schizophrenia'. *American Journal of Psychiatry, 154,* 1493–1495.

Fenwick, E., Klaxton, K. & Schulpher, M. (2001) Representing uncertainty: the role of cost-effectiveness acceptability curves. *Health Economics, 10,* 779–787.

Flanagan, R. J. (2006) Therapeutic monitoring of antipsychotic drugs. *CPD Clinical Biochemistry, 7,* 3–18.

Fleischhacker, W. W. & Hummer, M. (1997) Drug treatment of schizophrenia in the 1990s. Achievements and future possibilities in optimising outcomes. *Drugs, 53,* 915–929.

Ford, R., Raferty, J., Ryan, P., *et al.* (1997) Intensive case management for people with serious mental illness – site 2: cost effectiveness. *Journal of Mental Health,* 6, 191–199.

Ford, R., Minghella, E., Chalmers, C., *et al.* (2001) Cost consequences of home-based and in-patient based acute psychiatric treatment: results of an implementation study. *Journal of Mental Health,* 10, 467–476.

Foster, K., Meltzer, H., Gill, B., *et al.* (1996) Adults with a psychotic disorder living in the community. *OPCS Surveys of Psychiatric Morbidity in Great Britain,* Report 8. London: HMSO.

Francois, I., Gadreau, M., Gisselmann, A., *et al.* (1993) Contribution to the economic evaluation in psychiatry – a comparison of two establishments for chronic schizophrenic patients in the CHRU of Dijon [in French]. *Journal d'Economie Médicale, 11,* 185–199.

Freeman, D. & Garety, P. A. (2003) Connecting neurosis and psychosis: the direct influence of emotion on delusions and hallucinations. *Behaviour Research and Therapy, 41,* 923–947.

Freud, S. (1914; reprinted, 1953–1974) *On Narcissism: An Introduction.* In *The Standard Edition of the Complete Psychological Works of Sigmund Freud* (trans. and ed. J. Strachey), vol. 14. London: Hogarth Press.

Freud, S. (1933; reprinted, 1953–1974) *New Introductory Lectures on Psycho-Analysis.* In *The Standard Edition of the Complete Psychological Works of Sigmund Freud* (trans. and ed. J. Strachey), vol. 22. London: Hogarth Press.

Frith, C. D. (1992) *The Cognitive Neuropsychology of Schizophrenia.* Hillsdale, NJ: Lawrence Erlbaum.

Fromm-Reichmann, F. (1950) *Principles of Intensive Psychotherapy.* Chicago, Illinois: University of Chicago Press.

Gabbard, G. O. (1994) *Psychodynamic Psychiatry in Clinical Practice: The DSM-IV Edition.* Washington, D.C.: American Psychiatric Press.

Gaebel, W. & Frommann, N. (2000) Long-term course in schizophrenia: concepts, methods and research strategies. *Acta Psychiatrica Scandinavica, 102,* 49–53.

Gaertner, I., Gaertner, H. J., Vonthein, R. I., *et al.* (2001) Therapeutic drug monitoring of clozapine in relapse prevention: a five-year prospective study. *Journal of Clinical Psychopharmacology, 21,* 305–310.

Galletly, C. A., Clark, C. R. & MacFarlane, A. C. (2000) Treating cognitive dysfunction in patients with schizophrenia. *Journal of Psychiatry and Neuroscience, 25,* 117–124.

Galster, G. C., Champney, T. F. & Williams, Y. (1995) Costs of caring for persons with long-term mental illness in alternative residential settings. *Evaluation and Program Planning, 17,* 3.

Ganguly, R., Miller, L. S., Martin, B. C. (2003) Future employability, a new approach to cost-effectiveness analysis of antipsychotic therapy. *Schizophrenia Research, 63,* 111–119.

Garety, P. A. & Hemsley, D. R. (1994) *Delusions. Investigations into the Psychology of Delusional Reasoning.* UK: Psychology Press.

Garety, P. A., Fowler, D. & Kuipers, E. (2000) Cognitive-behavioral therapy for medication-resistant symptoms. *Schizophrenia Bulletin, 26,* 73–86.

Garety, P. A., Kuipers, E., Fowler, D., *et al.* (2001) A cognitive model of the positive symptoms of psychosis. *Psychological Medicine, 31,* 189–195.

Garety, P. A., Bebbington, P., Fowler, D., *et al.* (2007) Implications for neurobiological research of cognitive models of psychosis: a theoretical paper. *Psychological Medicine, 37,* 1377–1391.

Garety, P. A., Fowler, D. G., Freeman, D., *et al.* (2008) A randomised controlled trial of cognitive behavioural therapy and family intervention for the prevention of relapse and reduction of symptoms in psychosis. *British Journal of Psychiatry, 192,* 412–423.

Gater, R., Goldberg, D., Jackson, G., *et al.* (1997) The care of patients with chronic schizophrenia: a comparison between two services. *Psychological Medicine, 27,* 1325–1336.

Geddes, J., Freemantle, N., Harrison, P., *et al.* (2000) Atypical antipsychotics in the treatment of schizophrenia: systematic overview and meta-regression analysis. *British Medical Journal, 321,* 1371–1376.

Geitona, M., Kousoulakou, H., Ollandezos, M., *et al.* (2008) Costs and effects of paliperidone extended release compared with alternative oral antipsychotic agents in patients with schizophrenia in Greece: a cost effectiveness study. *Annals of General Psychiatry, 7,* 16.

Gelder, M., Mayou, R. & Geddes, J. (1997) *Oxford Textbook of Psychiatry.* Oxford: Oxford University Press.

Genc, Y., Taner, E. & Candansayar, S. (2007) Comparison of clozapine-amisulpride and clozapine-quetiapine combinations for patients with schizophrenia who are partially responsive to clozapine: a single-blind randomized study. *Advances in Therapy, 24,* 1–13.

Gilbert, P. L., Harris, M. J., McAdams, L. A., *et al.* (1995) Neuroleptic withdrawal in schizophrenic patients. A review of the literature. *Archives of General Psychiatry, 52,* 173–188.

Gillies, C. L., Lambert, P. C., Abrams, K. R., *et al.* (2008) Different strategies for screening and prevention of type 2 diabetes in adults: cost effectiveness analysis. *British Medical Journal, 336,* 1180–1185.

Gilroy, A. & McNeilly, G. (2000) *The Changing Shape of Art Therapy.* London: Jessica Kingsley Publishers.

Glennie, J. L. (1997) Pharmacoeconomic evaluation in schizophrenia: clozapine in treatment-resistant schizophrenia and risperidone in chronic schizophrenia. Ottawa, Canada: Canadian Coordinating Office for Health Technology Assessment.

Glenny, A. M., Altman, D. G., Song, F., *et al.* (2005) Indirect comparisons of competing interventions. *Health Technology Assessment, 9,* 1–152.

Glover, G., Arts, G. & Babu, K. S. (2006) Crisis resolution/home treatment teams and psychiatric admission rates in England. *British Journal of Psychiatry, 189,* 441–445.

Godleski, L. S. & Sernyak, M. J. (1996) Agranulocytosis after addition of risperidone to clozapine treatment. *American Journal of Psychiatry, 153,* 735–736.

Goeree, R., Farahati, F., Burke, N., *et al.* (2005) The economic burden of schizophrenia in Canada in 2004. *Current Medical Research and Opinion*, *21*, 2017–2028.

Goldstein, M. J. (1996) Psychoeducational family programs in the United States. In *Handbook of Mental Health Economics and Health Policy*, vol. 1: *Schizophrenia.* (eds M. Moscarelli, A. Rupp & N. Sartorius). New York: John Wiley.

Gray, J., Feldon, J., Rawlins, J., *et al.* (1991) The neuropsychology of schizophrenia. *Behavioral and Brain Sciences*, *14*, 1–84.

Gray, R., Leese, M., Bindman, J., *et al.* (2006) Adherence therapy for people with schizophrenia: European multicentre randomised controlled trial. *British Journal of Psychiatry*, *189*, 508–514.

Green, B. (1987) Group art therapy as an adjunct to treatment for chronic outpatients. *Hospital and Community Psychiatry*, *38*, 988–991.

Green, M. F. (1992) Neuropsychological performance in the unaffected twin. *Archives of General Psychiatry*, *49*, 247.

Green, M. F. (1993) Cognitive remediation in schizophrenia: is it time yet? *American Journal of Psychiatry*, *150*, 178–187.

Greene, R., Pugh, R. & Roberts, D. (2008) *Black and Minority Ethnic Parents with Mental Health Problems and Their Children.* Research Briefing no. 29. London: Social Care Institute for Excellence.

Guest, J. F. & Cookson, R. F. (1999) Cost of schizophrenia to UK society. An incidence-based cost-of-illness model for the first 5 years following diagnosis. *Pharmacoeconomics*, *15*, 597–610.

Gulbinat, W., Dupont, A., Jablensky, A., *et al.* (1992) Cancer incidence of schizophrenic patients: results of linkage studies in three countries. *British Journal of Psychiatry*, *161* (Suppl. 18), 75–83.

Haddad, P. M. & Wieck, A. (2004) Antipsychotic-induced hyperprolactinaemia: mechanisms, clinical features and management. *Drugs*, *64*, 2291–2314.

Hallam, A. & Schneider, J. (1999) Sheltered work schemes for people with severe mental health problems: service use and costs. *Journal of Mental Health*, *8*, 171–186.

Hamilton, S. H., Revicki, D. A., Edgell, E. T., *et al.* (1999) Clinical and economic outcomes of olanzapine compared with haloperidol for schizophrenia. Results from a randomised clinical trial. *Pharmacoeconomics*, *15*, 469–480.

Haro, J. M., Suarez, D., Novick, D., *et al.* (2007) Three-year antipsychotic effectiveness in the outpatient care of schizophrenia: observational versus randomized studies results. *European Neuropsychopharmacology*, *17*, 235–244.

Harrigan, S., McGorry, P. & Krstev, H. (2003) Does treatment delay in first-episode psychosis really matter? *Psychological Medicine*, *33*, 97–110.

Harrington, M., Lelliot, P., Paton, C., *et al.* (2002) Variation between services in polypharmacy and combined high dose of antipsychotic drugs prescribed for in-patients. *Psychiatric Bulletin*, *26*, 418–420.

Harris, E. C. & Barraclough, B. (1998) Excess mortality of mental disorder. *British Journal of Psychiatry*, *173*, 11–53.

Harrison, G., Hopper, K., Craig, T., *et al.* (2001) Recovery from psychotic illness: a 15- and 25-year international follow-up study. *British Journal of Psychiatry*, *178*, 506–517.

Harrow, M., Grossman, L. S., Jobe, T. H., *et al.* (2005) Do patients with schizophrenia ever show periods of recovery? A 15 year multi-follow-up study. *Schizophrenia Bulletin, 31,* 723–734.

Hasselblad, V. (1998) Meta-analysis of multi-treatment studies. *Medical Decision Making, 18,* 37–43.

Hatfield, B., Huxley, P. & Mohamad, H. (1992) Accommodation and employment: a survey into the circumstances and expressed needs of users of mental health services in a northern town. *British Journal of Social Work, 22,* 60–73.

Healey, A., Knapp, M., Astin, J., *et al.* (1998) Cost-effectiveness evaluation of compliance therapy for people with psychosis. *British Journal of Psychiatry, 172,* 420–424.

Healthcare Commission (2008) *Count Me In 2008: Results of the 2008 National Census of Inpatients in Mental Health and Learning Disability Services in England and Wales.* London: Commission for Healthcare Audit and Inspection.

Healthtalkonline (2008) http://www.healthtalkonline.org.uk [accessed December 2008]

Healy, D. (2002) *The Creation of Psychopharmacology.* Cambridge, MA: Harvard University Press.

Heeg, B., Buskens, E., Knapp, M., *et al.* (2005) Modelling the treated course of schizophrenia: development of a discrete event simulation model. *Pharmacoeconomics, 23* (Suppl. 1), 17–33.

Heeg, B. M., Antunes, J., Figueira, M. L., *et al.* (2008) Cost-effectiveness and budget impact of long-acting risperidone in Portugal: a modelling exercise. *Current Medical Research Opinion, 24,* 349–358.

Heinrichs, D. W., Hanlon, T. E. & Carpenter, W. T. (1984) The quality of life scale: an instrument for rating the schizophrenic deficit syndrome. *Schizophrenia Bulletin, 10,* 338–398.

Hemsley, D. R. (1993) A simple (or simplistic?) cognitive model for schizophrenia. *Behavioural Research and Therapy, 31,* 633–645.

Hennekens, C. H., Hennekens, A. R., Hollar, D., *et al.* (2005) Schizophrenia and increased risks of cardiovascular disease. *American Heart Journal, 150,* 1115–1121.

Hersen, M. & Bellack, A. (1976) Social skills training for chronic psychiatric patients: rationale, research findings and future directions. *Comprehensive Psychiatry, 17,* 559–580.

Herz, M. I., Endicott, J., Spitzer, R. L., *et al.* (1971) Day versus in-patient hospitalization: a controlled study. *American Journal of Psychiatry, 10,* 1371–1382.

Higgins, J. P. T. & Green, S., eds. (2005) *Cochrane Handbook for Systematic Reviews of Interventions 4.2.5* [updated May 2005]. In *The Cochrane Library,* Issue 3. Chichester: John Wiley & Sons.

Higgins, J. P. T. & Thompson, S. G. (2002) Quantifying heterogeneity in a meta-analysis. *Statistics in Medicine, 21,* 1539–1558.

Higgins, J. P. T. & Whitehead, A. (1996) Borrowing strength from external trials in a meta-analysis. *Statistics in Medicine, 15,* 2733–2749.

Hirsch, S. R. & Barnes, T. R. E. (1995) The clinical treatment of schizophrenia with antipsychotic medication. In *Schizophrenia* (eds S. R. Hirsch & D. R. Weinberger), pp. 443–468. Oxford: Blackwell.

HMSO (2005) *The Mental Capacity Act 2005*. London: the Stationery Office. Available at: http://www.opsi.gov.uk/acts/acts2005/pdf/ukpga_20050009_en.pdf

HMSO (2007) *The Mental Health Act 2007*. London: the Stationery Office. Available at: http://www.opsi.gov.uk/acts/acts2007/pdf/ukpga_20070012_en.pdf

Hogarty, G. E., Ulrich, R. F., Mussare, F., *et al.* (1976) Drug discontinuation among long term, successfully maintained schizophrenic outpatients. *Diseases of the Nervous System, 37*, 494–500.

Hoge, M. A., Davidson, L., Leonard, H. W., *et al.* (1992) The promise of partial hospitalization: a reassessment. *Hospital and Community Psychiatry, 43*, 345–354.

Hollister, L. E. (1974) Clinical differences among phenothiazines in schizophrenics. Introduction: specific indications for antipsychotics: elusive end of the rainbow. *Advanced Biochemical Psychopharmacology, 9*, 667–673.

Holt, R. I. G., Bushe, C. & Citrome, L. (2005) Diabetes and schizophrenia 2005: are we any closer to understanding the link? *Journal of Psychopharmacology, 19*, 56–65.

Honer, W. G., Thornton, A. E., Chen, E. Y. H., *et al.* (2006) Clozapine alone versus clozapine and risperidone with refractory schizophrenia. *New England Journal of Medicine, 354*, 472–482.

Hosalli, P. & Davis, J. M. (2003) Depot risperidone for schizophrenia (Cochrane review). *The Cochrane Library*, Issue 4. Oxford: Update Software.

Hu, T. W. & Jerrell, J. M. (1998) Estimating the cost impact of three case management programmes for treating people with severe mental illness. *British Journal of Psychiatry*, Suppl. *36*, 26–32.

Iqbal, M. M., Rahman, A., Husain, Z., *et al.* (2003) Clozapine: a clinical review of adverse effects and management. *Annals of Clinical Psychiatry, 15*, 33–48.

Isaac, M. N. (1996) Trends in the development of psychiatric services in India. *Psychiatric Bulletin, 20*, 43–45.

Issakidis, C., Sanderson., K., Teesson, M., *et al.* (1999) Intensive case management in Australia: a randomised controlled trial. *Acta Psychiatrica Scandinavica, 99*, 360–367.

Jablensky, A., Sartorius, N., Ernberg, G., *et al.* (1992) Schizophrenia: manifestations, incidence and course in different cultures. A World Health Organization ten-country study. *Psychological Medicine Monograph Supplement, 20*, 1–97.

Jablensky, A., McGrath, J., Herrman, H., *et al.* (2000) Psychotic disorders in urban areas. *Australian and New Zealand Journal of Psychiatry, 34*, 221–236.

Jackson, H., McGorry, P., Edwards, J., *et al.* (2005) A controlled trial of cognitively oriented psychotherapy for early psychosis (COPE) with four-year follow-up readmission data. *Psychological Medicine, 35*, 1295–1306.

Jackson H. J., McGorry P. D., Killackey E., *et al.* (2008) Acute-phase and 1-year follow-up results of a randomized controlled trial of CBT versus befriending for first-episode psychosis: the ACE project. *Psychological Medicine, 38*, 725–735.

Jadad, A. R., Moore, R. A., Carroll, D., *et al.* (1996) Assessing the quality of reports of randomized clinical trials: is blinding necessary? *Controlled Clinical Trials, 17*, 1–12.

Janicak, P. G., Davis, J. M., Preskorn, S. H., *et al.* (1993) *Principles and Practice of Psychopharmacotherapy.* Baltimore, MD: Williams & Wilkins.

Jeffreys, S. E., Harvey, C. A., McNaught, A. S., *et al.* (1997) The Hampstead Schizophrenia Survey 1991. I: prevalence and service use comparisons in an inner London health authority, 1986–1991. *British Journal of Psychiatry, 170*, 301–306.

Jerrell, J. M. (1995) Toward managed care for persons with severe mental illness: implications from a cost-effectiveness study. *Health Affairs, 14*, 197–207.

Jerrell, J. M. (2002) Cost-effectiveness of risperidone, olanzapine, and conventional antipsychotic medications. *Schizophrenia Bulletin, 28*, 589–605.

Jeste, D. V., Dgladsjo, J. A., Lindamer, L. A., *et al.* (1996) Medical co-morbidity in schizophrenia. *Schizophrenia Bulletin, 22*, 413–420.

Jobe, T. H. & Harrow, M. (2005) Long-term outcome of patients with schizophrenia: a review. *Canadian Journal of Psychiatry, 50*, 892–900.

Johnson, S., Nolan, F., Pilling, S., *et al.* (2005) Randomised controlled trial of acute mental health care by a crisis resolution team: the north Islington crisis study. *British Medical Journal, 331*, 599–603.

Johnston, S., Salkeld, G., Sanderson, K., *et al.* (1998) Intensive case management: a cost effectiveness analysis. *Australian and New Zealand Journal of Psychiatry, 32*, 551–559.

Johnstone, E. C., Owen, D. G., Gold, A., *et al.* (1984) Schizophrenic patients discharged from hospital – a follow up study. *British Journal of Psychiatry, 145*, 586–590.

Jones, C., Cormac, I., Mota, J., *et al.* (1999) Cognitive behaviour therapy for schizophrenia (Cochrane review). *The Cochrane Library*, Issue 1. Oxford: Update Software.

Jones, P. (1996) *Drama as Therapy: Theatre as Living.* London: Routledge.

Jones, P. B., Barnes, T. R. E., Davies, L., *et al.* (2006) Randomized controlled trial of the effect on quality of life of second- versus first-generation antipsychotic drugs in schizophrenia: Cost Utility of the Latest Antipsychotic Drugs in Schizophrenia Study (CUtLASS 1). *Archives of General Psychiatry, 63*, 1079–1087.

Josiassen, R. C., Ashok, J., Kohegyi, E., *et al.* (2005) Clozapine augmented with risperidone in the treatment of schizophrenia: a randomized, double-blind, placebo-controlled trial. *American Journal of Psychiatry, 162*, 130–136.

Joy, C. B., Adams, C. E. & Rice, K. (2002) Crisis intervention for people with severe mental illnesses (Cochrane review). *Cochrane Library*, Issue 1. Oxford: Update Software.

Kai, J., Crosland, A. & Drinkwater, C. (2000) Prevalence of enduring and disabling mental illness in the inner city. *British Journal of General Practice, 50*, 922–924.

Kane, J. M. (1987) Treatment of schizophrenia. *Schizophrenia Bulletin, 13*, 133–156.

Kane, J. M. (1990) Treatment programme and long-term outcome in chronic schizophrenia. *Acta Psychiatrica Scandanvica Supplement, 82*, 151–157.

Kane, J. M. & Marder, S. R. (1993) Psychopharmacologic treatment of schizophrenia. *Schizophrenia Bulletin, 19*, 287–302.

Kane, J. M., Woerner, M. & Lieberman, J. (1985) Tardive dyskinesia: prevalence, incidence, and risk factors. *Psychopharmacology Supplementum, 2*, 72–78.

Kane, J. M., Honigfeld, G., Singer, J., *et al.* (1988) Clozapine for treatment resistant schizophrenic: a double blind comparison with chlorpromazine. *Archives of General Psychiatry, 45*, 789–796.

Kane, J. M., Schooler, N. R., Marder, S., *et al.* (1996) Efficacy of clozapine versus haloperidol in a long-term clinical trial. *Schizophrenia Research, 18*, 127.

Kane, J. M., Marder, S. R., Schooler, N. R., *et al.* (2001) Clozapine and haloperidol in moderately refractory schizophrenia. *Archives of General Psychiatry, 58*, 965–972.

Kapur, S. (2003) Psychosis as a state of aberrant salience: a framework linking biology, phenomenology, and pharmacology in schizophrenia. *American Journal of Psychiatry, 160*, 13–23.

Kapur, S. & Remington, G. (2001) Dopamine D(2) receptors and their role in atypical antipsychotic action: still necessary and may even be sufficient. *Biological Psychiatry, 50*, 873–883.

Karunakaran, K., Tungaraza, T. E. & Harborne, G. (2006) Is clozapine-aripiprazole combination a useful regime in the management of treatment-resistant schizophrenia? *Journal of Psychopharmacology, 21*, 453–456.

Kasckow, J. W., Twamley, E., Mulchahey, J. J., *et al.* (2001) Health-related quality of well-being in chronically hospitalized patients with schizophrenia: comparison with matched outpatients. *Psychiatry Research, 103*, 69–78.

Kasper, S. & Winkler, D. (2006) Addressing the limitations of the CATIE study. *World Journal of Biological Psychiatry, 7*, 126–127.

Kavanagh, S., Opit, L., Knapp, M., *et al.* (1995) Schizophrenia: shifting the balance of care. *Social Psychiatry and Psychiatric Epidemiology, 30*, 206–212.

Kemp, R., Hayward, P., Applewhaite, G., *et al.* (1996) Compliance therapy in psychotic patients: a randomised controlled trial. *British Medical Journal, 312*, 345–349.

Kemp, R., Kirov, G., Everitt, B., *et al.* (1998) Randomised controlled trial of compliance therapy. 18-month follow-up. *British Journal of Psychiatry, 172*, 413–419.

Kendrick, T., Sibbald, B., Burns, T., *et al.* (1991) Role of general practitioners in care of long term mentally ill patients. *British Medical Journal, 302*, 508–510.

Kendrick, T., Burns, T., Garland, C., *et al.* (2000) Are specialist mental health services being targeted on the most needy patients? The effects of setting up specialist services in general practice. *British Journal of General Practice, 50*, 121–126.

Khan, I. & Pillay, K. (2003) Users' attitudes towards home and hospital treatment: a comparative study between South Asian and white residents of the British Isles. *Journal of Psychiatric and Mental Health Nursing, 10*, 137–146.

Killaspy, H., Bebbington, P., Blizard, R., *et al.* (2006) REACT: a randomised evaluation of assertive community treatment in North London. *British Medical Journal, 332*, 815–820.

Kinon, B. J., Kane, J. M., Johns, C., *et al.* (1993) Treatment of neuroleptic-resistant schizophrenia relapse. *Psychopharmacology Bulletin*, 29, 309–314.

Kirkbride, J. B., Fearon, P., Morgan, C., *et al.* (2006) Heterogeneity in incidence rates of schizophrenia and other psychotic syndromes: findings from the 3-center AeSOP study. *Archives of General Psychiatry*, *63*, 250–258.

Kissling, W. (1991) The current unsatisfactory state of relapse prevention in schizophrenic psychoses: suggestions for improvement. *Clinical Neuropharmacology*, *14* (Suppl. 2), S33–S44.

Klein, D. F. & Davis, J. M. (1969) *Diagnosis and Drug Treatment of Psychiatric Disorders*. Baltimore, MD: Williams & Wilkins.

Kleinman, A. & Benson, P. (2006) Anthropology in the clinic: the problem of cultural competency and how to fix it. *PLoS Medicine*, *3*, e294. Available at: http://medicine.plosjournals.org/perlserv/?request=get-document&doi=10.1371/journal.pmed.0030294&ct=1&SESSID=db116b1403c2772db8f82dff9283573f [accessed December 2008].

Knapp, M. (1997) Costs of schizophrenia. *British Journal of Psychiatry*, *171*, 509–518.

Knapp, M., Marks, I. M., Wolstenholme, J., *et al.* (1998) Home-based versus hospital-based care for serious mental illness: controlled cost-effectiveness study over four years. *British Journal of Psychiatry*, *172*, 506–512.

Knapp, M., Chisholm, D., Leese, M., *et al.* (2002) EPSILON. European Psychiatric Services: Inputs Linked to Outcome Domains and Needs. Comparing patterns and costs of schizophrenia care in five European countries: the EPSILON study. *Acta Psychiatrica Scandinavica*, *105*, 42–54.

Knapp, M., King, D., Pugner, K., *et al.* (2004a) Non-adherence to antipsychotic medication regimens: associations with resource use and costs. *British Journal of Psychiatry*, *184*, 509–516.

Knapp, M., Mangalore, R. & Simon, J. (2004b). The global costs of schizophrenia. *Schizophrenia Bulletin*, *30*, 279–293.

Knapp, M., Windmeijer, F., Brown, J., *et al.* (2008) Cost-utility analysis of treatment with olanzapine compared with other antipsychotic treatments in patients with schizophrenia in the pan-European SOHO study. *Pharmacoeconomics*, *26*, 341–358.

König, H.-H., Roick, C. & Angermeyer, M. C. (2007) Validity of the EQ-5D in assessing and valuing health status in patients with schizophrenic, schizotypal or delusional disorders. *European Psychiatry: the Journal of the Association of European Psychiatrists*, *22*, 177–187.

Kontaxakis, V. P., Havati-Kontaxakis, B. J., Stamouli, S. S., *et al.* (2002) Toxic interaction between risperidone and clozapine: a case report. *Progress in Neuro-psychopharmacology and Biological Psychiatry*, *26*, 407–409.

Kontaxakis, V. P., Ferentinos, P. P., Havaki-Kontaxaki, B. J., *et al.* (2005) Randomised controlled augmentation trials in clozapine-resistant schizophrenic patients: a critical review. *European Psychiatry*, *20*, 409–415.

Koro, C. E., Fedder, D. O., L'Italien, G. J., *et al.* (2002) Assessment of independent effect of olanzapine and risperidone on risk of diabetes among patients with schizophrenia: population based nested case-control study. *British Medical Journal, 325*, 243.

Krabbendam, L. & van Os, J. (2005) Affective processes in the onset and persistence of psychosis. *European Archives of Psychiatry and Clinical Neuroscience, 255*, 185–189.

Kreyenbuhl, J. A., Valensteen, M., McCarthy, J. F., *et al.* (2007) Long-term antipsychotic polypharmacy in the VA health system: patient and treatment patterns. *Psychiatric Services, 58*, 489–495.

Kris, E. B. (1965) Day hospitals. *Current Therapeutic Research, 7*, 320–323.

Kuipers, E., Fowler, D., Garety, P., *et al.* (1998) London–East Anglia randomised controlled trial of cognitive-behavioural therapy for psychosis. III: Follow-up and economic evaluation at 18 months. *British Journal of Psychiatry, 173*, 61–68.

Kurtz, M. M. & Mueser, K. T. (2008) A meta-analysis of controlled research on social skills training in schizophrenia. *Journal of Consulting and Clinical Psychology, 76*, 491–504.

Lambert, M., Naber, D., Schacht, A., *et al.* (2008) Rates and predictors of remission and recovery during 3 years in 392 never-treated patients with schizophrenia. *Acta Psychiatrica Scandinavia, 118*, 220–229.

Lamberti, J. S. & Herz, M. I. (1995) Psychotherapy, social skills training, and vocational rehabilitation in schizophrenia. In *Contemporary Issues in the Treatment of Schizophrenia* (eds C. L. Shriqui & H. A. Nasrallah). Washington DC: American Psychiatric Press.

Lang, F. H., Forbes, J. F., Murray, G. D., *et al.* (1997a) Service provision for people with schizophrenia. I. Clinical and economic perspective. *British Journal of Psychiatry, 171*, 159–164.

Lang, F., Johnstone, E. & Murray, D. (1997b) Service provision for people with schizophrenia. Role of the general practitioner. *British Journal of Psychiatry, 171*, 165–168.

Launois, R., Von Der Schulenburg, M. G., Knapp, M., *et al.* (1998) Cost-effectiveness of sertindole versus olanzapine or haloperidol: a comprehensive model. *International Journal of Psychiatry in Clinical Practice, 2* (Suppl. 2), S79–S86.

Laux, G., Heeg, B. M. S., van Hout, B. A., *et al.* (2005) Costs and effects of long-acting risperidone compared with oral atypical and conventional depot formulations in Germany. *Pharmacoeconomics, 23* (Suppl. 1), 49–61.

Lawrence, D. M., Holman, C. D., Jablensky, A. V., *et al.* (2003) Death rate from ischaemic heart disease in Western Australian psychiatric patients 1980–1998. *British Journal of Psychiatry, 182*, 31–36.

Lecomte, P., De Hert, M., van Dijk, M., *et al.* (2000) A 1-year cost-effectiveness model for the treatment of chronic schizophrenia with acute exacerbations in Belgium. *Value in Health, 3*, 1–11.

Leff, J. P., Kuipers, L., Berkowitz, R., *et al.* (1982) A controlled trial of social interventions in the families of schizophrenic patients. *British Journal of Psychiatry, 141*, 121–134.

Leff, J. P., Sharpley, M., Chisholm, D., *et al.* (2001) Training community psychiatric nurses in schizophrenia family work: a study of clinical and economic outcomes for patients and relatives. *Journal of Mental Health, 10,* 189–197.

Lehman, A. F., Dixon, L. B., Kernan, E., *et al.* (1995) Assertive treatment for the homeless mentally ill. In *Proceedings of the 148th Annual Meeting of the American Psychiatric Association.* Miami, FL: American Psychiatric Association.

Lehman, A. F., Steinwachs, D. M. & PORT Co-investigators (1998) Patterns of usual care for schizophrenia: initial survey results from the Schizophrenia Patient Outcomes Research Team (PORT) survey. *Schizophrenia Bulletin, 24,* 11–20.

Lehman, A. F., Dixon, L., Hoch, J. S., *et al.* (1999) Cost-effectiveness of assertive community treatment for homeless persons with severe mental illness. *British Journal of Psychiatry, 174,* 346–352.

Lenert, L. A., Sturley, A. P., Rapaport, M. H., *et al.* (2004) Public preferences for health states with schizophrenia and a mapping function to estimate utilities from positive and negative symptom scale scores. *Schizophrenia Research, 71,* 155–165.

Leucht, S. & Hartung, B. (2002) Benperidol for schizophrenia (Cochrane review). *The Cochrane Library,* Issue 2. Oxford: Update Software.

Leucht, S., Barnes, T. R. E., Kissling, W., *et al.* (2003) Relapse prevention in schizophrenia with new generation antipsychotics: a systematic review and explorative meta-analysis of randomized controlled trials. *American Journal of Psychiatry, 160,* 1209–1222.

Lewis, S. W., Davies, L., Jones, P. B., *et al.* (2006a) Randomised controlled trials of conventional antipsychotic versus new atypical drugs, and new atypical drugs versus clozapine, in people with schizophrenia responding poorly to, or intolerant of, current drug treatment. *Health Technology Assessment, 10,* 1–165.

Lewis, S. W., Barnes, T. R. E., Davies, L., *et al.* (2006b) Randomised controlled trial of effect of prescription of clozapine versus other second generation antipsychotic drugs in resistant schizophrenia. *Schizophrenia Bulletin, 32,* 715–723.

Liberman, R. P., Cardin, V., McGill, C. W., *et al.* (1987) Behavioral family management of schizophrenia: clinical outcome and costs. *Psychiatric Annals, 17,* 610–619.

Liddel, J., Williamson, M. & Irwig, L. (1996) *Method for Evaluating Research and Guideline Evidence.* Sydney: New South Wales Health Department.

Lieberman, J. A. (2006) Comparative effectiveness of antipsychotic drugs. A commentary on: Cost Utility of the Latest Antipsychotic Drugs in Schizophrenia Study (CUtLASS 1) and Clinical Antipsychotic Trials of Intervention Effectiveness (CATIE). *Archives of General Psychiatry, 63,* 1069–1072.

Lieberman, J. A., Jody, D., Geisler, S., *et al.* (1989) Treatment outcome of first episode schizophrenia. *Psychopharmacology Bulletin, 25,* 92–96.

Lieberman, J. A., Alvir, J. M., Woerner, M., *et al.* (1992) Prospective study of psychobiology in first-episode schizophrenia at Hillside Hospital. *Schizophrenia Bulletin, 18,* 351–371.

Lieberman, J., Jody, D., Geisler, S., *et al.* (1993) Time course and biologic correlates of treatment response in first-episode schizophrenia. *Archives of General Psychiatry, 50,* 369–376.

Lieberman, J. A., Stroup, S., Clinical Antipsychotic Trials of Intervention Effectiveness (CATIE) Investigators, *et al.* (2005) Effectiveness of antipsychotic drugs in patients with chronic schizophrenia. *New England Journal of Medicine*, *353*, 1209–1223.

Lindenmayer, J. P., Czobor, P., Volavka, J., *et al.* (2002) Olanzapine in refractory schizophrenia after failure of typical or atypical antipsychotic treatment: an open-label switch study. *Journal of Clinical Psychiatry*, *63*, 931–935.

Lindenmayer, J. P., Czobor, P., Volavka, J., *et al.* (2003) Changes in glucose and cholesterol levels in patients with schizophrenia treated with typical or atypical antipsychotics. *American Journal of Psychiatry*, *160*, 290–296.

Lindsley, O. R. (1963) Direct measurement and functional definition of vocal hallucinatory symptoms. *Journal of Experimental Analysis of Behavior*, *2*, 269.

Linszen, D., Dingemans, P. & Lenoir, M. (2001) Early intervention and a five-year follow-up in young adults with a short duration of untreated psychosis: ethical implications. *Schizophrenia Research*, *51*, 55–61.

Llorca, P. M., Lancon, C., Disdier, B., *et al.* (2002) Effectiveness of clozapine in neuroleptic-resistant schizophrenia: clinical response and plasma concentrations. *Journal of Psychiatry and Neuroscience*, *27*, 30–37.

Loebel, A. D., Lieberman, J. A., Alvir, J. M., *et al.* (1992) Duration of psychosis and outcome in first-episode schizophrenia. *American Journal of Psychiatry*, *149*, 1183–1188.

Lu, G. & Ades, A. E. (2004) Combination of direct and indirect evidence in mixed treatment comparisons. *Statistics in Medicine*, *23*, 3105–3124.

Lu, G. & Ades, A. E. (2006) Assessing evidence inconsistency in mixed treatment comparisons. *Journal of the American Statistical Association*, *101*, 447–459.

Lunn, D. J., Thomas, A., Best, N., *et al.* (2000) WinBUGS – a Bayesian modelling framework: concepts, structure, and extensibility. *Statistics and Computing*, *10*, 325–337.

Mackin, P., Bishop, D., Watkinson, H., *et al.* (2007) Metabolic disease and cardiovascular risk in people treated with antipsychotics in the community. *British Journal of Psychiatry*, *191*, 23–29.

MacMillan, J. F., Crow, T. J., Johnson, A. L., *et al.* (1986) Short-term outcome in trial entrants and trial eligible patients. *British Journal of Psychiatry*, *148*, 128–133.

Malmberg, L. & Fenton, M. (2001) Individual psychodynamic psychotherapy and psychoanalysis for schizophrenia and severe mental illness (Cochrane review). *The Cochrane Library*, Issue 4. Oxford: Update Software.

Mangalore, R. & Knapp, M. (2007) Cost of schizophrenia in England. *The Journal of Mental Health Policy and Economics*, *10*, 23–41.

Mann, T. (1996) *Clinical Guidelines: Using Clinical Guidelines to Improve Patient Care Within the NHS*. London: Department of Health NHS Executive.

Marder, S. R. & Wirshing, D. A. (2003) Maintenance treatment. In *Schizophrenia*. 2nd edition (eds S.R. Hirsch & D.R. Weinberger). Oxford: Blackwell

Mari, J. & Streiner, D. (1999) Family intervention for schizophrenia (Cochrane review). *The Cochrane Library*, Issue 1. Oxford: Update Software.

Marks, I. M., Connolly, J., Muijen, M., *et al.* (1994) Home-based versus hospital-based care for people with serious mental illness. *British Journal of Psychiatry, 165*, 179–194.

Marshall, M. & Lockwood, A. (2002) Assertive community treatment for people with severe mental disorders (Cochrane review). *The Cochrane Library*, Issue 3. Oxford: Update Software.

Marshall, M., Crowther, R., Almaraz-Serrano, A., *et al.* (2001) Systematic reviews of the effectiveness of day care for people with severe mental disorders: (1) acute day hospital versus admission; (2) vocational rehabilitation; (3) day hospital versus outpatient care. *Health Technology Assessment, 5.* [Also available in Marshall, M., Crowther, R., Almaraz-Serrano, A. M., *et al.* (2002) Day hospital versus out-patient care for psychiatric disorders (Cochrane review). *The Cochrane Library*, Issue 3. Oxford: Update Software.]

Marshall, M., Gray, A., Lockwood, A., *et al.* (2002) Case management for people with severe mental disorders (Cochrane review). *The Cochrane Library*, Issue 3. Oxford: Update Software.

Marwaha, S. & Johnson, S. (2004) Schizophrenia and employment–a review. *Social Psychiatry and Psychiatric Epidemiology, 39*, 337–349.

May, P. R. A. (ed.) (1968) *Treatment of Schizophrenia.* New York: Science House.

McCabe, R. & Priebe, S. (2004) The therapeutic relationship in the treatment of severe mental illness: a review of methods and findings *International Journal of Social Psychiatry, 50*, 115–128.

McCarthy, R. H. (1994) Seizures following smoking cessation in a clozapine responder. *Pharmacopsychiatry, 27*, 210–211.

McCarthy, R. H. & Terkelsen, K. G. (1995) Risperidone augmentation of clozapine. *Pharmacopsychiatry, 28*, 61–63.

McCreadie, R. G. (1992) The Nithsdale schizophrenia surveys. An overview. *Social Psychiatry and Psychiatric Epidemiology, 27*, 40–45.

McCreadie, R., on behalf of The Scottish Schizophrenia Lifestyle Group (2003) Diet, smoking and cardiovascular risk in people with schizophrenia: descriptive study. *British Journal of Psychiatry, 183*, 534–539.

McCrone, P., Beecham, J. & Knapp, M. (1994) Community psychiatric nurse teams: cost-effectiveness of intensive support versus generic care. *British Journal of Psychiatry, 165*, 218–221.

McCrone, P., Thornicroft, G., Phelan, M., *et al.* (1998) Utilisation and costs of community mental health services. PRiSM Psychosis Study 5. *British Journal of Psychiatry, 173*, 391–398.

McEvoy, J. P., Schooler, N. R. & Wilson, W. H. (1991) Predictors of therapeutic response to haloperidol in acute schizophrenia. *Psychopharmacology Bulletin, 27*, 97–101.

McFarlane, W. R., Lukens, E., Link, B., *et al.* (1995a) Multiple-family groups and psychoeducation in the treatment of schizophrenia. *Archives of General Psychiatry, 52*, 679–687.

McFarlane, W. R., Link, B., Dushay, R., *et al.* (1995b) Psychoeducational multiple family groups: four-year relapse outcome in schizophrenia. *Family Processes, 34*, 127–144.

McGorry, P. D., Edwards, J., Mihalopoulos, C., *et al.* (1996) EPPIC: An evolving system of early detection and optimal management. *Schizophrenia Bulletin, 22,* 305–326.

McGorry, P. D., Yung, A. R., Phillips, L. J., *et al.* (2002) A randomized controlled trial of interventions designed to reduce the risk of progression to first episode psychosis in a clinical sample with subthreshold symptoms. *Archives of General Psychiatry, 59,* 921–928.

McGrath, J. J. (2006) Variations in the incidence of schizophrenia: data versus dogma. *Schizophrenia Bulletin, 32,* 195–197.

McGrath, J., Saha, S., Chant, D., *et al.* (2008) Schizophrenia: a concise overview of incidence, prevalence, and mortality. *Epidemiologic Reviews, 30,* 67–76.

McGrew, J. H. & Bond, G. R. (1995) Critical ingredients of assertive community treatment: judgments of the experts. *Journal of Mental Health Administration, 22,* 113–125.

McGrew, J. H., Bond, G. R, Dietzen, L., *et al.* (1994) Measuring the fidelity of implementation of a mental health program model. *Journal of Consulting and Clinical Psychology, 62,* 670–678.

McGurk, S. R., Twamley, E. W., Sitzer, D. I., *et al.* (2007) A meta-analysis of cognitive remediation in schizophrenia. *American Journal of Psychiatry, 164,* 1791–1802.

McIntosh, A. M., Conlon, L., Lawrie, S. M, *et al.* (2006) Compliance therapy for schizophrenia. (Cochrane review). *The Cochrane Library,* Issue 3. Oxford: Update Software.

McKenzie, K. & Bhui, K. (2007) Institutional racism in mental health care. *British Medical Journal, 31,* 649–650.

Meaney, A. M., Smith, S., Howes, O. D., *et al.* (2004) Effects of long-term prolactin-raising antipsychotic medication on bone mineral density in patients with schizophrenia. *British Journal of Psychiatry, 184,* 503–508.

Meekums, B. (2002) *Dance Movement Therapy: A Creative Psychotherapeutic Approach.* London: Sage

Meltzer, H. Y, Gill, B., Petticrew, M., *et al.* (1995) *Office of Population Censuses and Surveys: Surveys of Psychiatric Morbidity in Great Britain.* Vol. 2. London: HMSO.

Melzer, D., Hale, A. S., Malik, S. J., *et al.* (1991) Community care for patients with schizophrenia one year after hospital discharge. *British Medical Journal, 303,* 1023–1026.

Merson, S., Tyrer, P., Onyett, S., *et al.* (1992) Early intervention in psychiatric emergencies: a controlled clinical trial. *Lancet, 339,* 1311–1314.

Merson, S., Tyrer, P., Carlen, D., *et al.* (1996) The cost of treatment of psychiatric emergencies: a comparison of hospital and community services. *Psychological Medicine, 26,* 727–734.

Mihalopoulos, C., McGorry, P. D. & Carter, R. C. (1999) Is phase-specific, community-oriented treatment of early psychosis an economically viable method of improving outcome? *Acta Psychiatrica Scandinavica, 100,* 47–55.

Miller, W. R. & Rollnick, S. (1991) *Motivational Interviewing: Preparing People to Change Addictive Behaviour.* New York: Guilford Press.

471

Mind (2005) *Fact Sheet – Statistics 5: The Financial Aspects of Mental Health Problems*. Available at: http://www.mind.org.uk/help/social_factors/statistics_5_the_financial_aspects_of_mental_health_problem [accessed September 2007]

Moffat, J., Sass, B., McKenzie, K., *et al.* (2008) Improving pathways into mental health care for black and ethnic minority groups: a systematic review of the grey literature. *International Review of Psychiatry, 21*, 439–449.

Mohan, R., McCrone, P., Szmukler, G., *et al.* (2006) Ethnic differences in mental health service use among patients with psychotic disorders. *Social Psychiatry and Psychiatric Epidemiology, 41*, 771–776.

Möller, H. J. (2008) Do effectiveness ('real world') studies on antipsychotics tell us the real truth? *European Archives of Psychiatry and Clinical Neuroscience, 258*, 257–270.

Möller, H. J. & van Zerssen, D. (1995) Course and outcome of schizophrenia. In *Schizophrenia* (eds S. R. Hirsch & D. R. Weinberger), pp. 106–127. Oxford: Blackwell.

Moore, T. H. M., Zammit, S., Lingford-Hughes, A., *et al.* (2007) Cannabis use and risk of psychotic or affective mental health outcomes: a systematic review. *Lancet, 370*, 319–328.

Morrison, A. P., French, P., Walford, L., *et al.* (2004) Cognitive therapy for the prevention of psychosis in people at ultra-high risk. Randomised controlled trial. *British Journal of Psychiatry, 185*, 291–297.

Mossaheb, I., Sacher, J., Wiesegger, G., *et al.* (2006) Haloperidol in combination with clozapine in treatment-refractory patients with schizophrenia. *European Neuropsychopharmacology, 16* (Suppl. 4), 416.

Muijen, M., Cooney, M., Strathdee, G., *et al.* (1994) Community psychiatric nurse teams: intensive support versus generic care. *British Journal of Psychiatry, 165*, 211–217.

Murray, C. J. L. & Lopez, A. D. (1996) *The Global Burden of Disease: a Comprehensive Assessment of Mortality and Disability from Diseases, Injuries, and Risk Factors in 1990 and Projected to 2020*. Cambridge, MA: Harvard University Press.

Nadeem, Z., McIntosh, A. & Lawrie, S. (2004) EBMH notebook: schizophrenia. *Evidence-Based Mental Health, 7*, 2–3.

Nasrallah, H. (2003) A review of the effect of atypical antipsychotics on weight. *Psychoneuroendocrinology, 28* (Suppl. 1), 83–96.

Nasrallah, H. A. (2008) Atypical antipsychotic-induced metabolic side effects: insights from receptor-binding profiles. *Molecular Psychiatry, 13*, 27–35.

Nasrallah, H. A., Meyer, J. M., Goff, D. C., *et al.* (2006) Low rates of treatment for hypertension, dyslipidemia and diabetes in schizophrenia: data from the CATIE schizophrenia trial sample at baseline. *Schizophrenia Research, 86*, 15–22.

National Institute for Mental Health in England (2003) *NIMHE Inside Outside. Improving Mental Health Services for Black and Minority Ethnic Communities*. London: Department of Health. Available at: www.nimhe.org.uk/downloads/inside_outside.pdf

National Institute for Mental Health in England (2005) *NIMHE Guiding Statement on Recovery*. London: National Institute for Mental Health in England.

Nazareth, I., King, M., Haines, A., *et al.* (1993) Accuracy of diagnosis of psychosis on a general practice computer system. *British Medical Journal, 307*, 32–34.

NCCMH (2003) *Schizophrenia: Full National Clinical Guideline on Core Interventions in Primary and Secondary Care*. London: Gaskell.

NCCMH (2006) *The Management of Bipolar Disorder in Adults, Children and Adolescents, in Primary and Secondary Care*. Leicester & London: The British Psychological Society and Gaskell.

NEPP (2002) *National Early Psychosis Project*. Available at: http://www.earlypsychosis.org/index.htm

Newcomer, J. W. (2007) Antipsychotic medications: metabolic and cardiovascular risk. *Journal of Clinical Psychiatry, 68* (Suppl. 4), 8–13.

Newcomer, J. W. & Haupt, D. W. (2006) The metabolic effects of antipsychotic medications. *Canadian Journal of Psychiatry, 51*, 480–491.

NHS, Business Services Authority, Prescription Pricing Division (2008) *Electronic Drug Tariff for England and Wales, June 2008*. Compiled on behalf of the Department of Health. Available at: http://www.ppa.org.uk/edt/June_2008/mindex.htm [accessed December 2008]

NHS Employers (2006) *Pay Circular (AforC) 1/2006. Pay and Conditions for NHS Staff Covered by the Agenda for Change Agreement*. London: NHS Employers.

NHS, The Information Centre (2008a). *Hospital Episode Statistics 2006–07*. London: The NHS Information Centre. Available at: http://www.hesonline.nhs.uk

NHS, The Information Centre (2008b) *Prescription Cost Analysis England 2007*. London: The NHS Information Centre, Prescribing Support Unit, NHS. Available at: http://www.ic.nhs.uk/pubs/prescostanalysis2007

NHS, The Information Centre (2008c) *Average Daily Quantity Values, 2008*. London: The NHS Information Centre, Prescribing Support Unit, NHS. Available at: http://www.ic.nhs.uk/webfiles/Services/PSU/adqs_2007_08.pdf

NICE (2002) *Guidance on the Use of Newer (Atypical) Antipsychotic Drugs for the Treatment of Schizophrenia*. Technology Appraisal No. 43. London: NICE.

NICE (2006) *Obesity: Guidance on the Prevention, Identification, Assessment and Management of Overweight and Obesity in Adults and Children*. NICE clinical guideline 43. London: NICE

NICE (2007) *The Guidelines Manual*. London: NICE. Available at: www.nice.org.uk

NICE (2008a) *Guide to the Methods of Technology Appraisal*. London: NICE.

NICE (2008b) *Social Value Judgements. Principles for the Development of NICE Guidance*. 2nd edition. London: NICE.

Nicholls, C. J., Hale, A. S. & Freemantle, N. (2003) Cost-effectiveness of amisulpride compared with risperidone in patients with schizophrenia. *Journal of Drug Assessment, 6*, 79–89.

The Nordic Cochrane Centre, The Cochrane Collaboration (2003) *Review Manager (RevMan)*. Version 4.2.10 for Windows. Copenhagen: The Nordic Cochrane Centre, The Cochrane Collaboration. [Computer programme]

References

The Nordic Cochrane Centre, The Cochrane Collaboration (2008) *Review Manager* (RevMan). Version 5.0. Copenhagen: The Nordic Cochrane Centre, The Cochrane Collaboration. [Computer programme]

Nosè, M., Barbui, C. & Tansella, M. (2003) How often do patients with psychosis fail to adhere to treatment programme? A systematic review. *Psychological Medicine*, *33*, 1149–1160.

Nuechterlein, K. H. (1987) Vulnerability models for schizophrenia: state of the art. In *Search for the Causes of Schizophrenia* (eds H. Hafner, W. F. Gattaz & W. Janzarik), pp. 297–316. Heidelberg: Springer.

Nuechterlein, K. H. & Dawson, M. E. (1984) A heuristic vulnerability/stress model of schizophrenic episodes. *Schizophrenia Bulletin*, *10*, 300–312.

Nuechterlein, K. H., Barch, D. M., Gold, J. M., *et al.* (2004) Identification of separable cognitive factors in schizophrenia. S*chizophrenia Research*, *72*, 29–39.

Office for National Statistics (1998) *Labour Force Survey (1997/8)*. London: Office for National Statistics.

Office for National Statistics (2008) *Population Trends 131. Deaths: Age and Sex, Numbers and Rates, 1976 Onwards (England and Wales)*. London: Office for National Statistics. Available at: http://www.statistics.gov.uk/STATBASE/ssdataset.asp?vlnk=9552&More=Y

Oh, P. I., Mittmann, N., Iskedjian, M., *et al.* (2001) Cost-utility of risperidone compared with standard conventional antipsychotics in chronic schizophrenia. *Journal of Medical Economics*, *4*, 137–156.

Oltmanns, T. F. & Neale, J. M. (1975) Schizophrenic performance when distractors are present: attentional deficit or differential task difficulty? *Journal of Abnormal Psychology*, *84*, 205–209.

Oosthuizen, P., Emsley, R. A., Turner, J., *et al.* (2001) Determining the optimal dose of haloperidol in first-episode psychosis. *Journal of Psychopharmacology*, *15*, 251–255.

Osborn, D. P. J. (2001) The poor physical health of people with mental illness. *Western Journal of Medicine*, *175*, 329–332.

Osborn, D. P. J., King, M. B. & Nazareth, I. (2003) Participation in cardiovascular risk screening by people with schizophrenia or similar mental illnesses: a cross sectional study in general practice. *British Medical Journal*, *326*, 1122–1123.

Osborn, D. P. J., King, M. B. & Nazareth, I. (2006) Risk of cardiovascular disease in people with severe mental illness: a cross sectional comparative study in primary care. *British Journal of Psychiatry*, *188*, 271–277.

Osborn, D. P. J., King, M. B., Nazareth, I., *et al.* (2007a) Physical activity, dietary habits and coronary heart disease risk factor knowledge amongst people with severe mental illness. A cross sectional comparative study in primary care. *Social Psychiatry and Psychiatric Epidemiology*, *42*, 787–793.

Osborn, D. P. J., Levy, G., Nazareth, I., *et al.* (2007b) Relative risk of cardiovascular and cancer mortality in people with severe mental illness from the United Kingdom's General Practice Research Database. *Archives of General Psychiatry*, *64*, 242–249.

Osser, D. N. & Sigadel, R. (2001) Short-term in-patient pharmacotherapy of schizophrenia. *Harvard Review of Psychiatry*, *9*, 89–104.

Ozdemir, V., Kalow, W., Posner, P., *et al.* (2002) CYP1A2 activity as measured by a caffeine test predicts clozapine and active metabolite norclozapine steady-state concentration in patients with schizophrenia. *Journal of Clinical Psychopharmacology*, *21*, 398–407.

Palmer, C. S., Revicki, D. A., Genduso, L. A., *et al.* (1998) A cost-effectiveness clinical decision analysis model for schizophrenia. *American Journal of Managed Care*, *4*, 345–355.

Palmer, C. S., Brunner, E., Ruiz-Flores, L. G., Paez-Agraz, F., Revicki, D. A. (2002) A cost-effectiveness clinical decision analysis model for treatment of Schizophrenia. *Archives of Medical Research*, *33*, 572–580.

Pantelis, C. & Lambert, T. J. (2003) Managing patients with 'treatment-resistant' schizophrenia. *Medical Journal of Australia*, *178* (Suppl.), 62–66.

Pantelis, C., Taylor, J. & Campbell, P. (1988) The South Camden Schizophrenia Survey. An experience of community based research. *Bulletin of the Royal College of Psychiatry*, *12*, 98–101.

Papadopoulous, I., Tilki, M. & Lees, S. (2004) Promoting cultural competence in healthcare through a research-based intervention in the UK. *Diversity in Health and Social Care*, *1*, 107–115.

Patel, M. X. & David, A. S. (2005) Why aren't depot antipsychotics prescribed more often and what can be done about it? *Advances in Psychiatric Treatment*, *11*, 203–213.

Paton, C., Lelliott, P., Harrington, M., *et al.* (2003) Patterns of antipsychotic and anticholinergic prescribing for hospital inpatients. *Journal of Psychopharmacology*, *17*, 223–229.

Paton, C., Whittington, C., Barnes, T. R. E. (2007) Augmentation with a second antipsychotic in patients with schizophrenia who partially respond to clozapine: a meta-analysis. *Journal of Clinical Psychopharmacology*, *27*, 198–204.

Paton, C., Barnes, T. R. E., Cavanagh, M.-R., *et al.* (2008) POMH-UK project team. High-dose and combination antipsychotic prescribing in acute adult wards in the UK; the challenges posed by PRN. *British Journal of Psychiatry*, *192*, 435–439.

Pekkala, E. & Merinder, L. (2002) Psychoeducation for schizophrenia (Cochrane review). *The Cochrane Library*, Issue 2. Oxford: Update Software.

Pierides, M. (1994) Mental health services in Cyprus. *Psychiatric Bulletin*, *18*, 425–427.

Pilling, S., Bebbington, P., Kuipers, E., *et al.* (2002) Psychological treatments in schizophrenia: II. Meta-analyses of randomized controlled trials of social skills training and cognitive remediation. *Psychological Medicine*, *32*, 783–791.

Piper, W. E., Rosie, J. S., Azim, H. F. A., *et al.* (1993) A randomized trial of psychiatric day treatment for patients with affective and personality disorders. *Hospital and Community Psychiatry*, *44*, 757–763.

Potter, W. Z., Ko, G. N., Zhang, L. D., *et al.* (1989) Clozapine in China: a review and preview of US/PRC collaboration. *Psychopharmacology*, *99*, S87–S91.

Preston, N. J. & Fazio, S. (2000) Establishing the efficacy and cost effectiveness of community intensive case management of long-term mentally ill: a matched control group study. *Australian and New Zealand Journal of Psychiatry, 34*, 114–121.

Quinlivan, R., Hough, R., Crowell, A., *et al.* (1995) Service utilisation and costs of care for severely mentally ill clients in an intensive case management program. *Psychiatric Services, 46*, 365–371.

Rathod, S., Kingdon, D., Smith, P., *et al.* (2005) Insight into schizophrenia: the effects of cognitive behavioural therapy on the components of insight and association with sociodemographics – data on a previously published randomised controlled trial. *Schizophrenia Research, 74*, 211–219.

Read, J., van Os, J., Morrison, A. P., *et al.* (2005) Childhood trauma, psychosis and schizophrenia: a literature review with theoretical and clinical implications. *Acta Psychiatrica Scandinavica, 112*, 330–350.

Rector, N. A., Seeman, M. V. & Segal, Z. V. (2003) Cognitive therapy for schizophrenia: a preliminary randomized controlled trial. *Schizophrenia Research, 63*, 1–11.

Remington, G., Kapur, S. & Zipursky, R. B. (1998) Pharmacotherapy of first-episode schizophrenia. *British Journal of Psychiatry Suppl., 172*, 66–70.

Repper J. & Perkins R. (2003) *Social Inclusion and Recovery – a Model for Mental Health Practice.* London: Bailliere Tindall.

Rethink (2003) *Just One Per Cent – the Experiences of People Using Mental Health Services.* Kingston upon Thames: Rethink.

Revicki, D.A., Shakespeare, A. & Kind, P. (1996) Preferences for schizophrenia-related health states: a comparison of patients, caregivers and psychiatrists. *International Clinical Psychopharmacology, 11*, 101–108.

Ridgeway, P. & Rapp, C. (1998) *Critical Ingredients Series.* Lawrence, Kansas: Kansas Department of Social and Rehabilitation Services, Commission on Mental Health and Developmental Disabilities.

Roberts, D., Bernard, M., Misca, G., *et al.* (2008) *Experiences of Children and Young People Caring for a Parent with a Mental Health Problem.* Research Briefing no. 24. London: Social Care Institute for Excellence.

Roberts, L., Roalfe, A., Wilson, S., *et al.* (2007) Physical health care of patients with schizophrenia in primary care: a comparative study. *Family Practice, 24*, 34–40.

Robinson, D. G., Woerner, M. G., Alvir, J. M. J., *et al.* (1999a) Predictors of relapse following response from a first episode of schizophrenia or schizoaffective disorder. *Archives of General Psychiatry, 56*, 241–247.

Robinson, D. G., Woerner, M. G., Alvir, J. M., *et al.* (1999b) Predictors of treatment response from a first episode of schizophrenia or schizoaffective disorder. *American Journal of Psychiatry, 156*, 544–549.

Robinson, D. G., Woerner, M. G., Alvir, J. M. J., *et al.* (2002) Predictors of medication discontinuation by patients with first-episode schizophrenia and schizoaffective disorder. *Schizophrenia Research, 57*, 209–219.

Rodgers, J., Black, G., Stobbart, A., *et al.* (2003) Audit of primary care of people schizophrenia in general practice in Lothian. *Quality in Primary Care, 11*, 133–140.

Rogers, S. E., Sciarappa, K., MacDonald-Wilson, K., *et al.* (1995) A benefit-cost analysis of a supported employment model for persons with psychiatric disabilities. *Evaluation and Program Planning, 18,* 105–115.

Rohricht, F. & Priebe, S. (2006) Effect of body-oriented psychological therapy on negative symptoms in schizophrenia: a randomised controlled trial. *Psychological Medicine, 36,* 669–678.

Rosenheck, R. A. & Neale, M. S. (1998) Cost-effectiveness of intensive psychiatric community care for high users of inpatient services. *Archives of General Psychiatry, 55,* 459–466.

Rosenheck, R., Neale, M. & Frisman, L. (1995) Issues in estimating the cost of innovative mental health programs. *Psychiatric Quarterly, 66,* 9–31.

Rosenheck, R., Cramer, J., Xu, W., *et al.* (1997) A comparison of clozapine and haloperidol in hospitalized patients with refractory schizophrenia. *The New England Journal of Medicine, 337,* 809–815.

Rosenheck, R., Perlick, D., Bingham, S., *et al.* (2003) Effectiveness and cost of olanzapine and haloperidol in the treatment of schizophrenia: a randomized controlled trial. *Journal of the American Medical Association, 290,* 2693–2702.

Rosenheck, R. A., Leslie, D. L., Sindelar, J., *et al.* (2006) Cost-effectiveness of second-generation antipsychotics and perphenazine in a randomized trial of treatment for chronic schizophrenia. *American Journal of Psychiatry, 163,* 2080–2089.

Rosser, R., Cottee, M., Rabin, R., *et al.* (1992) Index of health-related quality of life. In *Measures of the Quality of Life and the Uses to Which Such Measures May Be Put* (ed A. Hopkins). London: The Royal College of Physicians.

Rossler, W., Loffler, W., Fatkenheuer, B., *et al.* (1992) Does case management reduce rehospitalisation rates? *Acta Psychiatrica Scandinavica, 86,* 445–449.

Rostami-Hodjegan, A., Amin, A. M., Spencer, E. P., *et al.* (2004) Influence of dose, cigarette smoking, age, sex, and metabolic activity on plasma clozapine concentrations: a predictive model and nomograms to aid clozapine dose adjustment and to assess compliance in individual patients. *Journal of Clinical Psychopharmacology, 24,* 70–78.

Roth, A., Fonagy, P., Parry, G., *et al.* (1996) *What Works for Whom? A Critical Review of Psychotherapy Research.* New York: Guilford.

Royal College of Psychiatrists (2006) *Consensus Statement on High-Dose Antipsychotic Medication.* College Report 138. London: Royal College of Psychiatrists.

Royal College of Psychiatrists (2007) *Improving Services for Refugees and Asylum Seekers: Position Statement.* Available at: http://www.rcpsych.ac.uk/docs/Refugee% 20asylum%20seeker%20consensus%20final.doc [accessed August 2008]

Royal College of Psychiatrists (2008) Personal communication with the Prescribing Observatory for Mental Health [2005 data]. *Regular Oral Daily Prescriptions,* 2006.

Royal College of Psychiatrists' Centre for Quality Improvement (2007) *Accreditation for Acute Inpatient Mental Health Services (AIMS).* Available at: http://www.rcpsych.ac.uk/AIMS [accessed September 2007]

References

Saari, K., Koponen, H., Laitinen, J., *et al.* (2004) Hyperlipidemia in persons using antipsychotic medication: a general population-based birth cohort study. *Journal of Clinical Psychiatry*, *65*, 547–550.

Saddichha, S., Manjunatha, N., Ameen, S., *et al.* (2008) Diabetes and schizophrenia – effect of disease or drug? Results from a randomized, double-blind, controlled prospective study in first-episode schizophrenia. *Acta Psychiatrica Scandinavica*, *117*, 342–347.

Saha, S., Chant, D. & McGrath, J. (2008) Meta-analyses of the incidence and prevalence of schizophrenia: conceptual and methodological issues. *International Journal of Methods in Psychiatric Research*, *17*, 55–61.

Sainsbury Centre for Mental Health (2003) *Policy Paper 3: The Economic and Social Costs of Mental Illness.* London: The Sainsbury Centre for Mental Health. Available at: http://www.scmh.org.uk/80256FBD004F3555/vWeb/flKHAL6XCJ3V/$file/costs_of_mental_illness_policy_paper_3.pdf [accessed October 2007]

Salkever, D., Domino, M. E., Burns, B. J., *et al.* (1999) Assertive community treatment for people with severe mental illness: the effect on hospital use and costs. *Health Services Research*, *34*, 577–601.

Sartorius, N. (2002) Iatrogenic stigma of mental illness. *British Medical Journal*, *324*, 1470–1471.

Sass, B., Moffat, J., Bhui, K., *et al.* (2009) Enhancing pathways to care for black and minority ethnic populations: a systematic review. *International Review of Psychiatry*, *21*, 430–438.

Schizophrenia Patient Outcomes Research Team (1998) *Treatment Recommendations.* Rockville, MD: Agency for Healthcare Quality and Research. Available at: http://www.ahrq.gov/clinic/schzrec.htm

Schooler, N. R. (2003) Relapse and rehospitalisation: comparing oral and depot antipsychotics. *Journal of Clinical Psychiatry*, *64* (Suppl. 16), 14–17.

Sciolla, A., Patterson, T. L., Wetherell, J. L., *et al.* (2003) Functioning and well-being of middle-aged and older patients with schizophrenia: measurement with the 36-item short-form (SF-36) health survey. *American Journal of Geriatric Psychiatry*, *11*, 629–637.

Scottish Intercollegiate Guidelines Network (2001) *SIGN 50: A Guideline Developer's Handbook.* Edinburgh: Scottish Intercollegiate Guidelines Network.

Selten, J. P. & Cantor-Graae, E. (2005) Social defeat: risk factor for schizophrenia? *British Journal of Psychiatry*, *187*, 101–102.

Sevy, S., Nathanson, K., Schechter, C., *et al.* (2001) Contingency valuation and preferences of health states associated with side effects of antipsychotic medications in schizophrenia. *Schizophrenia Bulletin*, *27*, 643–652.

Shalev, A., Hermesh, H., Rothberg, J., *et al.* (1993) Poor neuroleptic response in acutely exacerbated schizophrenic patients. *Acta Psychiatrica Scandinavica*, *87*, 86–91.

Shepherd, G. (1978) Social skills training: the generalisation problem – some further data. *Behavioural Research and Therapy*, *16*, 297–299.

Shepherd, G., Murray A. & Muijen, M. (1994) *Relative Values: The Different Views of Users, Family Carers and Professionals on Services for People with Schizophrenia.* London: Sainsbury Centre for Mental Health.

Shiloh, R., Zemishlany, Z., Aizenberg, D., *et al.* (1997) Sulpiride augmentation in people with schizophrenia partially responsive to clozapine. A double-blind, placebo-controlled study. *British Journal of Psychiatry, 171,* 569–573.

Singleton, N., Bumpstead, R., O'Brien, M., *et al.* (2000) *Psychiatric Morbidity Among Adults Living in Private Households, 2000.* Report of a survey carried out by the Social Survey Division of the Office for National Statistics on behalf of the Department of Health, the Scottish Executive and the National Assembly for Wales. London: HMSO.

Slade, M., Rosen, A. & Shankar, R. (1995) Multidisciplinary mental health teams. *International Journal of Social Psychiatry, 41,* 180–189.

Slade, P. D. & Bentall, R. P. (1988) *Sensory Deception: A Scientific Analysis of Hallucination.* London: Croom Helm.

Sledge, W. H., Tebes, J., Wolff N., *et al.* (1996) Day hospital/crisis respite care versus inpatient care, part II: service utilization and costs. *American Journal of Psychiatry, 153,* 1074–1083.

Smith, M., Hopkins, D., Peveler, R.C., *et al.* (2008) First- v. second-generation antipsychotics and risk for diabetes in schizophrenia: systematic review and meta-analysis. *British Journal of Psychiatry, 192,* 406–411.

Snyder, S. H., Greenberg, D. & Yamumura, H. I. (1974) Antischizophrenic drugs: affinity for muscarinic cholinergic receptor sites in the brain predicts extrapyramidal effects. *Journal of Psychiatric Research, 11,* 91–95.

Soares, B. G. O., Fenton, M. & Chue, P. (2002) Sulpiride for schizophrenia (Cochrane review). *The Cochrane Library,* Issue 2. Oxford: Update Software.

Spiegelhalter, D. J., Thomas, A., Best, N. G., *et al.* (2001) WinBUGS *User Manual: Version 1.4.* Cambridge: MRC Biostatistics Unit.

Stack-Sullivan, H. (1947) *Conceptions of Modern Psychiatry.* Washington, D.C.: William Alanson White Psychiatric Foundation.

Stack-Sullivan, H. (1974) *Schizophrenia as a Human Process.* London: Norton.

Stahl, S. M. (2004) Focus on antipsychotic polypharmacy: evidence-based prescribing or prescribing-based evidence? *International Journal of Neuropsychopharmacology, 7,* 113–116.

Startup, M., Jackson, M. C. & Bendix, S. (2004) North Wales randomized controlled trial of cognitive behaviour therapy for acute schizophrenia spectrum disorders: outcomes at 6 and 12 months. *Psychological Medicine, 34,* 413–422.

Startup, M., Jackson, M. C., Evans, K. E., *et al.* (2005) North Wales randomized controlled trial of cognitive behaviour therapy for acute schizophrenia spectrum disorders: two-year follow-up and economic evaluation. *Psychological Medicine, 35,* 1307–1316.

Stein, L. I., Test, M. A. & Marx, A. J. (1975) Alternative to the hospital: a controlled study. *American Journal of Psychiatry, 132,* 517–522.

Steingard, S., Allen, M. & Schooler, N. R. (1994) A study of the pharmacologic treatment of medication-compliant schizophrenics who relapse. *Journal of Clinical Psychiatry, 55,* 470–472.

Strakowski, S. M., Johnson, J. L., DelBello, M. P., *et al.* (2005) Quality of life during treatment with haloperidol or olanzapine in the year following a first psychotic episode. *Schizophrenia Research, 78,* 161–169.

Stratton, I. M., Adler, A. I., Neil, H. A. W., *et al.* (2000) Association of glycaemia with macrovascular and microvascular complications of type 2 diabetes (UKPDS 35): prospective observational study. *British Medical Journal, 321*, 405–412.

Stroup, T. S., McEvoy, J. P., Swartz, M. S., *et al.* (2003) The National Institute of Mental Health Clinical Antipsychotic Trials of Intervention Effectiveness (CATIE) project: schizophrenia trial design and protocol development. *Schizophrenia Bulletin, 29*, 15–31.

Sultana, A. & McMonagle, T. (2002) Pimozide for schizophrenia or related psychoses (Cochrane review). *The Cochrane Library*, Issue 2. Oxford: Update Software.

Sultana, A., Reilly, J. & Fenton, M. (2002) Thioridazine for schizophrenia (Cochrane review). *The Cochrane Library*, Issue 2. Oxford: Update Software.

Sun, S. X., Liu, G. G., Christensen, D. B., *et al.* (2007) Review and analysis of hospitalization costs associated with antipsychotic nonadherence in the treatment of schizophrenia in the United States. *Current Medical Research and Opinion, 23*, 2305–2312.

Suvisaari, J. M., Saarni, S. I., Perala, J., *et al.* (2007) Metabolic syndrome among persons with schizophrenia and other psychotic disorders in a general population survey. *Journal of Clinical Psychiatry, 68*, 1045–1055.

Talwar, N., Crawford, M. J., Maratos, A., *et al.* (2006) Music therapy for in-patients with schizophrenia: exploratory randomised controlled trial. *British Journal of Psychiatry, 189*, 405–409.

Tang, Y.-L., Mao, P., Li, F.-M., *et al.* (2007) Gender, age, smoking behaviour and plasma clozapine concentrations in 193 Chinese inpatients with schizophrenia. *British Journal of Clinical Pharmacology, 64*, 49–56.

Tantam, D. & McGrath, G. (1989) Psychiatric day hospitals – another route to institutionalization? *Social Psychiatry and Psychiatric Epidemiology, 24*, 96–101.

Tarrier, N., Lownson, K. & Barrowclough, C. (1991) Some aspects of family interventions in schizophrenia. II. Financial considerations. *British Journal of Psychiatry, 159*, 481–484.

Tarrier, N., Beckett, R., Harwood, S., *et al.* (1993) A trial of two cognitive-behavioural methods of treating drug-resistant residual psychotic symptoms in schizophrenic patients: 1. Outcome. *British Journal of Psychiatry, 162*, 524–532.

Tarrier, N., Yusupoff, L., Kinney, C., *et al.* (1998) Randomised controlled trial of intensive cognitive behavioural therapy for patients with chronic schizophrenia. *British Medical Journal, 317*, 303–307.

Tauscher, J. & Kapur, S. (2001) Choosing the right dose of antipsychotics in schizophrenia: lessons from neuroimaging studies. *CNS Drugs, 15*, 671–678.

Taylor, D., Mace, S., Mir, S., *et al.* (2000) A prescription survey of the use of atypical antipsychotics for hospital in-patients in the United Kingdom. *International Journal of Psychiatry in Clinical Practice, 4*, 41–46.

Taylor, D., Mir, S., Mace, S., *et al.* (2002) Co-prescribing of atypical and typical antipsychotics prescribing sequence and documented outcome. *Psychiatric Bulletin, 26*, 170–172.

Taylor, D., Young, C., Esop, R., *et al.* (2005) Undiagnosed impaired fasting glucose and diabetes mellitus amongst inpatients receiving antipsychotic drugs. *Journal of Psychopharmacology*, *19*, 182–186.

Taylor, P. J. & Gunn, J. (1999) Homicides by people with mental illness: myth and reality. *British Journal of Psychiatry*, *174*, 9–14.

Test, M. A. & Stein, L. I. (1978) Training in community living: research design and results. In *Alternatives to Mental Hospital Treatment* (eds L. I. Stein & M. A. Test), pp. 57–74. New York: Plenum.

Thakore, J. H. (2005) Metabolic syndrome and schizophrenia. *British Journal of Psychiatry*, *186*, 435–436.

Thieda, P., Beard, S., Richter, A., *et al.* (2003) An economic review of compliance with medication therapy in the treatment of schizophrenia. *Psychiatric Services*, *54*, 508–516.

Thompson, K. S., Griffity, E. E. H. & Leaf, P. J. (1990) A historical review of the Madison Model of community care. *Hospital and Community Psychiatry*, *41*, 625–634.

Thorne, B. (1992) *Carl Rogers*. London: Sage.

Thornicroft, G. (2006) *Shunned: Discrimination Against People with Mental Illness*. Oxford: Oxford University Press.

Thornicroft, G., Wykes, T., Holloway, F., *et al.* (1998) From efficacy to effectiveness in community mental health services. PRiSM Psychosis Study. 10. *British Journal of Psychiatry, 173*, 423–427.

Thornicroft, G., Tansella, M., Becker, T., *et al.* (2004) The personal impact of schizophrenia in Europe. *Schizophrenia Research*, *69*, 125–132.

Tiihonen, J., Wahlbeck, K., Lonnqvist, J., *et al.* (2006) Effectiveness of antipsychotic treatments in a nationwide cohort of patients in community care after first hospitalization due to schizophrenia and schizoaffective disorder: observational follow-up study. *British Medical Journal*, *333*, 224.

Tilden, D., Aristides, M., Meddis, D., Burns, T. (2002) An economic assessment of quetiapine and haloperidol in patients with schizophrenia only partially responsive to conventional antipsychotics. *Clinical Therapeutics*, *24*, 1648–1667.

Trower, P., Birchwood, M., Meaden, A., *et al.* (2004) Cognitive therapy for command hallucinations: randomised controlled trial. *British Journal of Psychiatry*, *184*, 312–320.

Tunis, S. L., Croghan, T. W., Heilman, D. K., *et al.* (1999) Reliability, validity, and application of the medical outcomes study 36-item short-form health survey (SF-36) in schizophrenic patients treated with olanzapine versus haloperidol. *Medical Care*, *37*, 678–691.

Tunis, S. L., Faries, D. E., Nyhuis, A. W., *et al.* (2006) Cost-effectiveness of olanzapine as first-line treatment for schizophrenia: results from a randomized, open-label, 1-year trial. *Value in Health*, *9*, 77–89.

Turkington, D., Kingdon, D. & Turner, T. (2002) Effectiveness of a brief cognitive-behavioural therapy intervention in the treatment of schizophrenia. *British Journal of Psychiatry*, *180*, 523–527.

Tyrer, P. J. & Remington, M. (1979) Controlled comparison of day-hospital and out-patient treatment for neurotic disorders. *Lancet*, *1*, 1014–1016.

Tyrer, P. J., Evans, K., Gandhi, N., *et al.* (1998) Randomised controlled trial of two models of care for discharged psychiatric patients. *British Medical Journal, 316*, 106–109.

Tyrer, P. J., Coid, J., Simmonds, S., *et al.* (2002) Community mental health teams (CMHTs) for people with severe mental illnesses and disordered personality (Cochrane review). *The Cochrane Library*, Issue 1. Oxford: Update Software.

Ulrich, G. (2007) The additional therapeutic effect of group music therapy for schizophrenic patients: a randomized study *Acta Psychiatrica Scandinavica, 166*, 362–370.

Van Nimwegen, L. J., Storosum, J. G., Blumer, R. M., *et al.* (2008) Hepatic insulin resistance in antipsychotic naive schizophrenic patients: stable isotope studies of glucose metabolism. *The Journal of Clinical Endocrinology and Metabolism, 93*, 572–577.

Van Os, J., Krabbendam, L., Myin-Germeys, I., *et al.* (2005) The schizophrenia envirome. *Current Opinion in Psychiatry, 58*, 141–145.

Van Winkel, R., De Hert, M., Van Eyck, D., *et al.* (2006) Screening for diabetes and other metabolic abnormalities in patients with schizophrenia and schizoaffective disorder: evaluation of incidence and screening methods. *Journal of Clinical Psychiatry, 67*, 1493–1500.

Van Winkel, R., De Hert, M., Wampers, M., *et al.* (2008) Major changes in glucose metabolism, including new-onset diabetes, within 3 months after initiation of or switch to atypical antipsychotic medication in patients with schizophrenia and schizoaffective disorder. *Journal of Clinical Psychiatry, 69*, 472–479.

Vaughn, C. E. & Leff, J. P. (1976) The influence of family and social factors on the course of psychiatric illness. A comparison of schizophrenic and depressed neurotic patients. *British Journal of Psychiatry, 129*, 125–137.

Vera-Llonch, M., Delea, T. E., Richardson, E., *et al.* (2004) Outcomes and costs of risperidone versus olanzapine in patients with chronic schizophrenia or schizoaffective disorders: a Markov model. *Value in Health, 7*, 569–584.

Viguera, A. C., Baldessarini, R. J., Hegarty, J. D., *et al.* (1997) Clinical risk following abrupt and gradual withdrawal of maintenance neuroleptic treatment. *Archives of General Psychiatry, 54*, 49–55.

Wahlbeck, K., Cheine, M.V. & Essali, A. (1999) Clozapine versus typical neuroleptic medication for schizophrenia (Cochrane review). *The Cochrane Library*, Issue 3. Oxford: Update Software

Walburn, J., Gray, R., Gournay, K., *et al.* (2001) Systematic review of patient and nurse attitudes to depot antipsychotic medication. *British Journal of Psychiatry, 179*, 300–307.

Wallace, C. J., Nelson, C. J., Liberman, R. P., *et al.* (1980) A review and critique of social skills training with schizophrenic patients. *Schizophrenia Bulletin, 6*, 42–63.

Waller, S. & Finn, H. (2004) *Enhancing the Healing Environment – A Guide for NHS Trust.* London: King's Fund.

Warner, R. (1994) *Recovery from Schizophrenia.* 2nd edn. New York: Routledge.

Warner, R., Huxley, P. & Berg, T. (1999) An evaluation of the impact of clubhouse membership on quality of life and treatment utilization. *International Journal of Social Psychiatry, 45*, 310–320.

Weinberger, D. R., Berman, K. F. & Illowsky, B. P. (1988) Physiological dysfunction of dorsolateral prefrontal cortex in schizophrenia. III. A new cohort and evidence for a monoaminergic mechanism. *Archives of General Psychiatry, 45*, 609–615.

Weisbrod, B. A., Test, M. A. & Stein, L. I. (1980) Alternative to mental hospital treatment. II. Economic benefit-cost analysis. *Archives of General Psychiatry, 37*, 400–405.

Wiersma, D., Kluiter, H., Nienhuis, F., *et al.* (1989) *Day-treatment with Community Care as an Alternative to Standard Hospitalization: An Experiment in The Netherlands. A Preliminary Communication.* Groningen: Department of Social Psychiatry, University of Groningen.

Wiersma, D., Nienhuis, F. J., Slooff, C. J., *et al.* (1998) Natural course of schizophrenic disorders: a 15-year follow up of a Dutch incidence cohort. *Schizophrenia Bulletin, 24*, 75–85.

Wiersma, D., Wanderling, J., Dragomirecka, E., *et al.* (2000) Social disability in schizophrenia: its development and prediction over 15 years in incidence cohorts in six European countries. *Psychological Medicine, 30*, 1155–1167.

Wolff, N., Helminiak, T. W., Morse, G. A., *et al.* (1997) Cost-effectiveness evaluation of three approaches to case management for homeless mentally ill clients. *American Journal of Psychiatry, 154*, 341–348.

Wood, C. (1997) The history of art therapy 1938–95. In *Art, Psychotherapy and Psychosis* (eds K. Killick & S. Schaverien). London: Routledge.

World Health Organization (1990) *International Classification of Diseases.* 10th edn. Geneva: World Health Organization.

World Health Organization (1992) *International Statistical Classification of Diseases and Related Health Problems* (ICD–10). Geneva: World Health Organization.

Wu, E. Q., Birnbaum, H. G., Shi, L., *et al.* (2005) The economic burden of schizophrenia in the United States in 2002. *Journal of Clinical Psychiatry, 66*, 1122–1129.

Wykes, T. & Reeder, C. (2005) *Cognitive Remediation Therapy for Schizophrenia: Theory and Practice.* London: Routledge.

Wykes, T. & van der Gaag, M. (2001) Is it time to develop a new cognitive therapy for psychosis – cognitive remediation therapy (CRT)? *Clinical Psychology Review, 8*, 1227–1256.

Yagcioglu, A. E. A., Akdede, B. B. K., Turgut, T. I., *et al.* (2005) A double-blind controlled study of adjunctive treatment with risperidone in schizophrenic patients partially responsive to clozapine: efficacy and safety. *Journal of Clinical Psychiatry, 66*, 63–72.

Yang, W. Y., Zheng, L., Yong-Zhen, W., *et al.* (1998) Psychosocial rehabilitation effects of music therapy in chronic schizophrenic patients. *Hong Kong Journal of Psychiatry, 8*, 38–40.

Young, J. L., Zonana, H. V. & Shepler, L. (1986) Medication noncompliance in schizophrenia: codification and update. *Bulletin of the American Academy of Psychiatry and the Law, 14*, 105–122.

Young, J. L., Spitz, R. T., Hillbrand, M., *et al.* (1999) Medication adherence failure in schizophrenia: a forensic review of rates, reasons, treatments and prospects. *Journal of the American Academy of Psychiatry and the Law, 27*, 426–444.

References

Zhu, B., Ascher-Svanum, H., Shi, L. B., *et al.* (2008) Time to discontinuation of depot and oral first-generation antipsychotics in the usual care of schizophrenia. *Psychiatric Services*, *59*, 315–317.

Ziegenbein, M. I., Wittmann, G. & Kropp, S. (2006) Aripiprazole augmentation of clozapine in treatment-resistant schizophrenia: a clinical observation. *Clinical Drug Investigation*, *26*, 117–124.

Zubin, J. & Spring, B. (1977) Vulnerability – a new view of schizophrenia. *Journal of Abnormal Psychology*, *86*, 103–126.

Zullino, D. F., Delessert, D., Eap, C. B., *et al.* (2007) Tobacco and cannabis smoking cessation can lead to intoxication with clozapine or olanzapine. *International Clinical Psychopharmacololgy*, *17*, 141–143.

13   ABBREVIATIONS

Please note that abbreviations included in the appendices on the CD are also listed here.

ABPI	Association of the British Pharmaceutical Industry Association of the British Pharmaceutical Industry
ABPS	Awareness of Being a Patient Scale
AC	attention control
ACE	active cognitive therapy for early psychosis
ACES	Agitation-Calmness Evaluation Scale
ACT	assertive community treatment (also acceptance and commitment therapy in Appendix 15)
ADL	activities of daily living
ADQ	average daily quantity
AE	adverse event
AGREE	Appraisal of Guidelines for Research and Evaluation Instrument
AIMS	Abnormal Involuntary Movement Scale (in Appendix 15 only)
AIPSS	Assessment of Interpersonal Problem Solving Skills
AMDP	Association for Methodology and Documentation in Psychiatry
AMED	Allied and Alternative Medicine Database
AMHP	approved mental health professional
AMI	amisulpride
AP	antipsychotic
APA	American Psychiatric Association
APES	Adapted Pleasant Events Schedule
APT	attention process training
ARI	aripiprazole
ARS	Association for Research on Schizophrenia
BADS	Behavioural Assessment of the Dysexecutive Syndrome
BARS/BAS	Barnes Akathisia Rating Scale
BAT	Behavioural Assessment Task
B&C	board and care
BDI	Beck Depression Inventory
BFT	behavioural family therapy
BMC	BioMed Central
BME	black and minority ethnic
BMI	body mass index
BNF	British National Formulary
BP	bipolar disorder

BPRS	Brief Psychiatric Rating Scale
BPT	body-orientated psychological therapy
BRC	Biomedical Research Centre
BRMES	Bech-Rafaelsen Melancholia Scale
BSI	Brief Symptom Inventory
CA	cost analysis
CACR	computer-assisted cognitive rehabilitation
CARS-M	Clinicians Administered Rating Scale for Mania
CAT	cognitive adaptation training/Client's Assessment of Treatment Scale
CATIE	Clinical Antipsychotic Trials of Intervention Effectiveness
CBA	cost-benefit analysis
CBST/CBSST	cognitive behavioural social skills training
CBT	cognitive behavioural therapy
CBTp	CBT for psychosis
CCA	cost-consequences analysis
CCMD	Chinese Classification of Mental Disorders
CDS(S)	Calgary Depression Scale (for Schizophrenia)
CEA	cost-effectiveness analysis
CEAC	cost effectiveness acceptability curve
CEAF	cost-effectiveness acceptability frontier
CET	cognitive enhancement therapy
CGI	Clinical Global Impressions Scale
CGI-I	Clinical Global Impressions Improvement Scale
CGI-S	Clinical Global Impressions Severity Scale
CHL/CPZ	chlorpromazine
CI	confidence interval
CINAHL	Cumulative Index to Nursing and Allied Health Literature
CL/CLZ	clozapine
CM	case management
CMA	cost-minimisation analysis
CMHC	community mental health centre
CMHT	community mental health team
CMRS	Case Manager Rating Scale
CNI	cognitive nursing intervention
COAST	Croydon Outreach and Assertive Support Team
COPE	cognitively oriented psychotherapy for early psychosis
COSTART	Coding Symbols for a Thesaurus for Adverse Reaction Terms
CPA	care programme approach
CPN	community psychiatric nurse
CPRS	Comprehensive Psychiatric Rating Scale
CPT	Continuous Performance Test
CR	cognitive rehabilitation (or cognitive remediation depending on context)

CREP	cognitive rehabilitation intervention for severely impaired schizophrenia patients
CRHTT	crisis resolution and home treatment team
CRM	community re-entry module
CRT	cognitive remediation therapy
CS	computer skills component
CSIP	Community Services Improvement Partnership
CUA	cost-utility analysis
CUtLASS	Cost Utility of the Latest Antipsychotic Drugs in Schizophrenia Study
CVLT	California Verbal Learning Test
DAI	Drug Attitude Inventory
DALY	disability adjusted life years
DDQ	Desire for Drug Questionnaire
DIC	deviance information criterion
DLP	Daily Living Programme
DNA	did not attend
DOTES	Dosage Record Treatment Emergent Symptom Scale
DS	Delusions Scale
DSAS	Defective Symptoms Assessment Scale
ds-CPT	degraded stimulus Continuous Performance Test
DSDT	Digit Span Distractibility Test
DSM	*Diagnostic and Statistical Manual of Mental Disorders* (American Psychiatric Association)
DST	Digit Symbol Test
DTP	day treatment programme
DUP	duration of untreated psychosis
DVP	scale for rating treatment emergent symptoms in psychiatry
EABCT	European Association for Behavioural and Cognitive Therapies
EAS	Homeless Engagement and Acceptance Scale
ECG/EKG	electrocardiogram
ECT	electroconvulsive therapy
EE	expressed emotion
EEG	electroencephalogram
EIPS	early intervention in psychosis services
EIS	early intervention services
EM	expectation maximisation
EM Insight Scale	Explanatory Model Scale
EMBASE	Excerpta Medica Database
EPPIC	Early Psychosis Prevention and Intervention Centre (Melbourne, Australia)

EPPI-Centre	Evidence for Policy and Practice Information and Co-ordinating Centre
EPS	extrapyramidal side effects
EPSILON	European Psychiatric Services: Inputs Linked to Outcome Domains and Needs
EQ-5D	EuroQol five dimensions
ER	extended release
ERT	Emotion Recognition Test
ESRS	extrapyramidal symptom rating scale
EST	enriched supportive therapy
ETAU	enhanced treatment as usual
EUROQOL	European Quality of Life
Ext domin.	extendedly dominated
FACT	family-aided assertive community treatment
FAST	functional adaptation skills training
FBIS	Family Burden Interview Scale
FDA	Food and Drug Administration (US)
FES	first episode of schizophrenia
FGA	first-generation antipsychotic drug
FI	family intervention
FL1/FLUPE	flupentixol
FL2/FLUPHE	fluphenazine
FSSI	Family Support Service Index
FU	follow-up
GAF (-DIS)	Global Assessment of Functioning (-Disability Scale)
GAS	Global Assessment Scale
GDG	Guideline Development Group
GES	general environment support
GI	gastrointestinal
GP	general practitioner
GPS	General Psychopathology Scale
GPSF	Global Psychosocial Functioning
GTFm	Gießentest Observer Assessment
GTS	Gießentest Self-Assessment
HAM-D	Hamilton Rating Scale for Depression
HAS	Hillside Akathisia Scale
HAL	haloperidol
HCHS	hospital and community health services
HCQoL	Heinreich-Carpenter Quality of Life
HDL	high density lipoprotein
HDRS	Hamilton Depression Rating Scale
HES	hospital episode statistics

Hgb A$_{1C}$	glycosylated haemoglobin
HIT	hallucination-focused integrated treatment
HLM	hierarchical linear models
HMSO	Her Majesty's Stationary Office
HONOS	Health of the Nation Outcome Scales
HPC	Health Professions Council
HRQoL	health-related quality of life
IAPSRS	International Association of Psychosocial Rehabilitation Services
IAS	Interaction Anxiousness Scale
IBR	intensive behavioural rehabilitation
ICD	*International Statistical Classification of Diseases and Related Health Problems* (World Health Organization)
ICER	incremental cost-effectiveness ratio
ICM	intensive case management
ICP	International Congress of Pscyhology
IG	information group
IHRQoL	Index of Health-Related Quality of Life
IIP	Inventory of Interpersonal Problems
ILSS	Independent Living Skills Survey
IM	Intramuscular
IS	Insight Scale
ISPS	International Society for the Psychological Treatments of Schizophrenia and other Psychoses
ITAQ	Insight and Treatment Attitudes Questionnaire
ITT	intention to treat
IV	intravenous/inverse variance
KASQ	Knowledge About Schizophrenia Questionnaire
LAI	long-acting injectable
LDL (-C)	low density lipoprotein (-cholesterol)
LOCF	last observation carried forward
LQLS	Lancashire Quality of Life Scale
LSP	Life Skills Profile
LUNSERS	Liverpool University Neuroleptic Side-Effect Rating Scale
MADRS	Montgomery Asberg Depression Rating Scale
MANSA	Manchester Short Assessment of Quality of Life
MAQ	Medication Adherence Questionnaire
MATISSE	Multicentre study of Art Therapy In Schizophrenia: Systematic Evaluation
MATRICS	Measurement and Treatment Research to Improve Cognition in Schizophrenia consensus panel
MCAS	Multnomah Community Ability Scale

PAS	Psychotic Anxiety Scale
PC	paired comparisons
PE	psychoeducation
PEF	Psychiatric Evaluation Form
PER	perphenazine
Perc QoL	Lancashire Quality of Life Profile
PFQ	Personal Functioning Questionnaire
PGI	Patient Global Impression
PGWB	Psychological General Well-Being Scale
PI	principal investigator
PICO	patient, intervention, comparison and outcome
PLB	placebo
POMH-UK	National Prescribing Observatory for Mental Health
PORT	Patient Outcomes Research Team
p.r.n.	*pro re nata* [prescription taken as required]
PriMHE	Primary Mental Health Care and Education
PSE	Present State Examination
PSP	Personal and Social Functioning Scale
PSS	Personal Social Services
PSST	psychosocial skills training
PsycINFO	Psychological Information Database
PSYRATS	Psychotic Symptom Rating Scales
PT	personal therapy
QALY	quality adjusted life year
QLS	Quality of Life Scale
QOF	Quality and Outcomes Framework
QOLI	Quality of Life Inventory
QTcLD	QT interval corrected for heart rate using a linear formula
QUE	quetiapine
QWB	Quality of Well-Being scale
r	Number of events
R/RIS/RI	risperidone
RAVLT	Rey Auditory Verbal Learning Test
RCT	randomised controlled trial
RDC	research diagnostic criteria
RG	relatives' group
RMO	responsible medical officer
ROMI	Rating of Medication Influences
RR	relative risk, or risk ratio
RS	rating scales
RSCQ	Robson Self-Concept Questionnaire

RSE(S)	Rosenberg Self-Esteem Scale
RSWG	Remission in Schizophrenia Working Group
SADS (-C)	Schedule for Affective Disorders and Schizophrenia (-Change Version)
SAFTEE	a technique for the systematic assessment of side effects in clinical trials
SAI (-C, -E)	Schedule for the Assessment of Insight (-Compliance, -Expanded)
SANS	Scale for the Assessment of Negative Symptoms
SAPS	Scale for the Assessment of Positive Symptoms
SAS/SARS	Simpson-Angus Rating Scale
SAT	Span of Apprehension Test
SBS/SBAS	Social Behaviour (Assessment) Scale
SBST	Social Behavior Sequencing Task
SC	standard care
SCD	Schizophrenic Communication Disorder
SCET	Social Cognition Enhancement Training for Schizophrenia
SCM	standard case management
SCON	Conversation with a Stranger Task
SD	standard deviation
SDO	service delivery and organisation
SDS	Schedule for the Deficit Syndrome
SDSI	Social Disability Schedule for In-patients
SDSS	Social Disability Screening Schedule
SE	standard error
SER	sertindole
SES	Self-Esteem Scale
SF-36	Short-form health survey
SFS	Social Functioning Scale
SFT	systemic family therapy
SG	standard gamble/support group
SGA	second-generation antipsychotic
SGOT	serum glutamic oxaloacetic transaminase
SGPT	serum glutamic pyruvic transaminase
SIGN	Scottish Intercollegiate Guidelines Network
SKT	Syndrom-Kurztest Short Cognitive Performance Test
SLOF	Specified Level of Functioning Scale
SM	symptom management
SMD	Standardised mean difference
SMI	severe mental illness
SMR	standardised mortality ratio
SOFAS	Social and Occupational Functioning Assessment Scale
SPC	*Summary of Product Characteristics*

SPG	Skalen zur psychischen gesundheit (Scales about mental health)
SPSS	Statistical Package for Social Sciences
SPT	supportive psychotherapy
S-QoL	Schizophrenia Quality of Life questionnaire
SSIT	Simulated Social Interaction Test
SSPA	Social Skills Performance Assessment
SSQ	Social Support Questionnaire
SSRI	selective serotonin reuptake inhibitor
SST	social skills training
ST	supportive therapy
SUL	sulpiride
SUMD	Scale to Assess Unawareness of Mental Disorder
SWAM	Satisfaction with Antipsychotic Medication Scale
TA	Technology Appraisal
TAU	treatment as usual
TCI	Treatment Compliance Interview
TD	tardive dyskinesia
TESS	Treatment Emergent Symptom Scale
TMT	Trail Making Test
ToM	Theory of Mind
TRIP	Transforming Relapse and Instilling Prosperity
TRS	treatment-resistant schizophrenia
TSCKAS	Team Solutions Comprehensive Knowledge Assessment Scale
TTO	time trade-off
UC	usual care
UCSD	University of California, San Diego
UKAN	UK Advocacy Network
UKPDS	United Kingdom Prospective Diabetes Study
UKU	Udvalg for Kliniske Undersøgelser Side Effect Rating Scale
UPSA	University of California, San Diego Performance-Based Skills Assessment
VSSS	Verona Service Satisfaction Scale
WACP	World Assocation of Cultural Psychiatry
WAIS	Wechsler Adult Intelligence Scale
WCST-Cat	Wisconsin Card Sorting Test Category
WHO	World Health Organization
WHOQOL	World Health Organization Quality of Life
WISC-R	Weschler Intelligence Scale for Children (Revised)
WMD	Weighted mean difference

Abbreviations

WMS (-LM)	Wechsler Memory Scale (–Revised Logical Memory)
WONCA	World Organisation of General Practitioners
WOT	Ward occupational therapy
WPA	World Psychiatric Association
WTP	willingness to pay
ZIP	ziprasidone
ZOT	zotepine
ZUC (-A, -D)	Zuclopenthixol (-acetate, -dihydrochloride)